Microsoft®
ACCESS® 2010
COMPREHENSIVE

Microsoft®
ACCESS® 2010
COMPREHENSIVE

Gary B. Shelly

Philip J. Pratt

Mary Z. Last

COURSE TECHNOLOGY
CENGAGE Learning™

SHELLY
CASHMAN
SERIES®

Australia • Brazil • Japan • Korea • Mexico • Singapore • Spain • United Kingdom • United States

Microsoft® Access® 2010: Comprehensive
Gary B. Shelly, Philip J. Pratt, Mary Z. Last

Vice President, Publisher: Nicole Pinard

Executive Editor: Kathleen McMahon

Product Manager: Jon Farnham

Associate Product Manager: Aimee Poirier

Editorial Assistant: Angela Giannopoulos

Director of Marketing: Cheryl Costantini

Marketing Manager: Tristen Kendall

Marketing Coordinator: Adrienne Fung

Print Buyer: Julio Esperas

Director of Production: Patty Stephan

Content Project Manager: Jennifer Feltri

Development Editor: Amanda Brodkin

Copyeditor: Troy Lilly

Proofreader: Karen Annett

Indexer: Rich Carlson

QA Manuscript Reviewers: Chris Scriver,
    John Freitas, Serge Palladino, Susan Pedicini,
    Danielle Shaw

Art Director: Marissa Falco

Cover Designer: Lisa Kuhn, Curio Press, LLC

Cover Photo: Tom Kates Photography

Text Design: Joel Sadagursky

Compositor: PreMediaGlobal

© 2012 Course Technology, Cengage Learning

For product information and technology assistance, contact us at
Cengage Learning Customer & Sales Support, 1-800-354-9706

For permission to use material from this text or product,
submit all requests online at **cengage.com/permissions**
Further permissions questions can be emailed to
permissionrequest@cengage.com

Library of Congress Control Number: 2010938583

ISBN-13: 978-1-4390-7902-7

ISBN-10: 1-4390-7902-1

Course Technology
20 Channel Center Street
Boston, MA 02210
USA

Cengage Learning is a leading provider of customized learning solutions with office locations around the globe, including Singapore, the United Kingdom, Australia, Mexico, Brazil, and Japan. Locate your local office at:
international.cengage.com/region

Cengage Learning products are represented in Canada by Nelson Education, Ltd.

Visit our Web site **www.cengage.com/ct/shellycashman** to share and gain ideas on our textbooks!

To learn more about Course Technology,
visit **www.cengage.com/coursetechnology**

Purchase any of our products at your local college bookstore or at our preferred online store at **www.cengagebrain.com**

We dedicate this book to the memory of James S. Quasney (1940 – 2009), who for 18 years co-authored numerous books with Tom Cashman and Gary Shelly and provided extraordinary leadership to the Shelly Cashman Series editorial team. As series editor, Jim skillfully coordinated, organized, and managed the many aspects of our editorial development processes and provided unending direction, guidance, inspiration, support, and advice to the Shelly Cashman Series authors and support team members. He was a trusted, dependable, loyal, and well-respected leader, mentor, and friend. We are forever grateful to Jim for his faithful devotion to our team and eternal contributions to our series.

The Shelly Cashman Series Team

Printed in the United States of America
2 3 4 5 6 7 13 12 11

Microsoft ACCESS 2010

COMPREHENSIVE

Contents

Appendices

What is the Microsoft® Office Specialist Program?

The Microsoft Office Specialist Program enables candidates to show that they have something exceptional to offer – proven expertise in certain Microsoft programs. Recognized by businesses and schools around the world, over 4 million certifications have been obtained in over 100 different countries. The Microsoft Office Specialist Program is the only Microsoft-approved certification program of its kind.

What is the Microsoft Office Specialist Certification?

 The Microsoft Office Specialist certification validates through the use of exams that you have obtained specific skill sets within the applicable Microsoft Office programs and other Microsoft programs included in the Microsoft Office Specialist Program. The candidate can choose which exam(s) they want to take according to which skills they want to validate.

The available Microsoft Office Specialist Program exams include*:

- Using Windows Vista®
- Using Microsoft® Office Word 2007
- Using Microsoft® Office Word 2007 – Expert
- Using Microsoft® Office Excel® 2007
- Using Microsoft® Office Excel® 2007 – Expert
- Using Microsoft® Office PowerPoint® 2007
- Using Microsoft® Office Access® 2007
- Using Microsoft® Office Outlook® 2007
- Using Microsoft SharePoint® 2007

The Microsoft Office Specialist Program 2010 exams will include*:

- Microsoft Word 2010
- Microsoft Word 2010 Expert
- Microsoft Excel® 2010
- Microsoft Excel® 2010 Expert
- Microsoft PowerPoint® 2010
- Microsoft Access® 2010
- Microsoft Outlook® 2010
- Microsoft SharePoint® 2010

What does the Microsoft Office Specialist Approved Courseware logo represent?

 The logo indicates that this courseware has been approved by Microsoft to cover the course objectives that will be included in the relevant exam. It also means that after utilizing this courseware, you may be better prepared to pass the exams required to become a certified Microsoft Office Specialist.

For more information:

To learn more about Microsoft Office Specialist exams, visit www.microsoft.com/learning/msbc

To learn about other Microsoft approved courseware from Cengage Learning, visit www.cengagebrain.com

*The availability of Microsoft Office Specialist certification exams varies by Microsoft program, program version and language. Visit www.microsoft.com/learning for exam availability.

Microsoft, Access, Excel, the Office Logo, Outlook, PowerPoint, SharePoint, and Windows Vista are either registered trademarks or trademarks of Microsoft Corporation in the United States and/or other countries. The Microsoft Office Specialist logo and the Microsoft Office Specialist Approved Courseware logo are used under license from Microsoft Corporation.

Preface

The Shelly Cashman Series® offers the finest textbooks in computer education. We are proud that since Mircosoft Office 4.3, our series of Microsoft Office textbooks have been the most widely used books in education. With each new edition of our Office books, we make significant improvements based on the software and comments made by instructors and students. For this Microsoft Access 2010 text, the Shelly Cashman Series development team carefully reviewed our pedagogy and analyzed its effectiveness in teaching today's Office student. Students today read less, but need to retain more. They need not only to be able to perform skills, but to retain those skills and know how to apply them to different settings. Today's students need to be continually engaged and challenged to retain what they're learning.

With this Microsoft Access 2010 text, we continue our commitment to focusing on the user and how they learn best.

Objectives of This Textbook

Microsoft Access 2010: Comprehensive is intended for a ten- to fifteen-week period in a course that teaches Access 2010 as the primary component. No experience with a computer is assumed, and no mathematics beyond the high school freshman level is required. The objectives of this book are:

- To offer a comprehensive presentation of Microsoft Access 2010

- To expose students to practical examples of the computer as a useful tool

- To acquaint students with the proper procedures to create databases suitable for coursework, professional purposes, and personal use

- To help students discover the underlying functionality of Access 2010 so they can become more productive

- To develop an exercise-oriented approach that allows learning by doing

New to This Edition

Microsoft Access 2010: Comprehensive offers a number of new features and approaches, which improve student understanding, retention, transference, and skill in using Access 2010. The following enhancements will enrich the learning experience:

- Office 2010 and Windows 7: Essential Concepts and Skills chapter presents basic Office 2010 and Windows 7 skills.

- Streamlined first chapter allows the ability to cover more advanced skills earlier.

- Chapter topic redistribution offers concise chapters that ensure complete skill coverage.

- New pedagogical elements enrich material, creating an accessible and user-friendly approach.

  - Break Points, a new boxed element, identify logical stopping points and give students instructions regarding what they should do before taking a break.

  - Within step instructions, Tab | Group Identifiers, such as (Home tab | Bold button), help students more easily locate elements in the groups and on the tabs on the Ribbon.

  - Modified step-by-step instructions tell the student what to do and provide the generic reason why they are completing a specific task, which helps students easily transfer given skills to different settings.

The Shelly Cashman Approach

A Proven Pedagogy with an Emphasis on Project Planning

Each chapter presents a practical problem to be solved, within a project planning framework. The project orientation is strengthened by the use of Plan Ahead boxes, which encourage critical thinking about how to proceed at various points in the project. Step-by-step instructions with supporting screens guide students through the steps. Instructional steps are supported by the Q&A, Experimental Step, and BTW features.

A Visually Engaging Book that Maintains Student Interest

The step-by-step tasks, with supporting figures, provide a rich visual experience for the student. Call-outs on the screens that present both explanatory and navigational information provide students with information they need when they need to know it.

Supporting Reference Materials (Appendices and Quick Reference)

The appendices provide additional information about the Application at hand and include such topics as project planning guidelines and certification. With the Quick Reference, students can quickly look up information about a single task, such as keyboard shortcuts, and find page references of where in the book the task is illustrated.

Integration of the World Wide Web

The World Wide Web is integrated into the Access 2010 learning experience by (1) BTW annotations; (2) BTW, Q&A, and Quick Reference Summary Web pages; and (3) the Learn It Online section for each chapter.

End-of-Chapter Student Activities

Extensive end-of-chapter activities provide a variety of reinforcement opportunities for students where they can apply and expand their skills.

Instructor Resources

The Instructor Resources include both teaching and testing aids and can be accessed via CD-ROM or at login.cengage.com.

Instructor's Manual Includes lecture notes summarizing the chapter sections, figures and boxed elements found in every chapter, teacher tips, classroom activities, lab activities, and quick quizzes in Microsoft Word files.

Syllabus Easily customizable sample syllabi that cover policies, assignments, exams, and other course information.

Figure Files Illustrations for every figure in the textbook in electronic form.

PowerPoint Presentations A multimedia lecture presentation system that provides slides for each chapter. Presentations are based on chapter objectives.

Solutions To Exercises Includes solutions for all end-of-chapter and chapter reinforcement exercises.

Test Bank & Test Engine Test Banks include 112 questions for every chapter, featuring objective-based and critical thinking question types, and including page number references and figure references, when appropriate. Also included is the test engine, ExamView, the ultimate tool for your objective-based testing needs.

Data Files For Students Includes all the files that are required by students to complete the exercises.

Additional Activities For Students Consists of Chapter Reinforcement Exercises, which are true/false, multiple-choice, and short answer questions that help students gain confidence in the material learned.

Book Resources

🔒 Additional Faculty Files
🔒 Blackboard Testbank
🔒 Data Files
🔒 Instructor's Manual
🔒 Lecture Success System
🔒 PowerPoint Presentations
🔒 Solutions to Exercises
🔒 Syllabus
🔒 Test Bank and Test Engine
🔒 WebCT Testbank
Chapter Reinforcement Exercises
Student Downloads

SAM: Skills Assessment Manager

SAM 2010 is designed to help bring students from the classroom to the real world. It allows students to train on and test important computer skills in an active, hands-on environment.

SAM's easy-to-use system includes powerful interactive exams, training, and projects on the most commonly used Microsoft Office applications. SAM simulates the Microsoft Office 2010 application environment, allowing students to demonstrate their knowledge and think through the skills by performing real-world tasks such as bolding word text or setting up slide transitions. Add in live-in-the-application projects, and students are on their way to truly learning and applying skills to business-centric documents.

Designed to be used with the Shelly Cashman Series, SAM includes handy page references so that students can print helpful study guides that match the Shelly Cashman textbooks used in class. For instructors, SAM also includes robust scheduling and reporting features.

Content for Online Learning

Course Technology has partnered with the leading distance learning solution providers and class-management platforms today. To access this material, instructors will visit our password-protected instructor resources available at login.cengage.com. Instructor resources include the following: additional case projects, sample syllabi, PowerPoint presentations per chapter, and more. For additional information or for an instructor user name and password, please contact your sales representative. For students to access this material, they must have purchased a WebTutor PIN-code specific to this title and your campus platform. The resources for students may include (based on instructor preferences), but are not limited to: topic review, review questions, and practice tests.

CourseNotes

Course Technology's CourseNotes are six-panel quick reference cards that reinforce the most important and widely used features of a software application in a visual and user-friendly format. CourseNotes serve as a great reference

tool during and after the student completes the course. CourseNotes are available for software applications such as Microsoft Office 2010, Word 2010, Excel 2010, Access 2010, PowerPoint 2010, and Windows 7. Topic-based CourseNotes are available for Best Practices in Social Networking, Hot Topics in Technology, and Web 2.0. Visit www.cengagebrain.com to learn more!

A Guided Tour

Add excitement and interactivity to your classroom with "*A Guided Tour*" product line. Play one of the brief mini-movies to spice up your lecture and spark classroom discussion. Or, assign a movie for homework and ask students to complete the correlated assignment that accompanies each topic. "*A Guided Tour*" product line takes the prep work out of providing your students with information about new technologies and applications and helps keep students engaged with content relevant to their lives; all in under an hour!

  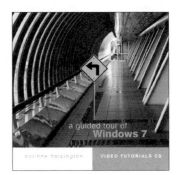

About Our Covers

The Shelly Cashman Series is continually updating our approach and content to reflect the way today's students learn and experience new technology. This focus on student success is reflected on our covers, which feature real students from the University of Rhode Island using the Shelly Cashman Series in their courses, and reflect the varied ages and backgrounds of the students learning with our books. When you use the Shelly Cashman Series, you can be assured that you are learning computer skills using the most effective courseware available.

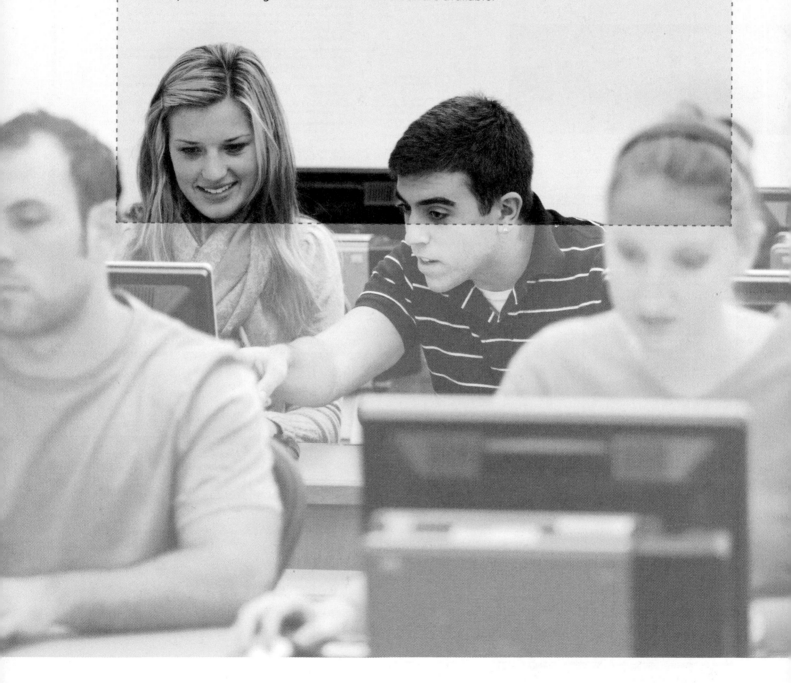

Textbook Walk-Through

The Shelly Cashman Series Pedagogy: Project-Based — Step-by-Step — Variety of Assessments

Plan Ahead boxes prepare students to create successful projects by encouraging them to think strategically about what they are trying to accomplish before they begin working.

Step-by-step instructions now provide a context beyond the point-and-click. Each step provides information on why students are performing each task, or what will occur as a result.

Overview

As you read this chapter, you will learn how to query a database by performing these general tasks:

- Create queries using Design view.
- Use criteria in queries.
- Create and use parameter queries.
- Sort data in queries.
- Join tables in queries.
- Create reports and forms from a query.
- Export data from a query.
- Perform calculations in queries.
- Create crosstab queries.

Plan Ahead

BTW Designing Queries
Before creating queries, examine the contents of the tables involved. You need to know the data type for each field and how the data for the field is stored. If a query includes a state, for example, you need to know whether state is stored as the two-character abbreviation of as the full state name.

Query Design Decisions

When posing a question to Access, you must design an appropriate query. In the process of designing a query, the decisions you make will determine the fields, tables, criteria, order, and special calculations included in the query. To design a query, you can follow these general guidelines:

1. **Identify the fields.** Examine the question or request to determine which fields from the tables in the database are involved. Examine the contents of these fields to make sure you understand the data type and format for storing the data.

2. **Identify restrictions.** Unless the question or request calls for the inclusion of all records, determine the restrictions or the conditions records must satisfy to be included in the results.

3. **Determine whether special order is required.** Examine the question or request to determine whether the results must appear in some specific order.

4. **Determine whether more than one table is required.** If all the fields identified in Step 1 are in the same table, no special action is required. If this is not the case, identify all tables represented by those fields.

5. **Determine whether calculations are required.** Examine the question or request to determine whether, in addition to the fields determined in Step 1, calculations must be included. Such calculations include individual record calculations (for example, adding the values in two fields) or group calculations (for example, finding the total of the values in a particular field for all the records).

6. **If data is to be summarized, determine whether a crosstab query would be appropriate.** If data is to be grouped by two different types of information, you can use a crosstab query. You will need to identify the two types of information. One of the types will form the row headings and the other will form the column headings in the query results.

When necessary, more specific details concerning the decisions and/or actions are presented at appropriate points in the chapter. The chapter also will identify the use of these guidelines in creating queries such as those shown in Figure 2–1.

Databases and Database Obj

To Use the Simple Query Wizard to Create a Query

Queries are simply questions, the answers to which are in the databa feature that helps you find the answers to a wide variety of questions. Once want to ask to determine the fields involved in the question, you can begin restrictions involved in the query, nor any special order or calculations, you

The following steps use the Simple Query Wizard to create a query t obtain financial information on its clients. The query displays the number, n hours YTD, and business analyst number of all clients.

1

- If the Navigation Pane is closed, click the Shutter Bar Open/Close Button to open the Navigation Pane.
- Be sure the Client table is selected.
- Click Create on the Ribbon to display the Create tab.
- Click the Query Wizard button (Create tab | Queries group) to display the New Query dialog box (Figure 1–60).

Figure 1–60

2

- Be sure Simple Query Wizard is selected, and then click the OK button (New Query dialog box) to display the Simple Query Wizard dialog box (Figure 1–61).

Q&A What would happen if the Business Analyst Table were selected instead of the Client table?
The list of available fields would contain fields from the Business Analyst Table rather than the Client table.

Q&A If the list contained Business Analyst Table fields, how could I make it contain Client table fields?
Click the arrow in the Tables/Queries box and then click the Client table in the list that appears.

Figure 1–61

Explanatory callouts summarize what is happening on screen.

Navigational callouts in red show students where to click.

6
- Click the Next button to move to the next Import Spreadsheet Wizard screen (Figure 1–57).

Q&A What happens if I later realize I have selected the wrong table?

If you have not yet clicked the Finish button, you can click the Back button to return to the screen where you selected the table, and then select the correct table.

Figure 1–57

7
- Because the table name is correct, click the Finish button to import the data (Figure 1–58).

Q&A I got an error message that stated that a particular field did not exist in the Client

1–58

Close button

Other Ways
1. Right-click table in Navigation Pane, click Import on shortcut menu.

5
- Press the TAB key to complete the entry for the field.
- Type 3450 in the Incentive YTD field, and then press the TAB key to complete the entry of the first record (Figure 1–25).

Q&A How and when do I save the record?

As soon as you have entered or modified a record and moved to another record, the original record is saved. This is different from other applications. The rows entered in an Excel worksheet, for example, are not saved until the entire worksheet is saved.

Figure 1–25

6
- Use the techniques shown in Steps 3 through 5 to enter the data for the second record (Figure 1–26).

🄿 **Experiment**
- Click the Salary YTD field on either of the records. Be sure the Table Tools Fields tab is selected. Click the Format box arrow and then click each of the formats in the Format box menu to see the effect on the values in the Salary YTD field. When finished, click Currency in the Format box menu.

Figure 1–26

Making Changes to the Data

As you enter data, check your entries carefully to ensure they are correct. If you make a mistake and discover it before you press the TAB key, correct it by pressing the BACKSPACE key until the incorrect characters are removed, and then type the correct characters. If you do not discover a mistake until later, you can use the following techniques to make the necessary corrections to the data:

- To undo your most recent change, click the Undo button on the Quick Access Toolbar. If there is nothing that Access can undo, this button will be dimmed, and clicking it will have no effect.
- To add a record, click the New (blank) record button, click the position for the Business Analyst Number field on the first open record, and then add the record. Do not worry about it being in the correct position in the table. Access will reposition the record based on the primary key, in this case, the Business Analyst Number.

BTW
Adding Records
You can add records in any order. When you close a table and re-open it, the records will be in order by primary key.

Textbook Walk-Through

Break Points identify logical breaks in the chapter if students need to stop before completing the project.

Break Point: If you wish to take a break, this is a good place to do so. You can quit Access now. To resume at a later time, start Access, open the database called Camashaly Design, and continue following the steps from this location forward.

Creating and Printing Reports

Camashaly Design wants to create the Client Financial Report shown in

Chapter Summary

In this chapter you have learned to design a database, create an Access database, create tables and add records to them, print the contents of tables, create queries, create forms, and create reports. You also have learned how to change database properties. The items listed below include all the new Access skills you have learned in this chapter.

Chapter Summary A concluding paragraph, followed by a listing of the tasks completed within a chapter together with the pages on which the step-by-step, screen-by-screen explanations appear.

1. Start Access (AC 12)
2. Create a Database (AC 13)
3. Create a Database Using a Template (AC 14)
4. Modify the Primary Key (AC 16)
5. Define the Remaining Fields in a Table (AC 19)
6. Save a Table (AC 21)
7. View the Table in Design View (AC 21)
8. Close the Table (AC 23)
9. Add Records to a Table (AC 23)
10. Quit Access (AC 26)
11. Open a Database from Access (AC 27)
12. Add Additional Records to a Table (AC 28)
13. Resize Columns in a Datasheet (AC 29)
14. Preview and Print the Contents of a Table (AC 31)
15. Create a Table in Design View (AC 33)
16. Import an Excel Worksheet (AC 38)
17. Use the Simple Query Wizard to Create a Query (AC 43)
18. Use a Criterion in a Query (AC 46)
19. Print the Results of a Query (AC 48)
20. Create a Form (AC 48)
21. Create a Report (AC 52)
22. Modify Column Headings and Resize Columns (AC 54)
23. Add Totals to a Report (AC 57)
24. Change Database Properties (AC 59)
25. Back Up a Database (AC 61)
26. Compact and Repair a Database (AC 61)
27. Open Another Database (AC 62)
28. Close a Database without Exiting Access (AC 62)
29. Save a Database with Another Name (AC 62)
30. Delete a Table or Other Object in the Database (AC 62)
31. Rename an Object in the Database (AC 62)

 If you have a SAM 2010 user profile, your instructor may have assigned an autogradable version of this assignment. If so, log into the SAM 2010 Web site at www.cengage.com/sam2010 to download the instruction and start files.

Learn It Online

Test your knowledge of chapter content and key terms.

Learn It Online Every chapter features a Learn It Online section that is comprised of six exercises. These exercises include True/False, Multiple Choice, Short Answer, Flash Cards, Practice Test, and Learning Games.

Instructions: To complete the Learn It Online exercises, start your browser, click the Address bar, and then enter the Web address `scsite.com/ac2010/learn`. When the Access 2010 Learn It Online page is displayed, click the link for the exercise you want to complete and then read the instructions.

Chapter Reinforcement TF, MC, and SA
A series of true/false, multiple choice, and short answer questions that test your knowledge of the chapter content.

Flash Cards
An interactive learning environment where you identify chapter key terms associated with displayed definitions.

Who Wants To Be a Computer Genius?
An interactive game that challenges your knowledge of chapter content in the style of a television quiz show.

Wheel of Terms
An interactive game that challenges your knowledge of chapter key terms in the style of the television show *Wheel of Fortune.*

Crossword Puzzle Challenge
A crossword puzzle that challenges your knowledge of key terms presented in the chapter.

Apply Your Knowledge

Reinforce the skills and apply the concepts you learned in this chapter.

Adding a Caption, Creating a Query, Creating a Form, and Creating a Report
Instructions: Start Access. Open the Babbage CPA Firm database. See the inside back cover of this book for instructions for downloading the Data Files for Students, or see your instructor for information on accessing the files required in this book.

The Babbage CPA Firm employs bookkeepers who maintain the books for those clients who need bookkeeping services. The Babbage CPA Firm has a database that keeps track of its bookkeepers and clients. Each client is assigned to a single bookkeeper, but each bookkeeper may be assigned many clients. The database has two tables. The Client table contains data on the clients who use the bookkeeping services of the Babbage CPA Firm. The Bookkeeper table contains data on the bookkeepers employed by Babbage CPA Firm.

Perform the following tasks:
1. Open the Bookkeeper table in Design view and add BKR # as the caption for Bookkeeper Number. Save the changes to the table.
2. Open the Bookkeeper table in Datasheet view and resize all columns to best fit the data. Save the changes to the layout of the table.
3. Use the Simple Query Wizard to create a query for the Client table that contains the Client Number, Client Name, Amount Paid, and Balance Due. Use the name, Client Query, for the query.
4. Create a simple form for the Bookkeeper table. Use the name, Bookkeeper, for the form.
5. Close the Bookkeeper form.

Apply Your Knowledge This exercise usually requires students to open and manipulate a file from the Data Files that parallels the activities learned in the chapter. To obtain a copy of the Data Files for Students, follow the instructions on the inside back cover of this text.

Extend Your Knowledge

Extend the skills you learned in this chapter and experiment with new skills. You may need to use Help to complete the assignment.

Using a Database Template to Create a Students Database

Instructions: Access includes a number of templates that you can use to create a beginning database that can be modified to meet your specific needs. You will create a Students database using the Students template. The database includes sample tables, queries, forms, and reports. You will change the database and create the Student Birthdays Query, shown in Figure 1–91.

Figure 1–91

Perform the following tasks:
1. Start Access.
2. With a USB flash drive connected to one of the computer's USB po[...] selected in the Backstage view and select Sample templates in the N[...]
3. Select the Students template and create a new database on your USB d[...]
4. Close the Student List form and change the organization of the Nav[...] Related Views .
5. Delete the Student Details form.
6. Use the Query Wizard to create the query shown in Figure 1–91. S[...] Birthdays Query.
7. Open the Student Phone List in Layout view and use the tools on th[...] Student Phone List title bold and change the font size to 24. Delete [...]
8. Save your changes to the report.
9. Compact the database.
10. Change the database properties, as specified by your instructor. Subr[...] format specified by your instructor.

Make It Right

Analyze a database and correct all errors and/or improve the design.

Correcting Errors in the Table Structure

Instructions: Start Access. Open the Beach Rentals database. See the inside back cover of this book for instructions for downloading the Data Files for Students, or see your instructor for information on accessing the files required in this book.

Beach Rentals is a database containing information on rental properties available at a beach resort. The Rentals table shown in Figure 1–92 contains a number of errors in the table structure. You are to correct these errors before any additional records can be added to the table. The Rental Code field is a Text field that contains a maximum of three characters. The field Address was omitted from the table. The Address field is a Text field with a maximum of 20 characters. It should appear after Rental Code. Only whole numbers should be allowed in the Bedrooms and Bathrooms fields. The column heading Weakly Rental is misspelled, and the field should contain monetary values. The Distance field represents the walking distance from the beach; the field should display two decimal places. The table name should be Rental Units, not Rentals.

Change the database properties, as specified by your instructor. Submit the revised database in the format specified by your instructor.

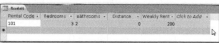

Figure 1–92

![SAM]

In the Lab

Design, create, modify, and/or use a database using the guidelines, concepts, and skills presented in this chapter. Labs are listed in order of increasing difficulty.

Lab 1: Creating Objects for the ECO Clothesline Database

Problem: ECO Clothesline is a local company that designs and manufactures eco-friendly casual wear, yoga clothing, and fitness apparel. All clothes are made from earth-friendly fabrics, such as bamboo, hemp, organic cotton, and natural silk. The company recently decided to store its customer and sales rep data in a database. Each customer is assigned to a single sales rep, but each sales rep may be assigned many customers. The database and the Customer table have been created, but there is no data in the Customer table. The Sales Rep table has not been created. The company plans to import the Customer data from an Excel workbook, shown in Figure 1–93a. The other Excel workbook (Figure 1–93b) contains information on the sales representatives that ECO employs. ECO would like to finish storing this data in a database and has asked for your help.

Instructions: Perform the following tasks: Start Access and open the ECO Clothesline database. See the inside back cover of this book for instructions for downloading the Data Files for Students, or see your instructor for information on accessing the files required in this book.
1. Import the Lab 1-1 Customer Data workbook into the Customer table.
2. Add the captions Cust # to the Customer Number field and SR # to the Sales Rep Number field in the Customer table and save the changes.
3. Open the Customer table in Datasheet view and resize the columns to best fit the data. Save the changes to the layout of the table.
4. Use Datasheet view to create a table in which to store the data related to sales reps. Use the name Sales Rep for the table. The fields and the data for the Sales Rep table are shown in Figure 1–93b.

Extend Your Knowledge projects at the end of each chapter allow students to extend and expand on the skills learned within the chapter. Students use critical thinking to experiment with new skills to complete each project.

Make It Right projects call on students to analyze a file, discover errors in it, and fix them using the skills they learned in the chapter.

Textbook Walk-Through

In the Lab

Lab 2: Creating the Walburg Energy Alternatives Database

Problem: Walburg Energy Alternatives is a nonprofit organization that promotes the use of energy alternatives such as solar power and wind power. The organization provides a variety of services and funds itself through donations. Recently, the organization decided to sell a small number of items in its education center to help fund programs. The store purchases the items from vendors that deal in energy-saving products. Currently, the information about the items and vendors is stored in the Excel workbook shown in Figure 1–95. Each item is assigned to a single vendor, but each vendor may be assigned many items. You volunteer part-time at the store, and the store manager has asked you to create a database that will store the item and vendor information. You have already determined that you need two tables in which to store the information: an Item table and a Vendor table.

Instructions: Perform the following tasks:

1. Design a new database in which to store all the objects related to the items for sale. Call the database Walburg Energy Alternatives.
2. Use the information shown in the Excel workbook in Figure 1–95 to determine the primary keys and determine additional fields. Then, determine the relationships between tables, the data types, and the field sizes.
3. Create the Item table using the information shown in Figure 1–95.
4. Create the Vendor table using the information shown in Figure 1–95. Be sure that the field size for the Vendor Code in the Item table is identical to the field size for the Vendor Code in the Vendor table. Add the caption, Phone, for the Telephone Number field.

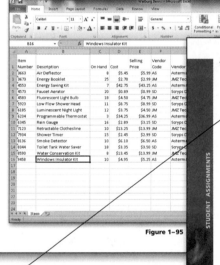

Figure 1–95

In the Lab Three all new in-depth assignments per chapter require students to utilize the chapter concepts and techniques to solve problems on a computer.

Cases and Places

Apply your creative thinking and problem solving skills to design and implement a solution.

See the inside back cover of this book for instructions for downloading the Data Files for Students, or see your instructor for information on accessing the files required in this book.

1: Design and Create an Advertising Database

Academic

You are a Marketing major currently doing an internship with the Chamber of Commerce in a local city. The Chamber publishes a Newcomer's Guide that contains advertisements from local businesses. Ad reps contact the businesses to arrange for advertising. Each advertiser is assigned to a single ad rep, but each ad rep may be assigned many advertisers. The Chamber would like your help in creating a database of advertisers and advertising representatives.

Based on the information in the Case 1-1 Chamber of Commerce workbook, use the concepts and techniques presented in this chapter to design and create a database to store the data that the Chamber needs. Submit your assignment in the format specified by your instructor.

2: Design and Create a Consignment Database

Personal

You are involved in a volunteer organization that provides clothing and school supplies to needy children. Recently, the Board of Directors decided to open a consignment shop as a way to raise additional funds. In a consignment shop, individuals bring in unwanted items, and the shop sells the items. Proceeds are split between the seller and the shop. The database must keep track of the items for sale in the shop as well as maintain data on the sellers. Each item is assigned to a single seller, but each seller may be assigned many items. The Board has asked you to create a database to store information about the consignment items.

Use the concepts and techniques presented in this chapter to design and create a database to store the consignment data. Then create the necessary tables and enter the data from the Case 1-2 Consignment workbook. Create an Available Items Report that lists the item number, description, price, and seller code. Submit your assignment in the format specified by your instructor.

3: Design and Create a Senior Care Database

Professional

You are co-owner of a company, Senior Care, that provides nonmedical services to older adults who need assistance with daily living. Helpers will drive individuals to appointments, do the grocery shopping, fill prescriptions, help with personal care, and provide companionship. Each client is assigned to a single helper, but each helper may be assigned many clients. The other owners have asked you to create a database of clients and helpers. Use the concepts and techniques presented in this chapter to design and create a database to meet Senior Care needs. Then create the necessary tables and enter the data from the Case 1-3 Senior Care workbook. Create a Client Report that lists each client's client number, client last name, client first name, balance, and helper number. Submit your assignment in the format specified by your instructor.

Cases & Places exercises call on students to create open-ended projects that reflect academic, personal, and business settings.

Microsoft® ACCESS® 2010
COMPREHENSIVE

Office 2010 and Windows 7: Essential Concepts and Skills

Objectives

You will have mastered the material in this chapter when you can:

- Perform basic mouse operations
- Start Windows and log on to the computer
- Identify the objects on the Windows 7 desktop
- Identify the programs in and versions of Microsoft Office
- Start a program
- Identify the components of the Microsoft Office Ribbon

- Create folders
- Save files
- Change screen resolution
- Perform basic tasks in Microsoft Office programs
- Manage files
- Use Microsoft Office Help and Windows Help

Office 2010 and Windows 7: Essential Concepts and Skills

Office 2010 and Windows 7

This introductory chapter uses Access 2010 to cover features and functions common to Office 2010 programs, as well as the basics of Windows 7.

Overview

As you read this chapter, you will learn how to perform basic tasks in Windows and Access by performing these general activities:

- Start programs using Windows.
- Use features in Access that are common across Office programs.
- Organize files and folders.
- Change screen resolution.
- Quit programs.

Introduction to the Windows 7 Operating System

Windows 7 is the newest version of Microsoft Windows, which is the most popular and widely used operating system. An **operating system** is a computer program (set of computer instructions) that coordinates all the activities of computer hardware such as memory, storage devices, and printers, and provides the capability for you to communicate with the computer.

The Windows 7 operating system simplifies the process of working with documents and programs by organizing the manner in which you interact with the computer. Windows 7 is used to run **application software**, which consists of programs designed to make users more productive and/or assist them with personal tasks, such as database management.

Windows 7 has two interface variations, Windows 7 Basic and Windows 7 Aero. Computers with up to 1 GB of RAM display the Windows 7 Basic interface (Figure 1a). Computers with more than 1 GB of RAM also can display the Windows Aero interface (Figure 1b), which provides an enhanced visual appearance. The Windows 7 Professional, Windows 7 Enterprise, Windows 7 Home Premium, and Windows 7 Ultimate editions have the capability to use Windows Aero.

Using a Mouse

Windows users work with a mouse that has at least two buttons. For a right-handed user, the left button usually is the primary mouse button, and the right mouse button is the secondary mouse button. Left-handed people, however, can reverse the function of these buttons.

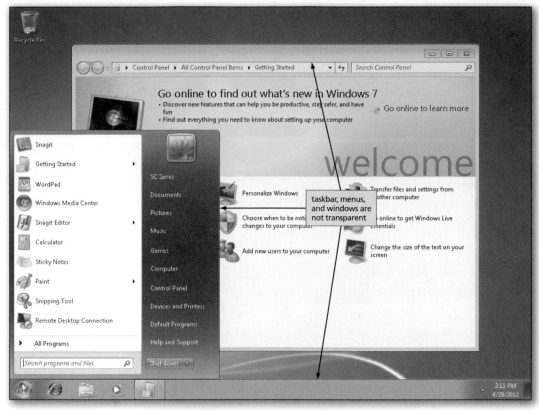

(a) Windows 7 Basic interface

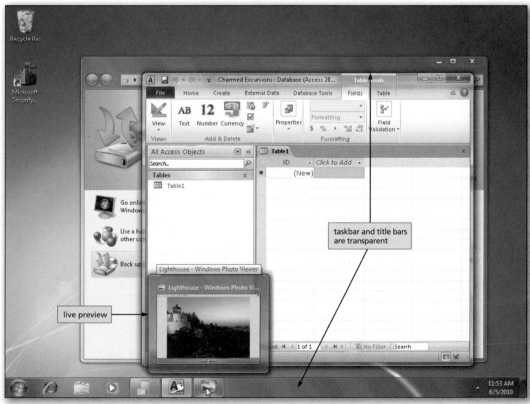

(b) Windows 7 Aero interface

Figure 1

Table 1 explains how to perform a variety of mouse operations. Some programs also use keys in combination with the mouse to perform certain actions. For example, when you hold down the CTRL key while rolling the mouse wheel, text on the screen becomes larger or smaller based on the direction you roll the wheel. The function of the mouse buttons and the wheel varies depending on the program.

Table 1 Mouse Operations		
Operation	**Mouse Action**	**Example***
Point	Move the mouse until the pointer on the desktop is positioned on the item of choice.	Position the pointer on the screen.
Click	Press and release the primary mouse button, which usually is the left mouse button.	Select or deselect items on the screen or start a program or program feature.
Right-click	Press and release the secondary mouse button, which usually is the right mouse button.	Display a shortcut menu.
Double-click	Quickly press and release the left mouse button twice without moving the mouse.	Start a program or program feature.
Triple-click	Quickly press and release the left mouse button three times without moving the mouse.	Select a paragraph.
Drag	Point to an item, hold down the left mouse button, move the item to the desired location on the screen, and then release the left mouse button.	Move an object from one location to another or draw pictures.
Right-drag	Point to an item, hold down the right mouse button, move the item to the desired location on the screen, and then release the right mouse button.	Display a shortcut menu after moving an object from one location to another.
Rotate wheel	Roll the wheel forward or backward.	Scroll vertically (up and down).
Free-spin wheel	Whirl the wheel forward or backward so that it spins freely on its own.	Scroll through many pages in seconds.
Press wheel	Press the wheel button while moving the mouse.	Scroll continuously.
Tilt wheel	Press the wheel toward the right or left.	Scroll horizontally (left and right).
Press thumb button	Press the button on the side of the mouse with your thumb.	Move forward or backward through Web pages and/or control media, games, etc.

*Note: The examples presented in this column are discussed as they are demonstrated in this chapter.

Scrolling

Minimize Wrist Injury Computer users frequently switch between the keyboard and the mouse during a database management session; such switching strains the wrist. To help prevent wrist injury, minimize switching. For instance, if your fingers already are on the keyboard, use keyboard keys to scroll. If your hand already is on the mouse, use the mouse to scroll.

A **scroll bar** is a horizontal or vertical bar that appears when the contents of an area may not be visible completely on the screen (Figure 2). A scroll bar contains **scroll arrows** and a **scroll box** that enable you to view areas that currently cannot be seen. Clicking the up and down scroll arrows moves the screen content up or down one line. You also can click above or below the scroll box to move up or down a section, or drag the scroll box up or down to move up or down to move to a specific location.

Shortcut Keys

In many cases, you can use the keyboard instead of the mouse to accomplish a task. To perform tasks using the keyboard, you press one or more keyboard keys, sometimes identified as

Figure 2

a **shortcut key** or **keyboard shortcut**. Some shortcut keys consist of a single key, such as the F1 key. For example, to obtain help about Windows 7, you can press the F1 key. Other shortcut keys consist of multiple keys, in which case a plus sign separates the key names, such as CTRL+ESC. This notation means to press and hold down the first key listed, press one or more additional keys, and then release all keys. For example, to display the Start menu, press CTRL+ESC, that is, hold down the CTRL key, press the ESC key, and then release both keys.

Starting Windows 7

It is not unusual for multiple people to use the same computer in a work, educational, recreational, or home setting. Windows 7 enables each user to establish a **user account**, which identifies to Windows 7 the resources, such as programs and storage locations, a user can access when working with a computer.

Each user account has a user name and may have a password and an icon, as well. A **user name** is a unique combination of letters or numbers that identifies a specific user to Windows 7. A **password** is a private combination of letters, numbers, and special characters associated with the user name that allows access to a user's account resources. A **user icon** is a picture associated with a user name.

When you turn on a computer, an introductory screen consisting of the Windows logo and copyright messages is displayed. The Windows logo is animated and glows as the Windows 7 operating system is loaded. After the Windows logo appears, depending on your computer's settings, you may or may not be required to log on to the computer. **Logging on** to a computer opens your user account and makes the computer available for use. If you are required to log on to the computer, the **Welcome screen** is displayed, which shows the user names of users on the computer (Figure 3). Clicking the user name or picture begins the process of logging on to the computer.

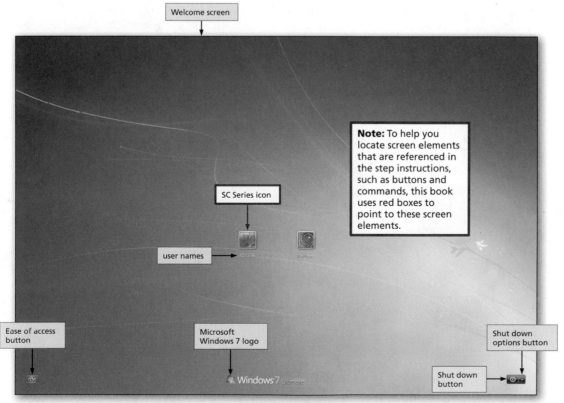

Figure 3

At the bottom of the Welcome screen is the 'Ease of access' button, the Windows 7 logo, a Shut down button, and a 'Shut down options' button. The following list identifies the functions of the buttons and commands that typically appear on the Welcome screen:

- Clicking the 'Ease of access' button displays the Ease of Access Center, which provides tools to optimize your computer to accommodate the needs of the mobility, hearing, and vision impaired users.

- Clicking the Shut down button shuts down Windows 7 and the computer.

- Clicking the 'Shut down options' button, located to the right of the Shut down button, displays a menu containing commands that perform actions such as restarting the computer, placing the computer in a low-powered state, and shutting down the computer. The commands available on your computer may differ.

  - The **Restart command** closes open programs, shuts down Windows 7, and then restarts Windows 7 and displays the Welcome screen.

  - The **Sleep command** waits for Windows 7 to save your work and then turns off the computer fans and hard disk. To wake the computer from the Sleep state, press the power button or lift a notebook computer's cover, and log on to the computer.

  - The **Shut down command** shuts down and turns off the computer.

To Log On to the Computer

After starting Windows 7, you might need to log on to the computer. The following steps log on to the computer based on a typical installation. You may need to ask your instructor how to log on to your computer. This set of steps uses SC Series as the user name. The list of user names on your computer will be different.

- Click the user icon (SC Series, in this case) on the Welcome screen (shown in Figure 3 on the previous page); depending on settings, this either will display a password text box (Figure 4) or will log on to the computer and display the Windows 7 desktop.

Q&A Why do I not see a user icon?

Your computer may require you to type a user name instead of clicking an icon.

Q&A What is a text box?

A text box is a rectangular box in which you type text.

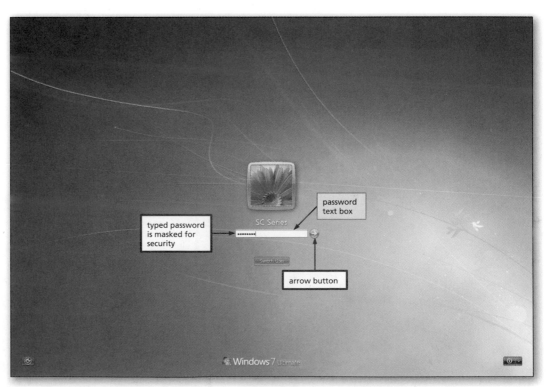

Figure 4

Q&A Why does my screen not show a password text box?

Your account does not require a password.

2

- If Windows 7 displays a password text box, type your password in the text box and then click the arrow button to log on to the computer and display the Windows 7 desktop (Figure 5).

Q&A

Why does my desktop look different from the one in Figure 5?

The Windows 7 desktop is customizable, and your school or employer may have modified the desktop to meet its needs. Also, your screen resolution, which affects the size of the elements on the screen, may differ from the screen resolution used in this book. Later in this chapter, you learn how to change screen resolution.

Figure 5

The Windows 7 Desktop

The Windows 7 desktop (Figure 5) and the objects on the desktop emulate a work area in an office. Think of the Windows desktop as an electronic version of the top of your desk. You can perform tasks such as placing objects on the desktop, moving the objects around the desktop, and removing items from the desktop.

When you start a program in Windows 7, it appears on the desktop. Some icons also may be displayed on the desktop. For instance, the icon for the **Recycle Bin**, the location of files that have been deleted, appears on the desktop by default. A **file** is a named unit of storage. Files can contain text, images, audio, and video. You can customize your desktop so that icons representing programs and files you use often appear on your desktop.

Introduction to Microsoft Office 2010

Microsoft Office 2010 is the newest version of Microsoft Office, offering features that provide users with better functionality and easier ways to work with the various files they create. These features include enhanced design tools, such as improved picture formatting tools and new themes, shared notebooks for working in groups, mobile versions of Office programs, broadcast presentation for the Web, and a digital notebook for managing and sharing multimedia information.

Microsoft Office 2010 Programs

Microsoft Office 2010 includes a wide variety of programs such as Word, PowerPoint, Excel, Access, Outlook, Publisher, OneNote, InfoPath, SharePoint Workspace, Communicator, and Web Apps:

- **Microsoft Word 2010**, or Word, is a full-featured word processing program that allows you to create professional-looking documents and revise them easily.
- **Microsoft PowerPoint 2010**, or PowerPoint, is a complete presentation program that allows you to produce professional-looking presentations.
- **Microsoft Excel 2010**, or Excel, is a powerful spreadsheet program that allows you to organize data, complete calculations, make decisions, graph data, develop professional-looking reports, publish organized data to the Web, and access real-time data from Web sites.
- **Microsoft Access 2010**, or Access, is a database management system that allows you to create a database; add, change, and delete data in the database; ask questions concerning the data in the database; and create forms and reports using the data in the database.
- **Microsoft Outlook 2010**, or Outlook, is a communications and scheduling program that allows you to manage e-mail accounts, calendars, contacts, and access to other Internet content.
- **Microsoft Publisher 2010**, or Publisher, is a desktop publishing program that helps you create professional-quality publications and marketing materials that can be shared easily.
- **Microsoft OneNote 2010**, or OneNote, is a note taking program that allows you to store and share information in notebooks with other people.
- **Microsoft InfoPath 2010**, or InfoPath, is a form development program that helps you create forms for use on the Web and gather data from these forms.
- **Microsoft SharePoint Workspace 2010**, or SharePoint, is collaboration software that allows you to access and revise files stored on your computer from other locations.
- **Microsoft Communicator** is communications software that allows you to use different modes of communications such as instant messaging, video conferencing, and sharing files and programs.
- **Microsoft Web Apps** is a Web application that allows you to edit and share files on the Web using the familiar Office interface.

Microsoft Office 2010 Suites

A **suite** is a collection of individual programs available together as a unit. Microsoft offers a variety of Office suites. Table 2 lists the Office 2010 suites and their components.

Programs in a suite, such as Microsoft Office, typically use a similar interface and share features. In addition, Microsoft Office programs use **common dialog boxes** for performing actions such as opening and saving files. Once you are comfortable working with these elements and this interface and performing tasks in one program, the similarity can help you apply the knowledge and skills you have learned to another Office program(s). For example, the process for saving a file in Word is the same in PowerPoint, Excel, and the other Office programs.

Table 2 Microsoft Office 2010 Suites	Microsoft Office Professional Plus 2010	Microsoft Office Professional 2010	Microsoft Office Home and Business 2010	Microsoft Office Standard 2010	Microsoft Office Home and Student 2010
Microsoft Word 2010	✔	✔	✔	✔	✔
Microsoft PowerPoint 2010	✔	✔	✔	✔	✔
Microsoft Excel 2010	✔	✔	✔	✔	✔
Microsoft Access 2010	✔	✔	✗	✗	✗
Microsoft Outlook 2010	✔	✔	✔	✔	✗
Microsoft Publisher 2010	✔	✔	✗	✔	✗
Microsoft OneNote 2010	✔	✔	✔	✔	✔
Microsoft InfoPath 2010	✔	✗	✗	✗	✗
Microsoft SharePoint Workspace 2010	✔	✗	✗	✗	✗
Microsoft Communicator	✔	✗	✗	✗	✗

Starting and Using a Program

To use a program, such as Access, you must instruct the operating system to start the program. Windows 7 provides many different ways to start a program, one of which is presented in this section (other ways to start a program are presented throughout this chapter). After starting a program, you can use it to perform a variety of tasks. The following pages use Access to discuss some elements of the Office interface and to perform tasks that are common to other Office programs.

Access

The term **database** describes a collection of data organized in a manner that allows access, retrieval, and use of that data. **Microsoft Access 2010**, usually referred to as simply **Access**, is a database management system. A **database management system** is software that allows you to use a computer to create a database; add, change, and delete data in the database; create queries that allow you to ask questions concerning the data in the database; and create forms and reports using the data in the database.

To Start a Program Using the Start Menu

Across the bottom of the Windows 7 desktop is the taskbar. The taskbar contains the **Start button**, which you use to access programs, files, folders, and settings on a computer. A **folder** is a named location on a storage medium that usually contains related documents. The taskbar also displays a button for each program currently running on a computer.

Clicking the Start button displays the Start menu. The **Start menu** allows you to access programs, folders, and files on the computer and contains commands that allow you to start programs, store and search for documents, customize the computer, and obtain help about thousands of topics. A **menu** is a list of related items, including folders, programs, and commands. Each **command** on a menu performs a specific action, such as saving a file or obtaining help.

The following steps, which assume Windows 7 is running, use the Start menu to start the Microsoft Access 2010 program based on a typical installation. You may need to ask your instructor how to start Access for your computer.

❶

- Click the Start button on the Windows 7 taskbar to display the Start menu (Figure 6).

Q&A Why does my Start menu look different?

It may look different depending on your computer's configuration. The Start menu may be customized for several reasons, such as usage requirements or security restrictions.

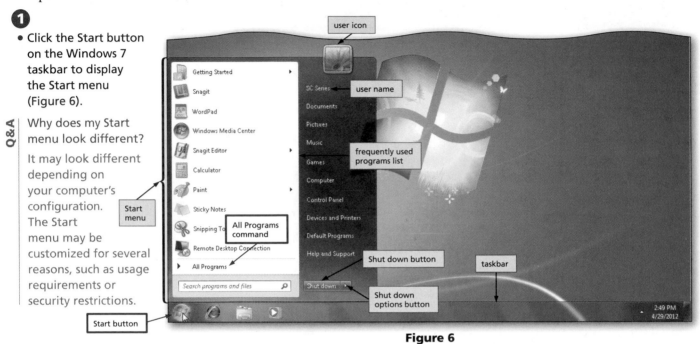

Figure 6

❷

- Click All Programs at the bottom of the left pane on the Start menu to display the All Programs list (Figure 7).

Q&A What is a pane?

A **pane** is an area of a window that displays related content. For example, the left pane on the Start menu contains a list of frequently used programs, as well as the All Programs command.

Q&A Why might my All Programs list look different?

Most likely, the programs installed on your computer will differ from those shown in Figure 7. Your All Programs list will show the programs that are installed on your computer.

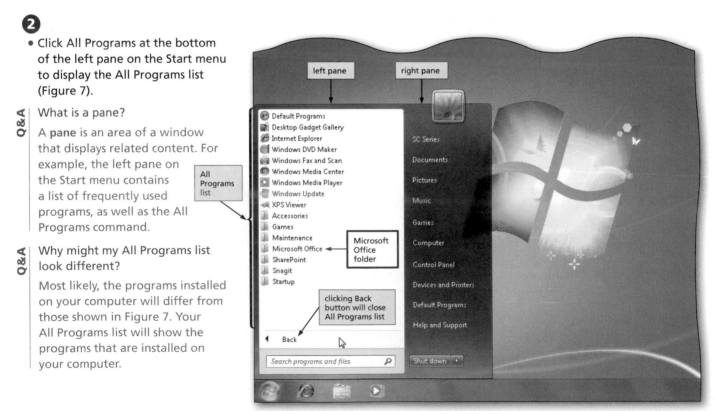

Figure 7

3

- If the program you want to start is located in a folder, click or scroll to and then click the folder (Microsoft Office, in this case) in the All Programs list to display a list of the folder's contents (Figure 8).

Q&A

Why is the Microsoft Office folder on my computer?

During installation of Microsoft Office 2010, the Microsoft Office folder was added to the All Programs list.

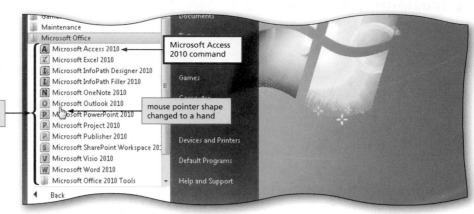

Figure 8

4

- Click, or scroll to and then click, the program name (Microsoft Access 2010, in this case) in the list to start the selected program (Figure 9).

Q&A

What happens when you start a program?

Many programs initially display a blank document in a program window, others provide a means for you to create a blank document or new database. A window is a rectangular area that displays data and information. The top of a window has a **title bar**, which is a horizontal space that contains the window's name.

Figure 9

Q&A

Why is my program window a different size?

The Access window shown in Figure 9 is not maximized. Your Access window already may be maximized. The steps on the next page maximize a window.

Other Ways

1. Double-click program icon on desktop, if one is present

2. Click program name in left pane of Start menu, if present

3. Display Start menu, type program name in search box, click program name

4. Double-click file created using program you want to start

To Maximize a Window

Sometimes content is not visible completely in a window. One method of displaying the entire contents of a window is to **maximize** it, or enlarge the window so that it fills the entire screen. The following step maximizes the Access window; however, any Office program's window can be maximized using this step.

- If the program window is not maximized already, click the Maximize button (shown in Figure 9 on the previous page) next to the Close button on the window's title bar (the Access window title bar, in this case) to maximize the window (Figure 10).

Q&A What happened to the Maximize button?

It changed to a Restore Down button, which you can use to return a window to its size and location before you maximized it.

Q&A How do I know whether a window is maximized?

A window is maximized if it fills the entire display area and the Restore Down button is displayed on the title bar.

Figure 10

Other Ways
1. Double-click title bar
2. Drag title bar to top of screen

Saving and Organizing Files

While you are creating a document, the computer stores it in memory. When you save a document, the computer places it on a storage medium such as a hard disk, USB flash drive, or optical disc. A saved document is referred to as a file. A **file name** is the name assigned to a file when it is saved. It is important to save a document frequently for the following reasons:

- The document in memory might be lost if the computer is turned off or you lose electrical power while a program is running.
- If you run out of time before completing a project, you may finish it at a future time without starting over.

When saving files, you should organize them so that you easily can find them later. Windows 7 provides tools to help you organize files.

Organizing Files and Folders

A file contains data. This data can range from a database to an accounting spreadsheet to an electronic math quiz. You should organize and store these files in folders to avoid misplacing a file and to help you find a file quickly.

If you are a freshman taking an introductory computer class (CIS 101, for example), you may want to design a series of folders for the different subjects covered in the class. To accomplish this, you can arrange the folders in a hierarchy for the class, as shown in Figure 11.

The hierarchy contains three levels. The first level contains the storage device, in this case a USB flash drive. Windows 7 identifies the storage device with a letter, and, in some cases, a name. In Figure 11, the USB flash drive is identified as REMOVABLE (E:). The second level contains the class folder (CIS 101, in this case), and the third level contains seven folders, one each for a different Office program that will be covered in the class (Word, PowerPoint, Excel, Access, Outlook, Publisher, and OneNote).

When the hierarchy in Figure 11 is created, the USB flash drive is said to contain the CIS 101 folder, and the CIS 101 folder is said to contain the separate Office folders (i.e., Word, PowerPoint, Excel, etc.). In addition, this hierarchy easily can be expanded to include folders from other classes taken during additional semesters.

Figure 11

The vertical and horizontal lines in Figure 11 form a pathway that allows you to navigate to a drive or folder on a computer or network. A **path** consists of a drive letter (preceded by a drive name when necessary) and colon, to identify the storage device, and one or more folder names. Each drive or folder in the hierarchy has a corresponding path.

Table 3 shows examples of paths and their corresponding drives and folders.

Table 3 Paths and Corresponding Drives and Folders	
Path	**Drive and Folder**
Computer ▶ RFMOVABLE (E:)	Drive E (REMOVABLE (E:))
Computer ▶ REMOVABLE (E:) ▶ CIS 101	CIS 101 folder on drive E
Computer ▶ REMOVABLE (E:) ▶ CIS 101 ▶ Access	Access folder in CIS 101 folder on drive E

The following pages illustrate the steps to organize folders for a class and save a file in a folder:

1. Create a folder identifying your class.
2. Create an Access folder in the folder identifying your class.
3. Save a file in the Access folder.
4. Verify the location of the saved file.

BTW

Saving Online
Instead of saving files on a USB flash drive, some people prefer to save them online so that they can access the files from any computer with an Internet connection.

To Create a Folder

When you create a folder, such as the CIS 101 folder shown in Figure 11, you must name the folder. A folder name should describe the folder and its contents. A folder name can contain spaces and any uppercase or lowercase characters, except a backslash (\), slash (/), colon (:), asterisk (*), question mark (?), quotation marks ("), less than symbol (<), greater than symbol (>), or vertical bar (I). Folder names cannot be CON, AUX, COM1, COM2, COM3, COM4, LPT1, LPT2, LPT3, PRN, or NUL. The same rules for naming folders also apply to naming files.

To store files and folders on a USB flash drive, you must connect the USB flash drive to an available USB port on a computer. The following steps create your class folder (CIS 101, in this case) on a USB flash drive.

1

- Connect the USB flash drive to an available USB port on the computer to open the AutoPlay window (Figure 12). (You may need to click the Windows Explorer program button on the taskbar to make the AutoPlay window visible.)

Q&A Why does the AutoPlay window not open?

Some computers are not configured to open an AutoPlay window. Instead, they might display the contents of the USB flash drive automatically, or you might need to access contents of the USB flash drive using the Computer window. To use the Computer window to display the USB flash drive's contents, click the Start button, click Computer on the Start menu, and then click the icon representing the USB flash drive and then proceed to Step 3 on the next page.

Q&A Why does the AutoPlay window look different from the one in Figure 12?

The AutoPlay window that opens on your computer might display different options. The type of USB flash drive, its contents, and the next available drive letter on your computer all will determine which options are displayed in the AutoPlay window.

Figure 12

2

- Click the 'Open folder to view files' link in the AutoPlay window to open the USB flash drive window (Figure 13).

Q&A Why does Figure 13 show REMOVABLE (E:) for the USB flash drive?

REMOVABLE is the name of the USB flash drive used to illustrate these steps. The (E:) refers to the drive letter assigned by Windows 7 to the USB flash drive. The name and drive letter of your USB flash drive probably will be different.

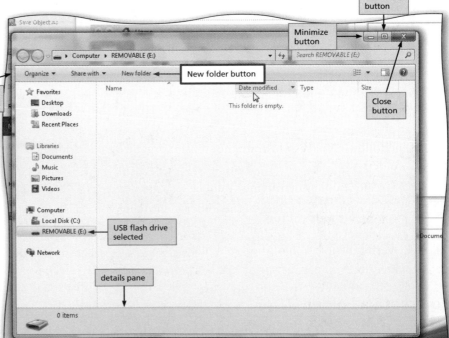

Figure 13

3

- Click the New folder button on the toolbar to display a new folder icon with the name, New folder, selected in a text box.

- Type CIS 101 (or your class code) in the text box to name the folder.

- Press the ENTER key to create a folder identifying your class on the selected drive (Figure 14). If the CIS 101 folder does not appear in the navigation pane, double-click REMOVABLE (E:) in the navigation pane to display the folder just added.

Q&A | What happens when I press the ENTER key?

The class folder (CIS 101, in this case) is displayed in the File list, which contains the folder name, date modified, type, and size.

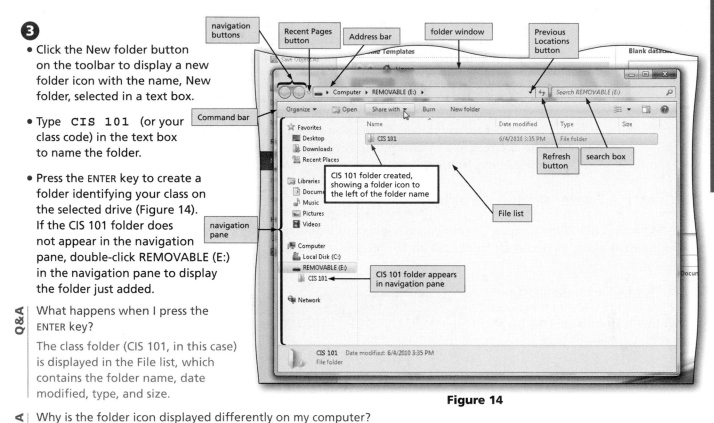

Figure 14

Q&A | Why is the folder icon displayed differently on my computer?

Windows might be configured to display contents differently on your computer.

Folder Windows

The USB flash drive window (shown in Figure 14) is called a folder window. Recall that a folder is a specific named location on a storage medium that contains related files. Most users rely on **folder windows** for finding, viewing, and managing information on their computer. Folder windows have common design elements, including the following (Figure 14):

- The **Address bar** provides quick navigation options. The arrows on the Address bar allow you to visit different locations on the computer.
- The buttons to the left of the Address bar allow you to navigate the contents of the left pane and view recent pages. Other buttons allow you to specify the size of the window.
- The **Previous Locations button** saves the locations you have visited and displays the locations when clicked.
- The **Refresh button** on the right side of the Address bar refreshes the contents of the right pane of the folder window.
- The **search box** to the right of the Address bar contains the dimmed word, Search. You can type a term in the search box for a list of files, folders, shortcuts, and elements containing that term within the location you are searching. A **shortcut** is an icon on the desktop that provides a user with immediate access to a program or file.
- The **Command bar** contains five buttons used to accomplish various tasks on the computer related to organizing and managing the contents of the open window.
- The **navigation pane** on the left contains the Favorites area, Libraries area, Computer area, and Network area.

• The **Favorites area** contains links to your favorite locations. By default, this list contains only links to your Desktop, Downloads, and Recent Places.
• The **Libraries area** shows links to files and folders that have been included in a library.

A **library** helps you manage multiple folders and files stored in various locations on a computer. It does not store the files and folders; rather, it displays links to them so that you can access them quickly. For example, you can save pictures from a digital camera in any folder on any storage location on a computer. Normally, this would make organizing the different folders difficult; however, if you add the folders to a library, you can access all the pictures from one location regardless of where they are stored.

To Create a Folder within a Folder

With the class folder created, you can create folders that will store the files you create using Access. The following steps create an Access folder in the CIS 101 folder (or the folder identifying your class).

1
• Double-click the icon or folder name for the CIS 101 folder (or the folder identifying your class) in the File list to open the folder (Figure 15).

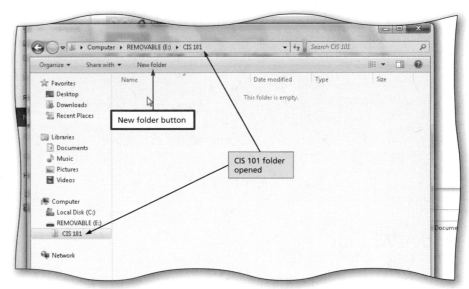

Figure 15

2
• Click the New folder button on the toolbar to display a new folder icon and text box for the folder.

• Type **Access** in the text box to name the folder.

• Press the ENTER key to create the folder (Figure 16).

Figure 16

To Expand a Folder, Scroll through Folder Contents, and Collapse a Folder

Folder windows display the hierarchy of items and the contents of drives and folders in the right pane. You might want to expand a drive in the navigation pane to view its contents, scroll through its contents, and collapse it when you are finished viewing its contents. When a folder is expanded, it lists all the folders it contains. By contrast, a collapsed folder does not list the folders it contains. The steps on the next page expand, scroll through, and then collapse the folder identifying your class (CIS 101, in this case).

1

- Double-click the folder identifying your class (CIS 101, in this case) in the navigation pane, which expands the folder to display its contents and displays a black arrow to the left of the folder icon (Figure 17).

Q&A Why is the Access folder indented below the CIS 101 folder in the navigation pane?

It shows that the folder is contained within the CIS 101 folder.

Q&A Why did a scroll bar appear in the navigation pane?

When all contents cannot fit in a window or pane, a scroll bar appears. As described earlier, you can view areas currently not visible by (1) clicking the scroll arrows, (2) clicking above or below the scroll bar, and (3) dragging the scroll box.

Figure 17

 Experiment

- If a scroll bar appears on your screen, click the down scroll arrow on the vertical scroll bar to display additional content at the bottom of the navigation pane.

- If a scroll bar appears on your screen, click the scroll bar above the scroll box to move the scroll box to the top of the navigation pane.

- If a scroll bar appears on your screen, drag the scroll box down the scroll bar until the scroll box is halfway down the scroll bar.

2

- Double-click the folder identifying your class (CIS 101, in this case) in the navigation pane to collapse the folder (Figure 18).

Figure 18

Other Ways	
1. Point in navigation pane to display arrows, click white arrow to expand or click black arrow to collapse	2. Select folder to expand or collapse using arrow keys, press RIGHT ARROW to expand; press LEFT ARROW to collapse

To Switch from One Program to Another

The next step is to create the database. Access, however, currently is not the active window. You can use the program button on the taskbar and live preview to switch to Access and then save the database in Access.

If Windows Aero is active on your computer, Windows displays a live preview window whenever you move your mouse on a button or click a button on the taskbar. If Aero is not supported or enabled on your computer, you will see a window title instead of a live preview. These steps use the Access program; however, the steps are the same for any active Office program currently displayed as a program button on the taskbar.

The next steps switch to the Access window.

- Point to the Access program button on the taskbar to see a live preview of the open document(s) or the window title(s) of the open document(s), depending on your computer's configuration (Figure 19).

Figure 19

- Click the program button or the live preview to make the program associated with the program button the active window (Figure 20).

Figure 20

To Create an Access Database

Unlike the other Office programs, Access saves a database when you first create it. When working in Access, you will add data to an Access database. As you add data to a database, Access automatically saves your changes rather than waiting until you manually save the database or quit Access. Recall that in Word and Excel, you entered the data first and then saved it.

Because Access automatically saves the database as you add and change data, you do not have to always click the Save button. In fact, the Save button in Access is used for saving the objects (including tables, queries, forms, reports, and other database objects) a database contains. You can use either the Blank database option or a template to create a new database. If you already know the organization of your database, you would use the Blank database option. If not, you can use a template. Templates can guide you by suggesting some commonly used databases that are available to use.

The following steps use the Blank database option to create a database named Charmed Excursions in the Access folder in the class folder (CIS 101, in this case) on a USB flash drive.

- If necessary, click the Blank database button in the New gallery (shown in Figure 20) in the Backstage view to select the template type.

- Click the File Name text box to select the default database name.

- Type **Charmed Excursions** in the File Name text box to enter the new file name. Do not press the ENTER key after typing the file name because you do not want to create the database at this time (Figure 21).

Figure 21

Why is the Backstage view automatically open when you start Access?

Unlike other Office programs, you first must save a database before adding any data. For this reason, the Backstage view opens automatically when you start Access.

- Click the 'Browse for a location to put your database' button to display the File New Database dialog box.

- Navigate to the desired save location (in this case, the Access folder in the CIS 101 folder [or your class folder] on the USB flash drive) by performing the tasks in Steps 2a, 2b, and 2c.

2a

- If the navigation pane is not displayed in the dialog box, click the Browse Folders button to expand the dialog box.

- If Computer is not displayed in the navigation pane, drag the navigation pane scroll bar until Computer appears.

- If Computer is not expanded in the navigation pane, double-click Computer to display a list of available storage devices in the navigation pane.

- If necessary, scroll through the dialog box until your USB flash drive appears in the list of available storage devices in the navigation pane (Figure 22).

Figure 22

2b

- If your USB flash drive is not expanded, double-click the USB flash drive in the list of available storage devices in the navigation pane to select that drive as the new save location and display its contents in the right pane.

2c

- If your class folder (CIS 101, in this case) is not expanded, double-click the CIS 101 folder to select the folder and display its contents in the right pane.

Q&A

What if I do not want to save in a folder?

Although storing files in folders is an effective technique for organizing files, some users prefer not to store files in folders. If you prefer not to save this file in a folder, skip all instructions in Step 2c and proceed to Step 3.

- Click the Access folder to select the folder and display its contents in the right pane (Figure 23).

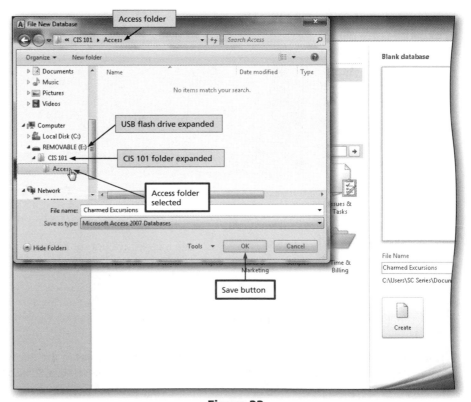

Figure 23

Q&A

Why does the 'Save as type' box say Microsoft Access 2007 Databases?

Microsoft Access database formats change with some new versions of Microsoft Access. The most recent format is the Microsoft Access 2007 Databases format, which was released with Access 2007.

3

• Click the OK button (File New Database dialog box) to select the Access folder as the location for the database and close the dialog box (Figure 24).

Figure 24

4

• Click the Create button in the Backstage view to create the database on the selected drive in the selected folder with the file name, Charmed Excursions. If necessary, click the Enable Content option button (Figure 25).

Q&A

How do I know that the Charmed Excursions database is created?

The name of the database appears on the title bar.

Figure 25

To Close an Office File Using the Backstage View

Sometimes, you may want to close an Office file, such as an Access database, entirely and start over with a new file. You also may want to close a file when you are finished working with it so that you can begin a new file. The following steps close the current active Office file, that is, the Charmed Excursions database, without quitting the active program (Access, in this case).

1

- Click File on the Ribbon to open the Backstage view (Figure 26).

2

- Click Close Database in the Backstage view to close the open file (Charmed Excursions, in this case) without quitting the active program.

Q&A What if the Office program displays a dialog box about saving?

Click the Save button if you want to save the changes, click the Don't Save button if you want to ignore the changes since the last time you saved, and click the Cancel button if you do not want to close the document.

Q&A Can I use the Backstage view to close an open file in other Office programs, such as Word and Excel?

Yes.

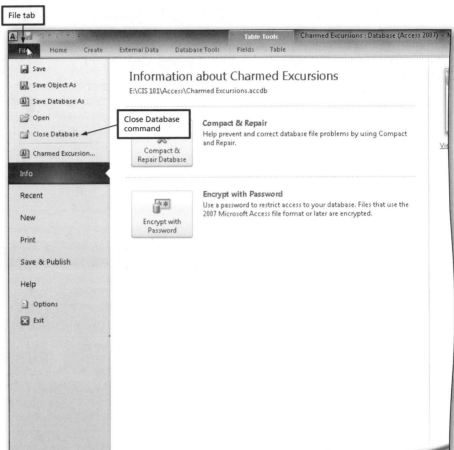

Figure 26

Unique Elements in Access

You work on objects such as tables, forms, and reports in the **Access work area**. In Figure 25 on the previous page, the Access window contains one open object. Figure 27 shows a work area with multiple objects open. **Object tabs** for the open objects appear at the top of the work area. You select an open object by clicking its tab. In the figure, the Suppliers Split Form is the selected object. To the left of the work area is the Navigation Pane, which contains a list of all the objects in the database. You use this pane to open an object. You also can customize the way objects are displayed in the Navigation Pane.

Because the Navigation Pane can take up space in the window, you may not have as much open space for working as you would with Word or Excel. You can use the Shutter Bar Open/Close Button to minimize the Navigation Pane when you are not using it, which allows more space to work with tables, forms, reports, and other database elements.

Figure 27

The Access Window, Ribbon, and Elements Common to Office Programs

Scroll Bars   You use a scroll bar to display different portions of an object in the work area. At the right edge of the work area is a vertical scroll bar. If an object is too wide to fit in the document window, a horizontal scroll bar also appears at the bottom of the work area. On a scroll bar, the position of the scroll box reflects the location of the portion of the object that is displayed in the work area.

Status Bar   The **Status bar**, located at the bottom of the Access window above the Windows 7 taskbar, presents information about the object as well as controls for viewing the document. As you type text or perform certain tasks, various indicators and buttons may appear on the Status bar.

The left side of the Status bar in Figure 25 shows the current object. The right side of the Status bar includes buttons you can use to change the view of an object.

Ribbon   The Ribbon, located near the top of the window below the title bar, is the control center in Access and other Office programs (Figure 28 on the next page). The Ribbon provides easy, central access to the tasks you perform while creating a document. The Ribbon consists of tabs, groups, and commands. Each **tab** contains a collection of groups, and each **group** contains related functions. When you start an Office program, such as Access, it initially displays several main tabs, also called default tabs. All Office programs have a **Home tab**, which contains the more frequently used commands.

In addition to the main tabs, Office programs display **tool tabs**, also called contextual tabs (Figure 28), when you perform certain tasks or work with objects such as forms, reports, or tables. If you are modifying the design of a form, for example, the Form Design Tools tab and its related subordinate Design tabs appear, collectively referred to as the Form Design Tools Design tab. When you are finished working with the form, the Form Design Tools tab disappears from the Ribbon. Access and other Office programs determine when tool tabs should appear and disappear based on tasks you perform. Some tool tabs, such as the Form Design Tools tab, have more than one related subordinate tab.

Items on the Ribbon include buttons, boxes (text boxes, check boxes, etc.), and galleries (Figure 28). A **gallery** is a set of choices, often graphical, arranged in a grid or in a list. You can scroll through choices in an in-Ribbon gallery by clicking the gallery's scroll arrows. Or, you can click a gallery's More button to view more gallery options on the screen at a time.

Figure 28

Some commands on the Ribbon display an image to help you remember their function. When you point to a command on the Ribbon, all or part of the command glows in shades of yellow and orange, and an Enhanced ScreenTip appears on the screen. An **Enhanced ScreenTip** is an on-screen note that provides the name of the command, available keyboard shortcut(s), a description of the command, and sometimes instructions for how to obtain help about the command (Figure 29). Enhanced ScreenTips are more detailed than a typical ScreenTip, which usually displays only the name of the command.

Some groups on the Ribbon have a small arrow in the lower-right corner, called a **Dialog Box Launcher**, that when clicked, displays a dialog box or a task pane with additional options for the group (Figure 30). When presented with a dialog box, you make selections and must close the dialog box before returning to the database. A **task pane**, in contrast to a dialog box, is a window that can remain open and visible while you work in the database.

Figure 29

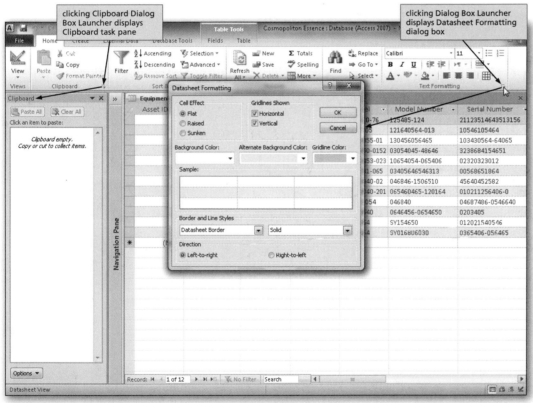

Figure 30

Quick Access Toolbar The **Quick Access Toolbar**, located initially (by default) above the Ribbon at the left edge of the title bar, provides convenient, one-click access to frequently used commands (Figure 29). The commands on the Quick Access Toolbar always are available, regardless of the task you are performing. The Quick Access Toolbar is discussed in more depth later in the chapter.

KeyTips If you prefer using the keyboard instead of the mouse, you can press the ALT key on the keyboard to display **KeyTips**, or keyboard code icons, for certain commands (Figure 31). To select a command using the keyboard, press the letter or number displayed in the KeyTip, which may cause additional KeyTips related to the selected command to appear. To remove KeyTips from the screen, press the ALT key or the ESC key until all KeyTips disappear, or click the mouse anywhere in the program window.

Figure 31

To Open an Existing Office File

Assume you want to continue working on an existing file, that is, a file you previously saved. Earlier in this chapter, you learned how to open a recently used file through the Backstage view. The following steps open a database, specifically the Charmed Excursions database, from the USB flash drive.

- With your USB flash drive connected to one of the computer's USB ports, if necessary, click File on the Ribbon to open the Backstage view.

- Click Open in the Backstage view to display the Open dialog box (Figure 32).

- Navigate to the location of the file to be opened (in this case, the USB flash drive, then to the CIS 101 folder [or your class folder], and then to the Access folder). For detailed steps about navigating, see Steps 2a – 2c on page OFF 20.

What if I did not save my file in a folder?

If you did not save your file in a folder, the file you want to open should be displayed in the Open dialog box before navigating to any folders.

Figure 32

• Click the file to be opened, Charmed Excursions in this case, to select the file (Figure 33).

• Click the Open button (Open dialog box) to open the selected file and display the opened file in the current program window.

Other Ways

1. Click File on the Ribbon, click Recent in Backstage view, double-click file
2. Press CTRL+O
3. Navigate to file in Windows Explorer, double-click file

Figure 33

To Display a Different Tab on the Ribbon

When you start Access, the Ribbon displays five main tabs: File, Home, Create, External Data, and Database Tools. The tab currently displayed is called the **active tab**.

The following step displays the External Data tab, that is, makes it the active tab.

• Click External Data on the Ribbon to display the External Data tab (Figure 34).

 Experiment

• Click the other tabs on the Ribbon to view their contents. When you are finished, click the External Data tab to redisplay the External Data tab.

Figure 34

Q&A

If I am working in a different Office program, such as PowerPoint or Word, how do I display a different tab on the Ribbon?

Follow this same procedure; that is, click the desired tab on the Ribbon.

To Minimize, Display, and Restore the Ribbon

To display more of a database or other item in the window of an Office program, some users prefer to minimize the Ribbon, which hides the groups on the Ribbon and displays only the main tabs. Each time you start an Office program, such as Access, the Ribbon appears the same way it did the last time you used that Office program. The chapters in this book, however, begin with the Ribbon appearing as it did at the initial installation of Access.

The following steps minimize, display, and restore the Ribbon in Access.

- Click the Minimize the Ribbon button on the Ribbon (shown in Figure 34) to minimize the Ribbon (Figure 35).

Q&A What happened to the groups on the Ribbon?

When you minimize the Ribbon, the groups disappear so that the Ribbon does not take up as much space on the screen.

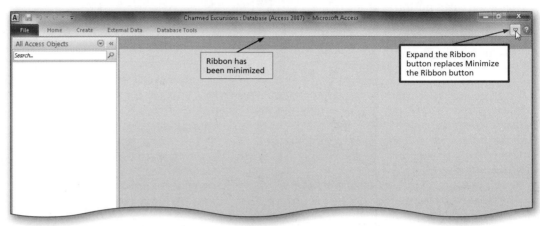

Figure 35

Q&A What happened to the Minimize the Ribbon button?

The Expand the Ribbon button replaces the Minimize the Ribbon button when the Ribbon is minimized.

- Click Home on the Ribbon to display the Home tab (Figure 36).

Q&A Why would I click the Home tab?

If you want to use a command on a minimized Ribbon, click the main tab to display the groups for that tab. After you select a command on the Ribbon, the groups will be hidden once again. If you decide not to use a command on the Ribbon, you can hide the groups by clicking the same main tab or clicking in the program window.

Figure 36

- Click Home on the Ribbon to hide the groups again (shown in Figure 35).

- Click the Expand the Ribbon button on the Ribbon (shown in Figure 35) to restore the Ribbon.

Other Ways

1. Double-click Home on the Ribbon
2. Press CTRL+F1

To Display and Use a Shortcut Menu

When you right-click certain areas of the Access and other program windows, a shortcut menu will appear. A **shortcut menu** is a list of frequently used commands that relate to the right-clicked object. When you right-click a scroll bar, for example, a shortcut menu appears with commands related to the scroll bar. When you right-click the Quick Access Toolbar, a shortcut menu appears with commands related to the Quick Access Toolbar. You can use shortcut menus to access common commands quickly. The following steps use a shortcut menu to move the Quick Access Toolbar, which by default is located on the title bar.

- Right-click the Quick Access Toolbar to display a shortcut menu that presents a list of commands related to the Quick Access Toolbar (Figure 37).

Figure 37

- Click Show Quick Access Toolbar Below the Ribbon on the shortcut menu to display the Quick Access Toolbar below the Ribbon (Figure 38).

Figure 38

- Right-click the Quick Access Toolbar to display a shortcut menu (Figure 39).

- Click Show Quick Access Toolbar Above the Ribbon on the shortcut menu to return the Quick Access Toolbar to its original position (shown in Figure 37).

Figure 39

To Customize the Quick Access Toolbar

The Quick Access Toolbar provides easy access to some of the more frequently used commands in Office programs. By default, the Quick Access Toolbar contains buttons for the Save, Undo, and Redo commands. You can customize the Quick Access Toolbar by changing its location in the window, as shown in the previous steps, and by adding more buttons to reflect commands you would like to access easily. The following steps add the Quick Print button to the Quick Access Toolbar in the Access window. They then remove the button from the Quick Access Toolbar. You can use these techniques to add or remove any of the available buttons.

- Click the Customize Quick Access Toolbar button to display the Customize Quick Access Toolbar menu (Figure 40).

Q&A

Which commands are listed on the Customize Quick Access Toolbar menu?

It lists commands that commonly are added to the Quick Access Toolbar.

Q&A

What do the check marks next to some commands signify?

Check marks appear next to commands that already are on the Quick Access Toolbar. When you add a button to the Quick Access Toolbar, a check mark will be displayed next to its command name.

Figure 40

- Click Quick Print on the Customize Quick Access Toolbar menu to add the Quick Print button to the Quick Access Toolbar (Figure 41).

Q&A

How would I remove a button from the Quick Access Toolbar?

You would right-click the button you want to remove and then click Remove from Quick Access Toolbar on the shortcut menu. If you want your screens to match the screens in the remaining chapters in this book, you would remove the Quick Print button from the Quick Access Toolbar.

- Click the Customize Quick Access Toolbar button to display the Customize Quick Access Toolbar menu, and then click Quick Print on the menu to remove the Quick Print button from the Quick Access Toolbar.

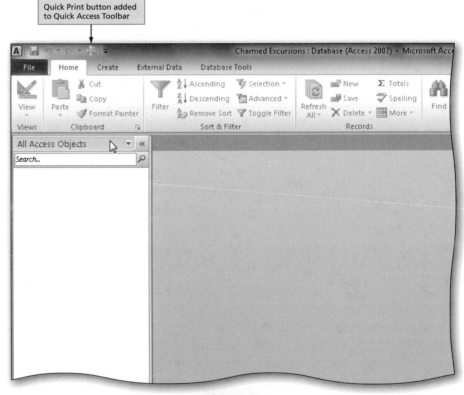

Figure 41

Screen Resolution

Screen resolution indicates the number of pixels (dots) that the computer uses to display the letters, numbers, graphics, and background you see on the screen. When you increase the screen resolution, Windows displays more information on the screen, but the information decreases in size. The reverse also is true; as you decrease the screen resolution, Windows displays less information on the screen, but the information increases in size.

Screen resolution usually is stated as the product of two numbers, such as 1024×768 (pronounced "ten twenty-four by seven sixty-eight"). A 1024×768 screen resolution results in a display of 1,024 distinct pixels on each of 768 lines, or about 786,432 pixels. Changing the screen resolution affects how the Ribbon appears in Office programs. Figure 42, for example, shows the Access Ribbon at screen resolutions of 1024×768 and 1280×800. All of the same commands are available regardless of screen resolution. Access, however, makes changes to the groups and the buttons within the groups to accommodate the various screen resolutions. The result is that certain commands may need to be accessed differently depending on the resolution chosen. A command that is visible on the Ribbon and available by clicking a button at one resolution may not be visible and may need to be accessed using its Dialog Box Launcher at a different resolution.

(a) Ribbon at Resolution of 1024 x 768

(b) Ribbon at Resolution of 1280 x 800

Figure 42

Comparing the two Ribbons in Figure 42, notice the changes in content and layout of the groups and galleries. In some cases, the content of a group is the same in each resolution, but the layout of the group differs. For example, the same gallery and buttons appear in the Text Formatting groups in the two resolutions, but the layouts differ. In other cases, the content and layout are the same across the resolution, but the level of detail differs with the resolution.

To Change the Screen Resolution

If you are using a computer to step through the chapters in this book and you want your screen to match the figures, you may need to change your screen's resolution. The figures in this book use a screen resolution of 1024 × 768. The following steps change the screen resolution to 1024 × 768. Your computer already may be set to 1024 × 768 or some other resolution. Keep in mind that many computer labs prevent users from changing the screen resolution; in that case, read the following steps for illustration purposes.

- Click the Show desktop button on the taskbar to display the Windows 7 desktop.

- Right-click an empty area on the Windows 7 desktop to display a shortcut menu that displays a list of commands related to the desktop (Figure 43).

Q&A
Why does my shortcut menu display different commands?

Depending on your computer's hardware and configuration, different commands might appear on the shortcut menu.

Figure 43

- Click Screen resolution on the shortcut menu to open the Screen Resolution window (Figure 44).

Figure 44

- Click the Resolution button in the Screen Resolution window to display the resolution slider.

Q&A

What is a slider?

A **slider** is an object that allows users to choose from multiple predetermined options. In most cases, these options represent some type of numeric value. In most cases, one end of the slider (usually the left or bottom) represents the lowest of available values, and the opposite end (usually the right or top) represents the highest available value.

4

- If necessary, drag the resolution slider until the desired screen resolution (in this case, 1024 × 768) is selected (Figure 45).

Q&A

What if my computer does not support the 1024 × 768 resolution?

Some computers do not support the 1024 × 768 resolution. In this case, select a resolution that is close to the 1024 × 768 resolution.

Figure 45

- Click an empty area of the Screen Resolution window to close the resolution slider.

- Click the OK button to change the screen resolution and display the Display Settings dialog box (Figure 46).

- Click the Keep changes button (Display Settings dialog box) to accept the new screen resolution.

Q&A

Why does a message display stating that the image quality can be improved?

Some computer monitors are designed to display contents better at a certain screen resolution, sometimes referred to as an optimal resolution.

Figure 46

Break Point: If you wish to take a break, this is a good place to do so. To resume at a later time, continue to follow the steps from this location forward.

Additional Common Features of Office Programs

The previous section used Access to illustrate common features of Office and some basic elements unique to Access. The following sections continue to use Access to present additional common features of Office.

In the following pages, you will learn how to do the following:

1. Start an Office program (Access) using the search box.
2. Open a database in an Office program (Access).
3. Close the database.
4. Reopen the database just closed.
5. Create a blank database from Windows Explorer and then open the file.
6. Save a database with a new file name.

To Start a Program Using the Search Box

The next steps, which assume Windows 7 is running, use the search box to start Access based on a typical installation; however, you would follow similar steps to start any program. You may need to ask your instructor how to start programs for your computer.

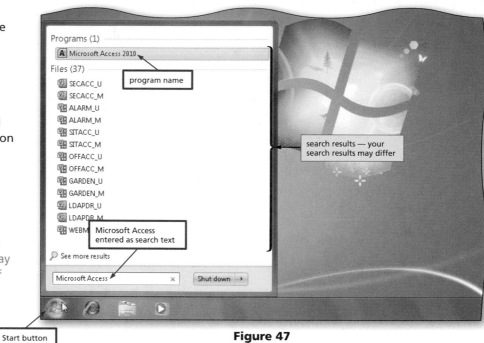

1

- Click the Start button on the Windows 7 taskbar to display the Start menu.

2

- Type **Microsoft Access** as the search text in the 'Search programs and files' text box and watch the search results appear on the Start menu (Figure 47).

Q&A

Do I need to type the complete program name or correct capitalization?

No, just enough of it for the program name to appear on the Start menu. For example, you may be able to type Access instead of Microsoft Access or access.

program name

search results — your search results may differ

Microsoft Access entered as search text

Start button

Figure 47

Restore Down button replaces Maximize button

3

- Click the program name, Microsoft Access 2010 in this case, in the search results on the Start menu.

- If the program window is not maximized, click the Maximize button on its title bar to maximize the window (Figure 48).

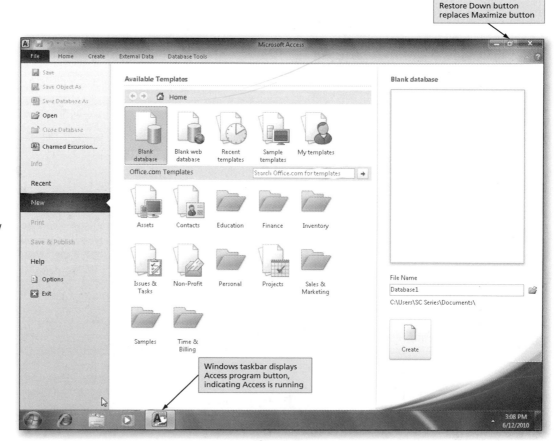

Windows taskbar displays Access program button, indicating Access is running

Figure 48

To Open a Recent Office File Using the Backstage View

You sometimes need to open a file that you recently modified. You may have more changes to make such as adding more content or correcting errors. The Backstage view allows you to access recent files easily. The following steps reopen the Charmed Excursions database.

- If necessary, click File on the Ribbon to open the Backstage view.

- Click the Recent tab in the Backstage view to display the Recent Databases Gallery (Figure 49).

- Click the desired file name in the Recent Databases Gallery, Charmed Excursions in this case, to open the database.

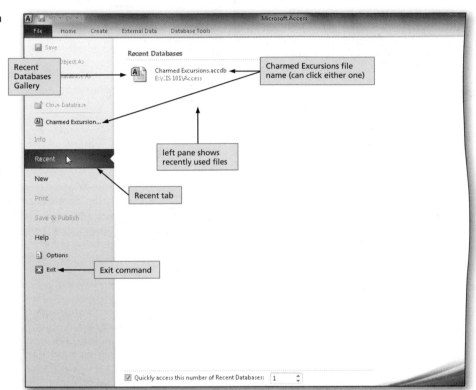

Figure 49

Q&A Can I use the Backstage view to open a recent file in other Office programs, such as Word and Excel?

Yes, as long as the file name appears in the list of recent files in the Recent gallery.

Q&A I see that there are two Charmed Excursions on the screen, one that is with the tabs and the other in the Recent Databases. Does it matter which one I click?

No. You could click either one. The advantage to the Recent Databases pane is that it can contain more databases.

Other Ways

1. Click Start button, point to program name, click file name on submenu
2. Click File on Ribbon, click Open in Backstage view, navigate to file (Open dialog box), click Open button

To Create a New Blank Database from Windows Explorer

Windows Explorer provides a means to create a blank database without ever starting an Office program. The following steps use Windows Explorer to create a blank database.

1

- Click the Windows Explorer program button on the taskbar to make the folder window the active window in Windows Explorer.

- If necessary, navigate to the desired location for the new file (in this case, the Access folder in the CIS 101 folder [or your class folder] on the USB flash drive).

- With the Access folder selected, right-click an open area in the right pane to display a shortcut menu.

- Point to New on the shortcut menu to display the New submenu (Figure 50).

Figure 50

2

- Click Microsoft Access Database on the New submenu to display an icon and text box for a new file in the current folder window (Figure 51).

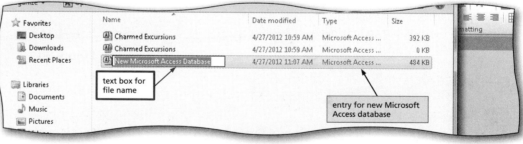

Figure 51

3

- Type **Charmed Excursions Northern** in the text box and then press the ENTER key to assign a name to the new file in the current folder (Figure 52).

Figure 52

To Start a Program from Windows Explorer and Open a File

Previously, you learned how to start an Office program (Access) using the Start menu and the search box. Another way start an Office program is to open an existing file from Windows Explorer, which causes the program in which the file was created to start and then open the selected file. The following steps, which assume Windows 7 is running, use Windows Explorer to start Access based on a typical installation. You may need to ask your instructor how to start Access for your computer.

- If necessary, display the file to open in the folder window in Windows Explorer (shown in Figure 52).

- Right-click the file icon or file name (Charmed Excursions Northern, in this case) to display a shortcut menu (Figure 53).

Figure 53

- Click Open on the shortcut menu to open the selected file in the program used to create the file, Microsoft Access in this case (Figure 54).

- If the program window is not maximized, click the Maximize button on the title bar to maximize the window.

Figure 54

To Use Save Database As to Change the Name of a File

You might want to save a file with a different name and even to a different location. For example, you might start a homework assignment with a data file and then save it with a final file name for submitting to your instructor, saving it to a location designated by your instructor. The following steps save a file with a different file name.

1 With your USB flash drive connected to one of the computer's USB ports, click File on the Ribbon to open the Backstage view.

2 Click Save Database As in the Backstage view to display the Save As dialog box.

3 Type `Charmed Excursions Western` in the File name text box (Save As dialog box) to change the file name. Do not press the ENTER key after typing the file name because you do not want to close the dialog box at this time.

4 If necessary, navigate to the desired save location (the Access folder in the CIS 101 folder [or your class folder] on the USB flash drive, in this case).

5 Click the Save button (Save As dialog box) to save the file in the selected folder on the selected drive with the new file name.

To Quit an Office Program

You are finished using Access. The following steps quit Access. You would use similar steps to quit other Office programs.

1 Click the Close button on the right side of the title bar to quit Access (you might need to do this twice).

2 If a dialog box appears, click the Save button to save any changes made to the object since the last save.

Moving, Renaming, and Deleting Files

Earlier in this chapter, you learned how to organize files in folders, which is part of a process known as **file management**. The following sections cover additional file management topics including renaming, moving, and deleting files.

To Rename a File

In some circumstances, you may want to change the name of, or rename, a file or a folder. For example, you may want to distinguish a file in one folder or drive from a copy of a similar file, or you may decide to rename a file to better identify its contents. The Access folder shown in Figure 53 contains the Access database, Charmed Excursions. The following steps change the name of the Charmed Excursions database in the Access folder to Charmed Excursions Southern.

1

- If necessary, click the Windows Explorer program button on the taskbar to display the folder window in Windows Explorer.

- If necessary, navigate to the location of the file to be renamed (in this case, the Access folder in the CIS 101 [or your class folder] folder on the USB flash drive) to display the file(s) it contains in the right pane.

- Right-click the Charmed Excursions icon or file name in the right pane to select the Charmed Excursions database and display a shortcut menu that presents a list of commands related to files (Figure 55).

Figure 55

- Click Rename on the shortcut menu to place the current file name in a text box.

- Type **Charmed Excursions Southern** in the text box and then press the ENTER key (Figure 56).

Q&A Are any risks involved in renaming files that are located on a hard disk?

If you inadvertently rename a file that is associated with certain programs, the programs may not be able to find the file and, therefore, may not execute properly. Always use caution when renaming files.

Q&A Can I rename a file when it is open?

No, a file must be closed to change the file name.

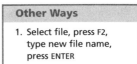

Figure 56

Other Ways

1. Select file, press F2, type new file name, press ENTER

To Move a File

At some time, you may want to move a file from one folder, called the source folder, to another, called the destination. When you move a file, it no longer appears in the original folder. If the destination and the source folders are on the same disk drive, you can move a file by dragging it. If the folders are on different disk drives, then you will need to right-drag the file. The following step moves the Charmed Excursions Southern from the Access folder to the CIS 101 folder.

- In Windows Explorer, if necessary, navigate to the location of the file to be moved (in this case, the Access folder in the CIS 101 folder [or your class folder] on the USB flash drive).

- If necessary, click the Access folder in the navigation pane to display the files it contains in the right pane.

- Drag the Charmed Excursions Southern in the right pane to the CIS 101 folder in the navigation pane and notice the ScreenTip as you drag the mouse (Figure 57).

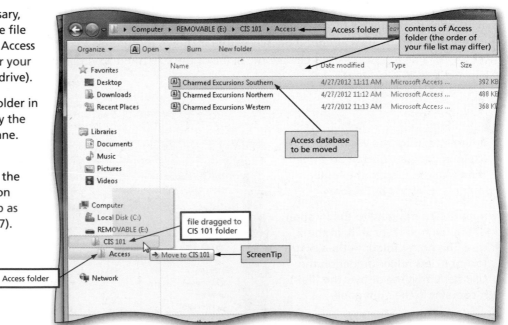

Figure 57

Other Ways

1. Right-click file, drag file to destination folder, click Move here

2. Right-click file to copy, click Cut on shortcut menu, right-click destination folder, click Paste on shortcut menu

3. Select file to copy, press CTRL+X, select destination folder, press CTRL+V

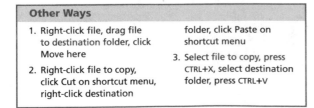

To Delete a File

A final task you may want to perform is to delete a file. Exercise extreme caution when deleting a file or files. When you delete a file from a hard disk, the deleted file is stored in the Recycle Bin where you can recover it until you empty the Recycle Bin. If you delete a file from removable media, such as a USB flash drive, the file is deleted permanently. The next steps delete the Charmed Excursions Southern database from the CIS 101 folder.

1

- In Windows Explorer, navigate to the location of the file to be deleted (in this case, the CIS 101 folder [or your class folder] on the USB flash drive).

- If necessary, click the CIS 101 folder in the navigation pane to display the files it contains in the right pane.

- Right-click the Charmed Excursions Southern icon or file name in the right pane to select the file and display a shortcut menu (Figure 58).

Figure 58

2

- Click Delete on the shortcut menu to display the Delete File dialog box (Figure 59).

- Click the Yes button (Delete File dialog box) to delete the selected file.

Q&A

Can I use this same technique to delete a folder?

Yes. Right-click the folder and then click Delete on the shortcut menu. When you delete a folder, all of the files and folders contained in the folder you are deleting, together with any files and folders on lower hierarchical levels, are deleted as well.

Figure 59

Other Ways

1. Select icon, press DELETE

Microsoft Office and Windows Help

At any time while you are using one of the Microsoft Office 2010 programs, such as Access, you can use Office Help to display information about all topics associated with the program. This section illustrates the use of Access Help. Help in other Office 2010 programs operates in a similar fashion.

In Office 2010, Help is presented in a window that has Web-browser-style navigation buttons. Each Office 2010 program has its own Help home page, which is the starting Help page that is displayed in the Help window. If your computer is connected to the Internet, the contents of the Help page reflect both the local Help files installed on the computer and material from Microsoft's Web site.

To Open the Help Window in an Office Program

The following step opens the Access Help window. The step to open a Help window in other Office programs is similar.

- Start Access.

- Click the Microsoft Access Help button near the upper-right corner of the program window to open the Access Help window (Figure 60).

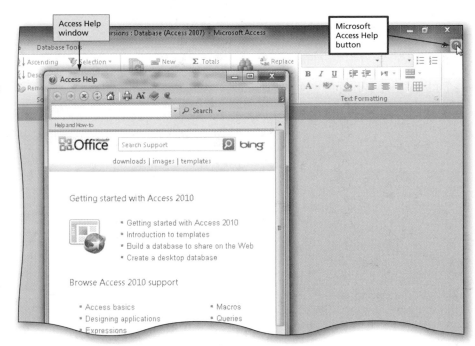

Figure 60

Other Ways
1. Press F1

Moving and Resizing Windows

Up to this point, this chapter has used minimized and maximized windows. At times, however, it is useful, or even necessary, to have more than one window open and visible on the screen at the same time. You can resize and move these open windows so that you can view different areas of and elements in the window. In the case of the Help window, for example, it could be covering document text in the Access window that you need to see.

To Move a Window by Dragging

You can move any open window that is not maximized to another location on the desktop by dragging the title bar of the window. The step on the next page drags the Access Help window to the top left of the desktop.

- Drag the window title bar (the Access Help window title bar, in this case) so that the window moves to the top left of the desktop, as shown in Figure 61.

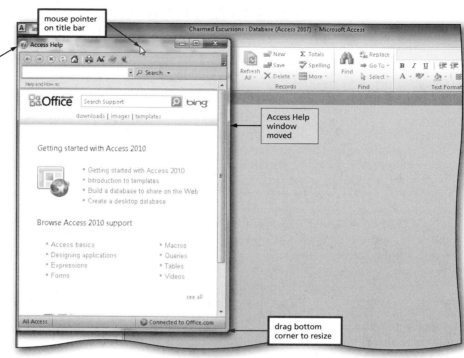

Figure 61

Other Ways
1. Right-click title bar, click Move on shortcut menu, drag window

To Resize a Window by Dragging

Sometimes, information is not visible completely in a window. A method used to change the size of the window is to drag the window borders. The following step changes the size of the Access Help window by dragging its borders.

1

- Point to the lower-right corner of the window (the Access Help window, in this case) until the mouse pointer changes to a two-headed arrow.

- Drag the bottom border downward to display more of the active window (Figure 62).

Q&A Can I drag other borders on the window to enlarge or shrink the window?

Yes, you can drag the left, right, and top borders and any window corner to resize a window.

Q&A Will Windows 7 remember the new size of the window after I close it?

Yes. When you reopen the window, Windows 7 will display it at the same size it was when you closed it.

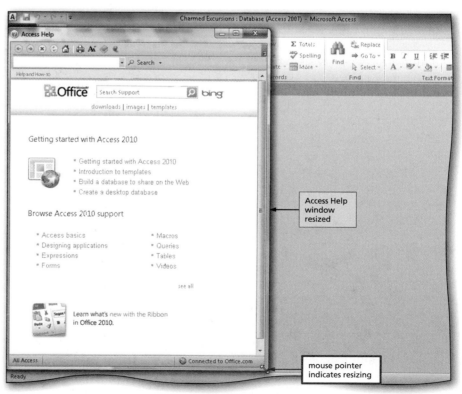

Figure 62

Using Office Help

Once an Office program's Help window is open, several methods exist for navigating Help. You can search for help by using any of the three following methods from the Help window:

1. Enter search text in the 'Type words to search for' text box.
2. Click the links in the Help window.
3. Use the Table of Contents.

To Obtain Help Using the 'Type words to search for' Text Box

Assume for the following example that you want to know more about the Backstage view. The following steps use the 'Type words to search for' text box to obtain useful information about the Backstage view by entering the word, Backstage, as search text.

1

- Type **Backstage** in the 'Type words to search for' text box at the top of the Access Help window to enter the search text.

- Click the Search button arrow to display the Search menu (Figure 63).

- If it is not selected already, click All Access on the Search menu, so that Help performs the most complete search of the current program (Access, in this case). If All Access already is selected, click the Search button arrow again to close the Search menu.

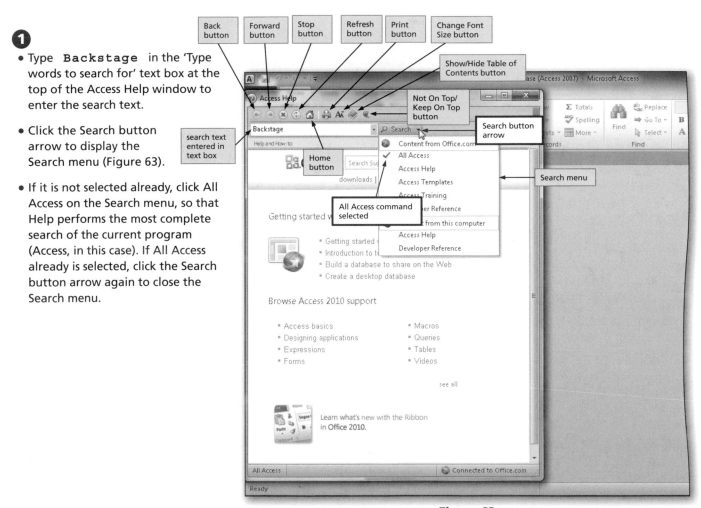

Figure 63

Q&A

Why select All Access on the Search menu?

Selecting All Access on the Search menu ensures that Access Help will search all possible sources for information about your search term. It will produce the most complete search results.

2

- Click the Search button to display the search results (Figure 64).

Q&A Why do my search results differ?

If you do not have an Internet connection, your results will reflect only the content of the Help files on your computer. When searching for help online, results also can change as material is added, deleted, and updated on the online Help Web pages maintained by Microsoft.

Q&A Why were my search results not very helpful?

When initiating a search, be sure to check the spelling of the search text; also, keep your search specific, with fewer than seven words, to return the most accurate results.

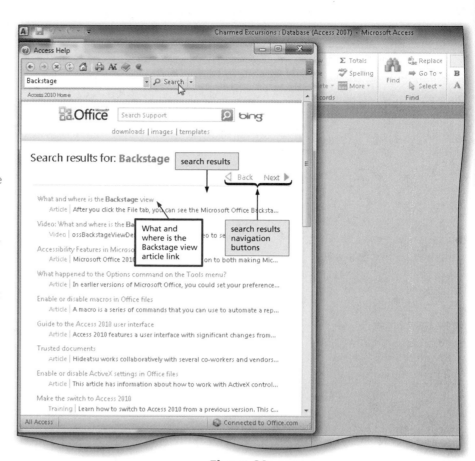

Figure 64

3

- Click the 'What and where is the Backstage view' link to open the Help document associated with the selected topic (Figure 65).

Figure 65

- Click the Home button on the toolbar to clear the search results and redisplay the Help home page (Figure 66).

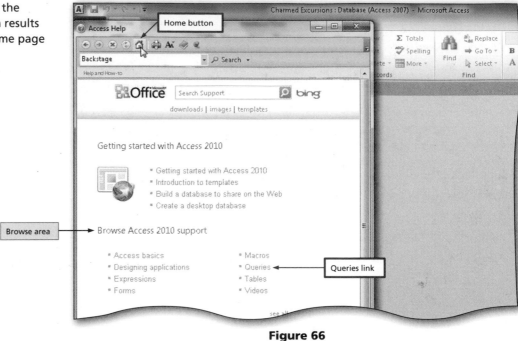

Figure 66

To Obtain Help Using the Help Links

If your topic of interest is listed in the Browse area of the Help window, you can click the link to begin browsing the Help categories instead of entering search text. You browse Help just as you would browse a Web site. If you know which category contains your Help information, you may want to use these links. The following step finds the Queries Help information using the category links from the Access Help home page.

1

- Click the Queries link on the Help home page (shown in Figure 66) to display the Queries page (Figure 67).

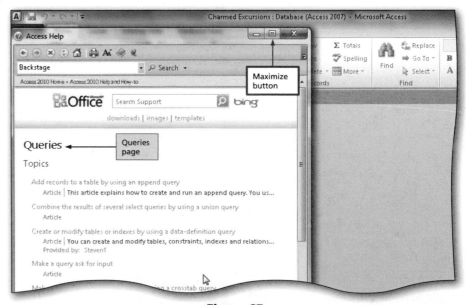

Figure 67

To Obtain Help Using the Help Table of Contents

A third way to find Help in Office programs is through the Help Table of Contents. You can browse through the Table of Contents to display information about a particular topic or to familiarize yourself with an Office program. The following steps access the Help information about fields by browsing through the Help Table of Contents.

1

- Click the Home button on the toolbar to display the Help home page.

- Click the Show Table of Contents button on the toolbar to display the Table of Contents pane on the left side of the Help window. If necessary, click the Maximize button on the Help title bar to maximize the window (Figure 68).

Q&A

Why does the appearance of the Show Table of Contents button change?

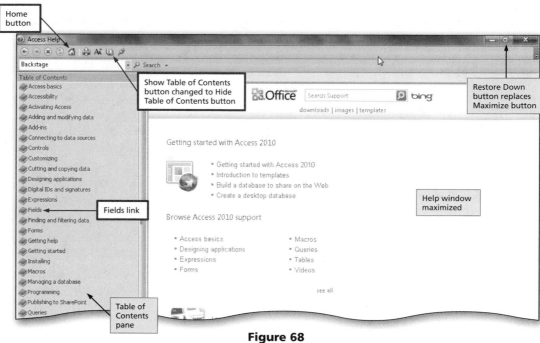

Figure 68

When the Table of Contents is displayed in the Help window, the Hide Table of Contents button replaces the Show Table of Contents button.

2

- Click the Fields link in the Table of Contents pane to view a list of Help subtopics.

- Click the 'Add a field to a table' link in the Table of Contents pane to view the selected Help document in the right pane (Figure 69).

- After reviewing the page, click the Close button to quit Help.

- Click the Access Close button to quit Access.

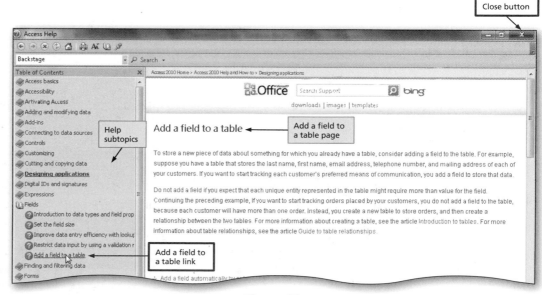

Figure 69

Q&A

How do I remove the Table of Contents pane when I am finished with it?

The Show Table of Contents button acts as a toggle. When the Table of Contents pane is visible, the button changes to Hide Table of Contents. Clicking it hides the Table of Contents pane and changes the button to Show Table of Contents.

Figure 70

Figure 71

Obtaining Help while Working in an Office Program

Help in Office programs, such as Access, provides you with the ability to obtain help directly, without the need to open the Help window and initiate a search. For example, you may be unsure about how a particular command works, or you may be presented with a dialog box that you are not sure how to use.

Figure 70 shows one option for obtaining help while working in Access. If you want to learn more about a command, point to the command button and wait for the Enhanced ScreenTip to appear. If the Help icon appears in the Enhanced ScreenTip, press the F1 key while pointing to the command to open the Help window associated with that command.

Figure 71 shows a dialog box that contains a Help button. Pressing the F1 key while the dialog box is displayed opens a Help window. The Help window contains help about that dialog box, if available. If no Help file is available for that particular dialog box, then the main Help window opens.

Using Windows Help and Support

One of the more powerful Windows 7 features is Windows Help and Support. **Windows Help and Support** is available when using Windows 7 or when using any Microsoft program running under Windows 7. This feature is designed to assist you in using Windows 7 or the various programs. Table 4 describes the content found in the Help and Support Center. The same methods used for searching Microsoft Office Help can be used in Windows Help and Support. The difference is that Windows Help and Support displays help for Windows 7, instead of for Microsoft Office.

Table 4 Windows Help and Support Center Content Areas	
Area	**Function**
Find an answer quickly	This area contains instructions about how to do a quick search using the search box.
Not sure where to start?	This area displays three topics to help guide a user: How to get started with your computer, Learn about Windows Basics, and Browse Help topics. Clicking one of the options navigates to corresponding Help and Support pages.
More on the Windows website	This area contains links to online content from the Windows Web site. Clicking the links navigates to the corresponding Web pages on the Web site.

To Start Windows Help and Support

The steps on the next page start Windows Help and Support and display the Windows Help and Support window, containing links to more information about Windows 7.

1

- Click the Start button on the taskbar to display the Start menu (Figure 72).

Why are the programs that are displayed on the Start menu different?

Windows adds the programs you have used recently to the left pane on the Start menu. You have started Access while performing the steps in this chapter, so that program now is displayed on the Start menu.

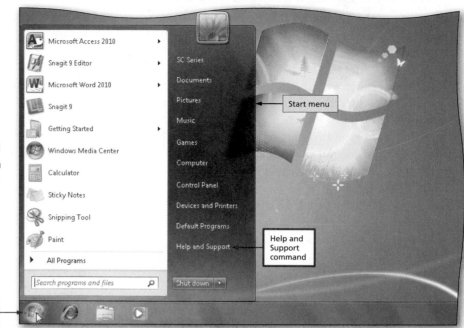

Figure 72

2

- Click Help and Support on the Start menu to open the Windows Help and Support window (Figure 73).

- After reviewing the Windows Help and Support window, click the Close button to quit Windows Help and Support.

Other Ways

1. Press CTRL+ESC, press RIGHT ARROW, press UP ARROW, press ENTER

2. Press WINDOWS+F1

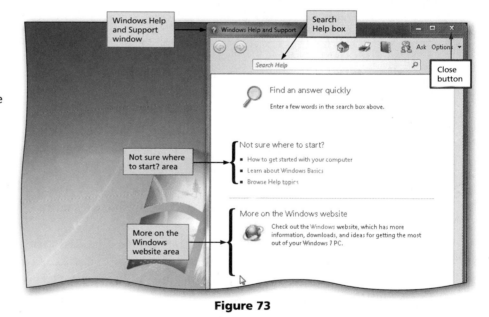

Figure 73

Chapter Summary

In this chapter, you learned about the Windows 7 interface. You started Windows 7, were introduced to the components of the desktop, and learned several mouse operations. You opened, closed, moved, resized, minimized, maximized, and scrolled a window. You used folder windows to expand and collapse drives and folders, display drive and folder contents, create folders, and rename and then delete a file.

You also learned some basic features of Microsoft Access 2010. As part of this learning process, you discovered the common elements that exist among Microsoft Office programs.

Microsoft Office Help was demonstrated using Access, and you learned how to use the Access Help window. You were introduced to the Windows 7 Help and Support Center and learned how to use it to obtain more information about Windows 7.

The items listed below include all of the new Windows 7 and Office 2010 skills you have learned in this chapter.

1. Log on to the Computer (OFF 6)
2. Start a Program Using the Start Menu (OFF 9)
3. Maximize a Window (OFF 12)
4. Create a Folder (OFF 13)
5. Create a Folder within a Folder (OFF 16)
6. Expand a Folder, Scroll through Folder Contents, and Collapse a Folder (OFF 17)
7. Switch from One Program to Another (OFF 18)
8. Create an Access Database (OFF 19)
9. Close an Office File Using the Backstage View (OFF 22)
10. Open an Existing Office File (OFF 26)
11. Display a Different Tab on the Ribbon (OFF 27)
12. Minimize, Display, and Restore the Ribbon (OFF 28)
13. Display and Use a Shortcut Menu (OFF 29)
14. Customize the Quick Access Toolbar (OFF 30)
15. Change the Screen Resolution (OFF 32)
16. Start a Program Using the Search Box (OFF 34)
17. Open a Recent Office File Using the Backstage View (OFF 36)
18. Create a New Blank Database from Windows Explorer (OFF 37)
19. Start a Program from Windows Explorer and Open a File (OFF 38)
20. Use Save Database As to Change the Name of a File (OFF 38)
21. Quit an Office Program (OFF 39)
22. Rename a File (OFF 39)
23. Move a File (OFF 40)
24. Delete a File (OFF 41)
25. Open the Help Window in an Office Program (OFF 42)
26. Move a Window by Dragging (OFF 42)
27. Resize a Window by Dragging (OFF 43)
28. Obtain Help Using the 'Type words to search for' Text Box (OFF 44)
29. Obtain Help Using the Help Links (OFF 46)
30. Obtain Help Using the Help Table of Contents (OFF 47)
31. Start Windows Help and Support (OFF 48)

 If you have a SAM 2010 user profile, your instructor may have assigned an autogradable version of this assignment. If so, log into the SAM 2010 Web site at www.cengage.com/sam2010 to download the instruction and start files.

Learn It Online

Test your knowledge of chapter content and key terms.

Instructions: To complete the Learn It Online exercises, start your browser, click the Address bar, and then enter the Web address `scsite.com/office2010/learn`. When the Office 2010 Learn It Online page is displayed, click the link for the exercise you want to complete and then read the instructions.

Chapter Reinforcement TF, MC, and SA
A series of true/false, multiple choice, and short answer questions that test your knowledge of the chapter content.

Flash Cards
An interactive learning environment where you identify chapter key terms associated with displayed definitions.

Practice Test
A series of multiple choice questions that test your knowledge of chapter content and key terms.

Who Wants To Be a Computer Genius?
An interactive game that challenges your knowledge of chapter content in the style of a television quiz show.

Wheel of Terms
An interactive game that challenges your knowledge of chapter key terms in the style of the television show *Wheel of Fortune*.

Crossword Puzzle Challenge
A crossword puzzle that challenges your knowledge of key terms presented in the chapter.

Apply Your Knowledge

Reinforce the skills and apply the concepts you learned in this chapter.

Creating a Folder and a Document

Instructions: You will create an Access folder and then create an Access database and save it in the folder.

Perform the following tasks:

1. Connect a USB flash drive to an available USB port and then open the USB flash drive window.
2. Click the New folder button on the toolbar to display a new folder icon and text box for the folder name.
3. Type `Access` in the text box to name the folder. Press the ENTER key to create the folder on the USB flash drive.
4. Start Access.
5. Use the Blank database option to create a database with the name Apply 1 in the Access folder.
6. Close the database and quit Access.
7. Rename the database to Apply 2.
8. Submit the database in the format specified by your instructor.

Extend Your Knowledge

Extend the skills you learned in this chapter and experiment with new skills. You will use Help to complete the assignment.

Using Help

Instructions: Use Access Help to perform the following tasks.

Perform the following tasks:

1. Start Access.
2. Click the Microsoft Access Help button to open the Access Help window (Figure 74).
3. Search Access Help to answer the following questions.
   a. What are three features new to Access 2010?
   b. What type of training courses are available through Help?
   c. What are the steps to add a new group to the Ribbon?
   d. What are Application Parts?
   e. What are document properties?
   f. What is a template?
   g. How do you back up a database?
   h. What is the purpose of compacting and repairing a database?
   i. What is the purpose of the Navigation Pane?
4. Submit the answers from your searches in the format specified by your instructor.
5. Quit Access.

Figure 74

Make It Right

Analyze a file structure and correct all errors and/or improve the design.

Organizing Vacation Photos

Note: To complete this assignment, you will be required to use the Data Files for Students. See the inside back cover of this book for instructions on downloading the Data Files for Students, or contact your instructor for information about accessing the required files.

Instructions: Traditionally, you have stored photos from past vacations together in one folder. The photos are becoming difficult to manage, and you now want to store them in appropriate folders. You

Figure 75

will create the folder structure shown in Figure 75. You then will move the photos to the folders so that they will be organized properly.

1. Connect a USB flash drive to an available USB port to open the USB flash drive window.

2. Create the hierarchical folder structure shown in Figure 75.

3. Move one photo to each folder in the folder structure you created in Step 2. The five photos are available in the Data Files for Students.

4. Submit your work in the format specified by your instructor.

In the Lab

Use the guidelines, concepts, and skills presented in this chapter to increase your knowledge of Windows 7 and Access 2010. Labs are listed in order of increasing difficulty.

Lab 1: Using Windows Help and Support

Problem: You have a few questions about using Windows 7 and would like to answer these questions using Windows Help and Support.

Instructions: Use Windows Help and Support to perform the following tasks:

1. Display the Start menu and then click Help and Support to start Windows Help and Support.

2. Use the Help and Support Content page to answer the following questions.

   a. How do you reduce computer screen flicker?

   b. Which dialog box do you use to change the appearance of the mouse pointer?

   c. How do you minimize all windows?

   d. What is a VPN?

3. Use the Search Help text box in Windows Help and Support to answer the following questions.

   a. How can you minimize all open windows on the desktop?

   b. How do you start a program using the Run command?

   c. What are the steps to add a toolbar to the taskbar?

   d. What wizard do you use to remove unwanted desktop icons?

4. The tools to solve a problem while using Windows 7 are called **troubleshooters**. Use Windows Help and Support to find the list of troubleshooters (Figure 76), and answer the following questions.

   a. What problems does the HomeGroup troubleshooter allow you to resolve?

   b. List five Windows 7 troubleshooters that are not listed in Figure 76.

5. Use Windows Help and Support to obtain information about software licensing and product activation, and answer the following questions.

   a. What is genuine Windows?

   b. What is activation?

   c. What steps are required to activate Windows?

   d. What steps are required to read the Microsoft Software License Terms?

   e. Can you legally make a second copy of Windows 7 for use at home, work, or on a mobile computer or device?

   f. What is registration?

6. Close the Windows Help and Support window.

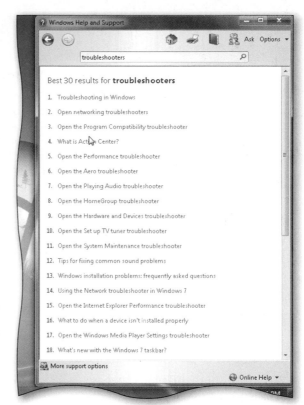

Figure 76

In the Lab

Lab 2: Creating Folders for a Pet Supply Store

Problem: Your friend works for Pete's Pet Supplies. He would like to organize his files in relation to the types of pets available in the store. He has five main categories: dogs, cats, fish, birds, and exotic. You are to create a folder structure similar to Figure 77.

Instructions: Perform the following tasks:

1. Connect a USB flash drive to an available USB port and then open the USB flash drive window.

2. Create the main folder for Pete's Pet Supplies.

3. Navigate to the Pete's Pet Supplies folder.

4. Within the Pete's Pet Supplies folder, create a folder for each of the following: Dogs, Cats, Fish, Birds, and Exotic.

5. Within the Exotic folder, create two additional folders, one for Primates and the second for Reptiles.

6. Submit the assignment in the format specified by your instructor.

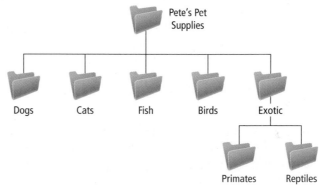

Figure 77

In the Lab

Lab 3: Creating Access Databases in Appropriate Folders

Problem: You are taking a class that requires you to complete three Access chapters. You will save the work completed in each chapter in a different folder (Figure 78).

Instructions: Create the folders shown in Figure 78. Then, using Access, create three small databases to save in each folder.

Figure 78

1. Connect a USB flash drive to an available USB port and then open the USB flash drive window.

2. Create the folder structure shown in Figure 78.

3. Navigate to the Chapter 1 folder.

4. Create an Access database named My Chapter 1 Access Database, and then save it in the Chapter 1 folder.

5. Navigate to the Chapter 2 folder.

6. Create another Access database named My Chapter 2 Access Database, and then save it in the Chapter 2 folder.

7. Navigate to the Chapter 3 folder.

8. Create another Access database named My Chapter 3 Access Database, and then save it in the Chapter 3 folder.

9. Quit Access.

10. Submit the assignment in the format specified by your instructor.

Cases and Places

Apply your creative thinking and problem solving skills to design and implement a solution.

To complete these assignments, you may be required to use the Data Files for Students. See the inside back cover of this book for instructions on downloading the Data Files for Students, or contact your instructor for information about accessing the required files.

1: Creating Beginning Files for Classes

Academic

You are taking the following classes: Introduction to Engineering, Beginning Psychology, Introduction to Biology, and Accounting. Create folders for each of the classes. Use the following folder names: Engineering, Psychology, Biology, and Accounting, when creating the folder structure. In the Engineering folder, use Access to create a database with the name of the class. In the Psychology folder, use Access to create a database named Behavioral Observations. In the Biology folder, use Access to create a database named Research. In the Accounting folder, create an Access database with the name, Tax Information. Use the concepts and techniques presented in this chapter to create the folders and files.

2: Using Help

Personal

Your parents enjoy working and playing games on their home computers. Your mother uses a notebook computer downstairs, and your father uses a desktop computer upstairs. They expressed interest in sharing files between their computers and sharing a single printer, so you offered to research various home networking options. Start Windows Help and Support, and search Help using the keywords, home networking. Use the link for installing a printer on a home network. Print the main steps for installing a printer. Use the link for setting up a HomeGroup and then print the main steps for creating a HomeGroup Access database. Use the concepts and techniques presented in this chapter to use Help.

3: Creating Folders

Professional

Your boss at the bookstore where you work part-time has asked for help with organizing her files. After looking through the files, you decided upon a file structure for her to use, including the following folders: books, magazines, tapes, DVDs, and general merchandise. Within the books folder, create folders for hardback and paperback books. Within magazines, create folders for special issues and periodicals. In the tapes folder, create folders for celebrity and major release. In the DVDs folder, create a folder for book to DVD. In the general merchandise folder, create folders for novelties, posters, and games. Use the concepts and techniques presented in this chapter to create the folders.

1 Databases and Database Objects: An Introduction

Objectives

You will have mastered the material in this chapter when you can:

- Design a database to satisfy a collection of requirements
- Describe the features of the Access window
- Create a database
- Create tables in Datasheet and Design views
- Add records to a table

- Close a database
- Open a database
- Print the contents of a table
- Create and use a query
- Create and use a form
- Create and print custom reports
- Modify a report in Layout view

1 | Databases and Database Objects: An Introduction

Introduction

The term **database** describes a collection of data organized in a manner that allows access, retrieval, and use of that data. Microsoft Access 2010, usually referred to as simply Access, is a database management system. A **database management system**, such as Access, is software that allows you to use a computer to create a database; add, change, and delete data in the database; ask and answer questions concerning the data in the database; and create forms and reports using the data in the database.

Project Planning Guidelines

The process of developing a database that communicates specific information requires careful analysis and planning. As a starting point, establish why the database is needed. Once the purpose is determined, analyze the intended users of the database and their unique needs. Then, gather information about the topic and decide what to include in the database. Finally, determine the database design and style that will be most successful at delivering the message. Details of these guidelines are provided in Appendix A. In addition, each project in this book provides practical applications of these planning considerations.

Project — Database Creation

Camashaly Design Group is a small company that provides custom marketing solutions for the service, nonprofit, and retail sectors. Alyssa Morgan, Camden Scott, and Ashton James started the business after they graduated from a local university. The three owners, all computer graphics design majors and business minors, worked on a service learning project during college that produced a Web site for a nonprofit organization. Alyssa, Camden, and Ashton worked well together. Upon researching the local area for competing businesses, they decided to form their own company. The company specializes in designing and maintaining Web sites and using social networking Web sites for online marketing. They also conduct market research and develop printed media. Camashaly already has received one award for its design work. Camashaly is also recognized for its efforts in providing work opportunities to individuals who want flexible schedules and to student interns.

BTWs
For a complete list of the BTWs found in the margins of this book, visit the Access 2010 BTW Web page (scsite.com/ac2010/btw).

Camashaly uses business analysts to work collaboratively with clients. Business analysts are employees who translate business requirements into marketing specifications and serve as the interface between clients and Camashaly. Business analysts are paid a base salary and can earn incentive pay for maintaining and expanding client relationships.

Camashaly charges a one-time fee for Web site development. Clients can pay for Web site maintenance by contracting for a specified number of hours or can pay for maintenance on an hour-by-hour basis. Other fees vary depending on the specific scope of work.

To ensure that operations run smoothly, Camashaly organizes data on its clients and business analysts in a database managed by Access. In this way, Camashaly keeps its data current and accurate while the owners can analyze the data for trends and produce a variety of useful reports. In this chapter, you will create the Camashaly database.

In a **relational database** such as those maintained by Access, a database consists of a collection of tables, each of which contains information on a specific subject. Figure 1–1 shows the database for Camashaly Design. It consists of two tables: the Client table (Figure 1–1a) contains information about the clients to whom Camashaly provides services, and the Business Analyst table (Figure 1–1b) contains information about the business analysts to whom these clients are assigned.

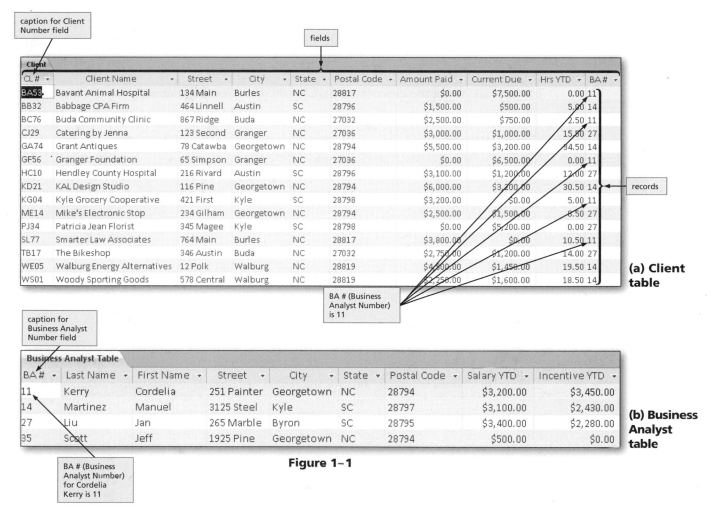

Figure 1–1

The rows in the tables are called **records**. A record contains information about a given person, product, or event. A row in the Client table, for example, contains information about a specific client, such as the client's name, address information, and other data.

The columns in the tables are called fields. A **field** contains a specific piece of information within a record. In the Client table, for example, the fourth field, City, contains the name of the city where the client is located.

The first field in the Client table is CL #, which is an abbreviation for Client Number. Camashaly Design assigns each client a client number. As is common to the way in which many organizations format client numbers, Camashaly Design calls it a number, although it actually contains letters. The Camashaly client numbers consist of two uppercase letters followed by a two-digit number.

The client numbers are unique; that is, no two clients are assigned the same number. Such a field can be used as a **unique identifier**. A unique identifier, as its name suggests, is a way of uniquely identifying each record in the database. A given client number will appear only in a single record in the table. Only one record exists, for example, in which the client number is BB32. A unique identifier also is called a **primary key**. Thus, the Client Number field is the primary key for the Client table.

The next eight fields in the Client table are Client Name, Street, City, State, Postal Code, Amount Paid, Current Due, and Hrs YTD, which is an abbreviation for Contract Hours YTD. YTD is an abbreviation for year to date. The Amount Paid column contains the amount that the client has paid Camashaly Design YTD prior to the current period. The Current Due column contains the amount due to Camashaly for the current period. The Hrs YTD column contains the number of hours the client has contracted for Web site maintenance so far this year. For example, client BB32 is Babbage CPA Firm. The address is 464 Linnell in Austin, South Carolina. The postal code is 28796. The client has paid $1,500.00 for services so far this year. The amount due for the current period is $500.00. The client has contracted for 5.00 hours of Web site maintenance.

Camashaly assigns a single business analyst to work with each client. The last column in the Client table, BA #, which is an abbreviation for Business Analyst Number, gives the number of the client's business analyst.

The first field in the Business Analyst table is also BA #, an abbreviation for Business Analyst Number. The business analyst numbers are unique, so the Business Analyst Number field is the primary key of the Business Analyst table.

The other fields in the Business Analyst table are Last Name, First Name, Street, City, State, Postal Code, Salary YTD, and Incentive YTD. The Salary YTD field gives the salary paid to the analyst thus far this year. The Incentive YTD gives the incentive for which the analyst qualified thus far this year. For example, business analyst 14 is Manuel Martinez. His address is 3125 Steel in Kyle, South Carolina. The Postal Code is 28797. So far this year, he has been paid $3,100.00 in salary. He has earned $2,430.00 in incentive pay.

The business analyst number appears in both the Client table and the Business Analyst table, and relates clients and business analysts. For example, in the Client table, you see that the business analyst number for client Babbage CPA Firm is 14. To find the name of this business analyst, look for the row in the Business Analyst table that contains 14 in the BA # column. After you have found it, you know the client is assigned to Manuel Martinez. To find all the clients assigned to Cordelia Kerry, you would first look in the Business Analyst table to find that her number is 11. You would then look through the Client table for all the clients that contain 11 in the BA # column. Her clients are BA53 (Bavant Animal Hospital), BC76 (Buda Community Clinic), GF56 (Granger Foundation), KG04 (Kyle Grocery Cooperative), and SL77 (Smarter Law Associates).

The last business analyst in the Business Analyst table, Jeff Scott, has not been assigned any clients yet; therefore, his business analyst number, 35, does not appear on any row in the Client table.

Overview

As you read this chapter, you will learn how to create the database shown in Figure 1–1 by performing these general tasks:

- Design the database.
- Create a new blank database.
- Create a table and add the records.
- Preview and print the contents of a table.
- Create a second table and import the records.
- Create a simple query.
- Create a simple form.
- Create and modify a report.

Database Design Guidelines

Plan
Ahead

Database design refers to the arrangement of data into tables and fields. In the example in this chapter, the design is specified, but in many cases, you will have to determine the design based on what you want the system to accomplish.

When designing a database to satisfy a given set of requirements, the actions you take and the decisions you make will determine the tables and fields that will be included in the database. As you create a database, such as the one shown in Figure 1–1 on page AC 3, you should follow these general guidelines:

1. **Identify the tables.** Examine the requirements for the database to identify the main objects that are involved. There will be a table for each object you identify.

    In one database, for example, the main objects might be departments and employees. Thus, there would be two tables: one for departments and the other for employees. In another database, the main objects might be clients and business analysts. In this case, there also would be two tables: one for clients and the other for business analysts. In still another database, the main objects might be books, publishers, and authors. This database would require three tables: one for books, a second for publishers, and a third for authors.

2. **Determine the primary keys.** Recall that the primary key is the unique identifier for records in the table. For each table, determine the unique identifier. In a Department table, for example, the unique identifier might be the Department Code. For a Book table, the unique identifier might be the ISBN.

3. **Determine the additional fields.** The primary key will be a field or combination of fields in a table. A table typically will contain many additional fields, each of which contains a type of data. Examine the project requirements to determine these additional fields. For example, in an Employee table, the additional fields might include such fields as Employee Name, Street Address, City, State, Postal Code, Date Hired, Salary, and so on.

4. **Determine relationships between the tables.** Examine the list of tables you have created to see which tables are related. When you determine that two tables are related, include matching fields in the two tables. For example, in a database containing employees and departments, there is a relationship between the two tables because one department can have many employees assigned to it. Department Code could be the matching field in the two tables.

5. **Determine data types for the fields.** For each field, determine the type of data the field can contain. One field, for example, might contain only numbers. Another field might contain currency amounts, while a third field might contain only dates. Some fields contain text data, meaning any combination of letters, numbers, and special characters (!, ;, ', &, and so on). For example, in an Employee table, the Date Hired field would contain dates, the Salary field would contain currency amounts, and the Hours Worked field would contain numbers. The other fields in the Employee table would contain text data, such as Employee Name and Department Code.

6. **Identify and remove any unwanted redundancy.** Redundancy is the storing of a piece of data in more than one place. Redundancy usually, but not always, causes problems, such as wasted space, difficulties with update, and possible data inconsistency. Examine each table you have created to see if it contains redundancy and, if so, determine whether the redundancy causes the problems described. If it does, remove the redundancy by splitting the table into two tables. For example, you might have a single table of employees. In addition to typical employee data (name, address, earnings, and so on), the table might contain Department Number and Department Name. If so, the Department Name could repeat multiple times. Every employee whose department number is 12, for example, would have the same department name. It would be better to split the table into two tables: one for Employees and one for Department. In the Department table, the Department Name is stored only once.

7. **Determine a storage location for the database.** The database you have designed will be stored in a single file. You need to determine a location in which to store the file.

8. **Determine additional properties for fields.** Before creating the database, determine any other properties you should specify for the fields. These could include a field size, which is

(continued)

(continued)

the maximum number of characters that can be stored in the field. If you want something other than the field name to appear at the top of a column (such as an abbreviation), you can change the caption to the desired heading. You also can add a description, which is a message that appears on the screen concerning a field whenever the field is selected.

9. **Determine the best method for distributing the database objects.** The traditional method of distributing database objects uses a printer to produce a hard copy of a table or report on paper. You also can distribute the table as an electronic image that mirrors the original table's appearance.

When necessary, more specific details concerning the above guidelines are presented at appropriate points in the chapter. The chapter also will identify the actions performed and decisions made regarding these guidelines during the creation of the database shown in Figure 1–1 on page AC 3.

Designing a Database

This section illustrates the database design process by showing how you would design the database for Camashaly Design from a set of requirements. In this section, you will use commonly accepted shorthand to represent the tables and fields that make up the database as well as the primary keys for the tables. For each table, you give the name of the table followed by a set of parentheses. Within the parentheses is a list of the fields in the table separated by columns. You underline the primary key. For example,

Product (<u>Product Code</u>, Description, On Hand, Price)

represents a table called Product. The Product table contains four fields: Product Code, Description, On Hand, and Price. The Product Code field is the primary key.

BTW

Determining Database Requirements
The determination of database requirements is part of a process known as systems analysis. A systems analyst examines existing and proposed documents, and examines organizational policies to determine exactly the type of data needs the database must support.

Database Requirements

The Camashaly Design database must maintain information on both clients and business analysts. The business currently keeps this data in two Word tables and two Excel workbooks, as shown in Figure 1–2. They use Word tables for address information and Excel workbooks for financial information.

Client Number	Client Name	Street	City	State	Postal Code
BA53	Bavant Animal Hospital	134 Main	Burles	NC	28817
BB32	Babbage CPA Firm	464 Linnell	Austin	SC	28796
BC76	Buda Community Clinic	867 Ridge	Buda	NC	27032
CJ29	Catering by Jenna	123 Second	Granger	NC	27036
GA74	Grant Antiques	78 Catawba	Georgetown	NC	28794
GF56	Granger Foundation	65 Simpson	Granger	NC	27036
HC10	Hendley County Hospital	216 Rivard	Austin	SC	28796
KD21	KAL Design Studio	116 Pine	Georgetown	NC	28794
KG04	Kyle Grocery Cooperative	421 First	Kyle	SC	28798
ME14	Mike's Electronic Stop	234 Gilham	Georgetown	NC	28794
PJ34	Patricia Jean Florist	345 Magee	Kyle	SC	28798
SL77	Smarter Law Associates	764 Main	Burles	NC	28817
TB17	The Bikeshop	346 Austin	Buda	NC	27032
WE05	Walburg Energy Alternatives	12 Polk	Walburg	NC	28819
WS01	Woody Sporting Goods	578 Central	Walburg	NC	28819

Figure 1–2   (a) Client Address Information (Word Table)

⬚	A	B	C	D	E	F	G	H
1	Client Number	Client Name	Amount Paid	Current Due	Contract Hours YTD			
2	BA53	Bavant Animal Hospital	0.00	7,500.00	0			
3	BB32	Babbage CPA Firm	1,500.00	500.00	5			
4	BC76	Buda Community Clinic	2,500.00	750.00	2.5			
5	CJ29	Catering by Jenna	3,000.00	1,000.00	15.5			
6	GA74	Grant Antiques	5,500.00	3,200.00	34.5			
7	GF56	Granger Foundation	0.00	6,500.00	0			
8	HC10	Hendley County Hospital	3,100.00	1,200.00	12			
9	KD21	KAL Design Studio	6,000.00	3,200.00	30.5			
10	KG04	Kyle Grocery Cooperative	3,200.00	0.00	5			
11	ME14	Mike's Electronic Stop	2,500.00	1,500.00	8.5			
12	PJ34	Patricia Jean Florist	0.00	5,200.00	0			
13	SL77	Smarter Law Associates	3,800.00	0.00	10.5			
14	TB17	The Bikeshop	2,750.00	1,200.00	14			
15	WE05	Walburg Energy Alternatives	4,500.00	1,450.00	19.5			
16	WS01	Woody Sporting Goods	2,250.00	1,600.00	18.5			

Figure 1–2 (b) Client Financial Information (Excel Worksheet)

Business Analyst Number	Last Name	First Name	Street	City	State	Postal Code
11	Kerry	Cordelia	251 Painter	Georgetown	NC	28794
14	Martinez	Manuel	3125 Steel	Kyle	SC	28797
27	Liu	Jan	265 Marble	Byron	SC	28795
35	Scott	Jeff	1925 Pine	Georgetown	NC	28794

Figure 1–2 (c) Business Analyst Address Information (Word Table)

⬚	A	B	C	D	E	F	G	H	I
1	Business Analyst Number	Last Name	First Name	Salary YTD	Incentive YTD				
2	11	Kerry	Cordelia	3,200.00	3,450.00				
3	14	Martinez	Manuel	3,100.00	2,430.00				
4	27	Liu	Jan	3,400.00	2,280.00				
5	35	Scott	Jeff	500.00	0.00				

Figure 1–2 (d) Business Analyst Financial Information (Excel Worksheet)

For clients, Camashaly needs to maintain address data. It currently keeps this address data in a Word table (Figure 1–2a). It also maintains financial data for each client. This includes the amount paid, current amount due, and contract hours YTD for the client. It keeps these amounts, along with the client name and number, in the Excel workbook shown in Figure 1–2b.

Camashaly keeps business analyst address data in a Word table, as shown in Figure 1–2c. Just as with clients, it keeps financial data for business analysts, including their salary YTD and incentive YTD, in a separate Excel workbook, as shown in Figure 1–2d.

Finally, it keeps track of which clients are assigned to which business analysts. Each client is assigned to a single business analyst, but each business analyst might be assigned many clients. Currently, for example, clients BA53 (Bavant Animal Hospital), BC76 (Buda Community Clinic), GF56 (Granger Foundation), KG04 (Kyle Grocery Cooperative), and SL77 (Smarter Law Associates) are assigned to business analyst 11 (Cordelia Kerry). Clients BB32 (Babbage CPA Firm), GA74 (Grant Antiques), KD21 (KAL Design Studio), WE05 (Walburg Energy Alternatives), and WS01 (Woody Sporting Goods) are assigned to business analyst 14 (Manuel Martinez). Clients CJ29 (Catering by Jenna), HC10 (Hendley County Hospital), ME14 (Mike's Electronic Stop), PJ34 (Patricia Jean Florist), and TB17 (The Bikeshop) are assigned to business analyst 27 (Jan Liu). Camashaly has an additional business analyst, Jeff Scott, whose number has been assigned as 35, but who has not yet been assigned any clients.

BTW

Additional Data for Camashaly
There are many other types of data that Camashaly could include in a database. For example, they might keep all employee information in a database as well as information on client contracts and an inventory of hardware and software.

Naming Tables and Fields

BTW

Naming Files
The following characters cannot be used in a file name: question mark (?), quotation mark ("), slash (/), backslash (\ ), colon (:), asterisk (*), vertical bar (|), greater than symbol (>), and less than symbol (<).

In designing your database, you must name the tables and fields. Thus, before beginning the design process, you must understand the rules Access applies to table and field names. These rules are:

1. Names can be up to 64 characters in length.
2. Names can contain letters, digits, and spaces, as well as most of the punctuation symbols.
3. Names cannot contain periods (.), exclamation points (!), accent graves (`), or square brackets ([ ]).
4. The same name cannot be used for two different fields in the same table.

The approach to naming tables and fields used in this text is to begin the names with an uppercase letter and to use lowercase for the other letters. In multiple-word names, each word begins with an uppercase letter, and there is a space between words (for example, Client Number). You should know that other approaches exist, all of which are acceptable in Access. Some people omit the space (ClientNumber). Still others use an underscore in place of the space (Client_Number). Finally, some use an underscore in place of a space, but use the same case for all letters (CLIENT_NUMBER or client_number).

Identifying the Tables

BTW

Naming Fields
Access 2010 has a number of reserved words, words that have a special meaning to Access. You cannot use these reserved words as field names. For example, Name is a reserved word and could not be used in the Client table to describe a client's name. For a complete list of reserved words in Access 2010, consult Access Help.

Now that you know the rules for naming tables and fields, you are ready to begin the design process. The first step is to identify the main objects involved in the requirements. For the Camashaly Design database, the main objects are clients and business analysts. This leads to two tables, which you must name. Reasonable names for these two tables are:

Client

Business Analyst

Determining the Primary Keys

The next step is to identify the fields that will be the unique identifiers, or primary keys. Client numbers uniquely identify clients, and business analyst numbers uniquely identify business analysts. Thus, the primary key for the Client table is the client number, and the primary key for the Business Analyst table is the business analyst number. Reasonable names for these fields would be Client Number and Business Analyst Number, respectively. Adding these primary keys to the tables gives:

Client (<u>Client Number</u>)
Business Analyst (<u>Business Analyst Number</u>)

Determining Additional Fields

After identifying the primary keys, you need to determine and name the additional fields. In addition to the client number, the Client Address Information shown in Figure 1–2a on page AC 6 contains the client name, street, city, state, and postal code. These would be fields in the Client table. The Client Financial Information shown in Figure 1–2b also contains the client number and client name, which are already included in the Client table. The financial information also contains the amount paid, current due, and contract hours YTD. Adding the amount paid, current due, and contract hours YTD fields to those already identified in the Client table and assigning reasonable names gives:

Client (<u>Client Number</u>, Client Name, Street, City, State, Postal Code,
      Amount Paid, Current Due, Contract Hours YTD)

Similarly, examining the Business Analyst Address Information in Figure 1–2c adds the last name, first name, street, city, state, and postal code fields to the Business Analyst table. In addition to the business analyst number, last name, and first name, the Business Analyst Financial Information in Figure 1–2d would add the salary YTD and Incentive YTD. Adding these fields to the Business Analyst table and assigning reasonable names gives:

Business Analyst (<u>Business Analyst Number</u>, Last Name, First Name, Street, City, State, Postal Code, Salary YTD, Incentive YTD)

Determining and Implementing Relationships Between the Tables

Determine relationships between the tables.
The most common type of relationship you will encounter between tables is the **one-to-many relationship**. This means that each row in the first table may be associated with many rows in the second table, but each row in the second table is associated with only one row in the first. The first table is called the "one" table and the second is called the "many" table. For example, there may be a relationship between departments and employees, in which each department can have many employees, but each employee is assigned to only one department. In this relationship, there would be two tables, Department and Employee. The Department table would be the "one" table in the relationship. The Employee table would be the "many" table.

To determine relationships between tables, you can follow these general guidelines:

- Identify the "one" table.

- Identify the "many" table.

- Include the primary key from the "one" table as a field in the "many" table.

Plan Ahead

According to the requirements, each client has one business analyst, but each business analyst can have many clients. Thus, the Business Analyst table is the "one" table, and the Client table is the "many" table. To implement this one-to-many relationship between business analysts and clients, add the Business Analyst Number field (the primary key of the Business Analyst table) to the Client table. This produces:

Client (<u>Client Number</u>, Client Name, Street, City, State, Postal Code, Amount Paid, Current Due, Contract Hours YTD, Business Analyst Number)
Business Analyst (<u>Business Analyst Number</u>, Last Name, First Name, Street, City, State, Postal Code, Salary YTD, Incentive YTD)

BTW

Database Design Language (DBDL)
DBDL is a commonly accepted shorthand representation for showing the structure of a relational database. You write the name of the table and then within parentheses you list all the columns in the table. If the columns continue beyond one line, indent the subsequent lines.

Determining Data Types for the Fields

Each field has a **data type**. This indicates the type of data that can be stored in the field. Three of the most commonly used data types are:

1. **Text** — The field can contain any characters. A maximum number of 255 characters is allowed in a field whose data type is Text.

2. **Number** — The field can contain only numbers. The numbers either can be positive or negative. Fields are assigned this type so they can be used in arithmetic operations. Fields that contain numbers but will not be used for arithmetic operations (such as postal codes) usually are assigned a data type of Text.

3. **Currency** — The field can contain only monetary data. The values will appear with currency symbols, such as dollar signs, commas, and decimal points, and with two digits following the decimal point. Like numeric fields, you can use currency fields in arithmetic operations. Access assigns a size to currency fields automatically.

Table 1–1 shows the other data types that are available in Access.

Table 1–1 Additional Data Types

Data Type	Description
Memo	Field can store a variable amount of text or combinations of text and numbers where the total number of characters may exceed 255.
Date/Time	Field can store dates and times.
AutoNumber	Field can store a unique sequential number that Access assigns to a record. Access will increment the number by 1 as each new record is added.
Yes/No	Field can store only one of two values. The choices are Yes/No, True/False, or On/Off.
OLE Object	Field can store an OLE object, which is an object linked to or embedded in the table.
Hyperlink	Field can store text that can be used as a hyperlink address.
Attachment	Field can contain an attached file. Images, spreadsheets, documents, charts, and so on can be attached to this field in a record in the database. You can view and edit the attached file.
Calculated	Field specified as a calculation based on other fields. The value is not actually stored.

In the Client table, because the Client Number, Client Name, Street, City, and State can all contain letters, their data types should be Text. The data type for Postal Code is Text instead of Number because postal codes are not used in arithmetic operations; you do not add postal codes or find an average postal code, for example. The Amount Paid and Current Due fields both contain monetary data, so their data types should be Currency. The Contract Hours YTD field contains a number that is not a currency amount, so its data type should be Number.

Similarly, in the Business Analyst table, the data type for the Business Analyst Number, Last Name, First Name, Street, City, State, and Postal Code fields all should be Text. The Salary YTD and Incentive YTD fields both contain monetary amounts, so their data types should be Currency.

Fields whose data type is Number often require you to change the field size, which is the storage space assigned to the field by Access. Table 1–2 shows the possible field sizes for Number fields. If the size were Byte, Integer, or Long Integer, for example, only integers could be stored. If you try to store a value that has decimal places, such as 2.50, the portion to the right of the decimal point would be removed, giving a result of 2. To address this problem, you would change to a size such as Single.

Table 1–2 Field Sizes for Number Fields

Field Size	Description
Byte	Integer value in the range of 0 to 255
Integer	Integer value in the range of –32,768 to 32,767
Long Integer	Integer value in the range of –2,147,483,648 to 2,147,483,647
Single	Numeric values with decimal places to seven significant digits — requires 4 bytes of storage
Double	Numeric values with decimal places to more accuracy than Single — requires 8 bytes of storage
Replication ID	Special identifier required for replication
Decimal	Numeric values with decimal places to more accuracy than Single or Double — requires 12 bytes of storage.

Identifying and Removing Redundancy

Redundancy means storing the same fact in more than one place. It usually results from placing too many fields in a table — fields that really belong in separate tables — and often causes serious problems. If you had not realized there were two objects, clients and business analysts, for example, you might have placed all the data in a single Client table. Figure 1–3 shows an example of a table that includes both client and business analyst information. Notice that the data for a given business analyst (number, name, address, and so on) occurs on more than one record. The data for analyst 11, Cordelia Kerry, is repeated in the figure.

Client Table

Client Number	Client Name	Street	...	Business Analyst Number	Last Name	First Name	...
BA53	Bavant Animal Hospital	134 Main	...	11	Kerry	Cordelia	...
BB32	Babbage CPA Firm	464 Linnell	...	14	Martinez	Manuel	...
BC76	Buda Community Clinic	867 Ridge	...	11	Kerry	Cordelia	...
...	...	...	...	...	...	...	...

business analyst numbers are 11

name of business analyst 11 appears more than once

Figure 1–3

Storing this data on multiple records is an example of redundancy, which causes several problems, including:

1. Wasted storage space. The name of business analyst 11, Cordelia Kerry, for example, should be stored only once. Storing this fact several times is wasteful.

2. More difficult database updates. If, for example, Cordelia Kerry's name is spelled wrong and needs to be changed in the database, her name would need to be changed in several different places.

3. A possibility of inconsistent data. Nothing prohibits the business analyst's last name from being Kerry on client BA53's record and Bronson on client BC76's record. The data would be inconsistent. In both cases, the business analyst number is 11, but the last names are different.

The solution to the problem is to place the redundant data in a separate table, one in which the data no longer will be redundant. If, for example, you place the data for business analysts in a separate table (Figure 1–4), the data for each business analyst will appear only once.

Client Table

Client Number	Client Name	Street	...	Business Analyst Number
BA53	Bavant Animal Hospital	134 Main	...	11
BB32	Babbage CPA Firm	464 Linnell	...	14
BC76	Buda Community Clinic	867 Ridge	...	11
...	...	...		

business analyst numbers are 11

Business Analyst Table

Business Analyst Number	Last Name	First Name	...
11	Kerry	Cordelia	...
14	Martinez	Manuel	...
...	...		...

name of business analyst 11 appears only once

Figure 1–4

BTW

Postal Codes
Some organizations with customers throughout the country have a separate table of postal codes, cities, and states. When placing an order, you typically are asked for your postal code (or ZIP code), rather than city, state, and postal code. You then are asked to confirm that the city and state correspond to that postal code.

Notice that you need to have the business analyst number in both tables. Without it, there would be no way to tell which business analyst is associated with which client. The remaining business analyst data, however, was removed from the Client table and placed in the Business Analyst table. This new arrangement corrects the problems of redundancy in the following ways:

1. Because the data for each business analyst is stored only once, space is not wasted.
2. Changing the name of a business analyst is easy. You have only to change one row in the Business Analyst table.
3. Because the data for a business analyst is stored only once, inconsistent data cannot occur. Designing to omit redundancy will help you to produce good and valid database designs.

You should always examine your design to see if it contains redundancy. If it does, you should decide whether you need to remove the redundancy by creating a separate table.

If you examine your design, you'll see that there is one area of redundancy (see the data in Figure 1–1 on page AC 3). Cities and states are both repeated. Every client whose postal code is 28794, for example, has Georgetown as the city and NC as the state. To remove this redundancy, you would create a table whose primary key is Postal Code and that contains City and State as additional fields. City and State would be removed from the Client table. Having City, State, and Postal Code in a table is very common, however, and usually you would not take such action. No other redundancy exists in your tables.

For an introduction to Windows 7 and instruction about how to perform basic Windows 7 tasks, read the Office 2010 and Windows 7 chapter at the beginning of this book, where you can learn how to resize windows, change screen resolution, create folders, move and rename files, use Windows Help, and much more.

To Start Access

If you are using a computer to step through the project in this chapter and you want your screens to match the figures in this book, you should change your screen's resolution to 1024 × 768. For information about how to change a computer's resolution, refer to the Office 2010 and Windows 7 chapter at the beginning of this book.

The following steps, which assume Windows 7 is running, start Access based on a typical installation. You may need to ask your instructor how to start Access for your computer. For a detailed example of the procedure summarized below, refer to the Office 2010 and Windows 7 chapter.

1 Click the Start button on the Windows 7 taskbar to display the Start menu.

2 Type **Microsoft Access** as the search text in the 'Search programs and files' text box and watch the search results appear on the Start menu.

3 Click Microsoft Access 2010 in the search results on the Start menu to start Access and display the Backstage view for Access.

4 If the Access window is not maximized, click the Maximize button next to the Close button on its title bar to maximize the window.

Creating a Database

In Access, all the tables, reports, forms, and queries that you create are stored in a single file called a database. Thus, you first must create the database to hold the tables, reports, forms, and queries. You can use either the Blank database option or a template to create a new database. If you already know the tables and fields you want in your database, you would use the Blank database option. If not, you can use a template. Templates can guide you by suggesting some commonly used databases.

Determine a storage location for the database.
When creating a database, you must decide which storage medium to use.

If you always work on the same computer and have no need to transport your database to a different location, then your computer's hard drive will suffice as a storage location. It is a good idea, however, to save a backup copy of your database on a separate medium in case the file becomes corrupted or the computer's hard drive fails.

If you plan to work on your database in various locations or on multiple computers, then you can consider saving your projects on a portable medium, such as a USB flash drive or CD. The projects in this book are stored on a USB flash drive, which saves files quickly and reliably and can be reused. CDs are easily portable and serve as good backups for the final versions of projects because they generally can save files only one time.

Plan Ahead

For an introduction to Office 2010 and instruction about how to perform basic tasks in Office 2010 programs, read the Office 2010 and Windows 7 chapter at the beginning of this book, where you can learn how to start a program, use the Ribbon, save a file, open a file, quit a program, use Help, and much more.

To Create a Database

Because you already know the tables and fields you want in the Camashaly Design database, you would use the Blank database option rather than using a template. The following steps assume you already have created folders for storing your files, for example, a CIS 101 folder (for your class) that contains an Access folder (for your assignments). Thus, these steps save the document in the Access folder in the CIS 101 folder on a USB flash drive using the file name, Camashaly Design. For a detailed example of the procedure summarized below, refer to the Office 2010 and Windows 7 chapter at the beginning of this book.

1 With a USB flash drive connected to one of the computer's USB ports, ensure the New tab is selected in the Backstage view and that Blank database is selected in the New gallery.

2 Click the Browse button in the right pane of the New gallery to display the File New Database dialog box.

3 Type `Camashaly Design` in the File New Database dialog box to change the file name. Do not press the ENTER key after typing the file name.

4 Navigate to the desired save location (in this case, the Access folder in the CIS 101 folder [or your class folder] on the USB flash drive).

5 Click the OK button, which returns you to the New gallery. (Your screen may show Camashaly Design.accdb.)

6 Click the Create button in the right pane of the New gallery to create the database on the selected drive with the entered file name (Figure 1–5).

BTW

Q&As
For a complete list of the Q&As found in many of the step-by-step sequences in this book, visit the Access 2010 Q&A Web page (scsite.com/ac2010/qa).

Q&A

The title bar for my Navigation Pane contains All Tables rather than All Access Objects, as in the figure. Is that a problem?

It is not a problem. The title bar indicates how the Navigation Pane is organized. You can carry out the steps in the text with either organization. To make your screens match the ones in the text, click the Navigation Pane arrow and then click Object Type.

Q&A

I do not have the Search bar that appears on the figure. Is that a problem?

It is not a problem. If your Navigation Pane does not display a Search bar and you want your screens to match the ones in the text, right-click the Navigation Pane title bar arrow to display a shortcut menu, and then click Search Bar.

Figure 1–5

TO CREATE A DATABASE USING A TEMPLATE

Ideally, you will design your own database, create a blank database, and then create the tables you have determined that your database should contain. If you are not sure what database design you will need, you could use a template. Templates can guide you by suggesting some commonly used databases. To create a database using a template, you would use the following steps.

1. After starting Access, be sure the Backstage view is open. If it is not, click File on the Ribbon to open it.
2. Click the New tab if it is not already selected.
3. Click Sample templates to display a list of templates stored locally or search Microsoft Office online for additional templates.
4. Click the template you want to use.
5. Enter a file name (or accept the suggested file name) and select a location for the database.
6. Click the Create button to create the database or the Download button to download the database and create the database, if necessary.

The Access Window

The Access window consists of a variety of components to make your work more efficient and documents more professional. These include the Navigation Pane, Access work area, Ribbon, shortcut menus, and Quick Access Toolbar. Some of these components are common to other Microsoft Office 2010 programs; others are unique to Access.

Navigation Pane and Access Work Area

You work on objects such as tables, forms, and reports in the **Access work area**. In the work area in Figure 1–5, a single table, Table1, is open in the work area. **Object tabs** for the open objects appear at the top of the work area. If you have multiple objects open at the same time, you can select one of the open objects by clicking its tab. To the left of the work area is the Navigation Pane. The **Navigation Pane** contains a list of all the objects in the database. You use this pane to open an object. You also can customize the way objects are displayed in the Navigation Pane.

The **status bar**, located at the bottom of the Access window, presents information about the database object, the progress of current tasks, and the status of certain commands and keys; it also provides controls for viewing the object. As you type text or perform certain commands, various indicators may appear on the status bar. The left edge of the status bar in Figure 1–5 shows that the table object is open in Datasheet view. Toward the right edge are View buttons, which you can use to change the view that currently is displayed.

Creating a Table

To create a table, you must describe the structure of the table to Access. That is, you must describe all the fields that make up the table and their characteristics. You must also indicate the primary key.

In Access, you can use two different views to create a table: Datasheet view and Design view. In **Datasheet view**, the data in the table is presented in rows and columns, similar to a spreadsheet. Although the main reason to use Datasheet view is to add or update records in a table, you can also use it to create a table or to later modify its structure. The other view, **Design view**, is only used to create a table or to modify the structure of the table.

As you might expect, Design view has more functionality for creating a table than Datasheet view. That is, there are certain actions that can only be performed in Design view. If creating your table requires such actions, you must use Design view. If not, you can choose either view. In this chapter, you will create the first table, the Business Analyst table, in Datasheet view. You will create the second table, the Client table, in Design view.

Whichever view you choose to use, before creating the table, you need to determine the names and data types of the fields that will make up the table. You already have determined the types for the Camashaly fields. You also need to determine additional properties for the fields.

BTW

The Ribbon and Screen Resolution
Access may change how the groups and buttons within the groups appear on the Ribbon, depending on the computer's screen resolution. Thus, your Ribbon may look different from the ones in this book if you are using a screen resolution other than 1024 × 768.

Plan
Ahead

Determine additional properties for fields.

- **Determine if a special caption is warranted.** Normally, the field name will appear as the label for a field on a form or report and as the column name in Datasheet view. If you would rather have a different name appear, you can change the field's caption to the desired name. One common use of captions is to shorten the column heading. If the data in a column is considerably shorter than the column heading, you could change the caption to a shorter heading. This would enable you to reduce the width of the column and yet still be able to see the entire column heading.

- **Determine if a special description is warranted.** Determine whether to include a description that would appear in the status bar whenever the field is selected.

- **Determine field sizes.** For Text fields, determine the field size; that is, the maximum number of characters that can be entered in the field. Users will be prohibited from entering a value that has more characters than the field size.

- **Determine formats.** Determine whether the data in the field should be formatted in any particular way. You could, for example, specify that a number field is to be formatted with precisely two decimal places.

BTW

Naming Tables
Database users typically have their own guidelines for naming tables. Some use the singular version of the object being described, while others use the prefix tbl with a table name. This book uses the singular version of the object (Client, Business Analyst) but adds the word Table to the name for the Business Analyst table to illustrate another possible approach. Including the word Table can assist visually impaired users when viewing the Navigation Pane.

The results of these decisions for the fields in the Business Analyst table are shown in Table 1–3. The table also shows the data types and field sizes of the fields as well as any special properties that need to be changed. The Business Analyst Number field has a caption of BA #, enabling the width of the Business Analyst Number column to be reduced in the datasheet.

Table 1–3 Structure of Business Analyst Table

Field Name	Data Type	Field Size	Description
Business Analyst Number	Text	2	**Primary Key** **Description:** Business Analyst Number **Caption:** BA #
Last Name	Text	15	
First Name	Text	15	
Street	Text	15	
City	Text	15	
State	Text	2	
Postal Code	Text	5	
Salary YTD	Currency		
Incentive YTD	Currency		

To Modify the Primary Key

When you first create your database, Access automatically creates a table for you. You can immediately begin defining the fields. If, for any reason, you do not have this table or inadvertently delete it, you can create the table by clicking Create on the Ribbon and then clicking the Table button (Create tab | Tables group). In either case, you are ready to define the fields.

The following steps define the first field, the Business Analyst Number field, which is the primary key. Access has already created a primary key field, which it has named ID. Thus, the steps will change the name, data type, and other properties of this field to match the Business Analyst field in Table 1–3.

1

- Right-click the column heading for the ID field to display a shortcut menu (Figure 1–6).

Q&A

Why does my shortcut menu look different?

You right-clicked within the column instead of right-clicking the column heading.

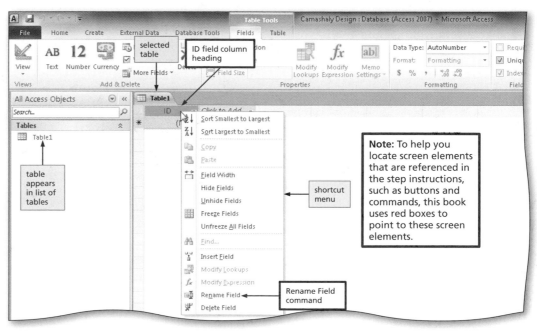

Figure 1–6

2

- Click Rename Field on the shortcut menu to highlight the current name.

- Type **Business Analyst Number** to assign a name to the new field.

- Click the white space immediately below the field name to complete the addition of the field (Figure 1–7).

Figure 1–7

Q&A

Why does the name not appear in its entirety?

The default column size is not large enough for Business Analyst Number to appear in its entirety. You will address this issue in later steps.

- Because the data type needs to be changed from AutoNumber to Text, click the Data Type box arrow (Table Tools Fields tab | Formatting group) to display a menu of available data types (Figure 1–8).

Figure 1–8

- Click Text to select the data type for the field (Figure 1–9).

Figure 1–9

- Click the Field Size text box (Table Tools Fields tab | Properties group) to select the current field size, use either the DELETE or BACKSPACE keys to erase the current field size, and then type 2 as the new field size.

- Click the Name & Caption button (Table Tools Fields tab | Properties group) to display the Enter Field Properties dialog box.

- Click the Caption text box (Enter Field Properties dialog box), and then type **BA #** as the caption.

Figure 1–10

- Click the Description text box, and then type **Unique identifier of business analyst** as the description (Figure 1–10).

- Click the OK button (Enter Field Properties dialog box) to change the caption and description (Figure 1–11).

Figure 1–11

To Define the Remaining Fields in a Table

To define an additional field, you click the Click to Add column heading, select the data type, and then type the field name. This is different from the process you used to modify the ID field, which was an existing field. The following steps define the remaining fields shown in Table 1–3 on page AC 16.

1

- Click the Click to Add column heading to display a menu of available data types (Figure 1–12).

Why did I follow a different process when I renamed this field?

The ID field was an existing field, created automatically by Access. For a new field, you need to click the Click to Add heading.

Figure 1–12

2

- Click Text in the menu of available data types to select the Text data type.

- Type Last Name to enter a field name.

- Click the white space below the field name to complete the change of the name. Click the white space a second time to select the field (Figure 1–13).

I realized after I entered the field name that I selected the wrong data type. How can I correct it?

Click the Data Type box arrow and then select the correct type.

Figure 1–13

I inadvertently clicked the white space before entering the field name. How can I correct the name?

Right-click the field name, click Rename Field on the shortcut menu, and then type the new name.

3

- Change the field size to 15 just as you changed the field size of the Business Analyst Number field.

- Using the same technique, add the remaining fields in the Business Analyst table. For the First Name, Street, City, State, and Postal Code fields, the Text data type is correct, but you will need to change the field size to match Table 1–3. For the Salary YTD and Incentive YTD fields, you need to change the data type to Currency. Before defining the Incentive YTD field, you may need to click the right scroll arrow to bring the column for the field to the screen (Figure 1–14).

Figure 1–14

Q&A

Why does Currency appear twice?

The second Currency is the format, which indicates how the data will be displayed. For the Currency data type, Access automatically sets the format to Currency, which is usually what you would want. You could change it to something else, if desired, by clicking the arrow and selecting the desired format.

Q&A

I have an extra row between the row containing the field names and the row that begins with the asterisk. What happened? Is this a problem? If so, how do I fix it?

You inadvertently added a record to the table by pressing some key. Even pressing the SPACEBAR would add a record. You now have a record you do not want. To fix it, you need to delete the record, which you will do in Step 4.

- If you have an additional record between the field names and the asterisk, press the ESC key to delete the record.

Making Changes to the Structure

When creating a table, check the entries carefully to ensure they are correct. If you discover a mistake while still typing the entry, you can correct the error by repeatedly pressing the BACKSPACE key until the incorrect characters are removed. Then, type the correct characters. If you do not discover a mistake until later, you can use the following techniques to make the necessary changes to the structure:

- To undo your most recent change, click the Undo button on the Quick Access Toolbar. If there is nothing that Access can undo, this button will be dim, and clicking it will have no effect.
- To delete a field, right-click the column heading for the field (the position containing the field name), and then click Delete Field on the shortcut menu.
- To change the name of a field, right-click the column heading for the field, click Rename Field on the shortcut menu, and then type the desired field name.
- To insert a field as the last field, click the Click to Add column heading, click the appropriate data type on the menu of available data types, type the desired field name, and, if necessary, change the field size.
- To insert a field between existing fields, right-click the column heading for the field that will follow the new field, and then click Insert Field on the shortcut menu. Right-click the column heading for the field, click Rename Field on the shortcut menu, and then type the desired field name.
- To move a field, click the column heading for the field to be moved to select the field, and then drag the field to the desired position.

As an alternative to these steps, you may want to start over. To do so, click the Close button for the table, and then click the No button in the Microsoft Access dialog box. Click Create on the Ribbon and then click the Table button to create a table. You then can repeat the process you used earlier to define the fields in the table.

BTW

Currency Symbols
To show the symbol for the Euro (€) instead of the dollar sign, change the Format property for the field whose data type is currency. To change the default symbols for currency, change the settings in the operating system using the control panel.

To Save a Table

The Business Analyst table structure now is complete. The final step is to save the table within the database. As part of the process, you will give the table a name. The following steps save the table, giving it the name, Business Analyst Table.

1

• Click the Save button on the Quick Access Toolbar to display the Save As dialog box (Figure 1–15).

Figure 1–15

2

• Type **Business Analyst Table** to change the name to be assigned to the table.

• Click the OK button (Save As dialog box) to save the table (Figure 1–16).

Other Ways

1. Click File on the Ribbon, click Save in the Backstage view
2. Right-click tab for table, click Save on shortcut menu
3. Press CTRL+S

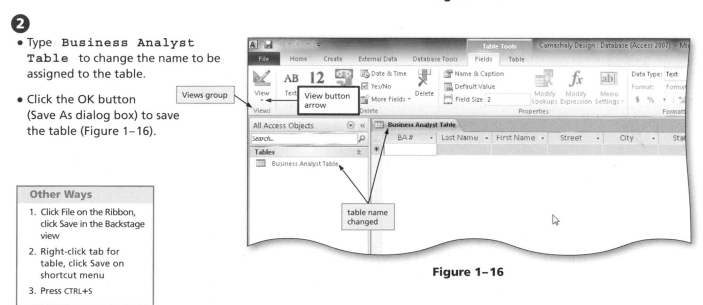

Figure 1–16

To View the Table in Design View

Even when creating a table in Datasheet view, Design view can be helpful. You should view the fields, data types, and properties to ensure you have entered them correctly. This viewing is easier to do in Design view. It is also easier to determine the primary key in Design view. The following steps view the structure of the Business Analyst Table in Design view so that you can verify the design is correct.

1

- Click the View button arrow (Table Tools Fields tab | Views group) to display the View button menu (Figure 1–17).

Q&A

Could I just click the View button rather than the arrow?

Yes. Clicking the button is equivalent to clicking the command represented by the icon currently appearing on the button. Because the icon on the button in Figure 1–17 is the icon for Design view, clicking the button would display the table in Design view. If you are uncertain, you can always click the arrow and select from the menu.

Figure 1–17

2

- Click Design View on the View button menu to view the table in Design view (Figure 1–18).

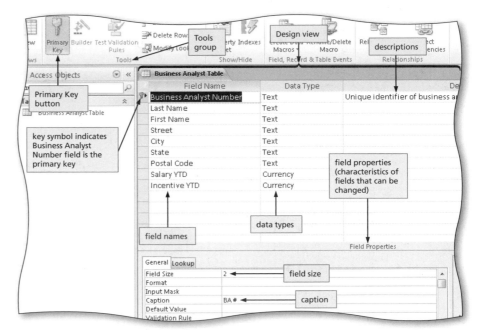

Figure 1–18

Other Ways

1. Click Design View button on status bar

Checking the Structure in Design View

You should use Design view to carefully check the entries you have made. In Figure 1–18, for example, you can see that the Business Analyst Number field is the primary key of the Business Analyst Table by the key symbol in front of the field name. If your table does not have a key symbol, you can click the Primary Key button (Table Tools Design tab | Tools group) to designate the field as the primary key. You also can check that the data type, the description, the field size, and the caption are all correct.

For the other fields, you can see the field name, data type, and description without taking any special action. To see the field size and/or caption for a field, click the field's **row selector**, the small box that precedes the field. Clicking the row selector for the Last Name field, for example, displays the field properties for the field (Figure 1–19). You then can check to see that the field size is correct. In addition, if the field has a caption, you can check to see if that is correct as well. If you find any mistakes, you can make the necessary corrections on this screen. When you have finished, you would click the Save button to save your changes.

To Close the Table

Once you are sure that your entries are correct and you have saved your changes, you can close the table. The following step closes the table.

- Click the Close button for the Business Analyst Table to close the table (Figure 1–19).

Figure 1–19

Other Ways

1. Right-click tab for table, click Close on shortcut menu

To Add Records to a Table

Creating a table by building the structure and saving the table is the first step in a two-step process. The second step is to add records to the table. To add records to a table, the table must be open. When making changes to tables, you work in Datasheet view. In Datasheet view, the table is represented as a collection of rows and columns called a **datasheet**.

You often add records in phases. For example, you might not have enough time to add all the records in one session. The following steps open the Business Analyst Table in Datasheet view and then add the first two records in the Business Analyst Table (Figure 1–20).

BA #	Last Name	First Name	Street	City	State	Postal Code	Salary YTD	Incentive YTD
11	Kerry	Cordelia	251 Painter	Georgetown	NC	28794	$3,200.00	$3,450.00
14	Martinez	Manuel	3125 Steel	Kyle	SC	28797	$3,100.00	$2,430.00

Figure 1–20

- Right-click the Business Analyst Table in the Navigation Pane to display the shortcut menu (Figure 1–21).

Figure 1–21

2

- Click Open on the shortcut menu to open the table in Datasheet view.

Q&A

What if I want to return to Design view?

You can open Design view by clicking Design View on the shortcut menu.

- Click the Shutter Bar Open/Close Button to close the Navigation Pane (Figure 1–22).

Figure 1–22

3

- Click the BA # field if necessary to display an insertion point, and type **11** to enter the first business analyst number (Figure 1–23).

Figure 1–23

4

- Press the TAB key to move to the next field.

- Enter the last name, first name, street, city, state, and postal code by typing the following entries, pressing the TAB key after each one: **Kerry** as the last name, **Cordelia** as the first name, **251 Painter** as the street, **Georgetown** as the city, **NC** as the state, and **28794** as the postal code.

- Type **3200** in the Salary YTD field (Figure 1–24).

Figure 1–24

Q&A

Do I need to type a dollar sign?

You do not need to type dollar signs or commas. In addition, because the digits to the right of the decimal point are both zeros, you do not need to type either the decimal point or the zeros.

5

- Press the TAB key to complete the entry for the field.

- Type 3 4 5 0 in the Incentive YTD field, and then press the TAB key to complete the entry of the first record (Figure 1–25).

Q&A

How and when do I save the record?

As soon as you have entered or modified a record and moved to another record, the original record is saved. This is different from other applications. The rows entered in an Excel worksheet, for example, are not saved until the entire worksheet is saved.

Figure 1–25

6

- Use the techniques shown in Steps 3 through 5 to enter the data for the second record (Figure 1–26).

Experiment

- Click the Salary YTD field on either of the records. Be sure the Table Tools Fields tab is selected. Click the Format box arrow and then click each of the formats in the Format box menu to see the effect on the values in the Salary YTD field. When finished, click Currency in the Format box menu.

Figure 1–26

Making Changes to the Data

As you enter data, check your entries carefully to ensure they are correct. If you make a mistake and discover it before you press the TAB key, correct it by pressing the BACKSPACE key until the incorrect characters are removed, and then type the correct characters. If you do not discover a mistake until later, you can use the following techniques to make the necessary corrections to the data:

- To undo your most recent change, click the Undo button on the Quick Access Toolbar. If there is nothing that Access can undo, this button will be dimmed, and clicking it will have no effect.

- To add a record, click the New (blank) record button, click the position for the Business Analyst Number field on the first open record, and then add the record. Do not worry about it being in the correct position in the table. Access will reposition the record based on the primary key, in this case, the Business Analyst Number.

BTW

Adding Records
You can add records in any order. When you close a table and reopen it, the records will be in order by primary key.

- To delete a record, click the record selector, shown in Figure 1–26, for the record to be deleted. Then press the DELETE key to delete the record, and click the Yes button when Access asks you to verify that you do indeed want to delete the record.

- To change the contents of one or more fields in a record, the record must be on the screen. If it is not, use any appropriate technique, such as the UP ARROW and DOWN ARROW keys or the vertical scroll bar, to move to it. If the field you want to correct is not visible on the screen, use the horizontal scroll bar along the bottom of the screen to shift all the fields until the one you want appears. If the value in the field is currently highlighted, you can simply type the new value. If you would rather edit the existing value, you must have an insertion point in the field. You can place the insertion point by clicking in the field or by pressing F2. You then can use the arrow keys, the DELETE key, and the BACKSPACE key for making the correction. You also can use the INSERT key to switch between Insert and Overtype mode. When you have made the change, press the TAB key to move to the next field.

If you cannot determine how to correct the data, you may find that you are "stuck" on the record, in which case Access neither allows you to move to another record nor allows you to close the table until you have made the correction. If you encounter this situation, simply press the ESC key. Pressing the ESC key will remove from the screen the record you are trying to add. You then can move to any other record, close the table, or take any other action you desire.

To Close a Table

Now that you have created and saved the Business Analyst Table, you can close it. The following step closes the table.

1 Click the Close button for the Business Analyst Table, shown in Figure 1–26, to close the table (Figure 1–27).

Figure 1–27

To Quit Access

The following steps quit Access. For a detailed example of the procedure summarized below, refer to the Office 2010 and Windows 7 chapter at the beginning of this book.

1 Click the Close button on the right side of the title bar to quit Access.

2 If a Microsoft Access dialog box appears, click the Save button to save any changes made to the object since the last save.

Break Point: If you wish to take a break, this is a good place to do so. To resume at a later time, continue following the steps from this location forward.

Starting Access and Opening a Database

Once you have created and later closed a database, you will need to open it in the future in order to use it. Opening a database requires that Access is running on your computer.

To Start Access

1 Click the Start button on the Windows 7 taskbar to display the Start menu.

2 Type `Microsoft Access` as the search text in the 'Search programs and files' text box and watch the search results appear on the Start menu.

3 Click Microsoft Access 2010 in the search results on the Start menu to start Access.

To Open a Database from Access

Earlier in this chapter, you saved your database on a USB flash drive using the file name, Camashaly Design. The following steps open the Camashaly Design database from the Access folder in the CIS 101 folder on the USB flash drive. For a detailed example of the procedure summarized below, refer to the Office 2010 and Windows 7 chapter at the beginning of this book.

1 With your USB flash drive connected to one of the computer's USB ports, click File on the Ribbon to open the Backstage view, if necessary.

2 Click Open in the Backstage view to display the Open dialog box.

3 Navigate to the location of the file to be opened (in this case, the USB flash drive, then to the CIS 101 folder [or your class folder], and then to the Access folder).

4 Click Camashaly Design to select the file to be opened.

5 Click the Open button (Open dialog box) to open the selected file and display the opened database in the Access window.

6 If a Security Warning appears, click the Enable Content button (Figure 1–28).

> **BTW**
>
> **Organizing Files and Folders**
> You should organize and store files in folders so that you easily can find the files later. For a discussion of folders and detailed examples of creating folders, refer to the Office 2010 and Windows 7 chapter at the beginning of this book.

Q&A

When would I not want to enable the content?

You would want to disable the content if you suspected that your database might contain harmful content or damaging macros. Because you are the one who created the database and no one else has used it, you should have no such suspicions.

Figure 1–28

Other Ways

1. Click File on the Ribbon, click Recent in the Backstage view, click file name

To Add Additional Records to a Table

You can add records to a table that already contains data using a process almost identical to that used to add records to an empty table. The only difference is that you place the insertion point after the last record before you enter the additional data. To do so, use the **Navigation buttons**, which are buttons used to move within a table, found near the lower-left corner of the screen when a table is open. The purpose of each of the Navigation buttons is described in Table 1–4.

Table 1–4 Navigation Buttons in Datasheet View	
Button	**Purpose**
First record	Moves to the first record in the table
Previous record	Moves to the previous record
Next record	Moves to the next record
Last record	Moves to the last record in the table
New (blank) record	Moves to the end of the table to a position for entering a new record

The following steps add the remaining records (Figure 1–29) to the Business Analyst table.

BA #	Last Name	First Name	Street	City	State	Postal Code	Salary YTD	Incentive YTD
27	Liu	Jan	265 Marble	Byron	SC	28795	$3,400.00	$2,280.00
35	Scott	Jeff	1925 Pine	Georgetown	NC	28794	$500.00	$0.00

Figure 1–29

 1

- If the Navigation Pane is closed, click the Shutter Bar Open/ Close Button, shown in Figure 1–27, to open the Navigation Pane (Figure 1–30).

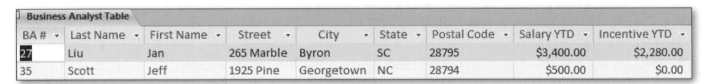

Figure 1–30

2

- Right-click the Business Analyst Table in the Navigation Pane to display a shortcut menu.

- Click Open on the short-cut menu to open the table in Datasheet view.

- Close the Navigation Pane by clicking the Shutter Bar Open/Close Button (Figure 1–31).

Figure 1–31

- Click the New (blank) record button to move to a position to enter a new record (Figure 1–32).

Q&A

Could you just click the Business Analyst Number (BA #) on the first open record and then add the record?

Yes, but it is a good habit to use the New (blank) Record button. Once a table contains more records than will fit on the screen, it is easier to click the New (blank) record button.

Figure 1–32

- Add the records shown in Figure 1–29, using the same techniques you used to add the first two records (Figure 1–33).

Other Ways

1. Click New button (Home tab | Records group)
2. Press CTRL+PLUS SIGN (+)

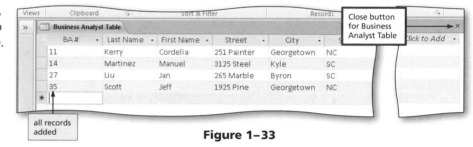

Figure 1–33

To Resize Columns in a Datasheet

Access assigns default column sizes, which do not always allow all the data in the field to appear. In some cases, the data might appear but not the entire field name. You can correct this problem by **resizing** the column (changing its size) in the datasheet. In some instances, you may want to reduce the size of a column. The State field, for example, is short enough that it does not require all the space on the screen that is allotted to it. Changing a column width changes the **layout**, or design, of a table.

The following steps resize the columns in the Business Analyst table and save the changes to the layout.

- Point to the right boundary of the field selector for the Business Analyst (BA #) field (Figure 1–34) so that the mouse pointer becomes a two-headed arrow.

Figure 1–34

2

- Double-click the right boundary of the field selector to resize the field so that it best fits the data.

- Use the same technique to resize all the other fields to best fit the data (Figure 1–35).

Figure 1–35

3

- Save the changes to the layout by clicking the Save button on the Quick Access Toolbar (Figure 1–35).

- Click the table's Close button (shown in Figure 1–33) to close the table.

Q&A What if I closed the table without saving the layout changes?

You would be asked if you want to save the changes.

Other Ways

1. Right-click field name, click Field Width

Plan Ahead

Determine the best method for distributing the database objects.

The traditional method of distributing database objects uses a printer to produce a hard copy of a table. A **hard copy** or **printout** is information that exists on a physical medium such as paper. For users who can receive fax documents, you can elect to print a hard copy on a remote fax machine. Hard copies can be useful for the following reasons:

- Many people prefer proofreading a hard copy of a document rather than viewing it on the screen to check for errors and readability.

- Hard copies can serve as reference material if your storage medium is lost or becomes corrupted and you need to re-create the document.

Instead of distributing a hard copy, users can choose to distribute the document as an electronic image that mirrors the original document's appearance. The electronic image of the document can be e-mailed, posted on a Web site, or copied to a portable medium such as a USB flash drive. Two popular electronic image formats, sometimes called fixed formats, are PDF by Adobe Systems and XPS by Microsoft. In Access, you can create PDF and XPS files through the External Data tab on the Ribbon. Electronic images of documents, such as PDF and XPS, can be useful for the following reasons.

- Users can view electronic images of documents without the software that created the original document (i.e., Access). Specifically, to view a PDF file, you use a program called Acrobat Reader, which can be downloaded free from Adobe's Web site. Similarly, to view an XPS file, you use a program called an XPS Viewer, which is included in the latest versions of Windows and Internet Explorer.

- Sending electronic documents saves paper and printer supplies. Society encourages users to contribute to **green computing**, which involves reducing the environmental waste generated when using a computer.

BTW

Changing Printers
To change the default printer that appears in the Print dialog box, click File on the Ribbon, click the Print tab in the Backstage view, click Print in the Print gallery, then click the Name box arrow and select the desired printer.

Previewing and Printing the Contents of a Table

When working with a database, you often will need to print a copy of the table contents. Figure 1–36 shows a printed copy of the contents of the Business Analyst table. (Yours may look slightly different, depending on your printer.) Because the Business Analyst table is substantially wider than the screen, it also will be wider than the normal printed page in portrait orientation. **Portrait orientation** means the printout is across the width of the page. **Landscape orientation** means the printout is across the height of the page. Thus, to print the wide database table, you might prefer to use landscape orientation. A convenient way to change to landscape orientation is to preview what the printed copy will look like by using Print Preview. This allows you to determine whether landscape orientation is necessary and, if it is, to change the orientation easily to landscape. In addition, you also can use Print Preview to determine whether any adjustments are necessary to the page margins.

			Business Analyst Table						4/12/2012

BA #	Last Name	First Name	Street	City	State	Postal Code	Salary YTD	Incentive YTD
11	Kerry	Cordelia	251 Painter	Georgetown	NC	28794	$3,200.00	$3,450.00
14	Martinez	Manuel	3125 Steel	Kyle	SC	28797	$3,100.00	$2,430.00
27	Liu	Jan	265 Marble	Byron	SC	28795	$3,400.00	$2,280.00
35	Scott	Jeff	1925 Pine	Georgetown	NC	28794	$500.00	$0.00

Figure 1–36

To Preview and Print the Contents of a Table

The following steps use Print Preview to preview and then print the contents of the Business Analyst table.

1

• If the Navigation Pane is closed, open the Navigation Pane by clicking the Shutter Bar Open/Close Button.

• Be sure the Business Analyst table is selected.

Q&A Why do I have to be sure the Business Analyst table is selected? It is the only object in the database.

When the database contains only one object, you do not have to worry about selecting the object. Ensuring that the correct object is selected is a good habit to form, however, to make sure that the object you print is the one you want.

Figure 1–37

• Click File on the Ribbon to open the Backstage view.

• Click the Print tab in the Backstage view to display the Print gallery (Figure 1–37).

2

• Click the Print Preview button in the Print gallery to display a preview of what the table will look like when printed.

• Close the Navigation Pane to free up more of the screen for the preview (Figure 1–38).

Q&A I cannot read the table. Can I magnify a portion of the table?

Yes. Point the mouse pointer, whose shape will change to a magnifying glass, at the portion of the table that you want to magnify, and then click. You can return the view of the table to the one shown in the figure by clicking a second time.

Figure 1–38

- Click the mouse pointer in the position shown in Figure 1–38 to magnify the upper-right section of the table (Figure 1–39).

My table was already magnified in a different area. How can I see the area shown in the figure?

One way is to use the scroll bars to move to the desired portion of the table. You also can click the mouse pointer anywhere in the table to produce a screen like the one in Figure 1–38, and then click in the location shown in the figure.

Figure 1–39

- Click the Landscape button to change to landscape orientation (Figure 1–40).

- Click the Print button (Print Preview tab | Print group) to display the Print dialog box.

- Click the OK button (Print dialog box) to print the table.

- When the printer stops, retrieve the hard copy of the Business Analyst Table.

- Click the Close Print Preview button (Print Preview tab | Close Preview group) to close the Print Preview window.

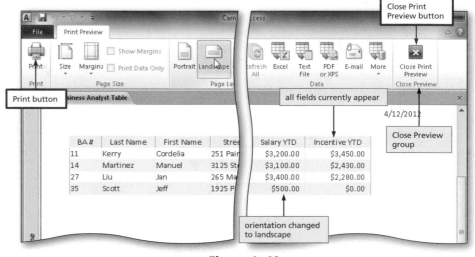

Figure 1–40

Other Ways

1. Press CTRL+P, click OK button (Print dialog box)

Creating Additional Tables

The Camashaly Design database contains two tables, the Business Analyst table and the Client table. You still need to create the Client table and add records to it. You created the Business Analyst table in Datasheet view. You will create the Client table in Design view.

Recall that the fields for the Client table are Client Number, Client Name, Street, City, State, Postal Code, Amount Paid, Current Due, Contract Hours YTD, and Business Analyst Number. The details that must be entered for these fields are shown in Table 1–5. The Client Number is the primary key. The Client Number field and the Business Analyst Number fields have both descriptions and captions. The Contract Hours YTD field has a caption.

Because the values in the Contract Hours YTD field have decimal places, only Single, Double, or Decimal would be possible field size choices. (See Table 1–2 on Page AC 10 for a description of the possible field sizes for Number fields.) The difference between these choices concerns the amount of accuracy. Double is more accurate than Single, for example, but requires more storage space. Because the rates are only two decimal places, Single is a perfectly acceptable choice.

In addition to changing the field size for the Contract Hours YTD, you will also change the format to Fixed (a fixed number of decimal places) and the number of decimal places to 2.

Table 1–5 Structure of Client Table			
Field Name	**Data Type**	**Field Size**	**Notes**
Client Number	Text	4	**Primary Key** **Description:** Client Number (two uppercase letters followed by 2-digit number) **Caption:** CL #
Client Name	Text	30	
Street	Text	15	
City	Text	15	
State	Text	2	
Postal Code	Text	5	
Amount Paid	Currency		
Current Due	Currency		
Contract Hours YTD	Number	Single	**Caption:** Hrs YTD **Format:** Fixed **Decimal Places:** 2
Business Analyst Number	Text	2	**Caption:** BA # **Description:** Business Analyst Number (number of business analyst for client)

To Create a Table in Design View

The next step in creating the table is to define the fields by specifying the required details in Design view. You will make entries in the Field Name, Data Type, and Description columns and enter additional information in the Field Properties box in the lower portion of the Table window. As you define the fields, the row selector (Figure 1–19 on page AC 23) indicates the field you currently are describing. Clicking the row selector selects the entire row. It is positioned on the first field, indicating Access is ready for you to enter the name of the first field in the Field Name column.

The following steps use Design view to define the fields in the table.

- Open the Navigation Pane.

- Click Create on the Ribbon to display the Create tab (Figure 1–41).

Figure 1–41

2

- Click the Table Design button (Create tab | Tables group) to create a new table in Design view (Figure 1–42).

Could I save the table now so I can assign it the name I want, rather than Table1?

You certainly could. Be aware, however, that you will still need to save it again once you have added all your fields.

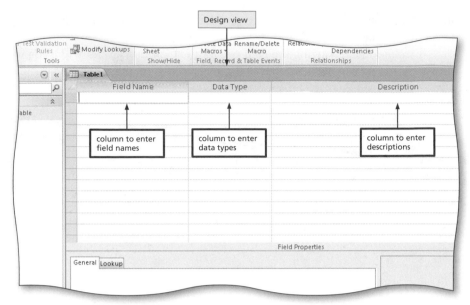

Figure 1–42

3

- Type **Client Number** (the name of the first field) in the Field Name column and then press the TAB key to accept the field name and move to the Data Type column (Figure 1–43).

Figure 1–43

4

- Because the Client Number field is the primary key, click the Primary Key button (Table Tools Design tab | Tools group) to designate the Client Number field as the primary key (Figure 1–44).

Figure 1–44

- Press the TAB key to move to the Description column, and then type **Client Number (two uppercase letters followed by a two-digit number)** as the description.

- Click the Field Size text box in the Field Properties pane to produce an insertion point, use either the BACKSPACE or DELETE key as necessary to erase the current entry (255), and then type **4** to change the field size.

- Click the Caption text box to produce an insertion point, and then type **CL #** to enter a caption (Figure 1–45).

Figure 1–45

- Click the Field Name column on the second row to produce an insertion point and then make the entries for the Client Name field.

- Use the techniques illustrated in Steps 1 through 5 to make the entries for the remaining fields in the Client table structure, shown in Table 1–5 on page AC 33, up through and including the name of the Amount Paid field.

- Click the Data Type box arrow to display a menu of available data types (Figure 1–46).

Figure 1–46

7

- Click Currency to select the data type.

- Enter the Current Due field and select the Currency data type.

- Enter the Contract Hours YTD field and select the Number data type (Figure 1–47).

Figure 1–47

8

- Click the Field Size box to display the Field Size box arrow.

- Click the Field Size box arrow to display the Field Size box menu (Figure 1–48).

Q&A

What would happen if I left the field size set to Integer?

If the field size is Integer, no decimal places can be stored. Thus a value of 2.50 would be stored as 2.

If you enter your hours and none of the values have decimal places, probably you did not change the field size.

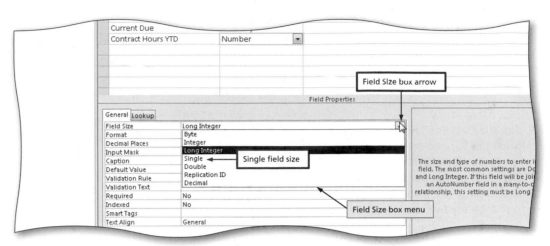

Figure 1–48

9

- Click Single to select single precision as the field size.

- Click the Format box to display the Format box arrow.

- Click the Format box arrow to display the Format box menu (Figure 1–49).

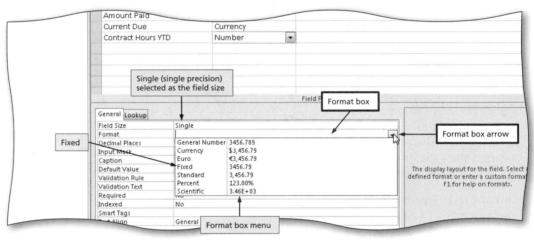

Figure 1–49

10

- Click Fixed to select fixed as the format.

- Click the Decimal Places box to display the Decimal Places box arrow.

- Click the Decimal Places box arrow to enter the number of decimal places.

- Click 2 to select 2 as the number of decimal places.

Figure 1–50

- Click the Caption text box to produce an insertion point, and then type **Hrs YTD** to enter a caption (Figure 1–50).

11

- Enter the Business Analyst Number field from Table 1–5. Be sure to change the description, field size, and caption to the ones shown in the table.

- Click the Save button on the Quick Access Toolbar to display the Save As dialog box, type Client as the name of the table, and then click the OK button (Save As dialog box) to save the table (Figure 1–51).

Figure 1–51

Other Ways

1. Press F6 to move between the upper pane and the lower pane in the Table Design window

Correcting Errors in the Structure

When creating a table, check the entries carefully to ensure they are correct. If you make a mistake and discover it before you press the TAB key, you can correct the error by repeatedly pressing the BACKSPACE key until the incorrect characters are removed. Then, type the correct characters. If you do not discover a mistake until later, you can click the entry, type the correct value, and then press the ENTER key. You can use the following techniques to make changes to the structure:

- If you accidentally add an extra field to the structure, select the field by clicking the row selector (the leftmost column on the row that contains the field to be deleted). Once you have selected the field, press the DELETE key. This will remove the field from the structure.

- If you forget to include a field, select the field that will follow the field you want to add by clicking the row selector, and then press the INSERT key. The remaining fields move down one row, making room for the missing field. Make the entries for the new field in the usual manner.

- If you made the wrong field a primary key field, click the correct primary key entry for the field and then click the Primary Key button (Table Tools Design tab | Tools group).

- To move a field, click the row selector for the field to be moved to select the field, and then drag the field to the desired position.

As an alternative to these steps, you may want to start over. To do so, click the Close button for the window containing the table, and then click the No button in the Microsoft Access dialog box. Click Create on the Ribbon and then click the Table Design button to create a table. You then can repeat the process you used earlier to define the fields in the table.

BTW

AutoCorrect Feature
The AutoCorrect feature of Access corrects common mistakes when entering text in a cell. AutoCorrect corrects two capital letters by changing the second letter to lowercase and capitalizes the first letter in the names of days. It also corrects more than 400 commonly misspelled words.

BTW

Other AutoCorrect Options
Using the Office AutoCorrect feature, you can create entries that will replace abbreviations with spelled-out names and phrases automatically. To specify AutoCorrect rules, click File on the Ribbon to open the Backstage view, click Options, and then click Proofing in the Access Options dialog box.

To Close the Table

Now that you have completed and saved the Client table, you can close it. The following step closes the table.

 Click the Close button for the Client table (see Figure 1–51) to close the table.

Importing Data from Other Applications to Access

Now that you have created the Client table, you could add the records to it just as you did with the Business Analyst table. Access provides an alternative, however, that is available because Camashaly Design has already stored the necessary data in an Excel workbook (Figure 1–52). The data is stored in the form of an Excel **list**; that is, the first row contains column headings describing the data in each of the columns, and the remaining rows contain the data. Camashaly can **import** the data, which means to make a copy of the data in a table in the Access database.

When importing data, you have two choices. You can create a new table, in which case the column headings in the worksheet become the field names in the table. Access will attempt to assign appropriate data types. You would need to review the data types, adjust field sizes, captions, descriptions, and formats after the data was imported. The other option is to add the records to an existing table. This method is appropriate if you have already created the table, provided the column headings in the worksheet match the field names in the table, as they do in the case of the Client table.

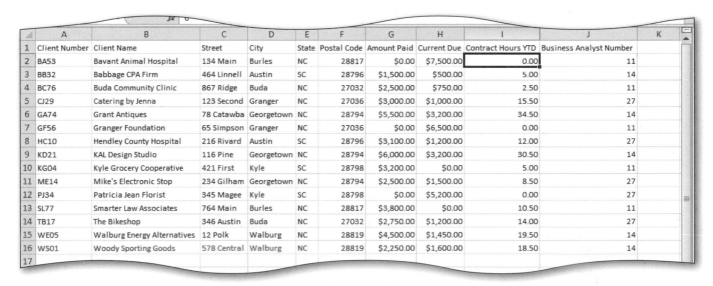

	A	B	C	D	E	F	G	H	I	J	K
1	Client Number	Client Name	Street	City	State	Postal Code	Amount Paid	Current Due	Contract Hours YTD	Business Analyst Number	
2	BA53	Bavant Animal Hospital	134 Main	Burles	NC	28817	$0.00	$7,500.00	0.00	11	
3	BB32	Babbage CPA Firm	464 Linnell	Austin	SC	28796	$1,500.00	$500.00	5.00	14	
4	BC76	Buda Community Clinic	867 Ridge	Buda	NC	27032	$2,500.00	$750.00	2.50	11	
5	CJ29	Catering by Jenna	123 Second	Granger	NC	27036	$3,000.00	$1,000.00	15.50	27	
6	GA74	Grant Antiques	78 Catawba	Georgetown	NC	28794	$5,500.00	$3,200.00	34.50	14	
7	GF56	Granger Foundation	65 Simpson	Granger	NC	27036	$0.00	$6,500.00	0.00	11	
8	HC10	Hendley County Hospital	216 Rivard	Austin	SC	28796	$3,100.00	$1,200.00	12.00	27	
9	KD21	KAL Design Studio	116 Pine	Georgetown	NC	28794	$6,000.00	$3,200.00	30.50	14	
10	KG04	Kyle Grocery Cooperative	421 First	Kyle	SC	28798	$3,200.00	$0.00	5.00	11	
11	ME14	Mike's Electronic Stop	234 Gilham	Georgetown	NC	28794	$2,500.00	$1,500.00	8.50	27	
12	PJ34	Patricia Jean Florist	345 Magee	Kyle	SC	28798	$0.00	$5,200.00	0.00	27	
13	SL77	Smarter Law Associates	764 Main	Burles	NC	28817	$3,800.00	$0.00	10.50	11	
14	TB17	The Bikeshop	346 Austin	Buda	NC	27032	$2,750.00	$1,200.00	14.00	27	
15	WE05	Walburg Energy Alternatives	12 Polk	Walburg	NC	28819	$4,500.00	$1,450.00	19.50	14	
16	WS01	Woody Sporting Goods	578 Central	Walburg	NC	28819	$2,250.00	$1,600.00	18.50	14	
17											

Figure 1–52

The process of importing into an Access database uses a wizard. Specifically, if the data is imported from an Excel worksheet, the process will use the Import Spreadsheet Wizard. The wizard takes you through some basic steps, asking a few simple questions. After you have answered the questions, the wizard will import or link the data.

To Import an Excel Worksheet

To import the data in the Camashaly Client Data workbook, you use the Import Spreadsheet Wizard to place the rows from an Excel worksheet into an existing table. The following steps import the Camashaly Client Data Excel workbook, which is provided as a data file. See the inside back cover of this book for instructions on downloading the Data Files for Students, or contact your instructor for more information about accessing the required files.

- Click External Data on the Ribbon to display the External Data tab (Figure 1–53).

Figure 1–53

2

- Click the Excel button (External Data tab | Import & Link group) to display the Get External Data – Excel Spreadsheet dialog box.

- Click the Browse button (Get External Data – Excel Spreadsheet dialog box) to display the File Open dialog box.

- Navigate to the USB flash drive (or the location of your data files).

- Double-click your USB flash drive, and then click Camashaly Client Data to select the file to be opened.

- Click the Open button (File Open dialog box), which will return you to the Get External Data dialog box with the Camashaly Client Data workbook selected.

3

- Click the option button to append a copy of records to a table (Figure 1–54).

Q&A

What happens if I select the option button to import records into a new table?

Instead of the records being added to an existing table, they will be placed in a new table. Access will assign all the data types. You would then need to ensure they are correct. You also would need to change any field sizes, descriptions, captions, formats, or number of decimal places to the ones you want.

Figure 1–54

4

- Click the arrow to produce a menu of available tables.

- Click the Client table to select the table to which a copy of the records will be appended (Figure 1–55).

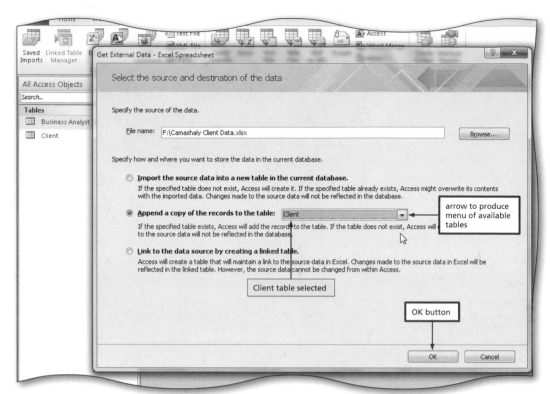

Figure 1–55

5

- Click the OK button to move to the next Import Spreadsheet Wizard screen (Figure 1–56).

Q&A

The First Row Contains Column Headings check box is checked, but it is dimmed. What if I want to remove the check mark?

When you are appending records to an existing table, the first row must contain column headings. If instead you were creating a new table, the first row might not contain column headings. In that case, you would have control over this check box.

Figure 1–56

6

- Click the Next button to move to the next Import Spreadsheet Wizard screen (Figure 1–57).

Q&A

What happens if I later realize I have selected the wrong table?

If you have not yet clicked the Finish button, you can click the Back button to return to the screen where you selected the table, and then select the correct table.

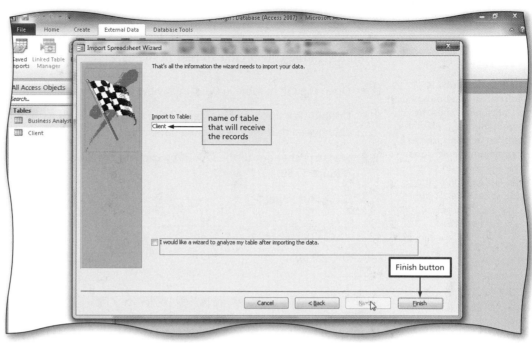

Figure 1–57

7

- Because the table name is correct, click the Finish button to import the data (Figure 1–58).

Q&A

I got an error message that stated that a particular field did not exist in the Client table. What did I do wrong? How do I fix it?

When you created the table, you did not name that particular field correctly. Open the table in Design view and change the field name to the correct name. Check other field names as well. When you are done, save and close the table. Then, repeat the import process.

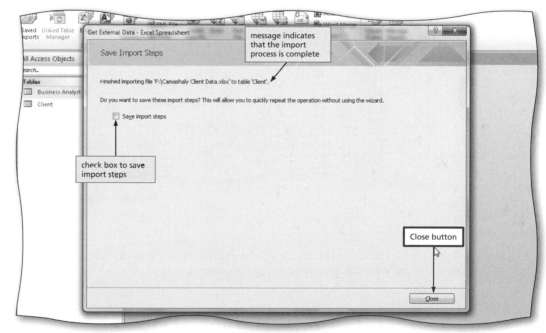

Figure 1–58

8

- Because you will not save the import steps, click the Close button.

Q&A

When would I save the import steps?

If you think you might need to repeat these steps in the future, you can save time by saving the steps.

Other Ways

1. Right-click table in Navigation Pane, click Import on shortcut menu

To Resize Columns in a Datasheet

You can resize the columns in the datasheet for the Client table just as you resized the columns in the datasheet for the Business Analyst table. The following steps resize the columns in the Client table to best fit the data.

BTW

Resizing Columns
To resize all columns in a datasheet to best fit simultaneously, select the column heading for the first column, hold down the SHIFT key and select the last column in the datasheet. Then, double-click the right boundary of any field selector.

1 Open the Client table in Datasheet view and then close the Navigation Pane.

2 Double-click the right boundary of the field selectors of each of the fields to resize the columns so that they best fit the data.

3 Save the changes to the layout by clicking the Save button on the Quick Access Toolbar (Figure 1–59).

4 Close the table.

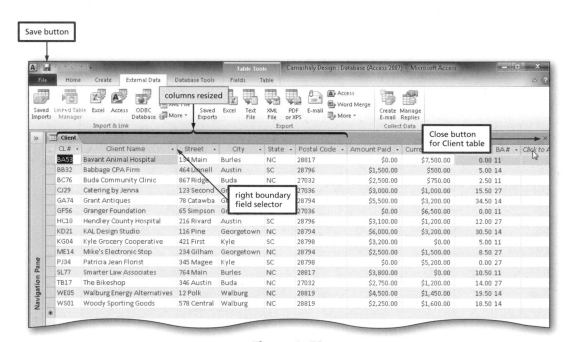

Figure 1–59

Break Point: If you wish to take a break, this is a good place to do so. You can quit Access now. To resume at a later time, start Access, open the database called Camashaly Design, and continue following the steps from this location forward.

Additional Database Objects

A computerized database such as Access contains many types of objects. Tables are the objects you use to store and manipulate data. Access supports other important types of objects as well; each of these objects has a specific purpose that assists in maximizing the benefits of a database. Through queries (questions), Access makes it possible to ask complex questions concerning the data in the database and then receive instant answers. Access also allows the user to produce attractive and useful forms for viewing and updating data. Additionally, Access includes report creation tools that make it easy to produce sophisticated reports for presenting data.

To Use the Simple Query Wizard to Create a Query

Queries are simply questions, the answers to which are in the database. Access contains a powerful query feature that helps you find the answers to a wide variety of questions. Once you have examined the question you want to ask to determine the fields involved in the question, you can begin creating the query. If there are no restrictions involved in the query, nor any special order or calculations, you can use the Simple Query Wizard.

The following steps use the Simple Query Wizard to create a query that Camashaly Design might use to obtain financial information on its clients. The query displays the number, name, amount paid, current due, contract hours YTD, and business analyst number of all clients.

1

- If the Navigation Pane is closed, click the Shutter Bar Open/Close Button to open the Navigation Pane.

- Be sure the Client table is selected.

- Click Create on the Ribbon to display the Create tab.

- Click the Query Wizard button (Create tab | Queries group) to display the New Query dialog box (Figure 1–60).

Figure 1–60

2

- Be sure Simple Query Wizard is selected, and then click the OK button (New Query dialog box) to display the Simple Query Wizard dialog box (Figure 1–61).

Q&A What would happen if the Business Analyst Table were selected instead of the Client table?

The list of available fields would contain fields from the Business Analyst Table rather than the Client table.

Q&A If the list contained Business Analyst Table fields, how could I make it contain Client table fields?

Click the arrow in the Tables/Queries box and then click the Client table in the list that appears.

Figure 1–61

- With the Client Number field selected, click the Add Field button to add the field to the query.

- With the Client Name field selected, click the Add Field button a second time to add the field.

- Click the Amount Paid field, and then click the Add Field button to add the field.

- In a similar fashion, add the Current Due, Contract Hours YTD, and Business Analyst Number fields (Figure 1–62).

Figure 1–62

- Click the Next button to move to the next screen.

- Ensure that the Detail (shows every field of every record) option button is selected (Figure 1–63).

Q&A

What is the difference between Detail and Summary?

Detail shows all the records and fields. Summary only shows computations (for example, the total amount paid).

Figure 1–63

- Click the Next button to move to the next screen.

- Ensure the title of the query is Client Query (Figure 1–64).

Figure 1–64

6

- Click the Finish button to create the query (Figure 1–65).

- Click the Close button for the Client Query to remove the query results from the screen.

Q&A

If I want to use this query in the future, do I need to save the query?

Normally you would. The one exception is a query created by the wizard. The wizard automatically saves the query it creates.

CL #	Client Name	Amount Paid	Current Due	Hrs YTD	BA #
BA53	Bavant Animal Hospital	$0.00	$7,500.00	0.00	11
BB32	Babbage CPA Firm	$1,500.00	$500.00	5.00	14
BC76	Buda Community Clinic	$2,500.00	$750.00	2.50	11
CJ29	Catering by Jenna	$3,000.00	$1,000.00	15.50	27
GA74	Grant Antiques	$5,500.00	$3,200.00	34.50	14
GF56	Granger Foundation	$0.00	$6,500.00	0.00	11
HC10	Hendley County Hospital	$3,100.00	$1,200.00	12.00	27
KD21	KAL Design Studio	$6,000.00	$3,200.00	30.50	14
KG04	Kyle Grocery Cooperative	$3,200.00	$0.00	5.00	11
ME14	Mike's Electronic Stop	$2,500.00	$1,500.00	8.50	27
PJ34	Patricia Jean Florist	$0.00	$5,200.00	0.00	27
SL77	Smarter Law Associates	$3,800.00	$0.00	10.50	11
TB17	The Bikeshop	$2,750.00	$1,200.00	14.00	27
WE05	Walburg Energy Alternatives	$4,500.00	$1,450.00	19.50	14
WS01	Woody Sporting Goods	$2,250.00	$1,600.00	18.50	14

Figure 1–65

Using Queries

After you have created and saved a query, Access stores it as a database object and makes it available for use in a variety of ways:

- To view the results of the query, open it by right-clicking the query in the Navigation Pane and clicking Open on the shortcut menu.

- To print the results with the query open, click File on the Ribbon, click the Print tab, and then click either Print or Quick Print.

- If you want to change the design of the query, right-click the query in the Navigation Pane and then click Design View on the shortcut menu to open the query in Design view.

- To print the query without first opening it, be sure the query is selected in the Navigation Pane and click File on the Ribbon, click the Print tab, and then click either Print or Quick Print.

You can switch between views of a query using the View button (Home tab | Views group). Clicking the arrow in the bottom of the button produces the View button menu. You then click the desired view in the menu. The two query views you will use in this chapter are Datasheet view (see the results) and Design view (change the design). You also can click the top part of the View button, in which case, you will switch to the view identified by the icon on the button. In the figure, the button contains the icon for Design view, so clicking the button would change to Design view. For the most part, the icon on the button represents the view you want, so you can usually simply click the button.

To Use a Criterion in a Query

After you have determined the fields to be included in a query, you will determine whether there are any restrictions on the records that are to be included. For example, you might only want to include those clients whose business analyst number is 14. In such a case, you need to enter the 14 as a **criterion**, which is a condition that the records to be included must satisfy. To do so, you will open the query in Design view, enter the criterion below the appropriate field, and then view the results of the query. The following steps enter a criterion to include only the clients of business analyst 14 and then view the query results.

- Right-click the Client Query in the Navigation Pane to produce a shortcut menu (Figure 1–66).

Figure 1–66

- Click Design View on the shortcut menu to open the query in Design view (Figure 1–67).

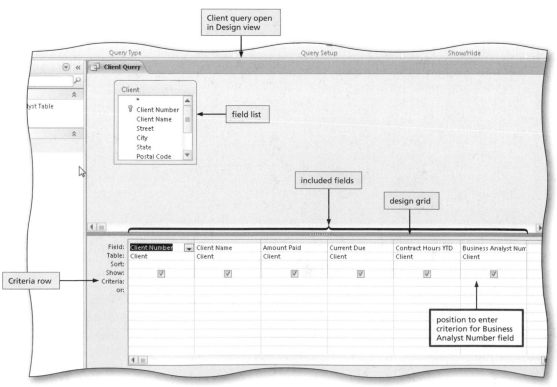

Figure 1–67

3

- Click the Criteria row in the Business Analyst Number column of the grid, and then type **14** as the criterion (Figure 1–68).

Q&A

The Business Analyst Number field is a text field. Do I need to enclose the value for a text field in quotation marks?

You could, but it is not necessary, because Access inserts the quotation marks for you automatically.

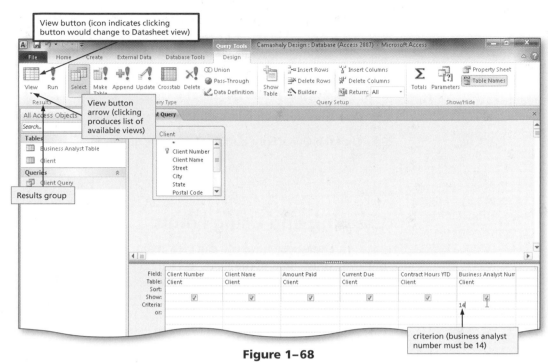

Figure 1–68

4

- Click the View button to display the query results in Datasheet view (Figure 1–69).

Q&A

Could I click the View button arrow and then click Datasheet view?

Yes, if the icon representing the view you want appears on the View button; however, it is easier just to click the button.

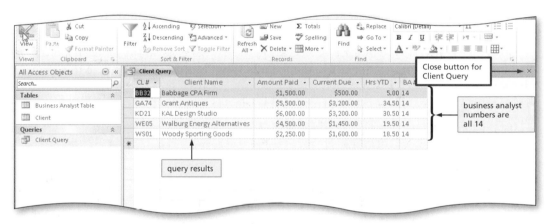

Figure 1–69

5

- Click the Close button for the Client Query to close the query.

- When asked if you want to save your changes, click the No button.

Q&A

If I saved the query, what would happen the next time I ran the query?

You would see only clients of business analyst 14.

Q&A

Could I save the query with another name?

Yes. To save the query with another name, click File on the Ribbon, click Save Object As, enter a new file name in the Save As dialog box and click the OK button (Save As dialog box).

Other Ways

1. Click Run button (Query Tools Design tab | Results group)

2. Click Datasheet View button on status bar

To Print the Results of a Query

The following steps print the results of a saved query.

1 With the Client Query selected in the Navigation Pane, click File on the Ribbon to open the Backstage view.

2 Click the Print tab in the Backstage view to display the Print gallery.

3 Click the Quick Print button to print the query.

Creating and Using Forms

In Datasheet view, you can view many records at once. If there are many fields, however, only some of the fields in each record might be visible at a time. In **Form view**, where data is displayed in a form on the screen, you usually can see all the fields, but only for one record.

To Create a Form

Like a paper form, a **form** in a database is a formatted document with fields that contain data. Forms allow you to view and maintain data. Forms also can be used to print data, but reports are more commonly used for that purpose. The simplest type of form in Access is one that includes all the fields in a table stacked one above the other. The following steps create a form, use the form to view records, and then save the form.

- Select the Client table in the Navigation Pane.

- If necessary, click Create on the Ribbon to display the Create tab (Figure 1–70).

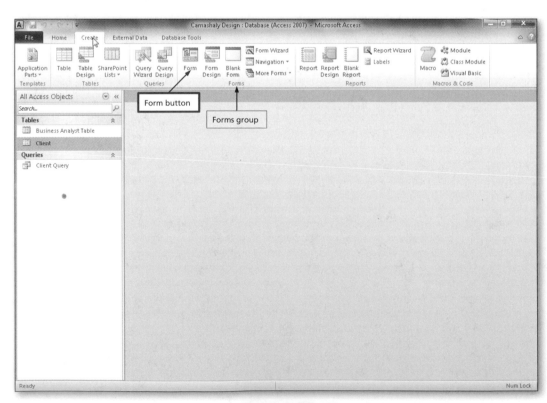

Figure 1–70

2

- Click the Form button (Create tab | Forms group) to create a simple form (Figure 1–71).

Q&A

A Field list appeared on my screen. What should I do?

Click the Add Existing Fields button (Form Layout Tools Design tab | Tools group) to remove the Field list from the screen.

Figure 1–71

3

- If the form appears in Layout view, click the Form View button on the Access status bar to display the form in Form view.

Q&A

How can I recognize Layout view?

Access identifies Layout view in three ways. The left side of the status bar will contain the words Layout View; there will be shading around the outside of the selected field in the form; and the Layout View button will be selected on the right side of the status bar.

- Click the Next Record button three times to move to record 4 (Figure 1–72).

Figure 1–72

4

- Click the Save button on the Quick Access Toolbar to display the Save As dialog box (Figure 1–73).

Figure 1–73

Did I have to click the Next Record button before saving?

No. The only reason you were asked to click the button was so that you could experience navigation within the form.

5

- Type **Client Form** as the form name, and then click the OK button to save the form.

- Click the Close button for the form to close the form.

Other Ways

1. Click View button (Form Layout Tools Design tab | Views group)

Using a Form

After you have saved a form, you can use it at anytime by right-clicking the form in the Navigation Pane and then clicking Open in the shortcut menu. In addition to viewing data in the form, you can also use it to enter or update data, a process that is very similar to updating data using a datasheet. If you plan to use the form to enter or revise data, you must ensure you are viewing the form in Form view.

Break Point: If you wish to take a break, this is a good place to do so. You can quit Access now. To resume at a later time, start Access, open the database called Camashaly Design, and continue following the steps from this location forward.

Creating and Printing Reports

Camashaly Design wants to create the Client Financial Report shown in Figure 1–74. Just as you can create a form containing all fields by clicking a single button, you can click a button to create a report containing all the fields. Doing so will not match the report shown in Figure 1–74, however, which does not contain all the fields. Some of the column headings are different. In addition, some of the headings in the report in Figure 1–74 are split over multiple lines, whereas the ones in the report created by clicking the button will not be split. Fortunately, you can later modify the report design to make it precisely match the figure. To do so, you use Layout view for the report.

Client Number	Client Name	Amount Paid	Current Due	Hrs YTD	Business Analyst Number
BA53	Bavant Animal Hospital	$0.00	$7,500.00	0.00	11
BB32	Babbage CPA Firm	$1,500.00	$500.00	5.00	14
BC76	Buda Community Clinic	$2,500.00	$750.00	2.50	11
CJ29	Catering by Jenna	$3,000.00	$1,000.00	15.50	27
GA74	Grant Antiques	$5,500.00	$3,200.00	34.50	14
GF56	Granger Foundation	$0.00	$6,500.00	0.00	11
HC10	Hendley County Hospital	$3,100.00	$1,200.00	12.00	27
KD21	KAL Design Studio	$6,000.00	$3,200.00	30.50	14
KG04	Kyle Grocery Cooperative	$3,200.00	$0.00	5.00	11
ME14	Mike's Electronic Stop	$2,500.00	$1,500.00	8.50	27
PJ34	Patricia Jean Florist	$0.00	$5,200.00	0.00	27
SL77	Smarter Law Associates	$3,800.00	$0.00	10.50	11
TB17	The Bikeshop	$2,750.00	$1,200.00	14.00	27
WE05	Walburg Energy Alternatives	$4,500.00	$1,450.00	19.50	14
WS01	Woody Sporting Goods	$2,250.00	$1,600.00	18.50	14
		$40,600.00	$34,800.00	176.00	

Client Financial Report — Thursday, April 12, 2012 — 5:17:00 PM

Figure 1–74

To Create a Report

You will first create a report containing all fields. The following steps create and save the initial report. They also modify the report title.

1

- Be sure the Client table is selected in the Navigation Pane.

- Click Create on the Ribbon to display the Create tab (Figure 1–75).

Why do I need to select the Client table prior to clicking Create on the Ribbon?

You do not need to select it at that point. You do need to select it prior to clicking the Report button at the next step because Access will include all the fields in whichever table or query is currently selected.

Figure 1–75

2

- Click the Report button (Create tab | Reports group) to create the report (Figure 1–76).

Why is the report title Client?

Access automatically assigns the name of the table or query as the title. It also automatically includes the date. You can change either of these later.

CL #	Client Name	Street	City	State
BA53	Bavant Animal Hospital	134 Main	Burles	NC
BB32	Babbage CPA Firm	464 Linnell	Austin	SC
BC76	Buda Community Clinic	867 Ridge	Buda	NC
CJ29	Catering by Jenna	123 Second	Granger	NC
GA74	Grant Antiques	78 Catawba	Georgetown	NC
GF56	Granger Foundation	65 Simpson	Granger	NC
HC10	Hendley County Hospital	216 Rivard	Austin	SC
KD21	KAL Design Studio	116 Pine	Georgetown	NC
KG04	Kyle Grocery Cooperative	421 First	Kyle	SC
ME14	Mike's Electronic Stop	234 Gilham	Georgetown	NC
PJ34	Patricia Jean Florist	345 Magee	Kyle	SC
SL77	Smarter Law Associates	764 Main	Burles	NC
TB17	The Bikeshop	346 Austin	Buda	NC
WE05	Walburg Energy Alternatives	12 Polk	Walburg	NC
WS01	Woody Sporting Goods	578 Central	Walburg	NC

Figure 1–76

3

- Click the Save button on the Quick Access Toolbar to display the Save As dialog box and then type **Client Financial Report** as the name of the report (Figure 1–77).

Figure 1–77

4

- Click the OK button (Save As dialog box) to save the report (Figure 1–78).

Q&A

The name of the report changed. Why did the report title not change too?

The report title just happens to begin with the same name as the report. If you change the name of the report, Access will not change the report title. You can change it at any time to any title you like.

Figure 1–78

5

- Close the report by clicking its Close button.

Using Layout View in a Report

When working with a report in Access, there are four different ways to view the report. They are Report view, Print Preview, Layout view, and Design view. Report view shows the report on the screen. Print Preview shows the report as it will appear when printed. Layout view is similar to Report view in that it shows the report on the screen, but it also allows you to make changes to the report. It is usually the easiest way to make such changes. Design view also allows you to make changes, but it does not show you the actual report. It is most useful when the changes you need to make are especially complex. In this chapter, you will use Layout view to modify the report.

To Modify Column Headings and Resize Columns

To make the report match the one in Figure 1–74, you need to change the title, remove some columns, modify the column headings, and also resize the columns. The following steps use Layout view to make the necessary modifications to the report.

- Right-click Client Financial Report in the Navigation Pane, and then click Layout View on the shortcut menu to open the report in Layout view.

- If a Field list appears, click the Add Existing Fields button (Report Layout Tools Design tab | Tools group) to remove the Field list from the screen.

- Close the Navigation Pane.

- Click the report title once to select it.

- Click the report title a second time to produce an insertion point (Figure 1–79).

Figure 1–79

Q&A

I clicked at a different position in the title and my insertion point is in the middle of Client. How do I produce an insertion point at the position shown in the figure?

You can use the RIGHT ARROW key to move the insertion point to the position in the figure or you can click the desired position.

- Press the SPACEBAR to insert a space and then type **Financial Report** to complete the title.

- Click the column heading for the Street field to select it.

- Hold the SHIFT key down and then click the column headings for the City field, the State field, and the Postal Code fields to select multiple column headings.

Q&A

What happens if I do not hold down the SHIFT key?

As soon as you click the column heading, it will be the only one that is selected. To select multiple objects, you need to hold the SHIFT key down for every object after the first one.

Figure 1–80

Q&A I selected the wrong collection of objects. What should I do?

You can click somewhere else on the report so that the objects you want are not selected, and then begin the process again. Alternatively, you can repeatedly click the Undo button on the Quick Access Toolbar to undo your selections. Once you have done so, you can select the objects you want.

- Click Arrange on the Ribbon to display the Arrange tab (Figure 1–80).

3

- Click the Select Column button (Report Layout Tools Arrange tab | Rows & Columns group) to select the entire columns corresponding to the column headings you selected in the previous step.

- Press the DELETE key to delete the columns.

- Click the column heading for the Client Number field twice, once to select it and the second time to produce an insertion point (Figure 1–81).

Q&A I inadvertently selected the wrong field. What should I do?

Click somewhere outside the various fields to deselect the one you have selected. Then, click the Client Number field twice.

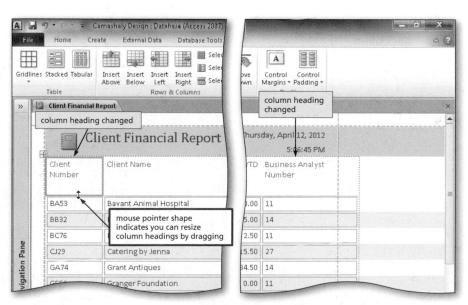

Figure 1–81

4

- Use the DELETE or BACKSPACE keys as necessary to erase the current entry and then type `Client Number` as the new entry.

- Click the heading for the Business Analyst Number field twice, erase the current entry, and then type `Business Analyst Number` as the new entry.

- Click the Client Number field heading to select it, point to the lower boundary of the heading for the Client Number field so that the mouse pointer changes to a two-headed arrow and then drag the lower boundary to the approximate position shown in Figure 1–82 to expand the column headings.

Figure 1–82

Q&A Do I have to be exact?

No. If you are in a slightly different position, your report would look a little different from the one in the figure, but the difference would not be significant.

5

● Point to the right boundary of the heading for the Client Number field so that the mouse pointer changes to a two-headed arrow and then drag the right boundary to the approximate position shown in Figure 1–83 to reduce the width of the column.

Q&A

Do I have to be exact?

No. Again, if you are in a slightly different position, the difference between your report and the one in the figure would not be significant.

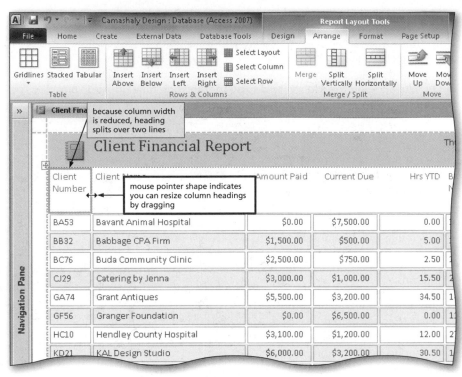

Figure 1–83

6

● Using the same technique, resize the other columns to the sizes shown in Figure 1–84.

Figure 1–84

To Add Totals to a Report

The report in Figure 1–74 contains totals for the Amount Paid, Current Due, and Hrs YTD columns. You can use Layout view to add these totals. The following steps use Layout view to include totals for these three columns.

1

- Click the Amount Paid field heading (shown in Figure 1–84) to select the field.

Q&A Do I have to click the heading? Could I click the field on one of the records?

You do not have to click the heading. You also could click the Amount Paid field on any record.

- Click Design on the Ribbon to display the Design tab.

- Click the Totals button (Report Layout Tools Design tab | Grouping & Totals group) to display the list of available calculations (Figure 1–85).

Figure 1–85

2

- Click Sum to calculate the sum of the amount of paid values.

Q&A Is Sum the same as Total?

Yes.

- Using the same technique, add totals for the Current Due and Hrs YTD columns.

- Scroll down to the bottom of the report to verify that the totals are included. If necessary, expand the size of the total controls so they appear completely.

- Click the Page number to select it and then drag it to the approximate position shown in Figure 1–86.

Figure 1–86

Q&A Why did I need to move the page number?

The dotted line near the right-hand edge of the screen indicates the right-hand border of the available space on the printed page, based on whatever margins and orientation are currently selected. A portion of the page number extends beyond this border. By moving the page number, it no longer extends beyond the border.

3

- Click the Save button on the Quick Access Toolbar to save your changes to the report layout.

- Close the report.

To Print a Report

The following steps print the report.

1 With the Client Financial Report selected in the Navigation Pane, click File on the Ribbon to open the Backstage view.

2 Click the Print tab in the Backstage view to display the Print gallery.

3 Click the Quick Print button to print the report.

Q&A How can I print multiple copies of my report?

Click File on the Ribbon to open the Backstage view. Click the Print tab, click Print in the Print gallery to display the Print dialog box, increase the number in the Number of Copies box, and then click the OK button (Print dialog box).

Q&A How can I print a range of pages rather than printing the whole report?

Click File on the Ribbon to open the Backstage view. Click the Print tab, click Print in the Print gallery to display the Print dialog box, click the Pages option button in the Print Range area, enter the desired page range, and then click the OK button (Print dialog box).

BTW

Tabbed Documents Versus Overlapping Windows
By default, Access 2010 displays database objects in tabbed documents instead of overlapping windows. If your database is in overlapping windows mode, click File on the Ribbon, click Options in the Backstage view, click Current Database in the Access Options dialog box, and select the Display Document Tabs check box and the Tabbed Documents option button.

Database Properties

Access helps you organize and identify your databases by using **database properties**, which are the details about a file. Database properties, also known as **metadata**, can include such information as the file's author, title, or subject. **Keywords** are words or phrases that further describe the database. For example, a class name or database topic can describe the file's purpose or content.

Five different types of document properties exist, but the more common ones used in this book are standard and automatically updated properties. **Standard properties** are associated with all Microsoft Office documents and include author, title, and subject. **Automatically updated properties** include file system properties, such as the date you create or change a file, and statistics, such as the file size.

To Change Database Properties

The Database Properties dialog box contains areas where you can view and enter database properties. You can view and change information in this dialog box at anytime while you are working on your database. It is a good idea to add your name and class name as database properties. You also can add keywords that further describe your database. The following steps use the Properties dialog box to change database properties.

1

• Click File on the Ribbon to open the Backstage view.

• If necessary, click the Info tab in the Backstage view to display the Info gallery (Figure 1–87).

Q&A

How do I close the Backstage view?

Click File on the Ribbon or click the preview of the document in the Info gallery to return to the Access database window.

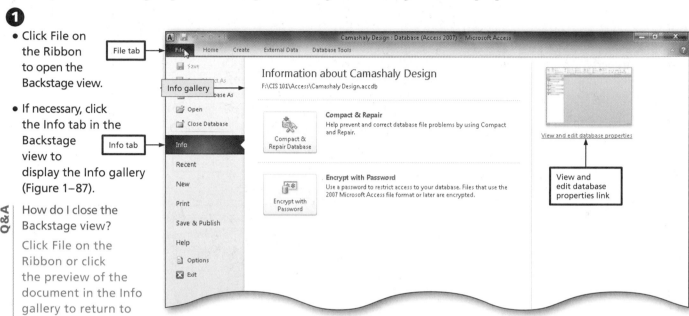

Figure 1–87

2

• Click the 'View and edit database properties' link in the right pane of the Info gallery to display the Camashaly Design.accdb Properties dialog box (Figure 1–88).

Q&A

Why are some of the database properties in my Properties dialog box already filled in?

The person who installed Microsoft Office 2010 on your computer or network may have set or customized the properties.

Figure 1–88

3

- If necessary, click the Summary tab.

- Click the Subject text box, if necessary delete any existing text, and then type `CIS 101, Section 20` as the Subject property.

- Click the Author text box and then type **`Trevor Wilkins`** as the Author property. If a name already is displayed in the Author text box, delete it before typing the new name.

- Click the Keywords text box, if necessary delete any existing text, and then type **`online marketing, Web site design`** as the Keywords property (Figure 1–89).

Q&A

What types of properties does Access collect automatically?

Access records such details as when the database was created, when it was last modified, total editing time, and the various objects contained in the database.

Figure 1–89

4

- Click the OK button to save your changes and remove the Camashaly Design.accdb Properties dialog box from the screen.

To Quit Access

The following steps quit Access.

1 Click the Close button on the right side of the title bar to quit Access.

2 If a Microsoft Access dialog box appears, click the Save button to save any changes made to the object since the last save.

Special Database Operations

The special operations involved in maintaining a database are backup, recovery, compacting a database, and repairing a database.

Backup and Recovery

It is possible to damage or destroy a database. Users can enter data that is incorrect; programs that are updating the database can end abnormally during an update; a hardware problem can occur; and so on. After any such event has occurred, the database may contain invalid data. It even might be totally destroyed.

Obviously, you cannot allow a situation in which data has been damaged or destroyed to go uncorrected. You must somehow return the database to a correct state. This process is called recovery; that is, you **recover** the database.

The simplest approach to recovery involves periodically making a copy of the database (called a **backup copy** or a **save copy**). This is referred to as **backing up** the database. If a problem occurs, you correct the problem by copying this backup copy over the actual database, often referred to as the **live database**.

To back up the database that is currently open, you use the Back Up Database command on the Save & Publish tab in the Backstage view. In the process, Access suggests a name that is a combination of the database name and the current date. For example, if you back up the Camashaly Design database on April 20, 2012, Access will suggest the name, Camashaly Design_2012-04-20. You can change this name if you desire, although it is a good idea to use this name. By doing so, it will be easy to distinguish between all the backup copies you have made to determine which is the most recent. In addition, if you discover that a critical problem occurred on April 18, 2012, you may want to go back to the most recent backup before April 18. If, for example, the database was not backed up on April 17 but was backed up on April 16, you would use Camashaly Design_2012-04-16.

TO BACK UP A DATABASE

You would use the following steps to back up a database to a file on a hard disk or high-capacity removable disk.

1. Open the database to be backed up.
2. Click File on the Ribbon to open the Backstage view, and then click the Save & Publish tab.
3. With Save Database As selected in the File Types area, click Back Up Database in the Save Database As area, and then click the Save As button.
4. Selected the desired location in the Save As box. If you do not want the name Access has suggested, enter the desired name in the File name text box.
5. Click the Save button to back up the database.

Access creates a backup copy with the desired name in the desired location. Should you ever need to recover the database using this backup copy, you can simply copy it over the live version.

Compacting and Repairing a Database

As you add more data to a database, it naturally grows larger. When you delete an object (records, tables, forms, or queries), the space previously occupied by the object does not become available for additional objects. Instead, the additional objects are given new space; that is, space that was not already allocated. To remove this wasted space from the database, you must **compact** the database. The same option that compacts the database also repairs problems that might have occurred in the database.

TO COMPACT AND REPAIR A DATABASE

You would use the following steps to compact and repair a database.

1. Open the database to be compacted.
2. Click File on the Ribbon to open the Backstage view, and then, if necessary, select the Info tab.
3. Click the Compact & Repair Database button in the Info gallery to compact and repair the database.

The database now is the compacted form of the original.

BTW

Access Help
At any time while using Access, you can find answers to questions and display information about various topics through Help. Used properly, this form of assistance can increase your productivity and reduce your frustrations by minimizing the time you spend learning how to use Access. For instruction about Access Help and exercises that will help you gain confidence in using it, read the Office 2010 and Windows 7 chapter at the beginning of this book.

BTW

Certification
The Microsoft Office Specialist (MOS) program provides an opportunity for you to obtain a valuable industry credential — proof that you have the Access 2010 skills required by employers. For more information, visit the Access 2010 Certification Web page (scsite.com/ac2010/cert).

BTW

Quick Reference
For a table that lists how to complete the tasks covered in this book using the mouse, Ribbon, shortcut menu, and keyboard, see the Quick Reference Summary at the back of this book, or visit the Access 2010 Quick Reference Web page (scsite.com/ac2010/qr).

Additional Operations

Additional special operations include opening another database, closing a database without quitting Access, and saving a database with another name. They also include deleting a table (or other object) as well as renaming an object. Finally, you can change properties of a table or other object, such as the object's description.

When you open another database, Access will automatically close the database that previously was open. Before deleting or renaming an object, you should ensure that the object has no dependent objects; that is, other objects that depend on the object you want to delete.

TO OPEN ANOTHER DATABASE

To open another database, you would use the following steps.

1. Click File on the Ribbon to open the Backstage view.
2. Click Open.
3. Select the database to be opened.
4. Click the Open button.

TO CLOSE A DATABASE WITHOUT QUITTING ACCESS

You would use the following steps to close a database without quitting Access.

1. Click File on the Ribbon to open the Backstage view.
2. Click Close Database.

TO SAVE A DATABASE WITH ANOTHER NAME

To save a database with another name, you would use the following steps.

1. Click File on the Ribbon to open the Backstage view, and then select the Save & Publish tab.
2. With Save Database As selected in the File Types area and Access Database selected in the Save Database As area, click the Save As button.
3. Enter a name and select a location for the new version.
4. Click the Save button.

TO DELETE A TABLE OR OTHER OBJECT IN THE DATABASE

You would use the following steps to delete a database object.

1. Right-click the object in the Navigation Pane.
2. Click Delete on the shortcut menu.
3. Click the Yes button in the Microsoft Access dialog box.

TO RENAME AN OBJECT IN THE DATABASE

You would use the following steps to rename a database object.

1. Right-click the object in the Navigation Pane.
2. Click Rename on the shortcut menu.
3. Type the new name and press the ENTER key.

Chapter Summary

In this chapter you have learned to design a database, create an Access database, create tables and add records to them, print the contents of tables, create queries, create forms, and create reports. You also have learned how to change database properties. The items listed below include all the new Access skills you have learned in this chapter.

1. Start Access (AC 12)
2. Create a Database (AC 13)
3. Create a Database Using a Template (AC 14)
4. Modify the Primary Key (AC 16)
5. Define the Remaining Fields in a Table (AC 19)
6. Save a Table (AC 21)
7. View the Table in Design View (AC 21)
8. Close the Table (AC 23)
9. Add Records to a Table (AC 23)
10. Quit Access (AC 26)
11. Open a Database from Access (AC 27)
12. Add Additional Records to a Table (AC 28)
13. Resize Columns in a Datasheet (AC 29)
14. Preview and Print the Contents of a Table (AC 31)
15. Create a Table in Design View (AC 33)
16. Import an Excel Worksheet (AC 38)
17. Use the Simple Query Wizard to Create a Query (AC 43)
18. Use a Criterion in a Query (AC 46)
19. Print the Results of a Query (AC 48)
20. Create a Form (AC 48)
21. Create a Report (AC 52)
22. Modify Column Headings and Resize Columns (AC 54)
23. Add Totals to a Report (AC 57)
24. Change Database Properties (AC 59)
25. Back Up a Database (AC 61)
26. Compact and Repair a Database (AC 61)
27. Open Another Database (AC 62)
28. Close a Database without Quitting Access (AC 62)
29. Save a Database with Another Name (AC 62)
30. Delete a Table or Other Object in the Database (AC 62)
31. Rename an Object in the Database (AC 62)

 If you have a SAM 2010 user profile, your instructor may have assigned an autogradable version of this assignment. If so, log into the SAM 2010 Web site at www.cengage.com/sam2010 to download the instruction and start files.

Learn It Online

Test your knowledge of chapter content and key terms.

Instructions: To complete the Learn It Online exercises, start your browser, click the Address bar, and then enter the Web address **scsite.com/ac2010/learn**. When the Access 2010 Learn It Online page is displayed, click the link for the exercise you want to complete and then read the instructions.

Chapter Reinforcement TF, MC, and SA
A series of true/false, multiple choice, and short answer questions that test your knowledge of the chapter content.

Flash Cards
An interactive learning environment where you identify chapter key terms associated with displayed definitions.

Practice Test
A series of multiple choice questions that test your knowledge of chapter content and key terms.

Who Wants To Be a Computer Genius?
An interactive game that challenges your knowledge of chapter content in the style of a television quiz show.

Wheel of Terms
An interactive game that challenges your knowledge of chapter key terms in the style of the television show *Wheel of Fortune*.

Crossword Puzzle Challenge
A crossword puzzle that challenges your knowledge of key terms presented in the chapter.

Apply Your Knowledge

Reinforce the skills and apply the concepts you learned in this chapter.

Adding a Caption, Creating a Query, Creating a Form, and Creating a Report

Instructions: Start Access. Open the Babbage CPA Firm database. See the inside back cover of this book for instructions for downloading the Data Files for Students, or see your instructor for information on accessing the files required in this book.

The Babbage CPA Firm employs bookkeepers who maintain the books for those clients who need bookkeeping services. The Babbage CPA Firm has a database that keeps track of its bookkeepers and clients. Each client is assigned to a single bookkeeper, but each bookkeeper may be assigned many clients. The database has two tables. The Client table contains data on the clients who use the bookkeeping services of the Babbage CPA Firm. The Bookkeeper table contains data on the bookkeepers employed by Babbage CPA Firm.

Perform the following tasks:

1. Open the Bookkeeper table in Design view and add BKR # as the caption for Bookkeeper Number. Save the changes to the table.

2. Open the Bookkeeper table in Datasheet view and resize all columns to best fit the data. Save the changes to the layout of the table.

3. Use the Simple Query Wizard to create a query for the Client table that contains the Client Number, Client Name, Amount Paid, and Balance Due. Use the name, Client Query, for the query.

4. Create a simple form for the Bookkeeper table. Use the name, Bookkeeper, for the form.

5. Close the Bookkeeper form.

6. Create the report shown in Figure 1–90 for the Client table. The report includes totals for both the Amount Paid and Balance Due fields. Be sure the totals appear completely. You might need to expand the size of the controls. Move the page number so that it is within the margins.

7. Compact the database.

8. Back up the database.

9. Change the database properties, as specified by your instructor. Submit the revised database in the format specified by your instructor.

Client Financial Report

Thursday, April 12, 2012
8:38:16 PM

Client Number	Client Name	Amount Paid	Balance Due	Bookkeeper Number
A54	Afton Mills	$575.00	$315.00	22
A62	Atlas Suppliers	$250.00	$175.00	24
B26	Blake-Scripps	$875.00	$250.00	24
D76	Dege Grocery	$1,015.00	$325.00	22
G56	Grand Cleaners	$485.00	$165.00	24
H21	Hill Shoes	$0.00	$285.00	34
J77	Jones Plumbing	$685.00	$0.00	22
M26	Mohr Crafts	$125.00	$185.00	24
S56	SeeSaw Industries	$1,200.00	$645.00	22
T45	Tate Repair	$345.00	$200.00	34
W24	Woody Sporting Goods	$975.00	$0.00	34
C29	Catering by Jenna	$0.00	$250.00	34
		$6,530.00	$2,795.00	

Figure 1–90

Extend Your Knowledge

Extend the skills you learned in this chapter and experiment with new skills. You may need to use Help to complete the assignment.

Using a Database Template to Create a Students Database

Instructions: Access includes a number of templates that you can use to create a beginning database that can be modified to meet your specific needs. You will create a Students database using the Students template. The database includes sample tables, queries, forms, and reports. You will change the database and create the Student Birthdays Query, shown in Figure 1–91.

Figure 1–91

Perform the following tasks:

1. Start Access.

2. With a USB flash drive connected to one of the computer's USB ports, ensure the New tab is selected in the Backstage view and select Sample templates in the New gallery.

3. Select the Students template and create a new database on your USB drive with the file name, Students.

4. Close the Student List form and change the organization of the Navigation Pane to Tables and Related Views .

5. Delete the Student Details form.

6. Use the Query Wizard to create the query shown in Figure 1–91. Save the query as Student Birthdays Query.

7. Open the Student Phone List in Layout view and use the tools on the Format tab to make the Student Phone List title bold and change the font size to 24. Delete the control containing the time.

8. Save your changes to the report.

9. Compact the database.

10. Change the database properties, as specified by your instructor. Submit the revised database in the format specified by your instructor.

Make It Right

Analyze a database and correct all errors and/or improve the design.

Correcting Errors in the Table Structure

Instructions: Start Access. Open the Beach Rentals database. See the inside back cover of this book for instructions for downloading the Data Files for Students, or see your instructor for information on accessing the files required in this book.

Beach Rentals is a database containing information on rental properties available at a beach resort. The Rentals table shown in Figure 1–92 contains a number of errors in the table structure. You are to correct these errors before any additional records can be added to the table. The Rental Code field is a Text field that contains a maximum of three characters. The field Address was omitted from the table. The Address field is a Text field with a maximum of 20 characters. It should appear after Rental Code. Only whole numbers should be allowed in the Bedrooms and Bathrooms fields. The column heading Weakly Rental is misspelled, and the field should contain monetary values. The Distance field represents the walking distance from the beach; the field should display two decimal places. The table name should be Rental Units, not Rentals.

Change the database properties, as specified by your instructor. Submit the revised database in the format specified by your instructor.

Figure 1–92

In the Lab

Design, create, modify, and/or use a database using the guidelines, concepts, and skills presented in this chapter. Labs are listed in order of increasing difficulty.

Lab 1: Creating Objects for the ECO Clothesline Database

Problem: ECO Clothesline is a local company that designs and manufactures eco-friendly casual wear, yoga clothing, and fitness apparel. All clothes are made from earth-friendly fabrics, such as bamboo, hemp, organic cotton, and natural silk. The company recently decided to store its customer and sales rep data in a database. Each customer is assigned to a single sales rep, but each sales rep may be assigned many customers. The database and the Customer table have been created, but there is no data in the Customer table. The Sales Rep table has not been created. The company plans to import the Customer data from an Excel workbook, shown in Figure 1–93a. The other Excel workbook (Figure 1–93b) contains information on the sales representatives that ECO employs. ECO would like to finish storing this data in a database and has asked for your help.

Instructions: Perform the following tasks: Start Access and open the ECO Clothesline database. See the inside back cover of this book for instructions for downloading the Data Files for Students, or see your instructor for information on accessing the files required in this book.

1. Import the Lab 1-1 Customer Data workbook into the Customer table.

2. Add the captions Cust # to the Customer Number field and SR # to the Sales Rep Number field in the Customer table and save the changes.

3. Open the Customer table in Datasheet view and resize the columns to best fit the data. Save the changes to the layout of the table.

4. Use Datasheet view to create a table in which to store the data related to sales reps. Use the name Sales Rep for the table. The fields and the data for the Sales Rep table are shown in Figure 1–93b.

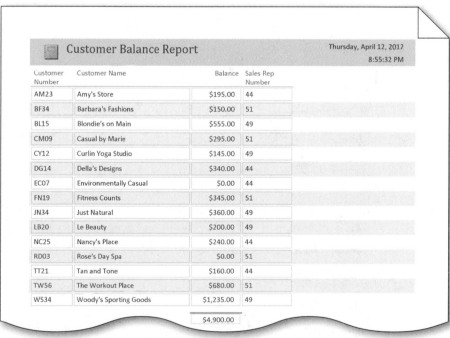

	A	B	C	D	E	F	G	H	I	J	K
1	Customer Number	Customer Name	Street	City	State	Postal Code	Balance	Amount Paid	Sales Rep Number		
2	AM23	Amy's Store	223 Johnson	Oxford	TN	37021	195.00	1,695.00	44		
3	BF34	Barbara's Fashions	1939 Jackson	Lowton	TN	37084	150.00	0.00	51		
4	BL15	Blondie's on Main	3294 Main	Oxford	TN	37021	555.00	1,350.00	49		
5	CM09	Casual by Marie	3140 Halsted	Ashton	VA	20123	295.00	1,080.00	51		
6	CY12	Curlin Yoga Studio	1632 Clark	Georgetown	NC	28794	145.00	710.00	49		
7	DG14	Della's Designs	312 Gilham	Granger	NC	27036	340.00	850.00	44		
8	EC07	Environmentally Casual	1805 Broadway	Pineville	VA	22503	0.00	1,700.00	44		
9	FN19	Fitness Counts	675 Main	Oxford	TN	37021	345.00	1,950.00	51		
10	JN34	Just Natural	2200 Lawrence	Ashton	VA	20123	360.00	700.00	49		
11	LB20	Le Beauty	13 Devon	Lowton	TN	37084	200.00	1,250.00	49		
12	NC25	Nancy's Place	1027 Wells	Walburg	NC	28819	240.00	550.00	44		
13	RD03	Rose's Day Spa	787 Monroe	Pineville	VA	22503	0.00	975.00	51		
14	TT21	Tan and Tone	1939 Congress	Ashton	VA	20123	160.00	725.00	44		
15	TW56	The Workout Place	34 Gilham	Granger	NC	27036	680.00	125.00	51		
16	WS34	Woody's Sporting Goods	578 Central	Walburg	NC	28819	1,235.00	0.00	49		
17											

(a) Customer Data (Excel Workbook)

	A	B	C	D	E	F	G	H	I	J
1	Sales Rep Number	Last Name	First Name	Street	City	State	Postal Code	Base Pay YTD	Comm Rate	
2	44	Jones	Pat	43 Third	Oxford	TN	37021	13,000.00	0.05	
3	49	Gupta	Pinn	678 Hillcrest	Georgetown	NC	28794	15,000.00	0.06	
4	51	Ortiz	Gabe	982 Victoria	Ashton	VA	20123	12,500.00	0.05	
5	55	Sinson	Terry	45 Elm	Walburg	NC	28819	500.00	0.04	
6										

(b) Sales Rep Data (Excel Workbook)

Figure 1–93

The primary key for the Sales Rep table is Sales Rep Number. Assign the caption SR # to the Sales Rep Number field. Comm Rate is a Number field, and Base Pay YTD is a Currency data type. The field size for Sales Rep Number is 2. The State field size is 2, and the Postal Code field size is 5. All other text fields have a field size of 15.

5. Open the Sales Rep table in Design view and change the field size for the Comm Rate field to Single, the format to Fixed, and the Decimal Places to 2.

6. Add the data shown in Figure 1–93b to the Sales Rep table. Resize the columns to best fit the data. Save the changes to the layout of the table.

7. Create a query using the Simple Query Wizard for the Customer table that displays the Customer Number, Customer Name, Balance, Amount Paid, and Sales Rep Number fields. Use the name Customer Query.

8. Create and save the report shown in Figure 1–94 for the Customer table. The report should include Customer Number, Customer Name, Balance, and Sales Rep Number fields. Include a total for the Balance field.

9. Change the database properties, as specified by your instructor. Submit the revised database in the format specified by your instructor.

Customer Balance Report

Thursday, April 12, 2012
8:55:32 PM

Customer Number	Customer Name	Balance	Sales Rep Number
AM23	Amy's Store	$195.00	44
BF34	Barbara's Fashions	$150.00	51
BL15	Blondie's on Main	$555.00	49
CM09	Casual by Marie	$295.00	51
CY12	Curlin Yoga Studio	$145.00	49
DG14	Della's Designs	$340.00	44
EC07	Environmentally Casual	$0.00	44
FN19	Fitness Counts	$345.00	51
JN34	Just Natural	$360.00	49
LB20	Le Beauty	$200.00	49
NC25	Nancy's Place	$240.00	44
RD03	Rose's Day Spa	$0.00	51
TT21	Tan and Tone	$160.00	44
TW56	The Workout Place	$680.00	51
WS34	Woody's Sporting Goods	$1,235.00	49
		$4,900.00	

Figure 1–94

In the Lab

Lab 2: Creating the Walburg Energy Alternatives Database

Problem: Walburg Energy Alternatives is a nonprofit organization that promotes the use of energy alternatives such as solar power and wind power. The organization provides a variety of services and funds itself through donations. Recently, the organization decided to sell a small number of items in its education center to help fund programs. The store purchases the items from vendors that deal in energy-saving products. Currently, the information about the items and vendors is stored in the Excel workbook shown in Figure 1–95. Each item is assigned to a single vendor, but each vendor may be assigned many items. You volunteer part-time at the store, and the store manager has asked you to create a database that will store the item and vendor information. You have already determined that you need two tables in which to store the information: an Item table and a Vendor table.

Instructions: Perform the following tasks:

1. Design a new database in which to store all the objects related to the items for sale. Call the database Walburg Energy Alternatives.

2. Use the information shown in the Excel workbook in Figure 1–95 to determine the primary keys and determine additional fields. Then, determine the relationships between tables, the data types, and the field sizes.

3. Create the Item table using the information shown in Figure 1–95.

4. Create the Vendor table using the information shown in Figure 1–95. Be sure that the field size for the Vendor Code in the Item table is identical to the field size for the Vendor Code in the Vendor table. Add the caption, Phone, for the Telephone Number field.

Figure 1–95

5. Add the appropriate data to the Item table. Resize the columns to best fit the data and save the changes to the layout.

6. Add the appropriate data to the Vendor table. Resize the columns to best fit the data and save the changes to the layout.

7. Create a query for the Item table. Include the Item Number, Description, Cost, Selling Price, and Vendor Code in the query. Save the query as Item Query.

8. Open the Item Query and add a criterion to limit retrieval to those items supplied by Scryps Distributors. Save the query as Item-Scryps Query.

9. Create a simple form for the Item table. Use the name, Item, for the form.

10. Create the report shown in Figure 1–96 for the Item table. Do not add any totals.

11. Change the database properties, as specified by your instructor. Submit the database in the format specified by your instructor.

Inventory Status Report

Thursday, April 12, 2012
8:56:19 PM

Item Number	Description	On Hand	Cost
3663	Air Deflector	8	$5.45
3673	Energy Booklet	25	$2.70
4553	Energy Saving Kit	7	$42.75
4573	Faucet Aerator	20	$0.89
4583	Fluorescent Light Bulb	18	$4.50
5923	Low Flow Shower Head	11	$8.75
6185	Luminescent Night Light	12	$3.75
6234	Programmable Thermostat	3	$34.25
6345	Rain Gauge	16	$2.89
7123	Retractable Clothesline	10	$13.25
7934	Shower Timer	15	$2.45
8136	Smoke Detector	10	$6.10
8344	Toilet Tank Water Saver	18	$3.35
8590	Water Conservation Kit	8	$13.45
9458	Windows Insulator Kit	10	$4.95

Figure 1–96

In the Lab

Lab 3: Creating the Philamar Training Database

Problem: Philamar Training provides business processes and information technology training to various companies and organizations. Philamar employs trainers who work with individual companies to determine training needs and then conduct the training. Currently, Philamar keeps data on clients and trainers in two Word documents and two Excel workbooks. Philamar also keeps track of which clients are assigned to which trainers. Each client is assigned to a single trainer, but each trainer might be assigned many clients. Currently, clients BS27, FI28, and MC28 are assigned to trainer 42, Belinda Perry. Clients CE16, CP27, FL93, HN83, and TE26 are assigned to trainer 48, Michael Stevens. Clients EU28 and PS82 are assigned to trainer 53, Manuel Gonzalez. Philamar has an additional trainer, Marty Danville, who has been assigned trainer number 67, but who has not yet been assigned any clients.

Instructions: Using the data shown in Figure 1–97 and the information in the previous paragraph, design the Philamar Training database. The data shown in Figure 1–97 is included in the Data Files for Students in the following files: Lab 1-3a.docx, Lab 1-3b.docx, Lab 1-3c.xlsx, and Lab 1-3d.xlsx. Use the database design guidelines in this chapter to help you in the design process.

Client Number	Client Name	Address	City	State	Postal Code
BS27	Blant and Sons	4806 Park	Kingston	TX	76653
CE16	Center Services	725 Mitchell	San Rita	TX	78364
CP27	Calder Plastics	7300 Cedar	Kingston	TX	76653
EU28	Elba's Furniture	1445 Hubert	Tallmadge	TX	77231
FI28	Farrow-Idsen	829 Wooster	Cedar Ridge	TX	79342
FL93	Fairland Lawn	143 Pangborn	Kingston	TX	76653
HN83	Hurley National	3827 Burgess	Tallmadge	TX	77231
MC28	Morgan-Alyssa	923 Williams	Crumville	TX	76745
PS82	PRIM Staffing	72 Crestview	San Rita	TX	78364
TE26	Telton-Edwards	5672 Anderson	Dunston	TX	77893

(a) Client Address Information (Word Table)

	A	B	C	D	E
1	Client Number	Client Name	Amount Paid	Current Due	
2	BS27	Blant and Sons	$11,876.00	$892.50	
3	CE16	Center Services	$12,512.00	$1,672.00	
4	CP27	Calder Plastics	$5,725.00	$0.00	
5	EU28	Elba's Furniture	$3,245.00	$202.00	
6	FI28	Farrow-Idsen	$8,287.50	$925.50	
7	FL93	Fairland Lawn	$976.00	$0.00	
8	HN83	Hurley National	$0.00	$0.00	
9	MC28	Morgan-Alyssa	$3,456.00	$572.00	
10	PS82	PRIM Staffing	$7,500.00	$485.00	
11	TE26	Telton-Edwards	$6,775.00	$0.00	
12					

(c) Client Financial Information (Excel Workbook)

Trainer Number	Last Name	First Name	Address	City	State	Postal Code
42	Perry	Belinda	261 Porter	Burdett	TX	76734
48	Stevens	Michael	3135 Gill	Rockwood	TX	78884
53	Gonzalez	Manuel	265 Maxwell	Camino	TX	76574
67	Danville	Marty	1827 Maple	Dunston	TX	77893

(b) Trainer Address Information (Word Table)

	A	B	C	D	E
1	Trainer Number	Last Name	First Name	Hourly Rate	YTD Earnings
2	42	Perry	Belinda	$23.00	$17,620.00
3	48	Stevens	Michael	$21.00	$13,567.50
4	53	Gonzalez	Manuel	$24.00	$19,885.00
5	67	Danville	Marty	$20.00	$0.00
6					

(d) Trainer Financial Information (Excel Workbook)

Figure 1–97

When you have completed the database design, create the database, create the tables, and add the data to the appropriate tables. Be sure to determine the correct data types and field sizes.

Finally, prepare the Client Query shown in Figure 1–98 and the Client Status Report shown in Figure 1–99. The report does not include totals. Change the database properties, as specified by your instructor. Submit the database in the format specified by your instructor.

Figure 1–98

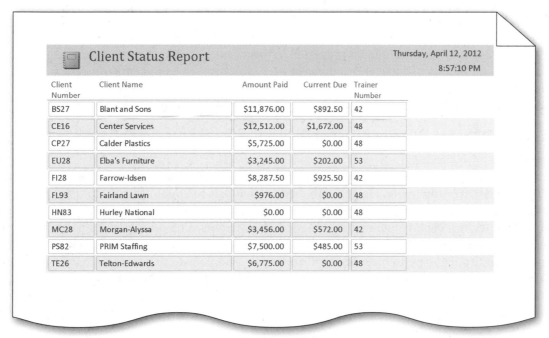

Figure 1–99

Cases and Places

Apply your creative thinking and problem solving skills to design and implement a solution.

See the inside back cover of this book for instructions for downloading the Data Files for Students, or see your instructor for information on accessing the files required in this book.

1: Design and Create an Advertising Database

Academic

You are a Marketing major currently doing an internship with the Chamber of Commerce in a local city. The Chamber publishes a Newcomer's Guide that contains advertisements from local businesses. Ad reps contact the businesses to arrange for advertising. Each advertiser is assigned to a single ad rep, but each ad rep may be assigned many advertisers. The Chamber would like your help in creating a database of advertisers and advertising representatives.

Based on the information in the Case 1-1 Chamber of Commerce workbook, use the concepts and techniques presented in this chapter to design and create a database to store the data that the Chamber needs. Submit your assignment in the format specified by your instructor.

2: Design and Create a Consignment Database

Personal

You are involved in a volunteer organization that provides clothing and school supplies to needy children. Recently, the Board of Directors decided to open a consignment shop as a way to raise additional funds. In a consignment shop, individuals bring in unwanted items, and the shop sells the items. Proceeds are split between the seller and the shop. The database must keep track of the items for sale in the shop as well as maintain data on the sellers. Each item is assigned to a single seller, but each seller may be assigned many items. The Board has asked you to create a database to store information about the consignment items.

Use the concepts and techniques presented in this chapter to design and create a database to store the consignment data. Then create the necessary tables and enter the data from the Case 1-2 Consignment workbook. Create an Available Items Report that lists the item number, description, price, and seller code. Submit your assignment in the format specified by your instructor.

3: Design and Create a Senior Care Database

Professional

You are co-owner of a company, Senior Care, that provides nonmedical services to older adults who need assistance with daily living. Helpers will drive individuals to appointments, do the grocery shopping, fill prescriptions, help with personal care, and provide companionship. Each client is assigned to a single helper, but each helper may be assigned many clients. The other owners have asked you to create a database of clients and helpers. Use the concepts and techniques presented in this chapter to design and create a database to meet Senior Care needs. Then create the necessary tables and enter the data from the Case 1-3 Senior Care workbook. Create a Client Report that lists each client's client number, client last name, client first name, balance, and helper number. Submit your assignment in the format specified by your instructor.

2 Querying a Database

Objectives

You will have mastered the material in this chapter when you can:

- Create queries using Design view
- Include fields in the design grid
- Use text and numeric data in criteria
- Save a query and use the saved query
- Create and use parameter queries
- Use compound criteria in queries
- Sort data in queries
- Join tables in queries

- Create a report and a form from a query
- Export data from a query to another application
- Perform calculations and calculate statistics in queries
- Create crosstab queries
- Customize the Navigation Pane

2 | Querying a Database

Introduction

BTW

Select Queries
The queries you create in this chapter are select queries. In a select query, you retrieve data from one or more tables using criteria that you specify and display the data in a datasheet.

One of the primary benefits of using a database management system such as Access is the ability to find answers to questions related to data stored in the database. When you pose a question to Access, or any other database management system, the question is called a query. A **query** is simply a question presented in a way that Access can process.

Thus, to find the answer to a question, you first create a corresponding query using the techniques illustrated in this chapter. After you have created the query, you instruct Access to display the query results, that is, to perform the steps necessary to obtain the answer. Access then displays the answer in Datasheet view.

Project — Querying a Database

Organizations and individuals achieve several benefits from storing data in a database and using Access to manage the database. One of the most important benefits is the capability of easily finding the answers to questions and requests such as those shown in Figure 2–1 and the following, which concern the data in the Camashaly Design database:

1. What are the number, name, amount paid, and current due for client BC76?
2. What are the number, name, amount paid, and current due for all clients whose name starts with Gr?
3. Give me the number, name, amount paid, current due, and business analyst number for all clients whose amount paid is more than $3,000 and whose business analyst number is 11.
4. List the client number, name, business analyst number, and amount paid for all clients. Sort the results by business analyst number and amount paid.
5. For each business analyst, list the number, last name, and first name. Also, list the client number and name for each of the business analyst's clients.
6. List the client number, client name, amount paid, current due, and the total amount (amount paid plus current due) for each client.
7. Give me the average amount paid by clients of each business analyst.
8. Summarize the total amount paid by city and by business analyst.

In addition to these questions, Camashaly Design managers need to find information about clients located in a specific city, but they want to enter a different city each time they ask the question. The company can use a parameter query to accomplish this task. Camashaly Design managers also want to summarize data in a specific way, and they can use a crosstab query to present the data in the desired form.

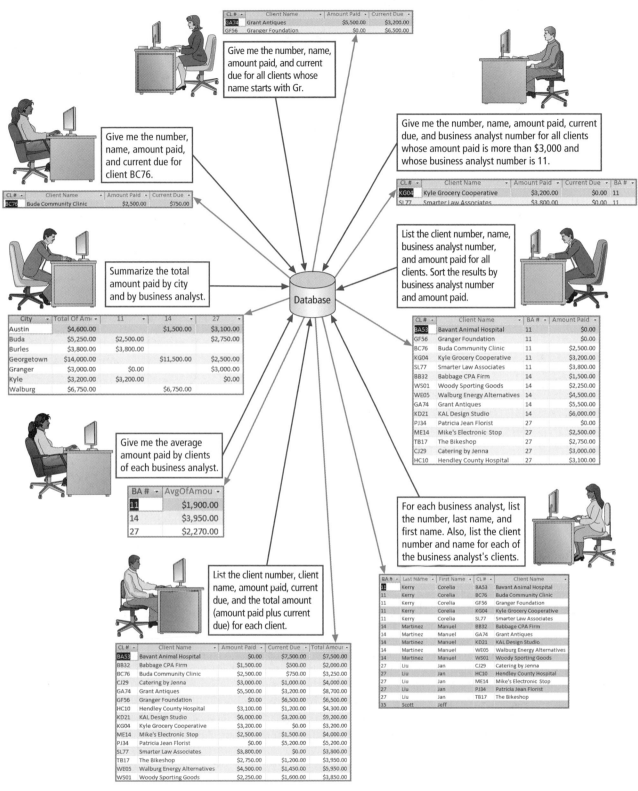

Figure 2–1

Overview

As you read this chapter, you will learn how to query a database by performing these general tasks:

- Create queries using Design view.
- Use criteria in queries.
- Create and use parameter queries.
- Sort data in queries.
- Join tables in queries.
- Create reports and forms from a query.
- Export data from a query.
- Perform calculations in queries.
- Create crosstab queries.

Plan Ahead

Designing Queries
Before creating queries, examine the contents of the tables involved. You need to know the data type for each field and how the data for the field is stored. If a query includes a state, for example, you need to know whether state is stored as the two-character abbreviation or as the full state name.

Query Design Decisions

When posing a question to Access, you must design an appropriate query. In the process of designing a query, the decisions you make will determine the fields, tables, criteria, order, and special calculations included in the query. To design a query, you can follow these general guidelines:

1. **Identify the fields.** Examine the question or request to determine which fields from the tables in the database are involved. Examine the contents of these fields to make sure you understand the data type and format for storing the data.

2. **Identify restrictions.** Unless the question or request calls for the inclusion of all records, determine the restrictions or the conditions records must satisfy to be included in the results.

3. **Determine whether special order is required.** Examine the question or request to determine whether the results must appear in some specific order.

4. **Determine whether more than one table is required.** If all the fields identified in Step 1 are in the same table, no special action is required. If this is not the case, identify all tables represented by those fields.

5. **Determine whether calculations are required.** Examine the question or request to determine whether, in addition to the fields determined in Step 1, calculations must be included. Such calculations include individual record calculations (for example, adding the values in two fields) or group calculations (for example, finding the total of the values in a particular field for all the records).

6. **If data is to be summarized, determine whether a crosstab query would be appropriate.** If data is to be grouped by two different types of information, you can use a crosstab query. You will need to identify the two types of information. One of the types will form the row headings and the other will form the column headings in the query results.

When necessary, more specific details concerning the decisions and/or actions are presented at appropriate points in the chapter. The chapter also will identify the use of these guidelines in creating queries such as those shown in Figure 2–1.

To Start Access

The following steps, which assume Windows 7 is running, start Access based on a typical installation. You may need to ask your instructor how to start Access for your computer. For a detailed example of the procedure summarized below, refer to the Office 2010 and Windows 7 chapter at the beginning of this book.

1 Click the Start button on the Windows 7 taskbar to display the Start menu.

2 Type `Microsoft Access` as the search text in the 'Search programs and files' text box and watch the search results appear on the Start menu.

3 Click Microsoft Access 2010 in the search results on the Start menu to start Access.

4 If the Access window is not maximized, click the Maximize button next to the Close button on its title bar to maximize the window.

For an introduction to Windows 7 and instruction about how to perform basic Windows 7 tasks, read the Office 2010 and Windows 7 chapter at the beginning of this book, where you can learn how to resize windows, change screen resolution, create folders, move and rename files, use Windows Help, and much more.

To Open a Database from Access

In the previous chapter, you saved your database on a USB flash drive using the file name, Camashaly Design. The following steps open the Camashaly Design database from the Access folder in the CIS 101 folder on the USB flash drive. For a detailed example of the procedure summarized below, refer to the Office 2010 and Windows 7 chapter at the beginning of this book.

1 With your USB flash drive connected to one of the computer's USB ports, click File on the Ribbon to open the Backstage view, if necessary.

2 Click Open in the Backstage view to display the Open dialog box.

3 Navigate to the location of the file to be opened (in this case, the USB flash drive, then to the CIS 101 folder [or your class folder], and then to the Access folder).

4 Click Camashaly Design to select the file to be opened.

5 Click the Open button (Open dialog box) to open the selected file and display the opened database in the Access window.

6 If a Security Warning appears, click the Enable Content button.

For an introduction to Office 2010 and instruction about how to perform basic tasks in Office 2010 programs, read the Office 2010 and Windows 7 chapter at the beginning of this book, where you can learn how to start a program, use the Ribbon, save a file, open a file, quit a program, use Help, and much more.

Creating Queries

Queries are simply questions, the answers to which are in the database. Access contains a powerful query feature. Through the use of this feature, you can find the answers to a wide variety of complex questions.

BTW

Q&As
For a complete list of the Q&As found in many of the step-by-step sequences in this book, visit the Access 2010 Q&A Web page (scsite.com/ac2010/qa).

Note: In this chapter, you will save each query example. When you use a query for another task, such as to create a form or report, you will assign a specific name to a query; for example, Analyst-Client Query. In situations in which you will not use the query again, you will assign a name using a convention that includes the chapter number and a query number; for example, Ch2q1. Queries are numbered consecutively.

To Create a Query in Design View

Most of the time, you will use Design view to create queries. Once you have created a new query in Design view, you can specify fields, criteria, sorting, calculations, and so on. The following steps create a new query in Design view.

- Close the Navigation Pane.
- Click Create on the Ribbon to display the Create tab.
- Click the Query Design button (Create tab | Queries group) to create a new query (Figure 2–2).

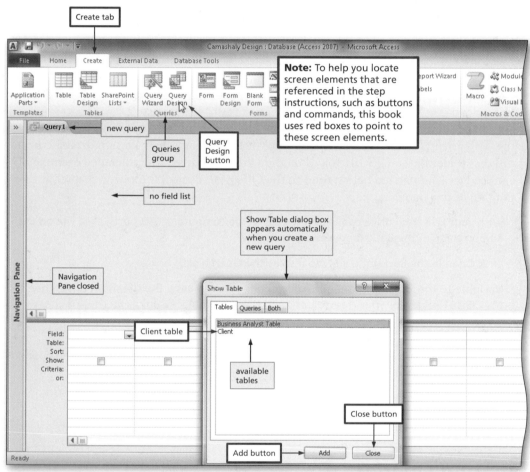

Figure 2–2

Q&A Is it necessary to close the Navigation Pane?

No. It gives you more room for the query, however, so it is usually a good practice to hide it.

②

- Click the Client table (Show Table dialog box) to select the table.

- Click the Add button to add the selected table to the query.

- Click the Close button to remove the dialog box from the screen.

Q&A | What if I inadvertently add the wrong table?

Right-click the table that you added in error and click Remove Table on the shortcut menu. You also can just close the query, indicate that you do not want to save it, and then start over.

- Drag the lower edge of the field list down far enough so all fields in the table appear (Figure 2–3).

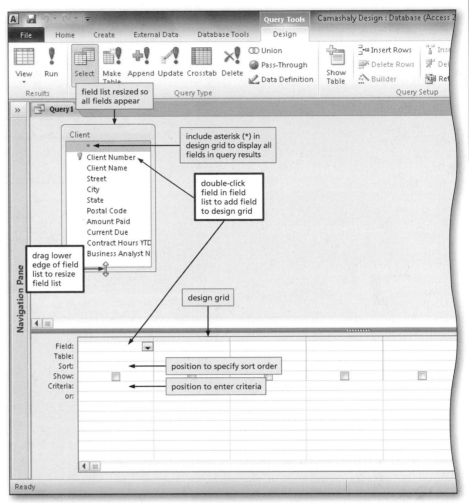

Figure 2–3

Q&A | How do I drag the lower edge?

Point to the lower edge, press and hold the left mouse button, move the mouse pointer to the new position for the lower edge, and then release the left mouse button. While the mouse pointer points to the lower edge of the field list, its shape changes to a two-headed arrow.

Q&A | Is it essential that I resize the field list?

No. You can always scroll through the list of fields using the scroll bar. It is usually more convenient to resize the field list so all fields appear.

To Add Fields to the Design Grid

Once you have a new query displayed in Design view, you are ready to make entries in the design grid, located in the lower pane of the window. You add the fields you want included in the query to the Field row in the grid. Only the fields that appear in the design grid will be included in the results of the query. The following steps begin the creation of a query that Camashaly Design might use to obtain the client number, client name, amount paid, and current due for a particular client. The following step selects the appropriate fields for the query.

1

- Double-click the Client Number field in the field list to add the field to the query.

Q&A

What if I add the wrong field?

Click just above the field name in the design grid to select the column and then press the DELETE key to remove the field.

- Double-click the Client Name field in the field list to add the field to the query.

- Add the Amount Paid field to the query.

- Add the Current Due field to the query (Figure 2–4).

Q&A

What if I want to include all fields? Do I have to add each field individually?

No. Instead of adding individual fields, you can double-click the asterisk (*) to add the asterisk to the design grid. The asterisk is a shortcut indicating all fields are to be included.

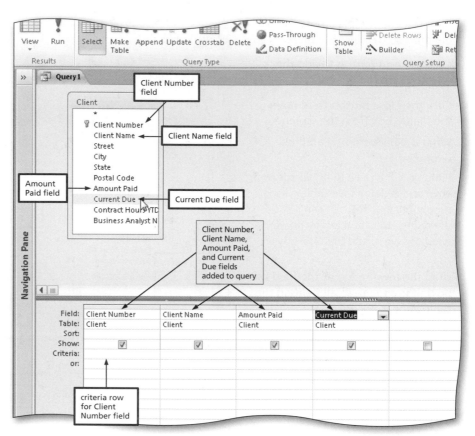

Figure 2–4

BTW

The Ribbon and Screen Resolution

Access may change how the groups and buttons within the groups appear on the Ribbon, depending on the computer's screen resolution. Thus, your Ribbon may look different from the ones in this book if you are using a screen resolution other than 1024 × 768.

Determining Criteria

When you use queries, usually you are looking for those records that satisfy some criterion. In the simple query you created in the previous chapter, for example, you entered a criterion to restrict the records that were included to those on which the business analyst number is 14. In another query, you might want the name, amount paid, and current due amounts of the client whose number is BC76, for example, or of those clients whose names start with the letters, Gr. You enter criteria in the Criteria row in the design grid below the field name to which the criterion applies. For example, to indicate that the client number must be BC76, you first must add the Client Number field to the design grid. You then would type BC76 in the Criteria row below the Client Number field.

To Use Text Data in a Criterion

To use **text data** (data in a field whose data type is Text) in criteria, simply type the text in the Criteria row below the corresponding field name. The following steps finish the creation of a query that Camashaly Design might use to obtain the client number, client name, amount paid, and current due amount of client BC76. These steps add the appropriate criterion so that only the desired client will appear in the results. The steps also save the query.

1

- Click the Criteria row for the Client Number field to produce an insertion point.

- Type **BC76** as the criterion (Figure 2–5).

Figure 2–5

2

- Click the View button (Query Tools Design tab | Results group) to display the query results (Figure 2–6).

Q&A I noticed that there is a View button on both the Home tab and the Design tab. Do they both have the same effect?

Yes. Use whichever one you find most convenient.

Figure 2–6

- Click the Save button on the Quick Access Toolbar to display the Save As dialog box.

- Type **Ch2q1** as the name of the query (Figure 2–7).

Can I also save from Design view?

Yes. You can save the query when you view it in Design view just as you can save the query when you view the query results in Datasheet view.

Figure 2–7

- Click the OK button (Save As dialog box) to save the query (Figure 2–8).

Figure 2–8

Other Ways

1. Right-click query tab, click Save on shortcut menu

Using Saved Queries

After you have created and saved a query, you can use it in a variety of ways:

- To view the results of the query that is not currently open, open it by right-clicking the query in the Navigation Pane and clicking Open on the shortcut menu.

- If you want to change the design of the query that is already open, return to Design view and make the changes.

- If you want to change the design of the query that is not currently open, right-click the query in the Navigation Pane and then click Design View on the shortcut menu to open the query in Design view.

- To print the results with the query open, click File on the Ribbon, click the Print tab in the Backstage view, and then click Quick Print.

- To print the query without first opening it, be sure the query is selected in the Navigation Pane and click File on the Ribbon, click the Print tab in the Backstage view, and then click Quick Print.

- You can switch between views of a query using the View button (Home tab | Views group). Clicking the arrow at the bottom of the button produces the View button menu. You then click the desired view in the menu. The two query views you use in this chapter are Datasheet view (see the results) and Design view (change the design). You can click the top part of the View button, in which case, you will switch to the view identified by the icon on the button. In the figure, the button contains the icon for Design view, so clicking the button would change to Design view. For the most part, the icon on the button represents the view you want, so you can usually simply click the button.

BTW

BTWs
For a complete list of the BTWs found in the margins of this book, visit the Access 2010 BTW Web page (scsite.com/ ac2010/btw).

To Use a Wildcard

Microsoft Access supports wildcards. **Wildcards** are symbols that represent any character or combination of characters. One common wildcard, the **asterisk** (*), represents any collection of characters. Thus Gr* represents the letters, Gr, followed by any collection of characters. Another wildcard symbol is the **question mark** (?), which represents any individual character. Thus T?m represents the letter, T, followed by any single character, followed by the letter, m; a search might return the names Tim or Tom.

The following steps modify the previous query so that Camashaly Design can select only those clients whose names begin with Gr. Because you do not know how many characters will follow the Gr, the asterisk wildcard symbol is appropriate. The steps also save the query with a new name using the Save As command.

1
- Click the View button (Home tab | Views group) to return to Design view.

- If necessary, click the Criteria row below the Client Number field to produce an insertion point.

Q&A

The text I entered now has quotation marks surrounding it. What happened?

Criteria for text data needs to be enclosed in quotation marks. You do not have to type the quotation marks; Access adds them automatically.

- Use the DELETE or BACKSPACE key as necessary to delete the current entry.

- Click the Criteria row below the Client Name field to produce an insertion point.

- Type **Gr*** as the criterion (Figure 2–9).

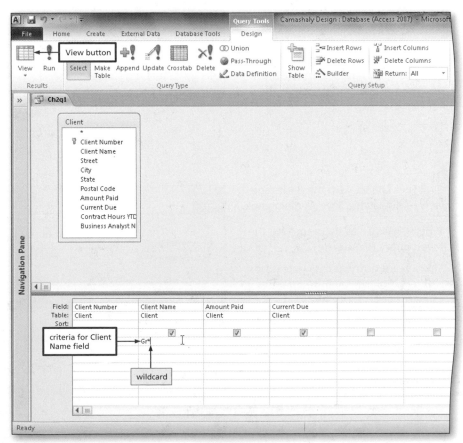

Figure 2–9

2

- View the query results by clicking the View button (Query Tools Design tab | Results group) (Figure 2–10).

 Experiment

- Vary the case of the letters in the criteria and view the results to determine whether case makes a difference when entering a wildcard.

Figure 2–10

3

- Click File on the Ribbon to open the Backstage view (Figure 2–11).

Q&A Why can I not just click the Save button on the Quick Access Toolbar like I did when I saved the previous query?

If you did, you would replace the previous query with the version you just created. Because you want to save both the previous query and the new one, you need to save the new version with a different name. To do so, you must use Save Object As, which is available through the Backstage view.

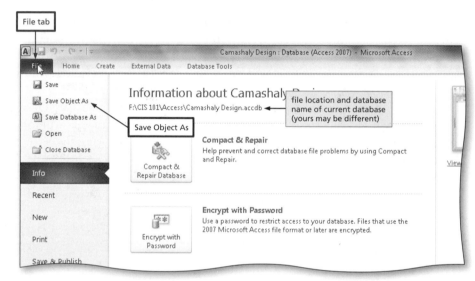

Figure 2–11

4

- Click Save Object As in the Backstage view to display the Save As dialog box.

- Type **Ch2q2** as the name for the saved query (Figure 2–12).

Q&A The current entry in the As text box is Query. Could I save the query as some other type of object?

Although you usually would want to save the query as another query, you also can save it as a form or report by changing the entry in the As text box. If you do, Access would create either a simple form or a simple report for the query.

Figure 2–12

5

- Click the OK button (Save As dialog box) to save the query with the new name, and then click File on the Ribbon to close the Backstage view (Figure 2–13).

Q&A

How can I tell that the query was saved with the new name?

The new name will appear on the tab.

Figure 2–13

To Use Criteria for a Field Not Included in the Results

In some cases, you might require criteria for a particular field that should not appear in the results of the query. For example, you may want to see the client number, client name, address, and amount paid for all clients located in Georgetown. The criteria involve the City field, but you do not want to include the City field in the results.

To enter a criterion for the City field, it must be included in the design grid. Normally, this also would mean it would appear in the results. To prevent this from happening, remove the check mark from its Show check box in the Show row of the grid.

The following steps modify the previous query so that Camashaly Design can select only those clients located in Georgetown. Camashaly does not want the city to appear in the results, however. The steps also save the query with a new name.

1

- Click the View button (Home tab | Views group), shown in Figure 2–13, to return to Design view.

Q&A

The text I entered is now preceded by the word, Like. What happened?

Criteria including wildcards need to be preceded by the word, Like. You do not have to type the word, Like, however. Access adds it automatically to any criterion involving a wildcard.

- Erase the criterion in the Client Name field.

- Add the City field to the query.

- Type **Georgetown** as the criterion for the City field (Figure 2–14).

Figure 2–14

2

• Click the Show check box for the City field to remove the check mark (Figure 2–15).

Q&A

Could I have removed the check mark before entering the criterion?

Yes. The order in which you perform the two operations does not matter.

Figure 2–15

3

• View the query results (Figure 2–16).

Experiment

• Click the View button to return to Design view, enter a different city name, and view the results. Repeat this process with a variety of city names, including at least one city name that is not in the database. When finished, change the criterion back to Georgetown.

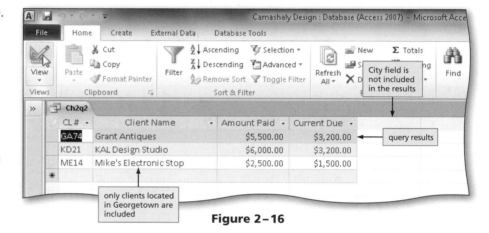

Figure 2–16

4

• Click File on the Ribbon to open the Backstage view.

• Click Save Object As in the Backstage view to display the Save As dialog box.

• Type **Ch2q3** as the name for the saved query.

• Click the OK button (Save As dialog box) to save the query with the new name.

• Click File on the Ribbon to close the Backstage view.

Creating a Parameter Query

BTW

Queries: Query-by-Example
Query-By-Example, often referred to as QBE, was a query language first proposed in the mid-1970s. In this approach, users asked questions by filling in a table on the screen. The Access approach to queries is based on Query-By-Example.

If you wanted to find clients located in Kyle instead of Georgetown, you would either have to create a new query or modify the existing query by replacing Georgetown with Kyle as the criterion. Rather than giving a specific criterion when you first create the query, on occasion, you may want to be able to enter part of the criterion when you view the query results and then have the appropriate results appear. For example, to include all the clients located in Kyle, you could enter Kyle as a criterion in the City field. From that point on, every time you ran the query, only the clients in Kyle would appear.

A better way is to allow the user to enter the city at the time the user wants to view the results. Thus, a user could view the query results, enter Kyle as the city, and then see all the clients in Kyle. Later, the user could use the same query but enter Georgetown as the city, and then see all the clients in Georgetown.

To enable this flexibility, you create a **parameter query**, which is a query that prompts for input whenever it is used. You enter a parameter (prompt for the user), rather than a specific value as the criterion. You create one by enclosing a value in a criterion in square brackets. It is important that the value in the brackets does not match the name of any field. If you enter a field name in square brackets, Access assumes you want that particular field and does not prompt the user for input. To prompt the user to enter the city name as the input, you could place [Enter City] as the criterion in the City field.

To Create and View a Parameter Query

The following steps create a parameter query that will prompt the users at Camashaly to enter a city, and then display the client number, name, address, and amount paid for all clients located in that city. The steps also save the query with a new name.

1

- Return to Design view.

- Erase the current criterion in the City column, and then type **[Enter City]** as the new criterion (Figure 2–17).

Q&A

What is the purpose of the square brackets?

The square brackets indicate that the text entered is not text that the value in the column must match. Without the brackets, Access would search for records on which the city is Enter City.

Figure 2–17

Q&A

What if I typed a field name in the square brackets?

Access would simply use the value in that field. To create a parameter query, you must not use a field name in the square brackets.

2

- Click the View button (Query Tools Design tab | Results group) to display the Enter Parameter Value dialog box (Figure 2–18).

Figure 2–18

3

- Type **Kyle** as the parameter value in the Enter City text box and then click the OK button (Enter Parameter Value dialog box) to close the dialog box and view the query (Figure 2–19).

 Experiment

- Try other characters between the square brackets. In each case, view the results. When finished, change the characters between the square brackets back to Enter City.

Figure 2–19

4

- Click File on the Ribbon to open the Backstage view.

- Click Save Object As in the Backstage view to display the Save As dialog box.

- Type **Client-City Query** as the name for the saved query.

- Click the OK button (Save As dialog box) to save the query with the new name and then click File on the Ribbon (Figure 2–20).

5

- Click the Close button for the Client-City query to close the query.

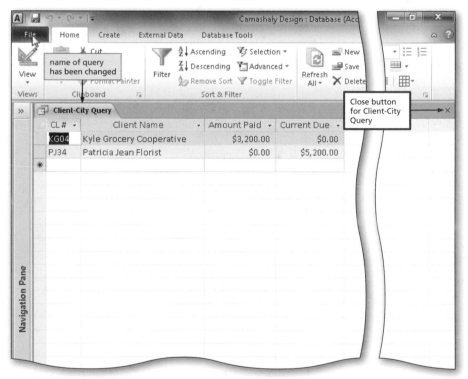

Figure 2–20

Break Point: If you wish to take a break, this is a good place to do so. You can quit Access now. To resume at a later time, start Access, open the database called Camashaly Design, and continue following the steps from this location forward.

To Use a Parameter Query

You use a parameter query like any other saved query. You can open it or you can print the query results. In either case, Access prompts you to supply a value for the parameter each time you use the query. As with other queries, the query always uses the data that is currently in the table. Thus, if changes have been made to the data since the last time you ran the query, the results of the query may be different, even if you enter the same value for the parameter. The following steps use the parameter query named Client-City Query.

1

- Open the Navigation Pane.

- Right-click the Client-City Query to produce a shortcut menu.

- Click Open on the shortcut menu to open the query and display the Enter Parameter Value dialog box (Figure 2–21).

The title bar for my Navigation Pane contains Tables and Related Views rather than All Access Objects as it did in Chapter 1. What should I do?

Click the Navigation Pane arrow and then click All Access Objects.

I do not have the Search bar at the top of the Navigation Pane that I had in Chapter 1. What should I do?

Right-click the Navigation Pane title bar arrow to display a shortcut menu, and then click Search Bar.

Figure 2–21

2

- Type **Kyle** in the Enter City text box, and then click the OK button (Enter Parameter Value dialog box) to display the results using Kyle as the city, as shown in Figure 2–20.

- Close the query.

To Use a Number in a Criterion

To enter a number in a criterion, type the number without any dollar signs or commas. The following steps create a query that Camashaly Design might use to display all clients whose current due amount is $0. The steps also save the query with a new name.

- Close the Navigation Pane.

- Click Create on the Ribbon to display the Create tab.

- Click the Query Design button (Create tab | Queries group) to create a new query.

- Click the Client table (Show Table dialog box) to select the table.

- Click the Add button to add the selected table to the query.

- Click the Close button to remove the dialog box from the screen.

- Drag the lower edge of the field list down far enough so all fields in the field list are displayed.

- Include the Client Number, Client Name, Amount Paid, and Current Due fields in the query.

- Type 0 as the criterion for the Current Due field (Figure 2–22).

Figure 2–22

Q&A   Do I need to enter a dollar sign and decimal point?

No. Access will interpret 0 as $0 because the data type for the Current Due field is currency.

- View the query results (Figure 2–23).

Q&A   Why did Access display the results as $0.00 when I only entered 0?

Access uses the format for the field to determine how to display the result. In this case, the format indicated that Access should include the dollar sign, decimal point, and two decimal places.

Figure 2–23

- Save the query as Ch2q4.

Q&A   How do I know when to use the Save button to save a query or use the Backstage view to perform a Save As?

If you are saving a new query, the simplest way is to use the Save button on the Quick Access Toolbar. If you are saving changes to a previously saved query but do not want to change the name, use the Save button. If you want to save a previously saved query with a new name, you must use the Backstage view and perform a Save Object As.

To Use a Comparison Operator in a Criterion

Unless you specify otherwise, Access assumes that the criteria you enter involve equality (exact matches). In the last query, for example, you were requesting those clients whose current due amount is equal to 0 (zero). If you want something other than an exact match, you must enter the appropriate **comparison operator**. The comparison operators are > (greater than), < (less than), >= (greater than or equal to), <= (less than or equal to), and NOT (not equal to).

The following steps use the > operator to create a query that Camashaly Design might use to find all clients whose amount paid is more than $3,000. The steps also save the query with a new name.

1
- Return to Design view.

- Erase the 0 in the Current Due column.

- Type >3000 as the criterion for the Amount Paid field (Figure 2–24).

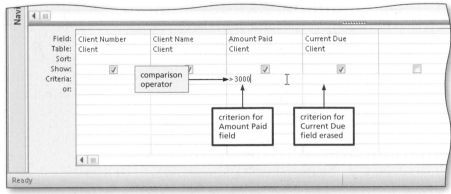

Figure 2–24

2
- View the query results (Figure 2–25).

  🔍 **Experiment**
- Return to Design view. Try a different criterion involving a comparison operator in the Amount Paid field and view the results. When finished, return to Design view, enter the original criterion (>3000) in the Amount Paid field, and view the results.

3
- Save the query as Ch2q5.

Figure 2–25

Using Compound Criteria

Often you will have more than one criterion that the data for which you are searching must satisfy. This type of criterion is called a **compound criterion**. Two types of compound criteria exist.

In an **AND criterion**, each individual criterion must be true in order for the compound criterion to be true. For example, an AND criterion would allow you to find those clients that have an amount paid greater than $3,000 and whose business analyst is business analyst 11.

Conversely, an **OR criterion** is true provided either individual criterion is true. An OR criterion would allow you to find those clients that have an amount paid greater than $3,000 and also those clients whose business analyst is business analyst 11 — either one criterion or the other is true. In this case, any client whose amount paid is greater than $3,000 would be included in the answer, regardless of whether the client's business analyst is business analyst 11. Likewise, any client whose business analyst is business analyst 11 would be included, regardless of whether the client had an amount paid greater than $3,000.

To Use a Compound Criterion Involving AND

To combine criteria with AND, place the criteria on the same row of the design grid. The following steps use an AND criterion to enable Camashaly to find those clients whose amount paid is greater than $3,000 and whose business analyst is analyst 11. The steps also save the query with a new name.

1

• Return to Design view.

• Include the Business Analyst Number field in the query.

• Type **11** as the criterion for the Business Analyst Number field (Figure 2–26).

Figure 2–26

2

• View the query results (Figure 2–27).

3

• Save the query as Ch2q6.

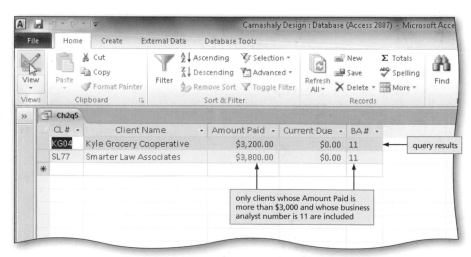

Figure 2–27

To Use a Compound Criterion Involving OR

To combine criteria with OR, the criteria must go on separate rows in the Criteria area of the grid. The following steps use an OR criterion to enable Camashaly to find those clients whose amount paid is greater than $3,000 or whose business analyst is analyst 11 (or both). The steps also save the query with a new name.

- Return to Design view.

- If necessary, click the Criteria entry for the Business Analyst Number field and then use the BACKSPACE key or the DELETE key to erase the entry ("11").

- Click the or row (the row below the Criteria row) for the Business Analyst Number field and then type **11** as the entry (Figure 2–28).

Figure 2–28

- View the query results (Figure 2–29).

- Save the query as Ch2q7.

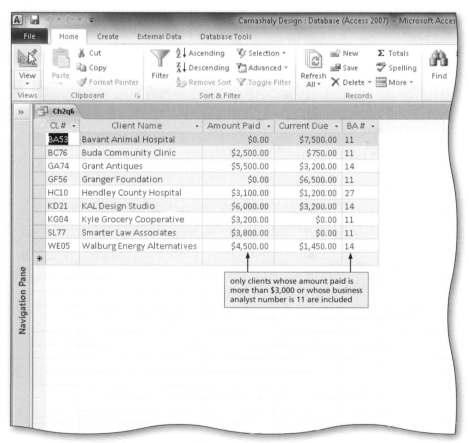

Figure 2–29

Special Criteria

There are three special criteria you can use in queries:

1. If you want to create a criterion involving a range of values in a single field, you can use the **AND operator**. You place the word AND between the individual conditions. For example, if you wanted to find all clients whose amount paid is >= $1,000 and <= $4,000, you would enter `>= 1000 AND <= 4000` as the criterion in the Amount Paid column.

2. You can select values in a given range by using the **BETWEEN operator**. This is often an alternative to the AND operator. For example, to find all clients whose amount paid is between $1,000 and $4,000, inclusive, you would enter `BETWEEN 1000 AND 4000` as the criterion in the Amount Paid column.

3. You can select values in a list by using the **IN operator**. You follow the word IN with the list of values in parentheses. For example, to find clients whose business analyst number is 11 or 14 using the IN operator, you would enter `IN ("11","14")` as the criterion in the Business Analyst Number column. Unlike when you enter a simple criterion, you must enclose text values in quotation marks.

Sorting

In some queries, the order in which the records appear is irrelevant. All you need to be concerned about are the records that appear in the results. It does not matter which one is first or which one is last.

In other queries, however, the order can be very important. You may want to see the cities in which clients are located and would like them arranged alphabetically. Perhaps you want to see the clients listed by business analyst number. Further, within all the clients of any given business analyst, you might want them to be listed by amount paid from largest amount to smallest.

To order the records in a query result in a particular way, you **sort** the records. The field or fields on which the records are sorted is called the **sort key**. If you are sorting on more than one field (such as sorting by amount paid within business analyst number), the more important field (Business Analyst Number) is called the **major key** (also called the **primary sort key**) and the less important field (Amount Paid) is called the **minor key** (also called the **secondary sort key**).

To sort in Microsoft Access, specify the sort order in the Sort row of the design grid below the field that is the sort key. If you specify more than one sort key, the sort key on the left will be the major sort key, and the one on the right will be the minor key.

The following are guidelines related to sorting in queries.

Plan
Ahead

Determine whether special order is required.
Examine the query or request to see if it contains words, such as order or sort, that would imply that the order of the query results is important. If so, you need to sort the query.

● **Determine the sort key(s).** If sorting is required, identify the field or fields on which the results are to be sorted. In the request, look for language such as ordered by or sort the results by, both of which would indicate that the specified field is a sort key.

● **If using two sort keys, determine major and minor key.** If you are using two sort keys, determine which one is the more important, or the major key. Look for language such as sort by amount paid within business analyst number, which implies that the overall order is by business analyst number. Thus, the Business Analyst Number field would be the major sort key and the Amount Paid field would be the minor sort key.

● **Determine sort order.** Words such as increasing, ascending, or low-to-high imply Ascending order. Words such as decreasing, descending, or high-to-low imply Descending order. Sorting in alphabetical order implies Ascending order. If there are no words to imply a particular order, you would typically use Ascending.

● **Determine restrictions.** Examine the query or request to see if there are any special restrictions. One common restriction is to exclude duplicates. Another common restriction is to list only a certain number of records, for example, to list only the first five records.

BTW

Clearing the Design Grid
You also can clear the design grid using the Ribbon. To do so, click the Home tab, click the Advanced button (Home tab | Sort & Filter group) to display the Advanced menu, and then click Clear Grid on the Advanced menu.

To Clear the Design Grid

If the fields you want to include in the next query are different from those in the previous query, it is usually simpler to start with a clear grid, one with no fields already in the design grid. You always can clear the entries in the design grid by closing the query and then starting over. A simpler approach to clearing the entries is to select all the entries and then press the DELETE key. The following steps return to Design view and clear the design grid.

1

● Return to Design view.

● Click just above the Client Number column heading in the grid to select the column.

Q&A I clicked above the column heading, but the column is not selected. What should I do?

You didn't point to the correct location. Be sure the mouse pointer changes into a down-pointing arrow and then click again.

● Hold the SHIFT key down and click just above the Business Analyst Number column heading to select all the columns (Figure 2–30).

2

● Press the DELETE key to clear the design grid.

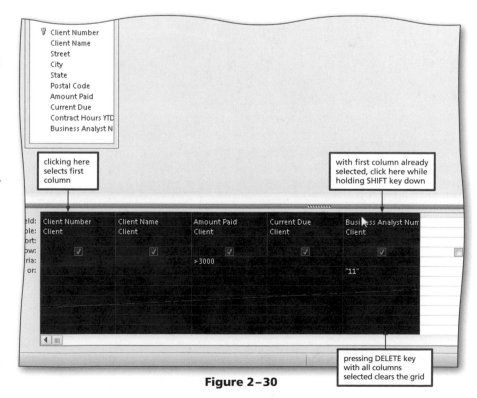

Figure 2–30

To Sort Data in a Query

After determining in the design process that a query is to be sorted, you will need to specify the sort key to Access. The following steps sort the cities in the Client table by indicating that the City field is to be sorted. The steps specify Ascending sort order.

- Include the City field in the design grid.

- Click the Sort row below the City field, and then click the Sort row arrow to display a menu of possible sort orders (Figure 2–31).

Figure 2–31

2

- Click Ascending to select the sort order (Figure 2–32).

Figure 2–32

3

- View the query results (Figure 2–33).

🔍 **Experiment**

- Return to Design view and change the sort order to Descending. View the results. Return to Design view and change the sort order back to Ascending. View the results.

Why do some cities appear more than once?

More than one client is located in those cities.

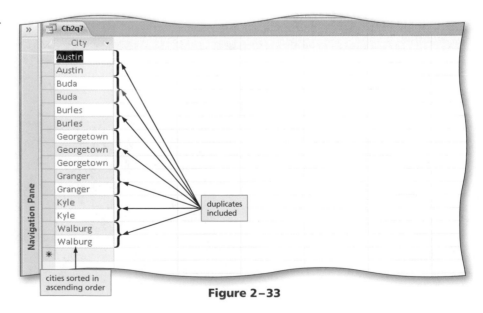

Figure 2–33

To Omit Duplicates

When you sort data, duplicates normally are included. In Figure 2–33, for example, Austin appeared twice, as did Buda, Burles, Granger, Kyle, and Walburg. Georgetown appeared three times. These duplicates do not add any value, so you should eliminate them from the results. To eliminate duplicates, display the query's property sheet. A **property sheet** is a window containing the various properties of the object. To omit duplicates, you will use the property sheet to change the Unique Values property from No to Yes.

The following steps create a query that Camashaly Design might use to obtain a sorted list of the cities in the Client table in which each city is listed only once. The steps also save the query with a new name.

1

- Return to Design view.

- Click the second field (the empty field to the right of City) in the design grid.

- If necessary, click Design on the Ribbon to display the Design tab.

- Click the Property Sheet button (Query Tools Design tab | Show/Hide group) to display the property sheet (Figure 2–34).

My property sheet looks different. What should I do?

If your sheet looks different, you clicked the wrong place and will have to close the property sheet and repeat this step.

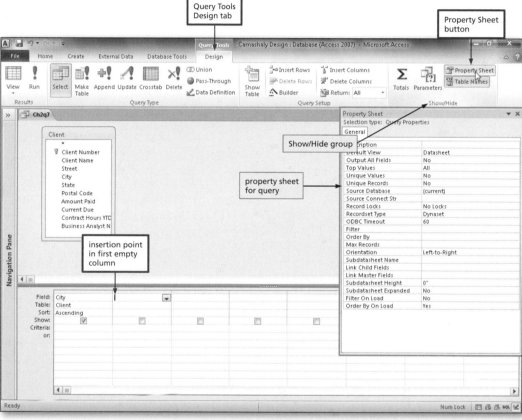

Figure 2–34

2

- Click the Unique Values property box, and then click the arrow that appears to produce a list of available choices (Figure 2–35).

Figure 2–35

- Click Yes and then close the Query Properties property sheet by clicking the Property Sheet button (Query Tools Design tab | Show / Hide group) a second time.

- View the query results (Figure 2–36).

- Save the query as Ch2q8.

Other Ways

1. Right-click second field in design grid, click Properties on shortcut menu

Figure 2–36

To Sort on Multiple Keys

The following steps sort on multiple keys. Specifically, Camashaly needs the data to be sorted by amount paid (low to high) within business analyst number, which means that the Business Analyst Number field is the major key and the Amount Paid field is the minor key. The steps also save the query with a new name.

- Return to Design view. Clear the design grid by clicking the first column in the grid, and then pressing the DELETE key to clear the design grid.

- In the following order, include the Client Number, Client Name, Business Analyst Number, and Amount Paid fields in the query.

- Select Ascending as the sort order for both the Business Analyst Number field and the Amount Paid field (Figure 2–37).

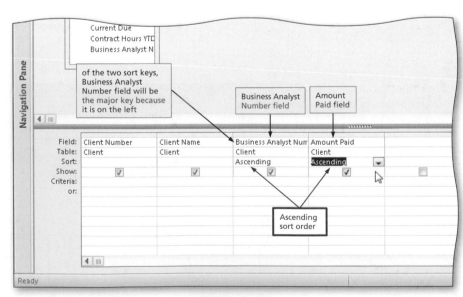

Figure 2–37

2

- View the query results (Figure 2–38).

🔍 **Experiment**

- Return to Design view and try other sort combinations for the Business Analyst Number and Amount Paid fields, such as Ascending for Business Analyst Number and Descending for Amount Paid. In each case, view the results to see the effect of the changes. When finished, select Ascending as the sort order for both fields.

 Q&A

What if the Amount Paid field is to the left of the Business Analyst Number field?

It is important to remember that the major sort key must appear to the left of the minor sort key in the design grid. If you attempted to sort by amount paid within business analyst number, but placed the Amount Paid field to the left of the Business Analyst Number field, your results would be incorrect.

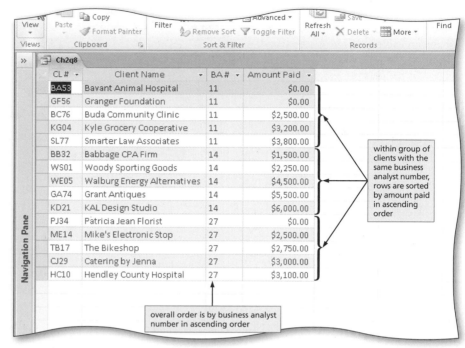

Figure 2–38

3

- Save the query as Ch2q9.

To Create a Top-Values Query

Rather than show all the results of a query, you may want to show only a specified number of records or a percentage of records. Creating a **top-values query** allows you to quantify the results. When you sort records, you can limit results to those records having the highest (descending sort) or lowest (ascending sort) values. To do so, first create a query that sorts the data in the desired order. Next, use the Return box on the Design tab to change the number of records to be included from All to the desired number or percentage. The following steps create a query for Camashaly Design that shows only the first five records that were included in the results of the previous query. The steps also save the resulting query with a new name.

1

- Return to Design view.

- If necessary, click Design on the Ribbon to display the Design tab.

- Click the Return box arrow (Query Tools Design tab | Query Setup group) to display the Return box menu (Figure 2–39).

Figure 2–39

2

- Click 5 in the Return box menu to specify that the query results should contain the first five rows.

Q&A

Could I have typed the 5? What about other numbers that do not appear in the list?

Yes, you could have typed the 5. For numbers not appearing in the list, you must type the number.

- View the query results (Figure 2–40).

3

- Save the query as Ch2q10.
- Close the query.

Figure 2–40

Q&A

Do I need to close the query before creating my next query?

Not necessarily. When you use a top-values query, however, it is important to change the value in the Return box back to All. If you do not change the Return value back to All, the previous value will remain in effect. Consequently, you might not get all the records you should in the next query. A good practice whenever you use a top-values query is to close the query as soon as you are done. That way, you will begin your next query from scratch, which guarantees that the value is reset to All.

Break Point: If you wish to take a break, this is a good place to do so. You can quit Access now. To resume at a later time, start Access, open the database called Camashaly Design, and continue following the steps from this location forward.

BTW

Join Line
If you do not get a join line automatically, there may be a problem with one of your table designs. Open each table in Design view and make sure that the data types are the same for the matching field in both tables and that one of the matching fields is the primary key in a table. Correct these errors and create the query again.

Joining Tables

In designing a query, you need to determine whether more than one table is required. If the question being asked involves data from both the Client and Business Analyst tables, for example, both tables are required for the query. For example, a query may require listing the number and name of each client along with the number and name of the client's business analyst. The client's name is in the Client table, whereas the business analyst's name is in the Business Analyst Table. Thus, this query cannot be completed using a single table; both the Client and Business Analyst tables are required. You need to **join** the tables; that is, to find records in the two tables that have identical values in matching fields (Figure 2–41). In this example, you need to find records in the Client table and the Business Analyst table that have the same value in the Business Analyst Number fields.

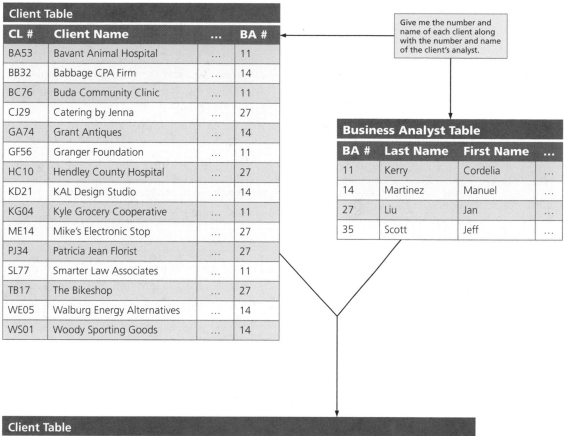

Give me the number and name of each client along with the number and name of the client's analyst.

Client Table

CL #	Client Name	...	BA #
BA53	Bavant Animal Hospital	...	11
BB32	Babbage CPA Firm	...	14
BC76	Buda Community Clinic	...	11
CJ29	Catering by Jenna	...	27
GA74	Grant Antiques	...	14
GF56	Granger Foundation	...	11
HC10	Hendley County Hospital	...	27
KD21	KAL Design Studio	...	14
KG04	Kyle Grocery Cooperative	...	11
ME14	Mike's Electronic Stop	...	27
PJ34	Patricia Jean Florist	...	27
SL77	Smarter Law Associates	...	11
TB17	The Bikeshop	...	27
WE05	Walburg Energy Alternatives	...	14
WS01	Woody Sporting Goods	...	14

Business Analyst Table

BA #	Last Name	First Name	...
11	Kerry	Cordelia	...
14	Martinez	Manuel	...
27	Liu	Jan	...
35	Scott	Jeff	...

Client Table

CL #	Client Name	...	BA #	Last Name	First Name	...
BA53	Bavant Animal Hospital	...	11	Kerry	Cordelia	...
BB32	Babbage CPA Firm	...	14	Martinez	Manuel	...
BC76	Buda Community Clinic	...	11	Kerry	Cordelia	...
CJ29	Catering by Jenna	...	27	Liu	Jan	...
GA74	Grant Antiques	...	14	Martinez	Manuel	...
GF56	Granger Foundation	...	11	Kerry	Cordelia	...
HC10	Hendley County Hospital	...	27	Liu	Jan	...
KD21	KAL Design Studio	...	14	Martinez	Manuel	...
KG04	Kyle Grocery Cooperative	...	11	Kerry	Cordelia	...
ME14	Mike's Electronic Stop	...	27	Liu	Jan	...
PJ34	Patricia Jean Florist	...	27	Liu	Jan	...
SL77	Smarter Law Associates	...	11	Kerry	Cordelia	...
TB17	The Bikeshop	...	27	Liu	Jan	...
WE05	Walburg Energy Alternatives	...	14	Martinez	Manuel	...
WS01	Woody Sporting Goods	...	14	Martinez	Manuel	...

Figure 2–41

BTW

Join Types
The type of join that finds records from both tables that have identical values in matching fields is called an inner join. An inner join is the default join in Access. Outer joins are used to show all the records in one table as well as the common records; that is, the records that share the same value in the join field. In a left outer join, all rows from the table on the left are included. In a right outer join, all rows from the table on the right are included.

The following are guidelines related to joining tables.

Determine whether more than one table is required.
Examine the query or request to see if all the fields involved in the request are in one table. If the fields are in two (or more) tables, you need to join the tables.

- **Determine the matching fields.** If joining is required, identify the matching fields in the two tables that have identical values. Look for the same column name in the two tables or for column names that are similar.

- **Determine whether sorting is required.** Queries that join tables often are used as the basis for a report. If this is the case, it may be necessary to sort the results. For example, the Analyst-Client Report is based on a query that joins the Business Analyst and Client tables. The query is sorted by business analyst number and client number.

- **Determine restrictions.** Examine the query or request to see if there are any special restrictions. For example, the user may only want clients whose current due amount is $0.00.

- **Determine join properties.** Examine the query or request to see if you only want records from both tables that have identical values in matching fields. If you want to see records in one of the tables that do not have identical values, then you need to change the join properties.

To Join Tables

If you have determined in the design process that you need to join tables, you will first bring field lists for both tables to the upper pane of the Query window while working in Design view. Access will draw a line, called a **join line**, between matching fields in the two tables, indicating that the tables are related. You then can select fields from either table. Access joins the tables automatically.

The first step is to create a new query and add the Business Analyst Table to the query. Then, add the Client table to the query. A join line will appear, connecting the Business Analyst Number fields in the two field lists. This join line indicates how the tables are related, that is, linked through these matching fields. If the names of the matching fields differ from one table to the other, Access will not insert the line. You can insert it manually, however, by clicking one of the two matching fields and dragging the mouse pointer to the other matching field.

The following steps create a query that Camashaly Design might use to display information from both the Client table and the Business Analyst Table.

1

- Click Create on the Ribbon to display the Create tab.

- Click the Query Design button (Create tab | Queries group) to create a new query.

- If necessary, click the Business Analyst Table (Show Table dialog box) to select the table.

- Click the Add button (Show Table dialog box) to add a field list for the Business Analyst Table to the query (Figure 2–42).

Figure 2–42

2

- Click the Client table (Show Table dialog box).

- Click the Add button (Show Table dialog box) to add a field list for the Client table.

- Close the Show Table dialog box by clicking the Close button.

- Expand the size of the two field lists so all the fields in the Business Analyst and Client tables appear (Figure 2–43).

Q&A I did not get a join line. What should I do?

Ensure that the names of the matching fields are exactly the same, the data types are the same, and the matching field is the primary key in one of the two tables. If all of these are true and you still do not have a join line, you can produce one by pointing to one of the matching fields, pressing the left mouse button, dragging to the other matching field, and releasing the left mouse button.

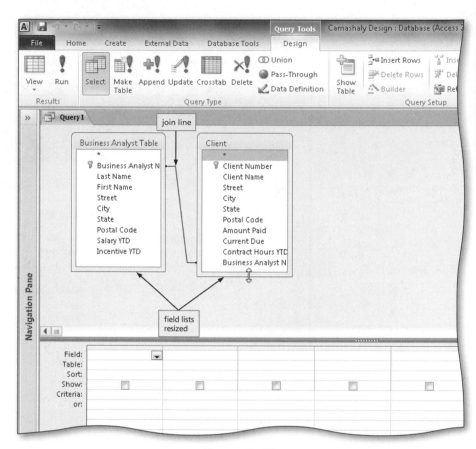

Figure 2–43

3

- In the design grid, include the Business Analyst Number, Last Name, and First Name fields from the Business Analyst Table as well as the Client Number and Client Name fields from the Client table.

- Select Ascending as the sort order for both the Business Analyst Number field and the Client Number field (Figure 2–44).

Figure 2–44

• View the query results
(Figure 2–45).

Figure 2–45

• Click the Save button
on the Quick Access
Toolbar to display the
Save As dialog box.

• Type **Analyst-
Client Query**
as the query name
(Figure 2–46).

6

• Click the OK button
(Save As dialog box)
to save the query.

Figure 2–46

To Change Join Properties

Normally, records that do not match do not appear in the results of a join query. For example, a business analyst such as Jeff Scott, for whom no clients currently exist, would not appear in the results. To cause such a record to be displayed, you need to change the **join properties**, which are the properties that indicate which records appear in a join. The following steps change the join properties of the Analyst-Client Query so that Camashaly can include all business analysts in the results, rather than only those analysts who have already been assigned clients.

1

- Return to Design view.

- Right-click the join line to produce a shortcut menu (Figure 2–47).

Q&A

I do not see Join Properties on my shortcut menu. What should I do?

If Join Properties does not appear on your shortcut menu, you did not point to the appropriate portion of the join line. You will need to point to the correct (middle) portion and right-click again.

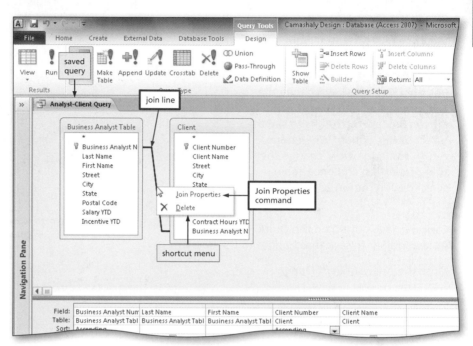

Figure 2–47

2

- Click Join Properties on the shortcut menu to display the Join Properties dialog box (Figure 2–48).

Figure 2–48

3

- Click option button 2 (Join Properties dialog box) to include all records from the Business Analyst Table regardless of whether they match any clients.

- Click the OK button (Join Properties dialog box) to modify the join properties.

- View the query results (Figure 2–49).

 Experiment

- Return to Design view, change the Join properties, and select option button 3. View the results to see the effect of this option. When done, return to Design view, change the Join properties, and once again select option button 2.

4

- Click the Save button on the Quick Access Toolbar to save the changes to the query.

- Close the Analyst-Client Query.

Q&A I see a dialog box that asks if I want to save the query. What should I do?

Click the OK button to save the query.

Figure 2–49

To Create a Report Involving a Join

The following steps use the Report Wizard to create the report for Camashaly Design that is shown in Figure 2–50.

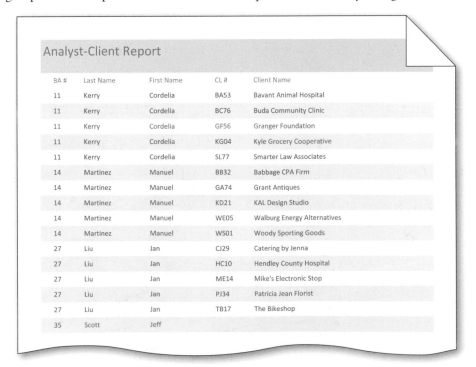

Figure 2–50

1

- Open the Navigation Pane, and then select the Analyst-Client Query in the Navigation Pane.

- Click Create on the Ribbon to display the Create tab.

- Click the Report Wizard button (Create tab | Reports group) to display the Report Wizard dialog box (Figure 2–51).

Figure 2–51

2

- Click the Add All Fields button (Report Wizard dialog box) to add all the fields in the Analyst-Client Query.

- Click the Next button to display the next Report Wizard screen (Figure 2–52).

Figure 2–52

3

- Because you will not specify any grouping, click the Next button in the Report Wizard dialog box to display the next Report Wizard screen.

- Because you already specified the sort order in the query, click the Next button again to display the next Report Wizard screen.

- Make sure that Tabular is selected as the Layout and Portrait is selected as the Orientation.

- Click the Next button to display the next Report Wizard screen.

- Erase the current title, and then type **Analyst-Client Report** as the new title.

- Click the Finish button to produce the report (Figure 2–53).

4

- Close the Analyst-Client Report.

Figure 2–53

To Print a Report

The following steps print a hard copy of the report.

1 With the Analyst-Client Report selected in the Navigation Pane, click File on the Ribbon to open the Backstage view.

2 Click the Print tab in the Backstage view to display the Print gallery.

3 Click the Quick Print button to print the report.

Creating a Form for a Query

In the previous chapter, you created a form for the Client table. You also can create a form for a query. Recall that a **form** in a database is a formatted document with fields that contain data. Forms allow you to view and maintain data.

To Create a Form for a Query

The following steps create a form and then save the form.

1

- If necessary, select the Analyst-Client Query in the Navigation Pane.

- Click Create on the Ribbon to display the Create tab (Figure 2–54).

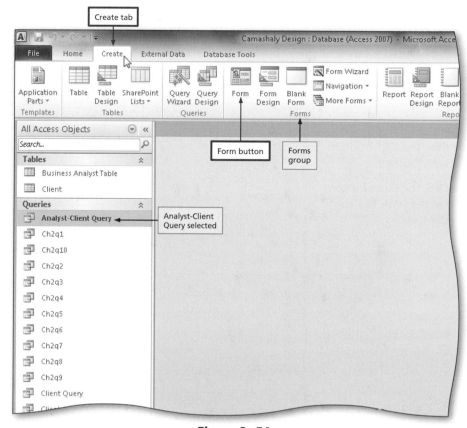

Figure 2–54

2

- Click the Form button (Create tab | Forms group) to create a simple form (Figure 2–55).

Figure 2–55

• Click the Save button on the Quick Access Toolbar to display the Save As dialog box.

• Type **Analyst-Client Form** as the form name (Figure 2–56).

Figure 2–56

• Click the OK button to save the form.

• Click the Close button for the form to close the form.

Using a Form

After you have saved a form, you can use it at any time by right-clicking the form in the Navigation Pane and then clicking Open on the shortcut menu. If you plan to use the form to enter data, you must ensure you are viewing the form in Form view.

Exporting Data from Access to Other Applications

You can **export**, or copy, data from an Access database so that another application (for example, Excel or Word) can use the data. The application that will receive the data determines the export process to be used. You can export to text files in a variety of formats. For applications to which you cannot directly export data, you often can export an appropriately formatted text file that the other application can import. Figure 2–57 shows the Analyst-Client Query exported to Excel.

Figure 2–57

To Export Data to Excel

For Camashaly Design to make the Analyst-Client Query available to Excel users, it needs to export the data. To export data to Excel, select the table or query to be exported, and then click the Excel button in the Export group on the External Data tab. The following steps export the Analyst-Client Query to Excel and save the export steps. By saving the export steps, you could easily repeat the export process whenever you like without going through all the following steps. You would use the saved steps to export data in the future by clicking the Saved Exports button (External Data tab | Export group) and then selecting the steps you saved.

1

• Click the Analyst-Client Query in the Navigation Pane to select it.

• Click External Data on the Ribbon to display the External Data tab (Figure 2–58).

Figure 2–58

2

- Click the Excel button (External Data tab | Export group) to display the Export - Excel Spreadsheet dialog box.

- Click the Browse button (Export - Excel Spreadsheet dialog box) to display the File Save dialog box, and select your USB flash drive as the file location.

- Be sure the file name is Analyst-Client Query and then click the Save button (File Save dialog box) (Figure 2–59).

Q&A Did I need to browse?

No. You could type the appropriate file location.

Q&A Could I change the name of the file?

You could change it. Simply replace the current file name with the one you want.

Q&A What if the file I want to export already exists?

Access will indicate that the file already exists and ask if you want to replace it. If you click the Yes button, the file you export will replace the old file. If you click the No button, you must either change the name of the export file or cancel the process.

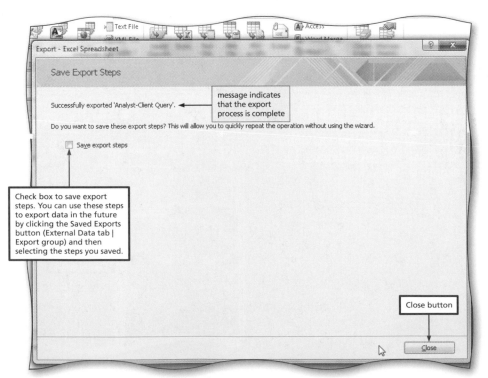

Figure 2–59

3

- Click the OK button (Export - Excel Spreadsheet dialog box) to export the data (Figure 2–60).

Figure 2–60

4

- Click the 'Save export steps' check box (Export - Excel Spreadsheet dialog box) to display the Save export steps options.

- If necessary, type **Export-Analyst-Client Query** in the Save as text box.

- Type **Export the Analyst-Client Query without formatting** in the Description text box (Figure 2–61).

5

- Click the Save Export button (Export - Excel Spreadsheet dialog box) to save the export steps.

Figure 2–61

To Export Data to Word

It is not possible to export data to the standard Word format. It is possible, however, to export the data as a rich text format (RTF) file, which Word can access. To export data from a query or table to an RTF file, you would use the following steps.

1. With the query or table to be exported selected in the Navigation Pane, click the More button (External Data tab | Export group) and then click Word on the More menu to display the Export - RTF File dialog box.

2. Select the name and location for the file to be created.

3. Click the Save button, and then click the OK button to export the data.

4. Save the export steps if you want, or simply click the Close button in the Export - RTF File dialog box to close the dialog box without saving the export steps.

Text Files

You also can export to text files. Text files contain unformatted characters, including alphanumeric characters, and some special characters, such as tabs, carriage returns, and line feeds.

In **delimited files**, each record is on a separate line, and the fields are separated by a special character, called the **delimiter**. Common delimiters are tabs, semicolons, commas, and spaces. You also can choose any other value that does not appear within the field contents. The comma-separated values (CSV) file often used in Excel is an example of a delimited file.

In **fixed-width files**, the width of any field is the same on every record. For example, if the width of the first field on the first record is 12 characters, the width of the first field on every other record also must be 12 characters.

To Export Data to a Text File

When exporting data to a text file, you can choose to export the data with formatting and layout. This option preserves much of the formatting and layout in tables, queries, forms, and reports. For forms and reports, this is the only option.

If you do not need to preserve the formatting, you can choose either delimited or fixed-width as the format for the exported file. The most common option, especially if formatting is not an issue, is delimited. You can choose the delimiter and also whether to include field names on the first row. In many cases, delimiting with a comma and including the field names is a good choice.

To export data from a table or query to a comma-delimited file in which the first row contains the column headings, you would use the following steps.

1. With the query or table to be exported selected in the Navigation Pane, click the Text File button (External Data tab | Export group) to display the Export - Text File dialog box.

2. Select the name and location for the file to be created.

3. If you need to preserve formatting and layout, be sure the 'Export data with formatting and layout' check box is checked. If you do not need to preserve formatting and layout, make sure the check box is not checked. Once you have made your selection, click the OK button in the Export - Text File dialog box.

4. To create a delimited file, be sure the Delimited option button is selected in the Export Text Wizard dialog box. To create a fixed-width file, be sure the Fixed Width option button is selected. Once you have made your selection, click the Next button.

5. a. If you are exporting to a delimited file, choose the delimiter that you want to separate your fields, such as a comma. Decide whether to include field names on the first row and, if so, click the Include Field Names on First Row check box. If you want to select a text qualifier, select it in the Text Qualifier list. When you have made your selections, click the Next button.

   b. If you are exporting to a fixed-width file, review the position of the vertical lines that separate your fields. If any lines are not positioned correctly, follow the directions on the screen to reposition them. When you have finished, click the Next button.

6. Click the Finish button to export the data.

7. Save the export steps if you want, or simply click the Close button in the Export - Text File dialog box to close the dialog box without saving the export steps.

Adding Criteria to a Join Query

Sometimes you will want to join tables, but you will not want to include all possible records. For example, you would like to create a report showing only those clients whose amount paid is greater than $3,000. In such cases, you will relate the tables and include fields just as you did before. You also will include criteria. To include only those clients whose amount paid is more than $3,000.00, you will include >3000 as a criterion for the Amount Paid field.

To Restrict the Records in a Join

The following steps modify the Analyst-Client Query so that the results for Camashaly Design only include those clients whose amount paid is more than $3,000.

- Open the Analyst-Client Query in Design view and close the Navigation Pane.

- Add the Amount Paid field to the query.

- Type >3000 as the criterion for the Amount Paid field (Figure 2–62).

Figure 2–62

- View the query results (Figure 2–63).

- Close the query.

- When asked if you want to save your changes, click the No button.

Q&A

What if I saved the changes?

The next time you used this query, you would only see clients whose amount paid is more than $3,000.

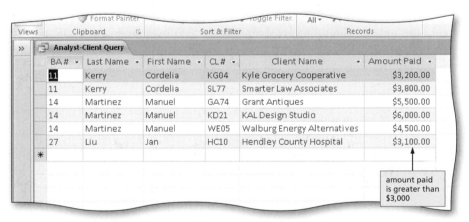

Figure 2–63

Calculations

If you have determined that a special calculation is required for a query, you then need to determine whether the calculation is an individual record calculation (for example, adding the values in two fields) or a group calculation (for example, finding the total of the values in a particular field on all the records).

Camashaly Design may want to know the total amount (amount paid and current due) from each client. This would seem to pose a problem because the Client table does not include a field for total amount. You can calculate it, however, because the total amount is equal to the amount paid plus the current due. A field that can be computed from other fields is called a **calculated field** or a **computed field**. A calculated field is an individual record calculation because each calculation only involves fields in a single record.

BTW

Expression Builder

Access includes a tool to help you create complex expressions. If you click Build on the shortcut menu (see Figure 2–64), Access displays the Expression Builder dialog box, which includes an expression box, operator buttons, and expression elements. You can type parts of the expression directly and paste operator buttons and expression elements into the box. You also can use functions in expressions.

Camashaly also may want to calculate the average amount paid for the clients of each business analyst. That is, they may want the average for the clients of business analyst 11, the average for the clients of business analyst 14, and so on. This type of calculation is called a **group calculation** because each calculation involves groups of records. In this example, the clients of business analyst 11 would form one group, the clients of business analyst 14 would be a second group, and the clients of business analyst 27 would form a third group.

The following are guidelines related to calculations in queries.

Plan Ahead

> **Determine whether calculations are required.**
> Examine the query or request to see if there are special calculations to be included. Look for words such as total, sum, compute, or calculate.
>
> • **Determine a name for the calculated field.** If calculations are required, decide on the name for the field. Assign a name that helps identify the contents of the field. For example, if you are adding the cost of a number of items, the name Total Cost would be appropriate. The name, also called an **alias**, becomes the column name when the query is run.
>
> • **Determine the format for the calculated field.** Determine how the calculated field should appear. If the calculation involves monetary amounts, you would use the currency format. If the calculated value contains decimals, determine how many decimal places to display.

To Use a Calculated Field in a Query

If you have determined that you need a calculated field in a query, you enter a name, or alias, for the calculated field, a colon, and then the calculation in one of the columns in the Field row of the design grid for the query. Any fields included in the expression must be enclosed in square brackets ([ ]). For example, for the total amount, you will type Total Amount:[Amount Paid]+[Current Due] as the expression.

You can type the expression directly into the Field row. You will not be able to see the entire entry, however, because the Field row is not large enough. The preferred way is to select the column in the Field row and then use the Zoom command on its shortcut menu. When Access displays the Zoom dialog box, you can enter the expression.

You are not restricted to addition in calculations. You can use subtraction (−), multiplication (*), or division (/). You also can include parentheses in your calculations to indicate which calculations should be done first.

The following steps create a query that Camashaly Design might use to obtain financial information on its clients, including the total amount (amount paid + current due), which is a calculated field.

• Create a query with a field list for the Client table.

• Add the Client Number, Client Name, Amount Paid, and Current Due fields to the query.

• Right-click the Field row in the first open column in the design grid to display a shortcut menu (Figure 2–64).

Figure 2–64

②

- Click Zoom on the shortcut menu to display the Zoom dialog box.

- Type **Total Amount: [Amount Paid]+ [Current Due]** in the Zoom dialog box (Figure 2–65).

Do I always need to put square brackets around field names?

If the field name does not contain spaces, square brackets are technically not necessary, although it is still acceptable to use the brackets. It is a good practice, however, to get in the habit of using the brackets.

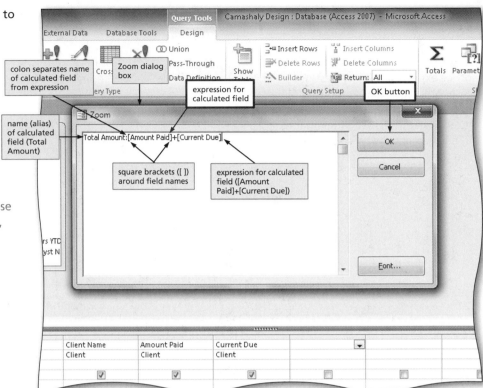

Figure 2–65

③

- Click the OK button (Zoom dialog box) to enter the expression (Figure 2–66).

Figure 2–66

4

- View the query results (Figure 2–67).

 Experiment

- Return to Design view and try other expressions. In at least one case, omit the Total Amount and the colon. In at least one case, intentionally misspell a field name. In each case, view the results to see the effect of your changes. When finished, reenter the original expression.

CL #	Client Name	Amount Paid	Current Due	Total Amour
BA53	Bavant Animal Hospital	$0.00	$7,500.00	$7,500.00
BB32	Babbage CPA Firm	$1,500.00	$500.00	$2,000.00
BC76	Buda Community Clinic	$2,500.00	$750.00	$3,250.00
CJ29	Catering by Jenna	$3,000.00	$1,000.00	$4,000.00
GA74	Grant Antiques	$5,500.00	$3,200.00	$8,700.00
GF56	Granger Foundation	$0.00	$6,500.00	$6,500.00
HC10	Hendley County Hospital	$3,100.00	$1,200.00	$4,300.00
KD21	KAL Design Studio	$6,000.00	$3,200.00	$9,200.00
KG04	Kyle Grocery Cooperative	$3,200.00	$0.00	$3,200.00
ME14	Mike's Electronic Stop	$2,500.00	$1,500.00	$4,000.00
PJ34	Patricia Jean Florist	$0.00	$5,200.00	$5,200.00
SL77	Smarter Law Associates	$3,800.00	$0.00	$3,800.00
TB17	The Bikeshop	$2,750.00	$1,200.00	$3,950.00
WE05	Walburg Energy Alternatives	$4,500.00	$1,450.00	$5,950.00
WS01	Woody Sporting Goods			$3,850.00

results are calculated by adding the amount paid and the current due

Total Amount field

Figure 2–67

Other Ways

1. Press SHIFT+F2

To Change a Caption

You can change the way items appear in the results of a query by changing their format. You also can change a query result's heading at the top of a column by changing the caption. Just as when you omitted duplicates, you will make this change by using a property sheet. In the property sheet, you can change the desired property, such as the format, the number of decimal places, or the caption. The following steps change the caption of the Amount Paid field to Paid and the caption of the Current Due field to Due. The steps also save the query with a new name.

1

- Return to Design view.

- If necessary, click Design on the Ribbon to display the Design tab.

- Click the Amount Paid field in the design grid, and then click the Property Sheet button (Query Tools Design tab | Show/Hide group) to display the properties for the Amount Paid field.

- Click the Caption box, and then type **Paid** as the caption (Figure 2–68).

 Q&A

My property sheet looks different. What should I do?

If your sheet looks different, you clicked the wrong place and will have to close the property sheet and repeat this step.

Figure 2–68

- Close the property sheet by clicking the Property Sheet button a second time.

- Click the Current Due field in the design grid, and then click the Property Sheet button (Query Tools Design tab | Show/Hide group).

- Click the Caption box, and then type **Due** as the caption.

- Close the Property Sheet by clicking the Property Sheet button a second time.

- View the query results (Figure 2–69).

3

- Save the query as Ch2q11.

- Close the query.

CL #	Client Name	Paid	Due	Total Amour
BA53	Bavant Animal Hospital	$0.00	$7,500.00	$7,500.00
BB32	Babbage CPA Firm	$1,500.00	$500.00	$2,000.00
BC76	Buda Community Clinic	$2,500.00	$750.00	$3,250.00
CJ29	Catering by Jenna	$3,000.00	$1,000.00	$4,000.00
GA74	Grant Antiques	$5,500.00	$3,200.00	$8,700.00
GF56	Granger Foundation	$0.00	$6,500.00	$6,500.00
HC10	Hendley County Hospital	$3,100.00	$1,200.00	$4,300.00
KD21	KAL Design Studio	$6,000.00	$3,200.00	$9,200.00
KG04	Kyle Grocery Cooperative	$3,200.00	$0.00	$3,200.00
ME14	Mike's Electronic Stop	$2,500.00	$1,500.00	$4,000.00
PJ34	Patricia Jean Florist	$0.00	$5,200.00	$5,200.00
SL77	Smarter Law Associates	$3,800.00	$0.00	$3,800.00
TB17	The Bikeshop	$2,750.00	$1,200.00	$3,950.00
WE05	Walburg Energy Alternatives	$4,500.00	$1,450.00	$5,950.00
WS01	Woody Sporting Goods	$2,250.00	$1,600.00	$3,850.00

captions changed

Figure 2–69

Other Ways

1. Right-click field in design grid, click Properties on shortcut menu

To Calculate Statistics

For group calculations, Microsoft Access supports several built-in statistics: COUNT (count of the number of records), SUM (total), AVG (average), MAX (largest value), MIN (smallest value), STDEV (standard deviation), VAR (variance), FIRST (first value), and LAST (last value). These statistics are called aggregate functions. An **aggregate function** is a function that performs some mathematical function against a group of records. To use any of these aggregate functions in a query, you include it in the Total row in the design grid. The Total row usually does not appear in the grid. To include it, click the Totals button on the Design tab.

The following steps create a new query for the Client table. The steps include the Total row in the design grid, and then calculate the average amount paid for all clients.

1

- Create a new query with a field list for the Client table.

- Click the Totals button (Query Tools Design tab | Show/Hide group) to include the Total row in the design grid.

- Add the Amount Paid field to the query (Figure 2–70).

Figure 2–70

- Click the Total row in the Amount Paid column to display the Total box arrow.

- Click the Total box arrow to display the Total list (Figure 2–71).

Figure 2–71

- Click Avg to select the calculation that Access is to perform (Figure 2–72).

Figure 2–72

- View the query results (Figure 2–73).

Experiment

- Return to Design view and try other aggregate functions. In each case, view the results to see the effect of your selection. When finished, select Avg once again.

Figure 2–73

To Use Criteria in Calculating Statistics

Sometimes calculating statistics for all the records in the table is appropriate. In other cases, however, you will need to calculate the statistics for only those records that satisfy certain criteria. To enter a criterion in a field, first you select Where as the entry in the Total row for the field, and then enter the criterion in the Criteria row. The following steps use this technique to calculate the average amount paid for clients of business analyst 11. The steps also save the query with a new name.

1

- Return to Design view.

- Include the Business Analyst Number field in the design grid.

- Click the Total box arrow in the Business Analyst Number column to produce a Total list (Figure 2–74).

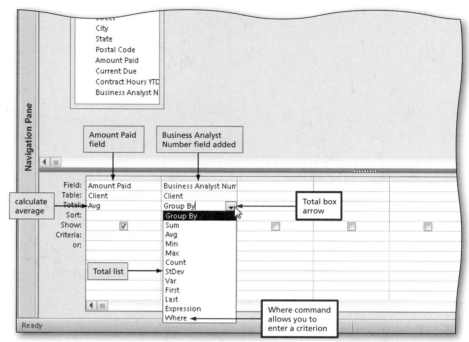

Figure 2–74

2

- Click Where.

- Type 11 as the criterion for the Business Analyst Number field (Figure 2–75).

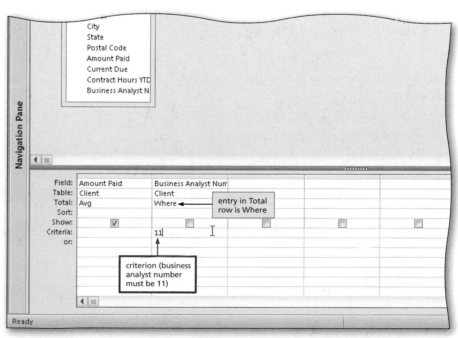

Figure 2–75

❸

• View the query results (Figure 2–76).

❹

• Save the query as Ch2q12.

Figure 2–76

To Use Grouping

Another way statistics often are used is in combination with grouping; that is, statistics are calculated for groups of records. You may, for example, need to calculate the average amount paid for the clients of each business analyst. You will want the average for the clients of business analyst 11, the average for clients of business analyst 14, and so on.

Grouping means creating groups of records that share some common characteristic. In grouping by Business Analyst Number, for example, the clients of business analyst 11 would form one group, the clients of business analyst 14 would form a second, and the clients of business analyst 27 would form a third group. The calculations then are made for each group. To indicate grouping in Access, select Group By as the entry in the Total row for the field to be used for grouping.

The following steps create a query that calculates the average amount paid for clients of each business analyst at Camashaly Design. The steps also save the query with a new name.

❶

• Return to Design view and clear the design grid.

• Include the Business Analyst Number field in the query.

• Include the Amount Paid field in the query.

• Select Avg as the calculation in the Total row for the Amount Paid field (Figure 2–77).

 Why was it not necessary for me to change the entry in the Total row for the Business Analyst Number field?

Group By, which is the initial entry in the Total row when you add a field, is correct. Thus, you did not need to change the entry.

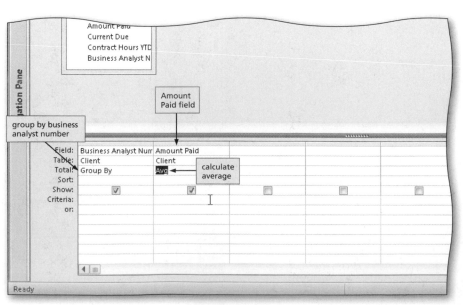

Figure 2–77

2

- View the query results (Figure 2–78).

3

- Save the query as Ch2q13.

- Close the query.

Figure 2–78

Crosstab Queries

A crosstab query calculates a statistic (for example, sum, average, or count) for data that is grouped by two different types of information. One of the types will appear down the side of the resulting datasheet, and the other will appear across the top. Crosstab queries are useful for summarizing data by category or group.

For example, if you have determined that a query must summarize the sum of the amounts paid grouped by both city and business analyst number, you could have cities as the row headings, that is, down the side. You could have business analyst numbers as the column headings, that is, across the top. The entries within the datasheet represent the total of the amounts paid. Figure 2–79 shows a crosstab in which the total of amount paid is grouped by both city and business analyst number with cities down the left side and business analyst numbers across the top. For example, the entry in the row labeled Georgetown and in the column labeled 14 represents the total of the amount paid by all clients of business analyst 14 who are located in Georgetown.

BTW

Certification
The Microsoft Office Specialist (MOS) program provides an opportunity for you to obtain a valuable industry credential — proof that you have the Access 2010 skills required by employers. For more information, visit the Access 2010 Certification Web page (scsite.com/ ac2010/cert).

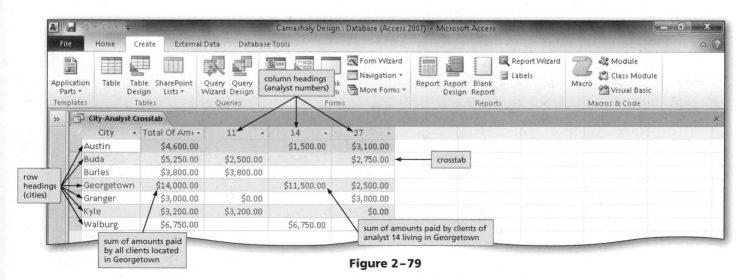

Figure 2–79

To Create a Crosstab Query

The following steps use the Crosstab Query Wizard to create a crosstab query for Camashaly Design that summarizes financial information by city and business analyst.

- Click Create on the Ribbon to display the Create tab.

- Click the Query Wizard button (Create tab | Queries group) to display the New Query dialog box (Figure 2–80).

Figure 2–80

- Click Crosstab Query Wizard (New Query dialog box).

- Click the OK button to display the Crosstab Query Wizard dialog box (Figure 2–81).

Figure 2–81

3

- With the Tables option button selected, click Table: Client to select the Client table, and then click the Next button to display the next Crosstab Query Wizard screen.

- Click the City field, and then click the Add Field button to select the City field for row headings (Figure 2–82).

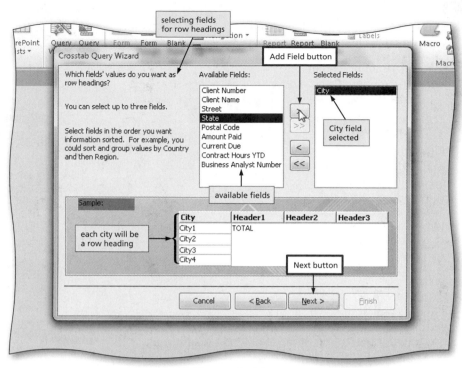

Figure 2–82

4

- Click the Next button to display the next Crosstab Query Wizard screen.

- Click the Business Analyst Number field to select the Business Analyst Number field for column headings (Figure 2–83).

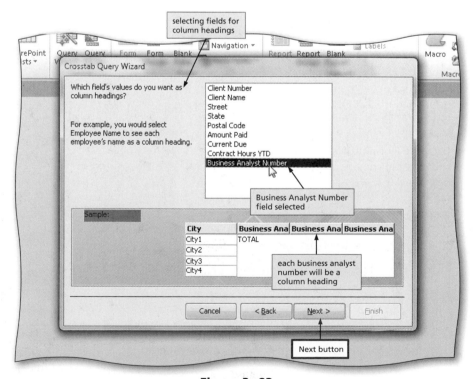

Figure 2–83

5

- Click the Next button to display the next Crosstab Query Wizard screen.

- Click the Amount Paid field to select the Amount Paid field for calculations.

Experiment

- Click other fields. For each field, examine the list of calculations that are available. When finished, click the Amount Paid field again.

- Click Sum to select Sum as the calculation to be performed (Figure 2–84).

My list of functions is different. What did I do wrong?

Either you clicked the wrong field, or the Amount Paid field has the wrong data type. For example, if you mistakenly assigned it the Text data type, you would not see Sum in the list of available calculations.

Figure 2–84

6

- Click the Next button to display the next Crosstab Query Wizard screen.

- Type **City-Analyst Crosstab** as the name of the query (Figure 2–85).

7

- Click the Finish button to produce the crosstab shown in Figure 2–79 on Page AC 123.

- Close the query.

If I want to view the crosstab at some future date, can I just open the query?

Yes.

Figure 2–85

To Customize the Navigation Pane

Currently, the entries in the Navigation Pane are organized by object type. That is, all the tables are together, all the queries are together, and so on. You might want to change the way the information is organized. For example, you might want to have the Navigation Pane organized by table, with all the queries, forms, and reports associated with a particular table appearing after the name of the table. You also can use the Search bar to restrict the objects that appear to only those that have a certain collection of characters in their name. For example, if you entered the letters, Cl, only those objects containing Cl somewhere within the name will be included.

The following steps change the organization of the Navigation Pane. They also use the Search bar to restrict the objects that appear.

1

- If necessary, click the Shutter Bar Open/Close Button to open the Navigation Pane.

- Click the Navigation Pane arrow to produce the Navigation Pane menu (Figure 2–86).

2

- Click Tables and Related Views to organize the Navigation Pane by table rather than by the type of object (Figure 2–87).

3

- Click the Navigation Pane arrow to produce the Navigation Pane menu.

- Click Object Type to once again organize the Navigation Pane by object type.

Figure 2–86

Figure 2–87

🔍 **Experiment**

- Select different Navigate To Category options to see the effect of the option. With each option you select, select different Filter By Group options to see the effect of the filtering. When you have finished experimenting, select the Object Type Navigate To Category option and the All Access Objects Filter By Group option.

• If the Search bar does not appear, right-click the Navigation Pane and click Search Bar on the shortcut menu.

• Click in the Search bar box to produce an insertion point.

• Type `Cl` as the search string to restrict the objects displayed to only those containing the desired string (Figure 2–88).

5

• Click the Clear Search String button to remove the search string and redisplay all objects.

Q&A Did I have to click the button to redisplay all objects? Could I simply have erased the current string to achieve the same result?

You did not have to click the button. You could have used the DELETE or BACKSPACE keys to erase the current search string.

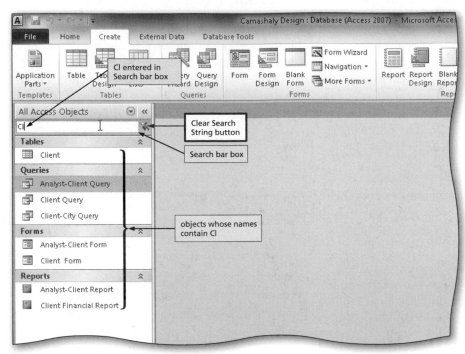

Figure 2–88

BTW **Quick Reference**
For a table that lists how to complete the tasks covered in this book using the mouse, Ribbon, shortcut menu, and keyboard, see the Quick Reference Summary at the back of this book, or visit the Access 2010 Quick Reference Web page (scsite.com/ac2010/qr).

To Quit Access

The following steps quit Access.

1 Click the Close button on the right side of the title bar to quit Access.

2 If a Microsoft Access dialog box appears, click the Save button to save any changes made to the object since the last save.

Chapter Summary

In this chapter you have learned to create queries, enter fields, enter criteria, use text and numeric data in queries, use wildcards, use compound criteria, create parameter queries, sort data in queries, join tables in queries, perform calculations in queries, and create crosstab queries. You also learned to create a report and a form that used a query, to export a query, and to customize the Navigation Pane. The items listed below include all the new Access skills you have learned in this chapter.

1. Create a Query in Design View (AC 78)
2. Add Fields to the Design Grid (AC 79)
3. Use Text Data in a Criterion (AC 80)
4. Use a Wildcard (AC 83)
5. Use Criteria for a Field Not Included in the Results (AC 85)
6. Create and View a Parameter Query (AC 87)
7. Use a Parameter Query (AC 89)
8. Use a Number in a Criterion (AC 90)
9. Use a Comparison Operator in a Criterion (AC 91)
10. Use a Compound Criterion Involving AND (AC 92)
11. Use a Compound Criterion Involving OR (AC 93)
12. Clear the Design Grid (AC 95)
13. Sort Data in a Query (AC 96)
14. Omit Duplicates (AC 97)
15. Sort on Multiple Keys (AC 98)
16. Create a Top-Values Query (AC 99)
17. Join Tables (AC 102)
18. Change Join Properties (AC 105)
19. Create a Report Involving a Join (AC 106)

If you have a SAM 2010 user profile, your instructor may have assigned an autogradable version of this assignment. If so, log into the SAM 2010 Web site at www.cengage.com/sam2010 to download the instruction and start files.

Learn It Online

Test your knowledge of chapter content and key terms.

Instructions: To complete the Learn It Online exercises, start your browser, click the Address bar, and then enter the Web address **scsite.com/ac2010/learn**. When the Access 2010 Learn It Online page is displayed, click the link for the exercise you want to complete and then read the instructions.

Chapter Reinforcement TF, MC, and SA

A series of true/false, multiple choice, and short answer questions that test your knowledge of the chapter content.

Flash Cards

An interactive learning environment where you identify chapter key terms associated with displayed definitions.

Practice Test

A series of multiple choice questions that test your knowledge of chapter content and key terms.

Who Wants To Be a Computer Genius?

An interactive game that challenges your knowledge of chapter content in the style of a television quiz show.

Wheel of Terms

An interactive game that challenges your knowledge of chapter key terms in the style of the television show *Wheel of Fortune*.

Crossword Puzzle Challenge

A crossword puzzle that challenges your knowledge of key terms presented in the chapter.

Apply Your Knowledge

Reinforce the skills and apply the concepts you learned in this chapter.

Using Wildcards in a Query, Creating a Parameter Query, Joining Tables, and Creating a Report

Instructions: Start Access. Open the Babbage CPA Firm database that you modified in Apply Your Knowledge in Chapter 1 on page AC 64. (If you did not complete this exercise, see your instructor for a copy of the modified database.)

Perform the following tasks:

1. Create a query for the Client table and add the Client Number, Client Name, City, and Amount Paid fields to the design grid. Find all clients who live in cities that start with Bu. Save the query as Apply 2 Step 1 Query.

Continued >

Apply Your Knowledge *continued*

2. Create a query for the Client table and add the Client Number, Client Name, Bookkeeper Number, and Balance Due fields to the design grid. Sort the records in descending order by Balance Due. Add a criterion for the Bookkeeper Number field that allows the user to enter a different bookkeeper each time the query is run. Save the query as Apply 2 Step 2 Query.

3. Create a query that joins the Bookkeeper and the Client tables. Add the Bookkeeper Number, First Name, and Last Name fields from the Bookkeeper table and the Client Number and Client Name fields from the Client table. Sort the records in ascending order by Bookkeeper Number and Client Number. All bookkeepers should appear in the result, even if they currently have no clients. Save the query as Bookkeeper-Client Query.

4. Create the report shown in Figure 2–89. The report uses the Bookkeeper-Client Query.

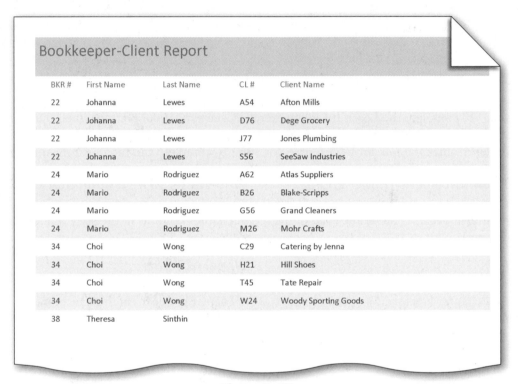

Bookkeeper-Client Report

BKR #	First Name	Last Name	CL #	Client Name
22	Johanna	Lewes	A54	Afton Mills
22	Johanna	Lewes	D76	Dege Grocery
22	Johanna	Lewes	J77	Jones Plumbing
22	Johanna	Lewes	S56	SeeSaw Industries
24	Mario	Rodriguez	A62	Atlas Suppliers
24	Mario	Rodriguez	B26	Blake-Scripps
24	Mario	Rodriguez	G56	Grand Cleaners
24	Mario	Rodriguez	M26	Mohr Crafts
34	Choi	Wong	C29	Catering by Jenna
34	Choi	Wong	H21	Hill Shoes
34	Choi	Wong	T45	Tate Repair
34	Choi	Wong	W24	Woody Sporting Goods
38	Theresa	Sinthin		

Figure 2–89

5. Submit the revised database in the format specified by your instructor.

Extend Your Knowledge

Extend the skills you learned in this chapter and experiment with new skills. You may need to use Help to complete the assignment.

Creating Crosstab Queries, Creating Queries Using Criteria, and Exporting a Query

Instructions: Start Access. Open the Natural Earthscapes database. See the inside back cover of this book for instructions for downloading the Data Files for Students, or see your instructor for information on accessing the files required in this book.

Natural Earthscapes is a small landscaping company that specializes in landscaping with native plants. The owners have created an Access database in which to store information about the customers they serve and the workers they employ. You will create the crosstab shown in Figure 2–90. You also will query the database using specified criteria.

Figure 2–90

Perform the following tasks:

1. Create the crosstab query shown in Figure 2–90. The crosstab query groups the total of customers' balances by city and worker number.

2. Create a query to find all customers who do not live in Kingston. Include the Customer Number, Last Name, Balance, and Amount Paid fields in the design grid. Save the query as Extend 2 Step 2 Query.

3. Create a query to find all customers where the customer's first name is either Frances or Francis. Include the Customer Number, Last Name, First Name, Street, and City fields in the query results. Save the query as Extend 2 Step 3 Query.

4. Create a query to find all customers where the worker number is 303 or 305 and the balance is greater than $40.00. Include the Customer Number, Last Name, First Name, Balance, and Worker Number fields in the design grid. Use the IN operator in your query design. Save the query as Extend 2 Step 4 Query.

5. Export the City-Worker Crosstab as a Word file with the name City-Worker Crosstab.rtf and save the export steps.

6. Open the Customer table and change the balance for AB10 to $90.

7. Use the saved export steps to export the City-Worker Crosstab again. When asked if you want to replace the existing file, click Yes.

8. Change the database properties, as specified by your instructor. Submit the revised database and the exported RTF file in the format specified by your instructor.

Make It Right

Analyze a database and correct all errors and/or improve the design.

Correcting Errors in the Query Design

Instructions: Start Access. Open the Retired Pet Sitters database. See the inside back cover of this book for instructions for downloading the Data Files for Students, or see your instructor for information on accessing the files required in this book.

Continued >

Make It Right *continued*

Retired Pet Sitters is a database maintained by a small pet-sitting business. The queries shown in Figure 2–91 contain a number of errors that need to be corrected before the queries run properly. The query shown in Figure 2–91a displays the query results in the proper order (Last Name, First Name, Balance, Sitter Number), but it is sorted incorrectly. The query results should be sorted by last name within sitter number in ascending order. Also, the caption for the Balance field should be Owed. Save the query with your changes.

When you try to run the query shown in Figure 2–91b, you get 0 results. You are trying to find all customers who live on Magee. Correct the error and save the query with your changes.

Figure 2–91 (a) Incorrect Sort Query

Figure 2–91 (b) Incorrect Criteria Query

Change the database properties, as specified by your instructor. Submit the revised database in the format specified by your instructor.

In the Lab

Design, create, modify, and/or use a database following the guidelines, concepts, and skills presented in this chapter. The assignments are listed in order of increasing difficulty.

Lab 1: Querying the ECO Clothesline Database

Problem: The management of ECO Clothesline has determined a number of questions it wants the database management system to answer. You must obtain answers to the questions posed by management.

Instructions: Use the database modified in the In the Lab 1 of Chapter 1 on page AC 66 for this assignment, or see your instructor for information on accessing the files required for this book.

Perform the following tasks:

1. Open the ECO Clothesline database and create a new query for the Customer table that includes the Customer Number, Customer Name, Amount Paid, and Sales Rep Number fields in the design grid for all customers where the sales rep number is 49. Save the query as Lab 2-1 Step 1 Query.

2. Create a query that includes the Customer Number, Customer Name, and Amount Paid fields for all customers located in Virginia (VA) with a paid amount greater than $1,000.00. Save the query as Lab 2-1 Step 2 Query.

3. Create a query that includes the Customer Number, Customer Name, Street, and City fields for all customers whose names begin with T. Save the query as Lab 2-1 Step 3 Query.

4. Create a query that lists all cities in ascending order. Each city should appear only once. Save the query as Lab 2-1 Step 4 Query.

5. Create a query that allows the user to enter the city to search when the query is run. The query results should display the Customer Number, Customer Name, Balance, and Amount Paid fields. Test the query by searching for those records where the client is located in Ashton. Save the query as Lab 2-1 Step 5 Query.

6. Include the Customer Number, Customer Name, and Balance fields in the design grid. Sort the records in descending order by the Balance field. Display only the top 25 percent of the records in the query result. Save the query as Lab 2-1 Step 6 Query.

7. Join the Sales Rep and the Customer table. Include the Sales Rep Number, First Name, and Last Name fields from the Sales Rep table. Include the Customer Number, Customer Name, and Balance from the Customer table. Sort the records in ascending order by sales rep's last name and customer name. All sales reps should appear in the result even if they currently have no customers. Save the query as Lab 2-1 Step 7 Query.

8. Open the Lab 2-1 Step 7 Query in Design view and remove the Sales Rep table. Add the Amount Paid field to the design grid. Calculate the total of the balance and amount paid amounts. Assign the alias Total Amount to the calculated field. Change the caption for the Balance field to Due. Save the query as Lab 2-1 Step 8 Query.

9. Create a query to display the average balance amount for all customers. Save the query as Lab 2-1 Step 9 Query.

10. Create a query to display the average balance amount for sales rep 51. Save the query as Lab 2-1 Step 10 Query.

11. Create a query to display the average balance amount for each sales rep. Save the query as Lab 2-1 Step 11 Query.

12. Create the crosstab shown in Figure 2–92. The crosstab groups the total of customers' amount paid amounts by state and sales rep number. Save the crosstab as State-Sales Rep Crosstab.

13. Submit the revised database in the format specified by your instructor.

State	Total Of Am	44	49	51
NC	$2,235.00	$1,400.00	$710.00	$125.00
TN	$6,245.00	$1,695.00	$2,600.00	$1,950.00
VA	$5,180.00	$2,425.00	$700.00	$2,055.00

Figure 2–92

In the Lab

Lab 2: Querying the Walburg Energy Alternatives Database

Problem:　The manager of the Walburg Energy Alternatives store has determined a number of questions he wants the database management system to answer. You must obtain answers to the questions posed by the manager.

Instructions:　Use the database created in the In the Lab 2 of Chapter 1 on page AC 67 for this assignment, or see your instructor for information on accessing the files required for this book.

Perform the following tasks:

1. Open the Walburg Energy Alternatives database and create a query that includes all fields and all records in the Item table. There should be only one column in the design grid. Name the query Lab 2-2 Step 1 Query.

2. Create a query that includes the Item Number, Description, Cost, and Vendor Code fields for all items where the vendor code is JM. Save the query as Lab 2-2 Step 2 Query.

3. Create a query that includes the Item Number and Description fields for all items where the description starts with the letters, En. Save the query as Lab 2-2 Step 3 Query.

4. Create a query that includes the Item Number and Description fields for all items with a cost less than $4.00. Save the query as Lab 2-2 Step 4 Query.

5. Create a query that includes the Item Number and Description fields for all items with a selling price greater than $20.00. Save the query as Lab 2-2 Step 5 Query.

6. Create a query that includes all fields for all items with a vendor code of AS and where the number on hand is fewer than 10. Save the query as Lab 2-2 Step 6 Query.

7. Create a query that includes all fields for all items that have a selling price greater than $10.00 or a vendor code of JM. Save the query as Lab 2-2 Step 7 Query.

8. Join the Vendor table and the Item table. Include the Vendor Code and Vendor Name fields from the Vendor table and the Item Number, Description, On Hand, and Cost fields from the Item table. Sort the records in ascending order by item number within vendor code. Save the query as Vendor-Item Query.

9. Create the form shown in Figure 2–93. The form uses the Vendor-Item Query.

Figure 2–93

10. Create a query that includes the Item Number, Description, On Hand, and Cost fields. Calculate the inventory value (on hand*cost) for all records in the table. Assign the alias Inventory Value to the calculated field. Change the caption for the On Hand column to In Stock. Format the Inventory Value field as currency with two decimal places. Sort the records in descending order by inventory value. Save the query as Lab 2-2 Step 10 Query.

11. Create a query that calculates and displays the average cost of all items. Save the query as Lab 2-2 Step 11 Query.

12. Create a query that calculates and displays the average cost of items grouped by vendor code. Save the query as Lab 2-2 Step 12 Query.

13. Submit the revised database in the format specified by your instructor.

In the Lab

Lab 3: Querying the Philamar Training Database

Problem: The management of Philamar Training has determined a number of questions it wants the database management system to answer. You must obtain answers to the questions posed by management.

Instructions: Use the database created in the In the Lab 3 of Chapter 1 on page AC 70 for this assignment, or see your instructor for information on accessing the files required for this book. For Part 1 and Part 3, save each query using a format similar to the following: Lab 2-3 Part 1a Query, Lab 2-3 Part 3a Query, and so on. Submit the revised database and the Trainer-Client Query.xlsx file in the format specified by your instructor.

Instructions Part 1: Create a new query for the Client table and include the Client Number, Client Name, Amount Paid, and Current Due fields in the design grid. Create queries that answer the following questions: (a) Which clients' names begin with F? (b) Which clients are located in Kingston? (c) Which clients have a current due amount of $0.00? (d) Which clients have an amount paid amount between $5,000.00 and $10,000.00? (e) Which two clients have the highest current due amounts? (f) For each client, what is the total of the current due and amount paid?

Instructions Part 2: Join the Trainer and the Client table. In the design grid, include the Trainer Number, First Name, and Last Name from the Trainer table and the Client Number, Client Name, and Amount Paid from the Client table. Sort the records in ascending order by trainer number and client number. All trainers should appear in the result, even if they currently have no clients. Save the query as Trainer-Client Query. Export the query to Excel and save the export steps.

Instructions Part 3: Create queries to calculate the following statistics: (a) What is the average current due amount for clients assigned to trainer 42? (b) What is the total current due amount for all clients? (c) What is the total amount paid for each trainer?

Cases and Places

Apply your creative thinking and problem solving skills to design and implement a solution.

Note: To complete these assignments, you may be required to use the Data Files for Students. See the inside back cover of this book for instructions on downloading the Data Files for Students, or contact your instructor for information about accessing the required files.

1: Querying the Chamber of Commerce Database

Academic

Use the Chamber of Commerce database you created in Cases and Places 1 in Chapter 1 on page AC 72 for this assignment. Use the concepts and techniques presented in this chapter to create queries for the following:

a. Find the advertiser name and address of all advertisers located on Main.

Continued >

Cases and Places *continued*

b. Find the advertiser number, advertiser name, balance, and amount paid for all advertisers whose balance is greater than $300 or whose amount paid is $0.00.

c. Find the total of the balance and amount paid amounts for each advertiser. Show the advertiser number, advertiser name, and total amount. Sort the results in descending order by total.

d. Find the advertiser number, advertiser name, balance, and amount paid for all advertisers whose balance is between $200 and $500.

e. Create a parameter query for the Advertiser table that will allow the user to enter a different postal code each time the query is run. The user should see all fields in the query result.

f. Find the ad rep for each advertiser. List the ad rep number, last name, first name, advertiser number, advertiser name, and balance. Sort the results in ascending order by ad rep number and advertiser number.

g. Determine the total of the balance amounts and amount paid amounts for all advertisers.

Submit the revised database in the format specified by your instructor.

2: Querying the Consignment Database

Personal

Use the Consignment database you created in Cases and Places 2 in Chapter 1 on page AC 72 for this assignment. Use the concepts and techniques presented in this chapter to create queries for the following:

a. Find the item number and description of all items that contain the word, Table.

b. Find the item number, description, condition, and date of the item that has the earliest posting date.

c. Find the total price (price*quantity) of each item available for sale. Show the item number, item description, and total price.

d. Find the seller of each item. Show the seller's first name and last name as well as the item description, price, quantity, and date posted. Sort the results by item description within seller last name.

e. Create a report based on the query you created in Step d. Include all fields in the report.

f. Modify the query you created in Step d to restrict retrieval to those items with a price greater than $50.00.

g. Find all items posted between March 1, 2012, and March 4, 2012. The user should see all fields in the query result.

Submit the revised database in the format specified by your instructor.

3: Querying the Senior Care Database

Professional

Use the Senior Care database you created in Cases and Places 3 in Chapter 1 on page AC 72 for this assignment. Use the concepts and techniques presented in this chapter to create queries for the following:

a. Find the first name, last name, and address of all clients where the street name begins with the letter U.

b. Find the client number, last name, first name, balance, and amount paid for all clients whose balance is $0.00 or whose amount paid is $0.00.

c. Find the total of the balance and amount paid amounts for each client. Show the client number, client last name, client first name, and total amount. Sort the results in descending order by total.

d. Find the helper for each client. List the helper number, helper last name, helper first name, client number, client last name, and client first name. Sort the results in ascending order by helper number and client number.

e. Create a report for the query created in Step d. Include all fields except the helper first name in the report. Create a form for the query created in Step d.

f. Export the query created in Step d as a text file.

g. Find the highest and lowest balances.

Submit the exported text file and revised database in the format specified by your instructor.

3 Maintaining a Database

Objectives

You will have mastered the material in this chapter when you can:

- Add, change, and delete records
- Search for records
- Filter records
- Update a table design
- Use action queries to update records
- Use delete queries to delete records
- Specify validation rules, default values, and formats

- Create and use single-valued lookup fields
- Create and use multivalued lookup fields
- Add new fields to an existing report
- Format a datasheet
- Specify referential integrity
- Use a subdatasheet
- Sort records

3 | Maintaining a Database

Introduction

Once a database has been created and loaded with data, it must be maintained. **Maintaining the database** means modifying the data to keep it up to date by adding new records, changing the data for existing records, and deleting records. Updating can include mass updates or mass deletions, that is, updates to, or deletions of, many records at the same time.

Maintenance of a database also can involve the need to **restructure the database** periodically, that is, to change the database structure. Restructuring can include adding new fields to a table, changing the characteristics of existing fields, and removing existing fields. Restructuring also includes the creation of validation rules and referential integrity. Validation rules ensure the validity of the data in the database, whereas referential integrity ensures the validity of the relationships. Maintaining a database also can include filtering records, a process that ensures that only the records that satisfy some criterion appear when viewing and updating the data in a table. Changing the appearance of a datasheet is a maintenance activity.

BTW

Database Backup
If you are doing mass changes to a database, be sure to back up the database prior to doing the updates.

Project — Maintaining a Database

BTW

The Ribbon and Screen Resolution
Access may change how the groups and buttons within the groups appear on the Ribbon, depending on the computer's screen resolution. Thus, your Ribbon may look different from the ones in this book if you are using a screen resolution other than 1024 × 768.

Camashaly Design faces the task of keeping its database up to date. As the company takes on new clients and business analysts, it will need to add new records, make changes to existing records, and delete records. Camashaly believes that it can serve its clients better by changing the structure of the database to categorize the clients by type. The company will do this by adding a Client Type field to the Client table. Business analysts believe they can maintain better client relationships if the database includes the services that are of interest to clients. The company will do so by adding a Services Needed field to the Client table. Because clients may need more than one service, this field will be a multivalued field, which is a field that can store multiple values or entries. Along with these changes, Camashaly staff wants to change the appearance of a datasheet when displaying data.

Camashaly would like the ability to make mass updates, that is, to update or delete many records in a single operation. It wants rules that make sure users can enter only valid, or appropriate, data into the database. Camashaly also wants to ensure that the database cannot contain the name of a client who is not associated with a specific business analyst. A final goal for Camashaly is to improve the efficiency of certain types of processing, specifically, sorting and retrieving data.

Figure 3–1 summarizes some of the various types of activities involved in maintaining the Camashaly Design database.

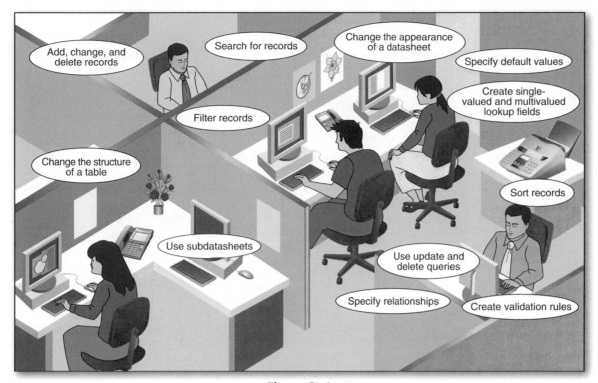

Figure 3–1

Overview

As you read through this chapter, you will learn how to maintain a database by performing these general tasks:

- Add, change, and delete records.
- Filter records so that only those records that satisfy some criterion appear in a datasheet or form.
- Change the structure of a table.
- Make mass changes to a table.
- Create validation rules to ensure that the database contains only valid data.
- Use single-valued and multivalued lookup fields.
- Update forms and reports to reflect changes to the table structure.
- Change the appearance of a datasheet.
- Enforce relationships by creating referential integrity.
- Order records.

Plan
Ahead

Database Maintenance Decisions

When maintaining a database in Access, you must consider how the database is being used and how it could be improved. The decisions you make will affect the modification of records, fields, default settings, formatting, and table relationships. To maintain a database, you should follow these general guidelines:

1. **Determine when it is necessary to add, change, or delete records in a database.** Decide how often updates are necessary. You might need to update the database on a regular schedule, or only as needed, depending on your needs. Also determine whether to make the updates to individual records or whether mass updates would be more efficient.

2. **Determine whether you should filter records.** For each situation where a user will be working with a table in the database, examine whether it might be desirable to have the records filtered, that is, to have only those records that satisfy some criterion appear.

3. **Determine whether additional fields are necessary or whether existing fields should be deleted.** Have there been any changes to the initial requirements that would require the addition of a field (or fields) to one of the tables? If so, you will need to add the field to the appropriate table. Also, now that the database has been in operation for a period of time, determine whether all the fields actually are being used. If some fields are not in use, verify that they are, in fact, no longer needed. If so, you can delete the field from the table.

4. **Determine whether validation rules, default values, and formats are necessary.** Can you improve the accuracy of the data entry process by enforcing data validation? What values are allowed for a particular field? For example, client name data should not be allowed in a city field. Are there some fields in which one particular value is used more than another? You can control the values that are entered in a field by modifying the table design to include default values, formats, and validation rules.

5. **Determine whether changes to the format of a datasheet are desirable.** Do you want to modify the appearance of the Datasheet view of your tables? It is a good idea to be consistent throughout all your tables except in special circumstances.

6. **Identify related tables in order to implement relationships between the tables.** Examine the database design you created earlier to identify related tables. Is there a one-to-many relationship between the tables? If so, which table is the one table? Which table is the many table? For each pair of related tables, you will need to make decisions about the implementation of the relationship between the tables.

When necessary, more specific details concerning the above decisions and/or actions are presented at appropriate points in the chapter. The chapter also will identify the use of these guidelines in database maintenance tasks such as those shown in Figure 3–1.

For an introduction to Windows 7 and instruction about how to perform basic Windows 7 tasks, read the Office 2010 and Windows 7 chapter at the beginning of this book, where you can learn how to resize windows, change screen resolution, create folders, move and rename files, use Windows Help, and much more.

To Start Access

The following steps, which assume Windows 7 is running, start Access based on a typical installation. You may need to ask your instructor how to start Access for your computer. For a detailed example of the procedure summarized below, refer to the Office 2010 and Windows 7 chapter at the beginning of this book.

1 Click the Start button on the Windows 7 taskbar to display the Start menu.

2 Type `Microsoft Access` as the search text in the 'Search programs and files' text box and watch the search results appear on the Start menu.

3 Click Microsoft Access 2010 in the search results on the Start menu to start Access.

4 If the Access window is not maximized, click the Maximize button next to the Close button on its title bar to maximize the window.

To Open a Database from Access

In Chapter 1, you created and saved your database on a USB flash drive using the file name, Camashaly Design. The following steps open the Camashaly Design database from the Access folder in the CIS 101 folder on the USB flash drive. For a detailed example of the procedure summarized below, refer to the Office 2010 and Windows 7 chapter at the beginning of this book.

1 With your USB flash drive connected to one of the computer's USB ports, click File on the Ribbon to open the Backstage view.

2 Click Open in the Backstage view to display the Open dialog box.

3 Navigate to the location of the file to be opened (in this case, the USB flash drive, then to the CIS 101 folder [or your class folder], and then to the Access folder).

4 Click Camashaly Design to select the file to be opened.

5 Click the Open button (Open dialog box) to open the selected file and display the opened database in the Access window.

6 If a Security Warning appears, click the Enable Content button.

For an introduction to Office 2010 and instruction about how to perform basic tasks in Office 2010 programs, read the Office 2010 and Windows 7 chapter at the beginning of this book, where you can learn how to start a program, use the Ribbon, save a file, open a file, quit a program, use Help, and much more.

Updating Records

Keeping the data in a database up to date requires updating records in three ways: adding new records, changing the data in existing records, and deleting existing records.

Adding Records

In Chapter 1, you added records to a database using Datasheet view; that is, as you added records, the records appeared on the screen in a datasheet. The data looked like a table. When you need to add additional records, you can use the same techniques.

In Chapter 1, you used a simple form to view records. You also can use a **split form**, a form that allows you to simultaneously view both simple form and datasheet views of the data. You can use either portion of a split form to add or update records. To add new records, change existing records, or delete records, you use the same techniques you used in Datasheet view.

BTW

Q&As
For a complete list of the Q&As found in many of the step-by-step sequences in this book, visit the Access 2010 Q&A Web page (scsite.com/ac2010/qa).

To Create a Split Form

The following steps create a split form.

1

- Open the Navigation Pane if it is currently closed.

- If necessary, click the Client table in the Navigation Pane to select it.

- Click Create on the Ribbon to display the Create tab.

- Click the More Forms button (Create tab | Forms group) to display the More Forms menu (Figure 3–2).

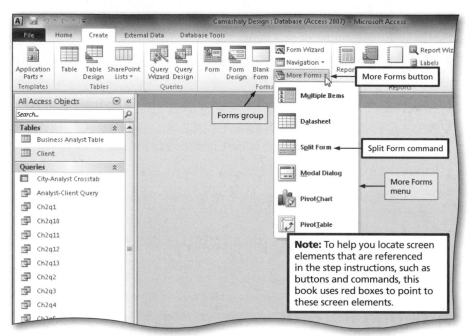

Figure 3–2

2

- Click Split Form to create a split form.

- Close the Navigation Pane (Figure 3–3).

Q&A

Is the form automatically saved the way the report was created when I used the Report Wizard?

No. You will need to take specific actions if you want to save the form.

Figure 3–3

3

- If the form appears in Layout view, click the Form View button on the Access status bar to display the form in Form view (Figure 3–4).

🔍 **Experiment**

- Click the various Navigation buttons (First record, Next record, Previous record, Last record, and New (blank) record) to see each button's effect. Click the Current Record box, change the record number, and press the ENTER key to see how to move to a specific record.

Figure 3–4

4

- Click the Save button on the Quick Access Toolbar to display the Save As dialog box.

- Type **Client Split Form** as the form name (Figure 3–5).

5

- Click the OK button (Save As dialog box) to save the form.

Figure 3–5

To Use a Form to Add Records

Once a form or split form is open in Form view, you can add records using the same techniques you used to add records in Datasheet view. The changes you make on the form are automatically made on the datasheet. You do not need to take any special action. The following steps use the split form that you just created to add records.

- Click the 'New (blank) record' button on the Navigation bar to enter a new record, and then type the data for the new record, as shown in Figure 3–6. Press the TAB key after typing the data in each field, except after typing the data for the final field (Business Analyst Number).

Figure 3–6

- Press the TAB key to complete the entry of the record.

- Close the form.

Other Ways

1. Click New button (Home tab | Records group)
2. Press CTRL+PLUS SIGN (+)

To Search for a Record

In the database environment, **searching** means looking for records that satisfy some criteria. Looking for the client whose number is GF56 is an example of searching. The queries in Chapter 2 also were examples of searching. Access had to locate those records that satisfied the criteria.

However, you can perform a search in Form view or Datasheet view without creating a query. To update client GF56, for example, first you need to find the client.

The following steps show how to search for the client whose number is GF56.

1

• Open the Navigation Pane.

• Scroll down in the Navigation Pane, if necessary, so that Client Split Form appears on your screen, right-click Client Split Form to display a shortcut menu, and then click Open on the shortcut menu to open the form in Form view.

Q&A
Which command on the shortcut menu gives me Form view? I see both Layout View and Design View, but no option for Form View.

The Open command opens the form in Form view.

• Close the Navigation Pane (Figure 3–7).

Figure 3–7

2

• Click the Find button (Home tab | Find group) to display the Find and Replace dialog box.

• Type **GF56** in the Find What text box (Find and Replace dialog box).

• Click the Find Next button to find client GF56 (Figure 3–8).

Q&A
Can I find records in Datasheet view or in Form view?

Yes. You use the same process to find records whether you are viewing the data with a split form, in Datasheet view, or in Form view.

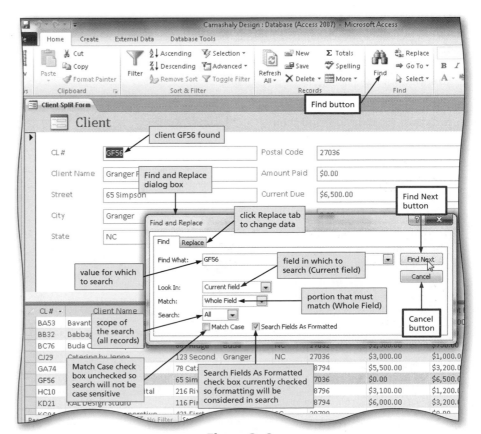

Figure 3–8

3

- Click the Cancel button (Find and Replace dialog box) to remove the dialog box from the screen.

Q&A Why does the button in the dialog box read, Find Next, rather than simply Find?

In some cases, after locating a record that satisfies a criterion, you might need to find the next record that satisfies the same criterion. For example, if you just found the first client whose business analyst number is 14, you then may want to find the second such client, then the third, and so on. To do so, click the Find Next button. You will not need to retype the value each time.

Q&A Can I replace one value with another using this dialog box?

Yes. Either click the Replace button (Home tab | Find group) or click the Replace tab in the Find and Replace dialog box. You then can enter both the value to find and the new value.

BTW BTWs
For a complete list of the BTWs found in the margins of this book, visit the Access 2010 BTW Web page (scsite.com/ac2010/btw).

Other Ways
1. Press CTRL+F

To Update the Contents of a Record

After locating the record to be changed, select the field to be changed by clicking the field. You also can press the TAB key repeatedly until the desired field is selected. Then make the appropriate changes. (Clicking the field automatically produces an insertion point. If you use the TAB key, you will need to press F2 to produce an insertion point.)

The following step uses Form view to change the name of client GF56 from Granger Foundation to Granger Family Foundation.

1

- Click in the Client Name field in the form for client GF56 immediately to the left of the F in the word, Foundation.

- Type the word **Family** before the word, Foundation, and then press the SPACEBAR to insert a space.

- Press the TAB key to complete the change and move to the next field (Figure 3–9).

Q&A Could I have changed the contents of the field in the datasheet portion of the split form?

Yes. You will first need to ensure the record to be changed appears in the datasheet. You then can change the value just as in the form.

Q&A Do I need to save my change?

No. Once you move to another record or close this form, the change to the name will become permanent.

Figure 3–9

To Delete a Record

When records no longer are needed, delete the records (remove them) from the table. If client GA74 no longer is served by Camashaly Design and its final payment has been received, the record can be deleted. The following steps delete client GA74.

1

- With the Client Split Form open, click the record selector in the datasheet, the small box that appears to the left of the first field of the record on which the client number is GA74 to select the record (Figure 3–10).

That technique works in the datasheet portion. How do I select the record in the form portion?

With the desired record appearing in the form, click the record selector (the triangle in front of the record) to select the entire record.

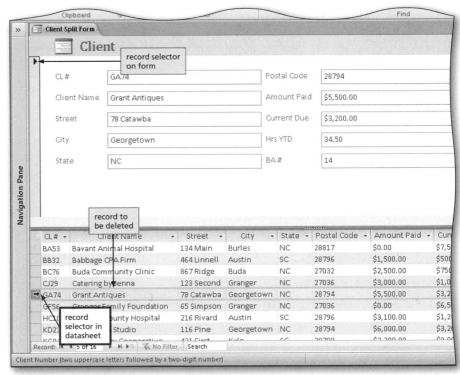

Figure 3–10

2

- Press the DELETE key to delete the record (Figure 3–11).

3

- Click the Yes button to complete the deletion.

- Close the Client Split Form.

Other Ways

1. Click Delete button (Home tab | Records group)

Figure 3–11

Filtering Records

You can use the Find button in either Datasheet view or Form view to locate a record quickly that satisfies some criterion (for example, the client number is GF56). All records appear, however, not just the record or records that satisfy the criterion. To have only the record or records that satisfy the criterion appear, use a **filter**. Four types of filters are available: Filter By Selection, Common Filters, Filter By Form, and Advanced Filter/Sort. You can use a filter in either Datasheet view or Form view.

Using the Find button
You can use the Find button (Home tab | Find group) to search for records in datasheets, forms, query results, and reports.

| Plan | **Determine whether to filter records.** |
| Ahead | If you determine that it is desirable to have only those records that satisfy some criterion appear, you have two choices: You can create a query or create a filter. The following guidelines apply to this decision. |

Determine whether to filter records.

If you determine that it is desirable to have only those records that satisfy some criterion appear, you have two choices: You can create a query or create a filter. The following guidelines apply to this decision.

- If you think that you will frequently want to display records that satisfy precisely this same criterion, you should consider creating a query whose results only contain the records that satisfy the criterion. To display those records in the future, simply open the query.

- If you are viewing data in a datasheet or form and decide you want to restrict the records to be included, it is easier to create a filter than a query. You can create and use the filter while you are viewing the data.

- If you have created a filter that you would like to be able to use again, you can save the filter as a query.

Once you have decided to use a filter, you need to decide which type of filter to use.

- If your criterion for filtering is that the value in a particular field matches or does not match a certain specific value, you can use Filter By Selection.

- If your criterion only involves a single field but is more complex (for example, the criterion specifies that the value in the field begins with a certain collection of letters) you can use a common filter.

- If your criterion involves more than one field, use Filter By Form.

- If your criterion involves more than a single And or Or, or if it involves sorting, you will probably find it simpler to use Advanced Filter/Sort.

To Use Filter By Selection

The simplest type of filter is called Filter By Selection. To use Filter By Selection, you give Access an example of the data you want by selecting the data within the table. You then choose the option you want on the Selection menu. For example, if you only want to display those clients located in Burles, Filter By Selection is appropriate. The following steps use Filter By Selection in Datasheet view to display only the records for clients in Burles.

- Open the Navigation Pane.

- Open the Client table, and close the Navigation Pane.

- Click the City field on the first record to select the city on that record as the city (Figure 3–12).

Could I have selected the City field on another record where the city is also Burles to select the same city?

Yes. It does not matter which record you select as long as the city is Burles.

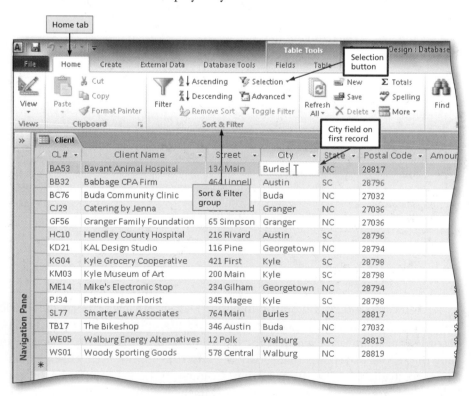

Figure 3–12

2

- Click the Selection button (Home tab | Sort & Filter group) to display the Selection menu (Figure 3–13).

Figure 3–13

3

- Click Equals "Burles" to select only those clients whose city is Burles (Figure 3–14).

Q&A Can I also filter in Form view?

Yes. Filtering works the same whether you are viewing the data with split form, in Datasheet view, or in Form view.

Experiment

- Try each of the other values in the Selection menu to see their effect. When done, once again select those clients whose city is Burles.

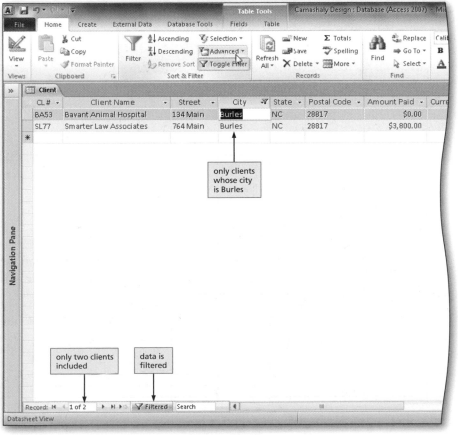

Figure 3–14

To Toggle a Filter

The Toggle Filter button toggles between filtered and unfiltered displays of the records in the table. That is, if only filtered records currently appear, clicking the Toggle Filter button will redisplay all records. If all records are currently displayed and there is a filter that is in effect, clicking the Toggle Filter button will display only the filtered records. If no filter is active, the Toggle Filter button will be dimmed, so clicking it would have no effect.

The following step toggles the filter to redisplay all records.

- Click the Toggle Filter button (Home tab | Sort & Filter group) to toggle the filter and redisplay all records (Figure 3–15).

Q&A Does that action clear the filter?

No. The filter is still in place. If you click the Toggle Filter button a second time, you will again see only the filtered records.

Figure 3–15

To Clear a Filter

Once you have finished using a filter, you can clear the filter. After doing so, you no longer will be able to use the filter by clicking the Toggle Filter button. The following steps clear the filter.

1 Click the Advanced button (Home tab | Sort & Filter group) to display the Advanced menu.

2 Click Clear All Filters on the Advanced menu.

To Use a Common Filter

You can filter individual fields by clicking the arrow to the right of the field name and using one of the common filters that are available for the field. If you have determined you want to include those clients whose city begins with G, Filter By Selection would not be appropriate. You could instead use the common filter for the field that would include only those records whose city begins with a particular value. The following steps use this common filter to include only those clients whose city begins with G.

1

- Click the City arrow to display the common filter menu.

- Point to the Text Filters command to display the custom text filters (Figure 3–16).

Q&A
I selected the City field and then clicked the Filter button on the Home tab | Sort & Filter group. My screen looks the same. Is this right?

Yes. That is another legitimate way to display the common filter menu.

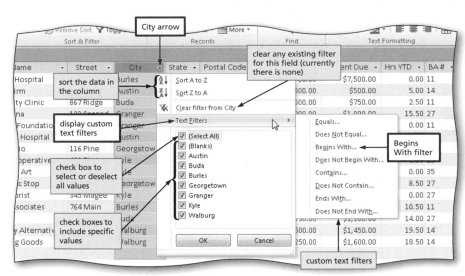

Figure 3–16

2

- Click Begins With to display the Custom Filter dialog box.

- Type G as the 'City begins with' value (Figure 3–17).

Q&A
If I wanted certain cities included, could I use the check boxes?

Yes. Be sure the cities you want are the only ones checked.

Experiment

- Try other options in the common filter menu to see their effects. When done, once again select those clients whose city begins with G.

Figure 3–17

3

- Click the OK button to filter the records (Figure 3–18).

Q&A
Can I use the same technique in Form view?

In Form view, you would need to click the field and then click the Filter button to display the Common Filter menu. The rest of the process would be the same.

4

- Click the Toggle Filter button (Home tab | Sort & Filter group) to toggle the filter and redisplay all records.

Figure 3–18

To Use Filter By Form

Filter By Selection and the common filter method you just used are quick and easy ways to filter by the value in a single field. For more complex criteria, however, these methods are not appropriate. Filter by Form allows you to filter based on multiple criteria, for example, to find only those clients whose postal code is 27036 and whose amount paid is 0. The following steps use Filter by Form to restrict the records that appear.

1

- Click the Advanced button (Home tab | Sort & Filter group) to display the Advanced menu (Figure 3–19).

Figure 3–19

2

- Click Clear All Filters on the Advanced menu to clear the existing filter.

- Click the Advanced button again to display the Advanced menu a second time.

- Click Filter By Form on the Advanced menu.

- Click the blank row in the Postal Code field, click the arrow that appears, and then click 27036.

- Click the Amount Paid field, click the arrow that appears, and then click 0 (Figure 3–20).

Q&A

Is there any difference in the process if I am viewing a table in Form view rather than in Datasheet view?

In Form view, you will make your entries in a form rather than a datasheet. Otherwise, the process is the same.

Figure 3–20

- Click the Toggle Filter button (Home tab | Sort & Filter group) to apply the filter (Figure 3–21).

🔑 **Experiment**

- Select Filter by Form again and enter different criteria. In each case, toggle the filter to see the effect of your selection. When done, once again select those clients whose postal code is 27036 and whose amount paid is $0.

Figure 3–21

To Use Advanced Filter/Sort

In some cases, your criteria may be too complex even for Filter By Form. You might decide you want to include any client for which the postal code is 27036 and the amount paid is $0. Additionally, you might want to include any client whose amount paid is greater than $4,000, no matter where the client is located. Further, you might want to have the results sorted by name. To filter records using complex criteria, you need to use Advanced Filter/Sort, as in the following steps.

1

- Click the Advanced button (Home tab | Sort & Filter group) to display the Advanced menu, and then click Clear All Filters on the Advanced menu to clear the existing filter.

- Click the Advanced button to display the Advanced menu a second time.

- Click Advanced Filter/Sort on the Advanced menu.

- Expand the size of the field list so all the fields in the Client table appear.

- Include the Client Name field and select Ascending as the sort order to specify the order in which the filtered records will appear.

- Include the Postal Code field and enter 27036 as the criterion.

- Include the Amount Paid field and enter 0 as the criterion in the Criteria row and >4000 as the criterion in the or row (Figure 3–22).

Figure 3–22

2

• Click the Toggle Filter button (Home tab | Sort & Filter group) to toggle the filter so that only records that satisfy the criteria will appear (Figure 3–23).

Q&A

Why are those particular records included?

The first record is included because the postal code is 27036 and the amount paid is $0.00. The other two records are included because the amount paid is over $4,000.

 Experiment

• Select Advanced Filter/Sort again and enter different sorting options and criteria. In each case, toggle the filter to see the effect of your selection. When done, change back to the sorting options and criteria you entered in Step 1.

Figure 3–23

3

• Close the Client table. When asked if you want to save your changes, click the No button.

Q&A

Should I not have cleared all filters before closing the table?

If you are closing a table and not saving the changes, it is not necessary to clear the filter. No filter will be active when you next open the table.

Filters and Queries

Now that you are familiar with how filters work, you might notice similarities between filters and queries. Filters and queries are related in three ways.

1. You can apply a filter to the results of a query just as you can apply a filter to a table.

2. When you have created a filter using Advanced Filter/Sort, you can save the filter settings as a query by using the Save as Query command on the Advanced menu.

3. You can restore filter settings that you previously saved in a query by using the Load from Query command on the Advanced menu.

Break Point: If you wish to take a break, this is a good place to do so. You can quit Access now. To resume at a later time, start Access, open the database called Camashaly Design, and continue following the steps from this location forward.

Changing the Database Structure

When you initially create a database, you define its **structure**; that is, you assign names and types to all the fields. In many cases, the structure you first define will not continue to be appropriate as you use the database.

Perhaps a field currently in the table no longer is necessary. If no one ever uses a particular field, it is not needed in the table. Because it is occupying space and serving no useful purpose, you should remove it from the table. You also would need to delete the field from any forms, reports, or queries that include it.

More commonly, an organization will find that it needs to maintain additional information that was not anticipated at the time the database was first designed. The organization's own requirements may have changed. In addition, outside regulations that the organization must satisfy may change as well. Either case requires the addition of fields to an existing table.

Although you can make some changes to the database structure in Datasheet view, it is usually easier and better to make these changes in Design view.

TO DELETE A FIELD

If a field in one of your tables no longer is needed, you should delete the field; for example, it may serve no useful purpose, or it may have been included by mistake. To delete a field, you would use the following steps.

1. Open the table in Design view.
2. Click the row selector for the field to be deleted.
3. Press the DELETE key.
4. When Access displays the dialog box requesting confirmation that you want to delete the field, click the Yes button.

BTW

Changing Data Types
It is possible to change the data type for a field that already contains data. Before you change a data type, however, you should consider what effect the change will have on other database objects, such as forms, queries, and reports. For example, you could convert a Text field to a Memo field if you find that you do not have enough space to store the data that you need. You also could convert a Number field to a Currency field or vice versa.

To Add a New Field

You can add fields to a table in a database. Camashaly Design has decided that it needs to categorize its clients. To do so requires an additional field, Client Type. The possible values for Client Type are NON (which indicates the client is a nonprofit organization), RET (which indicates the client is a retail organization), or SER (which indicates the client is a service organization). The following steps add the Client Type field to the Client table immediately after the Postal Code field.

 1

- If necessary, open the Navigation Pane.
- Open the Client table in Design view.
- Click the row selector for the Amount Paid field, and then press the INSERT key to insert a blank row above the selected field (Figure 3–24).

2

- Click the Field Name column for the new field.
- Type **Client Type** as the field name and then press the TAB key.

Figure 3–24

Other Ways

1. Click Insert Rows button (Table Tools Design tab | Tools group)

To Create a Lookup Field

Because there are only three possible values for the Client Type field, you should make it easy for users to enter the appropriate value. A **lookup field** allows the user to select from a list of values when updating the contents of the field.

The following steps make the Client Type field a lookup field.

- Click the Data Type column for the Client Type field, and then click the Data Type box arrow to display the menu of available data types (Figure 3–25).

Figure 3–25

- Click Lookup Wizard, and then click the 'I will type in the values that I want.' option button (Lookup Wizard dialog box) to indicate that you will type in the values (Figure 3–26).

Q&A

When would I use the other option button?

You would use the other option button if the data to be entered in this field is found in another table or query.

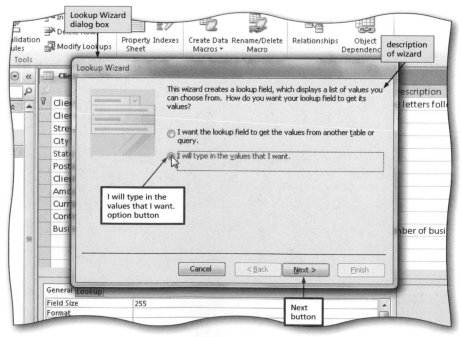

Figure 3–26

3

- Click the Next button to display the next Lookup Wizard screen (Figure 3–27).

Q&A

Why did I not change the field size for the Client Type field?

You could have changed the field size to 3 but it is not necessary. When you create a lookup field and indicate specific values for the field, you automatically restrict the field size.

Figure 3–27

4

- Click the first row of the table (below Col1), and then type **NON** as the value in the first row.

- Press the DOWN ARROW key, and then type **RET** as the value in the second row.

- Press the TAB key, and then type **SER** as the value in the third row (Figure 3–28).

Q&A

I notice you can press either the DOWN ARROW or the TAB key to move to the second row. Can you also press the ENTER key?

No. Pressing the ENTER key will exit the Lookup Wizard without finishing the process of adding a Lookup field.

Figure 3–28

5

- Click the Next button to display the next Lookup Wizard screen.

- Ensure Client Type is entered as the label for the lookup field and that the Allow Multiple Values check box is NOT checked (Figure 3–29).

6

- Click the Finish button to complete the definition of the lookup field.

Q&A

Why does the data type for the Client Type field still show Text?

The data type is still Text because the values entered in the wizard were entered as text.

Figure 3–29

To Add a Multivalued Field

Normally, fields contain only a single value. In Access, it is possible to have **multivalued fields**, that is, fields that can contain more than one value. Camashaly Design wants to use such a field to store the abbreviations of the various services its clients need (see Table 3–1 for the service abbreviations and descriptions). Unlike the Client Type, where each client only had one type, clients can require multiple service descriptions. One client might need Ad, Ban, Bill, and Logo (Ad Design, Banners, Billboards, and Logo Design). Another client might only need Host (Web Site Hosting).

Table 3–1 Service Abbreviations and Descriptions	
Service Abbreviation	**Description**
Ad	Ad Design
Ban	Banners
Bill	Billboards
Bus	Business Cards
ENews	Email Newsletter
Host	Web Site Hosting
Logo	Logo Design
Mkt	Marketing Research
News	Printed Newsletters
Pod	Podcasting
SE	Search Engine Visibility
Shop	Shopping Cart
Soc	Social Networking

Creating a multivalued field uses the same process as creating a lookup field, with the exception that you check the Allow Multiple Values check box. The following steps create a multivalued field.

1 Click the row selector for the Amount Paid field, and then press the INSERT key to insert a blank row.

2 Click the Field Name column for the new field, type `Services Needed` as the field name, and then press the TAB key.

3 Click the Data Type arrow to display the menu of available data types for the Services Needed field, and then click Lookup Wizard in the menu of available data types to start the Lookup Wizard.

4 Click the 'I will type in the values that I want.' option button to indicate that you will type in the values.

5 Click the Next button to display the next Lookup Wizard screen.

6 Click the first row of the table (below Col1), and then type `Ad` as the value in the first row.

7 Enter the remaining values from the first column in Table 3–1. Before typing each value, press the TAB key to move to a new row.

8 Click the Next button to display the next Lookup Wizard screen.

9 Ensure that Services Needed is entered as the label for the lookup field.

10 Click the Allow Multiple Values check box to allow the user to enter multiple values.

11 Click the Finish button to complete the definition of the Lookup Wizard field.

To Add a Calculated Field

A field that can be computed from other fields is called a **calculated field** or a **computed field**. In Chapter 2, you created a calculated field in a query that provided total amount data. With Access 2010, it is now possible to also include a calculated field in a table. Users will not be able to update this field. Instead, Access will automatically perform the necessary calculation whenever you display or use this field in any way. The following steps add a calculated field in the table.

- Click the row selector for the Contract Hours YTD field, and then press the INSERT key to insert a blank row above the selected field.

- Click the Field Name column for the new field.

- Type `Total Amount` as the field name and then press the TAB key.

- Click the Data Type box arrow to display the menu of available data types (Figure 3–30).

Figure 3–30

2

- Click Calculated to select the Calculated data type and display the Expression Builder dialog box (Figure 3–31).

Figure 3–31

3

- Double-click the Amount Paid field in the Expression Categories area (Expression Builder dialog box) to add the field to the expression.

Q&A I do not have the list of fields in the Expression Categories area. What should I do?

Click Client in the Expression Elements area.

- Type a plus sign (+).

Q&A Could I select the plus sign from a list rather than typing it?

Yes. Double-click Operators in the Expression Elements area to display available operators and then click the plus sign.

- Double-click the Current Due field in the Expression Categories area (Expression Builder dialog box) to add the field to the expression (Figure 3–32).

Figure 3–32

4

- Click the OK button (Expression Builder dialog box) to enter the expression in the Expression property of the selected field (Figure 3–33).

Q&A Could I have simply typed the expression in the Expression Builder dialog box rather than selecting the fields from a list?

Yes. You can use whichever technique you find more convenient.

Q&A When I entered a calculated field in a query, I typed the expression in the Zoom dialog box. Could I have used the Expression Builder instead?

Yes. To do so, you would click Build rather than Zoom on the shortcut menu.

Figure 3–33

To Save the Changes and Close the Table

The following steps save the changes; that is, they save the addition of the new fields and close the table.

1 Click the Save button on the Quick Access Toolbar to save the changes.

2 Close the Client table.

To Modify Single or Multivalued Lookup Fields

You may find that you later want to change the list of choices in a lookup field. If you find you need to modify a single or multivalued lookup field, you can use the following steps.

1. Open the table in Design view and select the field to be modified.

2. Click the Lookup tab in the Field Properties pane.

3. Change the list in the Row Source property to change the desired list of values.

BTW

Calculated Fields
Do not add a calculated field to a table if you plan to also use the database with Access 2007. Access 2007 does not recognize calculated fields. Also, if you modify the expression used to create the calculated field, the field may not update correctly.

Mass Changes

In some cases, rather than making individual changes to records, you will want to make mass changes. That is, you will want to add, change, or delete many records in a single operation. You can do this with action queries. Unlike the queries that you created in Chapter 2, which simply presented data in specific ways, an **action query** adds, deletes, or changes data in a table. An **update query** allows you to make the same change to all records satisfying some criterion. If you omit the criterion, you will make the same changes to all records in the table. A **delete query** allows you to delete all the records satisfying some criterion. You can add the results of a query to an existing table by using an **append query**. You also can add the query results to a new table by using a **make-table query**.

To Use an Update Query

The new Client Type field is blank on every record in the Client table. One approach to entering the information for the field would be to step through the entire table, assigning each record its appropriate value. If most of the clients have the same type, a simpler approach is available.

In the Camashaly Design database, for example, more clients are type NON. Initially, you can set all the values to NON. To accomplish this quickly and easily, you can use an **update query**, which is a query that makes the same change to all the records satisfying a criterion. Later, you can change the type for retail organizations and service organizations.

The following steps use an update query to change the value in the Client Type field to NON for all the records. Because all records are to be updated, criteria are not required.

1

- Create a new query for the Client table, and close the Navigation Pane.

- Click the Update button (Query Tools Design tab | Query Type group), double-click the Client Type field to select the field, click the Update To row in the first column of the design grid, and then type **NON** as the new value (Figure 3–34).

Q&A

Do I not have to enter a criterion?

If you only want the change to be made on some of the records, you would need to enter a criterion to identify those records. Without a criterion, the change will be made on all records, which is what you want in this update.

Figure 3–34

2

- Click the Run button (Query Tools Design tab | Results group) to run the query and update the records (Figure 3–35).

Q&A Why do I not click the View button to update the records?

The purpose of the View button is to simply view results. The Run button causes the updates specified by the query to take place.

Q&A Why would the dialog box not appear on my screen when I click the Run button?

If the dialog box does not appear, it means that you did not click the Enable Content button when you first opened the database. Close the database, open it again, and enable the content. Then, create and run the query again.

Figure 3–35

 Experiment

- Create an update query to change the client type to RET. Enter a criterion to restrict the records to be updated, and then run the query. Open the table to view your changes. When finished, create and run an update query to change the client type to NON on all records.

3

- Click the Yes button to make the changes.

Q&A Is there any way to see the records that will be updated before performing the update, in case you are not sure you are updating the correct records?

Yes. Click the Select button (Query Tools Design tab | Query Type group) to convert the query to a select query, add any additional fields that would help you identify the records, and then view the results. Return to Design view and make any necessary corrections to the query. When you are satisfied, click the Update button to once again convert the query to an update query.

Other Ways
1. Right-click any open area in upper pane, point to Query Type on shortcut menu, click Update Query on Query Type submenu

To Use a Delete Query

In some cases, you may need to delete several records at a time. If, for example, all clients in a particular postal code are to be serviced by another firm, the clients with this postal code can be deleted from the Camashaly Design database. Instead of deleting these clients individually, which could be very time consuming in a large database, you can delete them in one operation by using a **delete query**, which is a query that will delete all the records satisfying the criteria entered in the query.

The following steps use a delete query to delete any client whose postal code is 28819. (Two such clients currently exist in the database.)

● Click the column heading for the Client Type field and then press the DELETE key to clear the grid.

● Click the Delete button (Query Tools Design tab | Query Type group) to make the query a delete query.

● Double-click the Postal Code field to select the field.

● Click the Criteria row for the Postal Code field and type 28819 as the criterion (Figure 3–36).

2

● Run the query by clicking the Run button.

● Click the Yes button when Access displays a message indicating that there are two records which will be deleted to complete the deletion.

Figure 3–36

Q&A

Is there any way to see the records that will be deleted before performing the deletion, in case you are not sure you are deleting the correct records?

Yes. Prior to running the query, you would click the Select button (Query Tools Design tab | Query Type group) to convert the query to a select query, add any additional fields that would help you identify the records, and then view the results. You would then return to Design view and make any corrections to the query. When you are satisfied, click the Delete button to once again convert the query to a delete query.

● Close the Query window. Because you do not need to use this delete query again, do not save the query.

Other Ways

1. Right-click any open area in upper pane, point to Query Type on shortcut menu, click Delete Query on Query Type submenu

TO USE AN APPEND QUERY

An **append query** adds a group of records from one table to the end of another table. For example, suppose that Camashaly Design acquires some new clients and a database containing a table with those clients. To avoid entering all this information manually, you can append it to the Client table in the Camashaly Design database using the append query. To create an append query, you would use the following steps.

1. Create a query for the table containing the records to append.

2. In Design view, indicate the fields to include, and then enter any necessary criteria.

3. View the query results to be sure you have specified the correct data, and then return to Design view.

4. Click the Append button (Query Tools Design tab | Query Type group).

5. When Access displays the Append dialog box, specify the name of the table to receive the new records and its location. Run the query by clicking the Run button (Query Tools Design tab | Results group).

6. When Access indicates the number of records to be appended, click the OK button.

BTW

Delete Queries
If you do not specify any criteria in a delete query, Access will delete all the records in the table.

To Use a Make-Table Query

In some cases, you might want to copy the records from an existing table to a new table, that is, a table that has not yet been created. If so, use a **make-table query** to add the records to a new table. To create a make-table query, you would use the following steps.

1. Create a query for the table containing the records to add.
2. In Design view, indicate the fields to include, and then enter any necessary criteria.
3. View the query results to be sure you have specified the correct data, and then return to Design view.
4. Click the Make Table button (Query Tools Design tab | Query Type group).
5. When Access displays the Make Table dialog box, specify the name of the table to receive the new records and its location. Run the query by clicking the Run button (Query Tools Design tab | Results group).
6. When Access indicates the number of records to be inserted, click the OK button.

> **BTW**
>
> **Archive Tables**
> You can use a make table query to create an archive table. An **archive table** is a table that contains data that is no longer used in operations but that might still be needed by the organization.

Break Point: If you wish to take a break, this is a good place to do so. You can quit Access now. To resume at a later time, start Access, open the database called Camashaly Design, and continue following the steps from this location forward.

Validation Rules

You now have created, loaded, queried, and updated a database. Nothing you have done so far, however, restricts users to entering only valid data, that is, data that follows the rules established for data in the database. An example of such a rule would be that client types can only be NON, RET, or SER. To ensure the entry of valid data, you create these **validation rules,** that is, rules that a user must follow when entering the data. As you will see, Access will prevent users from entering data that does not follow the rules. The steps also specify **validation text**, which is the message that will appear if a user violates the validation rule.

> **BTW**
>
> **Database Design: Validation**
> In most organization, decisions about what is valid and what is invalid data are made during the requirements gathering process and the database design process.

Validation rules can indicate a **required field**, a field in which the user actually must enter data. Validation rules can restrict a user's entry to a certain **range of values**; for example, the values in the Amount Paid field must be between $0 and $30,000. They can specify a **default value**, that is, a value that Access will display on the screen in a particular field before the user begins adding a record. To make data entry of client numbers more convenient, you also can have lowercase letters appear automatically as uppercase letters. Finally, validation rules can specify a collection of acceptable values.

To Change a Field Size

The Field Size property for text fields represents the maximum number of characters a user can enter in the field. Because the field size for the Client Number field is 4, for example, a user would not be able to enter a fifth character in the field. Occasionally, you may find that the field size that seemed appropriate when you first created a table is no longer appropriate. In the Client table, there is now a name that is longer than 30 characters. To allow this name in the table, you need to change the field size for the Client Name field to a number that is large enough to accommodate the new name. The following step changes the field size for the Client Name field from 30 to 35.

1 Ensure that the Client table is open in Design view and that the Navigation Pane is closed.

2 Select the Client Name field by clicking its row selector.

3 Click the Field Size property to select it, delete the current entry (30), and then type 3 5 as the new field size.

To Specify a Required Field

To specify that a field is to be required, change the value for the Required property from No to Yes. The following step specifies that the Client Name field is to be a required field.

- Ensure that the Client Name field is still selected.

- Click the Required property box in the Field Properties pane, and then click the down arrow that appears.

- Click Yes in the list (Figure 3–37).

Q&A What is the effect of this change?

Users cannot leave the Client Name field blank when entering or editing records.

Figure 3–37

To Specify a Range

The following step specifies that entries in the Current Due field must be between $0 and $30,000. To indicate this range, the criterion specifies that the amount paid amount must be both >= 0 (greater than or equal to 0) and <= 30000 (less than or equal to 30,000).

- Select the Current Due field by clicking its row selector, click the Validation Rule property box to produce an insertion point, and then type `>=0 and <=30000` as the rule.

- Click the Validation Text property box to produce an insertion point, and then type `Must be at least $0.00 and at most $30,000.00` as the text (Figure 3–38).

Q&A What is the effect of this change?

Users now will be prohibited from entering a current due amount that either is less than $0.00 or greater than $30,000.00 when they add records or change the value in the Current Due field.

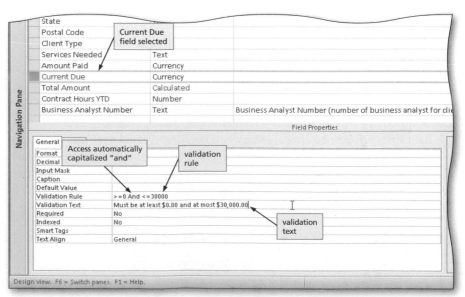

Figure 3–38

To Specify a Default Value

To specify a default value, enter the value in the Default Value property box. The following step specifies NON as the default value for the Client Type field. This simply means that if users do not enter a client type, the type will be NON.

1

- With the Client Type field selected, click the Default Value property box to produce an insertion point, and then type `=NON` as the value (Figure 3–39).

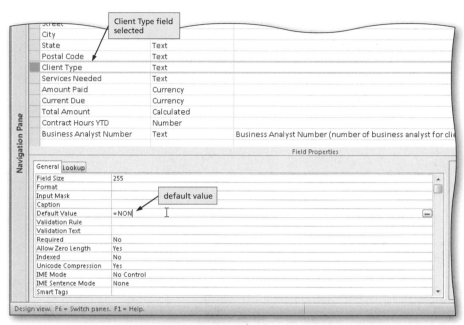

Figure 3–39

To Specify a Collection of Legal Values

The only **legal values, or allowable values,** for the Client Type field are NON, RET, and SER. An appropriate validation rule for this field prevents Access from accepting any entry other than these three possibilities. The following step specifies the legal values for the Client Type field.

1

- With the Client Type field selected, click the Validation Rule property box to produce an insertion point and then type `=NON or =RET or =SER` as the validation rule.

- Click the Validation Text property box and then type **Must be NON, RET, or SER** as the validation text (Figure 3–40).

Q&A

What is the effect of this change?

Users now will be allowed to enter only NON, RET, or SER in the Client Type field when they add records or make changes to this field.

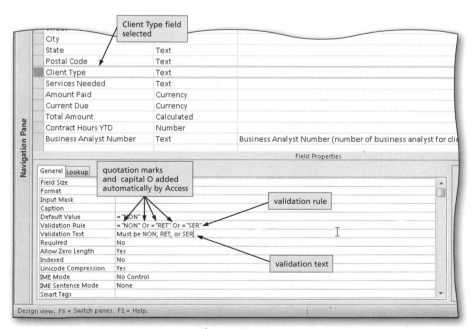

Figure 3–40

To Specify a Format

To affect the way data appears in a field, you can use a **format**. To use a format with a Text field, you enter a special symbol, called a **format symbol**, in the field's Format property box. The Format property uses different settings for different data types. The following step specifies a format for the Client Number field in the Client table and illustrates the way you enter a format. The format symbol used in the example is >, which causes Access to display lowercase letters automatically as uppercase letters. The format symbol < causes Access to display uppercase letters automatically as lowercase letters.

1

- Select the Client Number field.

- Click the Format property box and then type > (Figure 3–41).

Q&A What is the effect of this change?

From this point on, any lowercase letters will appear automatically as uppercase when users add records or change the value in the Client Number field.

Figure 3–41

To Save the Validation Rules, Default Values, and Formats

The following steps save the validation rules, default values, and formats.

1 Click the Save button on the Quick Access Toolbar to save the changes (Figure 3–42).

2 Click the No button to save the changes without testing current data.

3 Close the Client table.

Q&A Should I always click the No button when saving validation rules?

If this were a database used to run a business or to solve some other critical need, you would click Yes. You would want to be sure that the data already in the database does not violate the rules.

Figure 3–42

Updating a Table that Contains Validation Rules

When updating a table that contains validation rules, Access provides assistance in making sure the data entered is valid. It helps in making sure that data is formatted correctly. Entering a number that is out of the required range, for example, or entering a value that is not one of the possible choices, will produce an error message in the form of a dialog box. The database will not be updated until the error is corrected.

If the client number entered contains lowercase letters, such as wi12 (Figure 3–43), Access will display the data automatically as WI12 (Figure 3–44).

Figure 3–43

Figure 3–44

If the client type is not valid, such as xxx, Access will display the text message you specified (Figure 3–45) and prevent the data from entering the database.

Modifying Table Properties
You can change the properties of a table by opening the table in Design view and then clicking the Propery Sheet button. To display the records in a table in an order other than primary key (the default sort order), use the Order By property. For example, to display the Client table automatically in Client Name order, change the the Order By property box setting to **Client.Client Name** in the property box, close the property sheet, and save the change to the table design. When you open the Client table in Datasheet view, the records will be sorted in Client Name order.

BTW

Figure 3–45

If the amount paid value is not valid, such as 50000, which is too large, Access also displays the appropriate message (Figure 3–46) and refuses to accept the data.

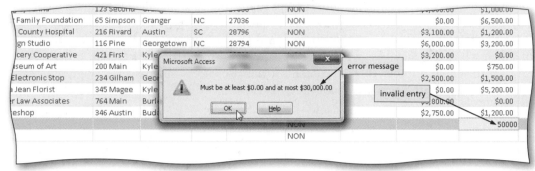

Figure 3–46

If a required field contains no data, Access indicates this by displaying an error message as soon as you attempt to leave the record (Figure 3–47). The field must contain a valid entry before Access will move to a different record.

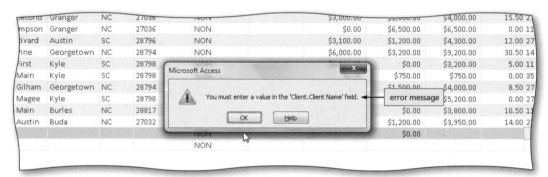

Figure 3–47

When entering data into a field with a validation rule, you may find that Access displays the error message and you are unable to make the necessary correction. It may be that you cannot remember the validation rule you created or it was created incorrectly. In such a case, you neither can leave the field nor close the table because you have entered data into a field that violates the validation rule.

If this happens, first try again to type an acceptable entry. If this does not work, repeatedly press the BACKSPACE key to erase the contents of the field and then try to leave the field. If you are unsuccessful using this procedure, press the ESC key until the record is removed from the screen. The record will not be added to the database.

Should the need arise to take this drastic action, you probably have a faulty validation rule. Use the techniques of the previous sections to correct the existing validation rules for the field.

To Change the Contents of a Field

Now that the size for the Client Name field has been increased, you can change the name for client HC10 to Hendley County Regional Hospital. Changing the field size for the field does not automatically increase the width of the corresponding column in the datasheet, however. You need to take the necessary action to resize the column, just as you resized columns in Chapter 1 on page AC 29. The following steps change the name and resize the column in the datasheet to accommodate the new name.

- Open the Client table in Datasheet view and ensure the Navigation Pane is closed.

- Click in the Client Name field for client HC10 immediately before the word, Hospital, to produce an insertion point.

- Change the name from Hendley County Hospital to Hendley County Regional Hospital by typing the word **Regional** and pressing the SPACEBAR.

2

- Resize the Client Name column to best fit the new data by double-clicking the right boundary of the field selector, that is, the column heading (Figure 3–48).

3

- Save the changes to the layout by clicking the Save button on the Quick Access Toolbar.

- Close the Client table.

Figure 3–48

To Use a Lookup Field

Earlier, you changed all the entries in the Client Type field to NON. You have created a rule that will ensure that only legitimate values (NON, RET, or SER) can be entered in the field. You also made Client Type a lookup field. You can make changes to a lookup field for individual records by clicking the field to be changed, clicking the arrow that appears in the field, and then selecting the desired value from the list.

The following steps change the Client Type values to the correct values.

1

- Open the Client table in Datasheet view and ensure the Navigation Pane is closed.

- Click in the Client Type field on the first record to display an arrow.

- Click the arrow to display the drop-down list of available choices for the Client Type field (Figure 3–49).

Q&A

I got the drop-down list as soon as I clicked. I did not need to click the arrow. What happened?

If you click in the position where the arrow would appear, you will get the drop-down list. If you click anywhere else, you would need to click the arrow.

Figure 3–49

Could I type the value instead of selecting it from the list?

Yes. Once you have either deleted the previous value or selected the entire previous value, you can begin typing. You do not have to type the full entry. When you begin with the letter, R, for example, Access will automatically add the ET.

Experiment

- Select the Client Type field on the first record. Try to change the client type by typing various values. Try to type an invalid client type (like MAN). When finished, change the value on the record to SER.

2

- Click SER to change the value.

- In a similar fashion, change the values on the other records to match those shown in Figure 3–50.

Figure 3–50

To Use a Multivalued Lookup Field

Using a multivalued lookup field is similar to using a regular lookup field. The difference is that when you drop down the list, the entries all will be preceded by check boxes. You then can check all the entries that you want. The appropriate entries are shown in Figure 3–51. As indicated in the figure, the services needed for client BA53 are Ad, Ban, Bill, and Logo.

CL #	Client Name	Services Needed
BA53	Bavant Animal Hospital	Ad, Ban, Bill, Logo
BB32	Babbage CPA Firm	Ad, Bus, ENews
BC76	Buda Community Clinic	Ban, Host, News
CJ29	Catering by Jenna	Bus, Host, Logo
GF56	Granger Family Foundation	Host
HC10	Hendley County Regional Hospital	ENews, News, Soc
KD21	KAL Design Studio	Host, Mkt, SE
KG04	Kyle Grocery Cooperative	Ad, Bill, Soc
KM03	Kyle Museum of Art	ENews, Host, Pod, Shop
ME14	Mike's Electronic Stop	Ad, Ban, Logo
PJ34	Patricia Jean Florist	Bus, Mkt, Shop
SL77	Smarter Law Associates	ENews, Pod
TB17	The Bikeshop	Ad, SE

Figure 3–51

The following steps make the appropriate entries for the Services Needed field.

1

- Click the Services Needed field on the first record to display the arrow.

- Click the arrow to display the list of available services (Figure 3–52).

All the services currently appear in the box. What if there were too many services to fit?

Access would automatically include a scroll bar that you could use to scroll through all the choices.

Figure 3–52

2

- Click the Ad, Ban, Bill, and Logo check boxes to select the services for the first client (Figure 3–53).

Figure 3–53

- Click the OK button to complete the selection.

- Using the same technique, enter the services given in Figure 3–51 on page AC 172 for the remaining clients.

- Double-click the right boundary of the field selector for the Services Needed field to resize the field so that it best fits the data (Figure 3–54).

- Save the changes to the layout by clicking the Save button on the Quick Access Toolbar.

- Close the Client table.

Q&A

What if I closed the table without saving the layout changes?

You would be asked if you want to save the changes.

Figure 3–54

To Update a Form to Reflect the Changes in the Table

In the first chapter, on page AC 48, you clicked the Form button (Create tab | Forms group) to create a simple form that contained all the fields in the Client table. Now that you have added additional fields, the form you created, Client Form, no longer contains all the fields in the table. Because creating the form required only clicking a single button, the simplest way to include all the fields from the Client table in the form is to delete the form and create it once again. The following steps delete the Client Form and then create it a second time. The form then will contain all the fields.

- Open the Navigation Pane, and then right-click the Client Form in the Navigation Pane to display a shortcut menu.

- Click Delete on the shortcut menu to delete the selected form, and then click the Yes button in the Microsoft Access dialog box to confirm the deletion.

- Click the Client table in the Navigation Pane to select the table.

- Click Create on the Ribbon to display the Create tab.

- Click the Form button (Create tab | Forms group) to create a simple form (Figure 3–55).

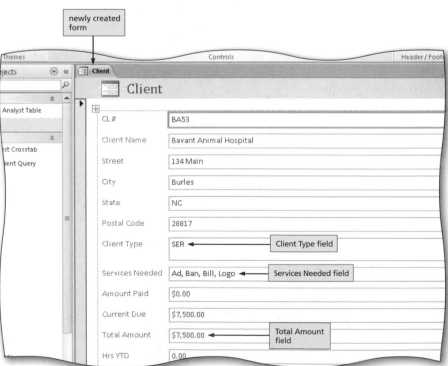

Figure 3–55

②

- Click the Save button on the Quick Access Toolbar to save the form.

- Type `Client Form` as the form name, and then click the OK button to save the form.

- Close the form.

To Update a Report to Reflect the Changes in the Table

You also may want to include the new fields in the Client Financial Report you created earlier. Just as you did with the form, you could delete the current version of the report and then create it all over again. There are several steps involved in creating a report, however, so it is more complicated than the process of recreating the form. An easier way is to modify the report in Layout view. In Layout view, you easily can resize columns and add new fields. The following steps modify the Client Financial Report by resizing the Client Name field so that the entire name of Hendley County Regional Hospital appears. They also add the Client Type and Total Amount fields. Finally, to accommodate the extra fields, the steps change the orientation of the report from Portrait to Landscape.

①

- Open the Navigation Pane, if necessary, and then right-click the Client Financial Report in the Navigation Pane to display a shortcut menu.

- Click Layout View on the shortcut menu to open the report in Layout view.

- Close the Navigation Pane.

- Click the column heading for the Client Name column, point to the right-hand border of the column heading so that the mouse pointer becomes a two-headed arrow, and then drag the pointer to the approximate position shown in Figure 3–56 to resize the column.

Q&A Do I have to be exact?

No. Make sure, however, that you can see all the data in the client name for client HC10. If not, you need to drag the border further to the right.

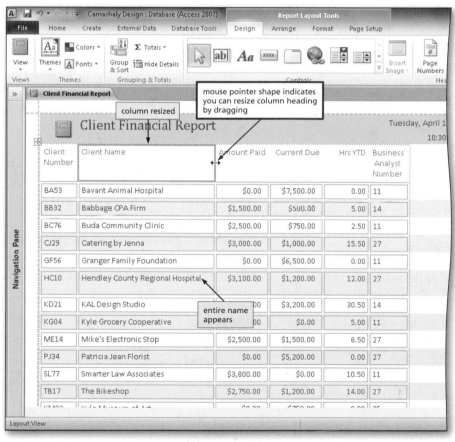

Figure 3–56

Q&A Did I have to select the column heading or could I have selected one of the entries in the column?

You could have selected any of the entries in the column.

2

- Click the Add Existing Fields button (Report Layout Tools Design tab | Tools group) to display a field list (Figure 3–57).

Q&A Why are there two Services Needed fields in the list?

They serve different purposes. If you were to select Services Needed, you would get all the services for a given client on one line. If you were to select Services Needed.Value, each service would be on a separate line. You are not selecting either one for this report.

Figure 3–57

3

- Point to the Client Type field in the field list, press and hold the left mouse button, and then drag the mouse pointer until the line to the left of the mouse pointer is between the Client Name and Amount Paid fields (Figure 3–58).

- Release the left mouse button to place the field.

Q&A What if I make a mistake?

You can delete the field by clicking the field and then pressing the DELETE key. You can move the field by dragging it to the correct position.

Figure 3–58

4

- Using the same technique, add the Total Amount field between the Current Due and Hrs YTD fields.

- Click the Add Existing Fields button (Report Layout Tools Design tab | Tools group) to remove the field list from the screen (Figure 3–59).

What would I do if the field list covered the portion of the report where I wanted to insert a new field?

You can move the field list to a different position on the screen by dragging its title bar.

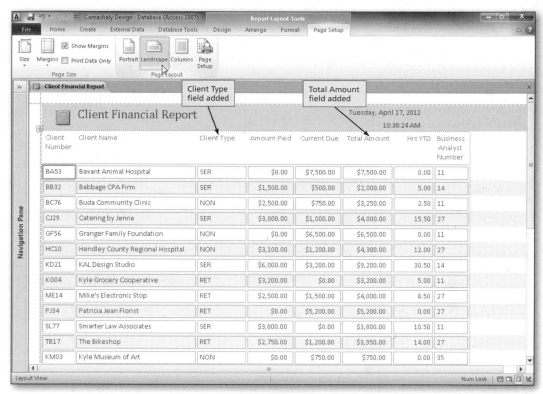

Figure 3–59

- Scroll the report, if necessary, so that the entire width of the report appears on the screen.

5

- Click Page Setup on the Ribbon to display the Page Setup tab.

- Click the Landscape button (Report Layout Tools Page Setup tab | Page Layout group) to change the orientation of the report to Landscape.

- Click the Save button on the Quick Access Toolbar to save your changes.

- Close the report.

To Include Totals in a Datasheet

It is possible to include totals and other statistics at the bottom of a datasheet in a special row called the Total row. The following steps display the total of the salary YTD and Incentive YTD for analysts in the Total row.

1

- Open the Business Analyst Table in Datasheet view and close the Navigation Pane.

- Click the Totals button (Home tab | Records group) to include the Total row in the datasheet.

- Click the Total row in the Salary YTD column to display an arrow.

- Click the arrow to display a menu of available calculations (Figure 3–60).

Q&A

Will I always get the same list?

No. You will only get the items that are applicable to the type of data in the column. You cannot calculate the sum of text data, for example.

Figure 3–60

2

- Click Sum to calculate the total of the salary YTD amounts.

- Click the Total row in the Incentive YTD column to display an arrow, click the arrow to display a menu of available calculations, and then click Sum to calculate the total of the incentive YTD amounts (Figure 3–61).

Experiment

- Experiment with other statistics. When finished, once again select the sum in both columns.

Figure 3–61

To Remove Totals from a Datasheet

If you no longer want the totals to appear as part of the datasheet, you can remove the Total row. The following step removes the Total row.

• Click the Totals button (Home tab | Records group), which is shown in Figure 3–60, to remove the Total row from the datasheet.

Changing the Appearance of a Datasheet

You can change the appearance of a datasheet in a variety of ways. For example, you can change the appearance of gridlines or change the text colors and font. Figure 3–62 shows the various buttons, found in the Text Formatting group on the Home tab, that are available to change the datasheet appearance.

Figure 3–62

The changes to the datasheet will be reflected not only on the screen, but also when you print or preview the datasheet.

Determine whether changes to the format of a datasheet are desirable.
You need to decide if changes to the format of a datasheet would improve its appearance and/or its usefulness. The following are the decisions you would make.

• Would totals or other calculations be useful in the datasheet? If so, include the Total row and select the appropriate computations.

• Would different gridlines make the datasheet more useful? If so, change to the desired gridlines.

• Would alternating colors in the rows make them easier to read? If so, change the alternate fill color.

• Would a different font and/or font color make the text stand out better? If so, change the font color and/or the font.

• Is the font size appropriate? Can you see enough data at one time on the screen and yet have the data be readable? If not, change the font size to an appropriate value.

• Is the column spacing appropriate? Are some columns wider than they need to be? Do some columns not display all the data? Change the column sizes as necessary.

As a general guideline, once you have decided on a particular look for a datasheet, all your datasheets should have the same look, unless there is a compelling reason for one of your datasheets to differ.

Plan Ahead

To Change Gridlines in a Datasheet

One of the changes you can make to a datasheet is which gridlines appear. You may feel that the appearance would be improved by having only horizontal gridlines. The following steps change the datasheet so that only horizontal gridlines are included.

- Open the Business Analyst Table in Datasheet view, if it is not already open.
- If necessary, close the Navigation Pane.
- Click the box in the upper-left corner of the datasheet to select the entire datasheet (Figure 3–63).

Figure 3–63

- Click the Gridlines button (Home tab | Text Formatting group) to display the Gridlines gallery (Figure 3–64).

Q&A
Does it matter whether I click the button or the arrow?

In this case, it does not matter. Either one will produce the same result.

Figure 3–64

- Click the Gridlines: Horizontal command in the Gridlines gallery to include only horizontal gridlines.

Experiment

- Experiment with other gridline options. When finished, once again select horizontal gridlines.

To Change the Colors and Font in a Datasheet

You may also decide to modify the appearance of the datasheet by changing the colors and the font. The following steps change the Alternate Fill color, a color that appears on every other row in the datasheet. They also change the font color, the font, and the font size.

1

- With the datasheet for the Business Analyst Table selected, click the Alternate Row Color button arrow (Home tab | Text Formatting group) to display the color palette (Figure 3–65).

Q&A Does it matter whether I click the button or the arrow?

Yes. Clicking the arrow produces a color palette. Clicking the button applies the currently selected color. When in doubt, you should click the arrow.

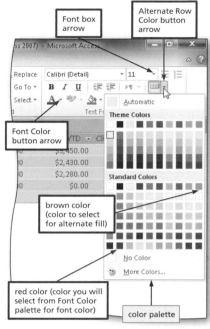

Figure 3–65

2

- Click Brown in the upper-right corner of Standard Colors to select brown as the alternate color.

- Click the Font Color button arrow, and then click Red (the second color in the bottom row) in the lower-left corner of Standard Colors to select Red as the font color.

- Click the Font box arrow, scroll down in the list until Bodoni MT appears, and then select Bodoni MT as the font. (If it is not available, select any font of your choice.)

- Click the Font Size box arrow, and select 10 as the font size (Figure 3–66).

Q&A Does the order in which I make these selections make a difference?

No. You could have made these selections in any order.

Experiment

- Experiment with other colors, fonts, and font sizes. When finished, return to the options selected in this step.

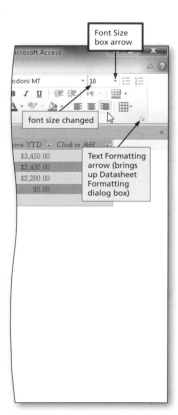

Figure 3–66

Using the Datasheet Formatting Dialog Box

As an alternative to using the individual buttons, you can click the Datasheet Formatting dialog box launcher to display the Datasheet Formatting dialog box (Figure 3–67). You can use the various options within the dialog box to make changes to the datasheet format. Once you are finished, click the OK button to apply your changes.

Figure 3–67

To Close the Datasheet without Saving the Format Changes

The following steps close the datasheet without saving the changes to the format. Because the changes are not saved, the next time you open the Business Analyst Table in Datasheet view, it will appear in the original format. If you had saved the changes, the changes would be reflected in its appearance.

1 Close the Business Analyst Table.

2 Click the No button in the Microsoft Access dialog box when asked if you want to save your changes.

Multivalued Fields in Queries

You can use multivalued fields in queries just as you can use other fields. You have a choice concerning how the multiple values appear. You can choose to have them on a single row or on multiple rows.

To Query a Multivalued Field Showing Multiple Values on a Single Row

To include a multivalued field in the results of a query, place the field in the query design grid just like any other field. The results will list all of the values for the multivalued field on a single row, just as in a datasheet. The following steps create a query to display the client number, client name, client type, and services needed for all clients.

1

- Create a query for the Client table and close the Navigation Pane.

- Include the Client Number, Client Name, Client Type, and Services Needed fields (Figure 3–68).

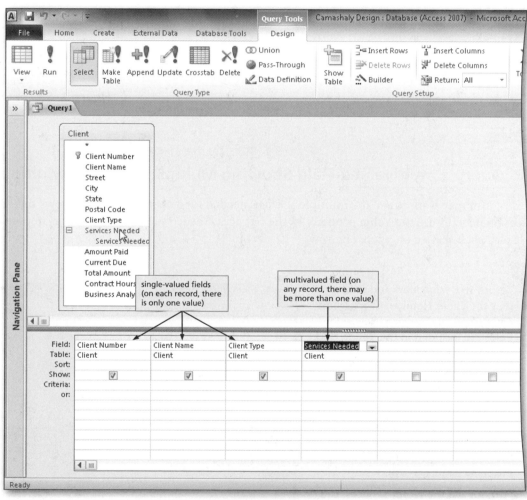

Figure 3–68

Using Criteria with Multivalued Fields
To enter criteria in a multivalued field, simply enter the criteria in the Criteria row. For example, to find all clients who need banners, enter **BAN** in the Criteria row.

● View the results (Figure 3–69).

Q&A

Can I include criteria for the multivalued field?

Yes. You can include criteria for the multivalued field.

Experiment

● Return to Design view and enter various criteria in the Services Needed field. Run the queries. When finished, return to the options selected in this step.

Figure 3–69

To Query a Multivalued Field Showing Multiple Values on Multiple Rows

You may want to see the multiple services needed for a client on separate rows rather than a single row. To do so, you need to use the Value property of the Services Needed field. The following steps use the Value property to display each service on a separate row.

● Return to Design view and ensure that the Client Number, Client Name, Client Type, and Services Needed fields are included in the design grid.

● Click the Services Needed field to produce an insertion point, press the RIGHT ARROW key as necessary to move the insertion point to the end of the field name, and then type a period and the word **Value** after the word, Needed, to use the Value property (Figure 3–70).

Q&A

I do not see the word, Services. Did I do something wrong?

No. There is not enough room to display the entire name. If you wanted to see it, you could point to the right boundary of the column selector and then either drag or double-click.

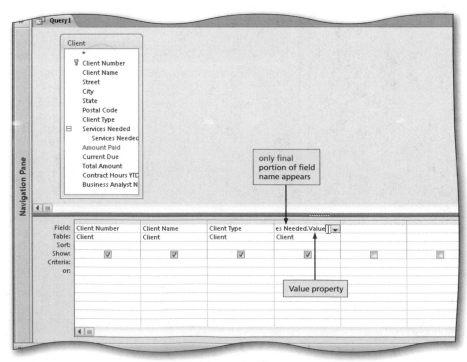

Figure 3–70

2

• View the results (Figure 3–71).

Q&A

Can I now include criteria for the multivalued field?

Yes. You could enter a criterion just like in any other query.

3

• Close the query.

• When asked if you want to save the query, click the No button.

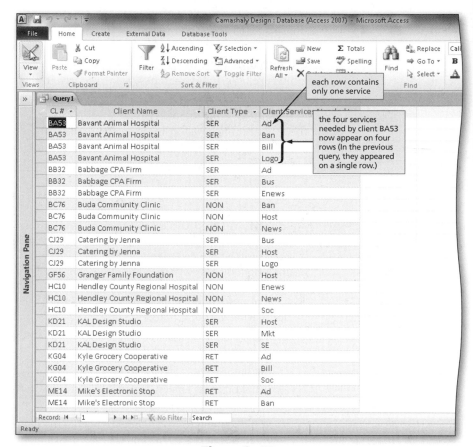

Figure 3–71

Break Point: If you wish to take a break, this is a good place to do so. You can quit Access now. To resume at a later time, start Access, open the database called Camashaly Design, and continue following the steps from this location forward.

Referential Integrity

When you have two related tables in a database, it is essential that the data in the common fields match. There should not be a client in the Client table whose business analyst number is 11, for example, unless there is a record in the Business Analyst Table whose number is 11. This restriction is enforced through **referential integrity**, which is the property that ensures that the value in a foreign key must match that of another table's primary key.

A **foreign key** is a field in one table whose values are required to match the *primary key* of another table. In the Client table, the Business Analyst Number field is a foreign key that must match the primary key of the Business Analyst Table; that is, the business analyst number for any client must be a business analyst currently in the Business Analyst Table. A client whose business analyst number is 92, for example, should not be stored because no such business analyst exists.

In Access, to specify referential integrity, you must define a relationship between the tables by using the Relationships button. Access then prohibits any updates to the database that would violate the referential integrity.

The type of relationship between two tables specified by the Relationships command is referred to as a **one-to-many relationship**. This means that *one* record in the first table is related to, or matches, *many* records in the second table, but each record in the second table is related to only *one* record in the first. In the Camashaly Design database, for example, a one-to-many relationship exists between the Business Analyst Table and the Client table. *One* business analyst is associated with *many* clients, but each client is associated with only a single business analyst. In general, the table containing the foreign key will be the *many* part of the relationship.

<table>
<tr>
<td>

Plan Ahead

</td>
<td>

Identify related tables in order to implement relationships between the tables. When specifying referential integrity, you need to decide how to handle deletions. In the relationship between clients and business analysts, for example, deletion of a business analyst for whom clients exist, such as business analyst number 14, would violate referential integrity. Any clients for business analyst 14 no longer would relate to any business analyst in the database. You can handle this in two ways. For each relationship, you need to decide which of the approaches is appropriate.

- The normal way to avoid this problem is to prohibit such a deletion.

- The other option is to **cascade the delete.** This means that Access would allow the deletion but then delete all related records. For example, it would allow the deletion of the business analyst from the Client table but then automatically delete any clients related to the deleted business analyst.

You also need to decide how to handle the update of the primary key. In the relationship between business analysts and clients, for example, changing the business analyst number for business analyst 14 to 41 in the Business Analyst Table would cause a problem because some clients in the Client table have business analyst number 14. These clients no longer would relate to any business analyst. You can handle this in two ways. For each relationship, you need to decide which of the approaches is appropriate.

- The normal way to avoid this problem is to prohibit this type of update.

- The other option is to **cascade the update.** This means to allow the change, but make the corresponding change in the foreign key on all related records. In the relationship between clients and business analysts, for example, Access would allow the update but then automatically make the corresponding change for any client whose business analyst number was 14. It now will be 41.

</td>
</tr>
</table>

To Specify Referential Integrity

The following steps use the Relationships button on the Database Tools tab to specify referential integrity by specifying a relationship between the Business Analyst and Client tables. The steps also ensure that update will cascade, but that delete will not.

1

• Click Database Tools
on the Ribbon to
display the Database
Tools tab.
(Figure 3–72).

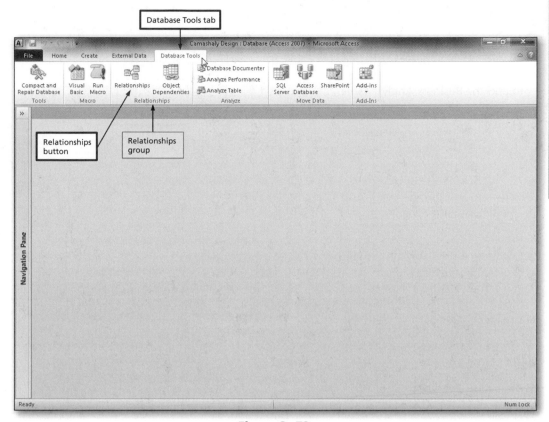

Figure 3–72

2

• Click the Relationships
button (Database Tools
tab | Relationships
group) to open the
Relationships window
and display the Show
Table dialog box
(Figure 3–73).

Figure 3–73

3

- If necessary, click the Business Analyst Table (Show Table dialog box) and then click the Add button to add the Business Analyst Table.

- Click the Client table and then click the Add button to add the Client table.

- Click the Close button (Show Table dialog box) to close the dialog box.

- Resize the field lists that appear so all fields are visible (Figure 3–74).

Q&A Do I need to resize the field lists?

No. You can use the scroll bars. Before completing the next step, however, you would need to make sure the Business Analyst Number fields in both tables appear on the screen.

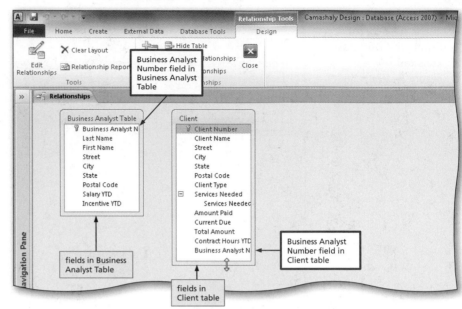

Figure 3–74

4

- Drag the Business Analyst Number field in the Business Analyst Table field list to the Business Analyst Number field in the Client table field list to display the Edit Relationships dialog box to create a relationship.

Q&A Do I actually move the field from the Business Analyst Table to the Client table?

No. The mouse pointer will change shape to indicate you are in the process of dragging, but the field does not move.

- Click the Enforce Referential Integrity check box (Edit Relationships dialog box).

- Click the Cascade Update Related Fields check box (Figure 3–75).

Q&A The Cascade check boxes were dim until I clicked the Enforce Referential Integrity check box. Is that correct?

Yes. Until you have chosen to enforce referential integrity, the cascade options are not applicable.

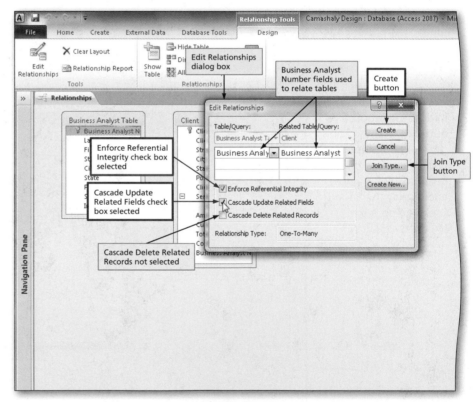

Figure 3–75

Q&A Can I change the join type like I can in queries?

Yes. Click the Join Type button in the Edit Relationships dialog box. Just as with queries, option button 1 creates an INNER join, option button 2 creates a LEFT join, and option button 3 creates a RIGHT join.

5

- Click the Create button (Edit Relationships dialog box) to complete the creation of the relationship (Figure 3–76).

Q&A | What is the symbol at the lower end of the join line?

It is the mathematical symbol for infinity. It is used here to denote the "many" end of the relationship.

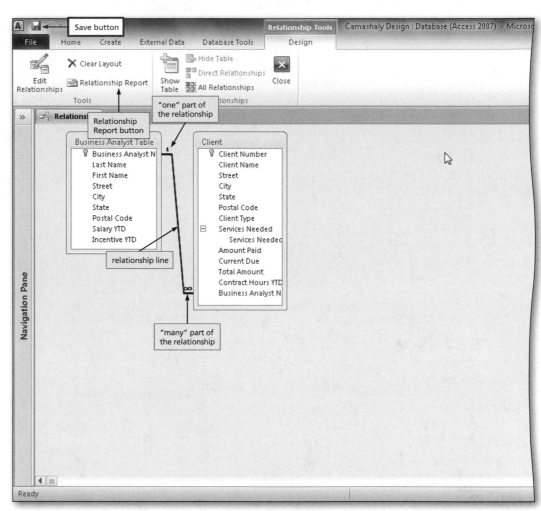

Figure 3–76

Q&A | Can I print a copy of the relationship?

Yes. Click the Relationship Report button (Relationship Tools Design tab | Tools group) to produce a report of the relationship. You can print the report. You also can save it as a report in the database for future use. If you do not want to save it, close the report after you have printed it and do not save the changes.

6

- Click the Save button on the Quick Access Toolbar to save the relationship you created.

- Close the Relationships window.

Q&A | Can I later modify the relationship if I want to change it in some way?

Yes. Click Database Tools on the Ribbon to display the Database Tools tab, and then click the Relationships button (Database Tools tab | Relationships group) to open the Relationships window. To add another table, click the Show Table button on the Design tab. To remove a table, click the Hide Table button. To edit a relationship, select the relationship and click the Edit Relationships button.

Effect of Referential Integrity

Referential integrity now exists between the Business Analyst and Client tables. Access now will reject any number in the Business Analyst Number field in the Client table that does not match a business analyst number in the Business Analyst Table. Attempting to change the business analyst number for a client to one that does not match any business analyst in the Business Analyst Table would result in the error message shown in Figure 3–77. Similarly, attempting to add a client whose business analyst number does not match would produce the same error message.

Figure 3–77

Access also will reject the deletion of a business analyst for whom related clients exist. Attempting to delete business analyst 11 from the Business Analyst Table, for example, would result in the message shown in Figure 3–78.

Figure 3–78

Access would, however, allow the change of a business analyst number in the Business Analyst Table. Then it automatically makes the corresponding change to the business analyst number for all the business analyst's clients. For example, if you changed the business analyst number of business analyst 14 to 41, the same 41 would appear in the business analyst number field for clients whose business analyst number had been 14.

To Use a Subdatasheet

Now that the Business Analyst Table is related to the Client table, it is possible to view the clients of a given business analyst when you are viewing the datasheet for the Business Analyst Table. The clients for the business analyst will appear below the business analyst in a **subdatasheet**. The availability of such a subdatasheet is indicated by a plus sign that appears in front of the rows in the Business Analyst Table. The following steps display the subdatasheet for business analyst 14.

1

- Open the Business Analyst Table in Datasheet view and close the Navigation Pane (Figure 3–79).

+ sign indicates subdatasheet available

click to display subdatasheet for analyst 14

Figure 3–79

2

- Click the plus sign in front of the row for business analyst 14 to display the subdatasheet (Figure 3–80).

Q&A How do I hide the subdatasheet when I no longer want it to appear?

When you clicked the plus sign, it changed to a minus sign. Click the minus sign.

 Experiment

- Display subdatasheets for other business analysts. Display more than one subdatasheet at a time. Remove the subdatasheets from the screen.

+ sign changed to - sign

subdatasheet for business analyst 14

click to hide subdatasheet

Figure 3–80

3

- Close the datasheet for the Business Analyst Table.

Handling Data Inconsistency

In many organizations, databases evolve and change over time. One department may create a database for its own internal use. Employees in another department may decide they need their own database containing much of the same information. For example, the Purchasing department may create a database of products that it buys and the Receiving department may create a database of products that it receives. Each department is keeping track of the same products. When the organization eventually merges the databases, they may find inconsistencies and duplication. The Find Duplicates Query Wizard and the Find Unmatched Query Wizard can assist in clearing the resulting database of duplication and errors.

TO FIND DUPLICATE RECORDS

One reason to include a primary key for a table is to eliminate duplicate records. A possibility still exists, however, that duplicate records can get into your database. The following steps illustrate how to use the Find Duplicates Query Wizard to find duplicate records.

1. Click Create on the Ribbon, and then click the Query Wizard button (Create tab | Queries group).
2. When Access displays the New Query dialog box, click the Find Duplicates Query Wizard and then click the OK button.
3. Identify the table and field or fields that might contain duplicate information.
4. Indicate any other fields you want displayed.
5. Finish the wizard to see any duplicate records.

TO FIND UNMATCHED RECORDS

Occasionally, you may want to find records in one table that have no matching records in another table. For example, you may want to determine which business analysts currently have no clients. The following steps illustrate how to find unmatched records using the Find Unmatched Query Wizard.

1. Click Create on the Ribbon, and then click the Query Wizard button (Create tab | Queries group).
2. When Access displays the New Query dialog box, click the Find Unmatched Query Wizard and then click the OK button.
3. Identify the table that might contain unmatched records and then identify the related table.
4. Indicate the fields you want displayed.
5. Finish the wizard to see any duplicate records.

Ordering Records

Normally, Access sequences the records in the Client table by client number whenever listing them because the Client Number field is the primary key. You can change this order, if desired.

To Use the Ascending Button to Order Records

To change the order in which records appear, use the Ascending or Descending buttons. Either button reorders the records based on the field in which the insertion point is located.

The following steps order the records by city using the Ascending button.

1

- Open the Client table in Datasheet view and close the Navigation Pane.

- Click the City field on the first record to select the field (Figure 3–81).

Q&A
Did I have to click the field on the first record?

No. Any other record would have worked as well.

Figure 3–81

BTW

Certification
The Microsoft Office Specialist (MOS) program provides an opportunity for you to obtain a valuable industry credential — proof that you have the Access 2010 skills required by employers. For more information, visit the Access 2010 Certification Web page (scsite.com/ac2010/cert).

②

• Click the Ascending button (Home tab | Sort & Filter group) to sort the records by City (Figure 3–82).

Q&A

What if I wanted the cities to appear in reverse alphabetical order?

Click the Descending button.

Experiment

• Sort the records by city in reverse order. When done, sort the records by city in the original order.

Figure 3–82

• Close the Client table.

• Click the No button (Microsoft Access dialog box) when asked if you want to save your changes.

> **Other Ways**
>
> 1. Right-click field name, click Sort A to Z (for ascending) or Sort Z to A (for descending)

TO USE THE ASCENDING BUTTON TO ORDER RECORDS ON MULTIPLE FIELDS

Just as you are able to sort the answer to a query on multiple fields, you also can sort the data that appears in a datasheet on multiple fields. To do so, the major and minor keys must be next to each other in the datasheet with the major key on the left. (If this is not the case, you can drag the columns into the correct position. Instead of dragging, however, usually it will be easier to use a query that has the data sorted in the desired order.)

To sort on a combination of fields where the major key is just to the left of the minor key, you would use the following steps.

1. Click the field selector at the top of the major key column to select the entire column.

2. Hold down the SHIFT key and then click the field selector for the minor key column to select both columns.

3. Click the Ascending button to sort the records.

To Quit Access

The following steps quit Access.

❶ Click the Close button on the right side of the title bar to quit Access.

❷ If a Microsoft Access dialog box appears, click the Save button to save any changes made to the object since the last save.

BTW

Quick Reference
For a table that lists how to complete the tasks covered in this book using the mouse, Ribbon, shortcut menu, and keyboard, see the Quick Reference Summary at the back of this book, or visit the Access 2010 Quick Reference Web page (scsite.com/ac2010/qr).

Chapter Summary

In this chapter you have learned how to use a form to add records to a table, search for records, delete records, filter records, create and use lookup fields, create calculated fields, create and use multivalued fields, make mass changes, create validation rules, change the appearance of a datasheet, specify referential integrity, and use subdatasheets. The items listed below include all the new Access skills you have learned in this chapter.

1. Create a Split Form (AC 142)
2. Use a Form to Add Records (AC 144)
3. Search for a Record (AC 144)
4. Update the Contents of a Record (AC 146)
5. Delete a Record (AC 147)
6. Use Filter By Selection (AC 148)
7. Toggle a Filter (AC 150)
8. Use a Common Filter (AC 150)
9. Use Filter By Form (AC 152)
10. Use Advanced Filter/Sort (AC 153)
11. Delete a Field (AC 155)
12. Add a New Field (AC 155)
13. Create a Lookup Field (AC 156)
14. Add a Calculated Field (AC 159)
15. Modify Single or Multivalued Lookup Fields (AC 161)
16. Use an Update Query (AC 162)
17. Use a Delete Query (AC 163)
18. Use an Append Query (AC 164)
19. Use a Make-Table Query (AC 165)
20. Specify a Required Field (AC 166)
21. Specify a Range (AC 166)
22. Specify a Default Value (AC 167)
23. Specify a Collection of Legal Values (AC 167)
24. Specify a Format (AC 168)
25. Change the Contents of a Field (AC 170)
26. Use a Lookup Field (AC 171)
27. Use a Multivalued Lookup Field (AC 172)
28. Update a Form to Reflect the Changes in the Table (AC 174)
29. Update a Report to Reflect the Changes in the Table (AC 175)
30. Include Totals in a Datasheet (AC 177)
31. Remove Totals from a Datasheet (AC 179)
32. Change Gridlines in a Datasheet (AC 180)
33. Change the Colors and Font in a Datasheet (AC 181)
34. Query a Multivalued Field Showing Multiple Values on a Single Row (AC 183)
35. Query a Multivalued Field Showing Multiple Values on Multiple Rows (AC 184)
36. Specify Referential Integrity (AC 186)
37. Use a Subdatasheet (AC 191)
38. Find Duplicate Records (AC 193)
39. Find Unmatched Records (AC 193)
40. Use the Ascending Button to Order Records (AC 194)
41. Use the Ascending Button to Order Records on Multiple Fields (AC 195)

 If you have a SAM 2010 user profile, your instructor may have assigned an autogradable version of this assignment. If so, log into the SAM 2010 Web site at www.cengage.com/sam2010 to download the instruction and start files.

Learn It Online

Test your knowledge of chapter content and key terms.

Instructions: To complete the Learn It Online exercises, start your browser, click the Address bar, and then enter the Web address `scsite.com/ac2010/learn`. When the Access 2010 Learn It Online page is displayed, click the link for the exercise you want to complete and then read the instructions.

Chapter Reinforcement TF, MC, and SA
A series of true/false, multiple choice, and short answer questions that test your knowledge of the chapter content.

Flash Cards
An interactive learning environment where you identify chapter key terms associated with displayed definitions.

Practice Test
A series of multiple choice questions that test your knowledge of chapter content and key terms.

Who Wants To Be a Computer Genius?
An interactive game that challenges your knowledge of chapter content in the style of a television quiz show.

Wheel of Terms
An interactive game that challenges your knowledge of chapter key terms in the style of the television show *Wheel of Fortune*.

Crossword Puzzle Challenge
A crossword puzzle that challenges your knowledge of key terms presented in the chapter.

Apply Your Knowledge

Reinforce the skills and apply the concepts you learned in this chapter.

Specifying Validation Rules, Updating Records, Formatting a Datasheet, and Creating Relationships
Instructions: Start Access. Open the Babbage CPA Firm database that you modified in Apply Your Knowledge in Chapter 2 on page AC 129. (If you did not complete this exercise, see your instructor for a copy of the modified database.)

Perform the following tasks:
1. Open the Client table in Design view, as shown in Figure 3–83 on page AC 198.
2. Format the Client Number field so any lowercase letters appear in uppercase and make the Client Name field a required field.
3. Specify that balance due amounts must be between $0 and $1,200. Include validation text.
4. Save the changes to the Client table.
5. Create a split form for the Client table and find the record for M26 and change the customer name to Mohr Craft Supplies.
6. Use the form to add the following record:

| L50 | Lou's Salon | 124 Fulton | Granger | 27036 | $0.00 | $325.00 | 38 |

Continued >

Apply Your Knowledge *continued*

Figure 3–83

7. Save the form as Client Split Form and close the form.

8. Open the Client table in Datasheet view and use Filter By Selection to find the record for H21. Delete the record. Remove the filter.

9. Add totals to the datasheet for the Amount Paid and Balance Due fields. Remove the gridlines from the datasheet.

10. Save the changes to the layout of the table. Close the Client table.

11. Establish referential integrity between the Bookkeeper table (the one table) and the Client table (the many table). Cascade the update but do not cascade the delete. Create a relationship report for the relationship. Save the report with the default report name Relationships for Babbage CPA Firm.

12. Submit the revised database in the format specified by your instructor.

Extend Your Knowledge

Extend the skills you learned in this chapter and experiment with new skills. You may need to use Help to complete the assignment.

Creating Action Queries and Changing Table Properties

Instructions: See the inside back cover of this book for instructions for downloading the Data Files for Students, or see your instructor for information on accessing the required files.

Generic Temp Services is a company that specializes in placing temporary workers in various administrative positions. Philamar Training has been approached about buying Generic Temp Services. Philamar is interested in knowing how many clients the companies have in common. Generic also needs to do some database maintenance by finding duplicates and finding unmatched records.

Perform the following tasks:

1. Open the Generic Temp Services database. Create and run a make-table query to create the Potential Clients table in the Generic Temp Services database shown in Figure 3–84. Save the query as Make Table Query.

Client Name	Street	City	Postal Code
Afton Manufac	612 Revere	Granger	27036
Atlas Distribut	227 Dandelion	Burles	28817
Blake-Scryps	557 Maum	Georgetown	28794
Dege Grocery C	446 Linton	Burles	28817
Grandston Clea	337 Abelard	Buda	27032
Hill Country Sh	247 Fulton	Granger	27036
Jones Plumbin	75 Getty	Buda	27032
Mohr Art Suppl	665 Maum	Georgetown	28794
SeeSaw Indust	31 Liatris	Walburg	28819
Tate Repair	824 Revere	Granger	27036
Woody Sportin	578 Central	Walburg	28819
Catering by Jer	123 Second	Granger	27036

Figure 3–84

2. Open the Potential Clients table, change the font size to 14, and resize the columns to best fit the data.

3. Save the changes to the layout of the table. Close the table.

4. Use the Find Duplicates Query Wizard to find duplicate information in the City field. Include the Client Name field in the query. Name the query City Duplicates Query. Close the query.

5. Use the Find Unmatched Query Wizard to find all records in the Worker table that do not match records in the Client table. Worker Number is the common field in both tables. Include the Worker Number, Last Name, and First Name in the query. Name the query Worker Unmatched Query. Close the query.

6. Submit the revised database in the format specified by your instructor.

Make It Right

Analyze a database and correct all errors and/or improve the design.

Correcting Table Design Errors

Instructions: Start Access. Open the Senior Jobbers database. See the inside back cover of this book for instructions for downloading the Data Files for Students, or see your instructor for information on accessing the required files.

Perform the following tasks:

Senior Jobbers provides a variety of small repairs and maintenance to homeowners. The owner of Senior Jobbers has decided that he could better manage the business if he added a multivalued field that lists the various types of repairs and maintenance that customers request. He created the field shown in Figure 3–85 but forgot to add Clean Gutters as one of the job types. Modify the multivalued lookup field to include Clean Gutters as a job type. By mistake, the owner also added the contact number field shown in Figure 3–85 to the Customer table. That field should be deleted.

Figure 3–85

Finally, he wanted to add referential integrity between the Worker table and the Customer table. The relationship shown in Figure 3–86 is not correct and must be fixed. The owner does not want to cascade the update or the delete.

Figure 3–86

Submit the revised database in the format specified by your instructor.

In the Lab

Design, create, modify, and/or use a database following the guidelines, concepts, and skills presented in this chapter. Labs 1, 2, and 3 are listed in order of increasing difficulty.

Lab 1: Maintaining the ECO Clothesline Database

Problem: ECO Clothesline is expanding rapidly and needs to make some database changes to handle the expansion. The company needs to know more about its customers, such as the type of business, and it needs to ensure that data that is entered is valid. It also needs to update the records in the database. Use the database modified in the In the Lab 1 of Chapter 2 on page AC 132 for this assignment, or see your instructor for information on accessing the files required for this book.

Perform the following tasks:

1. Open the ECO Clothesline database and then open the Customer table in Design view.

2. Add a Lookup field, Customer Type, to the Customer table. The field should appear after the Postal Code field. The field will contain data on the type of customer. The customer types are SAL (Salons, Studios, Fitness Clubs), SPG (Sporting Goods), and WMN (Women's Wear). Save these changes to the structure.

Continued >

3. Using a query, change all the entries in the Customer Type column to WMN. Save the query as Customer Type Update Query.

4. Open the Customer table and make the following changes. You can use either the Find button or Filter By Selection to locate the records to change:

    a. Change the customer type for customers CY12, FN19, LB20, RD03, TT21, and TW56 to SAL.

    b. Change the customer type for customer WS34 to SPG.

    c. Change the name of customer LB20 to Le Beauty Salon & Spa.

5. Change the alternate background color on the datasheet to white and remove the vertical gridlines. Save the changes to the layout of the table.

6. Create the following validation rules for the Customer table and save the changes.

    a. Specify the legal values SAL, SPT, and WMN for the Customer Type field. Include validation text.

    b. Assign a default value of WMN to the Customer Type field.

    c. Ensure that any letters entered in the Customer Number field appear as uppercase.

    d. Make Customer Name a required field.

7. Open the Customer table and use Filter By Form to find all records where the customer is located in Lowton and has a customer type of WMN, and then delete these records.

8. ECO Clothesline has signed up a sporting goods store, Ralph's (Customer Number RA21) and needs to add the record to the Customer table. Ralph's is at 72 Main in Lowton, TN 37084. Terry Sinson is the sales rep assigned to the account. To date, Ralph's has not been billed nor does the company owe for any services. Create a split form for the Customer table and use this split form to add the record. Save the split form as Customer Split Form.

9. Specify referential integrity between the Sales Rep table (the one table) and the Customer table (the many table). Cascade the update but not the delete.

10. Add the Customer Type field to the Customer Balance Report. The field should follow the Customer Name field. Save the changes to the report.

11. Submit the revised database in the format specified by your instructor.

In the Lab

Lab 2: Maintaining the Walburg Energy Alternatives Database

Problem: The management of the Walburg Energy Alternatives recently acquired some items from a store that is going out of business. You now need to append these new items to the current item table. You also need to change the database structure and add some validation rules to the database.

Use the database modified in the In the Lab 2 of Chapter 2 on page AC 134 for this assignment. You also will use the More Items database from the Data Files for Students. See the inside back cover of this book for instructions for downloading the Data Files for Students, or see your instructor for information on accessing the required files.

Perform the following tasks:

1. Open the More Items database from the Data Files for Students.

2. Create a new query for the Item table and add all fields to the query.

3. Using an append query, append all records in the More Items database to the Item table in the Walburg Energy Alternatives database, as shown in Figure 3–87.

Figure 3–87

4. Save the append query as Walburg Append Query and close the More Items database.

5. Open the Walburg Energy Alternatives database and then open the Item table in Datasheet view. There should be 20 records in the table.

6. The items added from the More Items database do not have a vendor assigned to them. Assign items 1234 and 2234 to vendor JM. Assign item 2216 to vendor AS. Assign items 2310 and 2789 to vendor SD.

7. Create an advanced filter for the Item table. The filter should display records with fewer than 10 items on hand and be sorted in ascending order by Description. Save the filter settings as a query and name the filter Reorder Filter.

8. Make the following changes to the Item table:

   a. Change the field size for the On Hand field to Integer. The Format should be fixed and the decimal places should be 0.

   b. Make Description a required field.

   c. Specify that the number on hand must be between 0 and 50. Include validation text.

   d. Add a calculated field Inventory Value (On Hand*Cost) following the Cost field. Format the field as currency.

9. Save the changes to the table design. If a dialog box appears indicating that some data may be lost, click the Yes button.

10. Add the Inventory Value field to the Inventory Status Report. Place the field after the Cost field. Save the changes to the report.

11. Specify referential integrity between the Vendor table (the one table) and the Item table (the many table). Cascade the update but not the delete.

12. Submit the revised More Items database and the Walburg Energy Alternatives database in the format specified by your instructor.

In the Lab

Lab 3: Maintaining the Philamar Training Database

Problem: Philamar Training is expanding rapidly and needs to make some database changes to handle the expansion. The company needs to know more about its clients, such as the type of business and the training services needed. You also are to add validation rules and update records in the database.

Use the Philamar Training database modified in the In the Lab 3 of Chapter 2 on page AC 135 for this assignment, or see your instructor for information on accessing the files required for this book. Submit the revised database in the format specified by your instructor.

Instructions Part 1: Several changes must be made to the database structure. For example, management would like a lookup field, Client Type, added to the Client table. The field should appear after the Postal Code field. The field will contain data on the type of client. The client types are MAN (Manufacturing), RET (Retail), and SER (Service). Philamar also needs a multivalued field that lists the general type of computer training of interest to each client. This knowledge can help Philamar better meet the needs of their clients. Add the field following the Client Type field. Table 3–2 lists the training abbreviations and descriptions that management would like in a Training Needed multivalued field.

Table 3–2 Training Abbreviations and Descriptions

Training Abbreviation	Description
APP	Application Software
HRD	Hardware
LAN	Local Area Networks
SEC	Security
WEB	Internet and World Wide Web
WIN	Windows

Management wants to ensure that an entry always appears in the Client Name field and that any letters entered in the Client Number field appear in uppercase. It also requires that the amount in the Current Due field is never less than 0 or greater than $5,000. The only values in the Client Type field are MAN, SER, and RET. Most clients are manufacturing organizations. Make the changes to the database structure.

Instructions Part 2: Use a query to assign the client type MAN to all records in the Client table. Save the query as Update Query. Clients EU28 and FI28 are retail organizations. Clients CE16, HN83, and PS82 are service organizations. The data for the Training Needed field shown in Figure 3–88 must be added to the database. The address for PRIM Staffing is incorrect. It should be 727 Crestview. Hurley National is really Hurley National Bank. A new retail organization, Ralph's, just became a Philamar client. The address for the store is 42 Main, Crumville, TX 76745. Ralph's is interested in application software and Windows training.

Management wants to use RA10 as the client number and Marty Danville as the trainer. The new client has not yet received any training and does not owe any money to Philamar.

CL #	Client Name	Training Needed
BS27	Blant and Sons	HRD, LAN, SEC
CE16	Center Services	APP, WEB, WIN
CP27	Calder Plastics	LAN, SEC, WEB
EU28	Elba's Furniture	APP, SEC, WEB
FI28	Farrow-Idsen	APP, WEB
FL93	Fairland Lawn	LAN, SEC, WEB
HN83	Hurley National Bank	APP, WIN
MC28	Morgan-Alyssa	HRD, LAN
PS82	PRIM Staffing	APP, WEB, WIN
RA10	Ralph's	APP, WIN
TE26	Telton-Edwards	SEC

Figure 3–88

Instructions Part 3: Management wants to make sure that clients are not assigned to a trainer who is not in the database. It also wants the ability to change a trainer number in the Trainer table and have the change applied to the Client table. Create the appropriate relationship that would satisfy management's needs.

Cases and Places

Apply your creative thinking and problem solving skills to design and implement a solution.

See the inside back cover of this book for instructions for downloading the Data Files for Students, or see your instructor for information on accessing the required files.

1: Maintaining the Chamber of Commerce Database

Academic

Use the Chamber of Commerce database you modified in Cases and Places 1 in Chapter 2 on page AC 135 for this assignment. Use the concepts and techniques presented in this chapter to modify the database as follows:

1. The chamber would like to categorize the businesses that advertise in the guide as retail, dining, or service establishments. These three types are the only valid category types. Most businesses are retail businesses.

2. Advertisers A228, C135, G346, H123, K109, M321, T167, and W456 are retail establishments. Advertisers C048, C234, D217, N007, and P124 are service establishments. The remaining advertisers are dining establishments.

3. An entry should always appear in the Advertiser Name field and any letters in the Advertiser Number field should appear in uppercase.

4. Chloe's Salon has changed its name to Chloe's Salon and Spa.

Continued >

Cases and Places *continued*

5. AAA Diner is a new restaurant in town and wants to advertise in the guide. Assign the Advertiser Number A245 to AAA Diner. The restaurant is located at 23 Berton, the postal code is 19363, and the telephone number is 555-0998. It has not yet made a payment and the balance is $75.00. Lars Tolbert is the ad rep.

6. Specify referential integrity. Cascade the update but not the delete.

7. Change the ad rep number for ad rep 26 to 22.

Submit the revised database in the format specified by your instructor.

2: Maintaining the Consignment Database

Personal

Use the Consignment database you modified in Cases and Places 2 in Chapter 2 on page AC 136 for this assignment. Use the concepts and techniques presented in this chapter to modify the database as follows:

1. Make the Condition field a lookup field. Only the current values in the database should be legal values. Most items are in good condition.

2. Update descriptions: A better description for the recliner is Leather Recliner. A better description for the bar stools is Kitchen Counter Stools.

3. The clothes hamper has been sold.

4. The minimum price of any item is $2.

5. The Description field always should contain data.

6. It would be easier to find items for sale if the default sort order for the Items table was by Description rather than by Item Number. Also, all descriptions should be displayed completely in Datasheet view.

7. Add the Condition field to the Available Items Report you created in Chapter 1. The field should follow the Description field. All descriptions should display completely.

8. Specify referential integrity. Cascade the delete but not the update.

Submit the revised database in the format specified by your instructor.

3: Maintaining the Senior Care Database

Professional

Use the Senior Care database you modified in Cases and Places 3 in Chapter 2 on page AC 136 for this assignment. Use the concepts and techniques presented in this chapter to modify the database as follows:

1. Senior Care could better serve its clients by adding a field that would list the type of services each client needs. Table 3–3 lists the service abbreviations and descriptions that should appear in the field.

Table 3–3 Service Abbreviations and Descriptions	
Service Abbreviation	**Description**
Bill	Bill/Mail/Correspondence Help
Cmp	Companionship
Hskp	Light Housekeeping
Hyg	Hygiene Assistance
Meal	Meal Planning/Preparation
Tran	Transportation/Errands

2. Add the data for this multivalued field shown in Figure 3–89 to the database.

3. This multivalued field also should appear in the Client Report you created in Chapter 1.

4. Senior Care is having trouble finding helpers willing to help with hygiene. Query the Client table to find all clients who require hygiene assistance. Save the query as Hygiene Needs Query.

5. Mike Preston has moved to assisted living and is no longer a client of Senior Care. Use Find or Filter By Selection to delete this record.

6. An entry should always appear in the client first and last name fields. Any letters in the Client Number field should appear in uppercase.

7. Specify referential integrity. Cascade the update but not the delete.

Client Number	Last Name	First Name	Services Needed
AB10	Alvarez	Francine	Bill, Cmp, Meal
BR18	Breeton	Alex	Hskp, Hyg
CH21	Chalmer	Ben	Cmp, Tran
FE47	Ferber	Jane	Cmp
GM50	Gammon	Fred	Hskp
HA15	Hammond	Lois	Bill, Hskp, Meal
HJ05	Heijer	Bill	Hyg, Tran
KL10	Klinger	Cynthia	Hskp, Meal
LA75	Last	Bill	Hyg, Tran
MA24	Manchester	Liz	Cmp, Tran
SA23	Santoro	Maria	Bill, Meal, Tran
TH41	Thomas	Albert	Bill, Tran
TR35	Trent	Jerry	Hskp, Hyg
WI87	Width	Evelyn	Cmp, Meal

Figure 3–89

Submit the revised database in the format specified by your instructor.

4 | Creating Reports and Forms

Objectives

You will have mastered the material in this chapter when you can:

- Create reports and forms using wizards
- Modify reports and forms in Layout view
- Group and sort in a report
- Add totals and subtotals to a report
- Conditionally format controls
- Resize columns
- Filter records in reports and forms

- Print reports and forms
- Apply themes
- Add a field to a report or form
- Include gridlines
- Add a date
- Change the format of a control
- Move controls
- Create and print mailing labels

4 | Creating Reports and Forms

BTW

Q&As
For a complete list of the Q&As found in many of the step-by-step sequences in this book, visit the Access 2010 Q&A Web page (scsite.com/ac2010/qa).

Introduction

One of the advantages to maintaining data in a database is the ability to present the data in attractive reports and forms that highlight certain information. Reports present specific data in an organized format that is usually printed. The data can come from one or more tables. You usually view forms on the screen, although you can print them. You often use forms to view specific data. You may use them to update data. Like reports, the data in the form can come from one or more tables. This chapter shows how to create reports and forms by creating two reports and a form. There are several ways to create both reports and forms. The most common is to use the Report or Form Wizard to create an initial report or form. If the layout created by the wizard is satisfactory, you are done. If not, you can use either Layout view or Design view to customize the report or form. In this chapter, you will use Layout view for this purpose. In later chapters, you will learn how to use Design view. You also will use the Label Wizard to produce mailing labels.

Project — Reports and Forms

Camashaly Design has realized several benefits from using the database of clients and analysts. Camashaly hopes to realize additional benefits using two custom reports that meet their specific needs. Figure 4–1 shows the first report, which is a modified version

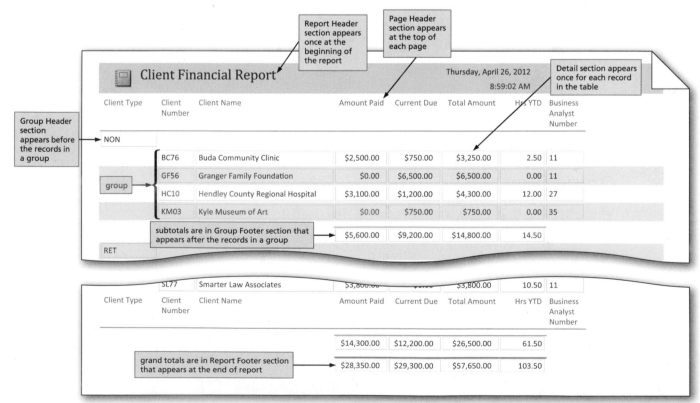

Figure 4–1

of an existing report. The report features grouping. The report shown in Figure 4–1 groups records by client types. There are three separate groups, one each for the three possible client types: NON, RET, and SER. The appropriate type appears before each group. The totals of the Amount Paid, Current Due, Total Amount, and Hrs YTD fields for the clients in the group (called a **subtotal**) appear after the group. At the end of the report are grand totals of the same fields.

Figure 4–2 shows the first page of the second report. This report encompasses data from both the Business Analyst Table and the Client table. Like the report in Figure 4–1, the data is grouped, although this time it is grouped by analyst number. Not only does the analyst number appear before each group, but the first name and last name of the analyst appear as well. Like the first report, this report contains subtotals.

Clients by Analyst

BA #	First Name	Last Name	CL #	Client Name	Amount Paid	Current Due
11	Cordelia	Kerry				
			BA53	Bavant Animal Hospital	$0.00	$7,500.00
			BC76	Buda Community Clinic	$2,500.00	$750.00
			GF56	Granger Family Foundation	$0.00	$6,500.00
			KG04	Kyle Grocery Cooperative	$3,200.00	$0.00
			SL77	Smarter Law Associates	$3,800.00	$0.00
Summary for 'Business Analyst Number' = 11 (5 detail records)						
Sum					$9,500.00	$14,750.00
14	Manuel	Martinez				
			BB32	Babbage CPA Firm	$1,500.00	$500.00
			KD21	KAL Design Studio	$6,000.00	$3,200.00
Summary for 'Business Analyst Number' = 14 (2 detail records)						
Sum					$7,500.00	$3,700.00
27	Jan	Liu				
			CJ29	Catering by Jenna	$3,000.00	$1,000.00
			HC10	Hendley County Regional Hospital	$3,100.00	$1,200.00
			ME14	Mike's Electronic Stop	$2,500.00	$1,500.00
			PJ34	Patricia Jean Florist	$0.00	$5,200.00
			TB17	The Bikeshop	$2,750.00	$1,200.00
Summary for 'Business Analyst Number' = 27 (5 detail records)						
Sum					$11,350.00	$10,100.00
35	Jeff	Scott				
			KM03	Kyle Museum of Art	$0.00	$750.00
BA #	First Name	Last Name	CL #	Client Name	Amount Paid	Current Due
Summary for 'Business Analyst Number' = 35 (1 detail record)						
Sum					$0.00	$750.00
Grand Total					$28,350.00	$29,300.00

Figure 4–2

Camashaly also wants to improve the data entry process by using a custom form, as shown in Figure 4–3. The form has a title and a date. It does not contain all the fields in the Client table, and the fields are in a different order than in the table. For this form, Camashaly likes the appearance of including the fields in a grid.

Figure 4–3

BTWs

For a complete list of the BTWs found in the margins of this book, visit the Access 2010 BTW Web page (scsite.com/ac2010/btw).

Camashaly also wants to be able to produce mailing labels for its clients. These labels must align correctly with the particular labels Camashaly uses and must be sorted by postal code (Figure 4–4).

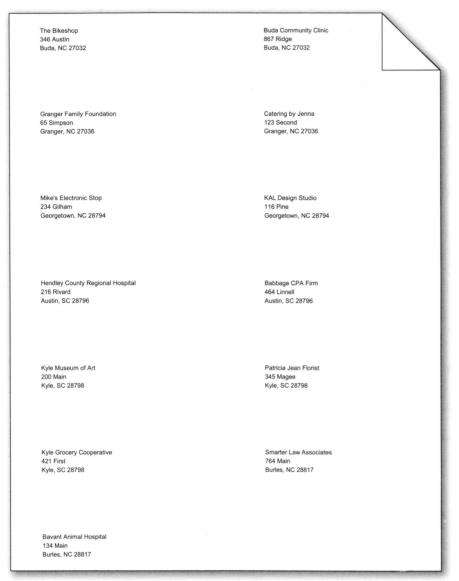

The Bikeshop
346 Austin
Buda, NC 27032

Buda Community Clinic
867 Ridge
Buda, NC 27032

Granger Family Foundation
65 Simpson
Granger, NC 27036

Catering by Jenna
123 Second
Granger, NC 27036

Mike's Electronic Stop
234 Gilham
Georgetown, NC 28794

KAL Design Studio
116 Pine
Georgetown, NC 28794

Hendley County Regional Hospital
216 Rivard
Austin, SC 28796

Babbage CPA Firm
464 Linnell
Austin, SC 28796

Kyle Museum of Art
200 Main
Kyle, SC 28798

Patricia Jean Florist
345 Magee
Kyle, SC 28798

Kyle Grocery Cooperative
421 First
Kyle, SC 28798

Smarter Law Associates
764 Main
Burles, NC 28817

Bavant Animal Hospital
134 Main
Burles, NC 28817

Figure 4–4

Overview

As you read this chapter, you will learn how to create reports and forms by performing these general tasks:

- Use Layout view to modify an existing report.
- Group and sort the report in Layout view.
- Add totals and subtotals to the report.
- Conditionally format a control.
- Filter records in the report.
- Use the Report Wizard to create a report on the Business Analyst and Client tables.
- Add a field to the report and include totals.
- Use the Form Wizard to create a form on the Client table.
- Include gridlines and a date in the form.
- Add a field to the form.
- Filter and sort records in the form.
- Create mailing labels.

Plan Ahead

Report and Form Design Guidelines

When creating reports and forms, you must identify the intended usage, audience, content, and formatting. To design reports and forms, you should follow these general guidelines:

1. **Determine whether the data should be presented in a report or a form.** Do you intend to print the data? If so, a report would be the appropriate choice. Do you intend to view the data on the screen? If so, a form would be the appropriate choice. Is the user going to update data? If so, a form would be the appropriate choice.

2. **Determine the intended audience for the report or form.** Who will use the report or form? Will the report or form be used by individuals external to the organization? For example, many government agencies require reports from organizations. If so, government regulations will dictate the report requirements. If the report is for internal use, the user will have specific requirements based on the intended use. The data required for a report or form depends on its use. Adding unnecessary data to a report or form can make the form or report unreadable. Include only data necessary for the intended use. What level of detail do they need? Reports used in day-to-day operations need more detail than weekly or monthly reports requested by management.

3. **Determine the tables that contain the data needed for the report or form.** Is all the data found in a single table, or does it come from multiple related tables?

4. **Determine the fields that should appear on the report or form.** What data items does the user of the report or form need?

5. **Determine the organization of the report or form.** In what order should the fields appear? How should they be arranged? Should the records in a report be grouped in some way?

6. **Determine the format of the report or form.** What should be in the report or form header? Do you want a title and date, for example? Do you want a logo? What should be in the body of the report and form? What should the style be? In other words, determine the visual characteristics that the various portions of the report or form should have.

7. **Review the report or form after it has been in operation to determine whether any changes are necessary.** Is the order of the fields still appropriate? Are any additional fields required?

8. **For mailing labels, determine the contents, order, and type of label.** What fields should appear on the label? How should they be arranged? Is there a certain order (for example, by postal code) in which the labels should be printed? Who is the manufacturer of the labels and what is the style number for the labels? What are the dimensions for each label? How many labels print across a page?

When necessary, more specific details concerning the above decisions and/or actions are presented at appropriate points in the chapter. The chapter also will identify the actions performed and decisions made regarding these guidelines in the design of the reports, forms, and labels such as those shown in Figures 4–1, 4–2, 4–3, and 4–4.

Consider Your Audience Always design reports and forms with your audience in mind. Make your reports and forms accessible to individuals who may have problems with color blindness or reduced vision.

To Start Access

The following steps, which assume Windows 7 is running, start Access based on a typical installation. You may need to ask your instructor how to start Access for your computer.

1 Click the Start button on the Windows 7 taskbar to display the Start menu.

2 Type **Microsoft Access** as the search text in the 'Search programs and files' text box and watch the search results appear on the Start menu.

3 Click Microsoft Access 2010 in the search results on the Start menu to start Access.

4 If the Access window is not maximized, click the Maximize button next to the Close button on its title bar to maximize the window.

To Open a Database from Access

The following steps open the Camashaly database from the Access folder in the CIS 101 folder on the USB flash drive.

1 With your USB flash drive connected to one of the computer's USB ports, click File on the Ribbon to open the Backstage view.

2 Click Open in the Backstage view to display the Open dialog box.

3 Navigate to the location of the file to be opened (in this case, the USB flash drive, then to the CIS 101 folder [or your class folder], and then to the Access folder).

4 Click Camashaly Design to select the file to be opened.

5 Click the Open button (Open dialog box) to open the selected file and display the opened database in the Access window.

6 If a Security Warning appears, click the Enable Content button.

BTW

The Ribbon and Screen Resolution
Access may change how the groups and buttons within the groups appear on the Ribbon, depending on the computer's screen resolution. Thus, your Ribbon may look different from the ones in this book if you are using a screen resolution other than 1024 × 768.

Report Creation

Unless you want a report that simply lists all the fields and all the records in a table, the simplest way to create a report design is to use the Report Wizard. In some cases, the Report Wizard can produce exactly the desired report. Other times, however, you first must use the Report Wizard to produce a report that is as close as possible to the desired report. Then, use Layout view to modify the report and transform it into the correct report. In either case, once you have created and saved the report, you can print it whenever you need to. Access will use the current data in the database for the report, formatting and arranging it in exactly the way you specified when you created the report.

Determine the tables and fields that contain the data needed for the report.
If you determine that data should be presented as a report, you then need to determine what tables and fields contain the data for the report. The following guidelines apply to this decision.

- **Examine the requirements for the report in general to determine the tables.** Do the requirements only relate to data in a single table, or does the data come from multiple tables? What is the relationship between the tables?

- **Examine the specific requirements for the report to determine the fields necessary.** Look for all the data items specified for the report. Each should correspond to a field in a table or be able to be computed from fields in a table. This information gives you the list of fields to include.

- **Determine the order of the fields.** Examine the requirements to determine the order in which the fields should appear. Be logical and consistent in your ordering. For example, in an address, the city should come before the state and the state should come before the postal code, unless there is some compelling reason for another order.

Plan Ahead

Using Layout View in a Report

When working with a report in Access, there are four different ways to view the report: Report view, Print Preview, Layout view, and Design view. Report view shows the report on the screen. Print Preview shows the report as it will appear when printed. Layout view is similar to Report view in that it shows the report on the screen, but it also allows you to make changes to the report. It is usually the easiest way to make such changes. Design view also allows you to make changes, but it does not show you the actual report. It is most useful when the changes you need to make are especially complex. In this chapter, you will use Layout view to modify the report.

Understanding Report Sections

A report is divided into various sections to help clarify the presentation of data. In Design view, which you will use in later chapters, the sections are labeled on the screen. Even though they are not labeled in Layout view, it is still useful to understand the purpose of the various sections. A typical report consists of a Report Header section, Page Header section, Detail section, Page Footer section, and Report Footer section (see Figure 4–1).

The contents of the Report Header section print once at the beginning of the report. In the Client Financial Report, the title is in the Report Header section. The contents of the Report Footer section print once at the end of the report. In the Client Financial Report, the Report Footer section contains the grand totals of Amount Paid, Current Due, Total Amount, and Hrs YTD. The contents of the Page Header section print once at the top of each page and typically contain the column headers. The contents of the Page Footer section print once at the bottom of each page and often contain a date and a page number. The contents of the Detail section print once for each record in the table; for example, once for Buda Community Clinic, once for Granger Family Foundation, and so on. In this report, they contain the client number, client name, amount paid, current due, total amount, hrs YTD, and business analyst number.

When the data in a report is grouped, there are two additional sections. The contents of the Group Header section are printed before the records in a particular group, and the contents of the Group Footer section are printed after the group. In the Client Financial Report, the Group Header section contains the Client Type, and the Group Footer section contains subtotals of Amount Paid, Current Due, Total Amount, and Hrs YTD.

Plan Ahead

> **Determine the organization of the report or form.**
> Determine various details concerning how the data in your report or form is to be organized.
>
> • **Determine sort order.** Is there a special order in which the records should appear?
>
> • **Determine grouping.** Should the records be grouped in some fashion? If so, what should appear before the records in a group? If, for example, clients are grouped by city, the name of the city should probably appear before the group. What should appear after the group? For example, are there some fields for which subtotals should be calculated? If so, the subtotals would come after the group. Determine whether you need multiple levels of grouping.

To Group and Sort in a Report

Camashaly has determined that the records in the report should be grouped by client type. That is, all the clients of a given type should appear together immediately after the type. Within the clients in a given type, the clients are to be ordered by client number. In Layout view of the report, you can specify both grouping and sorting by using the Group & Sort button on the Design tab. The following steps open the Client Financial Report in Layout view and then specify both grouping and sorting in the report.

1

- Right-click the Client Financial Report in the Navigation Pane to produce a shortcut menu.

- Click Layout View on the shortcut menu to open the report in Layout view.

- Close the Navigation Pane.

- If a field list appears, close the field list by clicking the Add Existing Fields button (Report Layout Tools Design tab | Tools group).

- Click the Group & Sort button (Report Layout Tools Design tab | Grouping & Totals group) to display the Group, Sort, and Total pane (Figure 4–5).

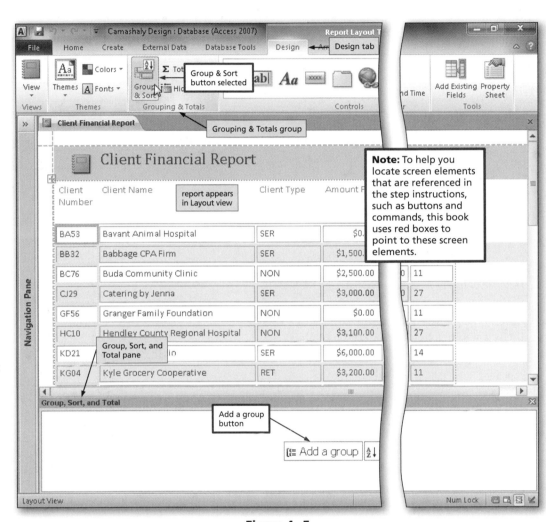

Figure 4–5

2

- Click the 'Add a group' button to add a group (Figure 4–6).

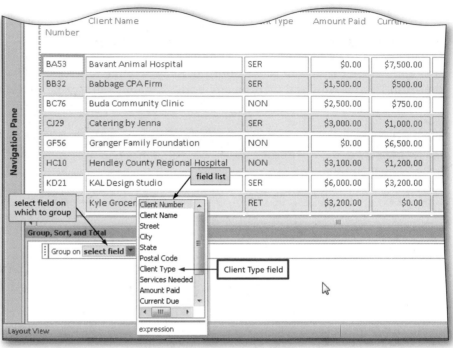

Figure 4–6

3

- Click the Client Type field in the field list to select a field for grouping and group the records on the selected field (Figure 4–7).

Q&A Does the field on which I group have to be the first field?

No. If you select a field other than the first field, Access will move the field you select into the first position.

Figure 4–7

4

• Click the 'Add a sort' button to add a sort (Figure 4–8).

Figure 4–8

5

• Click the Client Number field in the field list to specify the field on which the records in each group will be sorted (Figure 4–9).

I thought the report would be sorted by Client Type, because I chose to group on that field. What is the effect of choosing to sort by Client Number?

This sort takes place within groups. You are specifying that within the list of clients of the same type, the clients will be ordered by client number.

Figure 4–9

Other Ways

1. Right-click column header for field on which to group, click Group On (field name)

BTW

Grouping
You should allow sufficient white space between groups. If you feel the amount is insufficient, you can add more space by enlarging the group header or group footer.

Grouping and Sorting Options

For both grouping and sorting, you can click the More button to specify additional options (see Figure 4–10). The options you then could select are:

- Value. You can choose the amount of the value on which to group. Typically, you would group by the entire value, for example, the entire city name. You could choose, however, to only group on the first character, in which case all clients in cities that begin with the same letter would be considered a group. You also could group by the first two characters or by a custom number of characters.

- Totals. You can choose the values to be totaled. You can specify whether the totals are to appear in the group header or in the group footer and whether there is to be a grand total. You can also choose whether to show group totals as a percentage of the grand total.

- Title. You can customize the group title.

- Header section. You can include or omit a header section for the group.

- Footer section. You can include or omit a footer section for the group.

Figure 4–10

- Keep together. You can indicate whether Access is to attempt to keep portions of a group together on the same page. The default setting does not keep portions of a group together, but you can specify that Access should attempt to keep a whole group together on one page. If the group will not fit on the remainder of the page, Access will move the group header and the records in a group to the next page. Finally, you can choose to have Access keep the header and the first record together on one page. If the header would fit at the bottom of a page, but there would not be room for the first record, Access will move the header to the next page.

Understanding Report Controls

The various objects on a report are called **controls**. The report title, column headers, contents of various fields, subtotals, and so on are all contained in controls. When working in Layout view, as you will do in this chapter, Access handles details concerning these controls for you automatically. When working in Design view, you will see and manipulate the controls. Even when working in Layout view, however, it is useful to understand the concepts of controls.

The report has a control containing the title, Client Financial Report. Also included is a control containing each column header (Client Type, Client Number, Client Name, Amount Paid, Current Due, Total Amount, Hrs YTD, and Business Analyst Number). A control in the Group Header section displays the client type. There are four controls in the Group Footer section: One control displays the subtotal of Amount Paid, a second displays the subtotal of Current Due, a third displays the subtotal of Total Amount, and the fourth displays the subtotal of Hrs YTD. The Detail section has controls containing the client number, client name, amount paid, current due, total amount, hrs YTD, and business analyst number.

There are three types of controls: bound controls, unbound controls, and calculated controls. **Bound controls** are used to display data that comes from the database, such as the client number and name. **Unbound controls** are not associated with data from the database and are used to display such things as the report's title. Finally, **calculated controls** are used to display data that is calculated from other data, such as a total.

To Add Totals and Subtotals

Along with determining to group data in this report, Camashaly also determines that subtotals of the Amount Paid, Current Due, Total Amount, and Hrs YTD fields should be included. To add totals or other statistics, use the Totals button on the Design tab. You then select from a menu of aggregate functions, which are functions that perform some mathematical function against a group of records. The available aggregate functions, or calculations, are Sum (total), Average, Count Records, Count Values, Max (largest value), Min (smallest value), Standard Deviation, and Variance. The following steps add totals of the Amount Paid, Current Due, Total Amount, and Hrs YTD fields. Because the report is grouped, each group will have a subtotal, that is, a total for just the records in the group. At the end of the report, there will be a grand total, that is, a total for all records.

The following steps specify totals for the desired fields. Even though you previously specified totals for the Amount Paid, Current Due, and Hrs YTD fields, you need to do so again because of the grouping.

- Click the Amount Paid column header to select the field.

Q&A

Does it have to be the column header?

No, you could click the Amount Paid field on any record.

- Click the Totals button (Report Layout Tools Design tab | Grouping & Totals group) to display the list of available calculations (Figure 4–11).

Figure 4–11

- Click Sum to calculate the sum of amount paid values.

Q&A

Is Sum the same as Total?

Yes.

- If the total does not appear completely, drag the bottom of the control for the subtotal to the approximate position shown in Figure 4–12.

Figure 4–12

3

- Using the same technique as in Steps 1 and 2, add totals for the Current Due, Total Amount, and Hrs YTD fields (Figure 4–13).

Figure 4–13

To Remove the Group, Sort, and Total Pane

You have specified the grouping and sorting that you need for the report, so you no longer need the Group, Sort, and Total pane. The following step removes the Group, Sort, and Total pane from the screen.

1

- Click the Group & Sort button (Report Layout Tools Design tab | Grouping & Totals group) to remove the Group, Sort, and Total pane (Figure 4–14).

Q&A

Do I need to remove the Group, Sort, and Total pane?

Technically not. It gives more room on the screen for the report, however. You can easily display the pane whenever you need it by clicking the Group & Sort button again.

Figure 4–14

Plan Ahead	**Determine the format of the report or form.**
	Determine details concerning the appearance of the report.
	• **Determine the font or colors for the various sections of the reports.** Which combination of colors and fonts convey the best look for your report or form?
	• **Determine whether conditional formatting is appropriate.** Are there any fields in which you would like to emphasize certain values by giving them a different appearance?

To Conditionally Format Controls

You can emphasize values in a column that satisfy some criterion by formatting them differently from other values. This emphasis is called **conditional formatting**. Camashaly management would like to emphasize values in the Current Due field that are greater than or equal to $1,000 by making them red. The following steps conditionally format the Current Due field by specifying a **rule** that states that if the values in the field are greater than or equal to $1,000, such values will be formatted in red.

1

• Click Format on the Ribbon to display the Format tab.

• Click the Current Due field on the first record to select the field (Figure 4–15).

Does it have to be the first record?

No. You could click the field on any record.

Figure 4–15

2

- Click the Conditional Formatting button (Report Layout Tools Format tab | Control Formatting group) to display the Conditional Formatting Rules Manager dialog box (Figure 4–16).

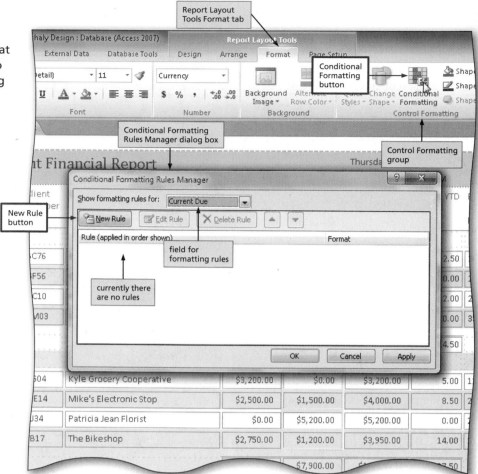

Figure 4–16

3

- Click the New Rule button (Conditional Formatting Rules Manager dialog box) to display the New Formatting Rule dialog box (Figure 4–17).

Q&A

I see that there are two boxes to enter numbers. I only have one number to enter, 1000. Am I on the right screen?

Yes. You will next change the comparison operator from between to 'greater than or equal to.' Once you have done so, Access will only display one box for entering a number.

Figure 4–17

- Click the box arrow (New Formatting Rule dialog box) to display the list of available comparison operators (Figure 4–18).

Figure 4–18

- Click 'greater than or equal to' to select the comparison operator.

- Click the box for the comparison value and then type 1 0 0 0 as the comparison value.

Q&A

What is the effect of selecting this comparison operator and entering this number?

Values in the field that are greater than or equal to 1000 satisfy this rule. Any formatting that you now specify will apply to those values and no others.

- Click the Font Color button arrow (New Formatting Rule dialog box) to display a color palette (Figure 4–19).

Figure 4–19

- Click the dark red color in the lower-left corner of the color palette to select the color (Figure 4–20).

Q&A

What other changes could I specify for those values that satisfy the rule?

You could specify that the value is bold, italic, and/or underlined. You could also specify a background color.

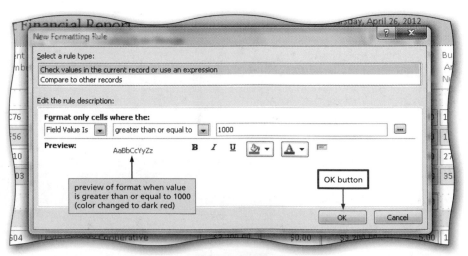

Figure 4–20

7

- Click the OK button (New Formatting Rule dialog box) to enter the rule (Figure 4–21).

What if I have more than one rule?

The rules are applied in order. If a value satisfies the first rule, the specified formatting will apply, and no further rules will be tested. If not, the value will be tested against the second rule. If it satisfies the rule, the formatting for the second rule would apply. If not, the value would be tested against the third rule, and so on.

Figure 4–21

Can I change this conditional formatting later?

Yes. Select the field for which you had applied conditional formatting on any record, click the Conditional Formatting button (Report Layout Tools Format tab | Control Formatting group), click the rule you want to change, click the Edit Rule button, and then make the necessary changes. You also can delete the selected rule by clicking the Delete Rule button or move the selected rule by clicking the up or down arrows.

8

- Click the OK button (Conditional Formatting Rules Manager dialog box) to complete the entry of the conditional formatting rules and apply the rule (Figure 4–22).

9

- Save your changes by clicking the Save button on the Quick Access Toolbar.

Experiment

- After saving your changes, experiment with different rules. Add a second rule that changes the format for any current due amount that is greater than or equal to $500 to a different color to see the effect of multiple rules. Change the order of rules to see the effect of a different order. When you have finished, delete any additional rules you have added so that the report contains only the one rule that you created earlier.

Figure 4–22

To Filter Records in a Report

You can filter records in a report. You can use the filter buttons in the Sort & Filter group on the Home tab in exactly the same way you did on a datasheet on page AC 148. If the filter involves only one field, however, right-clicking the field provides a simple way to filter. The following steps filter the records in the report to include only those records on which the amount paid is not $0.00.

1

- Right-click the Amount Paid field on the second record to display the shortcut menu (Figure 4–23).

Q&A

Did I have to pick the second record?

No. You could pick any record on which the Amount Paid is $0.00.

Figure 4–23

2

- Click 'Does Not Equal $0.00' on the shortcut menu to restrict the records to those on which the Amount Paid is not $0.00 (Figure 4–24).

Q&A

When would you use Number Filters?

You would use Number Filters if you need filters that are not on the main shortcut menu or if you need the ability to enter specific values other than the ones shown on the shortcut menu. If those filters are insufficient for your needs, you can use Advanced Filter/Sort, which is accessible through the Advanced button (Home tab | Sort & Filter group).

Other Ways

1. Click Selection button (Home tab | Sort & Filter group)

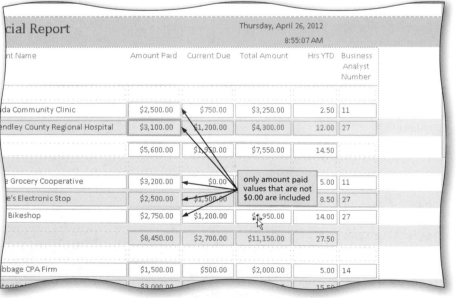

Figure 4–24

To Clear a Report Filter

When you no longer want the records to be filtered, you clear the filter. The following steps clear the filter on the Amount Paid field.

1
- Right-click the Amount Paid field on the second record to display the shortcut menu (Figure 4–25).

Figure 4–25

Q&A

Did I have to pick the second record?

No. You could pick the Amount Paid field on any record.

2
- Click 'Clear filter from Amount Paid' on the shortcut menu to clear the filter and redisplay all records.

Experiment
- Try other filters on the shortcut menu for the Amount Paid to see their effect. When done with each, clear the filter.

Other Ways

1. Click Advanced button (Home tab | Sort & Filter group), click Clear All Filters on Advanced menu

Conditional Formatting
Conditional formatting is available for forms as well as reports. To conditionally format controls on a form, open the Form in Layout view or Design view, select the control to format, click the Conditional Formatting button (Format tab | Control Formatting group), and then follow the steps on pages AC 225 through AC 227.

To Save and Close a Report

Now that you have completed your work on your report, you should save the report and close it. The following steps first save your work on the report and then close the report.

1 Click the Save button on the Quick Access Toolbar to save your work.

2 Close the Client Financial Report.

The Arrange and Page Setup Tabs

When working on a report in Layout view, you can make additional layout changes by using the Report Layout Tools Arrange and/or Page Setup tabs. The Arrange tab is shown in Figure 4–26. Table 4–1 shows the buttons on the Arrange tab along with the Enhanced ScreenTips that describe their function.

Figure 4–26

Using the Arrange tab
Because the commands located on the Arrange tab are actions associated with previously selected controls, be sure to select the desired control or controls first.

Table 4–1 Arrange Tab

Button	Enhanced ScreenTip
Gridlines	Gridlines
Stacked	Create a layout similar to a paper form, with labels to the left of each field.
Tabular	Create a layout similar to a spreadsheet, with labels across the top and data in columns below the labels.
Insert Above	Insert Above
Insert Below	Insert Below
Insert Left	Insert Left
Insert Right	Insert Right
Select Layout	Select Layout
Select Column	Select Column
Select Row	Select Row
Merge	Merge Cells
Split Vertically	Split the selected control into two rows.
Split Horizontally	Split the selected control into two columns.
Move Up	Move Up
Move Down	Move Down
Control Margins	Control Margins
Control Padding	Control Padding

The Report Layout Tools Page Setup tab is shown in Figure 4–27. Table 4–2 shows the buttons on the Page Setup tab along with the Enhanced ScreenTips that describe their function.

Figure 4–27

Table 4–2 Page Setup Tab	
Button	**Enhanced ScreenTip**
Size	Choose a paper size for the current section.
Margins	Select the margin sizes for the entire document or the current section.
Show Margins	Show Margins
Print Data Only	Print Data Only
Portrait	Change to portrait orientation.
Landscape	Change to landscape orientation.
Columns	Columns
Page Setup	Show the Page Setup dialog box.

To Print a Report

The following steps print the report.

1 If necessary, open the Navigation Pane.

2 With the Client Financial Report selected in the Navigation Pane, click File on the Ribbon to open the Backstage view.

3 Click the Print tab in the Backstage view to display the Print gallery.

4 Click the Quick Print button to print the report.

Q&A How can I print multiple copies of my report?

Click File on the Ribbon to open the Backstage view. Click the Print tab, click Print in the Print gallery to display the Print dialog box, increase the number in the Number of Copies box, and then click the OK button (Print dialog box).

Q&A How can I print a range of pages rather than printing the whole report?

Click File on the Ribbon to open the Backstage view. Click the Print tab, click Print in the Print gallery to display the Print dialog box, click the Pages option button in the Print Range area, enter the desired page range, and then click the OK button (Print dialog box).

Multitable Reports

You may determine that the data required for a report comes from more than one table. You can use the Report Wizard to create a report on multiple tables just as you can use it to create reports on single tables or queries.

BTW

Searching for Records in a Report
You can use the Find button to search for records in a report. To do so, open the report in Report view or Layout view and select the field in the report on which to search. Click the Find button (Home tab | Find group) to display the Find and Replace dialog box. Type the desired value on which to search in the Find What text box (Find and Replace dialog box) and then click the Find Next button.

To Create a Report that Involves Multiple Tables

Camashaly needs a report that includes the Business Analyst Number, First Name, and Last Name fields from the Business Analyst Table. In addition, for each client of the analyst, they need the Client Number, Client Name, Amount Paid, and Current Due fields from the Client table. The following steps use the Report Wizard to create a report that includes fields from both the Business Analyst and Client tables.

- Open the Navigation Pane if it is currently closed.

- Click the Business Analyst Table in the Navigation Pane to select it.

- Click Create on the Ribbon to display the Create tab.

- Click the Report Wizard button (Create tab | Reports group) to start the Report Wizard (Figure 4–28).

Q&A

My Navigation Pane does not look like the one in this screen. Is that a problem? How do I change it?

No, it is not a problem, but you should change it so it matches the screens in this chapter. To do so, click the Navigation Pane arrow and then click Object Type.

Figure 4–28

- Click the Add Field button to add the Business Analyst Number field to the report.

- Add the First Name field by clicking it and then clicking the Add Field button.

- Add the Last Name field in the same manner.

- Click the Tables/Queries arrow, and then click Table: Client in the Tables/Queries list box (Figure 4–29).

Figure 4–29

- Add the Client Number, Client Name, Amount Paid, and Current Due fields by clicking the field and then clicking the Add Field button.

- Click the Next button (Figure 4–30).

Figure 4–30

- Because the report is to be viewed by Business Analyst Table, and by Business Analyst Table already is selected, click the Next button (Figure 4–31).

Q&A I did not get this screen. Instead, I got an error message that said something about the tables not being related.

In Chapter 3, you create a relationship between the tables (page AC 188). That relationship must exist for the Report Wizard to be able to create the report. You will need to create the relationship and then begin these steps again.

Figure 4–31

5

- Click the Next button to move to the next Report Wizard screen.

- Click the box arrow in the text box labeled 1 and then click the Client Number field in the list to select the sort order (Figure 4–32).

Q&A When would I use the Summary Options button?

You would use the Summary Options button if you want to specify subtotals or other calculations within the wizard. You also can use it to produce a summary report by selecting Summary Only, which will omit all detail records from the report.

Figure 4–32

- Click the Summary Options button to display the Summary Options dialog box.
- Click the check boxes to calculate the sum of Amount Paid and the sum of Current Due (Figure 4–33).

Figure 4–33

- Click the OK button (Summary Options dialog box).
- Click the Next button, be sure the Stepped layout is selected, and then click the Landscape option button to select the orientation (Figure 4–34).

Figure 4–34

8

- Click the Next button to move to the next Report Wizard screen, and then type **Clients by Analyst** as the report title (Figure 4–35).

Figure 4–35

- Click the Finish button to produce the report (Figure 4–36).

Figure 4–36

- Click the magnifying glass mouse pointer somewhere within the report to view more of the report (Figure 4–37).

 Experiment

- Zoom in on various positions within the report. When finished, view a complete page of the report.

- Click the Save button on the Quick Access Toolbar to save your work.

- Click the Close button for the report to close the report and remove it from the screen.

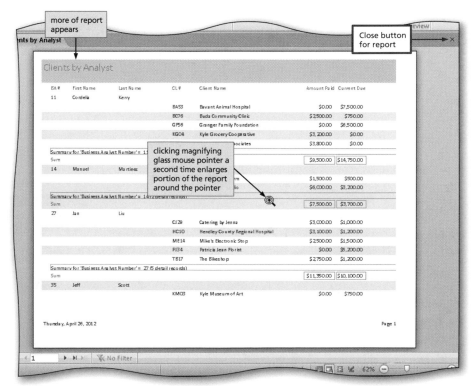

Figure 4–37

To Print a Report

The following steps print the Clients by Analyst report.

① Open the Navigation Pane, select the Clients by Analyst report, and then click File on the Ribbon to open the Backstage view.

② Click the Print tab in the Backstage view to display the Print gallery.

③ Click the Quick Print button to print the report.

Creating a Report in Layout View

You can use Layout view to create single- and multiple-table reports. To do so, you would first create a blank report and display a field list for the table containing the first fields you want to include on the report (Figure 4–38).

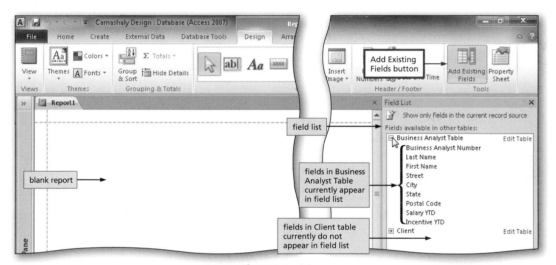

Figure 4–38

You would then drag any fields you want from the table onto the report in the order you want them to appear (Figure 4–39).

Figure 4–39

If there is a second table involved in the report, you would be sure a field list for the second table appears and then drag the fields from the second table onto the report in the desired order (Figure 4–40).

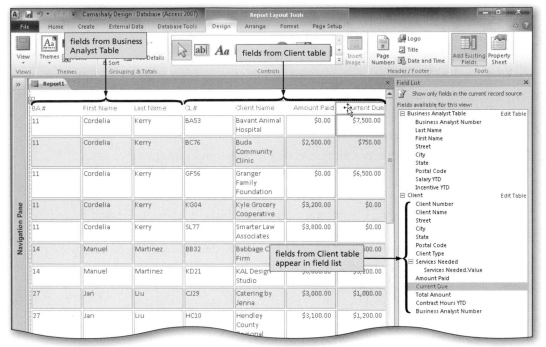

Figure 4–40

When you create a report in Layout view, the report does not automatically contain a title, but you can add one by clicking the Title button (Report Layout Tools Design tab | Header/Footer group) (Figure 4–41).

Figure 4–41

Once you have added the title, you can type whatever title you want for the report.

BTW

Multicolumn Reports
There are times when you may want to create a report that has multiple columns. For example, a telephone list with employee name and phone number could print in multiple columns. To do so, create the report using Layout view or Design view and then click the Page Setup button (Page Setup tab | Page Layout group), click the Columns tab, enter the number of columns, select the desired column layout, and then click the OK button (Page Setup dialog box).

TO CREATE A REPORT IN LAYOUT VIEW

If you want to create a report in Layout view, you would use the following steps.

1. Click Create on the Ribbon to display the Create tab.
2. Click the Blank Report button (Create tab | Reports group) to create a blank report.
3. If a field list does not appear, display a field list by clicking the Add Existing Fields button (Report Layout Tools Design tab | Tools group).
4. If the tables do not appear in the field list, click Show All Tables.
5. If the fields in a table do not appear, click the plus sign in front of the name of the table.
6. Drag the fields from the field list onto the report in the desired order.
7. If there is a second table, be sure the fields in the second table appear, and then drag the fields from the second table onto the report in the desired order. (If the field list covers the portion of the report where you want to drag the fields, you can move the field list to a different position by dragging its title bar.)
8. If you want to add a title to the report, click the Title button (Report Layout Tools Design tab | Header / Footer group) and then type the desired title.

BTW

Themes
Themes are standardized across all Office applications. You can download themes and share themes with others via Office Online or e-mail.

Using Themes

The most important characteristic of a report or form is that it contains the desired data arranged in an appropriate fashion. Another important characteristic, however, is the general appearance of the form. The colors and fonts that you use in the various sections of a report or form contribute to this look. There are two important goals to keep in mind when assigning colors and fonts. First, the various colors and fonts should complement each other. A clash of colors or two fonts that do not go well together can produce a report that looks unprofessional. Second, the choice of colors and fonts should be consistent. That is, all the reports and forms within a database should use the same colors and fonts unless there is some compelling reason for a report or form to look different from the others.

Fortunately, Access themes provide an easy way to achieve both goals. A **theme** consists of a selection of colors and fonts for the various sections in a report or form. The colors and fonts in any of the built-in themes are designed to complement each other. When you assign a theme, the theme immediately applies to all reports and forms, unless you specifically indicate otherwise. To assign a theme, you use the Theme picker, which is a menu of available themes (Figure 4–42).

If you point to any theme in the Theme picker, you will see a ScreenTip giving the name of the theme. When you select a theme, the colors and fonts represented by that theme will immediately apply to all reports and forms. If you later decide that you would prefer a different theme, simply repeat the process. That is, open any report or form and select a new theme. Its colors and fonts will then replace the colors and fonts of the old theme in all reports and forms.

Figure 4–42

You can also use the Browse for Themes command to browse for themes that are not listed but are available for download. If you have specified a combination of fonts and colors that you like but that is not already on the list of themes, you can use the Save Current Theme command to save your combination. If, after selecting a theme using the Themes button, you do not like the colors in the current theme, you can change the theme's colors. Click the Colors button (Report Layout Tools Design tab | Themes group) (Figure 4–43), and then select an alternative color scheme.

Figure 4–43

Similarly, if you do not like the fonts in the current theme, you can click the Fonts button (Report Layout Tools Design tab | Themes group) (Figure 4–44). You then can select an alternative font.

Figure 4–44

TO ASSIGN A THEME TO ALL OBJECTS

To assign a theme, it is easiest to use Layout view. You can use Design view as well, but it is easier to see the result of picking a theme when you are viewing the report or form in Layout view. To assign a theme to all reports and forms, you would use the following steps.

1. Open any report or form in Layout view.
2. Click the Themes button (Report Layout Tools Design tab | Themes group) to display the Theme picker.
3. Click the desired theme.

To ASSIGN A THEME TO A SINGLE OBJECT

In some cases, you might only want to apply a theme to the current report or form, while all other reports and forms would retain the characteristics from the original theme. To assign a theme to a single object, you would use the following steps.

1. Open the specific report or form to which you want to assign a theme in Layout view.
2. Click the Themes button (Report Layout Tools Design tab | Themes group) to display the Theme picker.
3. Right-click the desired theme to produce a shortcut menu.
4. Click the Apply Theme to This Object Only command on the shortcut menu to apply the theme to the single object on which you are working.

Live Preview for Themes

When selecting themes, Access furnishes a **live preview** of what the report or form will look like with the theme before you actually select the theme. The report or form will appear as it would in the theme to which you are currently pointing (Figure 4–45). If you like that theme, you then can select the theme by clicking the left mouse button.

Figure 4–45

To Create a Summary Report

You may determine that a report should be organized so that it only shows the overall group calculations, but not all the records. A report that includes the group calculations such as subtotals, but does not include the individual detail lines, is called a **summary report**. The following steps hide the detail lines in the Client Financial Report, thus creating a summary report.

1
- Open the Client Financial Report in Layout view and close the Navigation Pane.

2
- Click the Hide Details button (Report Layout Tools Design tab | Grouping & Totals group) to hide the details in the report (Figure 4–46).

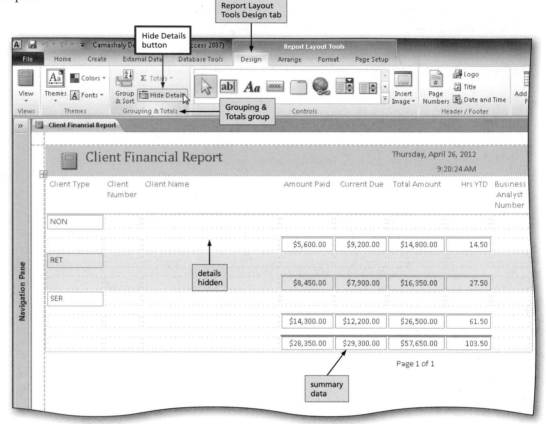

Figure 4–46

Q&A How can I see the details once I have hidden them?
Click the Hide Details button a second time.

Q&A There seems to be a lot of space before the Amount Paid and Current Due fields. Is that a problem?
The extra space is the space that would be occupied by the client number and name if you had not hidden the details. It is not a problem. If you wanted a report that was strictly a summary report, you would not have included those fields. If the fields were not included, hiding the details would not have produced this space.

BTW
Summary Reports
You can create a summary report in either Layout view or Design view.

3
- Close the report without saving your changes.

Q&A What would happen if I saved the report?
The next time you view the report, the details would still be hidden. If that happened and you wanted to show all the details, just click the Hide Details button a second time.

Break Point: If you wish to take a break, this a good place to do so. You can quit Access now. To resume at a later time, start Access, open the database called Camashaly Design, and continue following the steps from this location forward.

Form Creation

As with reports, it is usually simplest to begin creating a form by using the wizard. Once you have used the Form Wizard to create a form, you can modify that form in either Layout view or Design view.

To Use the Form Wizard to Create a Form

The following steps use the Form Wizard to create an initial version of the Client Financial Form. This initial version will contain the Client Number, Client Name, Client Type, Services Needed, Amount Paid, Current Due, Total Amount, and Business Analyst Number fields.

- Open the Navigation Pane and select the Client table.

- Click Create on the Ribbon to display the Create tab.

- Click the Form Wizard button (Create tab | Forms group) to start the Form Wizard (Figure 4–47).

Figure 4–47

2

- Add the Client Number, Client Name, Client Type, Services Needed, Amount Paid, Current Due, Total Amount, and Business Analyst Number fields to the form (Figure 4–48).

Figure 4–48

3

- Click the Next button to display the next Form Wizard screen (Figure 4–49).

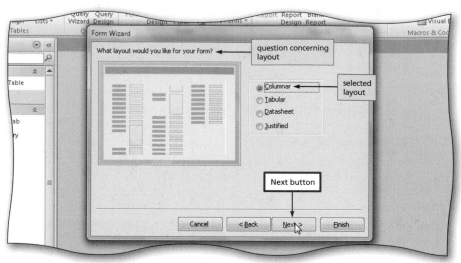

Figure 4–49

4

- Be sure the Columnar layout is selected, click the Next button to display the next Form Wizard screen, and then type **Client Financial Form** as the title for the form (Figure 4–50).

Figure 4–50

5

- Click the Finish button to complete and display the form (Figure 4–51).

6

- Click the Close button for the Client Financial Form to close the form.

Figure 4–51

Understanding Form Sections

A form typically has only three sections. The Form Header section appears at the top of the form and usually contains the form title. It also may contain a logo and/or a date. The body of the form is in the Detail section. The Form Footer section appears at the bottom of the form and is often empty.

Understanding Form Controls

Just as with reports, the various items on a form are called controls. Forms include the same three types of controls: bound controls, unbound controls, and calculated controls. Bound controls have attached labels that typically display the name of the field that supplies the data for the control. The **attached label** for the Client Number field, for example, is the portion of the screen immediately to the left of the field. It contains the words, Client Number.

Using Layout View in a Form

When working with a form in Access, there are three different ways to view the form. They are Form view, Layout view, and Design view. Form view shows the form on the screen and allows you to use the form to update data. Layout view is similar to Form view in that it shows the form on the screen. In Layout view, you cannot update the data, but you can make changes to the layout of the form, and it is the usually the easiest way to make such changes. Design view also allows you to make changes, but it does not show you the actual form. It is most useful when the changes you need to make are especially complex. In this chapter, you will use Layout view to modify the form.

To Place Controls in a Control Layout

To use Layout view with a form, the controls must be placed in a control layout, which is a set of controls grouped together so that they can be manipulated as a single unit. The following steps place the controls and their attached labels in a control layout.

1

- Open the Client Financial Form in Layout view and close the Navigation Pane.

- Click Arrange on the Ribbon to display the Form Layout Tools Arrange tab.

- Click the attached label for the Business Analyst Number control to select the control.

- While holding the SHIFT key down, click the remaining attached labels and all the controls (Figure 4–52).

Q&A

Did I have to select the attached labels and controls in that order?

No. As long as you select all of them, the order in which you selected them does not matter.

Figure 4–52

Q&A When I clicked some of the controls, they moved so they are no longer aligned as well as they are in the figure. What should I do?

You do not have to worry about it. Once you complete the next step, they will once again be aligned properly.

②

- Click the Stacked button (Form Layout Tools Arrange tab | Table group) to place the controls in a stacked layout (Figure 4–53).

Figure 4–53

Q&A How can I tell whether the controls are in a control layout?

Look for the Control Layout indicator in the upper-left corner of the control layout.

Q&A What is the difference between stacked layout and tabular layout?

In a stacked layout, which is more often used in forms, the controls are placed vertically with the labels to the left of the controls. In a tabular layout, which is more often used in reports, the controls are placed horizontally with the labels above the controls.

To Add a Date

You can add special items, such as a logo or title, to reports and forms. You can also add the date and/or the time. In the case of reports, you can add a page number as well. To add any of these items, you use the appropriate button in the Header/Footer group of the Design tab. The following steps use the Date and Time button to add a date to the Client Financial Form.

1

- Click Design on the Ribbon to display the Design tab.

- Click the Date and Time button (Form Layout Tools Design tab | Header/Footer group) to display the Date and Time dialog box (Figure 4–54).

Q&A

What is the relationship between the various check boxes and option buttons?

If the Include Date check box is checked, you must pick a date format from the three option buttons underneath the check box. If it is not checked, the option buttons will be dimmed. If the Include Time check box is checked, you must pick a time format from the three option buttons underneath the check box. If it is not checked, the option buttons will be dimmed.

Figure 4–54

2

- Click the option button for the second date format to select the format that shows the day of the month, followed by the abbreviation for the month, followed by the year.

- Click the Include Time check box to remove the check mark (Figure 4–55).

Figure 4–55

- Click the OK button (Date and Time dialog box) to add the date to the form (Figure 4–56).

Figure 4–56

To Change the Format of a Control

You can change the format of a control by clicking the control and then clicking the appropriate button on the Format tab. The following step uses this technique to bold the date.

- Click the Date control to select it.

- Click Format on the Ribbon to display the Form Layout Tools Format tab.

- Click the Bold button (Form Layout Tools Format tab | Font group) to bold the date (Figure 4–57).

Figure 4–57

To Move a Control

You can move a control by dragging the control. The following step moves the Date control to the lower edge of the form header.

1

- Point to the Date control so that the mouse pointer changes to a four-headed arrow and then drag the Date control to the lower boundary of the form header (Figure 4–58).

Figure 4–58

I moved my pointer a little bit and it became a two-headed arrow. Can I still drag the pointer?

If you drag when the pointer is a two-headed arrow, you will resize the control. To move the control, it must be a four-headed arrow.

Could I drag other objects as well? For example, could I drag the title to the center of the form header?

Yes. Just be sure you are pointing at the object and the pointer is a four-headed arrow. You can then drag the object to the desired location.

To Move Controls in a Control Layout

The controls for the fields are arranged in control layouts. A **control layout** is a guide that aligns the controls to give the form a uniform appearance. There are two types of control layouts. A **stacked layout** arranges the controls vertically with labels to the left of the control. A **tabular layout** arranges the controls horizontally with the labels across the top, typically in the Form Header section. The Client Financial Form contains a stacked layout.

Just as you moved the Date control in the previous section, you can move a control within a control layout by dragging the control to the location you want. As you move it, a line will indicate the position where the control will be placed when you release the left mouse button. You can move more than one control in the same operation by selecting both controls prior to moving them.

The following steps move the Client Type and Services Needed fields so that they follow the Business Analyst Number field.

1

- Click the label for the Client Type field to select it.

- Hold the SHIFT key down and click the control for the Client Type field, then click the label for the Services Needed field and the control for the Services Needed field to select both fields and their labels (Figure 4–59).

 Q&A Why did I have to hold the SHIFT key down when I clicked the remaining controls?

If you did not hold the SHIFT key down, you would only select the control for the Services Needed field (the last control selected). The other controls would no longer be selected.

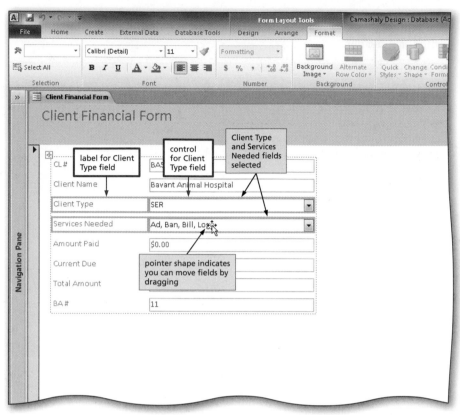

Figure 4–59

2

- Press the left mouse button and then drag the fields straight down to the position shown in Figure 4–60, making sure that the line by the mouse pointer is under the data.

Q&A What is the purpose of the line by the mouse pointer?

It shows you where the fields will be positioned.

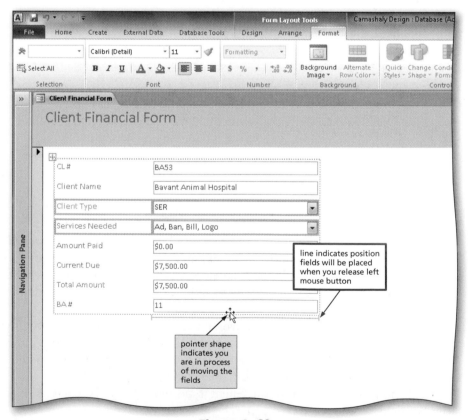

Figure 4–60

3

- Release the left mouse button to complete the movement of the fields (Figure 4–61).

Q&A

I inadvertently had the line under the label rather than the data when I released the mouse button. The data that I moved is now under the field names. How do I fix this?

You can try to move it back where it was, but that can be tricky. The easiest way is to click the Undo button on the Quick Access Toolbar to undo your change.

Q&A

I inadvertently moved my pointer so that the line became vertical and was located between a label and the corresponding data when I released the mouse button. It seemed to split the form. The data I moved appears right where the line was. It is between a label and the corresponding data. How do I fix this?

Just as in the previous answer, the easiest way is to click the Undo button on the Quick Access Toolbar to undo your change.

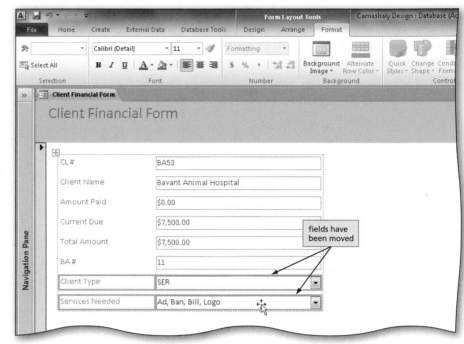

Figure 4–61

To Add a Field

Just as with a report, once you have created an initial form, you may decide that the form should contain an additional field. The following steps use a field list to add the City field to the Client Financial Form.

1

- Click Design on the Ribbon to display the Form Layout Tools Design tab.

- Click the Add Existing Fields button (Form Layout Tools Design tab | Tools group) to display a field list (Figure 4–62).

Figure 4–62

• Point to the City field in the field list, press the left mouse button, and then drag the pointer to the position shown in Figure 4–63.

Q&A Does it have to be exact?

The exact pointer position is not critical as long as the line is in the position shown in the figure.

Figure 4–63

• Release the left mouse button to place the field (Figure 4–64).

Q&A What if I make a mistake?

Just as when you are modifying a report, you can delete the field by clicking the field and then pressing the DELETE key. You can move the field by dragging it to the correct position.

• Click the Add Existing Fields button (Form Layout Tools Design tab | Tools group) to remove the field list.

Figure 4–64

To Filter and Sort Using a Form

Just as in a datasheet, you can filter and sort using Advanced Filter/Sort, which is a command on the Advanced menu. The following steps use Advanced Filter/Sort to filter the records to those records whose city begins with the letters, Gr. They also sort the records by client name. The effect of this filter and sort is that as you use the form to move through clients, you will only encounter those clients whose cities begin with Gr. In addition, you will encounter those clients in client name order.

- Click Home on the Ribbon to display the Home tab.

- Click the Advanced button (Home tab | Sort & Filter group) to display the Advanced menu (Figure 4–65).

Figure 4–65

❷

- Click Advanced Filter/Sort on the Advanced menu.

- Resize the field list so that all the fields appear.

- Add the Client Name field to the design grid and select Ascending sort order.

- Add the City field and type **Gr*** as the criterion for the City field (Figure 4–66).

Figure 4–66

3

- Click the Toggle Filter button (Home tab | Sort & Filter group) to filter the records (Figure 4–67).

Q&A

I can only see one record at a time in the form. How can I see which records are included?

You would have to scroll through the records. For example, you could repeatedly click the Next Record button.

Figure 4–67

To Clear a Form Filter

When you no longer want the records to be filtered, you clear the filter. The following steps clear the current filter for the Client Financial Form.

1 Click the Advanced button (Home tab | Sort & Filter group) to display the Advanced menu.

2 Click Clear All Filters on the Advanced menu to clear the filter.

To Save and Close a Form

Now that you have completed your work on your form, you should save the form and close it. The following steps first save your work on the form and then close the form.

1 Click the Save button on the Quick Access Toolbar to save your work.

2 Close the Client Financial Form.

To Print a Form

You can print all records, a range of records, or a selected record of a form by selecting the appropriate print range. To print the selected record, the form must be open. To print all records or a range of records, the form can simply be highlighted in the Navigation Pane. The following steps open the Client Financial Form and then print the first record in the form, which is the selected record.

1 Open the Navigation Pane, and then, if necessary, select the Client Financial Form.

2 Right-click the Client Financial Form and click Open on the shortcut menu.

3 Click File on the Ribbon to open the Backstage view.

4 Click the Print tab in the Backstage view to display the Print gallery.

5 Click the Print button to display the Print dialog box.

6 Click the Selected Record(s) option button in the Page Range box, and then click the OK button.

> **BTW**
>
> **Certification**
> The Microsoft Office Specialist (MOS) program provides an opportunity for you to obtain a valuable industry credential – proof that you have the Access 2010 skills required by employers. For more information, visit the Access 2010 Certification Web page (scsite.com/ac2010/cert).

The Arrange Tab

Forms, like reports, have an Arrange tab that you can use to modify the form's layout. However, the Page Setup tab is not available for forms. The buttons on the Arrange tab and the functions of those buttons are just like the ones described in Table 4–1 on page AC 230, with one exception. When working with a form, there is an extra button, the Anchoring button. The function of this button is to tie a control to a section or another control so that it moves or resizes in conjunction with the movement or resizing of its parent.

> **BTW**
>
> **Customizing Mailing Labels**
> Once you create mailing labels, you can customize them just as you can customize other reports. In Design view, you can add a picture to the label, change the font size, adjust the spacing between controls, or make any other desired changes.

Mailing Labels

Organizations need to send invoices and other correspondence to clients on a regular basis. Using preprinted mailing labels eliminates much of the manual labor involved in preparing mailings. In Access, mailing labels are a special type of report. When this report prints, the data appears on the mailing labels aligned correctly and in the order you specify.

To Create Labels

You create labels just as you create reports. The Label Wizard assists you in the process. Using the wizard, you can specify the type and dimensions of the label, the font used for the label, and the content of the label. The following steps create the labels.

1

- If necessary, open the Navigation Pane and select the Client table.

- Click Create on the Ribbon to display the Create tab.

- Click the Labels button (Create tab | Reports group) to display the Label Wizard dialog box.

- Ensure that English is selected as the Unit of Measure and that Avery is selected in the 'Filter by manufacturer' box.

- Scroll through the label types until C2163 appears and then click C2163 in the Product number list to select the specific type of labels (Figure 4–68).

Figure 4–68

2

- Click the Next button (Figure 4–69).

Q&A

Q&A What font characteristics could I change with this screen?

You could change the font, the font size, the font weight, and/or the font color. You could also specify italic or underlining.

Figure 4–69

3

- Click the Next button to accept the default font and color settings.

- Click the Client Name field and then click the Add Field button (Figure 4–70).

Q&A

What if I make a mistake?

You can erase the contents of any line in the label by clicking in the line to produce an insertion point and then using the DELETE or BACKSPACE keys to erase the current contents. You can then add the correct field by clicking the field and then clicking the Add Field button.

Figure 4–70

4

- Click the second line in the label, and then add the Street field.

- Click the third line of the label.

- Add the City field, type , (a comma), press the SPACEBAR, add the State field, press the SPACEBAR, and then add the Postal Code field (Figure 4–71).

Figure 4–71

5

- Because the label is now complete, click the Next button.

- Select the Postal Code field as the field to sort by, and then click the Add Field button (Figure 4–72).

Q&A

Why am I sorting by postal code?

When you need to do a bulk mailing, that is, mail a large number of items using a special mail rate, mail organizations often require that the mail be sorted in postal code order.

Figure 4–72

6

- Click the Next button.

- Ensure the name for the report (that is, the labels) is Labels Client (Figure 4–73).

Figure 4–73

7

- Click the Finish button to complete the labels (Figure 4–74).

8

- Close the Labels Client report.

Figure 4–74

To Print Labels

You print labels just as you print a report. The only difference is that you must load the labels in the printer before printing. The following steps print the labels once you have loaded labels in your printer.

1 With the Labels Client report selected in the Navigation Pane, click File on the Ribbon to open the Backstage view.

2 Click the Print tab in the Backstage view to display the Print gallery.

3 Click the Quick Print button to print the labels.

Q&A I want to load the correct number of labels. How do I know how many pages of labels will print?

If you are unsure how many pages of labels will print, open the label report in Print Preview first. Use the Navigation buttons in the status bar of the Print Preview window to determine how many pages of labels will print.

To Quit Access

The following steps quit Access.

1 Click the Close button on the right side of the title bar to quit Access.

2 If a Microsoft Access dialog box appears, click the Save button to save any changes made to the object since the last save.

BTW
Quick Reference
For a table that lists how to complete the tasks covered in this book using the mouse, Ribbon, shortcut menu, and keyboard, see the Quick Reference Summary at the back of this book, or visit the Access 2010 Quick Reference Web page (scsite.com/ac2010/qr).

Chapter Summary

In this chapter you have learned to use wizards to create reports and forms, modify the layout of reports and forms using Layout view, group and sort in a report, add totals to a report, conditionally format controls, filter records in reports and forms, resize and move controls, add fields to reports and forms, include gridlines, add a date, move controls in a control layout, apply themes, and create mailing labels. The items listed below include all the new Access skills you have learned in this chapter.

1. Group and Sort in a Report (AC 217)
2. Add Totals and Subtotals (AC 221)
3. Remove the Group, Sort, and Total Pane (AC 223)
4. Conditionally Format Controls (AC 224)
5. Filter Records in a Report (AC 228)
6. Clear a Report Filter (AC 229)
7. Create a Report that Involves Multiple Tables (AC 232)
8. Create a Report in Layout View (AC 238)
9. Assign a Theme to All Objects (AC 240)
10. Assign a Theme to a Single Object (AC 241)
11. Create a Summary Report (AC 242)
12. Use the Form Wizard to Create a Form (AC 243)
13. Place Controls in a Control Layout (AC 245)
14. Add a Date (AC 246)
15. Change the Format of a Control (AC 248)
16. Move a Control (AC 249)
17. Move Controls in a Control Layout (AC 249)
18. Add a Field (AC 251)
19. Filter and Sort Using a Form (AC 253)
20. Create Labels (AC 255)

 If you have a SAM 2010 user profile, your instructor may have assigned an autogradable version of this assignment. If so, log into the SAM 2010 Web site at www.cengage.com/sam2010 to download the instruction and start files.

Learn It Online

Test your knowledge of chapter content and key terms.

Instructions: To complete the Learn It Online exercises, start your browser, click the Address bar, and then enter the Web address **scsite.com/ac2010/learn**. When the Access 2010 Learn It Online page is displayed, click the link for the exercise you want to complete and then read the instructions.

Chapter Reinforcement TF, MC, and SA
A series of true/false, multiple choice, and short answer questions that test your knowledge of the chapter content.

Flash Cards
An interactive learning environment where you identify chapter key terms associated with displayed definitions.

Practice Test
A series of multiple choice questions that test your knowledge of chapter content and key terms.

Who Wants To Be a Computer Genius?
An interactive game that challenges your knowledge of chapter content in the style of a television quiz show.

Wheel of Terms
An interactive game that challenges your knowledge of chapter key terms in the style of the television show *Wheel of Fortune*.

Crossword Puzzle Challenge
A crossword puzzle that challenges your knowledge of key terms presented in the chapter.

Apply Your Knowledge

Reinforce the skills and apply the concepts you learned in this chapter.

Creating a Report and a Form

Instructions: Start Access. If you are using the Microsoft Access 2010 Complete or the Microsoft Access 2010 Comprehensive text, open the Babbage CPA Firm database that you used in Chapter 3. Otherwise, see your instructor for information on accessing the files required in this book.

Perform the following tasks:

1. Create the Clients by Bookkeeper report shown in Figure 4–75. The report is grouped by bookkeeper number and sorted by client number within bookkeeper number. Include totals for the Amount Paid and Balance Due fields. Change the orientation to landscape.

Clients by Bookkeeper

BKR #	First Name	Last Name	CL #	Client Name	Amount Paid	Balance Due
22	Johanna	Lewes				
			A54	Afton Mills	$575.00	$315.00
			D76	Dege Grocery	$1,015.00	$325.00
			J77	Jones Plumbing	$685.00	$0.00
			S56	SeeSaw Industries	$1,200.00	$645.00

Summary for 'Bookkeeper Number' = 22 (4 detail records)

Sum					$3,475.00	$1,285.00
24	Mario	Rodriguez				
			A62	Atlas Suppliers	$250.00	$175.00
			B26	Blake-Scripps	$875.00	$250.00
			G56	Grand Cleaners	$485.00	$165.00
			M26	Mohr Craft Supplies	$125.00	$185.00

Summary for 'Bookkeeper Number' = 24 (4 detail records)

Sum					$1,735.00	$775.00
34	Choi	Wong				
			C29	Catering by Jenna	$0.00	$250.00
			T45	Tate Repair	$345.00	$200.00
			W24	Woody Sporting Goods	$975.00	$0.00

Summary for 'Bookkeeper Number' = 34 (3 detail records)

Sum					$1,320.00	$450.00
38	Theresa	Sinthin				
			L50	Lou's Salon	$0.00	$325.00

Summary for 'Bookkeeper Number' = 38 (1 detail record)

Sum					$0.00	$325.00
Grand Total					$6,530.00	$2,835.00

Wednesday, June 02, 2010   Page 1

Figure 4–75

Continued >

Apply Your Knowledge *continued*

2. Create the Client Financial Form shown in Figure 4–76 for the Client table. The form includes the current date and is similar in style to that shown in Figure 4–3 on page AC 212.

Figure 4–76

3. Submit the revised database in the format specified by your instructor.

Extend Your Knowledge

Extend the skills you learned in this chapter and experiment with new skills. You may need to use Help to complete the assignment.

Creating a Summary Report and Assigning a Theme to a Form

Instructions: See the inside back cover of this book for instructions for downloading the Data Files for Students, or see your instructor for information on accessing the required files.

The College Helpers database contains data for a group of college students who perform miscellaneous jobs for homeowners to earn tuition money. You will create the summary report shown in Figure 4–77. You also will create the form shown in Figure 4–78.

Figure 4–77

Figure 4–78

Continued >

Extend Your Knowledge *continued*

Perform the following tasks:

1. Use the Report Wizard to create the summary report shown in Figure 4–77. Name the report Customer Summary Report. Group the report by city and sort by customer number within city. Include totals for the balance. Change the orientation to landscape.

2. Create the Customer Financial Form shown in Figure 4–78. The form has a stacked control layout. Apply the Austin theme to this form only.

3. Submit the revised database in the format specified by your instructor.

Make It Right

Analyze a database and correct all errors and/or improve the design.

Correcting Report and Form Design Errors

Instructions: Start Access. Open the WeClean4You database. See the inside back cover of this book for instructions for downloading the Data Files for Students, or see your instructor for information on accessing the required files.

The WeClean4You database contains data for a company that does residential cleaning. The owner of the company has created the report shown in Figure 4–79 using the Report Wizard, but she forgot to sort the report by customer number. She does not know how to total the Balance and Amount Paid fields. She would like to differentiate customers whose amount paid value is $0.00 by making the amount appear in a bold red font. *Hint:* Use Layout view to make the corrections.

Customers by Worker

Worker Number	Worker First Name	Worker Last Name	Customer Number	Customer First Name	Customer Last Name	Balance	Amount Paid
303	Joe	Levin					
			KL12	Cynthia	Klinger	$60.00	$104.00
			HJ07	Bill	Heijer	$29.00	$135.00
			AB10	Frances	Alvarez	$45.00	$305.00
305	Brad	Rogers					
			TR35	Gerry	Trent	$40.00	$223.00
			PR80	Martin	Prestz	$95.00	$168.00
			GM52	Frank	Gammort	$70.00	$0.00
			BR16	Alex	Breaton	$80.00	$280.00
307	Maria	Rodriguez					
			SA23	Maria	Santoro	$0.00	$0.00
			MA34	Lisa	Manston	$0.00	$145.00
			FE45	Jean	Ferdon	$0.00	$370.00

Figure 4–79

She also created the form shown in Figure 4–80 for the Customer table, but she forgot to add the Telephone Number field. The Telephone Number field should appear before the Balance field. She would like the customer first name to appear before the customer last name and she would like to add the date to the form header.

Figure 4–80

Submit the revised database in the format specified by your instructor.

In the Lab

Design, create, modify, and/or use a database following the guidelines, concepts, and skills presented in this chapter. Labs 1, 2, and 3 are listed in order of increasing difficulty.

Lab 1: Presenting Data in the ECO Clothesline Database

Problem: The management of ECO Clothesline already has realized the benefits from the database of customers and sales reps that you created. The management now would like to prepare reports and forms for the database.

Instructions: If you are using the Microsoft Access 2010 Complete or the Microsoft Access 2010 Comprehensive text, open the ECO Clothesline database that you used in Chapter 3. Otherwise, see your instructor for information on accessing the files required in this book.

Perform the following tasks:

1. Open in Layout view the Customer Balance Report you created in Chapter 1 and revised in Chapter 3. Modify the report to create the report shown in Figure 4–81. Group the report by Customer Type and sort by Customer Number within Customer Type. Add the Amount Paid field to the report and include totals for the Balance and Amount Paid fields.

Customer Balance Report

Thursday, April 26, 2(
2:50:13 PM

Customer Type	Customer Number	Customer Name	Balance	Amount Paid	Sales Rep Number
SAL					
	CY12	Curlin Yoga Studio	$145.00	$710.00	49
	FN19	Fitness Counts	$345.00	$1,950.00	51
	LB20	Le Beauty Salon & Spa	$200.00	$1,250.00	49
	RD03	Rose's Day Spa	$0.00	$975.00	51
	TT21	Tan and Tone	$160.00	$725.00	44
	TW56	The Workout Place	$680.00	$125.00	51
			$1,530.00	$5,735.00	
SPG					
	RA21	Ralph's	$0.00	$0.00	55
	WS34	Woody's Sporting Goods	$1,235.00	$0.00	49
			$1,235.00	$0.00	
WMN					
	AM23	Amy's Store	$195.00	$1,695.00	44
	BL15	Blondie's on Main	$555.00	$1,350.00	49
	CM09	Casual by Marie	$295.00	$1,080.00	51
	DG14	Della's Designs	$340.00	$850.00	44
	EC07	Environmentally Casual	$0.00	$1,700.00	44
	JN34	Just Natural	$360.00	$700.00	49
	NC25	Nancy's Place	$240.00	$550.00	44
			$1,985.00	$7,925.00	
			$4,750.00	$13,660.00	

Figure 4–81

2. Create the Customers by Sales Rep report shown in Figure 4–82. Include a total for the Balance field. Change the orientation to landscape. Make sure the total control displays completely. (*Hint:* Use Layout view to make this adjustment.)

Customers by Sales Rep

SR #	First Name	Last Name	Cust #	Customer Name	Balance
44	Pat	Jones			
			AM23	Amy's Store	$195.00
			DG14	Della's Designs	$340.00
			EC07	Environmentally Casual	$0.00
			NC25	Nancy's Place	$240.00
			TT21	Tan and Tone	$160.00

Summary for 'Sales Rep Number' = 44 (5 detail records)

Sum					$935.00
49	Pinn	Gupta			
			BL15	Blondie's on Main	$555.00
			CY12	Curlin Yoga Studio	$145.00
			JN34	Just Natural	$360.00
			LB20	Le Beauty Salon & Spa	$200.00
			WS34	Woody's Sporting Goods	$1,235.00

Summary for 'Sales Rep Number' = 49 (5 detail records)

Sum					$2,495.00
51	Gabe	Ortiz			
			CM09	Casual by Marie	$295.00
			FN19	Fitness Counts	$345.00
			RD03	Rose's Day Spa	$0.00
			TW56	The Workout Place	$680.00

Summary for 'Sales Rep Number' = 51 (4 detail records)

Sum					$1,320.00
55	Terry	Sinson			
			RA21	Ralph's	$0.00

Summary for 'Sales Rep Number' = 55 (1 detail record)

Sum					$0.00
Grand Total					$4,750.00

Thursday, April 26, 2012

Page 1

Figure 4–82

Continued >

In the Lab *continued*

3. Create the Customer Financial Form shown in Figure 4–83. The form includes the date.

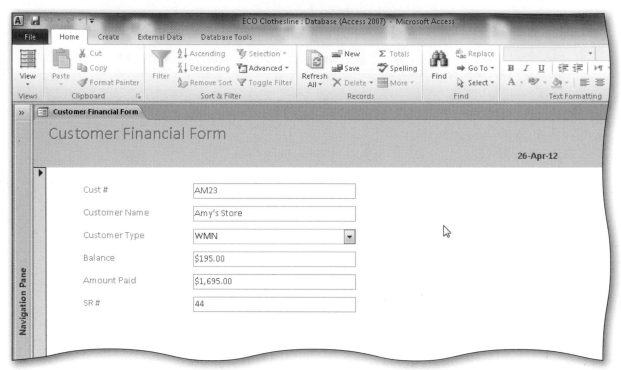

Figure 4–83

4. Create mailing labels for the Customer table. Use Avery labels C2163 and format the labels with customer name on the first line, street on the second line, and city, state, and postal code on the third line. Include a comma and a space after city and a space between state and postal code. Sort the labels by postal code.

5. Submit the revised database in the format specified by your instructor.

In the Lab

Lab 2: Presenting Data in the Walburg Energy Alternatives Database

Problem: The management of Walburg Energy Alternatives already has realized the benefits from the database of items and vendors that you created. The management now would like to prepare reports and forms for the database.

Instructions: If you are using the Microsoft Access 2010 Complete or the Microsoft Access 2010 Comprehensive text, open the Walburg Energy Alternatives database that you used in Chapter 3. Otherwise, see your instructor for information on accessing the files required in this book.

Perform the following tasks:

1. Open in Layout view the Inventory Status Report that you created in Chapter 1. Add a total for the Inventory Value field. Be sure the total is completely displayed. Display the average cost. If there are fewer than 10 items on hand, the value should appear in a red bold font. Filter the report for all items where the number on hand is 5 or less. Save the filtered report as Filtered Inventory Status Report.

2. Create the Items by Vendor report shown in Figure 4–84.

Items by Vendor

Vendor Code	Vendor Name	Item Number	Description	On Hand	Cost
AS	Asterman Industries				
		2216	Child Safety Caps	15	$2.89
		3663	Air Deflector	8	$5.45
		4553	Energy Saving Kit	7	$42.75
		6234	Programmable Thermostat	3	$34.25
		8136	Smoke Detector	10	$6.10
		9458	Windows Insulator Kit	10	$4.95
Summary for 'Vendor Code' = AS (6 detail records)					
Avg					$16.07
JM	JMZ Technologies				
		1234	Adhesive Door Sweep	5	$3.45
		2234	Clothes Dryer Heat Saver	4	$8.99
		3673	Energy Booklet	25	$2.70
		4583	Fluorescent Light Bulb	18	$4.50
		6185	Luminescent Night Light	12	$3.75
		7123	Retractable Clothesline	10	$13.25
		8590	Water Conservation Kit	8	$13.45
Summary for 'Vendor Code' = JM (7 detail records)					
Avg					$7.16
SD	Scryps Distributors				
		2310	Drip Counter	10	$1.79
		2789	Hot Water Gauge	6	$2.75
		4573	Faucet Aerator	20	$0.89
		5923	Low Flow Shower Head	11	$8.75
Vendor Code	Vendor Name	Item Number	Description	On Hand	Cost
		6345	Rain Gauge	16	$2.89
		7934	Shower Timer	15	$2.45
		8344	Toilet Tank Water Saver	18	$3.35
Summary for 'Vendor Code' = SD (7 detail records)					
Avg					$3.27

Figure 4–84

Continued >

In the Lab *continued*

3. Create the form shown in Figure 4–85. If there are fewer than 10 items on hand, the value should appear in a red bold font. Save the form as Item Update Form.

Figure 4–85

4. Filter the Item Update Form for all items where the cost is less than $3.00 and sort the results in descending order by cost. Save the form as Filtered Item Update Form.

5. Submit the revised database in the format specified by your instructor.

In the Lab

Lab 3: Presenting Data in the Philamar Training Database

Problem: The management of Philamar Training already has realized the benefits from the database you created. The management now would like to prepare reports and forms for the database.

Instructions: If you are using the Microsoft Access 2010 Complete or the Microsoft Access 2010 Comprehensive text, open the Philamar Training database that you used in Chapter 3. Otherwise, see your instructor for information on accessing the files required in this book. Submit the revised database in the format specified by your instructor.

Instructions Part 1: Modify the Client Status Report created in Chapter 1. Add the Client Type field to the report and group records by client type. Include totals for the Amount Paid and Current Due fields. If the amount due on any record is $0.00, the value should appear in a red bold font. The report should be similar to the Client Financial Report shown in Figure 4–1 on page AC 210.

Instructions Part 2: Create a Clients by Trainer report for Philamar Training. The report should be similar to the Clients by Analyst report shown in Figure 4–2 on page AC 211 with the records grouped by trainer number. Include the Trainer Number, First Name, and Last Name fields from the Trainer table. Include the Client Number, Client Name, Amount Paid, and Current Due fields from the Client table. Provide subtotals and a grand total for the Amount Paid and Current Due fields. Change the page layout to landscape.

Instructions Part 3: Create a Client Financial Form for Philamar Training that is similar to the form shown in Figure 4–3 on page AC 212. The form should include the Client Number, Client Name, Amount Paid, Current Due, Trainer Number, Client Type, and Training Needed fields.

Cases and Places

Apply your creative thinking and problem solving skills to design and implement a solution.

See the inside back cover of this book for instructions for downloading the Data Files for Students, or see your instructor for information on accessing the required files.

1: Presenting Data in the Chamber of Commerce Database

Academic

If you are using the Microsoft Access 2010 Complete or the Microsoft Access 2010 Comprehensive text, open the Chamber of Commerce database that you used in Chapter 3. Otherwise, see your instructor for information on accessing the files required in this book. Use the concepts and techniques presented in this chapter to perform each of the following tasks:

a. Create a report that groups advertisers by advertiser type. Include the Advertiser Type, Advertiser Number, Advertiser Name, Balance, Amount Paid, and Ad Rep Number fields in the report. Include totals for the two currency fields. Use conditional formatting to emphasize any values in the Balance field that are greater than $200.

b. Create a report that includes data from both the Ad Rep table and the Advertiser table. Include the Ad Rep Number, First Name, and Last Name fields from the Ad Rep table. Include the Advertiser Number, Advertiser Name, Balance, and Amount Paid fields from the Advertiser table. Group the report by ad rep number. Include totals for the two currency fields. Change the orientation to landscape.

Continued >

Cases and Places *continued*

c. Create a form for the Advertiser table. Include the Advertiser Number, Advertiser Name, Balance, Amount Paid, Advertiser Type, and Ad Rep Number fields on the form.

Submit the revised database in the format specified by your instructor.

2: Presenting Data in the Consignment Database

Personal

If you are using the Microsoft Access 2010 Complete or the Microsoft Access 2010 Comprehensive text, open the Consignment database that you used in Chapter 3. Otherwise, see your instructor for information on accessing the files required in this book. Use the concepts and techniques presented in this chapter to perform each of the following tasks:

a. Modify the Available Items Report you created in Chapter 1. Group the report by the condition of the item and sort by description. Include the average price.

b. Create a report that includes data from both the Seller and the Items table. Include the Seller Code, First Name, and Last Name fields from the Seller table. Include all fields except Seller Code from the Items table. Group the report by seller code and sort by description within group. Do not include any totals.

c. Create labels for the Items table. These labels will be used to tag items in the store. Include the seller code on the first line, the item number and description on the second line, the price on the third line, and the date posted on the fourth line. Use a font size and weight that will make it easy for individuals to read the label.

Submit the revised database in the format specified by your instructor.

3: Presenting Data in the Senior Care Database

Professional

If you are using the Microsoft Access 2010 Complete or the Microsoft Access 2010 Comprehensive text, open the Senior Care database that you used in Chapter 3. Otherwise, see your instructor for information on accessing the files required in this book. Use the concepts and techniques presented in this chapter to perform each of the following tasks:

a. Create a report that includes data from both the Helper table and the Client table. Include the Helper Number, First Name, and Last Name fields from the Helper table. Include the Client Number, First Name, Last Name, and Services Needed fields from the Client table. Group the report by helper number, and sort the report by client number. Change the page layout to Landscape.

b. Create a form for the Client table. Include the Client Number, First Name, Last Name, Amount Paid, Balance, Helper Number, and Services Needed fields.

Submit the revised database in the format specified by your instructor.

5 | Multitable Forms

Objectives

You will have mastered the material in this project when you can:

- Add Yes/No, Date/Time, Memo, OLE Object, and Attachment fields
- Use the Input Mask Wizard
- Update fields and enter data
- Change row and column size
- Create a form with a subform in Design view
- Modify a subform and form design

- Enhance the form title
- Change tab stops and tab order
- Use the form to view data and attachments
- View object dependencies
- Use Date/Time, Memo, and Yes/No fields in a query
- Create a form with a datasheet

5 Multitable Forms

Introduction

BTW

Q&As
For a complete list of the Q&As found in many of the step-by-step sequences in this book, visit the Access 2010 Q&A Web page (scsite.com/ac2010/qa).

This chapter adds several additional fields to the Camashaly database that require special data types. It then creates a form incorporating data from two tables. The two tables, Business Analyst and Client, are related in a one-to-many relationship. That is, one business analyst is related to *many* clients, but each client is related to only *one* business analyst. The Business Analyst Table is called the "one" table in the relationship and the Client table is called the "many" table. The form will show one business analyst at a time, but also will include the many clients of that business analyst. This chapter also creates queries that use the added fields.

Project — Multitable Forms

BTW

BTWs
For a complete list of the BTWs found in the margins of this book, visit the Access 2010 BTW Web page (scsite.com/ac2010/btw).

Camashaly Design uses its database to keep records about clients and business analysts. After using the database for several months, however, Camashaly has found that it needs to maintain additional data on its business analysts. The company wants to identify those business analysts who have a professional certificate in business analysis, store the start date of each business analyst in the database, and include notes about each business analyst as well as the business analyst's picture. Additionally, business analysts now maintain files about potential contacts. These files are separate from the database; some are maintained in Word and others in Excel. Camashaly would like a way to attach these files to the corresponding business analyst's record in the database. Finally, Camashaly wants to add the Phone Number field to the Business Analyst Table. Users should type only the digits in the telephone number and then have Access format the number appropriately. If the user enters 7195558364, for example, Access will format the number as (719) 555-8364.

After the proposed fields have been added to the database, Camashaly wants users to be able to use a form that incorporates the Client and Business Analyst tables and that includes the newly added fields as well as some of the existing fields. The form also should include the client number, name, amount paid, and current due amount for the clients of each business analyst. Camashaly would like to see multiple clients on the screen at the same time (Figure 5–1). The database should allow users to scroll through all the clients of a business analyst and to open any of the attachments concerning the business analyst's Client Notes. Finally, Camashaly requires queries that use the Certification, Start Date, and Comment fields.

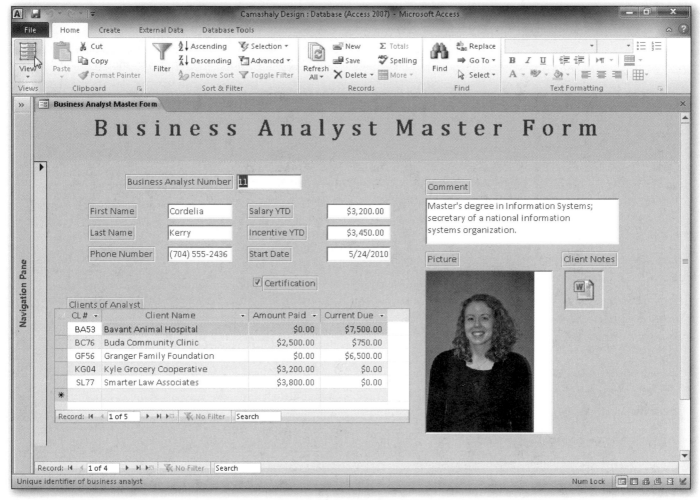

Figure 5–1

Overview

As you read through this chapter, you will learn how to create forms by performing these general tasks:

- Add the Certification, Start Date, Comment, Picture, and Client Notes fields to the Business Analyst Table and assign each field the appropriate data type.
- Add the Phone Number to the Business Analyst Table and create an appropriate input mask to automatically format the number.
- Create the Business Analyst Master Form and add the fields from the Business Analyst Table at the appropriate positions.
- Add a subform containing the Client Number, Client Name, Amount Paid, and Current Due fields from the Client table.
- Enhance the form by applying colors and various special effects.
- Create and run queries that involve the Certification, Start Date, and Comment fields.

Report and Form Design Guidelines

When designing reports and forms in Access, you must determine whether new fields are required and identify the source (table or tables) of the data. The decisions you make will affect the design of reports and forms. To design reports and forms, you should follow these general guidelines:

1. **When new fields are needed, determine the purpose of those fields to see if they need special data types.** Special data types will be needed for those fields that contain dates, contain values of Yes or No, or record an extended description of something. Fields containing pictures also require a special data type, as do fields containing attachments of files created in other applications.

2. **When a form is required, determine whether the form requires data from more than one table.** Determine whether all the data is found in a single table or whether it comes from multiple related tables.

3. **If the form requires data from more than one table, determine the relationship between the tables.** Identify one-to-many relationships. For each relationship, identify the "one" table and the "many" table.

4. **If the form requires data from more than one table, determine on which of the tables the form is to be based.** Which table contains data that is the focus of the form? For example, determine whether it is a form about business analysts that happens to require some client data to be effective or whether it is a form about clients that also includes some business analyst data as additional information. The table on which the form is based is the main table.

5. **Determine the fields from each table that need to be on the form.** Decide exactly how the form will be used and identify the fields that are necessary to support this use. Determine whether there are any additional fields that, while not strictly necessary, would make the form more functional. For example, if a user is entering a business analyst number on a form based on clients, it may be helpful to also see the name of the business analyst with that number.

When necessary, more specific details concerning the above decisions and/or actions are presented at appropriate points within the chapter. The chapter also will identify the use of these guidelines in the design of forms such as the one shown in Figure 5–1.

To Start Access

The following steps, which assume Windows 7 is running, start Access based on a typical installation. You may need to ask your instructor how to start Access for your computer.

1 Click the Start button on the Windows 7 taskbar to display the Start menu.

2 Type `Microsoft Access` as the search text in the 'Search programs and files' text box and watch the search results appear on the Start menu.

3 Click Microsoft Access 2010 in the search results on the Start menu to start Access.

4 If the Access window is not maximized, click the Maximize button next to the Close button on its title bar to maximize the window.

To Open a Database from Access

The following steps open the Camashaly Design database from the Access folder in the CIS 101 folder on the USB flash drive.

1 With your USB flash drive connected to one of the computer's USB ports, click File on the Ribbon to open the Backstage view.

2 Click Open in the Backstage view to display the Open dialog box.

3 Navigate to the location of the file to be opened (in this case, the USB flash drive, then to the CIS 101 folder [or your class folder], and then to the Access folder).

4 Click Camashaly Design to select the file to be opened.

5 Click the Open button (Open dialog box) to open the selected file and display the opened database in the Access window.

6 If a Security Warning appears, click the Enable Content button.

Adding Special Fields

Having analyzed its requirements, the management of Camashaly has identified a need for some new fields for the Business Analyst Table. They need a Phone Number field and they want to assist users in entering the correct format for a phone number, so the field will use an input mask. An **input mask** specifies how data is to be entered and how it will appear. Camashaly also needs a Certification field, which uses a value of Yes or No to indicate whether an analyst is certified; this field's data type will be Yes/No. They need a Start Date field, which will be a Date/Time field, that is, a field whose data type is Date/Time. They need a Comment field, which will be a Memo field. Because no special text formatting, such as bold or italic, is required in the Comment field, the value of the Text Format property will remain Plain Text rather than Rich Text. The Client Notes field, which must be able to contain multiple attachments for each business analyst, will be an Attachment field. The Picture field is the only field whose data type is uncertain — it could be either OLE Object, which can contain objects created by a variety of applications, or Attachment.

Certainly OLE Object is an appropriate data type for a picture, because when you store an image as an OLE object, the image stays with the database. On the other hand, if an Attachment field contains a picture, the field will display the picture. For other types of attachments, such as Word documents and Excel spreadsheets, however, the Attachment field displays an icon representing the attachment. Camashaly Design has decided to use OLE Object as the Picture field data type for two reasons. First, the form shown in Figure 5–1 contains another field that must be an Attachment field, the Client Notes field. In Datasheet view, an Attachment field appears as a paper clip rather than the field name. Thus, if the Picture field were also an Attachment field, the form would display two paper clips, leading to potential confusion. A second potential problem with using an Attachment field for pictures occurs when you have multiple attachments to a record. Only the first attachment routinely appears in the field on either a datasheet or form. Thus, if the picture were not the first attachment, it would not appear.

BTW

Memo Fields
If you need to keep a historical record of changes to a memo field, set the value for the Append Only property to yes.

<table>
<tr><td>Plan
Ahead</td><td>

Determine the purpose of new fields to see if they need special data types.
If you determine that you need new fields in a table, you then need to determine data types for these fields. Special data types include Yes/No, Date/Time, Memo, OLE Object, Attachment, and Hyperlink. To standardize the appearance of data, you can create an input mask, which applies common formatting to date, phone number, and other types of information.

- **Determine whether an input mask is appropriate.** Sometimes the data in the field should be displayed in a special way, for example, with parentheses and a hyphen like a phone number, or separated into three groups of digits like a Social Security number. If so, should Access assist the user in entering the data in the right format? For example, by including an input mask in a field, Access can automatically insert the parentheses and a hyphen when a user enters a phone number.

- **Determine whether the Yes/No data type is appropriate.** A field is a good candidate for the Yes/No data type if the only possible field values are Yes or No, True or False, or On or Off.

- **Determine whether the Date/Time data type is appropriate.** If a field contains a date, assigning it the Date/Time data type accomplishes several things. First, Access will ensure that the only values entered in the field are legitimate dates. Second, you can perform date arithmetic. For example, you can subtract one date from another to find the number of days between the two dates. Finally, you can sort the field and the dates will sort chronologically.

- **Determine whether the Memo data type is appropriate.** A field that contains text that is variable in length and potentially very lengthy is an appropriate use of the Memo data type. If you want to use special text effects, such as bold and italic, you can assign the field the Memo data type and change the value of the field's Text Format property from Plain Text to Rich Text. You can also collect history on the changes to a Memo field by changing the value of the field's Append Only property from No to Yes. If you do so, when you right-click the field and click Show Column History on the shortcut menu, you will see a record of all changes made to the field.

- **Determine whether the OLE Object data type is appropriate.** Does the field contain objects created by other applications that support **OLE (Object Linking and Embedding)** as a server? OLE is a feature of Microsoft Windows that creates a special relationship between Microsoft Access and the application that created the object. When you edit the object, Microsoft Access returns automatically to the application that created the object.

- **Determine whether the Attachment data type is appropriate.** Will the field contain one or more attachments that were created in other applications? If so, the Attachment data type is appropriate. It allows you to store multiple attachments on each record. You can view and manipulate these attachments in their original application.

- **Determine whether the Hyperlink data type is appropriate.** Will the field contain links to other Office documents or to Web pages? If so, Hyperlink is appropriate.

</td></tr>
</table>

To Add Fields with New Data Types to a Table

You add the new fields to the Business Analyst Table by modifying the design of the table and inserting the fields at the appropriate position in the table structure. The following steps add the Certification, Start Date, Comment, Picture, and Client Notes fields to the Business Analyst Table.

1

- If necessary, open the Navigation Pane.

- Right-click the Business Analyst Table to display a shortcut menu (Figure 5–2).

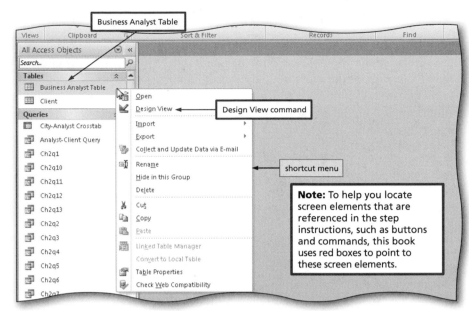

Figure 5–2

2

- Click Design View on the shortcut menu to open the table in Design view (Figure 5–3).

Figure 5–3

3

- Click the first open field to select the position for the first additional field.

- Type **Certification** as the field name, press the TAB key, select Yes/No as the data type, and then press the TAB key twice to move to the next field.

- In a similar fashion, add a field with **Start Date** as the field name and Date/Time as the data type, a field with **Comment** as the field name and Memo as the data type, a field with **Picture** as the field name and OLE Object as the data type, and a field with **Client Notes** as the field name and Attachment as the data type (Figure 5–4).

Figure 5–4

Q&A

Why use Date/Time as a data type for date fields rather than Text?

If you use Date/Time, the computer will ensure that only legitimate dates are entered in the field. In addition, you can perform appropriate arithmetic with dates. You also can sort by date.

4

- Click the Save button on the Quick Access Toolbar to save your changes.

To Use the Input Mask Wizard

An **input mask** specifies how data is to be entered and how it will appear. You can enter an input mask directly or you can use the Input Mask Wizard. The wizard assists you in the creation of the input mask by allowing you to select from a list of the most frequently used input masks.

To use the Input Mask Wizard, select the Input Mask property in the field's property sheet and then select the Build button. The following steps add the Phone Number field and then specify how the telephone number is to appear by using the Input Mask Wizard.

- Click the row selector for the Postal Code field (shown in Figure 5–4), and then press the INSERT key to insert a blank row above Postal Code.

- Click the Field Name column for the new field.

- Type **Phone Number** as the field name and then press the TAB key to enter the field.

- Click the Input Mask property box (Figure 5–5).

Q&A

Do I need to change the data type?

No. Text is the appropriate data type for the Phone Number field.

Figure 5–5

- Click the Build button to use a wizard to enter the input mask.

- If a dialog box appears asking you to save the table, click the Yes button. (If a dialog box displays a message that the Input Mask Wizard is not installed, check with your instructor before proceeding with the following steps.)

- Ensure that Phone Number is selected (Figure 5–6).

 Experiment

- Click different input masks and enter data in the Try It text box to see the effect of the input mask. When done, click the Phone Number input mask.

Figure 5–6

3

- Click the Next button to move to the next Input Mask Wizard screen, where you then are given the opportunity to change the input mask.

- Because you do not need to change the mask, click the Next button a second time (Figure 5–7).

Figure 5–7

4

- Be sure the 'Without the symbols in the mask, like this' option button is selected, click the Next button to move to the next Input Mask Wizard screen, and then click the Finish button (Figure 5–8).

Why does the data type not change to Input Mask?

The data type of the Phone Number field is still Text. The only thing that changed is one of the field properties, the Input Mask property.

Could I have typed the value in the Input Mask property myself, rather than using the wizard?

Yes. Input masks can be complex, however, so it is usually easier and safer to use the wizard.

5

- Click the Save button on the Quick Access Toolbar to save your changes.

- Close the Business Analyst Table.

Figure 5–8

Adding Fields in Datasheet View

BTW

Input Mask Characters
When you create an input mask, Access adds several characters. These characters control the literal values that appear when you enter data. For example, the first backslash in the input mask in Figure 5–8 displays the opening parenthesis. The double quotes force Access to display the closing parenthesis and a space. The second backslash forces Access to display the hyphen that separates the first and second part of the phone number.

You can also add fields in Datasheet view. One way to do so is to use the Add & Delete group on the Table Tools Fields tab (Figure 5–9). Select the field that precedes the position where you want to add the new field and then click the appropriate button. You can click the Text button to add a Text field, the Number button to add a Number field, the Currency button to add a Currency field, and so on. Alternatively, you can click the More Fields button as shown in the figure to display the Data Type gallery. You then can click a data type in the gallery to add a field with that type.

The gallery gives some additional control on the data type. For example, if you click the Check Box version of a Yes/No field, the field will be displayed as a check box, which is the common way to display such a field. If instead you click the Yes/No version of a Yes/No field, the value in the field will be displayed as either the word, Yes, or the word, No.

If you scroll down in the Data Type gallery, you will find a Quick Start section. The commands in this section give you quick ways of adding some common types of fields. For example, clicking Address in the Quick Start section immediately adds several fields: Address, City, State Province, Zip Postal, and Country Region. Clicking Start and End Dates immediately adds both a Start Date field and an End Date field.

In Datasheet view, you can rename fields by right-clicking the field name, clicking Rename Field on the shortcut menu, and then typing the new name. Delete a field by clicking the field and then clicking the Delete button (Table Tools Fields tab | Add & Delete group). Move a field from one location to another by dragging the field.

Figure 5–9

Updating the New Fields

After adding the new fields to the table, the next task is to enter data into the fields. The data type determines the manner in which this is accomplished. The following sections cover the methods for updating fields with an input mask, Yes/No fields, Date/Time fields, Memo fields, OLE fields, and Attachment fields. They also show how you would enter data in Hyperlink fields.

To Enter Data Using an Input Mask

When you are entering data in a field that has an input mask, Access will insert the appropriate special characters in the proper positions. This means Access automatically will insert the parentheses around the area code, the space following the second parenthesis, and the hyphen in the Phone Number field. The following steps use the input mask to add the telephone numbers.

1

- Open the Business Analyst Table and close the Navigation Pane.

- Click at the beginning of the Phone Number field on the first record to display an insertion point in the field (Figure 5–10).

Q&A I do not see the parentheses and hyphen as shown in the figure. Did I do something wrong?

It depends on exactly where you click as to whether you will see the symbols. In any case, as soon as you start typing in the field, the symbols should appear.

Figure 5–10

2

- Type 7045552436 as the telephone number (Figure 5–11).

Figure 5–11

- Use the same technique to enter the remaining telephone numbers, as shown in Figure 5–12.

Figure 5–12

To Enter Data in Yes/No Fields

Fields that are Yes/No fields contain check boxes. To set the value to Yes, place a check mark in the check box. To set a value to No, leave the check box blank. The following steps set the value of the Certification field, a Yes/No field, to Yes for the first and fourth records.

- Repeatedly click the right scroll arrow (shown in Figure 5–12) until the new fields appear.

- Click the check box in the Certification field on the first record to place a check mark in the box (Figure 5–13).

Figure 5–13

Q&A

What is the meaning of the check mark?

A check mark indicates the value in the Certification field is Yes. If there is no check mark, the value is No.

- Click the check box in the Certification field on the fourth record to place a check mark in the box.

To Enter Data in Date/Time Fields

To enter data in Date/Time fields, you can simply type the dates and include slashes (/). As an alternative, you can click the field, click the Date Picker that will appear next to the field, and then use the calendar to select the date. The following step adds the start dates for the business analysts.

1

- Click the Start Date field on the first record, type **5/24/2010** as the date on the first record, and then press the DOWN ARROW key.

- Type **2/1/2011** as the start date on the second record, and then press the DOWN ARROW key.

- Type **5/16/2011** as the start date on the third record, and then press the DOWN ARROW key.

- Type **1/9/2012** as the start date on the fourth record (Figure 5–14).

Q&A

How do I use the Date Picker?

Click the Date Picker to display a calendar. Scroll to the month and year you want and then click the desired day of the month.

Figure 5–14

Experiment

- Click the Date Picker on the last record and use it to assign a date. When finished, change the date to 1/9/2012.

BTW

Memo Fields
You also can enter data in a memo field using the Zoom dialog box. To do so, click the memo field and then press SHIFT+F2 to open the Zoom dialog box.

To Enter Data in Memo Fields

To update a memo field, simply type the data in the field. With the current row and column spacing on the screen, only a small portion of the memo will appear. To correct this problem, you will change the spacing later to allow more room for the memo. The following steps enter each business analyst's comment.

1

- If necessary, click the right scroll arrow (shown in Figure 5–12) so the Comment field appears.

- Click the Comment field on the first record, and then type **Master's degree in Information Systems; secretary of a national information systems organization.** as the entry (Figure 5–15).

Figure 5–15

2

- Click the Comment field on the second record, and then type `Bachelor's degree in Business Administration; veteran; has database experience.` as the entry.

- Click the Comment field on the third record, and then type `Working on a Master's degree in Business Administration; has a Bachelor's degree in Information Technology.` as the entry.

- Click the Comment field on the fourth record, and then type `Bachelor's degree in Computer Science; active in promoting CS as a major to young adults.` as the entry (Figure 5–16).

Figure 5–16

To Change the Row and Column Size

Only a small portion of the comments appears in the datasheet. To allow more of the information to appear, you can expand the size of the rows and the columns. You can change the size of a column by using the field selector. The **field selector** is the bar containing the field name. To change the size of a row, you use a record's **record selector**, which is the small box at the beginning of each record.

The following steps resize the column containing the Comment field and the rows of the table so a larger portion of the Comment field text will appear.

1

- Drag the right edge of the field selector for the Comment field to the right to resize the Comment column to the approximate size shown in Figure 5–17.

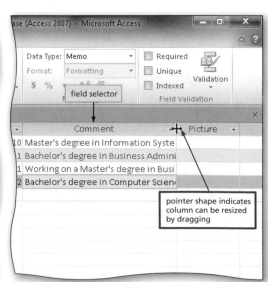

Figure 5–17

2

• Drag the lower edge of the record selector to approximately the position shown in Figure 5–18.

Q&A

Can rows be different sizes?

No. All rows must be the same size.

Figure 5–18

Other Ways	
1. Right-click record selector, click Row Height to change row spacing	2. Right-click field selector, click Field Width to change column size

Undoing Changes to Row Height and Column Width

If you later find that the changes you made to the row height or the column width are no longer appropriate, you can undo them. To undo changes to the row height, right-click the row selector, click Row Height on the shortcut menu, and then click the Standard Height check box in the Row Height dialog box. To undo changes to the column width, right-click the field selector, click Field Width on the shortcut menu, and then click the Standard Width check box in the Column Width dialog box.

To Enter Data in OLE Object Fields

To insert data into an OLE Object field, you use the Insert Object command on the OLE field's shortcut menu. The Insert Object command presents a list of the various types of objects that can be inserted. Access then opens the corresponding application to create the object; for example, Microsoft Excel Chart. If the object already is created and stored in a file, as is the case in this project, you simply insert it directly from the file.

The following steps insert pictures into the Picture field. The pictures will be visible as photographs in the form; however, the table will display the text, Bitmap Image, in the Picture field. The steps assume that the pictures are located in a folder called AccessData on your USB drive. If your pictures are located elsewhere, you will need to make the appropriate changes.

1

- Ensure the Picture field appears on your screen, and then right-click the Picture field on the first record to produce a shortcut menu (Figure 5–19).

Figure 5–19

2

- Click Insert Object on the shortcut menu to display the Microsoft Access dialog box (Figure 5–20).

Figure 5–20

3

- Click the 'Create from File' option button, and then click the Browse button to display the Browse dialog box.

- Navigate to the AccessData folder on your USB drive in the Browse dialog box. (If your pictures are located elsewhere, navigate to the folder where they are located instead of the AccessData folder.)

- Click Pict1 and then click the OK button (Browse dialog box) to select the appropriate picture (Figure 5–21).

Figure 5–21

4

- Click the OK button to insert the picture into the table.

Q&A

I do not see the picture. I just see the words, Bitmap Image. Is that correct?

Yes. You will see the actual picture when you use this field in a form.

Bitmap Image

The entries in the Picture field all should be the words, Bitmap Image. You will not see the actual picture of the business analyst. The entries may initially be something other than the words, Bitmap Image, but, if so, they should change to the words, Bitmap Image, after you move to another record. They also should change after you close and reopen the table.

TO CHANGE PICTURE FIELD ENTRIES TO BITMAP IMAGE

If the entries do not change to the words, Bitmap Image, there is a problem either with the graphics filters that are installed or with the file associations for BMP files. You would use a slightly different technique to add the pictures, as in the following steps:

1. Right-click the Picture field, click Insert Object, *and then* select the Bitmap Image object type from the Object Type list.
2. Click the OK button to open the Paint application. If necessary, maximize the Paint window.
3. Click the Paste button arrow (Home tab | Clipboard group), and then click the Paste from command.
4. Navigate to the location for the desired BMP file, select the file, and then click the Open button.
5. Click the Paint button, which is just to the left of the Home tab, and then click the 'Exit and return to document' command to return to the table.

> **BTW**
>
> **OLE Fields**
> OLE fields can occupy a great deal of space. To save space in your database, you can convert a picture from Bitmap Image to Picture (Device Independent Bitmap). To make the conversion, right-click the field, click Bitmap Image Object, click Convert, and then select Picture (Device Independent Bitmap) in the Convert dialog box.

To Enter the Remaining Pictures

The following step adds the remaining pictures. If you have the problem indicated in the previous section, you should use the suggested technique to add the pictures.

1 Insert the pictures into the second, third, and fourth records using the techniques illustrated in the previous set of steps. For the second record, select the picture named Pict2. For the third record, select the picture named Pict3. For the fourth record, select Pict4.

To Enter Data in Attachment Fields

To insert data into an Attachment field, you use the Manage Attachments command on the Attachment field's shortcut menu. The Manage Attachments command displays the Attachments dialog box, which you can use to attach as many files as necessary to the field. The following steps attach two files to the first business analyst and one file to the fourth business analyst. The second and third business analysts currently have no attachments.

1

- Ensure the Client Notes field, which has a paper clip in the field selector, appears on your screen, and then right-click the Client Notes field on the first record to produce a shortcut menu (Figure 5–22).

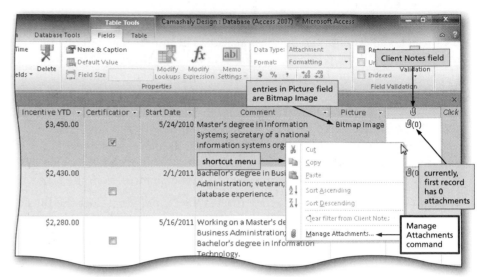

Figure 5–22

2

- Click Manage Attachments on the shortcut menu to display the Attachments dialog box (Figure 5–23).

Figure 5–23

3

- Click the Add button (Attachments dialog box) to add an attachment.

- Navigate to the AccessData folder on your USB drive in the Choose File dialog box. (If your files are located elsewhere, navigate to the folder where they are located instead of the AccessData folder.)

- Click Cordelia Kerry Clients, a Word file, and then click the Open button (Choose File dialog box) to attach the file.

- Click the Add button (Attachments dialog box).

- Click the Cordelia Kerry Potential Clients, an Excel file, and then click the Open button to attach the file (Figure 5–24).

Figure 5–24

4

- Click the OK button (Attachments dialog box) to close the Attachments dialog box.

- Using the same technique, attach the Jeff Scott Potential Clients file to the fourth record (Figure 5–25). (The second and third records have no attachments.)

Figure 5–25

To Enter Data in Hyperlink Fields

If you had a Hyperlink field, you would insert data by using the following steps.

1. Right-click the Hyperlink field in which you want to enter data to display a shortcut menu.

2. Click Hyperlink on the shortcut menu to display the Hyperlink submenu.

3. Click Edit Hyperlink on the Hyperlink submenu to display the Insert Hyperlink dialog box.

4. Type the desired Web address in the Address text box.

5. Click the OK button (Insert Hyperlink dialog box).

To Save the Properties and Close the Table

The row and column spacing are table properties. When changing any table properties, the changes apply only as long as the table is active *unless they are saved*. Once you have saved them, they will apply every time you open the table.

The following steps first save the properties and then close the table.

1 Click the Save button on the Quick Access Toolbar to save the changes to the table properties.

2 Close the table.

Break Point: If you wish to stop working through the chapter at this point, you can resume the project at a later time by starting Access, opening the database called Camashaly Design, and continuing to follow the steps from this location forward.

Viewing Pictures and Attachments in Datasheet View

Although the pictures do not appear on the screen, you can view them within the table. To view the picture of a particular business analyst, right-click the Picture field for the business analyst. Click Bitmap Image Object on the shortcut menu, and then click Open. The picture will appear. Once you have finished viewing the picture, close the window containing the picture by clicking its Close button.

You can view the attachments in the Client Notes field by right-clicking the field and then clicking Manage Attachments on the shortcut menu. The attachments then appear in the Attachments dialog box. To view an attachment, click the attachment and then click the Open button (Attachments dialog box). The attachment will appear in its original application. After you have finished viewing the attachment, close the original application and close the dialog box.

Multitable Form Techniques

With the additional fields in place, Camashaly Design management is ready to incorporate data from both the Business Analyst and Client tables in a single form. The form will display data concerning one business analyst. It also will display data concerning the many clients assigned to the business analyst. The relationship between business analysts and clients is a one-to-many relationship in which the Business Analyst Table is the "one" table and the Client table is the "many" table.

To include the data for the many clients of a business analyst on the form, the client data will appear in a **subform**, which is a form that is contained within another form. The form in which the subform is contained is called the main form. Thus, the **main form** will contain business analyst data, and the subform will contain client data.

Plan Ahead

> **Determine on which of the tables the form is to be based.**
> Once you determine that you need data from more than one table, you need to determine the main table and its relationship to any other table.
>
> - **Determine the main table the form is intended to view and/or update.** You need to identify the purpose of the form and the table it is really intended to show, which is the main table. If the database contains a table that could be omitted and still have the form make sense, that is *not* the main table.
>
> - **Determine how the additional table should fit into the form.** If the additional table is the "many" part of the relationship, the data should probably be in a subform or datasheet. If the additional table is the "one" part of the relationship, the data should probably appear simply as fields on the form.

Plan Ahead

> **Determine the fields from each table that need to be on the form.**
> After you decide on which tables the form is based, you need to decide which fields to include.
>
> - **Determine the fields from the main table that should be included on the form.** Identify the fields that users want on the form and determine whether a particular order for the fields would be most useful.
>
> - **Determine the fields from the additional table that should be included on the form.** Identify the fields from the additional table that would be helpful in updating or viewing the fields from the main table and determine whether users should be able to change these fields using the form. (Often they should not be able to change the fields.)

To Create a Form in Design View

You can create a form in Design view, which gives you the most flexibility in laying out the form using a blank design on which you place objects. The following steps create a form in Design view.

1

- If necessary, open the Navigation Pane and be sure the Business Analyst Table is selected.

- Click Create on the Ribbon to display the Create tab (Figure 5–26).

Figure 5–26

 2

- Click the Form Design button (Create tab | Forms group) to create a new form in Design view.

- Close the Navigation Pane.

- If a field list does not appear, click the Add Existing Fields button (Form Design Tools Design tab | Tools group) to display a field list (Figure 5–27). If you do not see the tables listed, click Show all tables. (Your list might show all fields in the Client table.)

Q&A How do I display the fields in the Business Analyst Table?

Click the expand indicator (+) in front of the Business Analyst Table to display the fields.

Figure 5–27

To Add a Control for a Field to the Form Design

To place a control for a field on a form, drag the field from the field list to the desired position. The following steps place the Business Analyst Number field on the form.

1

- If necessary, click the expand indicator for the Business Analyst Table to display the fields in the table. Point to the Business Analyst Number field in the field list for the Business Analyst Table, press the left mouse button, and then drag the field to the approximate position shown in Figure 5–28.

Q&A Do I have to be exact?

No. Just be sure you are in the same general location.

Figure 5–28

2

- Release the left mouse button to place a control for the field (Figure 5–29).

Figure 5–29

To Save the Form

Before continuing with the form creation, it is a good idea to save the form. The following steps save the form and assign it the name Business Analyst Master Form.

1 Click the Save button on the Quick Access Toolbar.

2 Type **Business Analyst Master Form** as the name of the form.

3 Click the OK button to save the form.

To Add Controls for Additional Fields

The following step places controls for the First Name, Last Name, Phone Number, Salary YTD, Incentive YTD, Start Date, and Certification fields on the form by dragging the fields from the field list.

1

- Drag the First Name, Last Name, Phone Number, Salary YTD, Incentive YTD, Start Date, and Certification fields and their labels to the approximate positions shown in Figure 5–30.

Q&A Do I have to align them precisely?

You can, but you do not need to. In the next steps, you will instruct Access to align the fields properly.

Q&A What if I drag the wrong field from the field list? Can I undo my action?

Yes. Click the Undo button.

Figure 5–30

To Align Controls on the Left

Often, you will want form controls to be aligned in some fashion. For example, the controls may be aligned so their right edges are even with each other. In another case, controls may be aligned so their top edges are even. To ensure that a collection of controls is aligned properly with each other, select all of the affected controls, and then use the appropriate alignment button on the Arrange tab.

There are two ways to select multiple controls. One way is to use a ruler. If you click a position on the horizontal ruler, you will select all the controls for which a portion of the control is under that position on the ruler. Similarly, if you click a position on the vertical ruler, you will select all the controls for which a portion of the control is to the right of that position on the ruler.

The second way to select multiple controls is to select the first control by clicking it. Then, select all the other controls by holding down the SHIFT key while clicking the control.

The following steps select the First Name, Last Name, and Phone Number controls and then align them so their left edges line up.

1

- Click the First Name control (the white space, not the label) to select the control.

- Hold the SHIFT key down and click the Last Name control to select an additional control.

- Hold the SHIFT key down, click the Phone Number control to select a third control, and then release the SHIFT key.

Q&A

I selected the wrong collection of fields. How can I start over?

Simply begin the process again, making sure you do not hold the SHIFT key down when you select the first field.

- Click Arrange on the Ribbon to display the Form Design Tools Arrange tab.

- Click the Align button (Form Design Tools Arrange tab | Sizing & Ordering group) to display the Align menu (Figure 5–31).

Figure 5–31

2

- Click the Left command on the Align menu to align the controls on the left (Figure 5–32).

3

- Click outside any of the selected controls to deselect the controls.

- Using the same technique, align the labels for the First Name, Last Name, and Phone Number fields on the left.

- Using the same technique, align the Salary YTD, Incentive YTD, and Start Date fields on the left.

- If necessary, align the labels for the Salary YTD, Incentive YTD, and Start Date fields on the left.

Figure 5–32

Other Ways
1. Right-click selected controls, click Align

To Align Controls on the Top and Adjust Vertical Spacing

You also can align controls so that their top edges line up. In addition, you can adjust spacing so that the vertical spacing between controls is the same. The following steps align the First Name and Salary YTD controls so that they are aligned on the top. Once these controls are aligned, you adjust the vertical spacing so that same amount of space separates each row of controls.

1

- Click the label for the First Name control to select the control.

- Hold the SHIFT key down and click the First Name control to select the additional control.

- Hold the SHIFT key down and click the label for the Salary YTD control to select the label as well.

- Hold the SHIFT key down and click the Salary YTD control to select an additional control.

- Click the Align button (Form Design Tools Arrange tab | Sizing & Ordering group) to display the Align menu (Figure 5–33).

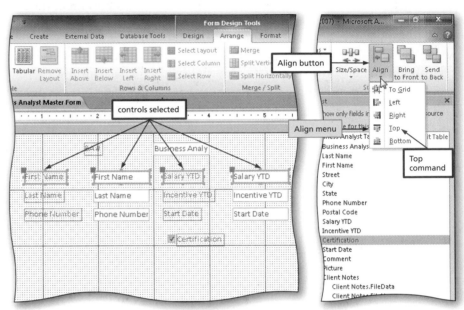

Figure 5–33

2

- Click the Top command on the Align menu to align the controls on the top.

- Click outside any of the selected controls to deselect the controls.

- Select the First Name, Last Name, Phone Number, Salary YTD, Incentive YTD, and Start Date fields.

- Click the Size/Space button (Form Design Tools Arrange tab | Sizing & Ordering group) to display the Size/Space menu (Figure 5–34).

3

- Click Equal Vertical on the Size/ Space menu to specify the spacing.

Figure 5–34

Q&A

What is the purpose of the other commands on the Size/Space menu?

You can adjust the spacing to fit the available space. You can adjust the space to match the tallest, shortest, widest, or narrowest section. You can adjust the space to match the closest grid points. You can specify equal horizontal spacing. Finally, you can increase or decrease either the vertical or the horizontal spacing.

To Move the Field List

Sometimes Access will obscure part of the form with the field list, making it difficult to place fields in the desired locations. To solve this problem, you can move the field list to a different location. The following step moves the field list in preparation for placing controls in the area it currently occupies.

1

• Move the field list to the approximate position shown in Figure 5–35 by dragging its title bar.

Q&A My field list changed size when I moved it. How can I return it to its original size?

Point to the border of the field list so that the mouse pointer changes to a double-headed arrow. You then can drag to adjust the size.

Q&A Can I make the field list smaller so I can see more of the screen?

Yes, you can adjust the size to whatever is most comfortable for you.

Figure 5–35

To Add Controls for the Remaining Fields

The following steps place controls for the Comment, Picture, and Client Notes fields and also move their attached labels to the desired position.

1

• Drag the control for the Comment field from the field list to the approximate position shown in Figure 5–36.

Figure 5–36

2

- Move the label for the Comment field to the position shown in Figure 5–37 by dragging its Move handle.

Q&A

I started to move the label and the control moved along with it. What did I do wrong?

You were not pointing at the handle to move the label independently of the control. Make sure you are pointing to the little box in the upper-left corner of the label.

Figure 5–37

3

- Using the same techniques, move the control for the Picture field to the approximate position shown in Figure 5–38 and move its label to the position shown in the figure.

Figure 5–38

4

- Click the control for the Picture field and drag the lower-right corner to the approximate position shown in Figure 5–39 to resize the control.

- Add the control for the Client Notes field in the position shown in the figure and move its attached label to the position shown in the figure.

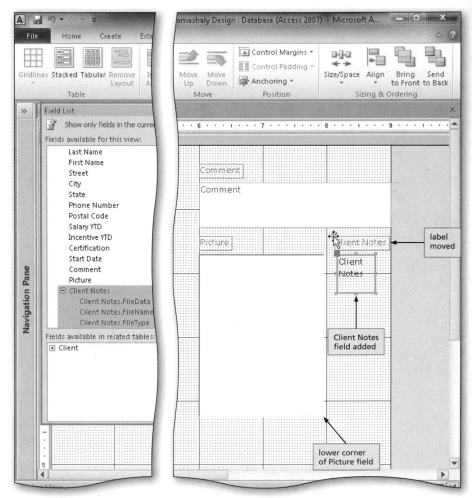

Figure 5–39

When would I need to click the expand indicator for the Client Notes field?

By clicking the expand indicator, you have access to three special properties of the field: FileData, FileName, and FileType. If you drag one of these onto the form, you will only get the corresponding information in the control. For example, if you drag Client Notes.FileName, the control will display the file name for the attachment. Most of the time, you want the field itself, so you would not use any of these properties.

5

- Close the field list by displaying the Design tab and then clicking the Add Existing Fields button (Form Design Tools Design tab | Tools group), which is shown in Figure 5–27.

Where will the field list be positioned the next time I display it?

Usually it will be in the position it was when you closed it. If that is the case and you want it in its typical position, move it there by dragging its title bar.

Other Ways
1. Click Close button for field list

To Use a Shortcut Menu to Change the Fill/Back Color

You can use the Background Color button on the Form Design Tools Format tab to change the background color of a form. In some cases, you also can use a shortcut menu. The following steps use a shortcut menu to change the background color of the form to gray.

1

- Right-click in the approximate position shown in Figure 5–40 to produce a shortcut menu.

Q&A

Does it matter where I right-click?

You can right-click anywhere on the form as long as you are outside of all the controls.

Figure 5–40

2

- Point to the Fill/Back Color command arrow on the shortcut menu to display a color palette (Figure 5–41).

3

- Click the gray color shown in Figure 5–41 to change the fill/back color to gray.

Figure 5–41

To Add a Title

A form should have a descriptive title. The following step adds a title to the form.

- Be sure the Design tab is selected.

- Click the Title button (Form Design Tools Design tab | Header/Footer group) to add a title to the form (Figure 5–42).

Q&A Why is there a new section?

The form title belongs in the Form Header section. When you clicked the Title button, Access added the Form Header section automatically and placed the title in it.

Q&A Could I add a Form Header section without having to click the Title button?

Yes. Right-click anywhere on the form background and click Form Header/Footer on the shortcut menu.

Figure 5–42

To Place a Subform

The Controls group on the Form Design Tools Design tab contains buttons called tools that you use to place a variety of types of controls on a form. To place a subform on a form, you use the Subform/Subreport tool. If the Use Control Wizards button is selected, a wizard will guide you through the process of adding the subform. The following steps use the Subform Wizard to place a subform.

- Click the More button (Form Design Tools Design tab | Controls group) to display a gallery of available tools (Figure 5–43).

Figure 5–43

2

- Be sure the Use Control Wizards button is selected, click the Subform/ Subreport tool on the Form Design Tools Design tab, and then move the mouse pointer to the approximate position shown in Figure 5–44.

Q&A How can I tell whether the Use Control Wizards button is selected?

The icon for the Use Control Wizards button will be highlighted, as shown in Figure 5–43. If it is not, click the Use Control Wizards button to highlight it, and then click the Subform/Subreport tool.

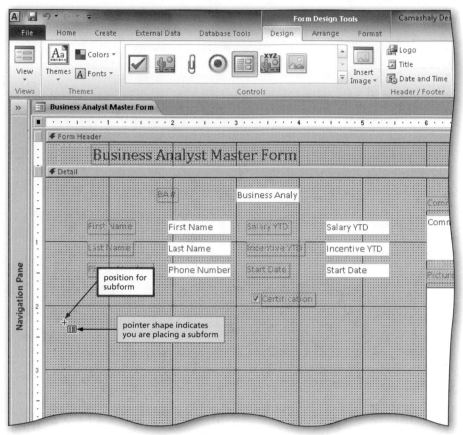

Figure 5–44

3

- Click the position shown in Figure 5–44 and then ensure the 'Use existing Tables and Queries' option button is selected (SubForm Wizard dialog box) (Figure 5–45).

Q&A My control is placed on the screen, but no wizard appeared. What should I do?

Press the DELETE key to delete the control you placed. Ensure that the Use Control Wizards button is selected, as described previously.

Figure 5–45

4

- Click the Next button.

- Click the Tables/Queries box arrow and then click the Client table to select the table that contains the fields for the subform.

- Add the Client Number, Client Name, Amount Paid, and Current Due fields by clicking the field and then clicking the Add Field button (SubForm Wizard dialog box) (Figure 5–46).

Figure 5–46

5

- Click the Next button to move to the next SubForm Wizard dialog box.

- Be sure the 'Choose from a list' option button is selected (Figure 5–47).

Q&A

Why do I use this option?

Most of the time, Access will have determined the appropriate fields to link the subform and the main form and placed an entry specifying those fields in the list. By choosing from the list, you can take advantage of the information that Access has created for you. The other option is to define your own, in which case you would need to specify the appropriate fields.

Figure 5–47

6

- Click the Next button.

- Type **Clients of Analyst** as the name of the subform (Figure 5–48).

Figure 5–48

7

- Click the Finish button to place the subform (Figure 5–49).

Figure 5–49

To View the Form

When working with a form in Design view, you can see the effect of the changes you have made by viewing the form in Form view. The following step views the form in Form view.

- Click the View button (Home tab | Views group) to view the form in Form view (Figure 5–50).

Q&A

Everything looks good except the subform. I do not see all the fields I should see. What should I do?

You need to modify the subform, which you will do in the upcoming steps.

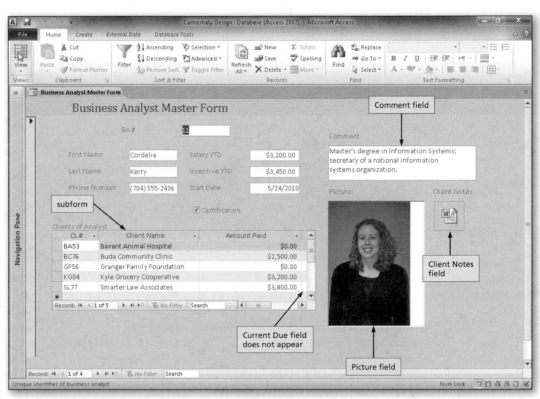

Figure 5–50

To Close and Save a Form

The following steps first save and then close the Business Analyst Master Form.

1 Click the Save button on the Quick Access Toolbar to save the form.

2 Close the Business Analyst Master Form by clicking the Close button for the form.

Break Point: If you wish to stop working through the chapter at this point, you can resume the project at a later time by starting Access, opening the database called Camashaly Design, and continuing to follow the steps from this location forward.

To Modify a Subform

The next task is to resize the columns in the subform, which appears on the form in Datasheet view. The subform exists as a separate object in the database; it is stored independently of the main form. The following steps open the subform and then resize the columns. They then center the data in the Client Number column.

1

- Open the Navigation Pane.

- Right-click the Clients of Analyst form to produce a shortcut menu.

- Click Open on the shortcut menu to open the form.

- Resize the columns to best fit the data by double-clicking the right boundaries of the field selectors (Figure 5–51).

Figure 5–51

2

- Click Home on the Ribbon to display the Home tab.

- Click the Client Number field on the first record.

Q&A

Did it have to be the first record?

No. The whole column will be aligned at once no matter which record you pick.

- Click the Center button (Home tab | Text Formatting group) to center the data in the column (Figure 5–52).

Figure 5–52

3

- Save your changes and then close the subform.

- Open the Business Analyst Master Form in Design view and then close the Navigation Pane.

- Click the boundary of the subform to select it.

- Adjust the approximate size and position of the subform to match the one shown in Figure 5–53.

Figure 5–53

4

- Click the View button (Form Design Tools Design tab | Views group) to view the form in Form view (Figure 5–54).

Q&A Could I have clicked the View button arrow and then clicked Form View?

Yes. You always can use the arrow. If the icon for the view you want appears on the face of the View button, however, you also can just click the button.

Q&A Could I have clicked the Form View button in the lower-right corner of the screen to move to Form view?

Yes. Those buttons are always an option. Use whichever approach you find most convenient.

Figure 5–54

To Change a Label

In Datasheet view, shortening the heading for the Business Analyst Number column to BA # made sense. With business analyst numbers only being two characters long, having a short column heading enabled the column to have a reasonable width. You accomplished that by changing the caption for the Business Analyst Number field to BA #. In the form, there is plenty of room for the full field name to appear in the label. The following steps change the contents of the label from BA # to Business Analyst Number.

- Return to Design view, and then click the label for the Business Analyst Number to select the label.

- Click the label a second time to produce an insertion point.

- Erase the current label (BA #) and then type **Business Analyst Number** as the new label (Figure 5–55).

Figure 5–55

- Click outside the label to deselect it.

- Click the label to select it.

Q&A

Why did I need to deselect the label and then select it again?

With the insertion point appearing in the label, you could not move the label. By deselecting it and then selecting it again, the label will be selected, but there will be no insertion point.

- Drag the Move handle in the upper-left corner to move the label to the approximate position shown in Figure 5–56.

- Save your changes.

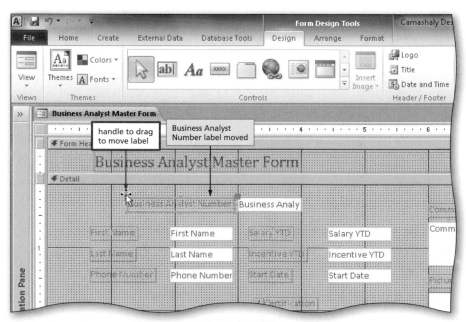

Figure 5–56

Size Mode for Pictures

The portion of a picture that appears as well as the way it appears is determined by the property called **size mode**. The possible size modes are as follows:

1. Clip — This size mode displays only the portion of the picture that will fit in the space allocated to it.

2. Stretch — This size mode expands or shrinks the picture to fit the precise space allocated on the screen. For photographs, usually this is not a good choice because fitting a photograph to the allocated space can distort the image, giving it a stretched appearance.

3. Zoom — This size mode does the best job of fitting the picture to the allocated space without changing the look of the picture. The entire picture will appear and be proportioned correctly. Some white space may be visible either above or to the right of the picture, however.

To Change the Size Mode

Currently, the size mode should be Zoom, which is appropriate. If it were not and you wanted to change it, you would use the following steps.

1. Click the control containing the picture, and then click the Property Sheet button (Form Design Tools Design tab | Tools group) to display the control's property sheet.

2. Click the Size Mode property, and then click the Size Mode property box arrow.

3. Click Zoom and then close the property sheet by clicking its Close button.

To Change Special Effects and Colors

Access allows you to change many of the characteristics of the labels in the form. You can change the border style and color, the background color, the font, and the font size. You also can apply special label effects, such as raised or sunken. The following steps change the font color and add special effects of the labels.

- Click the Business Analyst Number label to select it.

- Select each of the remaining labels by holding down the SHIFT key while clicking the label. Be sure to include the label for the subform (Figure 5–57).

Q&A

Does the order in which I select the labels make a difference?

No. The only thing that is important is that they are all selected when you are done.

Figure 5–57

2

- Display the Format tab.

- Click the Font Color arrow (Form Design Tools Format tab | Font group) to display a color palette (Figure 5–58).

Figure 5–58

3

- Click the blue color in the second position from the right in the bottom row of Standard Colors to change the font color for the labels.

 Experiment

- Try other colors by clicking the Font Color arrow and then clicking the other color to see which colors you think would be good choices for the font. When done, select the blue color.

- Display the Design tab.

Figure 5–59

- Click the Property Sheet button (Form Design Tools Design tab | Tools group) to produce the property sheet for the selected labels. If your property sheet still appears on the left side of the screen, drag it back to the right. Make sure the All tab is selected.

- Click the Border Style property box to display the Border Style property box arrow, and then click the arrow to display a menu of border styles (Figure 5–59).

Q&A The property sheet is too small to display the property box arrow. Can I change the size of the property sheet?

Yes. Point to the border of the property sheet so that the mouse pointer changes to a two-headed arrow. You then can drag to adjust the size.

4

- Click Solid in the menu of border styles to select a border style.

- Click the Border Width property box to display the Border Width property box arrow, and then click the arrow to display a menu of border widths.

- Click 3 pt to change the border width to 3 pt.

- Click the Special Effect property box to display the Special Effect property box arrow, and then click the arrow to display a menu of special effects (Figure 5–60).

Figure 5–60

5

- Click Etched in the menu of special effects to select a special effect.

 Experiment

- Try other special effects. In each case, view the form to see the special effect you selected and then return to Design view. When done, select Etched.

- Close the property sheet.

- Click the Business Analyst Number control (the white space, not the label) to select it.

- Select each of the remaining controls by holding down the SHIFT key while clicking the control. Do not include the subform.

- Display the property sheet.

- Select Sunken for the special effect (Figure 5–61).

Figure 5–61

• Close the property sheet by clicking the Property Sheet button (Form Design Tools Design tab | Tools group).

• Click the View button to view the form in Form view (Figure 5–62).

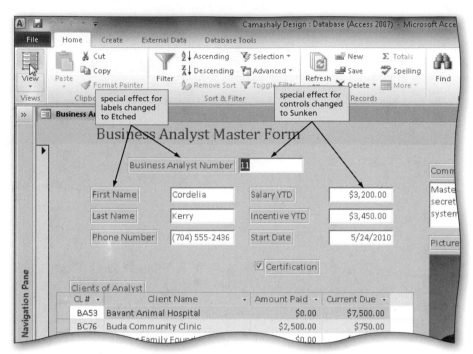

Figure 5–62

To Modify the Appearance of a Form Title

You can enhance the title in a variety of ways. These include moving it, resizing it, changing the font size, changing the font weight, and changing the alignment. The following steps enhance the form title.

• Return to Design view.

• Resize the Form Header section by dragging down the lower boundary of the section to the approximate position shown in Figure 5–63.

Figure 5–63

- Click the control containing the form title to select the control.

- Drag the lower-right sizing handle to resize the control to the approximate size shown in Figure 5–64.

Figure 5–64

- Click the Property Sheet button (Form Design Tools Design tab | Tools group) to display the control's property sheet.

- Click the Font Size property box, click the Font Size property box arrow, and then click 26 to change the font size.

- In a similar fashion, change the Text Align property value to Distribute and the Font Weight property value to Semi-bold (Figure 5–65).

- Close the property sheet by clicking the Property Sheet button (Form Design Tools Design tab | Tools group).

Figure 5–65

To Change a Tab Stop

Users may repeatedly press the TAB key to move through the controls on the form; however, they should bypass the Certification, Picture, and Client Notes controls. To omit these controls from the tab stop sequence, the following steps change the value of the Tab Stop property for the controls from Yes to No.

- Click the Certification control to select it.

- In addition, select the Picture control and the Client Notes control by holding down the SHIFT key while clicking each control (Figure 5–66).

- Click the Property Sheet button (Form Design Tools Design tab | Tools group) to display the property sheet.

- Make sure the All tab (Property Sheet) is selected, click the down scroll arrow until the Tab Stop property appears, click the Tab Stop property, click the Tab Stop property box arrow, and then click No.

- Close the property sheet.

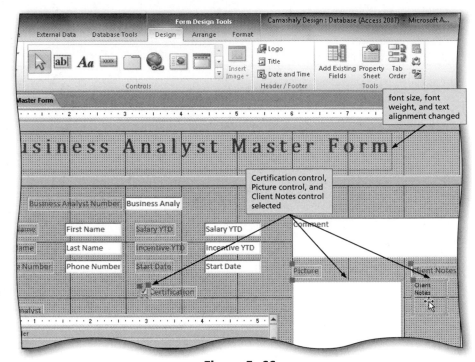

Figure 5–66

Q&A What is the effect of this change?

When a user tabs through the controls, he or she will bypass the Certification control, the Picture control, and the Client Notes control.

Q&A I do not see the Tab Stop property. What did I do wrong?

You clicked the labels for the controls, not the controls.

- Click the Save button on the Quick Access Toolbar to save your changes.

3

- Click the View button to view the form in Form view. It should look like the form shown in Figure 5–1.

- Close the form.

Break Point: If you wish to stop working through the chapter at this point, you can resume the project at a later time by starting Access, opening the database called Camashaly Design, and continuing to follow the steps from this location forward.

Changing the Tab Order

Users can repeatedly press the TAB key to move through the fields on a form. Access determines the order in which the fields are encountered in this process. If you prefer a different order, you can change the order by clicking the Tab Order button (Form Design Tools Design tab | Tools group). You can then use the Tab Order dialog box (Figure 5–67) to change the order by dragging rows to their desired position as indicated in the dialog box.

Figure 5–67

To Use the Form

To use a form to view data, right-click the form in the Navigation Pane, and then click Open on the shortcut menu that appears. You then can use the Navigation buttons at the bottom of the screen to move among business analysts. You can use the Navigation buttons in the subform to move among the clients of the business analyst currently shown on the screen. The following steps use the form to display desired data.

1

- Open the Navigation Pane if it is currently closed.

- Right-click the Business Analyst Master Form and then click Open on the shortcut menu.

- Close the Navigation Pane.

- Right-click the Client Notes field to display a shortcut menu (Figure 5–68).

Figure 5–68

2

- Click the Manage Attachments command on the shortcut menu to display the Attachments dialog box (Figure 5–69).

Q&A

How do I use this dialog box?

Select an attachment and click the Open button to view the attachment in its original application. Click the Add button to add a new attachment or the Remove button to remove the selected attachment. By clicking the Save button, you can save the selected attachment as a file in whatever location you specify. You can save all attachments at once by clicking the Save All button.

 Experiment

- Open both attachments to see how they look in the original applications. When finished, close each original application.

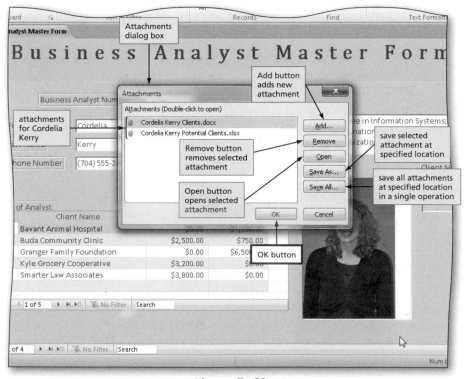

Figure 5–69

3

- Click the OK button to close the Attachments dialog box.

- Click the form's Next record button twice to display the data for business analyst 27 (Figure 5–70).

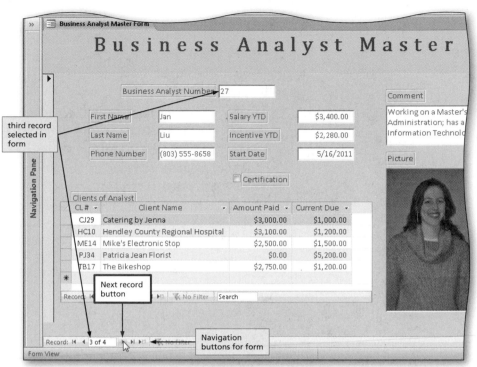

Figure 5–70

4

- Click the subform's Next record button twice to highlight the third client of business analyst 27 (Figure 5–71).

5

- Close the form.

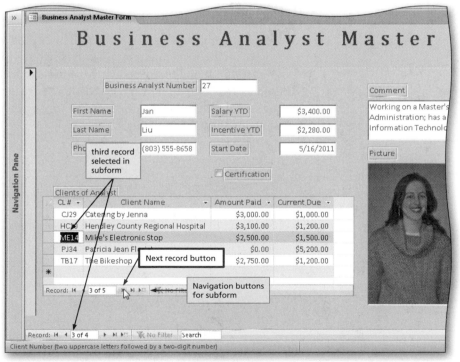

Figure 5–71

Other Ways
1. Double-click Attachments control

Navigation in the Form

The previous steps illustrated the way you work with a main form and subform. Clicking the Navigation buttons for the main form moves to a different business analyst. Clicking the Navigation buttons for the subform moves to a different client of the business analyst who appears in the main form. The following are other actions you can take within the form:

1. To move from the last field in the main form to the first field in the subform, press the TAB key. To move back to the last field in the main form, press CTRL+SHIFT+TAB.

2. To move from the last field in the subform to the first field in the next record's main form, press CTRL+TAB.

3. To switch from the main form to the subform using the mouse, click anywhere in the subform. To switch back to the main form, click any control in the main form. Clicking the background of the main form will not cause the switch to occur.

Object Dependencies

In Access, objects can depend on other objects. For example, a report depends on the table or query on which it is based. A change to the structure of the table or query could affect the report. You can view information on dependencies between database objects. Viewing a list of objects that use a specific object helps in the maintenance of a database and avoids errors when changes are made to the objects involved in the dependency. For example, many items, such as queries and forms, use data from the Client table and thus depend on the Client table. By clicking the Object Dependencies button, you can see what items are based on the object. You also can see the items on which the object depends.

If you are unfamiliar with a database, viewing object dependencies can help you better understand the structure of the database. Viewing object dependencies is especially useful after you have made changes to the structure of tables. An understanding of which reports, forms, and queries depend on a table can assist in making any necessary changes.

To View Object Dependencies

The following steps view the objects that depend on the Client table.

1

- Open the Navigation Pane and click the Client table.

- Display the Database Tools tab.

- Click the Object Dependencies button (Database Tools tab | Relationships group) to display the Object Dependencies pane.

- If necessary, click the 'Objects that depend on me' option button to select it (Figure 5–72).

 Experiment

- Click the 'Objects that I depend on' option button to see the objects on which the Client table depends. Then try both options for other objects in the database.

2

- Close the Object Dependencies pane by clicking the Object Dependencies button (Database Tools tab | Relationships group) a second time.

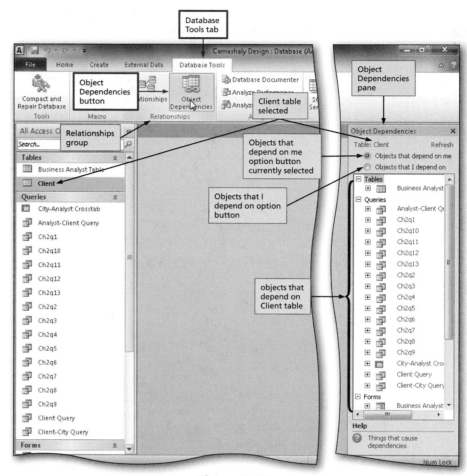

Figure 5–72

Date/Time, Memo, and Yes/No Fields in Queries

By specifying business analyst start dates using Date/Time fields, Camashaly Design can run queries to find business analysts hired before or after a certain date. Other uses of the date field might include calculating an analyst's length of service by subtracting the start date from the current date. Similarly, management can search for business analysts with specific qualifications by adding memos and Yes/No fields.

To use Date/Time fields in queries, you simply type the dates, including the slashes. To search for records with a specific date, you must type the date. You also can use comparison operators. To find all the business analysts whose start date is prior to January 1, 2011, for example, you type <1/1/2011 as the criterion.

You also can use Memo fields in queries. Typically, you will want to find all the records on which the Memo field contains a specific word or phrase. To do so, you use wildcards. For example, to find all the business analysts who have the word, Information, somewhere in the Comment field, you type *Information* as the criterion. The asterisk at the beginning indicates that any characters can appear before the word, Information. The asterisk at the end indicates that any characters can appear after the word, Information.

To use Yes/No fields in queries, type the word, Yes, or the word, No, as the criterion. The following steps create and run queries that use Date/Time, Memo, and Yes/No fields.

To Use Date/Time, Memo, and Yes/No Fields in a Query

The following steps use Date/Time, Memo, and Yes/No fields in queries to search for business analysts who meet specific criteria.

- Create a query for the Business Analyst Table and include the Business Analyst Number, Last Name, First Name, Start Date, Comment, and Certification fields in the query (Figure 5–73).

Figure 5–73

- Click the Criteria row under the Comment field and then type ***Information*** as the criterion.

- Click the Criteria row under the Start Date field, and then type **<1/1/2011** as the criterion (Figure 5–74).

Q&A

What happened to the criteria for the Comment field?

Access automatically reformatted it appropriately by adding the word, like, and placing quotation marks around the criterion.

Figure 5–74

3

- Click the View button to view the results (Figure 5–75).

Figure 5–75

4

- Click the View button to return to Design view (Figure 5–76).

Q&A Why does the date have number signs (#) around it?

This is the date format in Access. You usually do not have to enter the number signs because Access will insert them automatically.

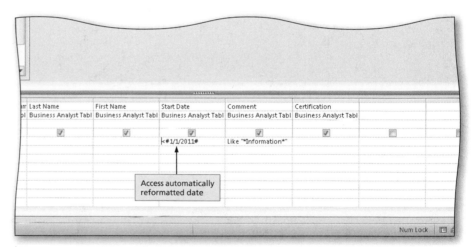

Figure 5–76

5

- Erase the criteria in the Start Date and Comment fields.

- Click the Criteria row under the Certification field and then type **Yes** as the criterion (Figure 5–77).

Q&A Do I have to type Yes?

You also could type True.

Figure 5–77

6

- Click the View button to view the results (Figure 5–78).

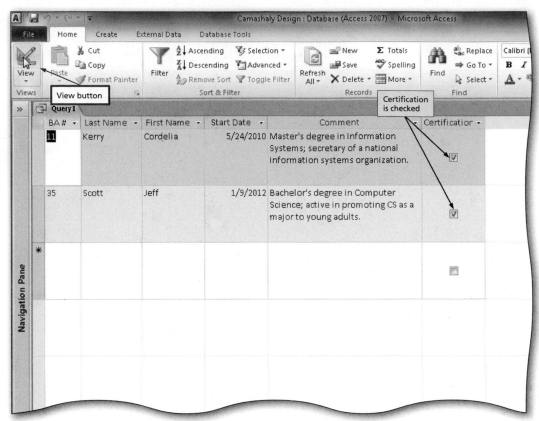

Figure 5–78

Experiment

- Try other combinations of values in the Start Date field, the Comment field, and/or the Certification field. In each case, view the results.

7

- Close the query without saving the results.

Datasheets in Forms

BTW

Date Fields in Queries
To test for the current date in a query, type Date() in the Criteria row of the appropriate column. Typing <Date() in the Criteria row for the Start Date, for example, finds those business analysts who started anytime before the date on which you run the query.

In forms created in Layout view, subforms are not available, but you can achieve similar functionality to subforms by including datasheets. Like subforms, the datasheets contain data for the "many" table in the relationship.

Creating a Simple Form with a Datasheet

If you create a simple form for a table that is the "one" table in a one-to-many relationship, Access automatically includes the "many" table in a datasheet within the form. If you create a simple form for the Business Analyst Table, for example, Access will include the Client table in a datasheet within the form, as in Figure 5–79. The clients in the datasheet will be the clients of the business analyst currently on the screen, in this case, Cordelia Kerry.

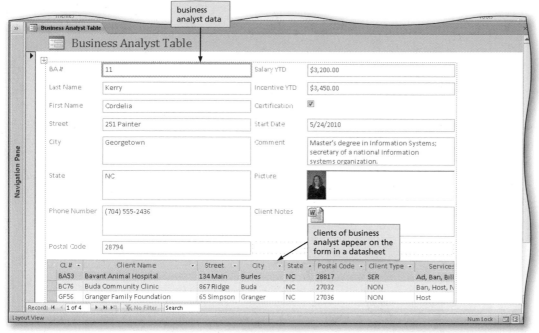

Figure 5–79

TO CREATE A SIMPLE FORM WITH A DATASHEET

To create a simple form with a datasheet, you would use the following steps.

1. Select the table in the Navigation Pane that is the "one" part of a one-to-many relationship.

2. Display the Create tab.

3. Click the Form button (Create tab | Forms group).

Creating a Form with a Datasheet in Layout View

You can create a form with a datasheet in Layout view. To do so, you would first use the field list to add any fields from the "one" table, as shown in Figure 5–80, in which fields from the Business Analyst Table have been added to the form.

Figure 5–80

Next, you would use the field list to add a single field from the "many" table, as shown in Figure 5–81, in which the Client Number field has been added. Access will automatically create a datasheet containing this field.

Figure 5–81

Finally, you would click the datasheet to select it and then use the field list to add the other fields from the "many" table that you want to be included in the form, as shown in Figure 5–82.

Figure 5–82

TO CREATE A FORM WITH A DATASHEET IN LAYOUT VIEW

Specifically, to create a form with a datasheet in Layout view, you would use the following steps.

1. Display the Create tab.

2. Click the Blank Form button (Create tab | Forms group) to create a form in Layout view.

3. If a field list does not appear, click the Add Existing Fields button (Form Design Tools Design tab | Tools group) to display a field list.

4. If necessary, click Show all tables to display the available tables.

5. Click the expand indicator (the plus sign) for the "one" table to display the fields in the table and then drag the fields to the desired positions.

6. Click the expand indicator for the "many" table and drag the first field for the datasheet onto the form to create the datasheet.

7. Select the datasheet and drag the remaining fields for the datasheet from the field list to the desired locations in the datasheet.

Creating a Multitable Form Based on the Many Table

All the forms discussed so far in this chapter were based on the "one" table, in this case, the Business Analyst Table. The records from the "one" table were included in a subform. You can also create a multitable form based on the "many" table, in this case, the Client table. Such a form is shown in Figure 5–83.

BTW

Placing Fields on a Datasheet
Be sure to select the datasheet before adding additional fields to the datasheet. When dragging a field from the field list to the datasheet, drag the field to the right boundary of the previous field. The mouse pointer will change to show that you are placing a control and you will see a vertical line.

BTW

Certification
The Microsoft Office Specialist (MOS) program provides an opportunity for you to obtain a valuable industry credential – proof that you have the Access 2010 skills required by employers. For more information, visit the Access 2010 Certification Web page (scsite.com/ac2010/cert).

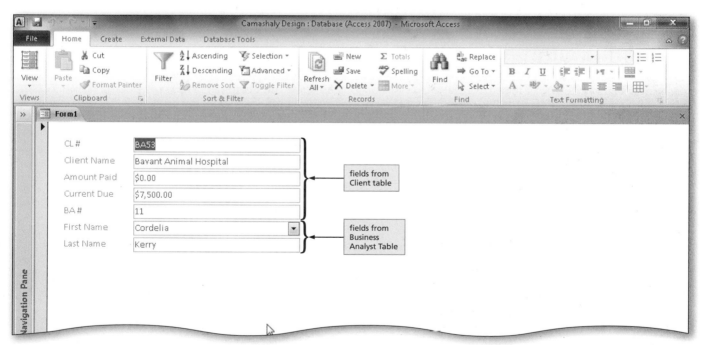

Figure 5–83

In this form, the Client Number, Client Name, Amount Paid, Current Due, and Business Analyst Number fields are in the Client table. The First Name and Last Name fields are found in the Business Analyst Table and are included in the form to help to identify the business analyst whose number appears in the Business Analyst Number field.

BTW

Quick Reference
For a table that lists how to complete the tasks covered in this book using the mouse, Ribbon, shortcut menu, and keyboard, see the Quick Reference Summary at the back of this book, or visit the Access 2010 Quick Reference Web page (scsite.com/ac2010/qr).

TO CREATE A MULTITABLE FORM BASED ON THE MANY TABLE

To create a multitable form based on the "many" table, you would use the following steps.

1. Click the Blank Form button (Create tab | Forms group) to create a form in Layout view.
2. If a field list does not appear, click the Add Existing Fields button on the Design tab to display a field list.
3. Drag the fields for the "many" table to the desired positions.
4. Drag the fields for the "one" table to the desired positions.

To Quit Access

The following steps quit Access.

1 Click the Close button on the right side of the title bar to quit Access.

2 If a Microsoft Access dialog box appears, click the Save button to save any changes made to the object since the last save.

Chapter Summary

In this chapter you have learned to use Yes/No, Date/Time, Memo, OLE Object, and Attachment data types; create and use an input mask; create a form and add a subform; enhance the look of the controls on a form; use a form with a subform; create queries involving Yes/No, Date/Time, and Memo fields; view object dependencies; and create forms containing datasheets in Layout view. The items listed below include all the new Access skills you have learned in this chapter.

1. Add Fields with New Data Types to a Table (AC 278)
2. Use the Input Mask Wizard (AC 280)
3. Enter Data Using an Input Mask (AC 283)
4. Enter Data in Yes/No Fields (AC 284)
5. Enter Data in Date/Time Fields (AC 285)
6. Enter Data in Memo Fields (AC 285)
7. Change the Row and Column Size (AC 286)
8. Enter Data in OLE Object Fields (AC 287)
9. Change Picture Field Entries to Bitmap Images (AC 289)
10. Enter Data in Attachment Fields (AC 289)
11. Enter Data in Hyperlink Fields (AC 291)
12. Create a Form in Design View (AC 292)
13. Add a Control for a Field to the Form Design (AC 293)
14. Add Controls for Additional Fields (AC 294)
15. Align Controls on the Left (AC 295)
16. Align Controls on the Top and Adjust Vertical Spacing (AC 296)
17. Move the Field List (AC 297)
18. Add Controls for the Remaining Fields (AC 297)
19. Use a Shortcut Menu to Change the Fill/Back Color (AC 299)
20. Add a Title (AC 301)
21. Place a Subform (AC 301)
22. View the Form (AC 305)
23. Modify a Subform (AC 305)
24. Change a Label (AC 308)
25. Change the Size Mode (AC 309)
26. Change Special Effects and Colors (AC 309)
27. Modify the Appearance of a Form Title (AC 312)
28. Change a Tab Stop (AC 314)
29. Use the Form (AC 315)
30. View Object Dependencies (AC 319)
31. Use Date/Time, Memo, and Yes/No Fields in a Query (AC 320)
32. Create a Simple Form with a Datasheet (AC 323)
33. Create a Form with a Datasheet in Layout View (AC 325)
34. Create a Multitable Form Based on the Many Table (AC 326)

If you have a SAM 2010 user profile, your instructor may have assigned an autogradable version of this assignment. If so, log into the SAM 2010 Web site at www.cengage.com/sam2010 to download the instruction and start files.

Learn It Online

Test your knowledge of chapter content and key terms.

Instructions: To complete the Learn It Online exercises, start your browser, click the Address bar, and then enter the Web address `scsite.com/ac2010/learn`. When the Access 2010 Learn It Online page is displayed, click the link for the exercise you want to complete and then read the instructions.

Chapter Reinforcement TF, MC, and SA
A series of true/false, multiple choice, and short answer questions that test your knowledge of the chapter content.

Flash Cards
An interactive learning environment where you identify chapter key terms associated with displayed definitions.

Practice Test
A series of multiple choice questions that test your knowledge of chapter content and key terms.

Who Wants To Be a Computer Genius?
An interactive game that challenges your knowledge of chapter content in the style of a television quiz show.

Wheel of Terms
An interactive game that challenges your knowledge of chapter key terms in the style of the television show *Wheel of Fortune*.

Crossword Puzzle Challenge
A crossword puzzle that challenges your knowledge of key terms presented in the chapter.

Apply Your Knowledge

Reinforce the skills and apply the concepts you learned in this chapter.

Adding Date/Time and OLE Fields, Using an Input Mask Wizard, and Querying Date/Time Fields

Instructions: Start Access. If you are using the Microsoft Access 2010 Complete or the Microsoft Access 2010 Comprehensive text, open the Babbage CPA Firm database that you used in Chapter 4. Otherwise, see your instructor for information on accessing the files required in this book.

Perform the following tasks:
1. Add the Start Date and Picture fields to the Bookkeeper table structure, as shown in Figure 5–84. Create an input mask for the Start Date field. Use the Short Date input mask type.

Figure 5–84

Continued >

Apply Your Knowledge *continued*

2. Add the data shown in Table 5–1 to the Bookkeeper table.

Table 5–1 Data for Bookkeeper Table		
Bookkeeper Number	Start Date	Picture
22	03/07/2011	Pict1.bmp
24	06/07/2010	Pict2.bmp
34	05/09/2011	Pict3.bmp
38	02/06/2012	Pict4.bmp

3. Query the Bookkeeper table to find all bookkeepers who started after January 1, 2012. Include the Bookkeeper Number, First Name, Last Name, Hourly Rate, and Earnings YTD in the query results. Save the query as Start Date Query.

4. Submit the revised database in the format specified by your instructor.

Extend Your Knowledge

Extend the skills you learned in this chapter and experiment with new skills. You may need to use Help to complete the assignment.

Adding Hyperlink Fields and Creating Multitable Forms Using Layout View

Instructions: Start Access. Open the Any School District database. See the inside back cover of this book for instructions on downloading the Data Files for Students, or contact your instructor for more information about accessing the required files.

The Human Resources director at Any School District has several job openings for the two high schools in the district. To keep track of teacher candidates, she created a database. She would like a Hyperlink field added to this database. You will add this field. You also will create the form shown in Figure 5–85.

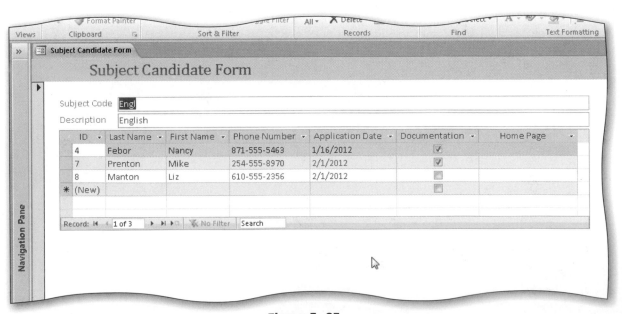

Figure 5–85

Perform the following tasks:

1. Open the Candidate table in Design view and add a Hyperlink field. Insert the field after the Documentation field. Use Home Page as the name of the field.

2. Open the Candidate table in Datasheet view and add data for the Hyperlink field to the first record. If the teachers at your school have individual Web pages, link to one of those pages. Otherwise, use your school home page as the URL. Resize the column to ensure that the complete URL is visible in the datasheet.

3. Use Layout view to create the multitable form shown in Figure 5–85. The Candidate table appears as a subform in the form. Use Subject Candidate Form as the title and save the form with the same name. Decrease the size of the subform.

4. Create a query for the Candidate table to find all candidates who have not submitted documentation. Include the ID, first name, last name, and phone number in the query results. Save the query as Documentation Query.

5. Submit the revised database in the format specified by your instructor.

Make It Right

Analyze a database and correct all errors and/or improve the design.

Correcting Form Design Errors

Instructions: Start Access. Open the LawnAndGarden database. See the inside back cover of this book for instructions on downloading the Data Files for Students, or contact your instructor for more information about accessing the required files.

The LawnAndGarden database contains data for a company that provides lawn and gardening services. The owner of the company has created the form shown in Figure 5–86 but he has encountered some problems with modifying the form.

Figure 5–86

Continued >

Make It Right *continued*

The Worker Master Form currently has the Raised special effect for the Worker Number label. All labels should have a raised special effect. The Worker Number control has a Sunken special effect. All other controls except the subform also should have the sunken special effect property. The subform is too big and needs to be resized. The Balance and Amount Paid fields should be right-aligned. The Last Name and YTD Earnings controls should be aligned to the top. The Hourly Rate and YTD Earnings labels should be aligned to the left. Finally, the form needs a title. The owner would like the title, Worker Master Form. The title should have a raised appearance, a text alignment of Distribute with a font size of 24, and a font weight of bold.

Submit the revised database in the format specified by your instructor.

In the Lab

Design, create, modify, and/or use a database following the guidelines, concepts, and skills presented in this chapter. Labs are listed in order of increasing difficulty.

Lab 1: Adding Fields and Creating Multitable Forms for the ECO Clothesline Database

Problem: ECO Clothesline needs to maintain additional data on each sales rep. The company needs to add the date each rep started as well as notes concerning the sales rep and a picture of the sales rep. The company wants a form that displays sales rep information and the customers for whom they are responsible.

Instructions: If you are using the Microsoft Access 2010 Complete or the Microsoft Access 2010 Comprehensive text, open the ECO Clothesline database that you used in Chapter 4. Otherwise, see the inside back cover of this book for instructions on downloading the Data Files for Students, or contact your instructor for more information about accessing the required files.

Perform the following tasks:
1. Add the Start Date, Notes, and Picture fields to the end of the Sales Rep table. Save the changes to the structure of the table.

2. Add the data shown in Table 5–2 to the Sales Rep table. Adjust the row and column spacing to best fit the data. Save the changes to the layout of the table.

Table 5–2 Data for Sales Rep Table			
Sales Rep Number	Start Date	Notes	Picture
44	5/10/2010	Excellent computer skills. Helps to train new employees.	Pict1.bmp
49	6/14/2010	Has a BBA in Marketing. Working on an MBA in Management.	Pict4.bmp
51	5/23/2011	Certified Personal Trainer. Enjoys working with health and fitness centers.	Pict2.bmp
55	1/16/2012	Has an AA degree. Working on a BBA in Management.	Pict3.bmp

3. Create the form shown in Figure 5–87. Use Sales Rep Master Form as the name of the form and Customers of Sales Rep as the name of the subform. Users should not be able to tab through the Picture control. The title is centered with a font size of 24 and a font weight of bold.

4. Query the Sales Rep table to find all sales reps who started before January 1, 2012, and who have computer skills. Include the Sales Rep Number, First Name, Last Name, and Notes fields in the query results. Save the query as Computer Skills Query.

5. Submit the revised database in the format specified by your instructor.

Figure 5–87

In the Lab

Lab 2: Adding Fields and Creating Multitable Forms for the Walburg Energy Alternatives Database

Problem: The management of Walburg Energy Alternatives has found that they need to maintain additional data on suppliers. Management needs to keep track of the last date an order was placed, whether the vendor accepts returns, and whether the vendor allows online ordering. Management also would like to attach to each vendor's record Excel files that contain historical cost data. Walburg Energy Alternatives requires a form that displays information about the vendor as well as the items that are purchased from vendors.

Instructions: If you are using the Microsoft Access 2010 Complete or the Microsoft Access 2010 Comprehensive text, open the Walburg Energy Alternatives database that you used in Chapter 4. Otherwise, see the inside back cover of this book for instructions on downloading the Data Files for Students, or contact your instructor for more information about accessing the required files.

Perform the following tasks:
1. Add the fields Last Order Date, Returns, Online Ordering, and Cost History to the end of the Vendor table structure. Last Order Date is a Date/Time field, Returns and Online Ordering are Yes/No fields, and Cost History is an Attachment field. Create an input mask for the Last Order Date that uses the Short Date input mask.

Continued >

In the Lab *continued*

2. Add the data shown in Table 5–3 to the Vendor table.

Table 5–3 Data for Vendor Table				
Vendor Code	Last Order Date	Returns	Online Ordering	Cost History
AS	3/30/2012	Yes	No	AS_History.xlsx
JM	3/26/2012	No	Yes	JM_History.xlsx
SD	4/4/2012	Yes	Yes	SD_History.xlsx

3. Create the form shown in Figure 5–88. Use Vendor Master Form as the name of the form and Items of Vendor as the name of the subform. The title is raised, semi-bold, and distributed with a font size of 24. The labels are blue, bold, and etched with a transparent border style. The fields have a sunken special effect.

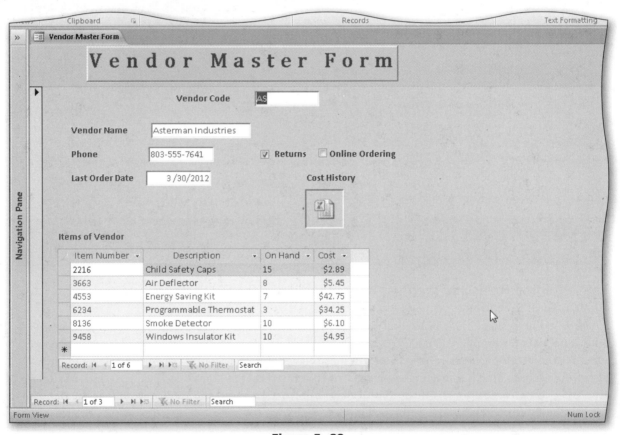

Figure 5–88

4. Open the Vendor Master Form and then open the cost history for Asterman Industries. Change the previous cost for item 4553 to $40.95. Save the change to the workbook.

5. Query the Vendor table to find all vendors that accept returns and allow online ordering. Include the Vendor Code and Name in the query results. Save the query as Returns-Online Query.

6. Submit the revised database in the format specified by your instructor.

In the Lab

Lab 3: Adding Fields and Creating Multitable Forms for the Philamar Training Database

Problem: The management of Philamar Training needs to maintain additional data on trainers. Management needs to store the date the trainer started, comments about each trainer, whether the trainer has MOS certification, and a picture of the trainer. Management wants a form that displays trainer information and the clients they represent.

Instructions: If you are using the Microsoft Access 2010 Complete or the Microsoft Access 2010 Comprehensive text, open the Philamar Training database that you used in Chapter 4. Otherwise, see the inside back cover of this book for instructions on downloading the Data Files for Students, or contact your instructor for more information about accessing the required files. Submit the revised database in the format specified by your instructor.

Instructions Part 1: Add the Start Date, Notes, MOS Certification, and Picture fields to the Trainer table and then add the data shown in Table 5–4 to the Trainer table. Be sure the datasheet displays the entire comment.

Table 5–4 Data for Trainer Table				
Trainer Number	Start Date	Notes	Mos Certification	Picture
42	5/10/2010	Has done corporate training for 5 years.	Yes	Pict1.bmp
48	10/11/2010	Specialist in database design and development.	No	Pict2.bmp
53	4/25/2011	Teaches computing courses at the community college.	Yes	Pict4.bmp
67	1/4/2012	Previous elementary school teacher.	No	Pict3.bmp

Instructions Part 2: Create a form for the Trainer table that is similar in design to the form shown in Figure 5–1 on page AC 275. Include all fields from the Trainer table except Address, City, State, and Postal Code. Include the Client Number, Client Name, Amount Paid, and Current Due fields from the Client table in the Clients of Trainer subform. Users should not be able to tab to the Picture field and should tab to the Notes field before the MOS Certification field. Save the form as Trainer Master Form.

Instructions Part 3: Find all trainers that have MOS certification and started before January 1, 2011. Include the Trainer Number, First Name, and Last Name fields in the query result. Save the query as Certification Query.

Cases and Places

Apply your creative thinking and problem solving skills to design and implement a solution.

See the inside back cover of this book for instructions for downloading the Data Files for Students, or see your instructor for information on accessing the required files.

1: Adding Fields and Creating Multitable Forms for the Chamber of Commerce Database

Academic

If you are using the Microsoft Access 2010 Complete or the Microsoft Access 2010 Comprehensive text, open the Chamber of Commerce database that you used in Chapter 4. Otherwise, see your instructor for more information about accessing the required files.

Continued >

Cases and Places *continued*

As part of your internship with the Chamber of Commerce, you worked temporarily as an ad rep when one of the reps was on vacation. This provided an opportunity to learn more about the marketing strategies of some of the advertisers. Now the Chamber has asked you to do some additional database work. Use the concepts and techniques presented in this chapter to perform each of the following tasks:

a. Add the Phone Number, Start Date, and Comment fields to the Ad Rep table. Place the Phone Number field after the Postal Code field and use an input mask of your choosing for both the Phone Number and the Start Date fields. Place the Start Date and Comment fields at the end of the table. Add the data shown in Table 5–5 to the Ad Rep table. Be sure the datasheet displays the entire comment.

Table 5–5 Data for Ad Rep Table			
Ad Rep Number	**Phone Number**	**Start Date**	**Comment**
22	215-555-1234	10/4/2010	Excellent copy editor.
29	610-555-2345	3/11/2011	Records radio advertisements for chamber.
32	215-555-8976	9/12/2011	Also works as a freelance journalist.
35	610-555-6578	3/15/2012	Semi-retired with extensive sales experience.

b. Create an Ad Rep Master Form for the Ad Rep table that is similar in design to the form shown in Figure 5–1 on page AC 275. Include all fields from Ad Rep table except Address, City, and Postal Code. Include an Advertisers of Ad Rep subform that includes the advertiser number, advertiser name, advertiser type, balance, and amount paid.

c. Create an Advertiser Update form for the Advertiser table. Include the advertiser number, advertiser name, balance, amount paid, advertiser type, and ad rep number. Include the first name and last name from the Ad Rep table. Users should not be able to change the ad rep name data.

Submit the revised database in the format specified by your instructor.

2: Creating Multitable Forms for the Consignment Database

Personal

If you are using the Microsoft Access 2010 Complete or the Microsoft Access 2010 Comprehensive text, open the Consignment database that you used in Chapter 4. Otherwise, see your instructor for more information about accessing the required files. Because many individuals volunteer at the consignment shop, you have been asked to simplify the task of entering data on sellers. Use the concepts and techniques presented in this chapter to perform each of the following tasks:

a. Create a Seller Master Form for the Seller table that is similar in design to the form shown in Figure 5–1 on page AC 275. Include all fields in the Seller table on the form. The Items of Seller subform should display all fields in the Items table except Seller Code. Customize the form by adding special effects to controls and labels as well as changing the background color of the form. Add the current date to the form header.

b. Create a query for the Items table to find all items posted during the month of March. Include the Item Number, Description, and Date Posted fields in the query results. Save the query as March Items Query.

Submit the revised database in the format specified by your instructor.

3: Adding Fields and Creating Multitable Forms for the Senior Care Database

Professional

If you are using the Microsoft Access 2010 Complete or the Microsoft Access 2010 Comprehensive text, open the Senior Care database that you used in Chapter 4. Otherwise, see your instructor for more information about accessing the required files. You and your co-owner have decided that you need to add some additional data to the Helper table. Use the concepts and techniques presented in this chapter to perform each of the following tasks:

a. Add a Phone Number and a Comment field to the Helper table. Add the Phone Number field after the First Name field. Create an input mask of your choosing for the Phone Number field. Add the Comment field to the end of the table. Change the Text Format property for the Comment field to Rich Text and the Append Only property to Yes.

b. Add the data shown in Table 5–6 to the Helper table. Make sure all data appears in the datasheet.

Table 5–6 Data for Helper Table		
Helper Number	Phone Number	Comment
203	803-555-3456	Has previous nursing home experience.
205	704-555-9876	Speaks Spanish. Has an AA degree.
207	704-555-2341	Excellent organizational skills.
209	803-555-4554	Has a chauffer's license.

c. Create a Helper Master Form for the Helper table. Include all fields from the Helper table. Include a Clients of Helper subform that includes the client number, client first name and last name, amount paid, and balance. Use your own design specifications for the form.

d. Open the Helper Master Form and bold the word Spanish in the Comment field for helper 205. Add the following sentence to the Comment field for helper 207: Working on an AA degree. Be sure the complete comment for helper 207 displays in the datasheet.

e. Create a query that finds all clients who need hygiene services and have a helper who speaks Spanish. Include the client number, client first and last names, helper number, and helper last name in the query results. Save the query as Hygiene-Spanish Query.

Submit the revised database in the format specified by your instructor.

6 | Advanced Report Techniques

Objectives

You will have mastered the material in this project when you can:

- Create and relate additional tables
- Create queries for reports
- Create reports in Design view
- Add fields and text boxes to a report
- Format report controls
- Group and ungroup report controls
- Update multiple report controls

- Add and modify a subreport
- Modify section properties
- Add a title, page number, and date
- Preview, print, and publish a report
- Add totals and subtotals
- Include a conditional value in a report

6 | Advanced Report Techniques

Introduction

BTW

Q&As
For a complete list of the Q&As found in many of the step-by-step sequences in this book, visit the Access 2010 Q&A Web page (scsite.com/ac2010/qa).

In this chapter, you will create two reports in Design view. Both reports feature grouping and sorting. The first report contains a subreport, which is a report that is contained within another report. The subreport contains data from a query and is related to data in the main report. The second report uses aggregate functions to calculate subtotals and grand totals. It also uses a function to calculate a value where the calculation will vary from record to record depending on whether a given criterion is true.

Project — Advanced Report Techniques

BTW

BTWs
For a complete list of the BTWs found in the margins of this book, visit the Access 2010 BTW Web page (scsite.com/ac2010/btw).

The owners of Camashaly Design want a master list of business analysts. This list should be available as an Access report. For each business analyst, the report is to include full details for all the clients assigned to the business analyst. In addition, Camashaly offers a range of educational courses designed to help clients understand the various marketing tools available to them. For clients who are taking courses, the report should list the specific courses being offered to the client. The actual report is shown in Figure 6–1a. The report is organized by business analyst, with the data for each analyst beginning on a new page. For each business analyst, the report lists the number, first name, and last name. Following the business analyst number and name, the report lists data for each client served by that business analyst. The client data includes the number, name, street, city, state, postal code, client type, services needed, amount paid, current due, and total amount. For each course the client is taking, the report lists the course number, description, total hours the course requires, hours already spent, and hours remaining.

BTW

The Ribbon and Screen Resolution
Access may change how the groups and buttons within the groups appear on the Ribbon, depending on the computer's screen resolution. Thus, your Ribbon may look different from the ones in this book if you are using a screen resolution other than 1024 × 768.

Many organizations offer discounts as a way of rewarding current clients and attracting new clients. The owners of Camashaly are considering offering a discount on the current due amount to its current clients. The exact amount of the discount depends on how much the client already has paid. If the amount paid is more than $4,000, the discount will be 4% of the current due amount. If the amount paid is $4,000 or less, then the discount will be 2% of the current due amount. To assist in determining the discount, Camashaly needs a report like the one shown in Figure 6–1b on page AC 340. The report groups clients by business analyst. It includes subtotals of both the Amount Paid and Current Due fields. Also, although not visible in the figure, it includes grand totals of both fields at the end of the report. Finally, it shows the discount amount, which is calculated by multiplying the current due amount by .04 (4%) for those clients for whom the amount paid is more than $4,000 and by .02 (2%) for all others.

Overview

As you read through this chapter, you will learn how to create the reports by performing these general tasks:

- Create and relate additional tables.
- Create queries for a report.
- Create a report, specify grouping and sorting, and add fields and text boxes to the report.
- Add a subreport to the report.
- Add a title, page number, and date to the report.
- Print and publish a report.
- Create a second report, specify grouping and sorting, and add fields and text boxes to the report.
- Add totals and subtotals to the report, and add a text box that uses a function.

Page 4   5/1/2012

Analyst Number	14	Analyst Name	Manuel Martinez

Client Number	BB32

Client Name	Babbage CPA Firm	Client Type	SER
Street	464 Linnell	Services Needed	Ad, Bus, Enews
City	Austin	Amount Paid	$1,500.00
State	SC	Current Due	$500.00
Postal Code	28796	Total Amount	$2,000.00

Course Number	Course Description	Total Hours	Hours Spent	Hours Remaining
C01	Using the Content Management System	8	4	4

Client Number	KD21

Client Name	KAL Design Studio	Client Type	SER
Street	116 Pine	Services Needed	Host, Mkt, SE
City	Georgetown	Amount Paid	$6,000.00
State	NC	Current Due	$3,200.00
Postal Code	28794	Total Amount	$9,200.00

Course Number	Course Description	Total Hours	Hours Spent	Hours Remaining
C03	Digital Image Management	6	0	6
C07	Understanding Cascading Style Sheets	8	4	4

(a) Business Analyst Master List – Page 4

Figure 6–1

D i s c o u n t   R e p o r t

Analyst Number	First Name	Last Name	Client Numbe	Client Name	Amount Paid	Current Due	Discount
11	Cordelia	Kerry					
			BA53	Bavant Animal Hospital	$0.00	$7,500.00	$150.00
			BC76	Buda Community Clinic	$2,500.00	$750.00	$15.00
			GF56	Granger Family Foundation	$0.00	$6,500.00	$130.00
			KG04	Kyle Grocery Cooperative	$3,200.00	$0.00	$0.00
			SL77	Smarter Law Associates	$3,800.00	$0.00	$0.00
				Subtotals	$9,500.00	$14,750.00	
14	Manuel	Martinez					
			BB32	Babbage CPA Firm	$1,500.00	$500.00	$10.00
			KD21	KAL Design Studio	$6,000.00	$3,200.00	$128.00
				Subtotals	$7,500.00	$3,700.00	
27	Jan	Liu					
			CJ29	Catering by Jenna	$3,000.00	$1,000.00	$20.00
			HC10	Hendley County Regional Hospital	$3,100.00	$1,200.00	$24.00
			ME14	Mike's Electronic Stop	$2,500.00	$1,500.00	$30.00
			PJ34	Patricia Jean Florist	$0.00	$5,200.00	$104.00
			TB17	The Bikeshop	$2,750.00	$1,200.00	$24.00

5/1/2012

(b) Discount Report

Figure 6 – 1

Plan
Ahead

Report Design Guidelines

When designing a report, the requirements of the users and the decisions you make will affect the appearance of the report. As you create reports and subreports, such as the ones shown in Figure 6–1, you should follow these general guidelines:

1. **Determine the intended audience and purpose of the report.** Identify the user or users of the report and determine how they will use it. Specify the necessary data and level of detail to include in the report.

2. **Determine the source of data for the report.** Determine whether all the data is in a single table or whether it comes from multiple related tables. The data may be found in a query. You might need to create multiple reports for a query where the criterion for a field changes, in which case, you would use a parameter query and enter the criterion when you run the report. If the data comes from multiple related tables, you might want to create a query and use the query as a source of data.

3. **Determine the fields that belong on the report.** Identify the data items that are needed by the user of the report.

4. **Determine the organization of the report.** The report may be enhanced by displaying the fields in a particular order and arranged in a certain way. Should the records in the report be grouped in some way? Should the report contain any subreports?

5. **Determine any calculations required for the report.** Should the report contain totals or subtotals? Are there any special calculations? If so, you may need to include functions to handle calculations. For example, the Business Analyst Master List contains a Total Amount field that is calculated by adding the contents of the Amount Paid field and the Current Due field. The Discount Report contains a Discount field, which is calculated by multiplying the amount in the Current Due field by 4% if the amount in the Amount Paid field is greater than $4,000 and by 2% otherwise.

6. **Determine the format and style of the report.** What information should be in the report heading? Do you want a title and date, for example? Do you want a logo? What should be in the body of the report? What should the style be? In other words, what visual characteristics should the various portions of the report have? Does the organization have specific style requirements for reports?

When necessary, more specific details concerning the above decisions and/or actions are presented at appropriate points in the chapter. The chapter also will identify the use of these guidelines in the design of the reports such as the ones shown in Figure 6–1.

To Start Access

The following steps, which assume Windows 7 is running, start Access based on a typical installation. You may need to ask your instructor how to start Access for your computer.

1 Click the Start button on the Windows 7 taskbar to display the Start menu.

2 Type `Microsoft Access` as the search text in the 'Search programs and files' text box and watch the search results appear on the Start menu.

3 Click Microsoft Access 2010 in the search results on the Start menu to start Access.

4 If the Access window is not maximized, click the Maximize button next to the Close button on its title bar to maximize the window.

To Open a Database from Access

BTW

Copy the Structure of a Table
If you want to create a table that has a structure similar to an existing table, you can copy the structure of the table only. Select the table in the Navigation Pane and click Copy, then click Paste. In the Paste Table As dialog box, type the new table name and click the Structure Only option button. Then, click the OK button. To modify the new table, open it in Design view.

The following steps open the Camashaly Design database from the Access folder in the CIS 101 folder on the USB flash drive.

❶ With your USB flash drive connected to one of the computer's USB ports, click File on the Ribbon to open the Backstage view.

❷ Click Open in the Backstage view to display the Open dialog box.

❸ Navigate to the location of the file to be opened (in this case, the USB flash drive, then to the CIS 101 folder [or your class folder], and then to the Access folder).

❹ Click Camashaly Design to select the file to be opened.

❺ Click the Open button (Open dialog box) to open the selected file and display the opened database in the Access window.

❻ If a Security Warning appears, click the Enable Content button.

Additional Tables

BTW

Many-to-Many Relationships
There is a many-to-many relationship between the Client table and the Course table. To implement a many-to-many relationship in a relational database management system such as Access, you create a third table, often called a junction or intersection table, that has as its primary key the combination of the primary keys of each of the tables involved in the many-to-many relationship. The primary key of the Course Offerings table is the combination of the Client Number and the Course Number fields.

Because the business analysts at Camashaly work collaboratively with clients, they are frequently asked to present courses on various Internet and Web development topics. Camashaly would like to incorporate this data in the Camashaly Design database.

Before creating the reports, you need to create two additional tables for the Camashaly Design database. The first table, Course, is shown in Tables 6–1a and 6–1b. As described in Table 6–1a, each course has a number and a description. The table also includes the total hours for which the course usually is offered and its increments; that is, the standard time blocks in which the course usually is offered. Table 6–1b contains the specific courses that the business analysts at Camashaly Design offer to their clients. The first row, for example, indicates that course C01 is called Using the Content Management System. It typically is offered in two-hour increments for a total of eight hours.

Table 6–1a Structure of Course Table

Field Name	Data Type	Field Size	Comments
Course Number	Text	3	Primary Key
Course Description	Text	40	
Hours	Number	Integer	
Increments	Number	Integer	

Table 6–1b Course Table

Course Number	Course Description	Hours	Increments
C01	Using the Content Management System	8	2
C02	HTML Basics	4	1
C03	Digital Image Management	6	3
C04	JavaScript Basics	12	3
C05	Understanding Social Networks	2	2
C06	Using Shopping Carts	4	2
C07	Understanding Cascading Style Sheets	8	2
C08	Podcasting	6	3

The second table is Table 6–2a, Course Offerings, which contains a client number, a course number, the total number of hours that the course is scheduled for the client, and the number of hours already spent in the course. The primary key of the Course Offerings table is a combination of the Client Number and Course Number fields.

Table 6–2b gives the data for the Course Offerings table. For example, the first record shows that client number BA53 currently has scheduled course C05 (Understanding Social Networks). The course is scheduled for 2 hours, and they have not yet spent any hours in class.

If you examine the data in Table 6–2b, you see that the Client Number field cannot be the primary key for the Course Offerings table. The fourth and fifth records, for example, both have a client number of HC10. The Course Number field also cannot be the primary key. The first and fifth records, for example, both have course number C05. Rather, the primary key is the combination of both Client Number and Course Number.

Table 6–2a Structure of Course Offerings Table

Field Name	Data Type	Field Size	Description
Client Number	Text	4	Part of Primary Key
Course Number	Text	3	Part of Primary Key
Total Hours	Number	Integer	
Hours Spent	Number	Integer	

Table 6–2b Course Offerings Table

Client Number	Course Number	Total Hours	Hours Spent
BA53	C05	2	0
BB32	C01	8	4
CJ29	C03	6	3
HC10	C04	12	6
HC10	C05	2	1
KD21	C03	6	0
KD21	C07	8	4
KG04	C01	8	6
KG04	C05	2	0
KG04	C08	6	4
ME14	C06	4	2
PJ34	C06	4	2
SL77	C04	12	9
SL77	C08	6	2
TB17	C02	4	2

BTW

AutoNumber Field as Primary Key
When you create a table in Datasheet view, Access automatically creates an ID field with the AutoNumber data type as the primary key field. As you add records to the table, Access increments the ID field so that each record will have a unique value in the field. AutoNumber fields are useful when there is no data field in a table that is a suitable primary key.

To Create the New Tables

You can create new Access tables in either Datasheet view or Design view. In Design view, you define the structure of the tables. The steps to create the new tables are similar to the steps you used previously to add fields to an existing table and to define primary keys. The only difference is the way you specify a primary key consisting of more than one field. First, you select both fields that make up the primary key by clicking the row selector for the first field, and then hold down the SHIFT key while clicking the row selector for the second field. Once the fields are selected, you can use the Primary Key button to indicate that the primary key consists of both fields.

The following steps create the tables in Design view.

1

- If necessary, close the Navigation Pane.

- Display the Create tab (Figure 6–2).

2

- Click the Table Design button (Create tab | Tables group) to create a table in Design view.

- Enter the information for the fields in the Course table as indicated in Table 6–1a on page AC 342, selecting Course Number as the primary key.

- Save the table using the name **Course** and close the table.

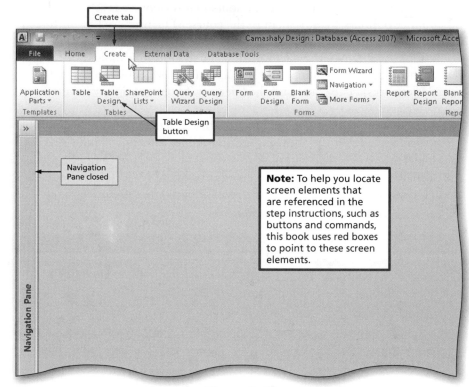

Figure 6–2

3

- Display the Create tab and then click the Table Design button (Create tab | Tables group) to create a second table in Design view.

- Enter the information for the fields in the Course Offerings table as indicated in Table 6–2a on page AC 343.

- Click the row selector for the Client Number field.

- Hold down the SHIFT key and then click the row selector for the Course Number field so both fields are selected.

- Click the Primary Key button (Table Tools Design tab | Tools group) to select the combination of the two fields as the primary key (Figure 6–3).

4

- Save the table using the name **Course Offerings** and close the table.

Figure 6–3

To Import the Data

Now that the tables have been created, you need to add data to them. You could enter the data manually, or if the data is already in electronic form, you could import the data. The data for the Course and Course Offerings tables is included in the Data Files for Students. The files are text files formatted as delimited files. The Course data is in a tab-delimited text (.txt) file, and the Course Offerings data is in a comma-separated values (.csv) file. The following steps import the data.

1 With the Camashaly Design database open, display the External Data tab and then click the Text File button (External Data tab | Import & Link group) to display the Get External Data – Text File dialog box.

2 Click the Browse button (Get External Data – Text File dialog box) and select the location of the file to be imported (for example, the folder called AccessData on drive F:). Select the Course file and click the Open button.

3 Select the 'Append a copy of records to the table' option button, select the Course table from the drop-down list, and then click the OK button. With the Delimited option button selected, click the Next button.

4 With the Tab option button selected, click the 'First Row Contains Field Names' check box, click the Next button, and then click the Finish button.

5 Click the Close button to close the Get External Data – Text Box dialog box without saving the import steps.

6 Use the technique shown in Steps 1 through 5 to import the Course Offerings.csv file into the Course Offerings table. Be sure the Comma option button is selected and there is a check mark in the 'First Row Contains Field Names' check box.

Q&A

I got an error message after I clicked the Finish button that indicated there were errors. The data was not imported. What should I do?

First, click the Cancel button to terminate the process. Then, review the structure of the table in Design view to ensure that the field names are all spelled correctly and that the data types are correct. Correct any errors you find, save your work, and then redo the steps to import the data.

Linking versus Importing

When an external table or worksheet is imported, or converted, into an Access database, a copy of the data is placed in a table in the database. The original data still exists, just as it did before, but no further connection exists between it and the data in the database. Changes to the original data do not affect the data in the database. Likewise, changes in the database do not affect the original data.

It also is possible to link data stored in a variety of formats to Access databases. To do so, you would select the 'Link to the data source by creating a linked table' option button when importing data, rather than the 'Import the source data into a new table in the current database' or 'Append a copy of the records to the table' option buttons. With linking, the connection is maintained; changes made to the data in the external table or worksheet affect the Access table.

To identify that a table is linked to other data, Access displays an arrow in front of the table in the Navigation Pane. In addition, an icon is displayed in front of the name that indicates the type of file to which the data is linked. For example, an Excel icon in front of the name indicates that the table is linked to an Excel worksheet.

BTW

Importing and Linking Files
You can import and link Excel workbooks, Access databases, ODBC databases such as SQL Server, text files, SharePoint lists, HTML documents, Outlook folders, and dBASE files. You can import but not link XML files.

BTW

Importing
You do not need to create a table before you import data. Instead, you can have Access automatically create a table to contain the imported data. To import an Excel workbook to an Access database without first creating the table, click the External Data tab on the Ribbon and then click the Excel button (External Data tab | Import & Link group) to display the Get External Data – Excel Spreadsheet dialog box. Click the Browse button (Get External Data – Excel Spreadsheet dialog box), select the file to be imported, and click the Open button. Select the 'Import the source data into a new table in the current database' option button, and then click the OK button. Follow the directions in the dialog box to finish importing the file.

BTW

Linking
Two of the primary reasons to link data from another program to Access are to use the query and report features of Access. When you link an Access database to data in another program, all changes to the data must be made in the source program. For example, if you link an Excel workbook to an Access database, you cannot edit the linked table in Access. You must make all changes to the data in Excel.

The Linked Table Manager

After you link tables between a worksheet and a database or between two databases, you can modify many of the linked table's features. For example, you can rename the linked table, set view properties, and set links between tables in queries. If you move, rename, or modify linked tables, you can use the Linked Table Manager within the Database Tools tab to update the links.

To Relate Several Tables

The new tables need to be related to the existing tables in the Camashaly Design database. The Client and Course Offerings tables are related through the Client Number fields in both. The Course and Course Offerings tables are related through the Course Number fields in both. The following steps illustrate the process of relating the tables.

1

- If necessary, close any open datasheet on the screen by clicking its Close button, and then display the Database Tools tab.

- Click the Relationships button (Database Tools tab | Relationships group) to open the Relationships window (Figure 6–4).

Q&A

I only see one table, did I do something wrong?

Click the All Relationships button to display all tables in relationships.

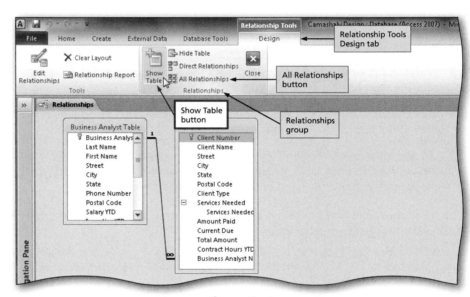

Figure 6–4

2

- Click the Show Table button (Relationship Tools Design tab | Relationships group) to display the Show Table dialog box (Figure 6–5).

3

- Click the Course Offerings table, click the Add button (Show Table dialog box), click the Course table, click the Add button again, and then click the Close button.

Q&A

I cannot see the Course Offerings table. Should I repeat the step?

If you can't see the table, it is behind the dialog box. You do not need to repeat the step.

Figure 6–5

- Point to the Client Number field in the Client table, press the left mouse button, drag to the Client Number field in the Course Offerings table, and then release the left mouse button to display the Edit Relationships dialog box. Click the Enforce Referential Integrity check box (Edit Relationships dialog box) and then click the Create button to create the relationship.

- Drag the Course Number field from the Course table to the Course Number field in the Course Offerings table. Click the Enforce Referential Integrity check box (Edit Relationships dialog box) and then click the Create button to create the relationship (Figure 6–6).

- Click the Save button to save the changes and then click the Close button (Relationship Tools Design tab | Relationships group).

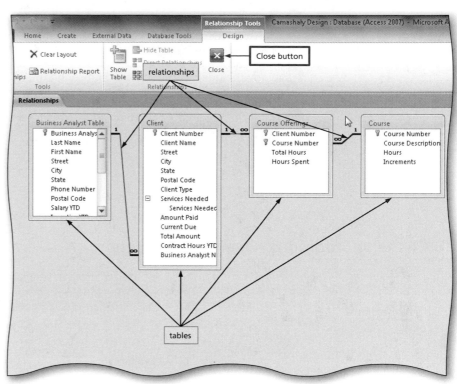

Figure 6–6

Creating Reports in Design View

Previously, you have used both Layout view and the Report Wizard to create reports. However, you simply can create the report in Design view. You also can use Design view to modify a report created by the wizard. If you do not use the wizard before moving to Design view, the design will be empty. It is then up to you to place all the fields in the desired locations. It is also up to you to specify any sorting or grouping that is required.

Whether you use the wizard or simply use Design view, you must determine on which table or query to base the report. If the report is to be based on a query, you first must create the query, unless, of course, it already exists.

To Create a Query for the Report

Camashaly's requirements for the reports specify that it would be convenient to use two queries for the report. These queries do not yet exist. You will need to create the two queries. The first query relates business analysts and clients, and the second query relates courses and course offerings. The following steps create the Business Analysts and Clients query.

1 If necessary, close the Navigation Pane, display the Create tab, and then click the Query Design button (Create tab | Queries group) to create a new query.

2 If necessary click the Business Analyst Table, click the Add button (Show Table dialog box), click the Client table, click the Add button, close the Show Table dialog box by clicking its Close button, and then resize the field lists to display as many fields as possible.

3 Double-click the Business Analyst Number, First Name, and Last Name fields from the Business Analyst Table to display them in the design grid.

BTW

Modify Composite Primary Keys
To change part of a composite primary key, open the table in Design view, click any field that participates in the primary key, and click the Primary Key button to remove the primary key. If the fields are adjacent to each other, click the row selector for the first field, hold down the SHIFT key and click the row selector for the second field. Then click the Primary Key button.

4 Double-click the Client Number, Client Name, Street, City, State, Postal Code, Client Type, Services Needed, Amount Paid, and Current Due fields from the Client table to add the fields to the design grid.

5 View the query results and scroll through the fields to make sure you have included all the necessary fields. If you have omitted a field, return to Design view and add it.

6 Click the Save button on the Quick Access Toolbar to save the query, type `Business Analysts and Clients` as the name of the query, and then click the OK button.

7 Close the query.

To Create an Additional Query for the Report

Camashaly Design needs to include in the Business Analyst Master List the number of hours that remain in a course offering. The following steps create the Course Offerings and Courses query that includes a calculated field for hours remaining. The hours remaining are calculated by subtracting hours spent from total number of hours.

1

- Display the Create tab and then click the Query Design button (Create tab | Queries group) to create a new query.

- Click the Course table, click the Add button (Show Table dialog box), click the Course Offerings table, click the Add button, and then click the Close button to close the Show Table dialog box.

- Double-click the Client Number and Course Number fields from the Course Offerings table to add the fields to the design grid.

- Double-click the Course Description field from the Course table.

- Double-click the Total Hours and Hours Spent fields from the Course Offerings table to add the fields to the design grid.

- Click the first open column in the design grid to select it.

- Click the Builder button (Query Tools Design tab | Query Setup group) to display the Expression Builder dialog box (Figure 6–7).

Figure 6–7

2

- Double-click Camashaly Design in the Expression Elements section to display the categories of objects within the Camashaly Design database, and then double-click Tables to display a list of tables.

- Click the Course Offerings table to select it.

- Double-click the Total Hours field to add it to the expression.

- Type a minus sign (–) to add it to the expression.

- Double-click the Hours Spent field to add it to the expression (Figure 6–8).

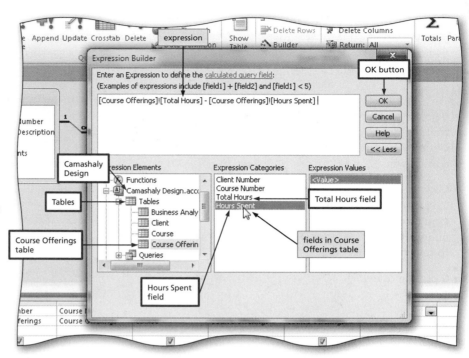

Q&A Why are the fields preceded by a table name and an exclamation point?

This notation qualifies the field; that is, it indicates to which table the field belongs.

Figure 6–8

Q&A Could I type the expression instead of using the Expression Builder?

Yes. You could type it directly into the design grid. You could also right-click the column and click Zoom to allow you to type the expression in the Zoom dialog box. Finally, you could use the Expression Builder, but simply type the expression rather than clicking any buttons. Use whichever method you find most convenient.

3

- Click the OK button (Expression Builder dialog box).

- With the field in the grid where you entered the expression selected, click the Property Sheet button (Query Tools Design tab | Show/Hide group) to display the property sheet for the new field.

Q&A The wrong property sheet appeared. What went wrong? What should I do?

You either did not click in the right location, or you have not yet completed entering the expression. The easiest way to ensure you have done both is to click any other column in the grid and then click the column with the expression.

- Click the Caption property box and type **Hours Remaining** as the caption (Figure 6–9).

Figure 6–9

- Close the property sheet and then view the results of the query (Figure 6–10). (Your results might be in a different order.)

- Verify that your query results match those in the figure. If not, return to Design view and make the necessary corrections.

- Click the Save button, type **Course Offerings and Courses** as the name of the query, and then click the OK button to save the query.

- Close the query.

Client Numb	Course Num	Course Desc	Total Hours	Hours Spent	Hours Rema
BB32	C01	Using the Cont	8	4	4
KG04	C01	Using the Cont	8	6	2
TB17	C02	HTML Basics	4	2	2
CJ29	C03	Digital Image N	6	3	3
KD21	C03	Digital Image N	6	0	6
HC10	C04	Javascript Basi	12	6	6
SL77	C04	Javascript Basi	12	9	3
BA53	C05	Understanding	2	0	2
HC10	C05	Understanding	2	1	1
KG04	C05	Understanding	2	0	2
ME14	C06	Using Shopping	4	2	2
PJ34	C06	Using Shopping	4	2	2
KD21	C07	Understanding	8	4	4
KG04	C08	Podcasting	6	4	2
SL77	C08	Podcasting	6	2	4

query results

results of calculation

Figure 6–10

Plan Ahead

Determine the fields that belong on the report.
If you determine that data should be presented as a report, you then need to determine what tables and fields contain the data for the report.

- **Examine the requirements for the report in general to determine the tables.** Do the requirements only relate to data in a single table, or does the data come from multiple tables? Is the data in a query, or could you create a query that contains some or all of the fields necessary for the report?

- **Examine the specific requirements for the report to determine the fields necessary.** Look for all the data items that are specified for the report. Each item should correspond to a field in a table, or it should be able to be computed from a field in a table. This information gives you the list of fields to include in the query.

- **Determine the order of the fields.** Examine the requirements to determine the order in which the fields should appear. Be logical and consistent in your ordering. For example, in an address, the city should come before the state, and the state should come before the postal code, unless there is some compelling reason for another order.

Plan Ahead

Determine the organization of the report.
Determine various details concerning how the data in your report is to be organized.

- **Determine sort order.** Is there a special order in which the records should appear?

- **Determine grouping.** Should the records be grouped in some fashion? If so, what information should appear before the records in a group? If, for example, clients are grouped by business analyst number, the number of the business analyst should probably appear before the group. Should the business analyst name also appear? What should appear after the group? For example, are there some fields for which subtotals should be calculated? If so, the subtotals would come after the group.

(continued)

(continued)

Plan
Ahead

- **Determine whether to include a subreport.** Rather than use grouping, you may choose to include a subreport, as shown in the Business Analyst Master List on page AC 339. The data concerning course offerings for the client could have been presented by grouping the course offerings' data by client number. The headings currently in the subreport would have appeared in the group header. Instead, it is presented in a subreport. Subreports, which are reports in their own right, offer more flexibility in formatting than group headers and footers. More important, in the Business Analyst Master List, some clients do not have any course offerings. If this information were presented using grouping, the group header will still appear for these clients. With a subreport, clients who have no course offerings do not appear.

To Create an Initial Report in Design View

Creating the report shown in Figure 6–1a on page AC 339 from scratch involves creating the initial report in Design view, adding the subreport, modifying the subreport separately from the main report, and then making the final modifications to the main report.

When you want to create a report from scratch, you use Design view rather than the Report Wizard. The Report Wizard is suitable for simple, customized reports. With Report Design, you can make advanced design changes, such as adding subreports. The following steps create the initial version of the Business Analyst Master List and select the **record source** for the report; that is, the table or query that will furnish the data for the report. The steps then specify sorting and grouping for the report.

- Display the Create tab.

- Click the Report Design button (Create tab | Reports group) to create a report in Design view.

- Ensure the selector for the entire report, the box in the upper-left corner of the report, is selected.

- Click the Property Sheet button (Report Design Tools Design tab | Tools group) to display a property sheet.

- With the All tab (Property Sheet) selected, click the Record Source property box arrow to display the list of available tables and queries (Figure 6–11).

Q&A Can I make the property sheet box wider so I can see more of the items in the Record Source list?

Yes, you can make the property sheet wider by dragging its right border.

Q&A The right side of the property sheet is cut off. Can I move the property sheet?

Yes, you can move the property sheet by dragging its title bar.

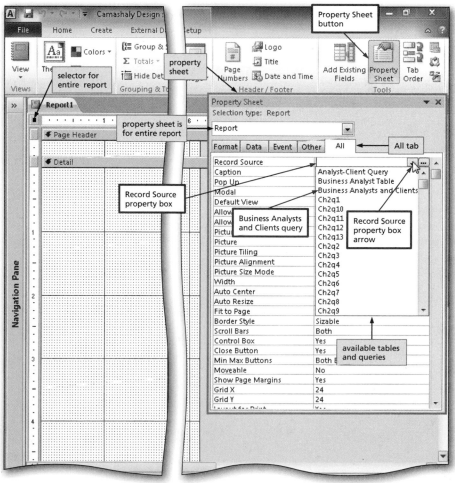

Figure 6–11

2

- Click the Business Analysts and Clients query to select the query as the record source for the report.

- Close the property sheet by clicking the Property Sheet button (Report Design Tools Design tab | Tools group).

- Click the Group & Sort button (Report Design Tools Design tab | Grouping & Totals group) to display the Group, Sort, and Total pane (Figure 6–12).

Figure 6–12

3

- Click the 'Add a group' button to display the list of available fields for grouping (Figure 6–13).

Figure 6–13

4

- Click the Business Analyst Number field to group by business analyst number (Figure 6–14).

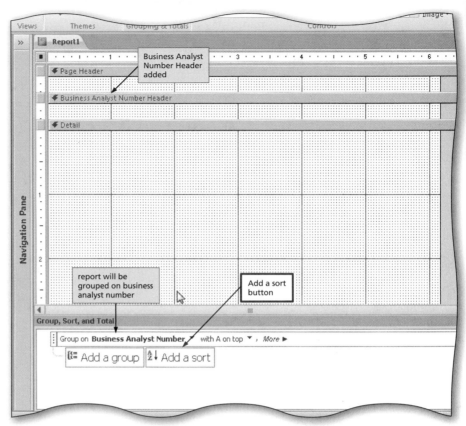

Figure 6–14

5

- Click the 'Add a sort' button to display the list of available fields for sorting (Figure 6–15).

6

- Click the Client Number field to sort by client number.

Figure 6–15

To Save the Report

Before proceeding with the next steps in the modification of the report, it is a good idea to save your work. The following steps save the report as Business Analyst Master List.

1 Click the Save button on the Quick Access Toolbar.

2 Type `Business Analyst Master List` as the report name.

3 Click the OK button.

BTW

Expression Builder
The Expression Builder provides easy access to built-in functions, table names, and field names. In Access 2010, the Expression Builder was enhanced to include IntelliSense that shows you options as you type. It also displays help for the currently selected expression value.

Recall from Chapter 4 that a report contains three types of controls: bound controls, unbound controls, and calculated controls. As you learned previously, reports contain standard sections, including the Report Header, Report Footer, Page Header, Page Footer, and Detail sections. When the data in a report is grouped, there are two additional possible sections. The contents of the **Group Header section** are printed before the records in a particular group, and the contents of the **Group Footer section** are printed after the group. In the Discount Report (Figure 6–1b), for example, which is grouped by business analyst number, the Group Header section contains the business analyst number and name, and the Group Footer section contains subtotals of the Amount Paid and Current Due fields.

To Add Fields to the Report in Design View

When you have determined the fields that are necessary for the report, you need to add them. You can add the fields to the report by dragging them from the field list to the appropriate position on the report. The following steps add the fields to the report.

1

- Remove the Group, Sort, and Total pane by clicking the Group & Sort button (Report Design Tools Design tab | Grouping & Totals group).

- Click the Add Existing Fields button (Report Design Tools Design tab | Tools group) to display a field list.

- Drag the Business Analyst Number field to the approximate position shown in Figure 6–16.

Q&A My field list does not look like the one in the figure. It has several tables listed, and at the top it has Show only fields in the current record source. Yours has Show all tables. What should I do?

Click the 'Show only field in the current record source' link. Your field list should then match the one in the figure.

Figure 6–16

- Release the left mouse button to place the field (Figure 6–17).

Figure 6–17

- Place the remaining fields in the positions shown in Figure 6–18.

- Display the Arrange tab.

- Adjust the positions of the labels to those shown in the figure. If any field is not in the correct position, drag it to its correct location. To move the control or the attached label separately, drag the large handle in the upper-left corner of the control or label. You can align controls using the Align button (Report Design Tools Arrange tab | Sizing & Ordering group) or adjust spacing by using the Size/Space button (Report Design Tools Arrange tab | Sizing & Ordering group).

Figure 6–18

 Experiment

- Select more than one control and then experiment with the Size/Space and the Align buttons (Report Design Tools Arrange tab | Sizing & Ordering group) to see their effects. After trying each one, click the Undo button to undo the change.

- Display the Design tab.

- Remove the field list by clicking the Add Existing Fields button (Report Design Tools Design tab | Tools group), which is shown in Figure 6–16.

To Change Labels

The labels for the Business Analyst Number and Client Number fields currently contain the captions BA # and CL # for the fields. Because there is plenty of room on the report to display longer names for both fields, you can make the report more descriptive by changing the labels. The following step changes the contents of the label for the Business Analyst Number field from BA # to Analyst Number. They also change the contents of the label for the Client Number field from CL # to Client Number.

- Click the label for the Business Analyst Number field twice, once to select it and the second time to produce an insertion point.

- Use the BACKSPACE or DELETE key to erase the current entry in the label and then type **Analyst Number** as the new entry.

- Click the label for the Client Number field twice to produce an insertion point.

- Use the BACKSPACE or DELETE key to erase the current entry in the label and then type **Client Number** as the new entry (Figure 6–19).

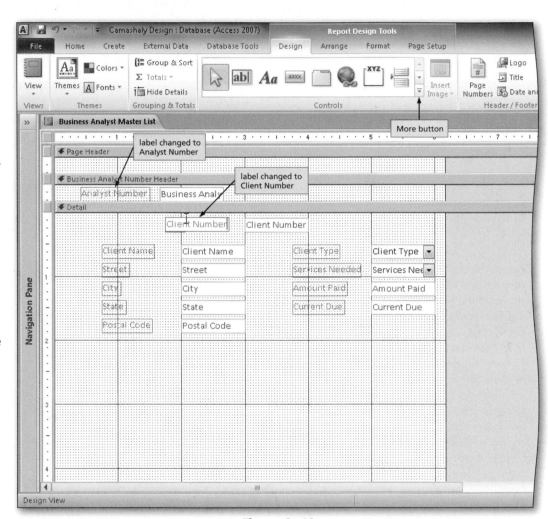

Figure 6–19

Using Other Tools in the Controls Group

Previously, you used the Subform/Subreport tool within the Controls group on the Design tab to place special controls on a form. The Controls group has additional tools available that can be used with forms and reports. A description of the additional tools appears in Table 6–3.

Table 6–3 Additional Tools in the Controls Group

Tool	Description	Button
Select	Enables sizing, moving, or editing of existing controls. If you click another tool and then want to cancel the effect of the tool before using it, you can click the Select tool.	
Text Box	Creates a text box for entering, editing, and displaying data. You can also bind the text box to a field in the underlying table or query.	
Label	Creates a label, a box containing identifying text that is independent of other controls, such as a title.	
Button	Creates a command button.	
Tab Control	Creates a tab control, which contains a series of tabbed pages. Each tabbed page can contain its own controls.	
Hyperlink	Inserts a hyperlink to an existing file, Web page, database object, or e-mail address.	
Option Group	Creates an option group, a rectangle containing a collection of option buttons. To select an option, you simply click the corresponding option button.	
Insert or Remove Page Break	Inserts or removes a physical page break (typically in a report).	
Combo box	Creates a combo box, which is a combination of a text box and a list box.	
Chart	Creates a chart.	
Line	Draws a line on a form or report.	
Toggle Button	Adds a toggle button. With a toggle button, a user can make a Yes/No selection by clicking the button. The button either appears to be pressed (for Yes) or not pressed (for No).	
List Box	Creates a list box, a box that allows the user to select from a list of options.	
Rectangle	Creates a rectangle.	
Check Box	Inserts a check box. With a check box, a user can make multiple Yes/No selections.	
Unbound Object Frame	Inserts an OLE object (for example, a graph, picture, sound file, or video) that is not contained in a field in a table within the database.	
Attachment	Inserts an Attachment field.	
Option Button	Inserts an option button. With an option button, a user can make a single Yes/No selection from among a collection of at least two choices.	
Subform/ Subreport	Creates a subform (a form contained within another form) or a subreport (a report contained within another report).	
Bound Object Frame	Inserts an OLE object (for example, a graph, picture, sound file, or video) that is contained in a field in a table within the database.	
Image	Inserts a frame into which you can insert a graphic. The graphic will be the same for all records.	

BTW

Use Control Wizards Button
Many of the tools shown in Table 6-3 have a wizard associated with them to assist you in specifying options and values for the control. To use the wizard, make sure the Use Control Wizards button is selected before you add a control to a form or report.

BTW

Hyperlink Controls
You can add a hyperlink to tables, forms, and reports. To add a hyperlink, which provides single-click access to Web pages, to a report, click the Hyperlink tool (Report Design Tools Design tab | Controls group), enter the hyperlink in the Address text box (Insert Hyperlink dialog box) and click the OK button. If necessary, move the hyperlink control to the desired location on the report.

BTW

Drop Down Controls
Drop down boxes can be combo boxes or list boxes. To add a combo box to a report, click the Combo Box tool (Report Design Tools Design tab | Controls group), move the mouse pointer to the desired location, and click the position to place the combo box. Follow the directions in the Combo Box Wizard dialog box to specify the options and values for the combo box. To add a list box to a report, click the List Box tool (Report Design Tools Design tab | Controls group) and follow the steps listed above for a combo box.

BTW

Graphs
You can add graphs (charts) to a report using the Chart tool. To add a graph (chart) to a report, click the Chart tool (Report Design Tools Design tab | Controls group), move the mouse pointer to the desired location, and click the position to place the graph. Follow the directions in the Chart Wizard dialog box to specify the data source for the chart, the values for the chart, and the chart type.

To Add Text Boxes

You can place a text box on a report or form by using the Text Box tool in the Controls group on the Design tab. The text box consists of a control that is initially unbound and an attached label. When you enter an expression in the text box, it becomes a calculated control. If the expression is just a single field (for example, =[Amount Paid]), it would be a bound control. Expressions also can be arithmetic operations; for example, calculating the sum of amount paid and current due. Many times, you need to **concatenate**, or combine, two or more text data items into a single expression; the process is called **concatenation**. To concatenate strings, you use the **ampersand (&)** operator. The process of converting an unbound control to a bound control is called **binding**.

The following steps add text boxes and create calculated controls.

1
- Click the Text Box tool (Report Design Tools Design tab | Controls group) and move the pointer to the approximate position shown in Figure 6–20.

Figure 6–20

2
- Click the position shown in Figure 6–20 to place a text box on the report (Figure 6–21).

Figure 6–21

3

- Click in the text box to produce an insertion point (Figure 6–22).

Q&A I inadvertently clicked somewhere else, so the text box was no longer selected. When I clicked the text box a second time, it was selected, but there was no insertion point. What should I do?

Simply click another time.

Figure 6–22

4

- In the text box, type
  `=[First Name]&' '&[Last Name]` as the entry.

Q&A What is the result of the expression I just entered?

The expression will display the first name of the business analyst, followed by a space, and then the last name of the business analyst. Any extra spaces at the end of the first name will be removed.

Q&A Could I use the Expression Builder instead of typing the expression?

Yes. Click the Property Sheet button and then click the Build button, which contains three dots, next to the Control Source property.

Q&A Do I need to use single quotes (')?

No. You also could use double quotes (").

- Click in the text box label to select the label and then click the label a second time to produce an insertion point (Figure 6–23).

Figure 6–23

5

- Use the BACKSPACE or DELETE key to erase the current entry in the label and then type **Analyst Name** as the new entry.

- Click outside the label to deselect it and then drag the label to the position shown in the figure by dragging the Move handle in the upper-left corner of the label (Figure 6–24).

Figure 6–24

6

- Use the techniques in Steps 1 to 5 to place a second text box in the position indicated in Figure 6–24. Type **=[Amount Paid]+[Current Due]** as the expression in the text box, drag the label to the position shown in the figure, erase the contents of the label, and type **Total Amount** in the label (Figure 6–25).

Q&A My label is not in the correct position. What should I do?

Click outside the label to deselect it, click the label, and then drag it to the desired position.

Q&A Total Amount already is a calculated field in the Client table. Why am I adding it to the report?

Access 2007 does not recognize calculated fields. If you want to share this report with individuals who use Access 2007, you will need to add the calculated control to the report.

Figure 6–25

To View the Report in Print Preview

As you are working on a report in Design view, it is useful to periodically view the report to gauge how it will look containing data. One way to do so is to use Print Preview. The following steps view the report in Print Preview.

- Click the View button arrow (Report Design Tools Design tab | Views group) to produce the View button menu.

- Click Print Preview on the View button menu to view the report in Print Preview (Figure 6–26).

Q&A What would happen if I clicked the View button instead of the View button arrow?

The icon on the View button is the icon for Report View, so you would view the results in Report view. This is another useful way to view a report, but compared with Print Preview, Report View does not give as accurate a picture of how the final printed report will look.

Q&A The total amount does not appear as currency, and the Services Needed field does not display all the values. How can I fix these issues?

You will see how to fix these issues in the next sections.

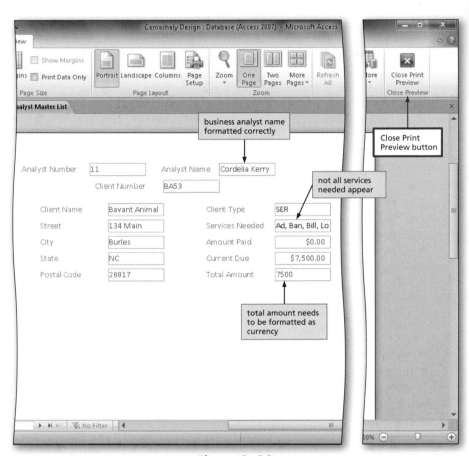

Figure 6–26

2
- Click the Close Print Preview button on the Print Preview tab to return to Design view.

To Format a Control

When you add a calculated control to a report, you often need to format the control. You can use a control's property sheet to change the value in the appropriate property. If a property does not appear on the screen, you have two choices. You can click the tab on which the property is located. For example, if it were a control related to data, you would click the Data tab to only show data-related properties. Many people, however, prefer to click the All tab, which shows all properties, and then simply scroll through the properties, if necessary, until locating the appropriate property. The following steps change the format of the Total Amount control to Currency by changing the value of the Format property and the Decimal Places property.

1

- Click the control containing the expression for Total Amount to select it and then click the Property Sheet button (Report Design Tools Design tab | Tools group) to display the property sheet.

- If necessary, click the All tab (Figure 6–27).

🔍 **Experiment**

- Click the other tabs in the property sheet to see the types of properties on each tab. When finished, once again click the All tab.

2

- Click the Format property box, click the arrow that appears, and then click Currency to select Currency as the format.

- Click the Decimal Places property box, click the arrow that appears, and then click 2 to select two decimal places.

- Remove the property sheet by clicking the Property Sheet button (Report Design Tools Design tab | Tools group) a second time.

- Preview the report using Print Preview to see the effect of the property changes.

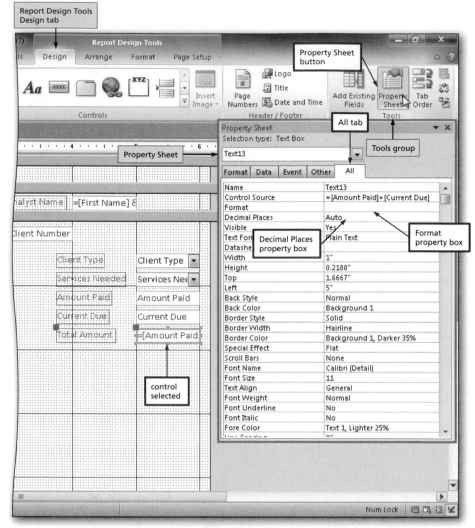

Figure 6–27

Other Ways

1. Right-click control, click Properties

To Group Controls

If your report contains a collection of controls that you frequently will want to modify in the same way, you can simplify the process of selecting all the controls by grouping them. Once they are grouped, selecting any control in the group automatically selects all of the controls in the group. You then can apply the desired change to all the controls.

The following steps group the controls within the Detail section.

1

- Click the Client Number control to select it.

Q&A Do I click the white space or the label?

The white space.

- While holding the SHIFT key down, click all the other controls in the Detail section to select them.

Q&A Does it matter in which order I select the other controls?

No. It is only important that you ultimately select all the controls.

- Release the SHIFT key.

- Display the Arrange tab.

- Click the Size/Space button (Report Design Tools Arrange tab | Sizing & Ordering group) to display the Size/ Space button menu (Figure 6–28).

Figure 6–28

2

- Click Group on the Size/Space button menu to group the controls.

Q&A What if I make a mistake and group the wrong collection of controls?

Ungroup the controls using the steps shown in the next section, and then group the correct collection of controls.

To UNGROUP CONTROLS

If you no longer need to simultaneously modify all the controls you have placed in a group, you can ungroup the controls. To do so, you would use the following steps.

1. Click any of the controls in a group to select the entire group.

2. Display the Arrange tab.

3. Click the Size/Space button (Report Design Tools Arrange tab | Sizing & Ordering group) to display the Size/Space button menu.

4. Click the Ungroup button on the Size/Space button menu to ungroup the controls.

To Modify Grouped Controls

To modify grouped controls, click any control in the group to select the entire group. Any change you then make affects all controls in the group. The following steps bold the controls in the group, resize them, and then change the border style.

1

- If necessary, click any one of the grouped controls to select the group.

- Display the Format tab.

- Click the Bold button (Report Design Tools Format tab | Font group) to bold all the controls in the group (Figure 6–29).

Figure 6–29

2

- Display the Design tab.

- Drag the right sizing handle of the Services Needed field to the approximate position shown in Figure 6–30 to resize all the controls in the group.

How do I change only one control in the group?

Double-click the control to select just the one control and not the entire group. You then can make any change you want to that control.

Figure 6–30

3

- Click the Property Sheet button (Report Design Tools Design tab | Tools group) to display the property sheet for the grouped controls.

- With the All tab (Property Sheet) selected, ensure the Border Style property is set to Solid. If it is not, click the Border Style property box to display an arrow, click the arrow to display the list of available border styles, and click Solid.

- Click the Border Width property box to display an arrow and then click the arrow to display the list of available border widths (Figure 6–31).

Figure 6–31

4

- Click 1 pt to select the border width.

 Experiment

- Try the other border styles and widths to see their effects. In each case, view the report and then return to Design view. When finished, once again select Solid as the border style and 1 pt as the border width.

- Close the property sheet.

To Modify Multiple Controls That Are Not Grouped

To modify multiple controls that are not grouped together, you must simultaneously select all the controls you want to modify. To do so, click one of the controls and then hold the SHIFT key down while selecting the others. The following steps italicize all the labels in the Detail section and then bold all the controls and labels in the Business Analyst Number Header section. Finally, the steps increase the size of the Business Analyst Name control so that the entire name will be visible.

1

- Click the label for the Client Number control to select it.

- While holding the SHIFT key down, click the labels for all the other controls in the Detail section to select them.

- Release the SHIFT key.

- Display the Format tab.

- Click the Italic button (Report Design Tools Format tab | Font group) to italicize the labels (Figure 6–32).

Figure 6–32

2

- Click in the vertical ruler to the left of the Business Analyst Number Header section to select all the controls in the section.

Q&A What exactly is selected when I click in the vertical ruler?

If you picture a horizontal line through the point you clicked, any control that intersects that horizontal line would be selected.

- Click the Bold button (Report Design Tools Format tab | Font group) to bold all the selected controls (Figure 6–33).

Figure 6–33

③

- Click outside the selected controls to deselect them. Click the control containing the expression for the business analyst's name to select it.

Q&A Why do I have to deselect the controls and then select one of them a second time?

If you do not do so, any action you take would apply to all the selected controls rather than just the one you want.

- Drag the right sizing handle of the selected control to the approximate position shown in Figure 6–34.

- View the report and then make any necessary adjustments.

Figure 6–34

Undoing and Saving

Remember that if you make a mistake, you often can correct it by clicking the Undo button on the Quick Access Toolbar. Clicking the Undo button will reverse your most recent change. You also can click the Undo button more than once to reverse multiple changes.

You should save your work frequently. That way, if you have problems that the Undo button will not fix, you can close the report without saving it and open it again. The report will be in exactly the state it was in at the time you saved it.

To Add a Subreport

To add a subreport to a report, you use the Subform/Subreport tool on the Design tab. Provided the Use Control Wizards button is selected, a wizard will guide you through the process of adding the subreport. The following steps add a subreport to display the course data.

- Display the Design tab.

- Click the More button (Report Design Tools Design tab | Controls group) (shown in Figure 6–31) to display a menu of available tools (Figure 6–35).

Figure 6–35

❷

- Be sure the Use Control Wizards button is selected, click the Subform/ Subreport tool, and then move the mouse pointer, which has changed to a plus sign with a subreport, to the approximate position shown in Figure 6–36.

Figure 6–36

3

- Click the position shown in Figure 6–36 to place the subreport and display the SubReport Wizard dialog box. Be sure the 'Use existing Tables and Queries' option button is selected (Figure 6–37).

Figure 6–37

4

- Click the Next button.

- Click the Tables/Queries box arrow.

- Scroll down until Query: Course Offerings and Courses is visible, click Query: Course Offerings and Courses, and then click the Add All Fields button to select all the fields in the query (Figure 6–38).

Figure 6–38

- Click the Next button and then ensure the 'Choose from a list' option button is selected (Figure 6–39).

Q&A

What is the purpose of this dialog box?

You use this dialog box to indicate the fields that link the main report (referred to as "form") to the subreport (referred to as "subform"). If the fields have the same name, as they often will, you can simply select Choose from a list and then accept the selection Access already has made.

Figure 6–39

- Click the Next button, type **Course Offerings by Client** as the name of the subreport, and then click the Finish button to add the subreport to the Business Analyst Master List report (Figure 6–40).

- Click outside the subreport to deselect the subreport.

- Click the Save button on the Quick Access Toolbar to save your changes.

- Close the Business Analyst Master List report.

Figure 6–40

Break Point: If you wish to stop working through the chapter at this point, you can resume the project at a later time by starting Access, opening the database called Camashaly Design, and continuing to follow the steps from this location forward.

To Open the Subreport in Design View

The subreport appears as a separate report in the Navigation Pane. It can be modified just like any other report. The following step opens the subreport in Design view.

1

- Open the Navigation Pane, scroll down so that the Course Offerings by Client report appears, and then right-click the Course Offerings by Client report to produce a shortcut menu.

- Click Design View on the shortcut menu to open the subreport in Design view.

- Close the Navigation Pane (Figure 6–41).

Figure 6–41

Print Layout Issues

If there is a problem with your report, for example, a report that is too wide for the printed page, you will get a green triangular symbol in the upper-left corner of the report. The green triangle is called an error indicator. Clicking it displays an Error Checking Options button. Clicking the Error Checking Options button produces the Error Checking Options menu, as shown in Figure 6–42.

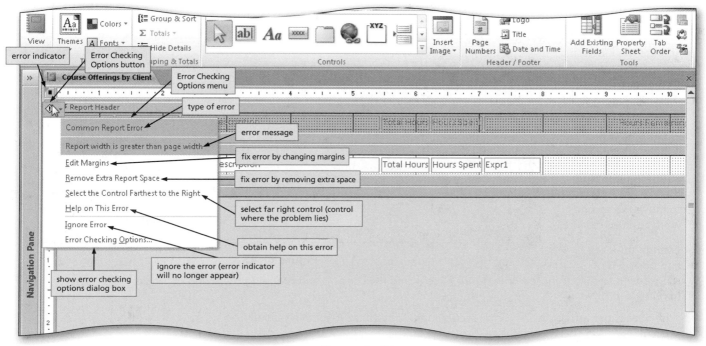

Figure 6–42

BTW

Subreports
Subreports provide more control in presenting data effectively than multiple levels of grouping can. Because grouping places headers in columns, it often can be difficult to determine the relationship between the group header and the detail. Also, you might want to present subreports side by side. You cannot do that with grouping.

The first line in the menu is simply a statement of the type of error that occurred. The second is a description of the specific error; in this case, the fact that the report width is greater than the page width. This situation could lead to data not appearing where you expect it to, as well as the printing of some blank pages.

The next three lines provide alternatives for addressing the error. You could change the margins to allow more space for the report. You could remove some extra space. You could select the control farthest to the right and move it. The fourth line gives more detailed help on the error. The Ignore Error command instructs Access to not consider this situation an error. Selecting Ignore Error would cause the error indicator to disappear. The final line displays the Error Checking Options dialog box, where you can make other changes.

Later in this chapter, you will fix the problem by changing the width of the report, so you do not need to take any action at this time.

To Modify the Controls in the Subreport

Because the client number appears in the main report, it does not need to be duplicated in the subreport. In addition, the column headers in the subreport should extend over two lines, as shown in Figure 6–1a on page AC 339. The following step modifies the subreport by deleting the Client Number control and revising the column headings.

1

• Click the Client Number control in the Detail section to select the control. Hold the SHIFT key down and click the Client Number control in the Report Header section to select both controls.

• With both controls selected, press the DELETE key to delete the controls.

• Change the labels in the Report Header section to match those shown in Figure 6–43. To extend a heading over two lines, click in front of the second word to produce an insertion point and then press SHIFT+ENTER to move the second word to a second line.

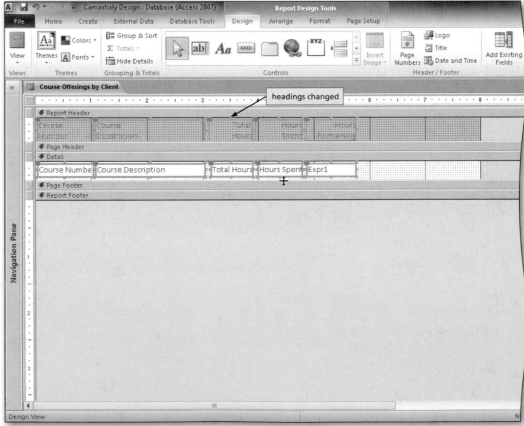

Figure 6–43

• Change the sizes and positions of the controls to match those in the figure by selecting the controls and dragging the sizing handles.

Q&A

Why does Expr1 appear in the Detail section under the Hours Remaining label?

Expr1 indicates that Hours Remaining is a calculated control.

Experiment

- There is currently a space between the two names in the Report Header labels. To delete the space, click immediately after the first word to produce an insertion point and then press the DELETE key. Try the various alignments (left, right, and center) before removing the space. Remove the space and try the various alignments again to see if the removal of the space makes any difference. When finished, make sure your labels look like the one in the figure.

To Change the Can Grow Property

If you preview the report, you will see that some of the course descriptions are too long to fit in the available space. This problem can be addressed in several ways.

1. Move the controls to allow more space in between controls. Then, drag the appropriate handles on the controls that need to be expanded to enlarge them.

2. Use the Font Size property to select a smaller font size. This will allow more data to fit in the same space.

3. Use the Can Grow property. By changing the value of this property from No to Yes, the data can be spread over two lines, thus allowing all the data to print. Access will split data at natural break points, such as commas, spaces, and hyphens.

The third approach is the easiest to use and also produces a very readable report. The following steps change the Can Grow property for the Course Description field. First, you preview the report to verify that there are some course descriptions that are too long for the available space and then make the necessary corrections.

1

- Click the View button arrow and then click Print Preview to preview the report (Figure 6–44).

Figure 6–44

- Click the Close Print Preview button to return to Design view.

- Click the Course Description control to select it.

- Click the Property Sheet button (Report Design Tools Design tab | Tools group) to display the property sheet.

- With the All tab selected, scroll down until the Can Grow property appears, and then click the Can Grow property box arrow to display the list of possible values for the Can Grow property (Figure 6–45).

What is the effect of the Can Shrink property?

If the value of the Can Shrink property is set to Yes, Access will remove blank lines that occur when the field is empty.

- Click Yes in the list to allow the Course Description control to grow as needed.

- Close the property sheet.

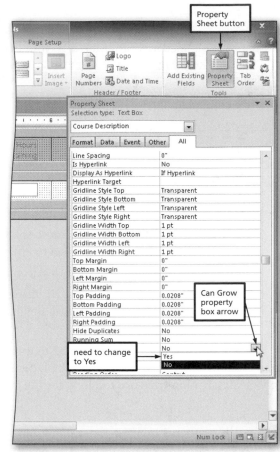

Figure 6–45

To Change the Appearance of the Controls in the Subreport

The following steps change the controls in the Detail section to Bold and the controls in the Report Header section to italic. They also change the background color in the Report Header section to white.

- Drag the right boundary of the subreport to the approximate position shown in Figure 6–46.

Figure 6–46

2

- Display the Format tab.

- Click the ruler to the left of the controls in the Detail section to select the controls, and then click the Bold button (Report Design Tools Format tab | Font group) to bold the controls.

- Click the ruler to the left of the controls in the Report Header section to select the controls, and then click the Italic button (Report Design Tools Format tab | Font group) to italicize the controls.

- Click the title bar for the Report Header to select the header without selecting any of the controls in the header.

- Click the Background Color button arrow (Report Design Tools Format tab | Font group) to display a color palette (Figure 6–47).

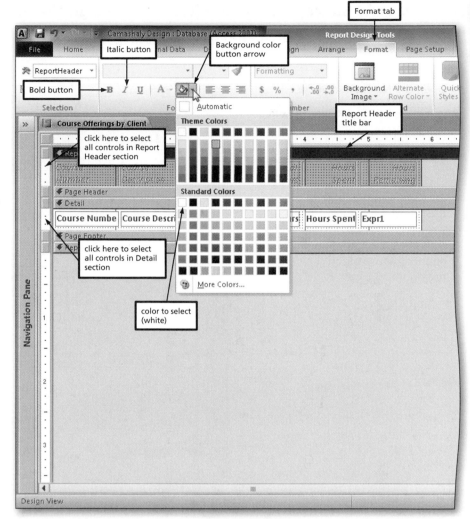

Figure 6–47

3

- Click White in the first row, first column of the Standard Colors to change the background color to white.

Q&A

What is the difference between clicking a color in the Theme colors and clicking a color in the Standard Colors?

The theme colors are specific to the currently selected theme. The first column, for example, represents "background 1," one of the selected background colors in the theme. The various entries in the column represent different intensities of the color at the top of the column. The colors would be different if a different theme were selected. If you select one of the theme colors and a different theme is selected in the future, the color you selected would change to the color in the same location. On the other hand, if you select a standard color, a change of theme would have no effect on the color.

- Click the Save button on the Quick Access Toolbar to save the changes.

- Close the Course Offerings by Client subreport.

To Resize the Subreport and the Report in Design View

The following steps resize the subreport control in the main report and then resize the main report.

1

- Open the Navigation Pane.

- Open the Business Analyst Master List in Design view.

- Close the Navigation Pane.

- Click the subreport and then drag the right sizing handle to change the size to the approximate size shown in Figure 6–48, and then drag the subreport to the approximate position shown in the figure.

Figure 6–48

2

- Scroll down in the main report so that the lower boundary of the Detail section appears, and then drag the lower boundary of the section so that there is approximately the same amount of space below the subreport as that shown in Figure 6–49.

 Q&A

I scrolled down to see the lower boundary of the Detail section and the controls are no longer on the screen. What is the easiest way to drag the boundary when the position to which I want to drag it is not visible?

You do not need to see the location to drag to it. As you get close to the top of the visible portion of the screen, Access will automatically scroll. You might find it easier, however, to drag the boundary near the top of the visible portion of the report, use the scroll bar to scroll up, and then drag some more. You might have to scroll a couple of times.

Figure 6–49

To Modify Section Properties

The following step first deletes the label for the subreport and then makes two modifications to the Business Analyst Number Header section. The first modification, which causes the contents of the Group Header section to appear at the top of each page, changes the Repeat Section property to Yes. Without this change, the business analyst number and name would only appear at the beginning of the group of clients of that business analyst. If the list of clients occupies more than one page, it would not be apparent on subsequent pages which business analyst is associated with those clients. The second modification changes the Force New Page property to Before Section, causing each section to begin at the top of a page.

- If necessary, scroll back up to the top of the report, and then click the label for the subreport (the label that reads Course Offerings by Client), and then press the DELETE key to delete the label.

- Click the Business Analyst Number Header bar to select the header, and then click the Property Sheet button (Report Design Tools Design tab | Tools group) to display the property sheet.

- With the All tab selected, click the Repeat Section property box, click the arrow that appears, and then click Yes to cause the contents of the group header to appear at the top of each page of the report.

Figure 6–50

- Click the Force New Page property box, and then click the arrow that appears to display the menu of possible values (Figure 6–50).

- Click Before Section to cause a new group to begin at the top of the next page.

- Close the property sheet.

To Add a Title, Page Number, and Date

You can add a title, a page number, and a date to a report or apply other formatting using buttons on the Design tab. The following steps add a title, page number, and date to the Business Analyst Master List report. The date is automatically added to the report header. The steps move the date to the page header by first cutting the date from its original position and then pasting it into the page header.

1

- Display the Design tab, and then click the Title button (Report Design Tools Design tab | Header/Footer group) to add a title.

The title is the same as the name of the report object. Can I change the report title without changing the name of the report object in the database?

Yes. The report title is a label, and you can change it using any of the techniques that you used for changing column headings and other labels.

- Click the Page Numbers button (Report Design Tools Design tab | Header/Footer group) to display the Page Numbers dialog box.

- Be sure the Page N and Top of Page [Header] option buttons are selected.

- If necessary, click the Alignment arrow and select Left (Figure 6–51).

Figure 6–51

2

- Click the OK button (Page Numbers dialog box) to add the page number.

- Click the Date and Time button (Report Design Tools Design tab | Header/Footer group) to display the Date and Time dialog box.

- Click the option button for the third date format and click the Include Time check box to remove the check mark (Figure 6–52).

Figure 6–52

3

- Click the OK button (Date and Time dialog box) to add the date to the Report Header and display the Home tab (Figure 6–53).

Figure 6–53

4

- With the control containing the date selected, click the Cut button (Home tab | Clipboard group) to cut the date, click the title bar for the page header to select the page header, and then click the Paste button (Home tab | Clipboard group) to paste the Date control at the beginning of the page header.

- Drag the Date control, which is currently sitting on top of the Page Number control, to the position shown in Figure 6–54.

Figure 6–54

To Remove the Alternate Color

An **alternate color** is a color different from the main color and appears on every other line in a datasheet or report. Using alternate colors can sometimes make a datasheet or report more readable. In reports with multiple sections, however, the alternate colors can be confusing. Access automatically assigns alternate colors within the report. If you do not want these alternate colors, you must remove them. The following steps remove the alternate colors from the various sections in the report, starting with the Detail section.

1
- Right-click the Detail section to produce a shortcut menu.
- Point to the Alternate Fill/Back Color arrow to produce a color palette (Figure 6–55).

2
- Click None on the color palette to specify that there is to be no alternate color for the selected section.
- Using the same techniques, remove the alternate color from all other sections, including the subreport. (For some sections, the command may be dimmed.)

Figure 6–55

BTW

Dates
The Access default theme assigns a blue color to the date. To change the date color, select the control and click the Property Sheet button. Click the Fore Color property box, click the arrow that appears and select the color of your choice.

To Save and Close the Report

The following steps save the final report and then close the report.

1 Click the Save button on the Quick Access Toolbar to save the report.

2 Close the report by clicking the Close 'Business Analyst Master List' button.

To Print the Report

The following steps print the Business Analyst Master List report.

1 With the Business Analyst Master List selected in the Navigation Pane, click File on the Ribbon to open the Backstage view.

2 Click the Print tab in the Backstage view to display the Print gallery.

3 Click the Quick Print button to print the report.

TO PUBLISH A REPORT

You can make a report available through e-mail by publishing the report as either a PDF or XPS file. If you wanted to do so, you would use the following steps.

1. Select the report to be published in the Navigation Pane.

2. Display the External Data tab.

3. Click the PDF or XPS button (External Data tab | Export group) to display the Publish as PDF or XPS dialog box.

4. Select the appropriate Save as type (either PDF or XPS).

5. Select either 'Standard (publishing online and printing)' or 'Minimum size (publishing online).'

6. If you want to publish only a range of pages, click the Options button and select the desired range.

7. Click the Publish button to publish the report in the desired format.

8. If you want to save the export steps, click the Save button and then click the 'Save export steps' check box. If not, click the Close button.

BTW

Page Breaks
You can force a page break to occur at a particular position in a report by adding a page break to the report. To do so, click the Insert Page Break tool (Report Design Tools Design tab | Controls group), move the mouse pointer to the desired position, and click the position to place the page break.

Break Point: If you wish to stop working through the chapter at this point, you can resume the project at a later time by starting Access, opening the database called Camashaly Design, and continuing to follow the steps from this location forward.

To Create a Second Report

Camashaly Design also would like a report that groups clients by business analyst. The report should include subtotals and grand totals. Finally, it should show the discount amount for each client. The discount amount is based on the current due amount. Clients who owe more than $4,000 will receive a 4% discount, and clients who owe $4,000 or less will receive a 2% discount. The following steps create the Discount Report, select the record source, and specify grouping and sorting options.

1 Close the Navigation Pane.

2 Display the Create tab and then click the Report Design button (Create tab | Reports group) to create a report in Design view.

3 Ensure the selector for the entire report, which is the box in the upper-left corner of the report, is selected, and then click the Property Sheet button (Report Design Tools Design tab | Tools group) to display a property sheet.

4 With the All tab selected, click the Record Source property box arrow, and then click the Business Analysts and Clients query to select the query as the record source for the report.

5 Close the property sheet.

6 Click the Group & Sort button (Report Design Tools Design tab | Grouping & Totals group) to display the Group, Sort, and Total pane.

7 Click the 'Add a group' button to display the list of available fields for grouping, and then click the Business Analyst Number field to group by business analyst number.

8 Click the 'Add a sort' button to display the list of available fields for sorting, and then click the Client Number field to sort by client number.

9 Remove the Group, Sort, and Total pane by clicking the Group & Sort button (Report Design Tools Design tab | Grouping & Totals group).

10 Click the Save button on the Quick Access Toolbar, type `Discount Report` as the report name, and click the OK button to save the report.

Q&A

Why save it at this point?

You do not have to save it at this point. It is a good idea to save it often, however. Doing so will give you a convenient point from which to restart if you have problems. If you have problems, you could close the report without saving it. When you reopen the report, it will be in the state it was in when you last saved it.

To Add and Move Fields in a Report

As with the previous report, you can add a field to the report by dragging the field from the field list. You can drag an attached label separately from the control to which it is attached by dragging the Move handle in its upper-left corner. This technique does not work, however, if you want to drag the attached label to a different section from the control's section. If you want the label to be in a different section, you must select the label, cut the label, select the section to which you want to move the label, and then paste the label. You then can move the label to the desired location.

The following steps add the Business Analyst Number field to the Business Analyst Number Header section and then move the label to the Page Header section.

1

• Click the Add Existing Fields button (Report Design Tools Design tab | Tools group) to display a field list. (Figure 6–56).

Q&A

My field list displays Show only fields in the current record source, not Show all tables, as in the figure. What should I do?

Click the 'Show only fields in the current record source' link at the top of the field list to display only those fields in the Business Analysts and Clients query.

Figure 6–56

2

• Drag the Business Analyst Number field to the approximate position shown in Figure 6–57.

Figure 6–57

3

• Click the label for the Business Analyst Number control to select it (Figure 6–58).

Figure 6–58

4

- Display the Home tab.

- Click the Cut button (Home tab | Clipboard group) to cut the label.

- Click the Page Header bar to select the page header (Figure 6–59).

Q&A Do I have to click the bar, or could I click somewhere else within the section?

You also could click within the section. Clicking the bar is usually safer, however. If you click in a section intending to select the section, but click within one of the controls in the section, you will select the control rather than the section. Clicking the bar always selects the section.

Figure 6–59

5

- Click the Paste button (Home tab | Clipboard group) to paste the label in the Page Header section (Figure 6–60).

Q&A When would I want to click the Paste button arrow rather than just the button?

Clicking the arrow displays the Paste button menu, which includes the Paste command and two additional commands. Paste Special allows you to paste data into different formats. Paste Append, which is available if you have cut or copied a record, allows you to paste the record to a table with a similar structure. If you want the simple Paste command, you can just click the button.

Figure 6–60

6

- Click in the label to produce an insertion point, use the BACKSPACE or DELETE key to erase the current entry in the label, and then type **Analyst Number** as the new entry.

- Click in the label in front of the word, Number, to produce an insertion point.

- Press SHIFT+ENTER to move the word, Number, to a second line.

To Add the Remaining Fields

The following steps add the remaining fields by dragging them into the Detail section. They next save the report, move the labels into the Page Header section, and move the controls containing the fields to the appropriate locations.

- Resize and move the Business Analyst Number control to the approximate size and position shown in Figure 6–61.

- Resize the Business Analyst Number label to the size shown in the figure.

- Drag the First Name, Last Name, Client Number, Client Name, Amount Paid, and Current Due fields into the Detail section, as shown in the figure.

Q&A Why drag them to the positions shown in the figure? That is not where they appear on the report. Could I drag them all at once?

Dragging them gets them onto the report, where you can now move the controls and labels individually to the desired locations. You can drag multiple fields by selecting the first field, holding down the SHIFT key, and then selecting other adjacent fields. To select fields that are not adjacent to each other, use the CTRL key. How you choose to select fields and drag them onto the report is a matter of personal preference.

Figure 6–61

- Close the field list.

- One at a time, cut each of the labels, paste the label into the Page Header section, and then resize, reformat, and move the labels to the approximate positions shown in Figure 6–62.

Q&A When I paste the label, it always places it at the left edge, superimposing the Business Analyst Number control. Can I change where Access places it?

Unfortunately, when you paste to a different section, Access places the control at the left edge. You will need to drag each control to its proper location after pasting it into the Page Header section.

Figure 6–62

- One at a time, resize and move the First Name and Last Name controls to the approximate positions in the Business Analyst Number Header section shown in the figure.

- One at a time, resize and move the Client Number, Client Name, Amount Paid, and Current Due controls to the approximate positions in the Detail section shown in the figure.

- Display the Arrange tab.

- Use the Align button (Report Design Tools Arrange tab | Sizing & Ordering group) as necessary to align all the controls as shown in Figure 6–62 on the previous page.

To Change the Can Grow Property

The following steps change the Can Grow property for the Client Name control so that names that are too long to fit in the available space will extend to additional lines.

1 Select the Client Name control.

2 Display the property sheet and scroll down until the Can Grow property appears.

3 Click the Can Grow property box and then click the Can Grow property box arrow to display the menu of available values for the Can Grow property.

4 Click Yes to change the value for the Can Grow property.

5 Close the property sheet.

To Resize the Detail Section

The following step resizes the Detail section of the Discount Report to remove most of the extra space below the controls in the section.

- Scroll down so that the lower boundary of the Detail section appears, and then drag the lower boundary of the section to a position just slightly below the controls in the section.

Q&A

I scrolled down to see the lower boundary of the Detail section, and the controls are no longer on the screen. What is the easiest way to drag the boundary when the position to which I want to drag it is not visible?

You do not need to see the location to drag to it. As you get close to the top of the visible portion of the screen, Access will automatically scroll. You might find it easier, however, to drag it near the top of the visible portion of the report, use the scroll bar to scroll up, and then drag some more. You might have to scroll a couple of times.

Plan Ahead	**Determine any calculations required for the report.**
	Determine details concerning any calculations required for the report.
	• **Determine whether to include calculations in the group and report footers.** The group footers or report footers might require calculated data such as subtotals or grand totals. Determine whether the report needs other statistics that must be calculated (for example, average).
	• **Determine whether any additional calculations are required.** Are there any special calculations? If so, determine the fields that are involved and how they are to be combined. Determine whether any of the calculations depend on whether a criterion is true or false, in which case the calculations are conditional.

Totals and Subtotals

To add totals or other statistics to a footer, add a text box control. You can use any of the aggregate functions: COUNT, SUM, AVG (average), MAX (largest value), MIN (smallest value), STDEV (standard deviation), VAR (variance), FIRST, and LAST. To use a function, type an equal (=) sign, followed by the function name. You then include a set of parentheses containing the item for which you want to perform the calculation. If the item name contains spaces, such as Amount Paid, you must enclose it in square brackets. For example, to calculate the sum of the amount paid values, the expression would be =SUM([Amount Paid]).

Access will perform the calculation for the appropriate collection of records. If you enter this expression in the Business Analyst Number Footer section, Access only will calculate the total for clients with the given business analyst; that is, it will calculate the appropriate subtotal. If you enter the expression in the Report Footer section, Access will calculate the total for all clients.

To Add Totals and Subtotals

An analysis of requirements at Camashaly indicated that the Discount Report should contain subtotals and grand totals of amounts paid and current due. The following steps first display the Business Analyst Number Footer section and then add the total of amount paid and current due to both the Business Analyst Number Footer section and the Report Footer section. The steps label the totals in the Business Analyst Number Footer section as subtotals and the totals in the Report Footer section as grand totals. The steps change the format of the new controls to currency and the number of decimal places to 2.

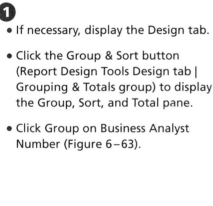

- If necessary, display the Design tab.

- Click the Group & Sort button (Report Design Tools Design tab | Grouping & Totals group) to display the Group, Sort, and Total pane.

- Click Group on Business Analyst Number (Figure 6–63).

Figure 6–63

- Click the More arrow to display additional options for grouping.
- Click the 'without a footer section' arrow to display the available options (Figure 6–64).

Figure 6–64

- Click 'with a footer section' to add a footer.
- Close the Group, Sort, and Total pane by clicking the Group & Sort button (Report Design Tools Design tab | Grouping & Totals group).
- Click the Text Box tool (Report Design Tools Design tab | Controls group), and then point to the position shown in Figure 6–65.

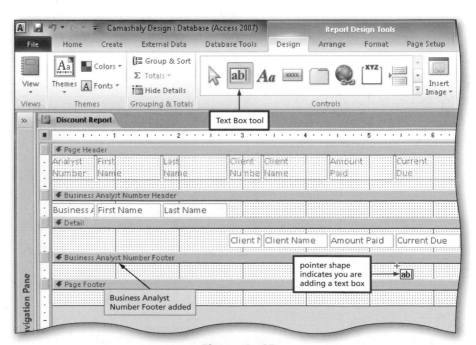

Figure 6–65

4

- Click the position shown in Figure 6–65 to place a text box (Figure 6–66).

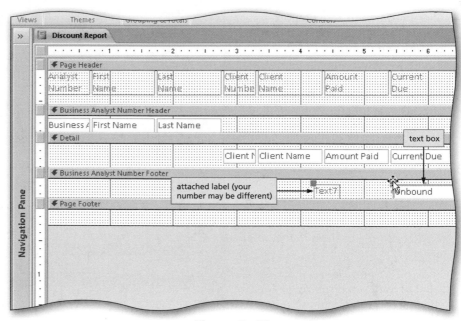

Figure 6–66

5

- Click the text box to produce an insertion point.

- Type =Sum([Current Due]) in the control to enter the expression calculation, and then press the ENTER key.

- Click the text box label to select it.

- Click the label a second time to produce an insertion point.

- Use the DELETE or BACKSPACE key to delete the Text7 (your number might be different).

- Type Subtotals as the label.

- Click outside the label to deselect it.

- Resize and align the Current Due controls in the Detail section and the Business Analyst Number Footer section as shown in Figure 6–67.

Figure 6–67

6

- Click the Text Box tool (Report Design Tools Design tab | Controls group), and then click in the Business Analyst Number Footer section just to the left of the control for the sum of Current Due to place another text box.

- Click the text box to produce an insertion point, type =Sum([Amount Paid]) in the control, and then press the ENTER key to enter the expression (Figure 6–68).

Q&A Could I add the controls in the other order?

Yes. The only problem is that the label of the second control overlaps the first control. Adding the controls in the order shown in the steps reduces the overlap. It is not a major difference, however.

Figure 6–68

7

- Click the label to select it, and then press the DELETE key to delete the label.

Q&A I inadvertently deleted the other control rather than the label. What should I do?

The first thing to try is to click the Undo button on the Quick Access Toolbar to reverse your deletion. You then can delete the correct control. If that does not work for you, you can simply delete the remaining control or controls in the section and start these steps over.

- Click the control for the sum of Amount Paid to select it and then hold down the SHIFT key and click the control for the sum of Current Due to select both controls.

- Click the Property Sheet button (Report Design Tools Design tab | Tools group) to display the property sheet.

- Change the format to Currency and the number of decimal places to 2 (Figure 6–69).

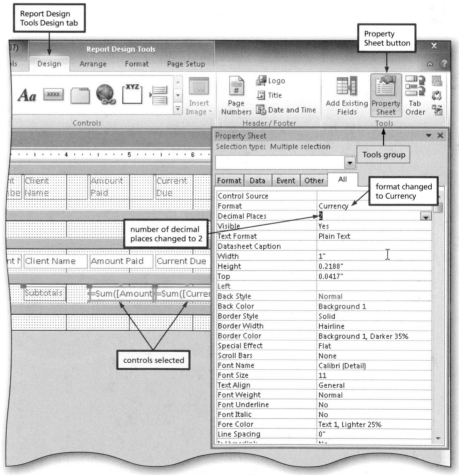

Figure 6–69

8

- Close the property sheet.

- Right-click any open area of the report to display a shortcut menu (Figure 6–70).

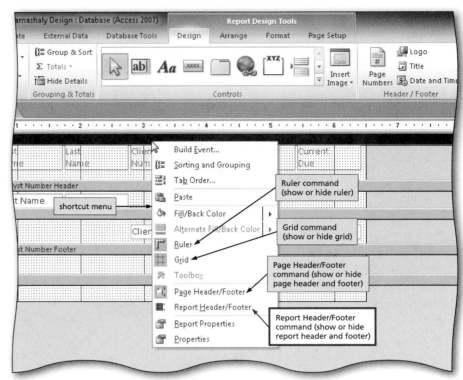

Figure 6–70

9

- Click Report Header/Footer to display the Report Header and Footer sections.

- Click the ruler in the Business Analyst Number Footer to the left of the controls in the section to select the controls.

- Display the Home tab.

- Click the Copy button (Home tab | Clipboard group) to copy the selected controls to the Clipboard (Figure 6–71).

Figure 6–71

⑩

- Click the Report Footer bar to select the footer and then click the Paste button (Home tab | Clipboard group) to paste a copy of the controls into the report footer.

- Move the controls to the positions shown in Figure 6–72.

- Click the label in the Report Footer section to select the label and then click a second time to produce an insertion point.

- Use the BACKSPACE or DELETE key to erase the current contents, and then type **Grand totals** to change the label (Figure 6–72).

Q&A

Could I enter the controls just as I did earlier rather than copying and pasting?

Yes. Copying and pasting is a little simpler, but it is a matter of personal preference.

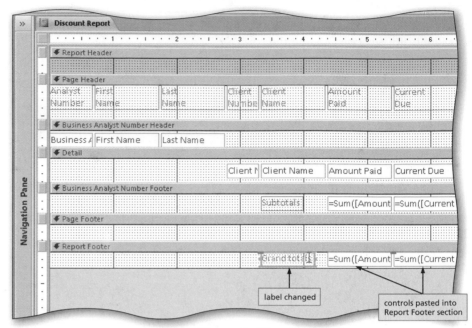

Figure 6–72

Grouping and Sorting Options

As you learned in Chapter 4, clicking the More button in the Group, Sort, and Total pane allows you to specify additional options for grouping and sorting. The additional options are: Value, which lets you choose the amount of the value on which to group; Totals, which lets you choose the values to be totaled; Title, which lets you customize the group title; Header section, which lets you include or omit a header section for the group; Footer section, which lets you include or omit a footer section for the group; and Keep together, which lets you specify whether Access is to attempt to keep portions of a group together on a page.

To View the Report

The following steps view the report in Report view, which is sometimes more convenient when you want to view the lower portion of the report.

① Click the View button arrow on the Home tab to display the View button menu.

② Click Report View on the View button menu to view the report in Report view.

③ Scroll down to the bottom of the report so that the grand totals appear on the screen (Figure 6–73).

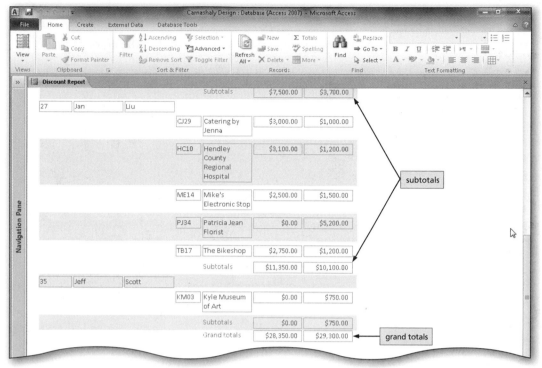

Figure 6–73

To Remove the Color from the Report Header

The following steps remove the color from the Report Header section by changing the background color for the header to white.

1
- Click the View button arrow and then click Design View to return to Design view.
- Right-click the report header to produce a shortcut menu.
- Point to the Fill/Back Color arrow on the shortcut menu to display a color palette (Figure 6–74).

2
- Click White in the first row, first column to change the background color to white.

Q&A

Why do I not see standard colors and theme colors like I did when I changed the background color in the other report?

When you use the Background Color button on the Ribbon, you see both standard colors and theme colors. When you use the shortcut menu, you only see the standard colors.

Figure 6–74

To Assign a Conditional Value

The Camashaly requirements for this report also involved a conditional value related to the amount of a client's discount. To assign a conditional value, you will use the IIf function. The IIf function consists of the letters IIf followed by three items, called **arguments**, in parentheses. The first argument is a criterion; the second and third arguments are expressions. If the criterion is true, the function assigns the value of the expression in the second argument. If the criterion is false, the function assigns the value of the expression in the third argument. The IIf function you will use is IIf([Amount Paid]>4000, .04*[Current Due], .02*[Current Due]). This function applies the following rules: If the amount paid is greater than $4,000, the value assigned is .04*[Current Due], that is, 4% of the current due amount. If the amount paid is not greater than $4,000, the value assigned is .02*[Current Due], that is, 2% of the current due amount.

The following steps add a text box and then use the Expression Builder to enter the appropriate IIf function in the text box. The steps then change the format of the text box. The steps modify and move the label for the text box. They also add a title, page number, and date, and then change the alignment of the title. The steps then change the size of the report.

1

- If necessary, display the Design tab.

- Click the Text Box tool (Report Design Tools Design tab | Controls group) and point to the approximate position shown in Figure 6–75.

Q&A How can I place the control accurately when there are no grid lines?

When you click the position for the control, Access automatically will expand the grid. You then can adjust the control using the grid.

Q&A Can I automatically cause controls to be aligned to the grid?

Yes. Click the Size/Space button (Report Design Tools Arrange tab | Sizing & Ordering group) and then click Snap to Grid on the Size/Space menu. From that point on, any controls you add will be automatically aligned to the grid.

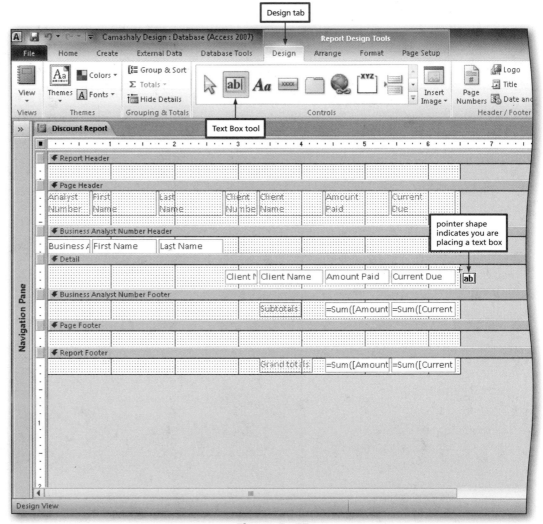

Figure 6–75

2

- Click the position shown in Figure 6–75 to place a text box.

- Click the attached label to select it and then press the DELETE key to delete the attached label.

- Click the text box to select it, and then click the Property Sheet button (Report Design Tools Design tab | Tools group) to display a property sheet.

- Click the Control Source property to select it (Figure 6–76).

Q&A Why did I choose Control Source, not Record Source?

You use Record Source to select the source of the records in a report, usually a table or a query. You use the Control Source property to specify the source of data for the control. This allows you to bind an expression or field to a control.

Figure 6–76

3

- Click the Build button to display the Expression Builder dialog box.

- Double-click Functions in the first column to display the function subfolders.

- Click Built-In Functions in the first column to display the various function categories in the second column.

- Scroll down in the second column so that Program Flow appears, and then click Program Flow to display the available program flow functions in the third column.

- Double-click IIf in the third column to select the IIf function (Figure 6–77).

Q&A Do I have to select Program Flow? Could I not just scroll down to IIf?

You do not have to select Program Flow. You could indeed scroll down to IIf. You will have to scroll through a large number of functions in order to get to IIf, however.

Figure 6–77

4

- Click the <expression> argument to select it and type `[Amount Paid]>4000` as the expression.

- Click the <truepart> argument to select it and type `.04*[Current Due]` as the true part.

- Click the <falsepart> argument to select it and type `.02*[Current Due]` as the false part (Figure 6–78).

Q&A Are there other ways I could enter the expression?

Yes. You could just type the whole expression. On the other hand, you could select the function just as in these steps, and, when entering each argument, you could select the fields from the list of fields and click the desired operators.

Figure 6–78

5

- Click the OK button (Expression Builder dialog box) to specify the expression as the control source for the text box.

Q&A My property sheet is covering my OK button. What should I do?

Click in the Expression Builder dialog box to bring the entire dialog box in front of the property sheet.

- Change the Format to Currency.

- Change the number of decimal places to 2.

- Close the property sheet by clicking the Property Sheet button.

- Click the Label tool on the Design tab and point to the approximate position shown in Figure 6–79.

Figure 6–79

6

• Press and hold the left mouse button, drag the pointer to the approximate position as the lower-right corner of the label shown in Figure 6–80, and then release the left mouse button to place the label.

Q&A

I made the label the wrong size. What should I do?

With the label selected, drag the sizing handles to resize the label as needed. Drag the control in a position away from the sizing handles if you need to move the label.

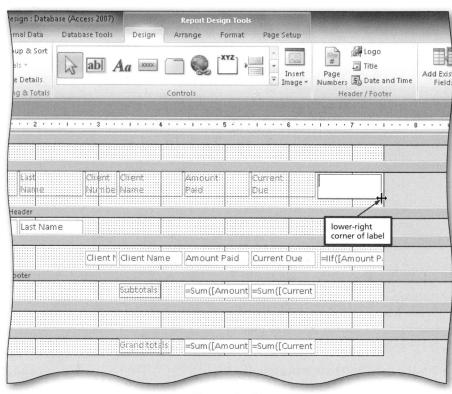

Figure 6–80

7

• Type `Discount` to enter the name of the label.

• Click outside the label to deselect the label and then select the Amount Paid, Current Due, and Discount labels.

• With the labels selected, display the Format tab and then click the Align Text Right button (Report Design Tools Format tab | Font group) to right-align the text within the labels.

• Move or resize the Discount label as necessary so that it aligns with the new text box and with the other controls in the Page Header section.

• Expand the Report Header section to the approximate size shown in Figure 6–81, place a label in the approximate position shown in the figure, and then type `Discount Report` in the label.

Figure 6–81

8

- Click outside the label to deselect it and then click the label in the report header a second time to select the entire label.

- Display the property sheet, change the font size to 20 and the text align property to Distribute, which spreads the letters evenly throughout the label. Change the font weight to Semi-bold, and then close the property sheet.

- If necessary, increase the size of the title control so that the entire title is displayed.

- Using the Design tab and the techniques on pages AC 378 through AC 379, add a page number to the page footer, and add a date (use the same format you have used previously in this chapter).

- Cut the date, and then paste it into the page footer. Drag the date so that the date is positioned in the approximate position shown in Figure 6–82.

- Drag the right boundary of the report to the position shown in the figure to reduce the width of the report.

Figure 6–82

To Change the Border Style

If you print or preview the report, you will notice that all the controls have boxes around them. The box is the border and you can select the border style. The following steps remove the boxes around the controls by changing the border style to transparent.

1 Select all controls in the report. You can click the first one, and then hold the SHIFT key down while clicking all the others. Alternatively, you can click in the ruler to the left of the Report Header section and then hold the SHIFT key down while clicking to the left of all the other sections.

2 Display the Design tab.

3 Click the Property Sheet button (Report Design Tools Design tab | Tools group) to display the property sheet.

4 Click the Border Style property box and then click the Border Style property box arrow to display the menu of available border styles.

5 Click Transparent to change the border style.

To Remove the Alternate Color

Just as with the Business Analyst Master List, the Discount Report also has alternate colors that need to be removed. The following steps remove the alternate colors from the various sections in the report, starting with the Detail section.

1 Right-click the Detail section to produce a shortcut menu.

2 Point to the Alternate Fill/Back Color arrow to produce a color palette.

3 Click None on the color palette to specify that there is to be no alternate color for the selected section.

4 Using the same techniques, remove the alternate color from all other sections. (For some sections, the command may be dimmed.)

Obtaining Help on Functions

There are many functions available in Access for a variety of purposes. To see the list of functions, use the Expression Builder. Double-click Functions in the first column and then click Built-In Functions. You then can scroll through the entire list of functions in the third column. Alternatively, you can click a function category in the second column, in which case the third column only will contain the functions in that category. To obtain detailed help on a function, highlight the function in the third column and click the Help button. The Help presented will show the syntax of the function, that is, the specific rule for how you must type the function and any arguments. It will give you general comments on the function as well as examples illustrating the use of the function.

BTW

Arguments
An argument is a piece of data on which a function operates. For example, in the expression =SUM ([Amount Paid]), Amount Paid is the argument because the SUM function will calculate the total of Amount Paid.

Page Setup Tab

You can use the buttons on the Page Setup tab to change margins, orientation, and other page setup characteristics of the report (Figure 6–83a). If you click the Margins button, you can choose from among some predefined margins or set your own custom margins (Figure 6–83b). If you click the Columns button, you will see the Page Setup dialog box with the Columns tab selected (Figure 6–83c). You can use this tab to specify multiple columns in a report as well as the column spacing. If you click the Page Setup button, you will see the Page Setup dialog box with the Print Options tab selected (Figure 6–83d). You can use this tab to specify custom margins. You can specify orientation by clicking the Page tab (Figure 6–83e). You also can select paper size, paper source, and printer using this tab.

(a) Page Setup tab
Figure 6–83

(b) Margins button menu

(c) Columns tab

(d) Print Options tab

(e) Page tab

Figure 6–83

To Change the Report Margins

If you look at the horizontal ruler in Figure 6–82 on page AC 398, you will notice that the report width is slightly over seven inches. Because the report probably will print on standard 8½" × 11" paper, a seven-inch report with one-inch margins on the left and right, which would result in a nine-inch width, will not fit. To allow the report to fit on the page, you need to reduce the margins. There are two ways to change the margins. You can click the Margins button on the Page Setup tab and then select from some predefined options. If you want more control, you can click the Page Setup button to display the Page Setup dialog box. You then can specify your own margins, change the orientation, and also specify multiple columns if you want a multicolumn report.

The following steps use the Margins button to select Narrow margins.

1 Display the Page Setup tab.

2 Click the Margins button (Report Design Tools Page Setup tab | Page Size group).

3 If necessary, click Narrow to specify the Narrow margin option.

Fine-Tuning a Report

When you have finished a report, you should review several of its pages in Print Preview to make sure the layout is precisely what you want. You may find that you need to increase the size of a control, which you can do by selecting the control and dragging the appropriate sizing handle. You may realize you need an additional control, which you could add by using the appropriate tool in the Controls group or by dragging a field from the field list.

In both cases, you have a potential problem. You may not have the room to increase the size or to add an additional control. If the control is part of a control layout that you had when you modified earlier reports in Layout view, you can resize controls or add new fields, and the remaining fields automatically adjust for the change. In Design view with individual controls, you must make any necessary adjustments manually.

TO MAKE ROOM FOR RESIZING OR ADDITIONAL CONTROLS

To make room for resizing a control or for adding additional controls, you would use the following steps.

1. Select all controls to the right of the control you want to resize or the position where you want to add another control.

2. Drag any of the selected controls to the right to make room for the change.

To Save and Close a Report

Now that you have completed your work on your report, you should save the report and close it. The following steps first save your work on the report and then close the report.

1 Click the Save button on the Quick Access Toolbar to save your work.

2 Close the Discount Report.

To Print a Report

The following steps print the report.

1 With the Discount Report selected in the Navigation Pane, click File on the Ribbon to open the Backstage view.

2 Click the Print tab in the Backstage view to display the Print gallery.

3 Click the Quick Print button to print the report and compare your results to Figure 6–1b on page AC 340.

BTW Certification
The Microsoft Office Specialist (MOS) program provides an opportunity for you to obtain a valuable industry credential — proof that you have the Access 2010 skills required by employers. For more information, visit the Access 2010 Certification Web page (scsite.com/ac2010/cert).

BTW Quick Reference
For a table that lists how to complete the tasks covered in this book using the mouse, Ribbon, shortcut menu, and keyboard, see the Quick Reference Summary at the back of this book, or visit the Access 2010 Quick Reference Web page (scsite.com/ac2010/qr).

To Quit Access

The following steps quit Access.

1 Click the Close button on the right side of the title bar to quit Access.

2 If a Microsoft Access dialog box appears, click the Save button to save any changes made to the object since the last save.

Chapter Summary

In this chapter you have learned to create and relate additional tables; create queries for a report; create reports in Design view; add fields and text boxes to a report; format controls; group and ungroup controls; modify multiple controls; add and modify a subreport; modify section properties; add a title, page number, and date; add totals and subtotals; use a function in a text box; and publish a report. The items listed below include all the new Access skills you have learned in this chapter.

1. Create the New Tables (AC 343)
2. Relate Several Tables (AC 346)
3. Create an Additional Query for the Report (AC 348)
4. Create an Initial Report in Design View (AC 351)
5. Add Fields to the Report in Design View (AC 354)
6. Change Labels (AC 356)
7. Add Text Boxes (AC 358)
8. View the Report in Print Preview (AC 361)
9. Format a Control (AC 361)
10. Group Controls (AC 362)
11. Ungroup Controls (AC 363)
12. Modify Grouped Controls (AC 364)
13. Modify Multiple Controls That Are Not Grouped (AC 365)
14. Add a Subreport (AC 368)
15. Open the Subreport in Design View (AC 371)
16. Modify the Controls in the Subreport (AC 372)
17. Change the Can Grow Property (AC 373)
18. Change the Appearance of the Controls in the Subreport (AC 374)
19. Resize the Subreport and the Report in Design View (AC 376)
20. Modify Section Properties (AC 377)
21. Add a Title, Page Number, and Date (AC 378)
22. Remove the Alternate Color (AC 380)
23. Publish a Report (AC 381)
24. Add and Move Fields in a Report (AC 382)
25. Add the Remaining Fields (AC 385)
26. Resize the Detail Section (AC 386)
27. Add Totals and Subtotals (AC 387)
28. Remove the Color from the Report Header (AC 393)
29. Assign a Conditional Value (AC 394)
30. Make Room for Resizing or Additional Controls (AC 401)

 If you have a SAM 2010 user profile, your instructor may have assigned an autogradable version of this assignment. If so, log into the SAM 2010 Web site at www.cengage.com/sam2010 to download the instruction and start files.

Learn It Online

Test your knowledge of chapter content and key terms.

Instructions: To complete the Learn It Online exercises, start your browser, click the Address bar, and then enter the Web address **scsite.com/ac2010/learn**. When the Access 2010 Learn It Online page is displayed, click the link for the exercise you want to complete and then read the instructions.

Chapter Reinforcement TF, MC, and SA
A series of true/false, multiple choice, and short answer questions that test your knowledge of the chapter content.

Flash Cards
An interactive learning environment where you identify chapter key terms associated with displayed definitions.

Practice Test
A series of multiple choice questions that test your knowledge of chapter content and key terms.

Who Wants To Be a Computer Genius?
An interactive game that challenges your knowledge of chapter content in the style of a television quiz show.

Wheel of Terms
An interactive game that challenges your knowledge of chapter key terms in the style of the television show *Wheel of Fortune*.

Crossword Puzzle Challenge
A crossword puzzle that challenges your knowledge of key terms presented in the chapter.

Apply Your Knowledge

Reinforce the skills and apply the concepts you learned in this chapter.

Adding a Table and Creating a Report with a Subreport
Instructions: Start Access. If you are using the Microsoft Access 2010 Complete or the Microsoft Access 2010 Comprehensive text, open the Babbage CPA Firm database that you used in Chapter 5. Otherwise, see your instructor for information on accessing the files required in this book.

Perform the following tasks:
1. Create a table in which to store data about bookkeeping services performed for clients. Use Accounts as the name of the table. The Accounts table has the structure shown in Table 6–4.

Table 6–4 Structure of Accounts Table			
Field Name	**Data Type**	**Field Size**	**Description**
Client Number	Text	3	Part of Primary Key
Service Date	Date/Time (Change Format property to Short Date)		Part of Primary Key
Hours Worked	Number (Change Format property to Fixed and Decimal Places to 2)	Single	

2. Import the Accounts.xlsx workbook to the Accounts table.
3. Create a one-to-many relationship between the Client table and the Accounts table.
4. Create a query that joins the Bookkeeper and Client tables. Include the Bookkeeper Number, First Name, and Last Name fields from the Bookkeeper table. Include all fields except the bookkeeper number from the Client table. Save the query as Bookkeepers and Clients.

Continued >

STUDENT ASSIGNMENTS

Apply Your Knowledge *continued*

5. Create the report shown in Figure 6–84. The report uses the query that you created in Step 4 and the Accounts table. Use the name Bookkeeper Master List for the report. The report is in the same style as the Business Analyst Master List shown in Figure 6–1a on page AC 339.

Bookkeeper Master List

Page 1   5/1/2012

| Bookkeeper Number | 22 | Bookkeeper Name | Johanna Lewes |

Client Number   A54

Client Name	Afton Mills	Amount Paid	$575.00
Street	612 Revere	Balance Due	$315.00
City	Granger		
Postal Code	27036		

Service Date	Hours Worked
3/26/2012	3.00

Client Number   D76

Client Name	Dege Grocery	Amount Paid	$1,015.00
Street	446 Linton	Balance Due	$325.00
City	Burles		
Postal Code	28817		

Service Date	Hours Worked
3/23/2012	3.00

Client Number   J77

Client Name	Jones Plumbing	Amount Paid	$685.00
Street	75 Getty	Balance Due	$0.00
City	Buda		
Postal Code	27032		

Service Date	Hours Worked
3/29/2012	3.50

Figure 6–84

6. Submit the revised database in the format specified by your instructor.

Extend Your Knowledge

Extend the skills you learned in this chapter and experiment with new skills. You may need to use Help to complete the assignment.

Modifying Reports

Instructions: Copy the Camashaly Design database and rename the database to Chapter 6 Camashaly Design. Start Access and open the database that you copied and renamed.

Perform the following tasks:

1. Open the Business Analyst Master List in Design view. Add your name to the report footer. Your name should appear on the left.

2. Change the report title from Business Analyst Master List to Business Analyst/Course Master List. Change the font color to red and underline the title. Change the report header background to white. Change the date format to Long Date. Change the border width for the subreport control to 4 pt.

3. Open the Discount Report in Design view. Calculate the average aggregate statistics for both the Amount Paid and Current Due columns. Place these statistics in the report footer only. Include an appropriate label for the statistics. Use conditional formatting to format the discount value in a bold red font for all records where the value is equal to or greater than $100.

4. Submit the revised database in the format specified by your instructor.

Make It Right

Analyze a database and correct all errors and/or improve the design.

Correcting Report Design Errors

Instructions: Start Access. Open the Condo Rentals database. See the inside back cover of this book for instructions on downloading the Data Files for Students, or contact your instructor for more information about accessing the required files.

The Condo Rentals database contains data about a company that rents condos in a popular resort community. The owner of the company has created the report shown in Design view in Figure 6–85, but there are a few problems. She really wanted to concatenate the first and last name of the owner with the label, Name. Bold the control and the label. The title of the report should be centered across the report and should appear in the report header, not in the page header. The page number and the date should appear in the page header, not the page footer. Finally, she would like to add a label to the report footer. The label should contain the text, End of Report, to indicate the end of the report. Bold the end-of-report label.

Continued >

Make It Right *continued*

Figure 6–85

Correct these errors and submit the revised database in the format specified by your instructor.

 In the Lab

Design, create, modify, and/or use a database following the guidelines, concepts, and skills presented in this chapter. Labs are listed in order of increasing difficulty.

Lab 1: Adding Tables and Creating Reports for the ECO Clothesline Database

Problem: ECO Clothesline needs to maintain data on a weekly basis on the open orders for its customers. These are orders that have not yet been delivered. To track this information requires a new table, an Open Orders table. The company also needs a report that displays sales rep information as well as information about customers and any open orders that the customer has. The company would like to show its appreciation to current customers by discounting the amount customers currently owe.

Instructions: If you are using the Microsoft Access 2010 Complete or the Microsoft Access 2010 Comprehensive text, open the ECO Clothesline database that you used in Chapter 5. Otherwise, see the inside back cover of this book for instructions on downloading the Data Files for Students, or contact your instructor for more information about accessing the required files.

Perform the following tasks:

1. Create the Open Orders table using the structure shown in Table 6–5.

Table 6–5 Structure of Open Orders Table			
Field Name	**Data Type**	**Field Size**	**Description**
Order Number	Text	4	Primary Key: Yes
Amount	Currency		
Customer Number	Text	4	Foreign Key: matches primary key of Customer table

2. Import the Open Orders.txt file into the Open Orders table.

3. Create a one-to-many relationship between the Customer table and the Open Orders table.

4. Create a query that joins the Sales Rep and the Customer tables. Include the Sales Rep Number, Last Name, and First Name fields from the Sales Rep table. Include all fields except the Sales Rep Number field from the Customer table. Save the query as Sales Reps and Customers.

5. Create the report shown in Figure 6–86. The report uses the Sales Reps and Customers query as the basis for the main report and the Open Orders table as the basis for the subreport. Use the name Sales Rep Master List for the report. The report title has a Text Align property value of Distribute. The Border Width property is hairline and the subreport label is Open Orders. The report is similar in style to the Business Analyst Master List shown in Figure 6–1a on page AC 339.

Sales Rep Master List

Page 1   5/1/2012

| Sales Rep Number | 44 | | Sales Rep Name | Pat Jones |

Customer Number **AM23**

Customer Name	**Amy's Store**	Customer Type	**WMN**
Street	**223 Johnson**	Balance	**$195.00**
City	**Oxford**	Amount Paid	**$1,695.00**
State	**TN**		
Postal Code	**37021**		

Open Orders

Order Number	Amount
303	**$175.00**
304	**$125.00**

Customer Number **DG14**

Customer Name	**Della's Designs**	Customer Type	**WMN**
Street	**312 Gilham**	Balance	**$340.00**
City	**Granger**	Amount Paid	**$850.00**
State	**NC**		
Postal Code	**27036**		

Open Orders

Figure 6–86

Continued >

In the Lab *continued*

6. Create the Customer Discount Report shown in Figure 6–87. The report uses the Sales Reps and Customers query. Customers who have paid $500 or more will receive a 3% discount on the remaining balance, and customers who have paid less than $500 will receive a 1% discount on the remaining balance. The report includes subtotals and grand totals for the Balance and Amount Paid fields. The report is similar in style to the Discount Report shown in Figure 6–1b on page AC 340.

7. Submit the revised database in the format specified by your instructor.

Customer Discount Report

Sales Rep Number	First Name	Last Name	Customer Number	Customer Name	Balance	Amount Paid	Discount
44	Pat	Jones					
			AM23	Amy's Store	$195.00	$1,695.00	$5.85
			DG14	Della's Designs	$340.00	$850.00	$10.20
			EC07	Environmentally Casual	$0.00	$1,700.00	$0.00
			NC25	Nancy's Place	$240.00	$550.00	$7.20
			TT21	Tan and Tone	$160.00	$725.00	$4.80
				Subtotals	$935.00	$5,520.00	
49	Pinn	Gupta					
			BL15	Blondie's on Main	$555.00	$1,350.00	$16.65
			CY12	Curlin Yoga Studio	$145.00	$710.00	$4.35
			JN34	Just Natural	$360.00	$700.00	$10.80
			LB20	Le Beauty Salon & Spa	$200.00	$1,250.00	$6.00
			WS34	Woody's Sporting Goods	$1,235.00	$0.00	$12.35
				Subtotals	$2,495.00	$4,010.00	
51	Gabe	Ortiz					
			CM09	Casual by Marie	$295.00	$1,080.00	$8.85
			FN19	Fitness Counts	$345.00	$1,950.00	$10.35
			RD03	Rose's Day Spa	$0.00	$975.00	$0.00

Figure 6–87

In the Lab

Lab 2: Adding Tables and Creating Reports for the Walburg Energy Alternatives Database

Problem: The manager of the Walburg Energy Alternatives store needs to track items that are being reordered from vendors. The manager must know when an item was ordered and how many were ordered. He also needs a report that displays vendor information as well as information about items and the order status of items. Walburg is considering an in-store sale and would like a report that shows the regular selling price as well as the sale price of all items.

Instructions: If you are using the Microsoft Access 2010 Complete or the Microsoft Access 2010 Comprehensive text, open the Walburg Energy Alternatives database that you used in Chapter 5. Otherwise, see the inside back cover of this book for instructions on downloading the Data Files for Students, or contact your instructor for more information about accessing the required files.

Perform the following tasks:
1. Create a table in which to store the item reorder information using the structure shown in Table 6–6. Use Reorder as the name of the table. Import the data from the Reorder.xlsx workbook.

Table 6–6 Structure of Reorder Table

Field Name	Data Type	Field Size	Description
Item Number	Text	4	Part of Primary Key
Date Ordered	Date/Time (Use Short Date format)		Part of Primary Key
Number Ordered	Number	Integer	

2. Add the Reorder table to the Relationships window and establish a one-to-many relationship between the Item table and the Reorder table.

3. Create the report shown in Figure 6–88. The report uses the Vendor-Item Query that was previously created as the basis for the main report and the Reorder table as the basis for the subreport. Use the name Vendor Master Report for the report. The report is the same style as that demonstrated in the project. Use conditional formatting to display the on hand value in bold red font color for all items with fewer than 10 items on hand. Change the Border Style property to Transparent. Change the Text Align property for the title to Distribute.

Continued >

STUDENT ASSIGNMENTS

In the Lab *continued*

Vendor Master Report

Page 1   5/1/2012

Vendor Code **AS**   Name   **Asterman Industries**

   Item Number   **2216**

Description   **Child Safety Caps**   *On Hand*   15

                                            Cost   **$2.89**

   Item Number   **3663**

Description   **Air Deflector**   *On Hand*   8

                                            Cost   **$5.45**

Date Ordered	*Number Ordered*
3/30/2012	**2**

   Item Number   **4553**

Description   **Energy Saving Kit**   *On Hand*   7

                                            Cost   **$42.75**

Date Ordered	*Number Ordered*
3/29/2012	**3**

Figure 6–88

4. Open the Vendor-Item Query in Design view and add the Selling Price field to the query. Save the query.

5. Create the Item Discount Report shown in Figure 6–89. The report uses the Vendor-Item Query and calculates the sale amount for each item. Items with a selling price of $10.00 or more have a 6% discount and 3% otherwise. Note that the report shows the sale price, not the discount. The report is similar to the Discount Report shown in Figure 6–1b on page AC 340. However, there are no group subtotals or report grand totals. The page number and the current date appear in the page footer. Change the Can Grow property for the Description field to Yes.

Item Discount Report

Vendor Code	Vendor Name	Item Number	Description	On Hand	Cost	Selling Price	Sale Price
AS	Asterman Industries						
		2216	Child Safety Caps	15	$2.89	$3.25	$3.15
		3663	Air Deflector	8	$5.45	$5.99	$5.81
		4553	Energy Saving Kit	7	$42.75	$43.25	$40.66
		6234	Programmable Thermostat	3	$34.25	$36.99	$34.77
		8136	Smoke Detector	10	$6.10	$6.50	$6.31
		9458	Windows Insulator Kit	10	$4.95	$5.25	$5.09
JM	JMZ Technologies						
		1234	Adhesive Door Sweep	5	$3.45	$3.89	$3.77
		2234	Clothes Dryer Heat Saver	4	$8.99	$9.19	$8.91
		3673	Energy Booklet	25	$2.70	$2.99	$2.90
		4583	Fluorescent Light Bulb	18	$4.50	$4.75	$4.61
		6185	Luminescent Night Light	12	$3.75	$4.50	$4.37
		7123	Retractable Clothesline	10	$13.25	$13.99	$13.15
		8590	Water Conservation Kit	8	$13.45	$13.99	$13.15
SD	Scryps Distributors						
		2310	Drip Counter	10	$1.79	$1.99	$1.93
		2789	Hot Water Gauge	6	$2.75	$2.99	$2.90
		4573	Faucet Aerator	20	$0.89	$0.99	$0.96
		5923	Low Flow Shower Head	11	$8.75	$8.99	$8.72
		6345	Rain Gauge	16	$2.89	$3.15	$3.06
		7934	Shower Timer	15	$2.45	$2.99	$2.90
		8344	Toilet Tank Water Saver	18	$3.35	$3.50	$3.40

Page 1   5/1/2012

Figure 6–89

6. Submit the revised database in the format specified by your instructor.

In the Lab

Lab 3: Adding Tables and Creating a Report for the Philamar Training Database

Problem: Philamar Training needs to track the classes its trainers offer to clients. The company also needs a report that displays trainer information as well as information about clients and class offerings.

Instructions: If you are using the Microsoft Access 2010 Complete or the Microsoft Access 2010 Comprehensive text, open the Philamar Training database that you used in Chapter 5. Otherwise, see the inside back cover of this book for instructions on downloading the Data Files for Students, or contact your instructor for more information about accessing the required files.

Instructions Part 1: Create two tables in which to store the data concerning classes and class offerings. The Class table contains data about the classes that Philamar offers. The Class Offerings table contains data about classes currently being offered by the trainers. The structure of the Class table is shown in Table 6–7, and the structure of the Class Offerings table is shown in Table 6–8.

Table 6–7 Structure of Class Table			
Field Name	**Data Type**	**Field Size**	**Description**
Class Code	Text	3	Primary Key
Class Description	Text	40	
Hours	Number	Integer	
Increments	Number	Integer	

Table 6–8 Structure of Class Offerings Table			
Field Name	**Data Type**	**Field Size**	**Description**
Client Number	Text	4	Part of Primary Key
Class Code	Text	3	Part of Primary Key
Total Hours	Number	Integer	
Hours Spent	Number	Integer	

The data for the Class table is in the Class.txt file, and the data for the Class Offerings table is in the Class Offerings.csv file. Add the data to the two tables and then update the relationships for the Philamar Training database.

Instructions Part 2: Create a query that joins the Trainer and Client tables. Include the trainer number, first name, and last name from the Trainer table. Include all fields except trainer number from the Client table. Save the query as Trainers and Clients. Create a query that joins the Class and Class Offerings table. Include the Client Number and Class Code fields from the Class Offerings table. Then, include the Class Description, Total Hours, and Hours Spent fields. Add a calculated field, Hours Remaining, that contains the difference between Total Hours and Hours Spent. Save the query as Class Offerings and Classes. The query should be similar to the Course and Course Offerings query created in the chapter.

Instructions Part 3: Create the report shown in Figure 6–90. The report is based on the two queries created in Part 2. The Date control uses the Long Date format, the title uses Distribute as the Text Align property, and there are no borders. The report is similar in style to the Business Analyst Master List shown in Figure 6–1a on page AC 339.

Trainer Master List

Page 1   Tuesday, May 01, 2012

Traininer Number 42   Trainer Name   Belinda Perry

Client Number   BS27

Client Name	**Blant and Sons**	*Client Type*	**MAN**	
City	**Kingston**	*Training Needed*	**HRD, LAN, SEC**	
State	**TX**	*Amount Paid*	**$11,876.00**	
Postal Code	**76653**	*Current Due*	**$892.50**	

Class Code	*Class Description*	*Total Hours*	*Hours Spent*	*Hours Remaining*
C01	**Beginning Windows 7**	**4**	**2**	**2**
C02	**Advanced Windows 7**	**4**	**0**	**4**

Client Number   FI28

Client Name	**Farrow-Idsen**	*Client Type*	**RET**	
City	**Cedar Ridge**	*Training Needed*	**APP, WEB**	
State	**TX**	*Amount Paid*	**$8,287.50**	
Postal Code	**79342**	*Current Due*	**$925.50**	

Figure 6–90

Cases and Places

Apply your creative thinking and problem solving skills to design and implement a solution.

See the inside back cover of this book for instructions for downloading the Data Files for Students, or see your instructor for information on accessing the required files.

1: Adding Tables and Creating a Report for the Chamber of Commerce Database

Academic

If you are using the Microsoft Access 2010 Complete or the Microsoft Access 2010 Comprehensive text, open the Chamber of Commerce database that you used in Chapter 5. Otherwise, see your instructor for more information about accessing the required files.

Your internship with the Chamber of Commerce has taught you the value of a good advertising strategy. Now the Chamber would like you to help them track active advertising accounts. Advertisers contract with the chamber to advertise for one month. The same ad may run for several months or be replaced monthly with an ad of a different size or design. The Chamber must track the active accounts for the current year. They also need a report grouped by ad rep that includes client and active account information. Use the concepts and techniques presented in this chapter to perform each of the following tasks:

a. Create the two tables necessary to track active accounts. The structure for the Ad Categories table is shown in Table 6–9, and the structure for the Active Accounts table is shown in Table 6–10. Import the Active Accounts text file into the Active Accounts table and the Ad Categories text file into the Ad Categories table. Then, update the relationships for the Chamber of Commerce database.

Table 6–9 Structure of Ad Categories Table			
Field Name	**Data Type**	**Field Size**	**Description**
Category Code	Text	2	Primary Key
Category Description	Text	40	

Table 6–10 Structure of Active Accounts Table			
Field Name	**Data Type**	**Field Size**	**Description**
Advertiser Number	Text	4	Part of Primary Key
Ad Month	Text	3	Part of Primary Key
Category Code	Text	3	Foreign Key: matches primary key of Ad Categories table

b. Create a query to join the Ad Rep table and the Advertiser table. Include the Ad Rep Number, First Name, and Last Name fields from the Ad Rep table. Include all fields from the Advertiser table except the Ad Rep Number fields. Save the query as Ad Reps and Advertisers. Create a query to join the Active Accounts and the Ad Categories table. Include the Advertiser Number, Ad Month, Category Code, and Category Description fields. Save the query as Ad Categories and Active Accounts.

c. Create an Ad Rep Master Report that uses the Ad Reps and Advertisers query as the basis for the main report and the Ad Categories and Active Accounts query as the basis for the subreport. The report should be similar to the report shown in Figure 6–1a on page AC 339. Concatenate the ad rep first and last names. Place the page number in the page footer.

Submit the revised database in the format specified by your instructor.

2: Adding Tables and Creating a Report for the Consignment Database

Personal

If you are using the Microsoft Access 2010 Complete or the Microsoft Access 2010 Comprehensive text, open the Consignment database that you used in Chapter 5. Otherwise, see your instructor for more information about accessing the required files. The volunteer group that manages the consignment shop would like you to prepare two reports for them. Both reports group data by seller code. They also would like to link to the database an Excel workbook that lists suggested prices for used items. Use the concepts and techniques presented in this chapter to perform each of the following tasks:

a. Create a query that joins the Seller table and Items table. Include the Seller Code, First Name, and Last Name fields from the Seller table. Include the Item Number, Description, Price, and Date Posted fields from the Items table. Save the query as Sellers and Items Query.

b. Create a report that is similar in style to the Discount Report shown in Figure 6–1b on page AC 340. Group the report by seller code and include the seller's first name and last name. The Detail section should include the item number, description, date posted, and price. Create a calculated control, Sale Price, that displays the sale price (not the discount) for all items. Items that have a price of $20.00 or more will have a 4% discount. Items that have a price of less than $20.00 will have a 2% discount. Do not include any subtotals or grand totals. Name the report Item Sale Report. Select your own fonts for the report.

c. Create a report that is similar in style to the Discount Report shown in Figure 6–1b on page AC 340. Group the report by seller code and include the seller's first name and last name. The Detail section should include the item number, description, date posted, and price. Create a calculated control, Reduced Price, that displays the Reduced Price (not the discount) for all items. Items that have a date posted earlier than March 4, 2012, will have a 5% discount. Items that have a date posted of March 4, 2012, or later will have a 3% discount. Do not include any subtotals or grand totals. Name the report Reduced Price Report. Select your own fonts for the report.

d. Link the Prices worksheet to the database. Rename the linked Prices table as Suggested Prices. Then, use the Linked Table Manager to update the link between the Excel worksheet and the Access table.

Submit the revised database in the format specified by your instructor.

3: Adding Tables and Creating a Report for the Senior Care Database

Professional

If you are using the Microsoft Access 2010 Complete or the Microsoft Access 2010 Comprehensive text, open the Senior Care database that you used in Chapter 5. Otherwise, see your instructor for more information about accessing the required files. You and your co-owner have decided that you need to better track the number of hours that helpers work. You also need a report that will list helpers as well as the clients they serve. Use the concepts and techniques presented in this chapter to perform each of the following tasks:

a. Create a table in which to store data about the services offered to clients. The table has the same structure as the Accounts table shown in Table 6–4, except that the field size for the Client Number field should be 4. (*Hint:* See the BTW on copying the structure of a table.) Name the table Services and import the Services.xlsx workbook. Update the relationships for the Senior Care database.

b. Create a query that joins the Helper and the Client tables. Include the Helper Number, First Name, and Last Name fields from the Helper table. Include all fields from the Client table except the Helper Number field. Save the query as Helpers and Clients.

c. Create a Helper Master Report that uses the Helpers and Clients query as the basis for the main report and the Services table as the basis for the subreport. The report should be similar to the report shown in Figure 6–1a on page AC 339. Add a Total Amount field to the main report that is the sum of Amount Paid and Balance. (*Hint:* This calculation is for each client record.) Concatenate the helper first and last names. (*Hint:* Because the fields First Name and Last Name are in both tables, you must qualify the field names in the concatenation formula.) Be sure to change the labels for client first name and client last name so that the table name is not included on the report.

Submit the revised database in the format specified by your instructor.

7 | Using SQL

Objectives

You will have mastered the material in this project when you can:

- Change the font or font size for SQL queries

- Create SQL queries

- Include fields in SQL queries

- Include simple and compound criteria in SQL queries

- Use computed fields and built-in functions in SQL queries

- Sort the results in SQL queries

- Use aggregate functions in SQL queries

- Group the results in SQL queries

- Join tables in SQL queries

- Use subqueries

- Compare SQL queries with Access-generated SQL

- Use INSERT, UPDATE, and DELETE queries to update a database

7 | Using SQL

Introduction

Q&A

Q&As
For a complete list of the Q&As found in many of the step-by-step sequences in this book, visit the Access 2010 Q&A Web page (scsite.com/ac2010/qa).

The language called **SQL (Structured Query Language)** is a very important language for querying and updating databases. It is the closest thing to a universal database language, because the vast majority of database management systems, including Access, use it in some fashion. Although some users will be able to do all their queries through the query features of Access without ever using SQL, those in charge of administering and maintaining the database system should be familiar with this important language. Access also can be used as an interface to other database management systems, such as SQL Server. To use or interface with SQL Server requires knowledge of SQL. SQL is supported by virtually every DBMS.

Project — Using SQL

BTW

BTWs
For a complete list of the BTWs found in the margins of this book, visit the Access 2010 BTW Web page (scsite.com/ac2010/btw).

The owners of Camashaly Design want to be able to use the extended data management capabilities available through SQL. In becoming familiar with SQL, Camashaly would like to create a wide variety of SQL queries.

Similar to creating queries in Design view, SQL provides a way of querying relational databases. In SQL, however, instead of making entries in the design grid, you type commands into SQL view to obtain the desired results, as shown in Figure 7–1a. You then can click the View button to view the results just as when you are creating queries in Design view. The results for the query in Figure 7–1a are shown in Figure 7–1b.

(a) Query in SQL

(b) Results

Figure 7–1

Overview

As you read through this chapter, you will learn how to create SQL queries by performing these general tasks:

- Create queries involving criteria.
- Sort the results of a query.
- Group records in a query and perform group calculations.
- Join tables in queries.
- Create a query that involves a subquery.
- Update data using the INSERT, UPDATE, and DELETE commands.

Plan
Ahead

SQL Query Guidelines.
When querying a database using SQL, you must design queries appropriately, identifying the required fields, tables, criteria, sorting, grouping, and operations to use. Querying in SQL also requires proper expression of queries using SQL clauses and formatting.

1. **Select the fields for the query.** Examine the requirements for the query you are constructing to determine which fields are to be included.

2. **Determine which table or tables contain these fields.** For each field, determine the table in which it is located.

3. **Determine criteria.** Determine any criteria that data must satisfy to be included in the results. If there are more than two tables in the query, determine the criteria to be used to ensure the data matches correctly.

4. **Determine sort order.** Is the data to be sorted in some way? If so, by what field or fields is it to be sorted?

5. **Determine grouping.** Is the data to be grouped in some way? If so, by what field is it to be grouped? Identify any calculations to be made for the group.

6. **Determine any update operations to be performed.** Determine whether rows need to be inserted, changed, or deleted. Determine the tables involved.

When necessary, more specific details concerning the above decisions and/or actions are presented at appropriate points in the chapter. The chapter also will identify the use of these guidelines in creating SQL queries such as the one shown in Figure 7–1.

To Start Access

The following steps, which assume Windows 7 is running, start Access based on a typical installation. You may need to ask your instructor how to start Access for your computer.

1 Click the Start button on the Windows 7 taskbar to display the Start menu.

2 Type `Microsoft Access` as the search text in the 'Search programs and files' text box and watch the search results appear on the Start menu.

3 Click Microsoft Access 2010 in the search results on the Start menu to start Access.

4 If the Access window is not maximized, click the Maximize button next to the Close button on its title bar to maximize the window.

BTW

The Ribbon and Screen Resolution
Access may change how the groups and buttons within the groups appear on the Ribbon, depending on the computer's screen resolution. Thus, your Ribbon may look different from the ones in this book if you are using a screen resolution other than 1024 × 768.

To Open a Database from Access

The following steps open the Camashaly Design database from the USB flash drive.

BTW

Datasheet Font Size
You also can use the
Access Options dialog box
to change the default
font and font size for
datasheets. To do so, click
Datasheet in the Access
Options dialog box and
make the desired changes
in the Default font area.

1 With your USB flash drive connected to one of the computer's USB ports, click File on the Ribbon to open the Backstage view.

2 Click Open in the Backstage view to display the Open dialog box.

3 Navigate to the location of the file to be opened (in this case, the USB flash drive, then to the CIS 101 folder [or your class folder], and then to the Access folder).

4 Click Camashaly Design to select the file to be opened.

5 Click the Open button (Open dialog box) to open the selected file and display the opened database in the Access window.

6 If a Security Warning appears, click the Enable Content button.

SQL Background

In this chapter, you query and update a database using the language called **SQL** (**Structured Query Language**). Similar to using the design grid in the Access Query window, SQL provides users with the capability of querying a relational database. Because SQL is a language, however, you must enter **commands** to obtain the desired results, rather than completing entries in the design grid. SQL uses commands to update tables and to retrieve data from tables. The commands that are used to retrieve data are usually called **queries**.

SQL was developed under the name SEQUEL at the IBM San Jose research facilities as the data manipulation language for IBM's prototype relational model DBMS, System R, in the mid-1970s. In 1980, it was renamed SQL to avoid confusion with an unrelated hardware product called SEQUEL. It is used as the data manipulation language for IBM's current production offerings in the relational DBMS arena — SQL/DS and DB2. Most relational DBMSs, including Microsoft Access and Microsoft SQL Server, use a version of SQL as a data manipulation language.

Some people pronounce SQL by pronouncing the three letters, that is, "ess-que-ell." It is very common, however to pronounce it as the name under which it was developed originally, that is, "sequel."

To Change the Font Size

You can change the font and/or the font size for queries using the Options button in the Backstage view and then Object Designers in the list of options in the Access Options dialog box. There usually is not a compelling reason to change the font, unless there is a strong preference for some other font. It often is worthwhile to change the font size, however. With the default size of 8, the queries can be hard to read. Increasing the font size to 10 can make a big difference. The following steps change the font size for queries to 10.

1

- Click File on the Ribbon to open the Backstage view.

- Click Options to display the Access Options dialog box.

- Click Object Designers to display the Object Designer options.

- In the Query design area, click the Size box arrow, and then click 10 in the list to change the size to 10 (Figure 7–2).

2

- Click the OK button to close the Access Options dialog box.

Figure 7–2

SQL Queries

When you query a database using SQL, you type commands in a blank window rather than filling in the design grid. When the command is complete, you can view your results just as you do with queries you create using the design grid.

To Create a New SQL Query

You begin the creation of a new **SQL query**, which is a query expressed using the SQL language, just as you begin the creation of any other query in Access. The only difference is that you will use SQL view instead of Design view. The following steps create a new SQL query.

- Close the Navigation Pane.
- Display the Create tab.
- Click the Query Design button (Create tab | Queries group) to create a query.
- Close the Show Table dialog box without adding any tables.
- Click the View button arrow (Query Tools Design tab | Results group) to display the View menu (Figure 7–3).

Q&A Why did the icon on the View button change to SQL, and why are there only two items on the menu instead of the usual five?

Without any tables selected, you cannot view any results. You only can use the normal Design view or SQL view.

Figure 7–3

- Click SQL View to view the query in SQL view (Figure 7–4).

Q&A What happened to the design grid?

In SQL view, you specify the queries by typing SQL commands rather than making entries in the design grid.

Figure 7–4

SQL Commands

The basic form of SQL expressions is quite simple: SELECT-FROM-WHERE. The command begins with a **SELECT clause**, which consists of the word, SELECT, followed by a list of those fields you want to include. The fields will appear in the results in the order in which they are listed in the expression. Next, the command contains a **FROM clause**, which consists of the word, FROM, followed by a list of the table or tables involved in the query. Finally, there is an optional **WHERE clause**, which consists of the word, WHERE, followed by any criteria that the data you want to retrieve must satisfy. The command ends with a semicolon (;), which in this text will appear on a separate line.

SQL has no special format rules for placement of terms, capitalization, and so on. The style used by this text is to place the word FROM on a new line, and then place the word WHERE, when it is used, on the next line. This makes the commands easier to read. This text also shows words that are part of the SQL language in uppercase and others in a combination of uppercase and lowercase. Because it is a common convention, and necessary in some versions of SQL, place a semicolon (;) at the end of each command.

Microsoft Access has its own version of SQL that, unlike some other versions of SQL, allows spaces within field names and table names. There is a restriction, however, to the way such names are used in SQL queries. When a name containing a space appears in SQL, it must be enclosed in square brackets. For example, Client Number must appear as [Client Number] because the name includes a space. On the other hand, City does not need to be enclosed in square brackets because its name does not include a space. For consistency, all names in this text are enclosed in square brackets. Thus, the City field would appear as [City] even though the brackets technically are not required by SQL.

BTW

SQL Standards
The International Organization for Standardization (ISO) and the American National Standards Institute (ANSI) recognize SQL as a standardized language. Different relational database management systems may support the entire set of standardized SQL commands or only a subset.

To Include Only Certain Fields

To include only certain fields in a query, list them after the word, SELECT. If you want to list all rows in the table, you do not need to include the word, WHERE. The following steps create a query for Camashaly Design that will list the number, name, amount paid, and current due amount of all clients.

BTW

Context-Sensitive Help in SQL
When you are working in SQL view, you can obtain context-sensitive help on any of the keywords in your query. To do so, click anywhere in the word about which you want to obtain help and press F1.

1

- Type `SELECT [Client Number],[Client Name],[Amount Paid],[Current Due]` as the first line of the command, and then press the ENTER key.

- Type `FROM [Client]` as the second line, press the ENTER key, and then type a semicolon (;) on the third line.

- Click the View button (Query Tools Design tab | Results group) to view the results (Figure 7–5).

Q&A My screen displays a dialog box that asks me to enter a parameter value. What did I do wrong?

You typed a field name incorrectly. Click Cancel to close the dialog box and then correct your SQL statement.

Q&A Why does CL # appear as the column heading for the Client Number field?

This is the caption for the field. If the field has a special caption defined, Access will use the caption rather than the field name. You will learn how to change this later in this chapter.

Q&A Can I save the query if I want to use it again?

You certainly can. Click the Save button on the Quick Access Toolbar and assign a name in the Save As dialog box.

2

- Click the Save button on the Quick Access Toolbar, type `Ch7q1` as the name in the Save As dialog box, and click the OK button to save the query as Ch7q1.

(a) Query

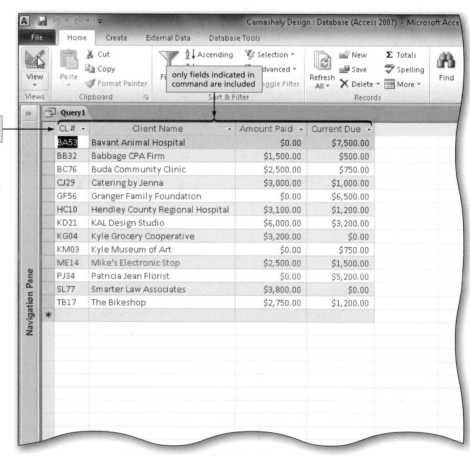

(b) Results

Figure 7–5

To Prepare to Enter a New SQL Query

To enter a new SQL query, you could close the window, click the No button when asked if you want to save your changes, and then begin the process from scratch. A quicker alternative is to use the View menu and then select SQL View. You then will be returned to SQL view with the current command appearing. At that point, you could erase the current command and then enter a new one. (If the next command is similar to the previous one, it might be simpler to modify the current command instead of erasing it and starting over.) The following steps show how to prepare to enter a new SQL query.

1

- Click the View button arrow (Home tab | Views group) to display the View button menu (Figure 7–6).

2

- Click SQL View to return to SQL view.

Figure 7–6

Could I just click the View button, or do I have to click the arrow?

Because the icon on the button is not the icon for SQL view, you must click the arrow.

To Include All Fields

To include all fields, you could use the same approach as in the previous steps, that is, list each field in the Client table after the word, SELECT. There is a shortcut, however. Instead of listing all the field names after SELECT, you can use the asterisk (*) symbol. This indicates that you want all fields listed in the order in which you described them to the system during data definition. The following steps list all fields and all records in the Client table.

- Press the DELETE key to delete the current command, type **SELECT *** as the first line of the command, and then press the ENTER key.

- Type **FROM [Client]** as the second line, press the ENTER key, and type a semicolon (**;**) on the third line.

- View the results (Figure 7–7).

Q&A Can I use copy and paste commands when I enter SQL commands?

Yes, you can use copy and paste as well as other editing techniques, such as replacing text.

- Click File on the Ribbon to open the Backstage view, click Save Object As to display the Save As dialog box, type **Ch7q2** as the name for the saved query, and click the OK button to save the query as Ch7q2. Click File on the Ribbon to close the Backstage view and return to the query.

Q&A Why can I not just click the Save button on the Quick Access Toolbar as I did when I saved the previous query?

If you did, you would replace the previous query with the version you just created. Because you want to save both the previous query and the new one, you need to save the new version with a different name. To do so, you must use Save Object As, which is available through the Backstage view.

(a) Query

(b) Results

Figure 7–7

Determine criteria.
Examine the query or request to determine any restrictions or conditions that records must satisfy to be included in the results.

- **Determine the fields involved in the criteria.** For any criterion, determine the fields that are included in the criterion. Determine the data types for these fields. If the criterion uses a value that corresponds to a Text field, enclose the value in single quotation marks. If the criterion uses a date, enclose the value between number signs (for example, #4/15/2012#).

- **Determine comparison operators.** When fields are being compared to other fields or to specific values, determine the appropriate comparison operator (equals, less than, greater than, and so on). If a wildcard is involved, then the query will use the LIKE operator.

- **Determine join criteria.** If tables are being joined, determine the fields that must match.

- **Determine compound criteria.** If more than one criterion is involved, determine whether all individual criteria are to be true, in which case you will use the AND operator, or whether only one individual criterion needs to be true, in which case you will use the OR operator.

Plan
Ahead

To Use a Criterion Involving a Numeric Field

To restrict the records to be displayed, include the word WHERE followed by a criterion as part of the command. If the field involved is a numeric field, you simply type the value. In typing the number, you do not type commas or dollar signs. The following steps create a query to list the client number and name of all clients whose current due amount is $0.00.

- Click the View button arrow, click SQL View to return to SQL view, and then delete the current command.

- Type **SELECT [Client Number],[Client Name]** as the first line of the command.

- Type **FROM [Client]** as the second line.

- Type **WHERE [Current Due]=0** as the third line, and then type a semicolon (**;**) on the fourth line.

- View the results (Figure 7–8).

Q&A

On my screen, the clients are listed in a different order. Did I do something wrong?

No. The order in which records display in a query result is random unless you specifically order the records. You will see how to order records later in this chapter.

(a) Query

(b) Results

Figure 7–8

- Save the query as Ch7q3. Return to the query.

Simple Criteria

The criterion following the word WHERE in the preceding query is called a simple criterion. A **simple criterion** has the form: field name, comparison operator, then either another field name or a value. The possible comparison operators are shown in Table 7–1. Note that there are two different versions for "not equal to" (<> and !=). You must use the one that is right for your particular implementation of SQL. If you use the wrong one, your system will let you know instantly. Simply use the other.

Table 7–1 Comparison Operators	
Comparison Operator	**Meaning**
=	equal to
<	less than
>	greater than
<=	less than or equal to
>=	greater than or equal to
<> or !=	not equal to

To Use a Comparison Operator

In the following steps, Camashaly Design uses a comparison operator to list the client number, client name, amount paid, and current due for all clients whose amount paid is greater than $3,000.

- Click the View button arrow, click SQL View to return to SQL view, and then delete the current command.

- Type **SELECT [Client Number],[Client Name],[Amount Paid],[Current Due]** as the first line of the command.

- Type **FROM [Client]** as the second line.

- Type **WHERE [Amount Paid]>3000** as the third line, and then type a semicolon (**;**) on the fourth line.

- View the results (Figure 7–9).

- Save the query as Ch7q4. Return to the query.

(a) Query

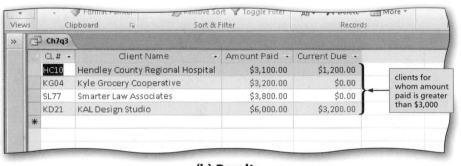

(b) Results

Figure 7–9

To Use a Criterion Involving a Text Field

If the criterion involves a text field, the value must be enclosed in single quotation marks. The following example lists the client number and name of all of Camashaly Design's clients located in Buda, that is, all clients for whom the value in the City field is Buda.

- Return to SQL view, delete the previous query, and type **SELECT [Client Number],[Client Name]** as the first line of the command.

- Type **FROM [Client]** as the second line.

- Type **WHERE [City]='Buda'** as the third line and type a semicolon (**;**) on the fourth line.

- View the results (Figure 7–10).

Q&A

Could I enclose the text field value in double quotation marks instead of single quotation marks?

Yes. It is usually easier, however, to use single quotes when entering SQL commands.

- Save the query as Ch7q5. Return to the query.

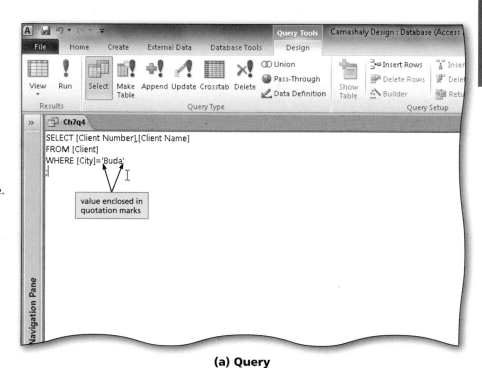

(a) Query

(b) Results

Figure 7–10

To Use a Wildcard

In most cases, the conditions in WHERE clauses involve exact matches, such as retrieving rows for each customer located in the city of Buda. In some cases, however, exact matches do not work. For example, you might know that the desired value contains only a certain collection of characters. In such cases, you use the LIKE operator with a wildcard symbol. Rather than testing for equality, the LIKE operator uses one or more wildcard characters to test for a pattern match. One common wildcard in Access, the **asterisk** (*), represents any collection of characters. Thus, B* represents the letter, B, followed by any string of characters. Another wildcard symbol is the question mark (?), which represents any individual character. Thus T?m represents the letter, T, followed by any single character, followed by the letter, m, such as in Tim or Tom.

The following steps use a wildcard to display the client number and name for every client of Camashaly Design whose city begins with the letter, B.

- Return to SQL view, delete the previous query, and type **SELECT [Client Number],[Client Name]** as the first line of the command.

- Type **FROM [Client]** as the second line.

- Type **WHERE [City] LIKE 'B*'** as the third line and type a semicolon (**;**) on the fourth line.

- View the results (Figure 7–11).

- Save the query as Ch7q6. Return to the query.

(a) Query

(b) Results

Figure 7–11

Break Point: If you wish to stop working through the chapter at this point, you can close Access now. You can resume the project at a later time by starting Access, opening the database called Camashaly Design, creating a new query in SQL view, and continuing to follow the steps from this location forward.

Compound Criteria

You are not limited to simple criteria. You also can use compound criteria. **Compound criteria** are formed by connecting two or more simple criteria using AND, OR, and NOT. When simple criteria are connected by the word AND, all the simple criteria must be true in order for the compound criterion to be true. When simple criteria are connected by the word OR, the compound criterion will be true whenever any of the simple criteria are true. Preceding a criterion by the word NOT reverses the truth or falsity of the original criterion. That is, if the original criterion is true, the new criterion will be false; if the original criterion is false, the new one will be true.

BTW

Wildcards
Other implementations of SQL do not use the asterisk (*) and question mark (?) wildcards. In SQL for Oracle and for SQL Server, the percent sign (%) is used as a wildcard to represent any collection of characters. In Oracle and SQL Server, the WHERE clause shown in Figure 7–11 on page AC 430 would be WHERE [City] LIKE 'B%'.

To Use a Compound Criterion Involving AND

The following steps use a compound criterion to allow Camashaly Design to impose two conditions. In particular, the steps display the number and name of those clients located in Buda who have a current due amount greater than $1,000.

- Return to SQL view, delete the previous query, and type **SELECT [Client Number],[Client Name]** as the first line of the command.

- Type **FROM [Client]** as the second line.

- Type **WHERE [City]='Buda'** as the third line.

- Type **AND [Current Due]>1000** as the fourth line and type a semicolon (**;**) on the fifth line.

- View the results (Figure 7–12).

(a) Query

2

- Save the query as Ch7q7. Return to the query.

(b) Results

Figure 7–12

To Use a Compound Criterion Involving OR

The following steps use a compound criterion to enable Camashaly Design to display the client number and name of those clients located in Buda or for whom the current due amount is greater than $1,000.

- Return to SQL view, delete the previous query, and type `SELECT [Client Number],[Client Name],[City]` as the first line of the command.

- Type `FROM [Client]` as the second line.

- Type `WHERE [City]='Buda'` as the third line.

- Type `OR [Current Due]>1000` as the fourth line and type a semicolon (;) on the fifth line.

- View the results (Figure 7–13).

- Save the query as Ch7q8. Return to the query.

(a) Query

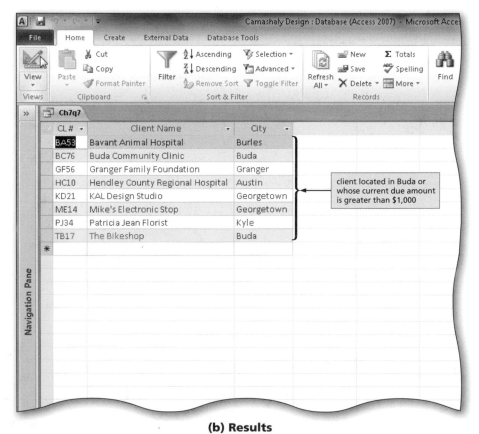

(b) Results

Figure 7–13

To Use NOT in a Criterion

To use the word NOT in a criterion, precede the criterion with the word NOT. The following steps list the numbers and names of the clients of Camashaly Design not located in Buda.

- Return to SQL view and delete the previous query.

- Type **SELECT [Client Number],[Client Name],[City]** as the first line of the command.

- Type **FROM [Client]** as the second line.

- Type **WHERE NOT [City]= 'Buda'** as the third line and type a semicolon (**;**) on the fourth line.

- View the results (Figure 7–14).

- Save the query as Ch7q9. Return to the query.

(a) Query

(b) Results

Figure 7–14

To Use a Computed Field

Just as with queries created in Design view, you can include fields in queries that are not in the database, but that can be computed from fields that are in the database. Such a field is called a computed or calculated field. Such computations can involve addition (+), subtraction (–), multiplication (*), or division (/). The query in the following steps computes the hours remaining, which is equal to the total hours minus the hours spent.

To indicate the contents of the new field (the computed field), you can name the field by following the computation with the word, AS, and then the name you want to assign the field. The following steps calculate the hours remaining for each course offered by subtracting the hours spent from the total hours and then assigning the name Hours Remaining to the calculation. The steps also list the Client Number, Course Number, Total Hours, and Hours Spent for all course offerings for which the number of hours spent is greater than 0.

1

- Return to SQL view and delete the previous query.

- Type **SELECT [Client Number],[Course Number], [Total Hours],[Hours Spent],[Total Hours]- [Hours Spent] AS [Hours Remaining]** as the first line of the command.

- Type **FROM [Course Offerings]** as the second line.

- Type **WHERE [Hours Spent]>0** as the third line and type a semicolon on the fourth line.

- View the results (Figure 7–15).

Q&A

The new name, Hours Remaining, is partially hidden. What should I do to see the entire name?

You could drag the right boundary of the field selector (the box containing Hours Remaining) to enlarge the field to the desired size. You also could double-click the right boundary of the field selector to resize the column so that it best fits the data.

2

- Save the query as Ch7q10. Return to the query.

(a) Query

(b) Results

Figure 7–15

Sorting

Sorting in SQL follows the same principles as when using Design view to specify sorted query results, employing a sort key as the field on which data is to be sorted. SQL uses major and minor sort keys when sorting on multiple fields. By following a sort key with the word DESC with no comma in between, you can specify descending sort order. If you do not specify DESC, the data will be sorted in ascending order.

To sort the output, you include an **ORDER BY clause**, which consists of the words ORDER BY followed by the sort key. If there are two sort keys, the major sort key is listed first. Queries that you construct in Design view require that the major sort key is to the left of the minor sort key in the list of fields to be included. In SQL, there is no such restriction. The fields to be included in the query are in the SELECT clause, and the fields to be used for sorting are in the ORDER BY clause. The two clauses are totally independent.

Determine sort order.
Examine the query or request to see if it contains words such as order or sort that would imply that the order of the query results is important. If so, you need to sort the query.

- **Determine whether data is to be sorted.** Examine the requirements for the query looking for words like sorted by, ordered by, arranged by, and so on.

- **Determine sort keys.** Look for the fields that follow sorted by, ordered by, or any other words that signify sorting. If the requirements for the query include the phrase, ordered by client name, then Client Name is a sort key.

- **If there is more than one sort key, determine which one will be the major sort key and which will be the minor sort key.** Look for words that indicate which field is more important. For example, if the requirements indicate that the results are to be ordered by amount paid within analyst number, Business Analyst Number is the more important sort key.

Plan
Ahead

To Sort the Results on a Single Field

The following steps list the client number, name, amount paid, current due, and analyst number for all clients. Camashaly Design wants this data to be sorted by client name.

❶

- Return to SQL view and delete the previous query.

- Type `SELECT [Client Number],[Client Name], [Amount Paid],[Current Due],[Business Analyst Number]` as the first line of the command.

- Type `FROM [Client]` as the second line.

- Type `ORDER BY [Client Name]` as the third line and type a semicolon (`;`) on the fourth line.

- View the results (Figure 7–16).

❷

- Save the query as Ch7q11. Return to the query.

(a) Query

(b) Results

Figure 7–16

To Sort the Results on Multiple Fields

The following steps list the client number, name, amount paid, current due, and analyst number for all clients. This time, Camashaly wants the data to be sorted by amount paid within analyst number. That is, the data is to be sorted by analyst number. In addition, within the group of clients that have the same analyst number, the data is to be sorted further by amount paid. This means that the Business Analyst Number field is the major (primary) sort key and the Amount Paid field is the minor (secondary) sort key.

1

- Return to SQL view and delete the previous query.

- Type `SELECT [Client Number],[Client Name],[Amount Paid],[Current Due],[Business Analyst Number]` as the first line of the command.

- Type `FROM [Client]` as the second line.

- Type `ORDER BY [Business Analyst Number],[Amount Paid]` as the third line and type a semicolon (`;`) on the fourth line.

- View the results (Figure 7–17).

 Experiment

- Try reversing the order of the sort keys to see the effect. Also, try to specify descending order for one or both of the sort keys. In each case, view the results to see the effect of your choice. When finished, return to the original sorting order for both fields.

2

- Save the query as Ch7q12. Return to the query.

(a) Query

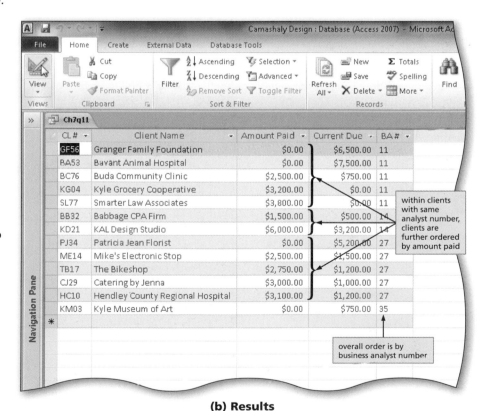

(b) Results

Figure 7–17

To Sort the Results in Descending Order

To sort in descending order, you follow the name of the sort key with the DESC operator. The following steps list the client number, name, amount paid, current due, and analyst number for all clients. Camashaly wants the data to be sorted by descending current due within analyst number. That is, within the clients having the same analyst number, the data is to be sorted further by current due in descending order.

1

- Return to SQL view and delete the previous query.

- Type **SELECT [Client Number],[Client Name],[Amount Paid],[Current Due],[Business Analyst Number]** as the first line of the command.

- Type **FROM [Client]** as the second line.

- Type **ORDER BY [Business Analyst Number],[Current Due] DESC** as the third line and type a semicolon (**;**) on the fourth line.

Q&A

Do I need a comma between [Current Due] and DESC?

No. In fact, you must not use a comma. If you did, SQL would assume that you want a field called DESC. Without the comma, SQL knows that the DESC indicates that the sort on the [Current Due] field is to be in descending order.

- View the results (Figure 7–18).

2

- Save the query as Ch7q13. Return to the query.

(a) Query

SELECT [Client Number],[Client Name],[Amount Paid],[Current Due],[Business Analyst Number]
FROM [Client]
ORDER BY [Business Analyst Number],[Current Due] DESC

order (sort) by Business Analyst Number field

within clients of the same analyst, further ordered by Current Due field in descending order

(b) Results

CL #	Client Name	Amount Paid	Current Due	BA #
BA53	Bavant Animal Hospital	$0.00	$7,500.00	11
GF56	Granger Family Foundation	$0.00	$6,500.00	11
BC76	Buda Community Clinic	$2,500.00	$750.00	11
SL77	Smarter Law Associates	$3,800.00	$0.00	11
KG04	Kyle Grocery Cooperative	$3,200.00	$0.00	11
KD21	KAL Design Studio	$6,000.00	$3,200.00	14
BB32	Babbage CPA Firm	$1,500.00	$500.00	14
PJ34	Patricia Jean Florist	$0.00	$5,200.00	27
ME14	Mike's Electronic Stop	$2,500.00	$1,500.00	27
TB17	The Bikeshop	$2,750.00	$1,200.00	27
HC10	Hendley County Regional Hospital	$3,100.00	$1,200.00	27
CJ29	Catering by Jenna	$3,000.00	$1,000.00	27
KM03	Kyle Museum of Art	$0.00	$750.00	35

within clients with the same analyst number, clients are further ordered by current due in descending order

overall order is by business analyst number

Figure 7–18

To Omit Duplicates When Sorting

When you sort data, duplicates normally are included. The query in Figure 7–19 sorts the client numbers in the Course Offerings table. Because any client can be offered many courses at a time, client numbers can be included more than once. Camashaly does not find this useful and would like to eliminate these duplicate client numbers.

(a) Query

(b) Results

Figure 7–19

The **DISTINCT operator** eliminates duplicate values in the results of a query. To use the operator, you follow the word DISTINCT with the field name in parentheses. The following steps display the client numbers in the Course Offerings table in client number order, but with any duplicates removed.

- Return to SQL view and delete the previous query.

- Type **SELECT DISTINCT ([Client Number])** as the first line of the command.

- Type **FROM [Course Offerings]** as the second line.

- Type **ORDER BY [Client Number]** as the third line and type a semicolon (**;**) on the fourth line.

- View the results (Figure 7–20).

- Save the query as Ch7q14. Return to the query.

(a) Query

(b) Results

Figure 7–20

Break Point: If you wish to stop working through the chapter at this point, you can close Access now. You can resume the project at a later time by starting Access, opening the database called Camashaly Design, creating a new query in SQL view, and continuing to follow the steps from this location forward.

To Use a Built-In Function

SQL has built-in functions, also called aggregate functions, to perform various calculations. Similar to the functions you learned about in Chapter 2, these functions in SQL are called COUNT, SUM, AVG, MAX, and MIN, respectively.

Camashaly uses the following steps to determine the number of clients assigned to analyst number 11 by using the COUNT function with an asterisk (*).

1

- Return to SQL view and delete the previous query.

- Type **SELECT COUNT(*)** as the first line of the command.

- Type **FROM [Client]** as the second line.

- Type **WHERE [Business Analyst Number]='11'** as the third line and type a semicolon (**;**) on the fourth line.

- View the results (Figure 7–21).

Q&A

Why does Expr1000 appear in the column heading of the results?

Because the column is a computed column, it does not have a name. Access assigns a generic expression name. You can add a name for the column by including the AS clause in the query, and it is good practice to do so.

2

- Save the query as Ch7q15. Return to the query.

(a) Query

(b) Results

Figure 7–21

To Assign a Name to the Results of a Function

Camashaly Design would prefer to have a more meaningful name than Expr1000 for the results of counting client numbers. Fortunately, just as you can assign a name to a calculation that includes two fields, you can assign a name to the results of a function. To do so, follow the expression for the function with the word AS and then the name to be assigned to the result. The following steps assign the name, Client Count, to the expression in the previous query.

- Return to SQL view and delete the previous query.

- Type `SELECT COUNT(*) AS [Client Count]` as the first line of the command.

- Type `FROM [Client]` as the second line.

- Type `WHERE [Business Analyst Number]='11'` as the third line and type a semicolon (;) on the fourth line.

- View the results (Figure 7–22).

(a) Query

- Save the query as Ch7q16. Return to the query.

(b) Results

Figure 7–22

To Use Multiple Functions in the Same Command

There are only two differences between COUNT and SUM, other than the obvious fact that they are computing different statistics. First, in the case of SUM, you must specify the field for which you want a total, instead of an asterisk (*); second, the field must be numeric. You could not calculate a sum of names or addresses, for example. The following steps use both the COUNT and SUM functions to count the number of clients and calculate the sum, or total, of their amount paid amounts.

- Return to SQL view and delete the previous query.

- Type **SELECT COUNT(*) AS [Client Count], SUM([Amount Paid]) AS [Sum Paid]** as the first line of the command.

- Type **FROM [Client]** as the second line and type a semicolon (;) on the third line.

- View the results (Figure 7–23).

🔎 **Experiment**

- Try using the other functions in place of SUM. In each case, view the results to see the effect of your choice. When finished, once again select SUM.

2

- Save the query as Ch7q17. Return to the query.

(a) Query

(b) Results

Figure 7–23

The use of AVG, MAX, and MIN is similar to SUM. The only difference is that a different statistic is calculated.

Grouping

Recall that grouping means creating groups of records that share some common characteristic. When you group rows, any calculations indicated in the SELECT command are performed for the entire group.

Plan
Ahead

Determine grouping.
Examine the query or request to determine whether records should be organized by some common characteristic.

- **Determine whether data is to be grouped in some fashion.** Examine the requirements for the query to see if they contain individual rows or information about groups of rows.

- **Determine the field or fields on which grouping is to take place.** By which field is the data to be grouped? Look to see if the requirements indicate a field along with several group calculations.

- **Determine which fields or calculations are appropriate to display.** When rows are grouped, one line of output is produced for each group. The only output that can appear are statistics that are calculated for the group or fields whose values are the same for all rows in a group. For example, it would make sense to display the analyst number, because all the clients in the group have the same analyst number. It would not make sense to display the client number, because the client number will vary from one row in a group to another. SQL could not determine which client number to display for the group.

To Use Grouping

Camashaly Design wants to calculate the totals of the Amount Paid field, called Total Paid, and the Current Due field, called Total Due, for the clients of each analyst. To calculate the totals, the command will include the calculations, SUM([Amount Paid]) and SUM([Current Due]). To get totals for the clients of each analyst, the command also will include a **GROUP BY clause**, which consists of the words, GROUP BY, followed by the field used for grouping, in this case, Business Analyst Number.

Including GROUP BY Business Analyst Number will cause the clients for each analyst to be grouped together; that is, all clients with the same analyst number will form a group. Any statistics, such as totals, appearing after the word SELECT will be calculated for each of these groups. Using GROUP BY does not mean that the information will be sorted.

The following steps use the GROUP BY clause to produce the results Camashaly wants. The steps also rename the total amount paid as Sum Paid and the total current due as Sum Due by including appropriate AS clauses; finally, the steps sort the records by business analyst number.

1

- Return to SQL view and delete the previous query.

- Type **SELECT [Business Analyst Number], SUM([Amount Paid]) AS [Sum Paid], SUM([Current Due]) AS [Sum Due]** as the first line of the command.

- Type **FROM [Client]** as the second line.

- Type **GROUP BY [Business Analyst Number]** as the third line.

- Type **ORDER BY [Business Analyst Number]** as the fourth line and type a semicolon (**;**) on the fifth line.

- View the results (Figure 7–24).

2

- Save the query as Ch7q18. Return to the query.

(a) Query

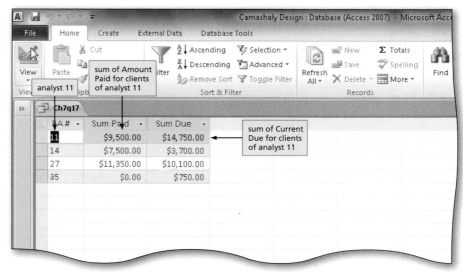

(b) Results

Figure 7–24

Grouping Requirements

When rows are grouped, one line of output is produced for each group. The only output that can be displayed are statistics that are calculated for the group or columns whose values are the same for all rows in a group. When rows are grouped by business analyst number, it is appropriate to display the business analyst number, because the number in one row in a group must be the same as the number in any other row in the group. It is appropriate to display the sum of the Amount Paid and Current Due fields because they are statistics calculated for the group. It would not be appropriate to display a client number, however, because the client number varies on the rows in a group; the analyst is associated with many clients. SQL would not be able to determine which client number to display for the group. SQL will display an error message if you attempt to display a field that is not appropriate, such as the client number.

To Restrict the Groups that Appear

In some cases, Camashaly Design may only want to display certain groups. For example, management may want to display only those analysts for whom the sum of the current due amounts are greater than $10,000. This restriction does not apply to individual rows, but instead to groups. Because WHERE applies only to rows, you cannot use a WHERE clause to accomplish the kind of restriction you have here. Fortunately, SQL provides a clause that is to groups what WHERE is to rows. The HAVING clause, which consists of the word HAVING followed by a criterion, is used in the following steps, which restrict the groups to be included to those on which the sum of the current due is greater than $10,000.00.

- Return to SQL view.

- Click the beginning of the fourth line (ORDER BY [Business Analyst Number]) and press the ENTER key to insert a new blank line.

- Click the beginning of the new blank line, and then type **HAVING SUM([Current Due])>10000** as the new fourth line.

- View the results (Figure 7–25).

(a) Query

- Save the query as Ch7q19. Return to the query.

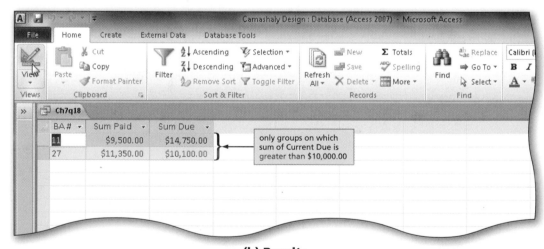

(b) Results

Figure 7–25

Break Point: If you wish to stop working through the chapter at this point, you can close Access now. You can resume the project at a later time by starting Access, opening the database called Camashaly Design, creating a new query in SQL view, and continuing to follow the steps from this location forward.

Joining Tables

Many queries require data from more than one table. Just as with creating queries in Design view, SQL should provide a way to **join** tables, that is, to find rows in two tables that have identical values in matching fields. In SQL, this is accomplished through appropriate criteria following the word WHERE.

If you want to list the client number, name, analyst number, first name of the analyst, and last name of the analyst for all clients, you need data from both the Client and Business Analyst tables. The Business Analyst Number field is in both tables, the Client Number field is only in the Client table, and the First Name and Last Name fields are only in the Business Analyst Table. You need to access both tables in your SQL query, as follows:

1. In the SELECT clause, you indicate all fields you want to appear.

2. In the FROM clause, you list all tables involved in the query.

3. In the WHERE clause, you give the criterion that will restrict the data to be retrieved to only those rows included in both of the two tables, that is, to the rows that have common values in matching fields.

BTW

Inner Joins
A join that compares the tables in the FROM clause and lists only those rows that satisfy the condition in the WHERE clause is called an inner join. SQL has an INNER JOIN clause. You could replace the FROM and WHERE clauses in the query shown in Figure 7–26a on page AC 448 with FROM Client INNER JOIN [Business Analyst] ON [Client].[Business Analyst Number]=[Business Analyst]. [Business Analyst Number] to get the same results as shown in Figure 7–26b.

Qualifying Fields

There is a problem in indicating the matching fields. The matching fields are both called Business Analyst Number. There is a field in the Client table called Business Analyst Number, as well as a field in the Business Analyst Table called Business Analyst Number. In this case, if you only enter Business Analyst Number, it will not be clear which table you mean. It is necessary to **qualify** Business Analyst Number, that is, to specify to which field in which table you are referring. You do this by preceding the name of the field with the name of the table, followed by a period. The Business Analyst Number field in the Client table, for example, is [Client].[Business Analyst Number].

Whenever there is potential ambiguity, you must qualify the fields involved. It is permissible to qualify other fields as well, even if there is no confusion. For example, instead of [Client Name], you could have typed [Client].[Client Name] to indicate the Client Name field in the Client table. Some people prefer to qualify all fields, and this is not a bad approach. In this text, you only will qualify fields when it is necessary to do so.

To Rename a Table

In Chapter 1, you assigned the name Business Analyst Table to the Business Analyst table. In this chapter, you will change the name to Business Analyst to make it easier to enter SQL commands. The following steps change the name.

1 Open the Navigation Pane and right-click the Business Analyst Table.

2 Click Rename on the shortcut menu.

3 Delete the current entry, type **Business Analyst** as the new table name, and press the ENTER key.

4 Close the Navigation Pane.

To Join Tables

Camashaly Design wants to list the client number, client name, analyst number, first name of the analyst, and last name of the analyst for all clients. Because the data comes from two tables, the following steps create a query to join the tables.

- Return to SQL view and delete the previous query.

- Type **SELECT [Client Number],[Client Name],[Client].[Business Analyst Number],[First Name],[Last Name]** as the first line of the command.

- Type **FROM [Client], [Business Analyst]** as the second line.

- Type **WHERE [Client]. [Business Analyst Number]=[Business Analyst].[Business Analyst Number]** as the third line and type a semicolon (**;**) on the fourth line.

Q&A

What is the purpose of the WHERE clause?

The WHERE clause specifies that only rows on which the analyst numbers match are to be included. In this case, the analyst number in the Client table ([Client].[Business Analyst Number]) must be equal to the analyst number in the Business Analyst table ([Business Analyst]. [Business Analyst Number]).

- View the results (Figure 7–26).

- Save the query as Ch7q20. Return to the query.

(a) Query

(b) Results

Figure 7–26

To Restrict the Records in a Join

You can restrict the records to be included in a join by creating a compound criterion. The criterion will include the criterion necessary to join the tables along with a criterion to restrict the records. The criteria will be connected with AND.

Camashaly would like to modify the previous query so that only analysts whose start date is prior to May 1, 2011, are included. The following steps modify the previous query appropriately. The date is enclosed between number signs (#).

1

- Return to SQL view.

- Click immediately prior to the semicolon on the last line.

- Type **AND [Start Date] <#5/1/2011#** and press the ENTER key.

Q&A

Could I use other formats for the date in the criterion?

Yes. You could type #May 1, 2011# or #1-May-2011#.

- View the results (Figure 7–27).

2

- Save the query as Ch7q21. Return to the query.

(a) Query

(b) Results

Figure 7–27

BTW

Outer Joins

Sometimes you need to list all the rows from one of the tables in a join, regardless of whether they match any rows in the other table. For example, you can perform a join on the Client and Course Offerings table but display all clients — even the ones without course offerings. This type of join is called an outer join. In a left outer join, all rows from the table on the left (the table listed first in the query) will be included regardless of whether they match rows from the table on the right (the table listed second in the query). Rows from the right will be included only if they match. In a right outer join, all rows from the table on the right will be included regardless of whether they match rows from the table on the left. The SQL clause for a left outer join is LEFT JOIN and the SQL clause for a right outer join is RIGHT JOIN.

Aliases

When tables appear in the FROM clause, you can give each table an **alias**, or an alternative name, that you can use in the rest of the statement. You create an alias by typing the name of the table, pressing the SPACEBAR, and then typing the name of the alias. No commas or periods are necessary to separate the two names.

You can use an alias for two basic reasons: for simplicity or to join a table to itself. Figure 7–28 shows the same query as in Figure 7–27, but with the Client table assigned the letter, C, as an alias and the Business Analyst table assigned the letter, B. The query in Figure 7–28 is less complex. Whenever you need to qualify a field name, you can use the alias. Thus, you only need to type B.[Business Analyst Number] rather than [Business Analyst].[Business Analyst Number].

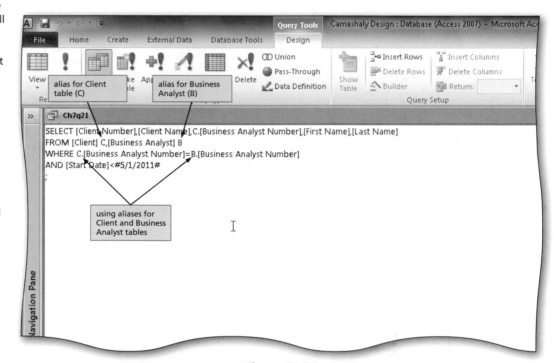

Figure 7–28

To Join a Table to Itself

The other use of aliases is in joining a table to itself. An example of this type of join would enable Camashaly to find client numbers and names for every pair of clients located in the same city. One such pair, for example, would be client CJ29 (Catering by Jenna) and client GF56 (Granger Family Foundation) because both clients are located in the same city (Granger). Another example would be client BA53 (Bavant Animal Hospital) and client SL77 (Smarter Law Associates) because both clients are located in the same city (Burles).

If there were two Client tables in the database, Camashaly could obtain the results they want by simply joining the two Client tables looking for rows where the cities were the same. Even though there is only one Client table, you actually can treat the Client table as two tables in the query by creating two aliases. You would change the FROM clause to:

```
FROM CLIENT F, CLIENT S
```

SQL treats this clause as a query of two tables. The clause assigns the first Client table the letter, F, as an alias. It also assigns the letter, S, as an alias for the Client table. The fact that both tables are really the single Client table is not a problem. The following steps assign two aliases (F and S) to the Client table and list the client number and client name of both clients as well as the city in which both are located.

1

- Return to SQL view and delete the previous query.

- Type **SELECT F.[Client Number],F.[Client Name],S.[Client Number],S.[Client Name],F.[City]** as the first line of the command.

- Type **FROM [Client] F,[Client] S** as the second line.

- Type **WHERE F.[City]=S.[City]** as the third line.

- Type **AND F.[Client Number]<S.[Client Number]** as the fourth line and type a semicolon (**;**) on the fifth line.

- View the results (Figure 7–29).

(a) Query

Q&A

Why is the criterion F.[Client Number] < S.[Client Number] included in the query?

If you did not include this criterion, the query

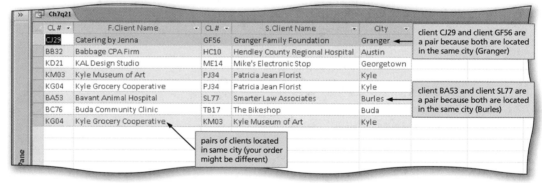

(b) Results

Figure 7–29

would contain four times as many results. On the first row in the results, for example, the first client number is CJ29 and the second is GF56. Without this criterion, there would be a row on which both the first and second client numbers are CJ29, a row on which both are GF56, and a row on which the first is GF56 and the second is CJ29. This criterion only selects the one row on which the first client number (CJ29) is less than the second client number (GF56).

2

- Save the query as Ch7q22. Return to the query.

Subqueries

It is possible to place one query inside another. Figure 7–30, on the following page, illustrates a **subquery**, which is an inner query, contained within parentheses, that is evaluated first. Then the outer query can use the results of the subquery to find its results. In some cases, using a subquery can be the simplest way to produce the desired results, as illustrated in the following query.

(a) Query

analysts with at least one client located in Buda

(b) Results

Figure 7–30

To Use a Subquery

The following steps use the query shown in Figure 7–30 as a subquery. This query selects analyst numbers from those records in the Client table on which the City is Buda. In other words, Camashaly Design can use this query to select analyst numbers for those analysts who have at least one client located in Buda.

After the subquery is evaluated, the outer query will select the analyst number, first name, and last name for those analysts whose analyst number is in the list produced by the subquery.

1

- Return to SQL view and delete the previous query.

- Type **SELECT [Business Analyst Number],[First Name],[Last Name]** as the first line of the command.

- Type **FROM [Business Analyst]** as the second line.

- Type **WHERE [Business Analyst Number] IN** as the third line.

- Type **(SELECT [Business Analyst Number]** as the fourth line.

- Type **FROM [Client]** as the fifth line.

- Type **WHERE [City]= 'Buda')** as the sixth line and type a semicolon (**;**) on the seventh line.

- View the results (Figure 7–31).

2

- Save the query as Ch7q23. Return to the query.

(a) Query

number, first name, and last name of analysts with clients located in Buda

formatting carries over from changes to format of Business Analyst table

(b) Results

Figure 7–31

Using an IN Clause

The query in Figure 7–31 uses an IN clause with a subquery. You can also use an IN clause with a list as an alternative to an OR criterion when the OR criterion involves a single field. For example, to find clients whose city is Buda, Georgetown, or Granger, the criterion using IN would be City IN ('Buda','Georgetown','Granger'). The corresponding OR criterion would be City='Buda' OR City='Georgetown' OR City='Granger'. The choice of which one to use is a matter of personal preference.

You also can use this type of IN clause when creating queries in Design view. To use the criterion in the previous paragraph, for example, include the City field in the design grid and enter the criterion in the Criteria row.

BTW

BETWEEN Operator
The BETWEEN operator allows you to search for a range of values in one field. For example, to find all clients whose amount paid amount is between $20,000 and $30,000, the WHERE clause would be WHERE Amount Paid BETWEEN 20000 AND 30000.

Comparison with Access-Generated SQL

When you create a query in Design view, Access automatically creates a corresponding SQL query that is similar to the queries you have created in this chapter. The Access query shown in Figure 7–32, for example, was created in Design view and includes the Client Number and Client Name fields. The City field has a criterion (Buda), but the City field will not appear in the results.

(a) Query

(b) Results

Figure 7–32

BTW

Union, Pass-Through, and Data Definition Queries
There are three queries that can only be created in SQL view. The Union query combines fields from more than one table into one query result set. The Pass-Through query enables you to send SQL commands directly to ODBC (Open Database Connectivity) databases using the ODBC database's SQL syntax. The Data Definition query allows you to create or alter database tables or create indexes in Access directly.

The SQL query that Access generates in correspondence to the Design view query is shown in Figure 7–33. The query is very similar to the queries you have entered, but there are three slight differences. First, the fields are qualified (Client.[Client Number] and Client.[Client Name]), even though they do not need to be; only one table is involved in the query, so no qualification is necessary. Second, the City field is not enclosed in square brackets. The field legitimately is not enclosed in square brackets because there are no spaces or other special characters in the field name. Finally, there are extra parentheses in the criteria.

Figure 7–33

Both the style used by Access and the style you have been using are legitimate. The choice of style is a personal preference.

Updating Data through SQL

Although SQL is often regarded as a language for querying databases, it also contains commands to update databases. You can add new records, update existing records, and delete records.

Plan Ahead

Determine any update operations to be performed. Examine the database to determine if records must be added, updated, and/or deleted.   • **Determine INSERT operations.** Determine whether new records need to be added. Determine to which table they should be added.   • **Determine UPDATE operations.** Determine changes that need to be made to existing records. Which fields need to be changed? Which tables contain these fields? What criteria identify the rows that need to be changed?   • **Determine DELETE operations.** Determine which tables contain records that are to be deleted. What criteria identify the rows that need to be deleted?

To Use an INSERT Command

You can add records to a table using the SQL INSERT command. The command consists of the words INSERT INTO followed by the name of the table into which the record is to be inserted. Next is the word VALUE followed by the values for the fields in the record. Values for Text fields must be enclosed within quotation marks. The following steps add a record that Camashaly Design wants to add to the Course Offerings table. The record is for client BA53 and Course C06, and indicates that the course will be offered for a total of 4 hours, of which 0 hours already have been spent.

❶

- If necessary, return to SQL view and delete the existing query.

- Type **INSERT INTO [Course Offerings]** as the first line of the command.

- Type **VALUES** as the second line.

- Type **('BA53','C06',4,0)** as the third line and type a semicolon (**;**) on the fourth line (Figure 7–34).

Figure 7–34

❷

- Run the query by clicking the Run button (Query Tools Design tab | Results group).

- When Access displays a message indicating the number of records to be inserted (appended), click the Yes button to insert the records.

Q&A | I clicked the View button and did not get the message. Do I need to click the Run button?

Yes. You are making a change to the database, so you must click the Run button, or the change will not be made.

Q&A | How can I see if the record was actually inserted?

Use a SELECT query to view the records in the Course Offerings table.

❸

- Save the query as Ch7q24. Return to the query.

To Use an UPDATE Command

You can update records in SQL by using the UPDATE command. The command consists of UPDATE, followed by the name of the table in which records are to be updated. Next, the command contains one or more SET clauses, which consist of the word SET, followed by a field to be updated, an equal sign, and the new value. The SET clause indicates the change to be made. Finally, the query includes a WHERE clause. When you execute the command, all records in the indicated table that satisfy the criterion will be updated. The following steps use the SQL UPDATE command to perform an update requested by Camashaly Design. Specifically, they change the Hours Spent to 2 on all records in the Course Offerings table on which the client number is BA53 and the course number is C06. Because the combination of the Client Number and Course Number fields is the primary key, only one record will be updated.

❶

- Delete the existing query.

- Type **UPDATE [Course Offerings]** as the first line of the command.

- Type **SET [Hours Spent]=2** as the second line.

- Type **WHERE [Client Number]='BA53'** as the third line.

- Type **AND [Course Number]='C06'** as the fourth line and type a semicolon (**;**) on the fifth line (Figure 7–35).

Figure 7–35

Q&A Do I need to change a field to a specific value like 2?

No. You could use an expression. For example, to add $100 to the Current Due amount, the SET clause would be SET [Current Due]=[Current Due]+100.

2

• Run the query.

• When Access displays a message indicating the number of records to be updated, click the Yes button to update the records.

Q&A How can I see if the update actually occurred?

Use a SELECT query to view the records in the Course Offerings table.

3

• Save the query as Ch7q25. Return to the query.

To Use a DELETE Command

You can delete records in SQL using the DELETE command. The command consists of DELETE FROM, followed by the name of the table from which records are to be deleted. Finally, you include a WHERE clause to specify the criteria. When you execute the command, all records in the indicated table that satisfy the criterion will be deleted. The following steps use the SQL DELETE command to delete all records in the Course Offerings table on which the client number is BA53 and the Course number is C06, as Camashaly Design has requested. Because the combination of the Client Number and Course Number fields is the primary key, only one record will be deleted.

• Delete the existing query.

• Type **DELETE FROM [Course Offerings]** as the first line of the command.

• Type **WHERE [Client Number]='BA53'** as the second line.

• Type **AND [Course Number]='C06'** as the third line and type a semicolon (;) on the fourth line (Figure 7–36).

Figure 7– 36

• Run the query.

• When Access displays a message indicating the number of records to be deleted, click the Yes button to delete the records.

Q&A How can I see if the deletion actually occurred?

Use a SELECT query to view the records in the Course Offerings table.

• Save the query as Ch7q26. Return to the query.

• Close the query.

To Restore the Font Size

Earlier you changed the font size from its default setting of 8 to 10 so the SQL queries would be easier to read. Unless you prefer to retain this new setting, you should change the setting back to the default. The following steps restore the font size to its default setting.

1 Click File on the Ribbon to open the Backstage view.

2 Click Options to display the Access Options dialog box.

3 Click Object Designers to display the Object Designer options.

4 In the Query design area, click the Size box arrow, and then click 8 in the list that appears to change the size back to 8.

5 Click the OK button to close the Access Options dialog box.

BTW

Quick Reference
For a table that lists how to complete the tasks covered in this book using the mouse, Ribbon, shortcut menu, and keyboard, see the Quick Reference Summary at the back of this book, or visit the Access 2010 Quick Reference Web page (scsite.com/ac2010/qr).

To Quit Access

The following steps quit Access.

1 Click the Close button on the right side of the title bar to quit Access.

2 If a Microsoft Access dialog box appears, click the Save button to save any changes made to the object since the last save.

Chapter Summary

In this chapter you have learned to create SQL queries; include fields in a query; use criteria involving both numeric and text fields as well as use compound criteria; use computed fields and rename the computation; sort the results of a query; use the built-in functions; group records in a query and also restrict the groups that appear in the results; join tables and restrict the records in a join; use subqueries; and use the INSERT, UPDATE, and DELETE commands to update data. Finally, you looked at the SQL that is generated automatically by Access. The items listed below include all the new Access skills you have learned in this chapter.

1. Change the Font Size (AC 421)
2. Create a New SQL Query (AC 422)
3. Include Only Certain Fields (AC 423)
4. Prepare to Enter a New SQL Query (AC 425)
5. Include All Fields (AC 426)
6. Use a Criterion Involving a Numeric Field (AC 427)
7. Use a Comparison Operator (AC 428)
8. Use a Criterion Involving a Text Field (AC 429)
9. Use a Wildcard (AC 430)
10. Use a Compound Criterion Involving AND (AC 431)
11. Use a Compound Criterion Involving OR (AC 432)
12. Use NOT in a Criterion (AC 433)
13. Use a Computed Field (AC 434)
14. Sort the Results on a Single Field (AC 435)
15. Sort the Results on Multiple Fields (AC 437)
16. Sort the Results in Descending Order (AC 438)
17. Omit Duplicates When Sorting (AC 439)
18. Use a Built-In Function (AC 441)
19. Assign a Name to the Results of a Function (AC 442)
20. Use Multiple Functions in the Same Command (AC 443)
21. Use Grouping (AC 444)
22. Restrict the Groups that Appear (AC 446)
23. Join Tables (AC 448)
24. Restrict the Records in a Join (AC 449)
25. Join a Table to Itself (AC 450)
26. Use a Subquery (AC 452)
27. Use an INSERT Command (AC 454)
28. Use an UPDATE Command (AC 455)
29. Use a DELETE Command (AC 456)

If you have a SAM 2010 user profile, your instructor may have assigned an autogradable version of this assignment. If so, log into the SAM 2010 Web site at www.cengage.com/sam2010 to download the instruction and start files.

Learn It Online

Test your knowledge of chapter content and key terms.

Instructions: To complete the Learn It Online exercises, start your browser, click the Address bar, and then enter the Web address **scsite.com/ac2010/learn**. When the Access 2010 Learn It Online page is displayed, click the link for the exercise you want to complete and then read the instructions.

Chapter Reinforcement TF, MC, and SA
A series of true/false, multiple choice, and short answer questions that test your knowledge of the chapter content.

Flash Cards
An interactive learning environment where you identify chapter key terms associated with displayed definitions.

Practice Test
A series of multiple choice questions that test your knowledge of chapter content and key terms.

Who Wants To Be a Computer Genius?
An interactive game that challenges your knowledge of chapter content in the style of a television quiz show.

Wheel of Terms
An interactive game that challenges your knowledge of chapter key terms in the style of the television show *Wheel of Fortune.*

Crossword Puzzle Challenge
A crossword puzzle that challenges your knowledge of key terms presented in the chapter.

Apply Your Knowledge

Reinforce the skills and apply the concepts you learned in this chapter.

Using Criteria, Joining Tables, and Sorting in SQL Queries
Instructions: Start Access. If you are using the Microsoft Access 2010 Complete or the Microsoft Access 2010 Comprehensive text, open the Babbage CPA Firm database that you used in Chapter 6. Otherwise, see your instructor for information on accessing the files required in this book.

Perform the following tasks using SQL:
1. Find all clients whose amount paid amount is greater than $1,000. Display all fields in the query result. Save the query as Apply 7 Step 1 Query.

2. Find all clients whose amount paid amount or balance due amount is $0.00. Display the Client Number, Client Name, Amount Paid, and Balance Due fields in the query result. Save the query as Apply 7 Step 2 Query.

3. Find all records in the Client table where the postal code is not 27036. Display the Client Number, Client Name, and City in the query result. Save the query as Apply 7 Step 3 Query.

4. Display the Client Number, Client Name, Bookkeeper Number, First Name, and Last Name for all clients. Sort the records in ascending order by bookkeeper number and client number. Save the query as Apply 7 Step 4 Query.

5. Submit the revised database in the format specified by your instructor.

Extend Your Knowledge

Extend the skills you learned in this chapter and experiment with new skills. You may need to use Help to complete the assignment.

Instructions: Start Access. Open the LawnYard Maintenance database. See the inside back cover of this book for instructions for downloading the Data Files for Students, or see your instructor for information on accessing the files required in this book.

LawnYard Maintenance is a small landscaping and maintenance company. The owners have created an Access database in which to store information about the customers they serve and the workers they employ. You will create SQL queries using the LIKE, IN, and BETWEEN operators. You also will create a query that uses a subquery.

Perform the following tasks:

1. Find all customers where the customer's first name is either Frances or Francis. Display the Customer Number, Last Name, First Name, and City fields in the result. Save the query as Extend 7 Step 1 Query.

2. Find all customers who live in Kingston or Anderson. Use the IN operator. Display the Customer Number, Last Name, First Name, and City fields in the result. Save the query as Extend 7 Step 2 Query.

3. Find all customers whose amount paid amount is greater than or equal to $200 and less than or equal to $300. Use the BETWEEN operator. (*Hint*: Use Help to solve this problem.) Display the Customer Number, Last Name, First Name, and Amount Paid fields in the result. Save the query as Extend 7 Step 3 Query.

4. Use a subquery to find all workers whose customers are located in Anderson. Display the worker number, first name, and last name. Save the query as Extend 7 Step 4 Query.

5. Submit the revised database and in the format specified by your instructor.

Make It Right

Analyze a database, correct all errors, and/or improve the design.

Correcting Errors in the Query Design

Instructions: Start Access. Open the College Pet Sitters database. See the inside back cover of this book for instructions for downloading the Data Files for Students, or see your instructor for information on accessing the files required in this book.

College Pet Sitters is a database maintained by a small pet-sitting business owned by college students. The queries shown in Figure 7–37 contain a number of errors that need to be corrected before the queries run properly. The query shown in Figure 7–37a displays the Enter Parameter Value dialog box, but this is not a parameter query. Also, the owners wanted to assign the name, Total Amount, to the Balance + Paid calculation. Save the query with your changes.

(a) Incorrect Field Name Query

Figure 7–37

Continued >

Make It Right *continued*

When you view the results for the query shown in Figure 7–37b, you get 30 records. You know this is wrong. Also, the query did not sort correctly. The query results should be sorted first by sitter number and then by descending balance. Correct the errors and save the query with your changes.

(b) Incorrect Join and Sort Query

Figure 7–37

Change the database properties, as specified by your instructor. Submit the revised database in the format specified by your instructor.

In the Lab

Design, create, modify, and/or use a database following the guidelines, concepts, and skills presented in this chapter. The assignments are listed in order of increasing difficulty.

Lab 1: Querying the ECO Clothesline Database Using SQL

Problem: The management of ECO Clothesline wants to learn more about SQL and has determined a number of questions it wants SQL to answer. You must obtain answers to the questions posed by management.

Instructions: If you are using the Microsoft Access 2010 Complete or the Microsoft Access 2010 Comprehensive text, open the ECO Clothesline database that you used in Chapter 6. Otherwise, see your instructor for information on accessing the files required in this book.

Perform the following tasks:
1. Find all customers where the customer type is SAL. Include the Customer Number, Customer Name, and Sales Rep Number fields in the result. Save the query as Lab 7-1 Step 1 Query.
2. Find all customers located in Tennessee (TN) with a paid amount greater than $1,500.00. Include the Customer Number, Customer Name, and Amount Paid fields in the result. Save the query as Lab 7-1 Step 2 Query.
3. Find all customers whose names begin with the letter, C. Include the Customer Number, Customer Name, and City fields in the result. Save the query as Lab 7-1 Step 3 Query.
4. List all cities in descending order. Each city should appear only once. Save the query as Lab 7-1 Step 4 Query.
5. Display the customer number, name, sales rep number, first name, and last name for all customers. Sort the results in ascending order by sales rep number and customer number. Save the query as Lab 7-1 Step 5 Query.
6. List the average balance amount grouped by sales rep number. Name the average balance as Average Billed. Save the query as Lab 7-1 Step 6 Query.
7. Find the customer number and name for every pair of customers who are located in the same city. Save the query as Lab 7-1 Step 7 Query.

8. Find the customer numbers, names, and sales rep numbers for all customers that have open orders. Use the alias O for the Open Orders table and C for the Customer table. Each customer should appear only once. Save the query as Lab 7-1 Step 8 Query.

9. Use a subquery to find all sales reps whose customers are located in Pineville. Save the query as Lab 7-1 Step 9 Query.

10. Find the average balance amount for sales rep 44. Save the query as Lab 7-1 Step 10 Query.

11. Submit the revised database in the format specified by your instructor.

In the Lab

Lab 2: Querying the Walburg Energy Alternatives Database Using SQL

Problem: The manager of the Walburg Energy Alternatives store would like to learn more about SQL and has determined a number of questions he wants SQL to answer. You must obtain answers to the questions posed by the manager.

Instructions: If you are using the Microsoft Access 2010 Complete or the Microsoft Access 2010 Comprehensive text, open the Walburg Energy Alternatives database that you used in Chapter 6. Otherwise, see your instructor for information on accessing the files required in this book.

Perform the following tasks:
1. Find all records in the Item table where the difference between the cost of the item and the selling price of the item is less than $0.25 (25 cents). Display the item number, description, cost, and selling price in the query result. Save the query as Lab 7-2 Step 1 Query.

2. Display the item number, description, and profit (selling price – cost) for all items. Name the computed field Profit. Save the query as Lab 7-2 Step 2 Query.

3. Find all items where the description begins with the letter, W. Include the item number and description in the result. Save the query as Lab 7-2 Step 3 Query.

4. Display the vendor name, item number, description, and cost for all items where the number on hand is less than 10. Sort the results in ascending order by vendor name and description. Save the query as Lab 7-2 Step 4 Query.

5. Find the average cost by vendor. Name the computed field Average Cost. Save the query as Lab 7-2 Step 5 Query.

6. Find the total number of reordered items for each item in the Reorder table. Name the computed field Total Ordered. Include the item number in the result. Save the query as Lab 7-2 Step 6 Query.

7. Add the following record to the Reorder table.

Item Number	Date Ordered	Number Ordered
8590	4/12/2012	3

Save the steps to add the record as Lab 7-2 Step 7 Query.

8. Update the Number Ordered field to 5 for those records where the Item Number is 8590 and the date ordered is 4/12/2012. Save the steps to update the record as Lab 7-2 Step 8 Query.

9. Delete all records where the Item Number is 8590 and the date ordered is 4/12/2012. Save the steps to delete the record as Lab 7-2 Step 9 Query.

10. Submit the revised database in the format specified by your instructor.

In the Lab

Lab 3: Querying the Philamar Training Database Using SQL

Problem: The management team of Philamar Training would like to learn more about SQL and has determined a number of questions it wants SQL to answer. You must obtain answers to the questions posed by management.

Instructions: If you are using the Microsoft Access 2010 Complete or the Microsoft Access 2010 Comprehensive text, open the Philamar Training database that you used in Chapter 6. Otherwise, see your instructor for information on accessing the files required in this book. Save each query using a format similar to the following: Lab 7-3 Part 1a Query, Lab 7-3 Part 2a Query, and so on. Submit the revised database in the format specified by your instructor.

Instructions Part 1: For all the queries in Part 1, include the Client Number, Client Name, Amount Paid, and Current Due fields in the query results. Create SQL queries that answer the following questions: (a) Which clients are located in cities that start with the letter, C? (b) Which clients have a client type other than MAN? (c) Which clients have a current due amount of $0.00 and an amount paid amount of $0.00? (d) Which clients have an amount paid amount between $3,000.00 and $6,000.00? (e) For each client, what is the total of the current due and amount paid? Display the total in the result as Total Amount.

Instructions Part 2: (a) Create a SQL query that includes the Trainer Number, First Name, Last Name, Client Number, Client Name, and Amount Paid fields. Sort the records in ascending order by trainer number and client number. (b) Restrict the records retrieved in part (a) to only those clients whose client type is MAN. (c) Find the client numbers and names for every pair of clients located in the same city. (d) In which cities does Philamar have clients? List each city only once.

Instructions Part 3: Create queries to calculate the following statistics: (a) How many clients does Philamar have, and what is the total of their amount paid amounts? Assign Client Count and Sum Paid as the names for the calculations. (b) What is the total current due amount and total amount paid amount for all clients grouped by trainer? Assign Sum Paid and Sum Due as the names for the calculations. (c) Restrict the records retrieved in (b) to those on which the sum of the current due is greater than $1,000.

Cases and Places

Apply your creative thinking and problem solving skills to design and implement a solution.

See the inside back cover of this book for instructions on downloading the Data Files for Students, or contact your instructor for information about accessing the required files.

1: Querying the Chamber of Commerce Database

Academic

If you are using the Microsoft Access 2010 Complete or the Microsoft Access 2010 Comprehensive text, open the Chamber of Commerce database that you used in Chapter 6. Otherwise, see your instructor for more information about accessing the required files. One of your courses at school requires that you learn to use SQL. The Chamber has agreed that you can use the database and create

SQL queries. Use the concepts and techniques presented in this chapter to create SQL queries for the following:

a. Find the advertiser names and addresses of all advertisers located on Berton Street.

b. Find the advertiser number, advertiser name, balance, and amount paid for all advertisers whose balance is less than $100 and whose amount paid is $0.00.

c. Find the total of the balance and amount paid amounts for each advertiser. Show the advertiser number, advertiser name, and total amount.

d. Use a subquery to find all ad reps whose advertisers have an advertiser type of RET. Display the ad rep number, first name, and last name.

e. Find the ad rep for each advertiser. List the ad rep number, first name, last name, advertiser number, advertiser name, and balance. Restrict retrieval to only those records where the balance is greater than $200. Sort the results in ascending order by ad rep number and advertiser number.

f. Add a record to the Active Accounts table for advertiser number G346. The advertiser would like to place a quarter-page ad for the month of Jun.

g. Change the category code to 3 for all records in the Active Accounts table where the advertiser number is G346 and the ad month is Jun.

h. Delete all records in the Active Accounts table where the advertiser number is G346 and the ad month is Jun.

Submit the revised database in the format specified by your instructor.

2: Querying the Consignment Database

Personal

If you are using the Microsoft Access 2010 Complete or the Microsoft Access 2010 Comprehensive text, open the Consignment database that you used in Chapter 6. Otherwise, see your instructor for more information about accessing the required files. You recently attended a seminar on the use of Access databases by nonprofit organizations. Now you would like to learn SQL to enhance your understanding of databases. Use the concepts and techniques presented in this chapter to create SQL queries for the following:

a. Find the item number and description of all items that contain the word, Kitchen.

b. Find the item number, description, condition, and date of all items with a date posted prior to March 1, 2012.

c. Find the total price (price * quantity) of each item available for sale. Show the item number, item description, and total price.

d. Find the seller of each item. Show the seller's first name and last name as well as the item number, item description, price, quantity, and date posted. Sort the results by item description within seller last name.

e. Modify the query you created in Step d to restrict retrieval to those items with a price less than $10.00.

f. Find all items in good or excellent condition. Use the IN operator and display all fields in the query result.

g. Find all items posted between March 4, 2012, and March 7, 2012. The user should see all fields in the query result.

Submit the revised database in the format specified by your instructor.

Continued >

Cases and Places *continued*

3: Querying the Senior Care Database

Professional

If you are using the Microsoft Access 2010 Complete or the Microsoft Access 2010 Comprehensive text, open the Senior Care database that you used in Chapter 6. Otherwise, see your instructor for more information about accessing the required files. You and your co-owner are interested in learning SQL. Use the concepts and techniques presented in this chapter to create SQL queries for the following:

a. Find the first names, last names, and addresses of all clients whose first name begins with the letters, Fr.

b. Find the total of the balance and amount paid amounts for each client. Show the client number, client first name, client last name, and total amount.

c. Restrict the records retrieved in Step b to only those records where the total amount is greater than $1,000.

d. Find the helper for each client. List the helper number, helper last name, helper first name, client number, client last name, and client first name. Assign aliases to the Client and Helper tables. Sort the results in ascending order by helper number and client number.

e. Restrict the records retrieved in Step d to only those helpers who speak Spanish.

f. Find the average balance amount grouped by helper number.

g. Restrict the records retrieved in Step f to only those groups where the average balance amount is greater than $125.

Submit the revised database in the format specified by your instructor.

8 | Advanced Form Techniques

Objectives

You will have mastered the material in this project when you can:

- Create a form in Design view
- Add combo boxes that include selection lists
- Add combo boxes for searching
- Format and resize controls
- Apply formatting characteristics with the Format Painter
- Add command buttons to a form
- Modify buttons and combo boxes

- Add a calculated field
- Use tab controls to create a multipage form
- Add and modify a subform
- Insert charts
- Modify a chart type
- Format a chart
- Use the Arrange tab on forms and reports

8 | Advanced Form Techniques

Introduction

BTW

Q&As
For a complete list of the Q&As found in many of the step-by-step sequences in this book, visit the Access 2010 Q&A Web page (scsite.com/ac2010/qa).

This chapter creates two new forms. The first form contains two combo boxes, one for selecting data from a related table and one for finding a record on the form. It also contains command buttons to accomplish various tasks.

The second form you will create is a **multipage form**, a form that contains more than one page of information. The form contains a tab control that allows you to access two different pages. Clicking the first tab displays a page containing a subform. Clicking the second tab displays a page containing two charts.

Project — Advanced Form Techniques

Camashaly Design wants two additional forms to use with its Client and Business Analyst tables. The first form, Client View and Update Form (Figure 8–1a), contains the fields in the Client table. The form has five command buttons: Next Record, Previous Record, Add Record, Delete Record, and Close Form. Clicking any of these buttons causes the action indicated on the button to take place.

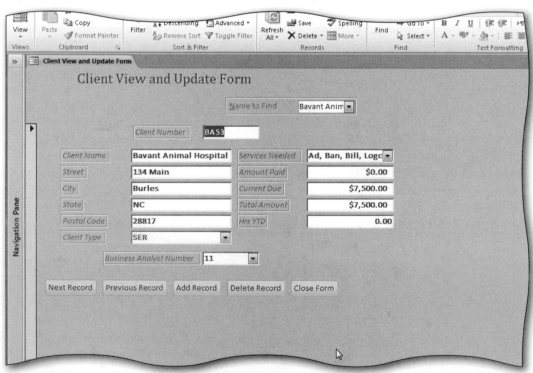

(a) Client View and Update Form

Figure 8–1

(b) Finding a Business Analyst Number

(c) Searching for a Client by Name
Figure 8–1

The form also contains a combo box for the Business Analyst Number field that assists users in selecting the correct analyst (Figure 8–1b).

To assist users in finding a client when they know the client's name, the form also includes a combo box they can use for this purpose (Figure 8–1c). After clicking the arrow, the user can simply click the client they want to find; Access then will locate the client and display that client's data in the form (Figure 8–1d).

(d) Client Has Been Found

Figure 8–1

For the second new form, Camashaly Design needs a multipage form that lists the numbers and names of analysts. Selecting the first tab, the one labeled Datasheet, displays a subform listing information about the course offerings for clients of the selected analyst (Figure 8–2a).

Selecting the other tab, the one labeled Charts, displays two charts that illustrate the total hours spent and hours remaining by the analyst for the various courses (Figure 8–2b). In both charts, the slices of the pie represent the various courses. They are color-coded and the legend at the bottom indicates the meaning of the various colors. The size of the pie slice gives a visual representation of the portion of the hours spent or hours remaining by the analyst for that particular course. The chart also includes specific percentages. If you look at the bottom purple slice in the Hours Spent by Course Offering chart, for example, you see that the color represents course C04. It signifies 42% of the total. Thus, for all the hours already spent on the various course offerings by analyst 11, 42% have been spent on course C04.

BTW

BTWs
For a complete list of the BTWs found in the margins of this book, visit the Access 2010 BTW Web page (scsite. com/ac2010/btw).

(a) Analyst Course Data Form with Datasheet Tab Selected

Figure 8–2

(b) Analyst Course Data Form with Charts Tab Selected
Figure 8–2

Overview

As you read through this chapter, you will learn how to create the forms by performing these general tasks:

- Create a form with a calculated field, a combo box for finding records in a related table, and a combo box for finding a record.
- Add command buttons to the form.
- Modify a macro for one of the buttons.
- Modify the combo box for finding a record so that it works correctly.
- Create a form with a tab control.
- Add a subform to one of the tabbed pages.
- Add charts to the other tabbed page.

Form Design Guidelines

Plan Ahead

When creating more complex forms, you must decide on the intended usage, audience, content, and formatting. To design and create forms, you should follow these general guidelines:

1. **Determine the intended audience and the purpose of the form.** Who will use the form? How will they use it? What data do they need? What level of detail do they need?

2. **Determine the source of data for the form.** Determine whether data will be found in a single table or from multiple related tables. Which table or tables contain the data?

3. **Determine the fields that belong on the form.** What data items are needed by the user of the form?

4. **Determine any calculations required for the form.** Decide whether the form should contain any special calculations. For example, you might want to display the results of adding the values in two fields, such as the Salary YTD and Incentive YTD fields in the Business Analyst table. The calculations can also involve text fields. For example, you could display the result of combining the contents of the First Name field and the Last Name field. Such a result, called a concatenated field, is really just a special type of calculation.

(continued)

(continued)

5. **Determine the organization of the form.** In what order should the fields appear? How should they be arranged?

6. **Determine any additional controls that should be on the form.** Should the form contain a subform? Should the form contain a chart? Should the form contain command buttons to assist the user in performing various functions? Should the form contain a combo box to assist the user in searching for a record?

7. **Determine the format and style of the form.** What should be in the form heading? Do you want a title, for example? Do you want a logo? What should be in the body of the form? What should the style be? In other words, what visual characteristics should the various portions of the form have?

When necessary, more specific details concerning the above decisions and/or actions are presented at appropriate points in the chapter. The chapter also will identify the use of these guidelines in the design of the forms such as the ones shown in Figure 8–1 and Figure 8–2.

To Start Access

BTW

The Ribbon and Screen Resolution
Access may change how the groups and buttons within the groups appear on the Ribbon, depending on the computer's screen resolution. Thus, your Ribbon may look different from the ones in this book if you are using a screen resolution other than 1024 × 768.

The following steps, which assume Windows 7 is running, start Access based on a typical installation. You may need to ask your instructor how to start Access for your computer.

1 Click the Start button on the Windows 7 taskbar to display the Start menu.

2 Type **Microsoft Access** as the search text in the 'Search programs and files' text box and watch the search results appear on the Start menu.

3 Click Microsoft Access 2010 in the search results on the Start menu to start Access.

4 If the Access window is not maximized, click the Maximize button next to the Close button on its title bar to maximize the window.

To Open a Database from Access

The following steps open the Camashaly database from the Access folder in the CIS 101 folder on the USB flash drive.

1 With your USB flash drive connected to one of the computer's USB ports, click File on the Ribbon to open the Backstage view if necessary.

2 Click Open in the Backstage view to display the Open dialog box.

3 Navigate to the location of the file to be opened (in this case, the USB flash drive, then to the CIS 101 folder [or your class folder], and then to the Access folder).

4 Click Camashaly Design to select the file to be opened.

5 Click the Open button (Open dialog box) to open the selected file and display the opened database in the Access window.

6 If a Security Warning appears, click the Enable Content option button.

Determine the fields that belong on the form. If you determine that data should be presented as a form, you then need to determine what tables and fields contain the data for the form.

- **Examine the requirements for the form in general to determine the tables.** Do the requirements only relate to data in a single table, or does the data come from multiple tables? How are the tables related?

- **Examine the specific requirements for the form to determine the fields necessary.** Look for all the data items that are specified for the form. Each item should correspond to a field in a table or be able to be computed from a field in a table. This information gives you the list of fields.

- **Determine whether there are any special calculations required.** Are there any special calculations? What are they? What fields are involved and how are they to be combined?

Determine the organization of the form. Determine various details concerning how the data in your form is to be organized.

- **Determine the order of the fields.** Examine the requirements to determine the order in which the fields should appear. Be logical and consistent in your ordering. For example, in an address, the city should come before the state, and the state should come before the postal code, unless there is some compelling reason for another order.

- **Determine whether to include a subform.** If the fields for the form come from exactly two tables, there is a one-to-many relationship between the two tables, and the form is based on the "one" table, you will often place the data for the "many" table in a subform. If there are more than two tables involved, you may be able to create a query on which you can base the subform.

- **Determine whether to include a chart.** Do you want to represent data in a visual manner? If so, you can include a chart. If you do decide to use a chart, which type of chart would best represent the data? If you want to represent total amounts, for example, a bar chart may be appropriate. If, instead, you want to represent portions of the whole, a pie chart may be better.

Determine any additional controls that should be on the form. After you determine the tables, fields, and organization for your form, you need to determine if there are any additional items to add to the form.

- **Determine whether the form should include any combo boxes.** A combo box is a combination of a text box, where users can type data, and a list box, where users can click an arrow to display a list. Would a combo box improve the functionality of the form? Is there a place where it would be convenient for users to enter data by selecting the data from a list, either a list of predefined items or a list of values from a related table? If users need to search for records, including a combo box can assist in the process.

- **Determine whether the form should include any command buttons.** Can you make certain actions more convenient for users by including command buttons? Buttons can carry out record navigation actions (for example, go to the next record), record operation actions (for example, add a record), form operation actions (for example, close a form), report operation actions (for example, print a report), application actions (for example, quit application), and some miscellaneous actions (for example, run a macro).

- **Determine whether the form should contain a tab control.** If the form contains more information than conveniently will fit on the screen at a time, consider adding a tab control. With a tab control, you can organize the information within a collection of tabbed pages. To access any of the tabbed pages, users need only click the corresponding tab.

Creating a Form with Combo Boxes and Command Buttons

BTW

Combo Boxes
You also can create combo boxes for reports.

After planning your form, you may decide that you need to use features such as combo boxes and command buttons. You can include such items while modifying the form in Design view. Provided the Use Control Wizards button is selected, a wizard will assist you in the process.

To Create a Form in Design View

You can create a form using several different form tools, such as the Form Wizard and the Form button. Creating a form in Design view gives you the most flexibility in laying out the form. You will be presented with a blank design on which to place objects. The following steps create a form in Design view.

1
- Display the Create tab.

- Click the Form Design button (Create tab | Forms group) to create a new form in Design view.

- If necessary, close the Navigation Pane.

- Ensure the selector for the entire form, the box in the upper-left corner of the form, is selected.

- Click the Property Sheet button (Form Design Tools Design tab | Tools group) to display a property sheet.

- With the All tab selected, click the Record Source arrow, and then click the Client table to select the Client table as the record source.

- Click the Save button on the Quick Access Toolbar, then type `Client Master Form` as the form name (Figure 8–3).

Figure 8–3

2

- Click the OK button (Save As dialog box) to save the form.

- Click the Caption property in the property sheet, and then type **Client View and Update Form** as the new caption.

- Close the property sheet by clicking the Property Sheet button on the Design tab.

- Click the Add Existing Fields button (Form Design Tools Design tab | Tools group) to display the field list (Figure 8–4).

Q&A Why doesn't the name on the tab change to the new caption, Client View and Update Form?

The name on the tab will change to the new caption in Form view. In Design view, you still see the name of the form object.

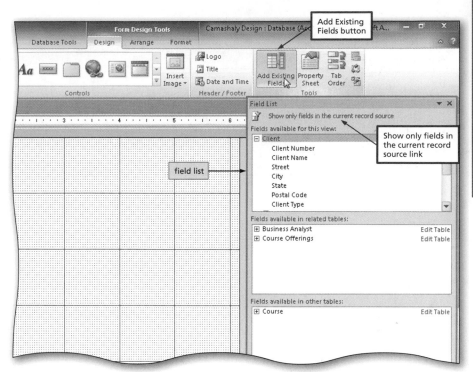

Figure 8–4

To Add Fields to the Form Design

After deciding which fields to add to the Client View and Update Form, you can place them on the form by dragging the fields from the field list to the desired position. The following steps place the Business Analyst Number field on the form.

1

- If necessary, click the 'Show only fields in the current record source' link at the top of the field list to change the link to 'Show all tables' and display only the fields in the Client table.

- Drag the Client Number field from the field list to the approximate position shown in Figure 8–5.

- Click the label once to select it and then click it a second time to produce an insertion point.

- Use the BACKSPACE or DELETE key as necessary to erase the current entry (CL #) and then type **Client Number** as the new label.

Figure 8–5

Q&A I thought the caption for Client Number was changed to CL # so that this short caption would appear in datasheets, on forms, and on reports. Why am I now changing it back?

In these forms, there is plenty of room for the entire field name. Thus, there is no need for the short captions.

2

- Click the Client Name field in the field list.

- While holding the SHIFT key down, click the Client Type field in the field list to select multiple fields (Figure 8–6).

Figure 8–6

3

- Drag the selected fields to the approximate position shown in Figure 8–7.

- Select the Services Needed through Contract Hours YTD fields and then drag the selected fields to the approximate position shown in the figure.

- Adjust the sizing and alignment of the controls to approximately match those in the figure. If controls for any of the fields are not aligned properly, align them by dragging them to the desired location or by using the alignment buttons on the Arrange tab.

- Close the field list.

Figure 8–7

Combo Boxes

When entering an analyst number, the value must match the number of an analyst currently in the Business Analyst table. To assist the users in entering this data, the form will contain a combo box. A **combo box** combines the properties of a **text box**, which is a box into which you can type an entry, and a **list box**, which is a box you can use to display a list from which to select a value. With a combo box, the user can either type the data or click the combo box arrow to display a list of possible values and then select an item from the list.

BTW

Drop-Down Boxes
Combo boxes also are called drop-down boxes because a list drops down when you click the combo box arrow.

To Add a Combo Box that Selects Values from a Related Table

If you have determined that a combo box displaying values from a related table would be useful on your form, you can add the combo box to a form using the Combo Box tool in the Controls group on the Design tab. If the Use Control Wizards button in the Controls group on the Design tab is selected, you can use a wizard to guide you through the process of creating the combo box. The following steps place on the form a combo box that displays values from a related table for the Business Analyst Number field.

1

• Click the More button (Form Design Tools Design tab | Controls group) (see Figure 8–7) to display all the available tools in the Controls group (Figure 8–8).

Figure 8–8

2

• With the Use Control Wizards button in the Controls group on the Design tab selected, click the Combo Box tool (Form Design Tools Design tab | Controls group), and then move the mouse pointer, whose shape has changed to a small plus symbol accompanied by a combo box, to the position shown in Figure 8–9.

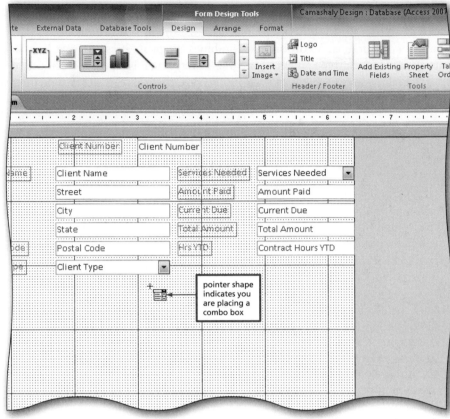

Figure 8–9

3

• Click the position shown in Figure 8–9 to place a combo box.

• If necessary, in the Combo Box Wizard dialog box, click the 'I want the combo box to get the values from another table or query.' option button (Figure 8–10).

Q&A

What is the purpose of the other options?

Use the second option if you want to type a list from which the user will choose. Use the third option if you want to use the combo box to search for a record.

Figure 8–10

• Click the Next button, and then, with the Tables option button selected, click Table: Business Analyst (Figure 8–11), if necessary, to specify that the combo box values will come from the Business Analyst table.

Figure 8–11

• Click the Next button to display the next Combo Box Wizard screen.

• Click the Add Field button to add the Business Analyst Number as a field in the combo box.

• Click the First Name field and then click the Add Field button.

• Click the Last Name field and then click the Add Field button (Figure 8–12).

Figure 8–12

- Click the Next button to display the next Combo Box Wizard screen.
- Click the arrow in the first text box, and then select the Business Analyst Number field (Figure 8–13).

Figure 8–13

- Click the Next button to display the next Combo Box Wizard screen (Figure 8–14).

Q&A What is the key column? Do I want to hide it?

The key column would be the Business Analyst Number, the column that identifies both a first name and a last name. Because the purpose of this combo box is to update analyst numbers, you certainly do not want them hidden.

Figure 8–14

8

• Click the 'Hide key column (recommended)' check box to remove the check mark so that the Business Analyst Number field will appear along with the First Name and Last Name fields.

• Click the Next button to display the next Combo Box Wizard screen (Figure 8–15).

Q&A Do I need to make any changes here?

No. The Business Analyst Number field, which is the field you want to store, is already selected.

Figure 8–15

9

• Click the Next button to display the next Combo Box Wizard screen.

• Click the 'Store that value in this field:' option button.

• Because you want to store the value in the Business Analyst Number field, click the 'Store that value in this field:' box arrow, and then click Business Analyst Number (Figure 8–16).

Figure 8–16

- Click the Next button to display the next Combo Box Wizard screen.

- Be sure Business Analyst Number is entered as the label for the combo box, and then click the Finish button to place the combo box.

Q&A Could I change the label to something else?

Yes. If you prefer a different label, you could change it.

- Move the Business Analyst Number label by dragging its Move handle to the position shown in Figure 8–17.

- Save your changes to the form.

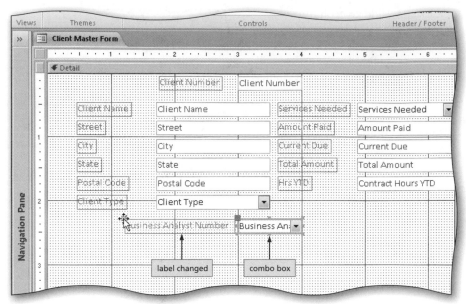

Figure 8–17

To Change the Background Color

You can use the Background Color button on the Format tab to change the background color of a form. The following steps change the background color of the form to a light gray.

1

- Click anywhere in the Detail section but outside all the controls to select the section.

- Display the Format tab.

- Click the Background Color button arrow (Form Design Tools Format tab | Font group) to display a color palette (Figure 8–18).

2

- Click the Light Gray 2 color, the first color in the third row under Standard Colors, to change the background color.

Experiment

- Try other colors to see their effect. When finished, once again select the Light Gray 2 color.

Figure 8–18

To Format a Control

You can use buttons on the Design tab to format a control in a variety of ways. You have even more control over the types of changes you can make, however, if you use the property sheet. The following steps make a variety of changes to the format of the Client Number control.

1

- Display the Design tab.

- Click the Client Number control (the white space, not the label) to select it.

- Click the Property Sheet button (Form Design Tools Design tab | Tools group) to display the property sheet.

- Change the value of the Font Weight property to Semi-bold.

- Change the value of the Special Effect property to Sunken.

- Click the Fore Color property box to select it, and then click the Build button (the three dots) to display a color palette (Figure 8–19).

Figure 8–19

2

- Click the Dark Blue color (the second color from the right in the bottom row under Standard Colors) to select it as the font color.

- Click the label for the Client Number field to select it.

- Change the value of the Font Italic property to Yes.

- Change the Special Effect property to Etched (Figure 8–20).

3

- Close the property sheet.

Figure 8–20

Q&A Shouldn't I have closed the property sheet before selecting a different control?

You could have, but you didn't need to. The property sheet displayed on the screen always applies to the currently selected controls.

To Use the Format Painter

Once you have formatted a control and its label the way you want, you can format other controls in exactly the same way by using the format painter. To do so, click the control whose format you want to copy, click the Format Painter button on the Format tab, and then click the other control to apply the characteristics of the selected control. If you want to copy the format to more than one other control, double-click the Format Painter button instead of simply clicking the button, and then click each of the controls that you want to change. The following steps copy the formatting of the Client Number control and label to the other controls.

- Display the Format tab.

- Click the Client Number control to select it, and then double-click the Format Painter button (Form Design Tools Format tab | Font group) to select the Format Painter.

- Point to the Client Name control (Figure 8–21).

Figure 8–21

- Click the Client Name control to assign it the same formatting as the Client Number control.

- Click all the other controls on the form to assign them the same formatting.

- Click the Format Painter button (Form Design Tools Format tab | Font group) to deselect the Format Painter (Figure 8–22).

Figure 8–22

Q&A
Do I always have to click the Format Painter button when I have finished copying the formatting?

If you double-clicked the Format Painter button to enable you to copy the formatting to multiple controls, you need to click the Format Painter button again to turn off the copying. If you simply clicked the Format Painter button to enable you to copy the formatting to a single control, you do not need to click the button again. As soon as you copy the formatting to the single control, the copying will be turned off.

Q&A
Does the order in which I click the other controls matter?

No. The only thing that is important is that you ultimately click all the controls whose formatting you want to assign.

To View the Form

As you are working on the design of a form, it is a good idea to periodically view the form in Form view to see the effects of your changes. The following steps view the form in Form view and then return to Design view.

- Display the Design tab.

- Click the View button (Form Design Tools Design tab | Views group) to view the form in Form view (Figure 8–23).

Q&A
Why did I have to change from the Format tab to the Design tab?

The Format tab does not have a View button.

- Click the View button arrow (Home tab | Views group) to produce the View button menu.

- Click Design View on the View button menu to return to Design view.

Q&A
Could I simply click the View button?

No. The icon on the View button is the one for Layout view. Clicking the button would show you the form in Layout view, but you are working on the form in Design view.

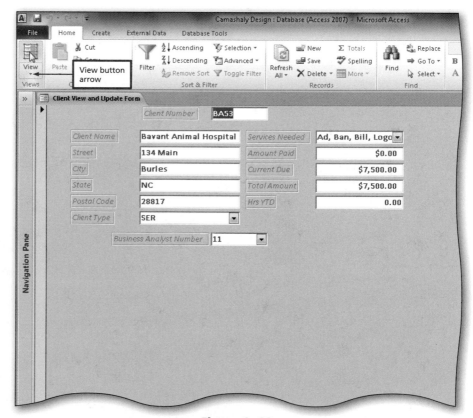

Figure 8–23

Other Ways

1. Click Form View button on Status bar to view form and click Design View button on Status bar to return to Design view

To Add a Title and Expand the Form Header Section

The form you are creating has a title, Client View and Update Form. The following steps add the title to the form. They also expand the Form Header section so that there will be sufficient room for the combo box you will add later.

1

- Click the Title button (Form Design Tools Design tab | Header/Footer group) to add a Form Header section and to add a control for the title to the Form Header section (Figure 8–24).

Q&A Why is the title Client View and Update Form rather than Client Master Form?

If you have changed the caption, the title will use the new value of the Caption property.

Q&A Could I add the Form Header section before adding the title? If I do, what happens when I add the title?

Access will place the title in the Form Header section that you already added.

Figure 8–24

2

- Drag the lower boundary of the Form Header section down to the approximate position shown in Figure 8–25.

Figure 8–25

To Change the Background Color of the Form Header

The background color of the form header in the form in Figure 8–1 is the same as the rest of the form. The following steps change the background color of the form header appropriately.

1 Click anywhere in the Form Header section but outside all the controls to select the section.

2 Display the Format tab.

3 Click the Background Color button arrow (Form Design Tools Format tab | Font group) to display a color palette.

4 Click the Light Gray 2 color, the first color in the third row under Standard Colors, to change the background color.

BTW

Background Images
You also can use a picture (image) as the background on a form or report. To do so, click anywhere in the form or report then click Background Image (Format tab | Background group). You can add a background image in either Design view or Layout view.

Break Point: If you wish to stop working through the chapter at this point, you can quit Access now. You can resume the project at a later time by starting Access, opening the database called Camashaly Design, opening the Client Master Form in Design view, and continuing to follow the steps from this location forward.

To Add Command Buttons to a Form

You may find that you can improve the functionality of your form by adding command buttons. To add command buttons, you use the Use Control Wizards button and the Button tool in the Controls group on the Design tab. When using the series of Command Button Wizard dialog boxes, you provide the action that should be taken when the command button is clicked, for example, go to the next record. Access includes several categories of commonly used actions within wizards.

In the Record Navigation category, you will select the Go To Next Record action for one of the command buttons. From the same category, you will select the Go To Previous Record action for another. Other buttons will use the Add New Record and the Delete Record actions from the Record Operations category. The Close Form button will use the Close Form action from the Form Operations category.

The following steps add command buttons to move to the next record, move to the previous record, add a record, delete a record, and close the form.

1

- Make sure the Use Control Wizards button is selected.

- Click the Button tool (Form Design Tools Design tab | Controls group) and then move the mouse pointer to the approximate position shown in Figure 8–26.

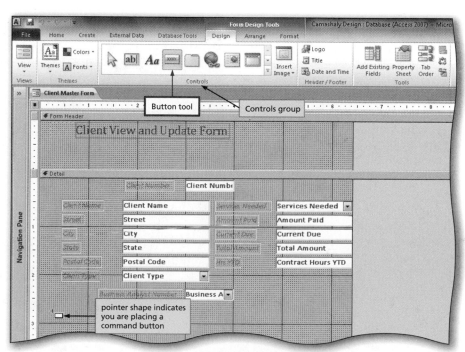

Figure 8–26

2

- Click the position shown in Figure 8–26 to display the Command Button Wizard dialog box.

- With Record Navigation selected in the Categories box, click Go To Next Record in the Actions box (Figure 8–27).

Figure 8–27

3

- Click the Next button to display the next Command Button Wizard screen.

- Click the Text option button (Figure 8–28).

Q&A

What is the purpose of these option buttons?

Choose the first option button to place text on the button. You then can specify the text to be included or accept the default choice. Choose the second option button to place a picture on the button. You then can select a picture.

Figure 8–28

4

- Because Next Record is the desired text and does not need to be changed, click the Next button.

- Type **Next Record** as the name of the button (Figure 8–29).

Figure 8–29

5

- Click the Finish button to finish specifying the button.

- Use the techniques in Steps 1 through 4 to place the Previous Record button directly to the right of the Next Record button. The action is Go To Previous Record in the Record Navigation category. Choose the Text option button and Previous Record on the button, and then type **Previous Record** as the name of the button.

- Use the techniques in Steps 1 through 4 to place a button directly to the right of the Previous Record button. The action is Add New Record in the Record Operations category. Choose the Text option button and Add Record on the button, and then type **Add Record** as the name of the button.

- Use the techniques in Steps 1 through 4 to place the Delete Record and Close Form buttons in the positions shown in Figure 8–30. For the Delete Record button, the category is Record Operations and the action is Delete Record. For the Close Form button, the category is Form Operations and the action is Close Form.

Figure 8–30

Q&A My buttons are not aligned like yours are. What should I do?

If your buttons are not aligned properly, you can drag them to the correct positions. You also can use the Arrange tab.

To Add a Combo Box that is Used to Find a Record

Although you can use the Find button (Home tab | Find group) to locate records on a form or a report, it may be more convenient to use a combo box. You could type the client's name directly into the box. Alternatively, you can click the Name to Find box arrow, and Access displays a list of client names. To select a name from the list, simply click the name.

To create a combo box, use the Combo Box tool in the Controls group on the Design tab. The Combo Box Wizard then will guide you through the steps of adding the combo box. The following steps place a combo box for names on the form.

1

- Click the More button (Form Design Tools Design tab | Controls group) to display all the controls.

- With the Use Control Wizards button selected, click the Combo Box tool (Form Design Tools Design tab | Controls group) and then move the mouse pointer, whose shape has changed to a small plus sign with a combo box, to the position shown in Figure 8–31.

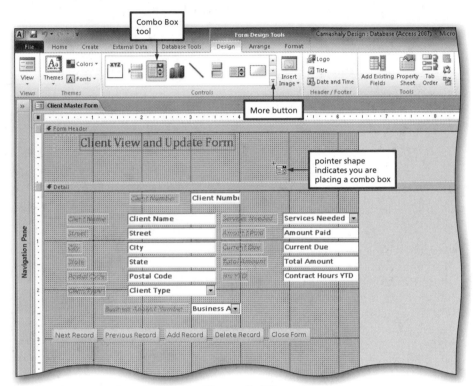

Figure 8–31

2

- Click the position shown in Figure 8–31 to display the Combo Box Wizard.

- Click the 'Find a record on my form based on the value I selected in my combo box.' option button to specify that the user will select from a list of values.

- Click the Next button, click the Client Name field, and then click the Add Field button to select the Client Name field for the combo box (Figure 8–32).

Figure 8–32

3

- Click the Next button.

- Drag the right boundary of the column heading to the approximate size shown in Figure 8–33.

Q&A Can I also resize the column to best fit the data by double-clicking the right boundary of the column heading?

Yes.

Figure 8–33

4

- Click the Next button, and then type **&Name to Find** as the label for the combo box.

Q&A What is the purpose of the ampersand in front of the letter, N?

The ampersand (&) in front of the letter, N, indicates that users can select the combo box by pressing ALT+N.

- Click the Finish button, and, if necessary, position the control and label in the approximate position shown in Figure 8–34.

Q&A Why is the letter, N, underlined?

The underlined letter, N, in the word, Name, indicates that you can press ALT+N to select the combo box. It is underlined because you preceded the letter, N, with the ampersand.

Figure 8–34

To Place a Rectangle

To emphasize the special nature of the combo box, you can place a rectangle around it as a visual cue. The following steps use the Rectangle tool to place a rectangle.

- Click the More button (Form Design Tools Design tab | Controls group) to display all the controls.

- Click the Rectangle tool, which is the far right tool in the second row, point to the position for the upper-left corner of the rectangle shown in Figure 8–35, press the left mouse button, drag the pointer to the lower-right corner of the rectangle, and then release the left mouse button to place the rectangle.

- Click the Property Sheet button (Form Design Tools Design tab | Tools group) to display the property sheet for the rectangle.

- Change the value of the Special Effect property to Etched.

- Make sure the value of the Back Style property is Transparent, so the combo box will appear within the rectangle.

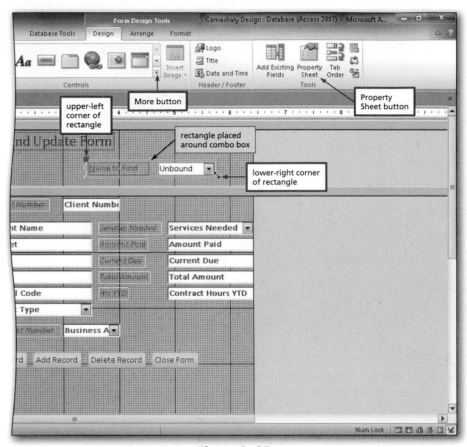

Figure 8–35

Q&A

What if the value is not Transparent?

If the value is not Transparent, the rectangle would cover the combo box completely and the combo box would not be visible.

- Close the property sheet.

- Save and then close the form.

To Open the Client Master Form

Once you have created the form, you can use it at any time by opening it. The following steps open the Client Master Form.

1 Open the Navigation Pane, and then right-click the Client Master Form to display the shortcut menu.

2 Click Open on the shortcut menu to open the form.

3 Close the Navigation Pane (Figure 8–36).

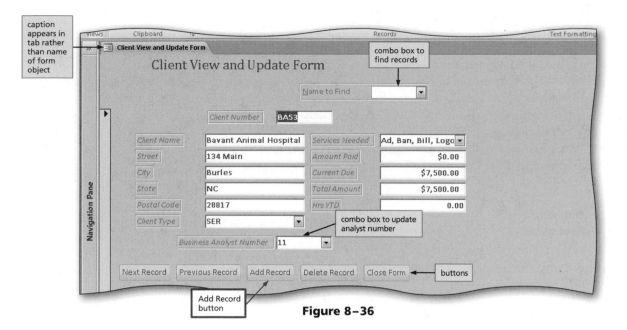

Figure 8–36

Using the Buttons

To move around on the form, you can use the buttons to perform the actions you specify. To move forward to the next record, click the Next Record button. Click the Previous Record button to move back to the previous record. Clicking the Delete Record button will delete the record currently on the screen. Access will display a message requesting that you verify the deletion before the record actually is deleted. Clicking the Close Form button will remove the form from the screen.

To Use the Add Record Button

Clicking the Add Record button will clear the contents of the form so you can add a new record. The following step uses the Add Record button.

1
- Click the Add Record button (Figure 8–37).

Q&A There is no insertion point in the Client Number field. How would I begin entering a new record?

To begin entering a record, you would have to click the Client Number field before you can start typing.

Q&A Why does NON appear in the Client Type field?

The value NON is the default value assigned to the Client Type field.

Experiment
- Try each of the other buttons to see their effects. Do not delete any records. After clicking the Close Form button, open the form once again.

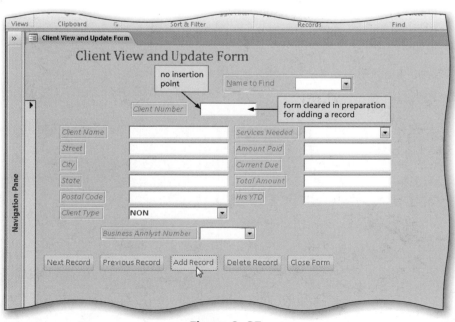

Figure 8–37

To Use the Combo Box

Using the combo box, you can search for a client in two ways. First, you can click the combo box arrow to display a list of client names, and then select the name from the list by clicking it. Alternatively, you can begin typing the name. As you type, Access will display automatically the name that begins with the letters you have typed. Once the correct name is displayed, select the name by pressing the TAB key. Regardless of the method you use, the data for the selected client appears on the form once the selection is made.

The following steps first locate the client whose name is KAL Design Studio, and then use the Next Record button to move to the next client.

1

- Click the Name to Find box arrow to display a list of client names (Figure 8–38).

The list is not in alphabetical order, because Bavant Animal Hospital is before Babbage CPA Firm. Wouldn't it be easier to use if the list was in alphabetical order?

Yes. You will change the combo box later so that the names appear in alphabetical order.

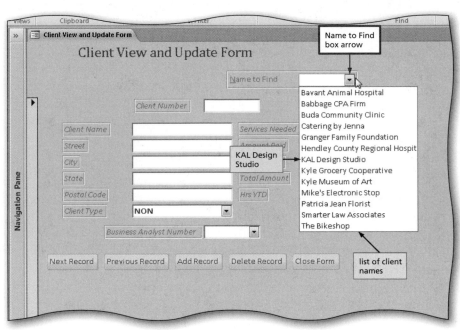

Figure 8–38

2

- Click KAL Design Studio to display the data for KAL Design Studio in the form (Figure 8–39).

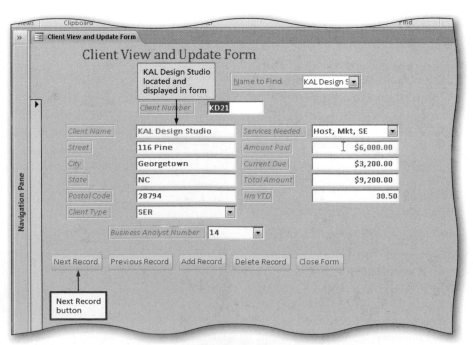

Figure 8–39

3

- Click the Next Record button to display the next record (Figure 8–40).

Q&A

Why does the combo box still contain KAL Design Studio, rather than Kyle Grocery Cooperative?

This is a problem with the combo box. You will address this issue later.

Experiment

- Select the entry in the combo box and enter the letters, sm, to find Smarter Law Associates. Try other client names in the combo box.

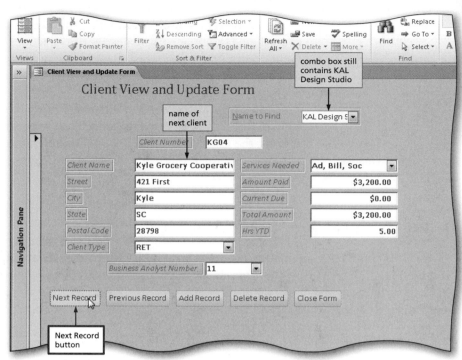

Figure 8–40

Issues with the Add Record Button

Although clicking the Add Record button does erase the contents of the form in preparation for adding a new record, there is a problem with it. After clicking the Add Record button, there should be an insertion point in the control for the first field — the Client Number field — but there is not. To display an insertion point automatically when you click the Add Record button, you need to change the focus. A control is said to have the **focus** when it becomes active; that is, when it becomes able to receive user input through mouse or keyboard actions. At any point in time, only one item on the form has the focus. In addition to adding a new record, clicking the Add Record button needs to update the focus to the Client Number field.

BTW

Focus
A visual way exists to determine which object on the screen has the focus. If a field has the focus, an insertion point will appear in the field. If a button has the focus, a small rectangle will appear inside the button.

Issues with the Combo Box

The combo box has the following issues. First, if you examine the list of names in Figure 8–38, you will see that they are not in alphabetical order (Bavant Animal Hospital comes before Babbage CPA Firm). Second, when you move to a record without using the combo box, such as when navigating using the buttons, the name in the combo box does not change to reflect the name of the client currently on the screen. Third, one way to change the focus from one field to another is to press the TAB key. As you repeatedly press the TAB key, the focus should move through all the fields on the form. It should not move to the combo box, however, because that does not represent a field to be updated.

BTW

Converting Macros to VBA Code
You can convert macros that are attached to forms to VBA (Visual Basic for Applications) code. To do so, open the form in Design view and click the Convert Form's Macros to Visual Basic button (Form Design Tools Design tab | Tools group). You also can convert macros that are attached to reports.

Macros

To correct the problem with the Add Record button not displaying an insertion point, you will update a **macro**, which is a series of actions that Access performs when a particular event occurs, in this case when the Add Record button is clicked. (In the next chapter, you will create macros on your own. In this case, Access has already created the macro; you just need to add a single action to it.)

Specifically, you need to add an action to the macro that will move the focus to the control for the Client Number field. The appropriate action is GoToControl. Like many actions, the GoToControl action requires additional information, called arguments. The argument for the GoToControl action is the name of the control, in this case, the Client Number control.

To Modify the Macro for the Add Record Button

When creating or modifying macros, it is necessary for control names not to contain spaces. In fact, if you are programming in VBA (Visual Basic for Applications), this is an absolute requirement. You can use different methods of changing the names so that they don't contain spaces. One approach is to simply remove the space. This approach would change Client Number to ClientNumber, for example. The approach you will use is to insert an underscore (_) in place of the space. For example, you will change Client Number to Client_Number.

The following steps first change the name of the controls to remove spaces. They then modify the macro that is associated with the clicking of the Add Record button by adding an action that will change the focus to the control for the Client Number field.

1

- Click the View button arrow and then click Design View to return to Design view.

- Click the control for the Client Number field (the white space, not the label), and then click the Property Sheet button (Form Design Tools Design tab | Tools group) to display the property sheet.

- If necessary, click the All tab. Ensure the Name property is selected, click immediately following the word, Client, press the DELETE key to delete the space, and then type an underscore (_) to change the name to Client_Number (Figure 8–41).

Q&A

Could I just erase the old name and type Client_Number?

Yes. Use whichever method you find most convenient.

Figure 8–41

2

• Click the control for the Client Name field to display its property sheet and then change the name to Client_Name.

• Close the property sheet and then right-click the Add Record button to display a shortcut menu (Figure 8–42).

Figure 8–42

3

• Click Build Event on the shortcut menu to display the macro associated with the On Click event that Access created automatically.

• If the Action Catalog does not appear, click the Action Catalog button (Macro Tools Design tab | Show/Hide group) to display the Action Catalog.

• If there is a plus sign in front of Actions, click the plus sign to display all actions.

• Click the plus sign in front of Database Objects to display all actions associated with Database Objects (Figure 8–43).

Figure 8–43

Q&A

How can I recognize actions? How can I recognize the arguments of the actions?

The actions are in bold. The arguments for the action follow the action and are not bold. The value for an argument appears to the right of the argument. The value for the 'Go to' argument of the OnError action is Next, for example.

Q&A What is the purpose of the three actions currently in the macro?

The first action indicates that, if there is an error, Access should proceed to the next action in the macro rather than immediately stopping the macro. The second action causes Access to go to the record indicated by the values in the arguments. The value, New, indicates that it is to go to a new record. Because the final action has a condition, the action will only be executed if the condition is true, that is, the error code contains a value other than 0. In that case, the MsgBox action will display a description of the error.

4

• Drag the GoToControl action from the Action Catalog to the position shown in Figure 8–44.

• Type **Client_ Number** as the Control Name argument (Figure 8–44).

Q&A What is the effect of the GoToControl action?

When Access executes this action, the focus will move to the control indicated in the Control Name argument, in this case, the Client_Number control.

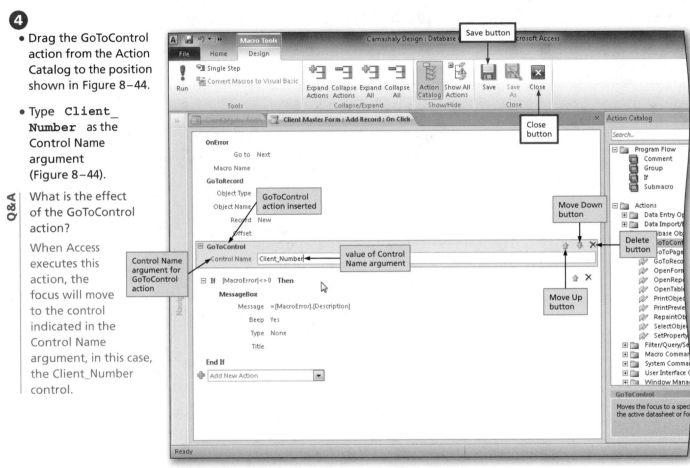

Figure 8–44

Q&A I added the GoToControl action to the wrong place in the macro. How do I move it?

To move it up in the list, click the Move Up button. To move it down, click the Move Down button.

Q&A I added the wrong action. What should I do?

Click the Delete button to delete the action you added, and then add the GoToControl action. If you decide you would rather start over instead, click the Close button (Macro Tools Design tab | Close group) and then click the No button when asked if you want to save your changes. You can then begin again from Step 3.

5

• Click the Save button (Macro Tools Design tab | Close group) to save your changes.

• Click the Close button (Macro Tools Design tab | Close group) to close the macro and return to the form design.

To Modify the Combo Box

You need to take special action to correct the issues with the combo box. To ensure the data is sorted in the correct order, you need to modify the query that Access has created for the combo box so the data is sorted by client name. You also need to modify the VBA (Visual Basic for Applications) code associated with what is termed the On Current event property of the entire form. The modification to the On Current event property will ensure that the combo box remains current with the rest of the form; that is, it contains the name of the client whose number currently appears in the Client Number field. The following steps modify the query and then the code associated with the On Current event property appropriately. The final step changes the Tab Stop property for the combo box from Yes to No.

- Click the Name to Find combo box (the white space, not the label), and then click the Property Sheet button (Form Design Tools Design tab | Tools group).

- Change the name to Name_to_Find.

- Scroll down in the property sheet so that the Row Source property appears, click the Row Source property, and then click the Build button (the three dots) to display the Query Builder.

- Click the Sort row in the Client Name field, click the box arrow that appears, and then click Ascending to change the order and display client names in alphabetical order in the combo box (Figure 8–45).

Figure 8–45

- Click the Save button on the Quick Access Toolbar to save your changes.

- Close the Query Builder window by clicking the Close button on the Design tab.

- Close the property sheet.

- Click the form selector (the box in the upper-left corner of the form) to select the form.

- Click the Property Sheet button (Form Design Tools Design tab | Tools group), scroll down until the On Current property appears, and then click the On Current property.

- Click the Build button (the three dots) to display the Choose Builder dialog box (Figure 8–46).

Figure 8–46

- Click Code Builder in the Choose Builder dialog box, and then click the OK button to display the VBA code generated for the form (Figure 8–47).

Figure 8–47

- Press the TAB key and then type **Name_to_Find = Client_ Number ' Update the combo box** as shown in Figure 8–48.

How would I construct a command like this in my own form?

Begin with the name you assigned to the combo box, followed by an equal sign, and then the name of the control containing the primary key of the table. The portion of the statement following the single quotation mark is a comment describing the purpose of the command. You could simply type the same thing that you see in this command.

Figure 8–48

- Click the Close button for the Microsoft Visual Basic for Applications – Camashaly Design window, and then close the Form property sheet.

- Click the Name to Find combo box and then click the Property Sheet button (Form Design Tools Design tab | Tools group).

- Scroll down until the Tab Stop property appears, click the Tab Stop property, and then click the Tab Stop property box arrow.

- Click No to change the value of the Tab Stop property, which skips over the combo box in the tab sequence, and then close the property sheet.

- Save your changes and then close the form.

Using the Modified Form

The problems with the combo box now are corrected. When you click the Add Record button, an insertion point appears in the Client Number field (Figure 8–49a). When you click the Name to Find box arrow, the list of names is in alphabetical order (Figure 8–49b). After using the Name to Find box to find a client (Figure 8–49c) and clicking the Next button, the Name to Find box is updated with the correct client name (Figure 8–49d).

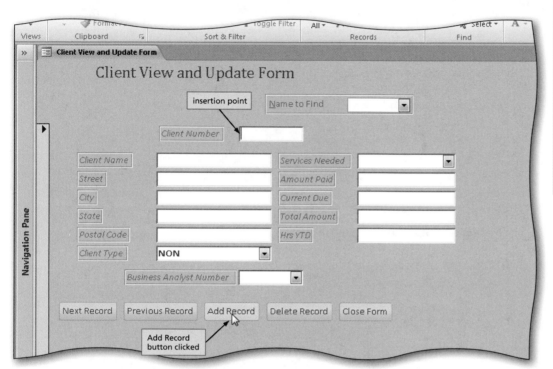

(a) Using the Add Record button

(b) Using the Name to Find box

Figure 8–49

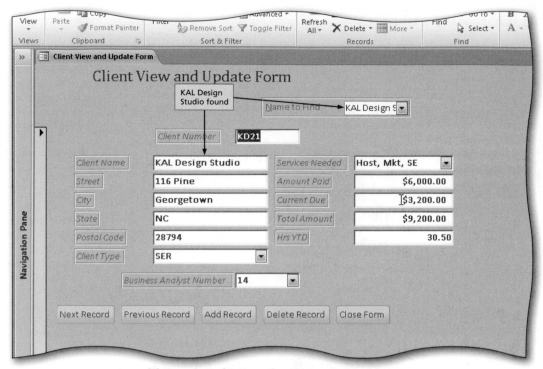

(c) Results of using the Name to Find box

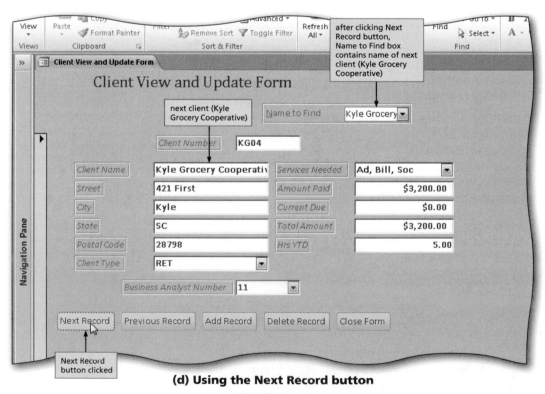

(d) Using the Next Record button

Figure 8–49

Break Point: If you wish to stop working through the chapter at this point, you can quit Access now. You can resume the project at a later time by starting Access, opening the database called Camashaly Design, and continuing to follow the steps from this location forward.

Creating a MultiPage Form

If you have determined that you have more data than will fit conveniently on one screen, you can create a **multipage form**, a form that includes more than a single page. There are two ways to create a multipage form. One way is to insert a page break at the desired location or locations. An alternative approach that produces a nice-looking and easy-to-use multipage form is to insert a tab control. The multiple pages are all within the tab control. To move from one page in the tab control to another, a user simply clicks the desired tab. The tab control shown in Figure 8–2 on page AC 468, for example, has a tab labeled Datasheet that contains a datasheet showing the relevant data. It has a second tab, labeled Charts, that displays the relevant data in two charts.

BTW

Adding Images to Forms
You can include a picture (image) on a form. To insert an image on a form, open the form in Design view or Layout view and click the Insert Image button (Design tab | Controls group) and place the image in the desired position on the form. You also can add images to reports.

To Create the Query

The second form you will create is based on a query. The following steps create the necessary query.

1

- Display the Create tab, and then click the Query Design button (Create tab | Queries group) to create a query.

- Click the Business Analyst table and then click the Add button to add the Business Analyst table to the query.

- Click the Client table and then click the Add button to add the Client table to the query.

- Click the Course Offerings table and then click the Add button to add the Course Offerings table to the query.

- Click the Close button (Show Table dialog box).

- Resize the Business Analyst and Client field lists so as many fields as possible appear (Figure 8–50).

Figure 8–50

- Double-click the Business Analyst Number field from the Business Analyst table and the Client Number field from the Client table.

- Double-click the Course Number and Hours Spent fields from the Course Offerings table.

- Right-click the Field row in the first open column of the design grid to produce a shortcut menu.

- Click Zoom on the shortcut menu to display the Zoom dialog box and then type **Hours Remaining:[Total Hours]-[Hours Spent]** in the Zoom dialog box to enter the expression for the field (Figure 8–51).

Figure 8–51

- Click the OK button and then click the View button (Query Tools Design tab | Results group) to ensure your results are correct.

- Click the Save button on the Quick Access Toolbar and type **Analysts and Course Offerings** as the name of the query (Figure 8–52).

- Click the OK button to save the query.

- Close the query.

Figure 8–52

To Create a Form with a Tab Control

The following step creates a form in Design view that contains a tab control. The form will include two tabs: one that displays a datasheet and another that displays two charts.

1

- If necessary, close the Navigation Pane.

- Display the Create tab.

- Click the Form Design button (Create tab | Forms group) to create a new form in Design view.

- Ensure the selector for the entire form — the box in the upper-left corner of the form — is selected.

- Click the Property Sheet button (Form Design Tools Design tab | Tools group) to display a property sheet.

- With the All tab selected, click the Record Source property, click the arrow that appears, and then click Business Analyst to select the Business Analyst table as the record source.

Figure 8–53

Q&A I see more than one choice that begins with the same letters as Business Analyst. How do I know I am selecting right one?

There are two ways to find out if you are selecting the right choice. You could click one of them to produce an insertion point and then repeatedly press the RIGHT ARROW key to see the remainder of the name. If it is not the correct one, select another. The other way is to expand the width of the property sheet so that it is large enough for the entire names to appear. You do so by dragging the left border further to the left.

- Close the property sheet.

- Click the Add Existing Fields button (Form Design Tools Design tab | Tools group) to display a field list and then drag the Business Analyst Number field to the approximate position shown in Figure 8–53.

- Change the label for the Business Analyst Number field from BA # to Analyst Number.

To Add a Calculated Field to the Form

If you have determined that a calculated field is appropriate for a form, you can create one by using the Text Box tool in the Controls group on the Design tab. Place the text box on the form and then indicate the calculation that is to be performed.

The following steps add a calculated field. In this case, the calculation involves two text fields, First Name and Last Name. The formal term for this type of calculation is **concatenation**, which simply means linking objects together in a series. In this calculation, you will concatenate the first name, a single space, and the last name.

1

- Click the Text Box tool (Form Design Tools Design Tab | Controls group) and then move the mouse pointer, which has changed shape to a small plus symbol accompanied by a text box, to the position shown in Figure 8–54.

Figure 8–54

2

- Click the position shown in Figure 8–54 to place a text box on the report.

- Click in the text box to produce an insertion point.

- Type `=[First Name]&' '& [Last Name]` as the entry in the text box.

- Click the attached label to select it (Figure 8–55).

Figure 8–55

- Press the DELETE key to delete the attached label.

- Resize the Business Analyst Number control to the approximate size shown in Figure 8–56.

- Click the text box to select it, drag it to the position shown in Figure 8–56, and then drag the right sizing handle to the approximate position shown in the figure.

- Close the field list by clicking the Add Existing Fields button (Form Design Tools Design tab | Tools group).

Figure 8–56

To Use Tab Controls to Create a Multipage Form

To use tabs on a form, you need to insert a tab control. The following steps insert a tab control with two tabs: Datasheet and Charts. Users will be able to click the Datasheet tab in the completed form to view course offerings in Datasheet view. Clicking the Charts tab will display two charts representing the same course data as in the Datasheet tab.

- Click the Tab Control tool (Form Design Tools Design Tab | Controls group) and move the mouse pointer to the approximate location shown in Figure 8–57.

Figure 8–57

2

- Click the position shown in Figure 8–57 to place a tab control on the form.

- Click the far left tab and then click the Property Sheet button (Form Design Tools Design tab | Tools group) to display a property sheet.

- Change the value for the Name property to `Datasheet` (Figure 8–58).

Figure 8–58

 Q&A My property sheet looks different. What should I do?

Be sure you clicked the far left tab before displaying the property sheet. The highlight should be within the border of the tab, as shown in the figure.

3

- Click the second tab without closing the property sheet.

- Change the value for the Name property to `Charts`.

- Close the property sheet.

- Save the form using the name, Analyst Course Data.

BTW

Tab Controls
You can change the order of tab controls. To do so, right-click any tab control and click Page Order on the shortcut menu. Use the Move Up and Move Down buttons to change to the desired order.

To Add a Subform

To add a subform to a form, you use the Subform/Subreport tool in the Controls group on the Design tab. Provided the Use Control Wizards button is selected, a wizard will guide you through the process of adding the subform. The following steps place a subform on the Datasheet tab.

1

- Click the Datasheet tab.

- Resize the tab control to the approximate size shown in Figure 8–59 by dragging the appropriate sizing handles.

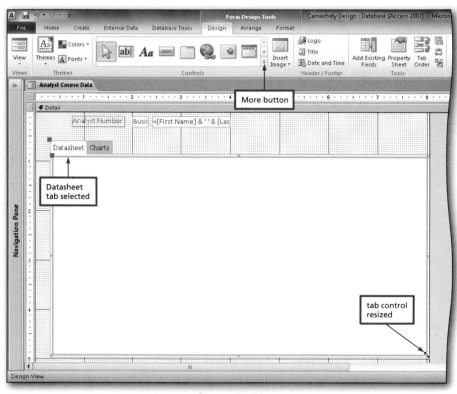

Figure 8–59

2

- Click the More button (Form Design Tools Design tab | Controls group).

- With the Use Control Wizards button selected, click the Subform/ Subreport tool (Form Design Tools Design tab | Controls group) and then move the mouse pointer to the approximate position shown in Figure 8–60.

Figure 8–60

3

- Click the position shown in Figure 8–60 to open the SubForm Wizard.

- Be sure the 'Use existing Tables and Queries' option button is selected.

- Click the Next button to display the next SubForm Wizard screen.

- Click the Tables/Queries box arrow and then click the Analysts and Course Offerings query.

- Click the Add All Fields button (Figure 8–61).

Figure 8–61

4

- Click the Next button.

- Be sure the 'Choose from a list' option button is selected.

- Click the Next button.

- Type **Course Offerings for Analyst** as the name of the subform and then click the Finish button to complete the creation of the subform (Figure 8–62).

5

- Save and then close the Analyst Course Data form.

Figure 8–62

To Modify a Subform

The next task is to modify the subform. The Business Analyst Number field needed to be included in the subform because it is used to link the data in the subform to the data in the main form. It is not supposed to appear in the form, however. In addition, the remaining columns need to be resized to appropriate sizes. The following steps first remove the Business Analyst Number field and then convert to Datasheet view to resize the remaining columns.

- Open the Navigation Pane, right-click the Course Offerings for Analyst form, and then click Design View on the shortcut menu.

- Click the Business Analyst Number control, and then press the DELETE key to delete the control.

- Change the label for the Client Number control from CL # to Client Number.

- Save the subform and close it.

- Right-click the subform in the Navigation Pane and click Open on the shortcut menu.

- Resize each column to best fit the data by double-clicking the right boundary of the column's field selector (Figure 8–63).

- Save the subform and then close it.

Figure 8–63

To Resize the Subform

The following step resizes the subform to the size shown in Figure 8–2a on page AC 468.

- If necessary, open the Navigation Pane, right-click Analyst Course Data and then click Design View on the shortcut menu.

- Close the Navigation Pane.

- Resize the subform to the size shown in Figure 8–64 by dragging the right sizing handle.

Figure 8–64

To Change the Background Color

The following steps change the background color of the form to a light gray.

1 Click anywhere in the Detail section but outside all the controls to select the section.

2 Display the Format tab.

3 Click the Background Color button arrow (Form Design Tools Format tab | Font group) to display a color palette (Figure 8–65).

4 Click the Light Gray 2 color, the first color in the third row under Standard Colors, to change the background color.

Figure 8–65

To Insert Charts

To visually represent data in a table or query, you can create a chart. To insert a chart, use the Chart tool on the Design tab. The Chart Wizard then will ask you to indicate the fields to be included on the chart and the type of chart you want to insert. The following steps insert a chart.

1
- Display the Design tab.
- Click the Charts tab on the tab control.
- Click the More button (Form Design Tools Design tab | Controls group).
- Click the Chart tool.
- Move the pointer to the approximate position shown in Figure 8–66.

Figure 8–66

- Click the position shown in Figure 8–66 to display the Chart Wizard dialog box.

- Click the Queries option button in the Chart Wizard dialog box, click the Analysts and Course Offerings query, and then click the Next button.

- Select the Course Number and Hours Spent fields by clicking them and then clicking the Add Field button (Figure 8–67).

Figure 8–67

3

- Click the Next button.

- Click the Pie chart, the chart in the lower-left corner (Figure 8–68).

🔎 **Experiment**

- Click the other chart types and read the descriptions of chart types in the lower-right corner of the Chart Wizard dialog box. When finished, click the Pie chart in the lower-left corner.

Figure 8–68

4

• Click the Next button (Figure 8–69).

Q&A What do these positions represent? Can I change them?

The field under the chart represents the data that will be summarized by slices of the pie. The other field is used to indicate the series. In this example, the field for the series is the course number, and the sizes of the slices of the pie will represent the sum of the number of hours spent. You can change these by dragging the fields to the desired locations.

Figure 8–69

Q&A These positions make sense for a pie chart. What if I selected a different chart type?

The items on this screen will be relevant to the particular chart type you select. Just as with the pie chart, the correct fields will often be selected automatically. If not, you can drag the fields to the correct locations.

5

• Click the Next button (Figure 8–70).

Q&A The Business Analyst Number field does not appear in my chart. Can I still use it to link the form and the chart?

Yes. Even though the Business Analyst Number does not appear, it is still included in the query on which the chart is based. In fact, it is essential that it is included so that you can link the document (that is, the form) and the chart. Linking the document and the chart ensures that the chart will reflect accurately the data for the correct analyst, that is, the analyst who currently appears in the form.

Figure 8–70

6

- Click the Next button, type **Hours Spent by Course Offering** as the title, and then click the Finish button (Figure 8–71).

Q&A

The data does not look right. What's wrong and what do I need to do to fix it?

The data in the chart is fictitious. The data simply represents the general way the chart will look. When you view the actual form, the data represented in the chart should be correct.

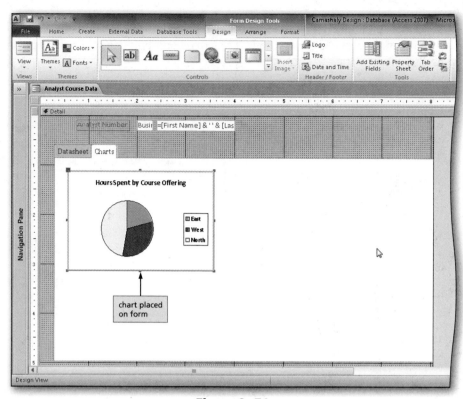

Figure 8–71

7

- Use the techniques shown in Steps 1 through 6 to add a second chart at the position shown in Figure 8–72. In this chart, select Hours Remaining instead of Hours Spent and type **Hours Remaining by Course Offering** as the title of the chart instead of Hours Spent by Course Offering.

- Resize the two charts to the size shown in the figure by clicking the chart and then dragging an appropriate sizing handle.

8

- Save your changes.

- Close the form.

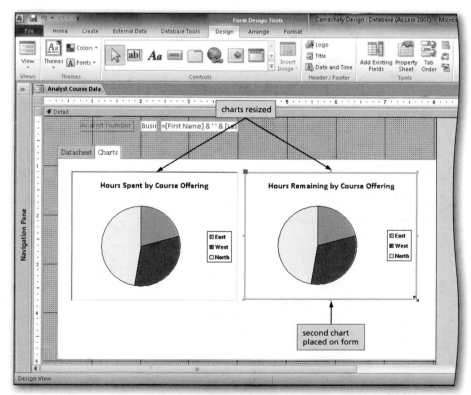

Figure 8–72

To Use the Form

You use this form just like the other forms you have created and used. To move from one tabbed page to another, simply click the desired tab. The corresponding page then will appear. The following steps use the form to view the course data.

1

- Open the Navigation Pane, open the Analyst Course Data form in Form view, and close the Navigation Pane (Figure 8–73).

What is the purpose of the navigation buttons in the subform?

These navigation buttons allow you to move within the records in the subform, that is, within the course offerings for the analyst whose number and name appear at the top of the form.

Figure 8–73

To Modify a Chart Type

When you first create a chart, you specify the chart type. You can later change the type by editing the chart and selecting the Chart Type command. The following steps change the chart type.

1

- Click the Charts tab to display the charts.

- Return to Design view.

- Click the Charts tab to display the charts in Design view (Figure 8–74).

Figure 8–74

2

- Right-click the Hours Spent by Course Offering chart to display a shortcut menu.

Q&A Does it matter where I right-click?
You should right-click within the rectangle but outside any of the items within the rectangle, in other words, in the white space.

Q&A My shortcut menu is very different. What should I do?
Click the View button arrow and then click Design View to ensure that you are viewing the form in Design view and then try again.

- Point to Chart Object on the shortcut menu to display the Chart Object submenu (Figure 8–75).

Figure 8–75

3

- Click Edit on the Chart Object submenu to edit the chart. Access will automatically display the underlying chart data in Datasheet view (Figure 8–76).

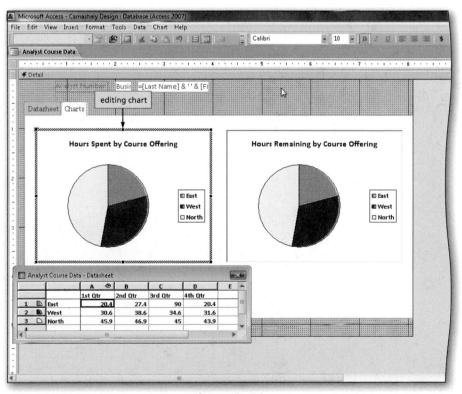

Figure 8–76

4

- Right-click the chart to display the shortcut menu for editing the chart (Figure 8–77).

 Does it matter where I right-click?

You should right-click within the rectangle but outside any of the items within the rectangle, in other words, in the white space.

 What types of changes can I make if I select Format Chart Area?

You can change such things as border style, color, fill effects, and fonts.

 How do I make other changes?

By clicking Chart Options on the shortcut menu, you can change titles, legends, and labels. For 3-D charts, by clicking 3-D View on the shortcut menu, you can change the elevation and rotation of the chart. You can also format specific items on the chart, as you will see in the next section.

Figure 8–77

5

- Click the Chart Type command on the shortcut menu to display the Chart Type dialog box (Figure 8–78).

 What is the relationship between the Chart type and the Chart sub-type?

You can think of Chart types as categories of charts. There are column charts, bar charts, line charts, and so on. Once you have selected a category, the chart sub-types are those charts in that category. If you have selected the Pie chart category, for example, the charts within the category are the ones shown in the list of chart sub-types in Figure 8–78.

Figure 8–78

6

• Click the chart sub-type in the middle of the first row of chart sub-types to select it as the chart sub-type.

 Experiment

• Click each of the chart types and examine the chart sub-types associated with that chart type. When finished, select Pie as the chart type and the sub-type in the middle of the first row as the chart sub-type.

• Click the OK button to change the chart sub-type.

• Click outside the chart and the datasheet to deselect the chart.

• Make the same change to the other chart (Figure 8–79).

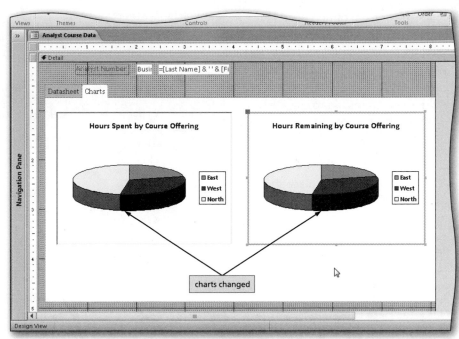

Figure 8–79

To Format a Chart

You can change the border style, color, fill effects, and fonts by using the Format Chart Area command. You can change titles, legends, and labels by using the Chart Options command. You can also format specific portions of a chart by right-clicking the portion you want to format and then clicking the appropriate command on the shortcut menu. The following steps use this technique to move the legend so that it is at the bottom of the chart and then include percentages in the chart.

1

• Right-click the Hours Spent by Course Offering chart to display a shortcut menu, point to Chart Object on the shortcut menu to display the Chart Object submenu, and then click Edit on the Chart Object submenu.

• Right-click the legend to display a shortcut menu, and then click Format Legend on the shortcut menu to display the Format Legend dialog box.

• Click the Placement tab (Figure 8–80).

Figure 8–80

2

- Click the Bottom option button to specify that the legend should appear at the bottom of the chart.

Q&A What other types of changes can I make in this dialog box?

Click the Patterns tab to change such things as border style, color, and fill effects. Click the Font tab to change the font and/or font characteristics.

- Click the OK button to place the legend at the location you selected.

- Right-click the pie chart to display a shortcut menu, and then click Format Data Series on the shortcut menu to display the Format Data Series dialog box.

- Click the Data Labels tab.

- Click the Percentage check box to specify that percentages are to be included (Figure 8–81).

Figure 8–81

Q&A I see a Patterns tab just as with the legend, but how would I use the Options tab? Also, does the fact that these are check boxes rather than option buttons mean that I can select more than one?

Use the Options tab to indicate whether the color is to vary by slice and to specify the angle of the first slice in the pie. Because these are check boxes, you can select as many as you want. Selecting too many can clutter the chart, however.

Q&A These options make sense for a pie chart, but what about other chart types?

The options that you see will vary from one chart type to another. They will be relevant for the selected chart type.

3

- Click the OK button to include percentages on the chart.

- Click outside the chart and the datasheet to deselect the chart.

- Make the same change to the other chart.

- Click the View button and then click the Charts tab to display the modified charts (Figure 8–82).

4

- Save and then close the form.

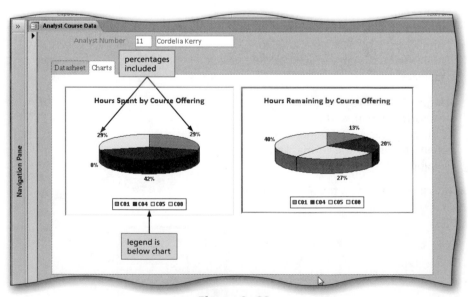

Figure 8–82

Using the Arrange Tab on Forms and Reports

In earlier chapters, you worked with control layouts in forms and reports. In a control layout, the data is aligned either horizontally or vertically. You can perform a variety of operations on the layout as a unit. The two types of layouts are stacked layouts, which are most commonly used in forms, and tabular layouts, which are most commonly used in reports (Figure 8–83).

(a) Stacked Layout

(b) Tabular Layout
Figure 8– 83

If you are creating a desktop database that will only be opened in Access, you do not need to use control layouts, so all the techniques you have learned in creating forms like the one you created earlier in this chapter are available. If, on the other hand, you plan to publish the database to the Web and use it in a browser, you must use layouts on all forms and reports. Forms or reports that do not use layouts cannot be used in a browser.

Thus, working with control layouts, as you have done earlier in the text, is very important. In working with control layouts, there are many functions you can perform using the Arrange tab. You can insert rows and columns, delete rows and columns, split and merge cells, and move rows. You also can change margins, which affects spacing within cells, and padding, which affects spacing between rows and columns. You can split a layout into two layouts and move layouts. Finally, you can anchor controls so that they maintain the same distance between the control and the anchor position as the form or report is resized. Refer to Table 4–1 on page AC 230 for more information about the functions available on the Arrange tab.

Creating or Removing a Layout

If you create a form using the Form button (Create tab | Forms group), Access automatically creates a stacked layout. If you create a report using the Report button (Create tab | Reports group), Access automatically creates a tabular layout. In other cases, you can create a layout using the Arrange tab. There are times when you no longer want controls to be in a control layout. If so, you can remove the layout.

To Create a Layout for a Form or Report

To create a layout in either a form or report, you would use the following steps.

1. Select all the controls that you want to place in a layout.
2. Click the Stacked button (Arrange tab | Table group) to create a stacked layout or the Tabular button (Arrange tab | Table group) to create a tabular layout.

To Remove a Layout for a Form or Report

To remove a layout from either a form or report, you would use the following steps.

1. Right-click any control in the layout you want to remove to produce a shortcut menu.
2. Point to Layout on the shortcut menu and then click Remove Layout on the submenu to remove the layout.

Using Undo

When making changes with the Arrange tab buttons, it is not uncommon to make a change that you did not intend. Sometimes taking appropriate action to reverse the change can prove difficult. If so, remember that you can undo the change by clicking the Undo button on the Quick Access Toolbar. It is also a good idea to save your work frequently. That way, you can always close the form or report without saving. When you reopen the form or report, it will not have any of your most recent changes.

Inserting Rows and Columns

You can insert a blank row either above or below a selected row (Figure 8–84). You can then fill in the row by either typing a value or dragging a field from a field list. In a similar fashion, you can insert a blank column either to the left or right of a selected column.

(a) Selecting a Row

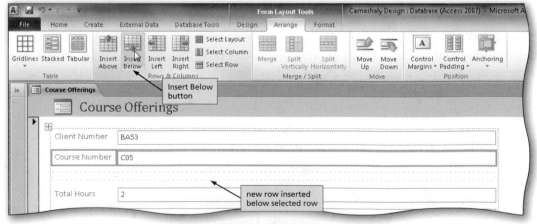

(b) Inserting a Row

Figure 8–84

To Insert a Row

You would use the following steps to insert a blank row.

1. Select any control in the row above or below which you want to insert a new row.
2. Click the Select Row button (Arrange tab | Rows & Columns group) to select the row.
3. Click the Insert Above button (Arrange tab | Rows & Columns group) to insert a blank row above the selected row or the Insert Below button (Arrange tab | Rows & Columns group) to insert a blank row below the selected row.

As you have seen earlier in the text, you also can insert a row containing a field by simply dragging the field from the field list to the desired location.

To Insert a Column

You would use the following steps to insert a new column.

1. Select any control in the column to the right or left of which you want to insert a new column.
2. Click the Select Column button (Arrange tab | Rows & Columns group) to select the column.
3. Click the Insert Left button (Arrange tab | Rows & Columns group) to insert a blank column to the left of the selected column or the Insert Right button (Arrange tab | Rows & Columns group) to insert a blank column to the right of the selected column.

Deleting Rows and Columns

You can delete any unwanted row or column from a control layout.

To Delete a Row

You would use the following steps to delete a row.

1. Click any control in the row you want to delete.
2. Click Select Row (Arrange tab | Rows & Columns group).
3. Press the DELETE key to delete the row.

To Delete a Column

You would use the following steps to delete a column.

1. Click any control in the column you want to delete.
2. Click Select Column (Arrange tab | Rows & Columns group).
3. Press the DELETE key to delete the column.

Splitting and Merging Cells

You can split a cell into two cells either horizontally, as shown in Figure 8–85, or vertically. You can then enter contents into the new cell. For example, in Figure 8–85, you could type text into the new cell that gives information about client numbers. You can also merge two cells into one.

Figure 8–85

To Split a Cell

To split a cell, you would use the following steps.

1. Click the cell to be split.
2. Click the Split Vertically button (Arrange tab | Merge / Split group) to split the selected cell vertically or the Split Horizontally button (Arrange tab | Merge / Split group) to split the selected cell horizontally.

To Merge Cells

You would use the following steps to merge cells.

1. Select the first cell to be merged.
2. While holding the CTRL key down, click all the other cells to be merged.
3. Click the Merge button (Arrange tab | Merge / Split group) to merge the cells.

Moving Cells

You can move a cell in a layout by dragging it to its new position. Most often, however, you will not want to move individual cells, but rather whole rows (Figure 8–86). You can move a row by selecting the row and then dragging it to the new position or you can use the Move buttons on the Arrange tab.

(a) Row Selected

BTW

Gridlines
You also can add gridlines to a form. To do so, select the control or controls for which you want to add gridlines, then click the Gridlines button (Form Layout Tools Arrange tab | Table group). When the Gridlines menu appears, select the desired option. You also can change the color, border style, and width of gridlines using the Gridlines menu.

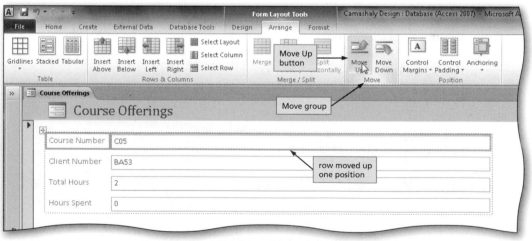

(b) Row Moved

Figure 8–86

To Move Rows Using the Move Buttons

You would use the following steps to move a row.

1. Select any cell in the row to be moved.
2. Click the Select Row button (Arrange tab | Rows & Columns group) to select the entire row.

3. Click the Move Up button (Arrange tab | Move group) to move the selected row up one row or the Move Down button (Arrange tab | Move group) to move the selected row down one row.

Margins and Padding

You can change the spacing within a layout by changing the control margins and the control padding. The control margins, which you change with the Control Margins button, affect the spacing around the text inside a control. Figure 8–87 shows the various options as well as samples of two of the options.

(a) Changing Control Margins

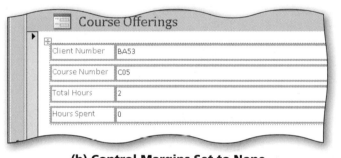

(b) Control Margins Set to None

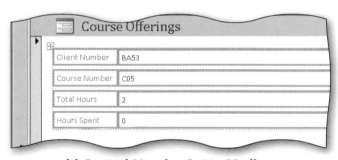

(c) Control Margins Set to Medium

Figure 8–87

The control padding, which you change with the Control Padding button, affects the spacing around the outside of a control. The options are the same as those for control margins. Figure 8–88 shows samples of two of the options.

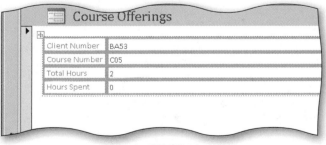

(a) Control Padding Set to None

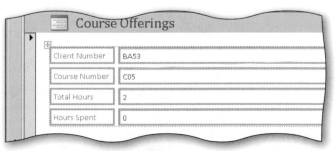

(b) Control Padding Set to Medium

Figure 8–88

To Change Control Margins

You would use the following steps to change a control's margins.

1. Select any cell in the layout.
2. Click the Select Layout button (Arrange tab | Rows & Columns group) to select the entire layout. (You also could have selected the layout by clicking the layout selector.)
3. Click the Control Margins button (Arrange tab | Position group) to display the available margin settings.
4. Click the desired margin setting.

To Change Control Padding

The following steps would change control padding.

1. Select the layout.
2. Click the Control Padding button (Arrange tab | Position group) to display the available padding settings.
3. Click the desired padding setting.

Although you can make the margin and padding changes for individual controls, it is much more common to do so for the entire layout. Doing so gives a more uniform appearance to the layout.

Splitting a Layout

You can split a single layout into two separate layouts (Figure 8–89) and then modify each layout separately. They can be moved to different locations and formatted differently.

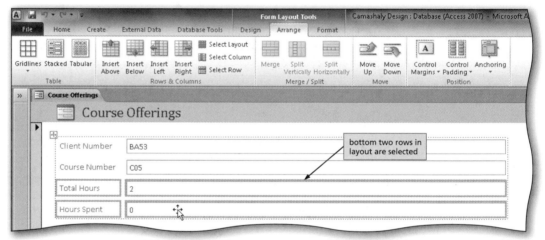

(a) Rows to be Moved to New Layout Selected

(b) Rows Moved to New Layout

Figure 8–89

TO SPLIT A LAYOUT

To split a layout, you would use the following steps.

1. Select all the cells that you want to move to a new layout.
2. Click the Stacked button (Arrange tab | Table group) to place the cells in a stacked layout or the Tabular button (Arrange tab | Table group) to place the cells in a tabular layout.

Moving a Layout

You can move a layout to a different location on the form (Figure 8–90).

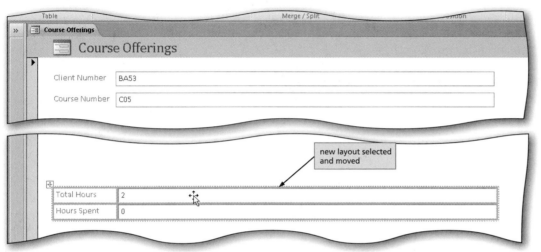

Figure 8–90

TO MOVE A LAYOUT

You would use the following steps to move a layout.

1. Click any cell in the layout to be moved and then click the Select Layout button (Arrange tab | Rows & Columns group) to select the layout.
2. Drag the layout to the new location.

Anchoring Controls

The Anchoring button allows you to tie (anchor) controls to a section or to other controls so that they maintain the same distance between the control and the anchor position as the form or report is resized. To anchor the controls you have selected, you use the Anchoring gallery (Figure 8–91).

Figure 8–91

The Top Left, Top Right, Bottom Left, and Bottom Right options anchor the control in the indicated position on the form. The other five operations also stretch the controls in the indicated direction.

TO ANCHOR CONTROLS

The following steps would be used to anchor controls.

1. Select the control or controls to be anchored.
2. Click the Anchoring button (Arrange tab | Position group) to produce the Anchoring gallery.
3. Select the desired Anchoring option from the Anchoring gallery.

The best way to see the effect of anchoring is to display objects in overlapping windows rather than tabbed documents. With overlapping windows, you can resize the object by dragging the border of the object. Anchored objects keep their same relative position (Figure 8–92).

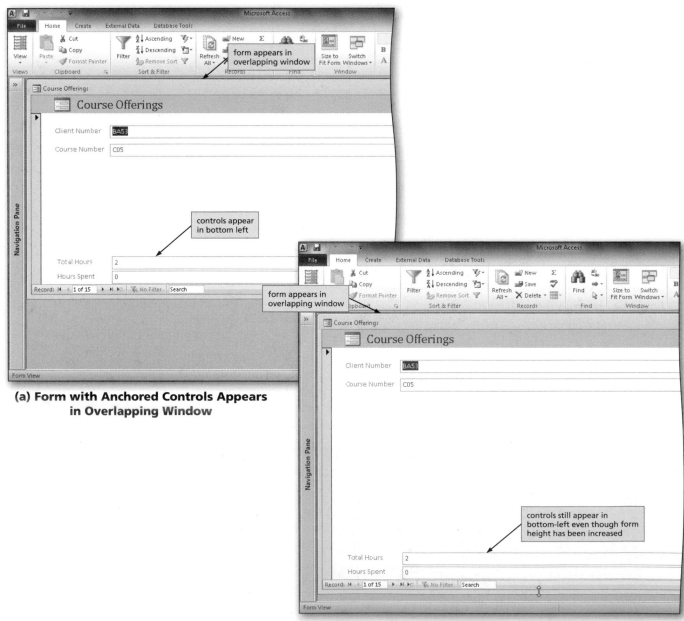

**(a) Form with Anchored Controls Appears
in Overlapping Window**

**(b) Resized Form with Anchored Controls Appears in
Overlapping Window**

Figure 8–92

If you want to display objects in overlapping windows, you have to modify the appropriate Access option.

TO DISPLAY OBJECTS IN OVERLAPPING WINDOWS

You would use the following steps to overlap windows.

1. Click File on the Ribbon to open the Backstage view.
2. Click Options to display the Access Options dialog box.
3. Click Current Database to display the Current Database options.
4. In the Application Options area, click the Overlapping Windows option button.
5. Click the OK button to close the Access Options dialog box.
6. For the changes to take effect, you will need to close and then reopen the database.

You use a similar process to return to displaying objects in tabbed documents.

TO DISPLAY OBJECTS IN TABBED DOCUMENTS

You would use the following steps to display tabbed documents.

1. Click File on the Ribbon to open the Backstage view.
2. Click Options to display the Access Options dialog box.
3. Click Current Database to display the Current Database options.
4. In the Application Options area, click the Tabbed Documents option button.
5. Click the OK button to close the Access Options dialog box.
6. For the changes to take effect, you will need to close and then reopen the database.

To Quit Access

The following steps quit Access.

1 Click the Close button on the right side of the title bar to quit Access.

2 If a Microsoft Access dialog box appears, click the Save button to save any changes made to the object since the last save.

BTW

Quick Reference
For a table that lists how to complete the tasks covered in this book using the mouse, Ribbon, shortcut menu, and keyboard, see the Quick Reference Summary at the back of this book, or visit the Access 2010 Quick Reference Web page (scsite.com/ac2010/qr).

Chapter Summary

In this chapter you have learned to create a form in Design view, add a combo box that displays information from a related table as well as a combo box that is used to find records on a form, format controls and use the Format Painter, add command buttons to a form, modify a button and a combo box, add a calculated field to a form, use a tab control to create a multipage form, add and modify a subform, insert charts, change chart types, and format charts. You also learned how to use the Arrange tab on forms and reports. The items listed below include all the new Access skills you have learned in this chapter.

1. Create a Form in Design View (AC 472)
2. Add Fields to the Form Design (AC 473)
3. Add a Combo Box that Selects Values from a Related Table (AC 475)
4. Change the Background Color (AC 480)
5. Format a Control (AC 481)
6. Use the Format Painter (AC 482)
7. View the Form (AC 483)
8. Add a Title and Expand the Form Header Section (AC 484)
9. Add Command Buttons to a Form (AC 485)
10. Add a Combo Box that is Used to Find a Record (AC 488)
11. Place a Rectangle (AC 490)
12. Use the Add Record Button (AC 491)
13. Use the Combo Box (AC 492)
14. Modify the Macro for the Add Record Button (AC 494)
15. Modify the Combo Box (AC 497)
16. Create the Query (AC 501)
17. Create a Form with a Tab Control (AC 503)
18. Add a Calculated Field to the Form (AC 503)
19. Use Tab Controls to Create a Multipage Form (AC 505)
20. Add a Subform (AC 506)
21. Modify a Subform (AC 509)
22. Resize the Subform (AC 509)

If you have a SAM 2010 user profile, your instructor may have assigned an autogradable version of this assignment. If so, log into the SAM 2010 Web site at www.cengage.com/sam2010 to download the instruction and start files.

Learn It Online

Test your knowledge of chapter content and key terms.

Instructions: To complete the Learn It Online exercises, start your browser, click the Address bar, and then enter the Web address **scsite.com/ac2010/learn**. When the Access 2010 Learn It Online page is displayed, click the link for the exercise you want to complete and then read the instructions.

Chapter Reinforcement TF, MC, and SA
A series of true/false, multiple choice, and short answer questions that test your knowledge of the chapter content.

Flash Cards
An interactive learning environment where you identify chapter key terms associated with displayed definitions.

Practice Test
A series of multiple choice questions that test your knowledge of chapter content and key terms.

Who Wants To Be a Computer Genius?
An interactive game that challenges your knowledge of chapter content in the style of a television quiz show.

Wheel of Terms
An interactive game that challenges your knowledge of chapter key terms in the style of the television show *Wheel of Fortune*.

Crossword Puzzle Challenge
A crossword puzzle that challenges your knowledge of key terms presented in the chapter.

Apply Your Knowledge

Reinforce the skills and apply the concepts you learned in this chapter.

Creating a Multipage Form for the Babbage CPA Firm Database
Instructions: Start Access. If you are using the Microsoft Access 2010 Comprehensive text, open the Babbage CPA Firm database that you used in Chapter 7. Otherwise, see your instructor for information on accessing the files required in this book.

Perform the following tasks:

1. Create a query that joins the Bookkeeper, Client, and Accounts tables. Include the Bookkeeper Number field from the Bookkeeper table, the Client Number field from the Client table, and the Service Date and Hours Worked fields from the Accounts table. Sort the query in ascending order by Bookkeeper Number, Client Number, and Service Date. Save the query as Bookkeepers and Accounts.

2. Create the Bookkeeper Account Data form shown in Figure 8–93. The Datasheet tab displays a subform listing information about services for clients of the bookkeeper (Figure 8–93a). Data for the subform is based on the Bookkeepers and Accounts query. Data for the Chart tab also is based on the Bookkeepers and Accounts query and displays the total number of hours worked for each client (Figure 8–93b).

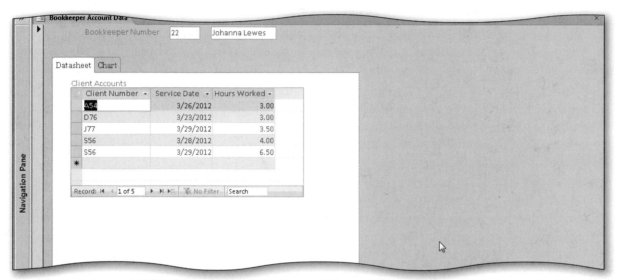

(a) Bookkeeper Account Data with Datasheet Tab Selected

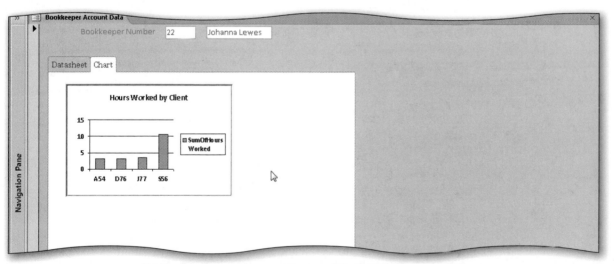

(b) Bookkeeper Account Data with Chart Tab Selected

Figure 8–93

3. Submit the revised database in the format specified by your instructor.

Extend Your Knowledge

Extend the skills you learned in this chapter and experiment with new skills. You may need to use Help to complete the assignment.

Modifying Forms

Instructions: Copy the Camashaly Design database and rename the database to Chapter 8 Camashaly Design. Start Access and open the Chapter 8 Camashaly Design database.

Perform the following tasks:
1. Open the Analyst Course Data Form in Design view. Add a title to the form and insert the current date in the form header.
2. Add a third tab control to the form. Name the tab control, Clients.
3. Add a subform to the Clients tab control. The Client table is the basis of the subform. Display the Client Number, Client Name, Client Type, and Total Amount fields in a datasheet on the subform. Accept the default name for the subform and delete the label that appears above the datasheet. Resize the datasheet so that all columns appear in the control.
4. Open the Client Master Form in Design view. Change the font color of the form title to Dark Red and format the title as bold. Add a background image to the form. You can create your own image or use one of the sample pictures included with Microsoft Access. (Hint: See the BTW on page AC 485 for assistance with this task.)
5. Open the Client Financial Form in Layout view. Horizontally split the control that displays data for the Client Number field. Type Client Number in the new cell. Change the control margins to narrow and the control padding to narrow, and the anchoring to top-left. Use the Move Up button to move the Current Due field above the Amount Paid field. Add an image to the form. You can create your own image or use one of the sample pictures included with Microsoft Access. (*Hint:* See the BTW on page AC 501 for assistance with this task.)
6. Submit the revised database in the format specified by your instructor.

Make It Right

Analyze a database and correct all errors and/or improve the design.

Correcting Form Design Errors

Instructions: Start Access. Open the YogaYoga database. See the inside back cover of this book for instructions on downloading the Data Files for Students, or contact your instructor for more information about accessing the required files.

The YogaYoga database contains data about a company that conducts yoga workshops. The owner of the company has created the form shown in Figure 8–94, but there are a few problems. The caption for the form should be Client View and Update Form. The name in the Name to Find combo box should change when the Next Record navigation button is clicked. Users should not be able to tab through the Name to Find combo box. Finally, the owner of the company would like you to place a rectangle around the Name to Find combo box and apply the Raised special effect.

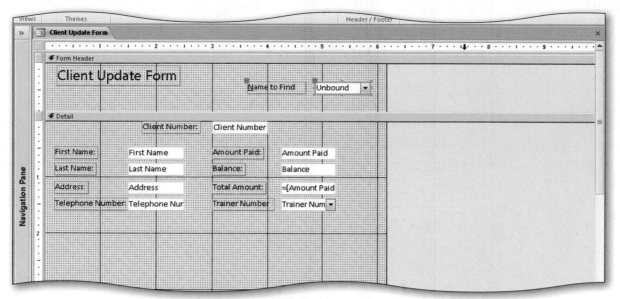

Figure 8-94

Correct these errors and submit the revised database in the format specified by your instructor.

In the Lab

Design, create, modify, and/or use a database following the guidelines, concepts, and skills presented in this chapter. Labs are listed in order of increasing difficulty.

Lab 1: Applying Advanced Form Techniques to the ECO Clothesline Database

Problem: ECO Clothesline needs a form for the Customer table that will allow users to update data in the table. ECO also needs a form to display open orders data for sales reps.

Instructions: If you are using the Microsoft Access 2010 Comprehensive text, open the ECO Clothesline database that you used in Chapter 7. Otherwise, see your instructor for information on accessing the files required in this book.

Perform the following tasks:
1. Create a query that includes the Sales Rep Number field from the Sales Rep table, the Customer Number field from the Customer table and the Order Number and Amount fields from the Open Orders table. Sort the query in ascending order by Sales Rep Number, Customer Number, and Order Number. Save the query as Sales Reps and Orders.
2. Create the form shown in Figure 8-95. Total Amount is a calculated control and is the sum of the Balance and Amount Paid amounts. Format the Total Amount control as Currency with two decimal places. (*Hint:* Use the property sheet for the control.) The form includes command buttons, a combo box for the Sales Rep Number field, and a combo box to search for customers by name. Be sure to sort the customer names in ascending order, place a rectangle around the combo box, and update the combo box. The user should not be able to tab to the combo box. When the Add Record button is clicked, the insertion point should be in the Customer Number field. The form is similar in style to the form shown in Figure 8-1 on page AC 466.

Continued >

In the Lab *continued*

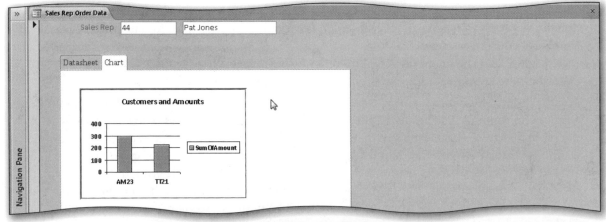

Figure 8–95

3. Create the Sales Rep Order Data form shown in Figure 8–96. The subform that appears in the Datasheet tab uses the Sales Reps and Orders query (Figure 8–96a). The chart that appears in the Chart tab uses the same query (Figure 8–96b).

(a) Sales Rep Order Data with Datasheet Tab Selected

(b) Sales Rep Order Data with Chart Tab Selected

Figure 8–96

4. Submit the revised database in the format specified by your instructor.

In the Lab

Lab 2: Applying Advanced Form Techniques to the Walburg Energy Alternatives Database

Problem: The management of the Walburg Energy Alternatives store needs a form that displays item information. The form should display the total cost of items on hand. It also should include command buttons to perform common operations, a combo box to search for items by description, and a combo box for vendor code. They also need a form that displays vendor information as well as items on order and all items associated with a vendor.

Instructions: If you are using the Microsoft Access 2010 Comprehensive text, open the Walburg Energy Alternatives database that you used in Chapter 7. Otherwise, see your instructor for information on accessing the files required in this book.

Perform the following tasks:

1. Create the Item View and Update Form shown in Figure 8–97. The form includes command buttons, a drop-down box (combo box) for the Vendor Code field, and a combo box to search for items by name. Be sure to sort the item names in ascending order, place a rectangle around the combo box, and update the combo box. The user should not be able to tab to the combo box. When the Add Record button is clicked, the insertion point should be in the Item Number field. The form is similar in style to that shown in Figure 8–1 on page AC 466.

Figure 8–97

2. Create a query that includes the Vendor Code field from the Vendor table, the Item Number and Description fields from the Item table, and the Number Ordered and Date Ordered fields from the Reorder table. Sort the query by Vendor Code, Item Number, and Date Ordered. Save the query as Vendors and Orders.

3. Create the Vendor Orders Data form shown in Figure 8–98. The On Order tab (Figure 8–98a) uses the Vendors and Orders query for the subform. The In Stock tab (Figure 8–98b) uses the Item table for the subform. Note that the labels for Vendor Code and Vendor Name have been changed and that there is a title on the form. The form's title is bold. Use red as the font for the labels with a font weight of bold and dark blue as the font for the text boxes with a font weight of semi-bold. You can use the Format Painter to copy formatting for text boxes and labels.

Continued >

In the Lab *continued*

(a) Vendor Orders Data with On Order Tab Selected

(b) Vendor Orders Data with In Stock Tab Selected

Figure 8–98

4. Submit the revised database in the format specified by your instructor.

In the Lab

Lab 3: Applying Advanced Form Techniques to the Philamar Training Database

Problem: Philamar Training needs a form that displays client information. The form should include command buttons to perform common operations, a combo box to search for clients by name, and a combo box for the Trainer Number field. The company also needs a form that displays trainer information as well as information about classes.

Instructions: If you are using the Microsoft Access 2010 Comprehensive text, open the Philamar Training database that you used in Chapter 7. Otherwise, see your instructor for information on accessing the files required in this book. Submit the revised database in the format specified by your instructor.

Instructions Part 1: Create a Client View and Update Form that is similar in style and appearance to the form shown in Figure 8–1 on page AC 466. The form should include a combo box to search for clients by name and a combo box for the Trainer Number field. Include command buttons to go to the next record, go to the previous record, add records, and delete records. Place pictures on the command buttons instead of text using the picture option in the Command Button Wizard. Be sure to sort the client names in ascending order, place a rectangle around the combo box, and update the combo box. The user should not be able to tab to the combo box. When the Add Record button is clicked, the insertion point should be in the Client Number field.

Instructions Part 2: Create a query that joins the Trainer, Client, and Class Offerings tables. Include the trainer number, client number, class code, and hours spent in the query. Create a calculated field, Hours Remaining, that subtracts Hours Spent from Total Hours. Sort the query by trainer number, client number, and class code. Save the query as Trainers and Class Offerings.

Instructions Part 3: Create the Trainer Data form shown in Figure 8–99. This form uses the query you created in Part 2. The Datasheet tab includes all fields in the query except Trainer Number. (*Hint:* Delete this field after you add the subform.)

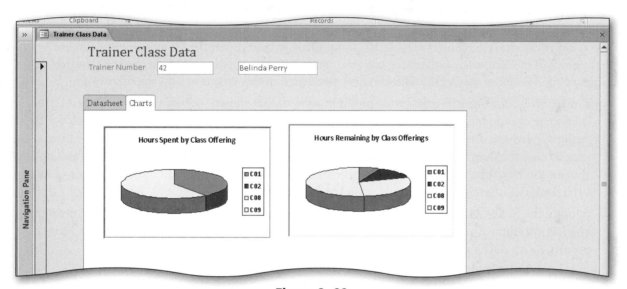

Figure 8–99

Cases and Places

Apply your creative thinking and problem solving skills to design and implement a solution.

1: Applying Advanced Form Techniques to the Chamber of Commerce Database

Academic

If you are using the Microsoft Access 2010 Comprehensive text, open the Chamber of Commerce database that you used in Chapter 7. Otherwise, see your instructor for more information about accessing the required files. As part of your internship, you worked temporarily as an ad rep. Based on that experience as well as the knowledge you have gained at school, you have suggested to the Chamber of Commerce that they add some forms to the database. Use the concepts and techniques presented in this chapter to do the following:

a. Create an Advertiser Master Form that is similar in style to that shown in Figure 8–1 on page AC 466. The form should include a combo box to search for advertisers by name and a combo box for the Ad Rep Number field. Include command buttons to add records, delete records, and close the form. Be sure to sort the advertiser names in ascending order, place a rectangle around the

Continued >

combo box, and update the combo box. The user should not be able to tab to the combo box. When the Add Record button is clicked, the insertion point should be in the Advertiser Number field.

b. Create a query that joins the Ad Rep table, the Advertiser table, and the Active Accounts table. Include the Ad Rep Number, Advertiser Number, Advertiser Name, Ad Month, and Category Code fields. Sort the query by Ad Rep Number, Advertiser Number, and Ad Month.

c. Create an Ad Rep Account Data form that is similar in style to that shown in Figure 8–2 on page AC 468. The form should have two tabs. Each tab will have a subform. The data for the first tab comes from the query created in Step b. The second tab should have a subform that displays a datasheet based on the Advertiser table and includes the Advertiser Number, Advertiser Name, and Advertiser Type fields.

Submit the revised database in the format specified by your instructor.

2: Applying Advanced Form Techniques to the Consignment Database

Personal

If you are using the Microsoft Access 2010 Comprehensive text, open the Consignment database that you used in Chapter 7. Otherwise, see your instructor for more information about accessing the required files. Use the concepts and techniques presented in this chapter to do the following:

a. Create an Item Master Form that is similar in style to that shown in Figure 8–1 on page AC 466. The form should include a combo box to search for items by description and a combo box for the Seller Code field. Include command buttons to add records, delete records, and close the form. Be sure to sort the description in ascending order, place a rectangle around the combo box, and update the combo box. The user should not be able to tab to the combo box. When the Add Record button is clicked, the insertion point should be in the Item Number field.

b. Modify the Seller Master Form by concatenating the seller first name and last name and changing the form so the name appears next to the seller code. Add command buttons to move to the next record, move to the previous record, and close the form.

Submit the revised database in the format specified by your instructor.

3: Applying Advanced Form Techniques to the Senior Care Database

Professional

If you are using the Microsoft Access 2010 Comprehensive text, open the Senior Care database that you used in Chapter 7. Otherwise, see your instructor for more information about accessing the required files. Use the concepts and techniques presented in this chapter to do the following:

a. Create a Client Master Form that is similar in style and appearance to the form shown in Figure 8–1a on page AC 466. The form should include a combo box to search for clients by name and a combo box for the Helper Number field. Include command buttons to go to the next record, go to the previous record, add records, delete records, and close the form. Be sure to sort the client names in ascending order and update the combo box. The user should not be able to tab to the combo box. When the Add Record button is clicked, the insertion point should be in the Client Number field.

b. Create a query that joins the Helper, Client, and Services tables. Include the Helper Number field from the Helper table, the Client Number field from the Client table, and the Service Date and Hours Worked fields from the Services table. Sort the query in ascending order by helper number, Client Number, and Service Date. Save the query.

c. Create a form for the Helper table that is similar to the form shown in Figure 8–2a on page 468. The form should have two tabs; a Datasheet tab and a Chart tab. The Datasheet tab displays a subform listing information about services for clients of the helper. Data for the subform is based on the query you created in Step b. Data for the Chart tab also is based on the query created in Step b.

Submit the revised database in the format specified by your instructor.

9 | Macros, Navigation Forms, PivotTables, and PivotCharts

Objectives

You will have mastered the material in this project when you can:

- Create and modify macros and submacros
- Create a menu form with command buttons
- Create a menu form with option groups
- Create datasheet forms and user interface (UI) macros
- Create navigation forms

- Create data macros
- Create a PivotTable
- Change properties in a PivotTable
- Use a PivotTable
- Create a PivotChart and add a legend
- Change properties in a PivotChart
- Use a PivotChart

9 | Macros, Navigation Forms, PivotTables, and PivotCharts

Introduction

Q&As

For a complete list of the Q&As found in many of the step-by-step sequences in this book, visit the Access 2010 Q&A Web page (scsite.com/ac2010/qa).

In this chapter, you will learn how to create and test macros. You will use a menu form with command buttons as well as a menu form with an option group. You also will create and use user interface (UI) macros in forms. Camashaly Design requires a navigation form that will allow users to open forms and reports simply by clicking appropriate tabs and buttons. You will learn about the use of data macros for ensuring that updates to the database are valid. Finally, you will create and use both a PivotTable and a PivotChart to organize and display data.

Project — Macros, Navigation Forms, PivotTables, and PivotCharts

The owners of Camashaly Design have heard about navigation forms that enable users to access forms and reports by simply clicking tabs and buttons. A **navigation form** like the one shown in Figure 9–1a is a form that includes tabs to display forms and reports. This navigation form contains several useful features. With the Client tab selected, you can click the client number on any row to see the data for the selected client displayed in the Client View and Update Form (Figure 9–1b). The form does not appear in a tabbed sheet, the way tables, queries, forms, and reports normally do. Rather, it appears as a **pop-up form**, a form that stays on top of other open objects, even when another object is active. Clicking the Business Analyst tab displays business analyst data. As with clients, clicking the business analyst number on any record displays data for that analyst in a pop-up form. Clicking the Forms tab in the Camashaly Design navigation form displays buttons for each of the available forms (Figure 9–1c). You can open the desired form by clicking the appropriate button. Clicking the Reports tab displays an option group for displaying reports (Figure 9–1d). You can preview or export any of the reports one at a

BTWs

For a complete list of the BTWs found in the margins of this book, visit the Access 2010 BTW Web page (scsite.com/ac2010/btw).

(a) Navigation Form for Camashaly Design

Figure 9–1

(b) Clicking a Client Number in the Navigation Form Displays the Client Data in the Client View and Update Form

(c) Forms Tab

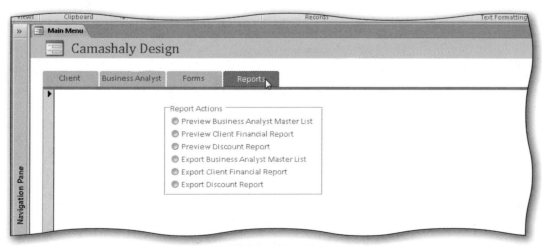

(d) Reports Tab

Figure 9–1

time by clicking the corresponding option button. Camashaly would like such a navigation form because they believe it will improve the user-friendliness of the database, thereby improving employee satisfaction and efficiency.

Before creating the navigation form, Camashaly will create **macros**, which are collections of actions designed to carry out specific tasks. To perform the actions in a macro, you run the macro. When a macro is run, Access will execute the various steps, called **actions**, in the order indicated by the macro. The navigation form macros are run by clicking certain buttons in the form.

Chapter 2 showed how to create a crosstab query, which is a query that calculates a statistic (for example, sum, average, or count) for data that is grouped by two different types of information. A PivotTable is similar to a crosstab query. The PivotTable in Figure 9–2a, displays the sum of hours spent and hours remaining, grouped by course number and analyst number. Unlike a crosstab, however, a PivotTable is dynamic, a feature that appeals to Camashaly. By clicking the plus or minus signs, Camashaly can expand and contract the level of detail that appears in the table. They can dynamically filter the data so that only certain courses or analysts are included. They can even use additional fields to filter the data. For example, they could specify that the data should only reflect courses offered to certain clients. Finally, they can change the organization. They might prefer to reverse the roles of the rows and columns, having the rows represent analysts and the columns represent courses. Accomplishing this is a simple matter of dragging the fields to the desired positions.

They can represent the same data graphically by using a PivotChart like the one in Figure 9–2b. In this particular chart, the colors of the sections of the bars represent the different courses, as indicated by the legend on the right of the chart. Across the bottom of the chart are the analysts' numbers. The bars represent the hours spent or hours remaining for the analyst. The total bar, ignoring colors, would thus represent the total hours spent or remaining by the analyst. Unlike a regular chart, the PivotChart has the same dynamic capabilities as a PivotTable. You can change to a different chart type, you can reverse the roles of the rows and columns, and you can filter data with the same ease you can in a PivotTable.

PivotTables and PivotCharts are normally associated with Microsoft Excel. You could always export data from an Access database to Excel and then use Excel to create a PivotTable or PivotChart. Having PivotTable and PivotChart capabilities within Access, however, means that you do not have to go through that process.

Course Number ▾		Business Analyst Number ▾						Grand Total	
		11		14		27			
		Spent	Remaining	Spent	Remaining	Spent	Remaining	Spent	Remaining
C01		6	2	4	4			10	6
C02						2	2	2	2
C03				0	6	3	3	3	9
C04		9	3			6	6	15	9
C05		0	4			1	1	1	5
C06						4	4	4	4
C07				4	4			4	4
C08		6	6					6	6
Grand Total		21	15	8	14	16	16	45	45

(a) PivotTable for Analysts and Course Offerings Query

Figure 9–2

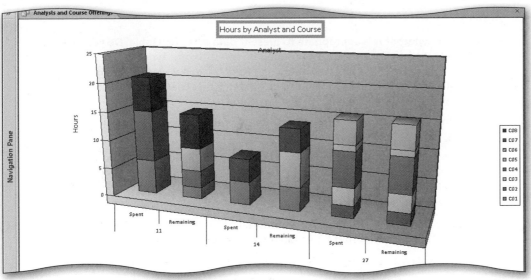

(b) PivotChart for Analysts and Course Offerings Query
Figure 9–2

Overview

As you read through this chapter, you will learn how to create macros, navigation forms, PivotTables, and PivotCharts by performing these general tasks:

- Create a macro containing submacros.
- Create a menu form with command buttons.
- Create a menu form with an option group and create a macro for the option group.
- Create a datasheet form and create user interface (UI) macros for the form.
- Create a navigation form and add tabs to the navigation form.
- Create a data macro.
- Create and use a PivotTable.
- Create and use a PivotChart.

Plan
Ahead

Macro, Navigation Form, PivotTable, and PivotChart Design Guidelines
When creating macros, navigation forms, PivotTables, and PivotCharts, the requirements of the users and the decisions you make will affect the ease of use of the database. As you create macros, navigation forms, and PivotTables and PivotCharts such as those shown in Figures 9–1 and 9–2, you should follow these general guidelines:

1. **Determine when it would be beneficial to automate tasks in a macro.** Are there tasks involving multiple steps that would be more conveniently accomplished by running a macro than by carrying out all the individual steps? For example, to open a form in read-only mode could be accomplished conveniently through a macro. Are there tasks that are to be performed when the user clicks buttons on a menu form? Are there tasks to be performed when a user clicks a control on a form? Are there tasks to be performed when a user updates a table? These tasks can be placed in a macro that can be run when the button is clicked.

2. **Determine whether it is appropriate to create a navigation form.** If you want to make it easy and convenient for users to perform a variety of tasks just by clicking tabs and buttons, consider creating a navigation form. You can associate the performance of the various tasks with the tabs and buttons in the navigation form.

3. **Determine the organization of the navigation form.** Determine the various tasks that need to be performed by clicking tabs and buttons. Decide the logical grouping of the tabs and buttons.

(continued)

Plan
Ahead

(continued)

4. **Determine whether it is appropriate to present data as a PivotTable.** Do you need to calculate a statistic for data that is grouped by two different types of information? If so, you can consider either a crosstab query or a PivotTable. If you want the presentation to be interactive, that is, if you want to be able to easily change the organization of the data as well as to filter the data, then a PivotTable is appropriate.

5. **Determine the organization of the PivotTable.** Determine the fields for the rows, columns, data, and filters.

6. **Determine whether it is appropriate to present data as a PivotChart.** Do you want to summarize the same type of data as in a PivotTable, but graphically? Do you need the same ability to be able to change the organization of the presentation as well as to filter the data? If so, a PivotChart is appropriate.

7. **Determine the organization of the PivotChart.** Determine the fields for the *x*-axis and the *y*-axis. Decide which chart type would best display the data.

When necessary, more specific details concerning the above decisions and/or actions are presented at appropriate points in the chapter. The chapter also will identify the use of these guidelines in the design of navigation forms, such as the ones shown in Figure 9–1a through 9–1d on pages AC 538 and AC 539, as well as PivotTables and PivotCharts, such as the ones shown in Figure 9–2a and 9–2b on pages AC 540 and AC 541.

To Start Access

BTW

The Ribbon and Screen Resolution
Access may change how the groups and buttons within the groups appear on the Ribbon, depending on the computer's screen resolution. Thus, your Ribbon may look different from the ones in this book if you are using a screen resolution other than 1024 × 768.

The following steps, which assume Windows 7 is running, start Access based on a typical installation. You may need to ask your instructor how to start Access for your computer.

1 Click the Start button on the Windows 7 taskbar to display the Start menu.

2 Type **Microsoft Access** as the search text in the 'Search programs and files' text box and watch the search results appear on the Start menu.

3 Click Microsoft Access 2010 in the search results on the Start menu to start Access.

4 If the Access window is not maximized, click the Maximize button next to the Close button on its title bar to maximize the window.

To Open a Database from Access

The following steps open the Camashaly database from the Access folder in the CIS 101 folder on the USB flash drive.

1 With your USB flash drive connected to one of the computer's USB ports, click File on the Ribbon to open the Backstage view if necessary.

2 Click Open in the Backstage view to display the Open dialog box.

3 Navigate to the location of the file to be opened (in this case, the USB flash drive, then to the CIS 101 folder [or your class folder], and then to the Access folder).

4 Click Camashaly Design to select the file to be opened.

5 Click the Open button (Open dialog box) to open the selected file and display the opened database in the Access window.

6 If a Security Warning appears, click the Enable Content button.

Creating and Using Macros

Like other applications, Access allows you to create and use macros. A macro consists of a series of actions that Access performs when the macro is run. When you create a macro, you specify these actions. Once you have created a macro, you can simply run the macro, and Access will perform the various actions you specified. For example, the macro might open a form in read-only mode, a mode where changes to the table are prohibited. Another macro might export a report as a PDF file.

To create a macro, you enter the actions in a special window called the Macro Builder window. Once a macro is created, it exists as an object in the database, and you can run it from the Navigation Pane by right-clicking the macro and then clicking Run on the shortcut menu. Macros also can be associated with buttons on forms. When you click the corresponding button on the form, Access will run the macro. Whether a macro is run from the Navigation Pane or from a form, the effect is the same: Access will execute the actions in the order in which they occur in the macro.

In this chapter, you will create macros for a variety of purposes. As you enter actions, you will select them from a list presented to you by the Macro Builder. The names of the actions are self-explanatory. The action to open a form, for example, is OpenForm. Thus, it is not necessary to memorize the specific actions that are available.

To Begin Creating a Macro

The following steps begin creating a macro. You will later add the appropriate actions to the macro.

- If necessary, close the Navigation Pane.

- Display the Create tab (Figure 9–3).

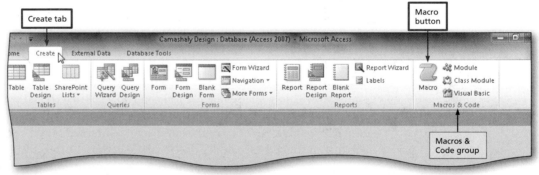

Figure 9–3

- Click the Macro button (Create tab | Macros & Code group) to create a new macro (Figure 9–4).

Figure 9–4

BTW

Saving a Macro as a VBA Module
You can save a macro as a VBA module using the Save Object As command in the Backstage view. Select the macro in the Navigation Pane, click File on the Ribbon to open the Backstage view, and then click Save Object As. When the Save As dialog box appears, click Module in the As text box and then click the OK button.

The Macro Builder Window

You create a macro by adding actions in the macro window, shown in Figure 9–4. You can add actions by clicking the arrow and selecting the desired action. You can also use the Action Catalog, which is a list of macro actions organized by type. The list is searchable. If the Action Catalog does not appear, click the Action Catalog button (Macro Tools Design tab | Show/Hide group) to display it. You can add an action by double-clicking the action in the Action Catalog or by dragging it.

The available actions are arranged in categories. To see the actions in a category, click the plus sign (+) in front of the category. The actions within the category will appear, and the plus sign will change to a minus sign (–). To hide the actions in a category, click the minus sign.

Many actions require additional information; these additional pieces of information are called the **arguments** of the action. For example, if the action is OpenForm, Access needs to know which form is to be opened. You indicate the form to be opened by setting the value of the Form Name argument to the desired form. If the value for the Form Name argument for the OpenForm action is Analyst Course Data, then Access will open the Analyst Course Data form when it executes this action.

Actions can have more than one argument. For example, the OpenForm action has a Data Mode argument. If the value of the Data Mode argument is Read Only, then the form will be opened in Read Only mode, which indicates users will be able to view but not change data. When you select an action, the arguments will appear along with the action, and you can make any necessary changes to them.

In the forms you will create later in this chapter, you need macros for opening the Analyst Course Data form as read-only (no update possible), opening the Business Analyst Master Form, opening the Client Master Form, previewing the Business Analyst Master List, previewing the Client Financial Report, previewing the Discount Report, exporting the Business Analyst Master List as a PDF file, exporting the Client Financial Report as a PDF file, and exporting the Discount Report as a PDF file. You could create nine separate macros to accomplish these tasks. A simpler way, however, is to make each of these a submacro within a single macro. You can run a submacro just as you can run a macro.

You will create a macro called Forms and Reports that contains these nine submacros. Table 9–1 shows the submacros. Submacros can contain many actions, but each one in this table includes only a single action. For each submacro, the table gives the action, those arguments that need to be changed, and the values you need to assign to those arguments. If an argument is not listed, then you do not need to change the value from the default value that is assigned by Access.

Table 9–1 Forms and Reports Macro

Submacro	Action	Arguments to be Changed
Open Analyst Course Data		
	OpenForm	Form Name: Analyst Course Data Data Mode: Read Only
Open Business Analyst Master Form		
	OpenForm	Form Name: Business Analyst Master Form
Open Client Master Form		
	OpenForm	Form Name: Client Master Form
Preview Business Analyst Master List		
	OpenReport	Report Name: Business Analyst Master List View: Print Preview

Table 9–1 Forms and Reports Macro (continued)

Submacro	Action	Arguments to be Changed
Preview Client Financial Report		
	OpenReport	Report Name: Client Financial Report View: Print Preview
Preview Discount Report		
	OpenReport	Report Name: Discount Report View: Print Preview
Export Business Analyst Master List		
	ExportWithFormatting	Object Type: Report Object Name: Business Analyst Master List Output Format: PDF Format (*.pdf)
Export Client Financial Report		
	ExportWithFormatting	Object Type: Report Object Name: Client Financial Report Output Format: PDF Format (*.pdf)
Export Discount Report		
	ExportWithFormatting	Object Type: Report Object Name: Discount Report Output Format: PDF Format (*.pdf)

To Add an Action to a Macro

To continue creating the Forms and Reports macro, enter the actions in the Macro Builder. To enter an action, double-click the action in the Action Catalog. Access will add the action to the Add New Action box. If there is more than one Add New Action box, you need to ensure that the one where you want to add the action is selected before you double-click.

The following steps add the first action. They also make the necessary changes to any arguments. Finally, the steps save the macro.

1

- Double-click the Submacro element from the Program Flow section of the Action Catalog to add a submacro and then type **Open Analyst Course Data** as the name of the submacro (Figure 9–5).

 How can I tell the purpose of the various actions?

If necessary, expand the category containing the action so that the action appears. Point to the action. An expanded ScreenTip will appear, giving you a description of the action.

Figure 9–5

- Click the expand indicator for the Database Objects category of actions (the plus sign in front of the category) to display the actions within the category.

- Double-click the OpenForm action to add it to the submacro (Figure 9–6).

Q&A

What should I do if I add an action in the wrong position? What should I do if I add the wrong action?

If you add an action in the wrong position, use the Move Up or Move Down buttons to move it to the correct position. If you added the wrong action, click the Delete button to delete the action, and then fix the error by adding the correct action.

Figure 9–6

- Click the drop-down arrow for the Form Name argument and then select Analyst Course Data.

- Click the drop-down arrow for the Data Mode argument and then select Read Only (Figure 9–7).

Q&A

What is the effect of selecting Read Only? What are the other options?

Read Only means that users can view the data using the form but cannot change it. Other options are Add and Edit. Add allows viewing records and adding new records, but not updating records. Edit allows viewing records, adding new records, and updating existing records.

Figure 9–7

4

- Click the Save button on the Quick Access Toolbar, type **Forms and Reports** as the name of the macro, and then click the OK button to save the macro.

To Add Additional Actions to a Macro

To complete the macro, you need to add the additional actions shown in Table 9–1 on page AC 544 – AC 545. You add the additional actions just as you added the first action. Initially, Access displays all the actions you have added with their arguments clearly visible. After you have added several actions, you might want to collapse some or all of the actions, thus making it easier to get an overall view of your macro. You can always expand any action later to see details concerning the arguments. The following steps add additional actions to a macro, collapsing existing actions when necessary to provide a better view of the overall macro structure.

 1

- Point to the minus sign (–) in front of the OpenForm action and then click the minus sign to collapse the action (Figure 9–8).

Q&A Could I also use the buttons on the Ribbon?

Yes, you can use the buttons in the Collapse/Expand group on the Macro Tools Design tab. Click the Expand Actions button to expand the selected action, or click the Collapse Actions button to collapse the selected action. You can expand all actions at once by clicking the Expand All button, or you can collapse all actions at once by clicking the Collapse All button.

Figure 9–8

2

- Double-click the Submacro element from the Program Flow section of the Action Catalog to add a submacro and then type **Open Business Analyst Master Form** as the name of the submacro.

- Double-click the OpenForm action to add it to the submacro.

- Click the drop-down arrow for the Form Name argument and then select Business Analyst Master Form.

- In a similar fashion, add the Open Client Master Form submacro.

- Add the OpenForm action to the submacro.

- Select Client Master Form as the value for the Form Name argument (Figure 9–9).

Q&A Do I have to change the values of any of the other arguments?

No. The automatic values that Access sets are appropriate.

Figure 9–9

3

- For each of the three submacros, point to the minus sign (–) in front of the submacro and then click the minus sign to collapse the submacro.

- Add a submacro named Preview Business Analyst Master List.

- Add the OpenReport action to the macro.

- Select Business Analyst Master List as the report name.

- Select Print Preview as the view (Figure 9–10).

Figure 9–10

4

- Collapse the Preview Business Analyst Master List submacro.

- Add the Preview Client Financial Report submacro. Include the action described in Table 9–1. The report name is Client Financial Report and the view is Print Preview.

- Add the Preview Discount Report submacro. Include the action described in Table 9–1. The report name is Discount Report and the view is Print Preview.

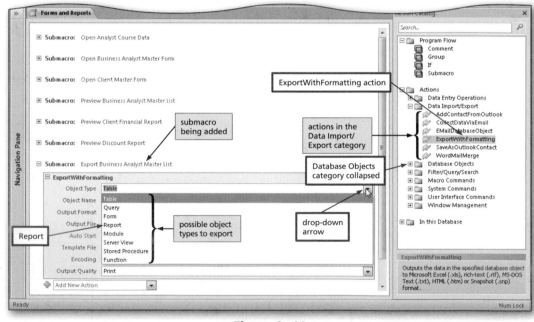

Figure 9–11

- Collapse the Preview Client Financial Report and Preview Discount Report submacros.

- Collapse the Database Objects category and then expand the Data Import/Export category.

- Add a submacro called Export Business Analyst Master List.

- Add the ExportWithFormatting action.

- Click the drop-down arrow for the Object Type argument to display a list of possible object types (Figure 9–11).

5

- Click Report in the list to indicate that Access is to export a report.

- Click the drop-down arrow for the Object Name argument and select Business Analyst Master List as the object name.

- Click the drop-down arrow for the Output Format argument and then select PDF Format (*.pdf) as the Output Format to export the report in PDF format (Figure 9–12).

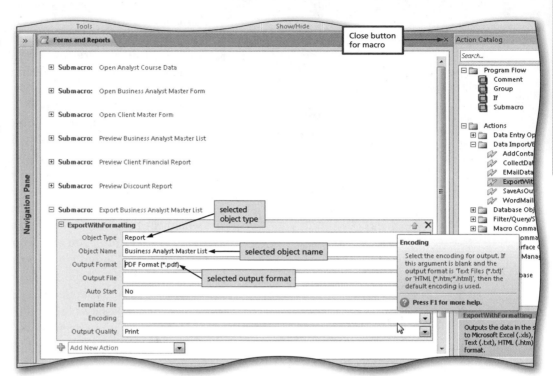

Figure 9–12

6

- Add the Export Client Financial Report submacro.

- Include the action described in Table 9–1 and select Client Financial Report as the report name.

- Select PDF Format (*.pdf) as the Output Format to export the report in PDF format.

- Add the Export Discount Report submacro.

- Select Discount Report as the report name.

- Select PDF Format (*.pdf) as the Output Format to export the report in PDF format.

- Save the macro.

- Close the macro by clicking its Close button, shown in Figure 9–12.

Opening Databases Containing Macros

It is possible that a macro stored in a database can contain a computer virus. By default, Access disables macros when it opens a database and displays a Security Warning. If the database comes from a trusted source and you are sure that it does not contain any macro viruses, click the Enable Content button. You can make adjustments to Access security settings by clicking File on the Ribbon to open the Backstage view, and then clicking Options to display the Access Options dialog box, clicking Trust Center, clicking Trust Center Settings, and then clicking Macro Settings.

Errors in Macros

Macros can contain errors. The macro may abort. It may open the wrong table or produce a wrong message. If you have problems with a macro, you can **single-step the macro,** that is, proceed through a macro a step at a time in Design view.

Figure 9–13

Figure 9–13 shows a macro open in Design view. This macro first has an action to open the Course table in Datasheet view in Read Only mode. It then changes the view to Print Preview. Next, it opens the Client table in Datasheet view in Edit mode. Finally, it opens the Analyst-Client Query in Datasheet view in Read Only mode. The macro in the figure is a common type of macro that opens several objects at once. To open all these objects, the user only has to run the macro. Unfortunately, this macro contains an error. The name of the Client table is misspelled as "Clients" in the second OpenTable action.

To run this macro in single-step mode, you first would click the Single Step button (Macro Tools Design tab | Tools group). You next would click the Run button (Macro Tools Design tab | Tools group) to run the macro. Because you clicked the Single Step button, Access would display the Macro Single Step dialog box (Figure 9–14). The dialog box shows the action to be executed and the values of the various arguments. You can click the Step button to proceed to the next step.

Figure 9–14

With this macro, after you clicked the Step button twice, you would arrive at the screen shown in Figure 9–15. Access is about to execute the OpenTable command. The arguments are Clients, Datasheet, and Edit. At this point, you might spot the fact that "Clients" is misspelled. It should be "Client." If so, you could click the Stop All Macros button and then make the necessary changes.

Figure 9–15

If you instead click the Step button, the misspelled name will cause the macro to abort. Access would display the appropriate error message in the Microsoft Access dialog box (Figure 9–16). This error indicates that Access could not find the object named Clients. Armed with this knowledge, you can click the OK button, stop the macro, and then make the necessary change.

BTW

Converting a Macro to VBA Code
If you want to use many of the resources provided by Windows or communicate with another Windows application, you will need to convert any macros to VBA (Visual Basic for Applications) code. To convert a macro to VBA code, open the macro in the Macro Builder window and click the Convert Macros to Visual Basic button (Macro Tools Design tab | Tools group). When the Convert Macro dialog box appears, select the appropriate options, and then click Convert.

BTW

Viewing VBA Code
You can view VBA code that is attached to a form or report. To do so, open the form or report in Design view and click the View Code button (Report Design Tools Design tab | Tools group) for reports or (Form Design Tools Design tab | Tools group) for forms.

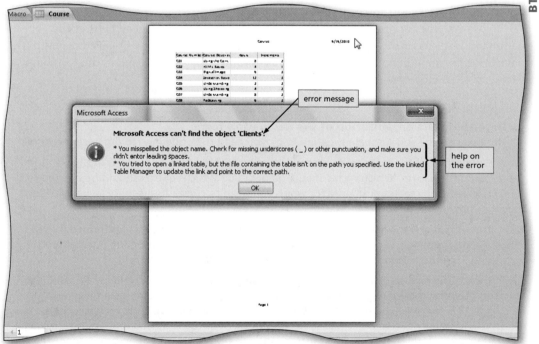

Figure 9–16

You do not need to step through a macro to discover the error. You can simply run the macro, either by clicking the Run button (Macro Tools Design tab | Tools group) with the macro open, or by right-clicking the macro in the Navigation Pane and clicking Run. In either case, Access will run the macro until it encounters the error. When it does, it will display the same message shown in Figure 9–16. Just as with stepping through the macro, you would click the OK button, stop the macro, and then make the necessary change.

Break Point: If you wish to stop working through the chapter at this point, you can resume the project at a later time by starting Access, opening the database called Camashaly Design, and continuing to follow the steps from this location forward.

Creating and Using a Navigation Form

Figure 9–1a on page AC 538 showed a navigation form for Camashaly Design. A **navigation form** is a form that contains a **navigation control**, a control that can display a variety of forms and reports. Like the form in Figure 9–1a, navigation controls contain tabs. Clicking the tab displays the corresponding form or report. The tabs can be arranged across the top and/or down the sides.

BTW

Navigation Forms
In Access 2010, the navigation form replaces the switchboard manager. A navigation form contains a navigation control and a subform control. After you create a navigation form, you can use the Navigation Where Clause property associated with a navigation control to automatically apply a filter.

You only can include forms and reports on the tabs; you cannot include either tables or queries. The navigation form in Figure 9–1a, however, appears to have a tab corresponding to the Client table. There is a technique you can use to make it appear as though the navigation form contains tables or queries. You create a datasheet form based on the table or query. Figure 9–1a actually shows a datasheet form based on the Client table and does not show the Client table itself.

You also might want the users to be able to click a tab in the navigation form and then be presented with a list of forms or reports from which they could choose. Figure 9–1c on page AC 539 shows a list of forms presented as buttons where the user would click the button for the desired form. Figure 9–1d shows a list of reports presented in an option group where the user would click the desired option button. Notice that the user could click an option button to preview a report. The user could click a different option button to export the report as a PDF file.

To implement options like these, you create a blank form and add either the command buttons or the option group. You then include the form you have created in the navigation form. When users click the corresponding tab, Access displays the form and users can then click the appropriate button.

**Plan
Ahead**

Determine the organization of the navigation form.
Once you decide you want a navigation form, you need to decide how to organize the form.

- **Determine all the tasks to be accomplished by clicking tabs or buttons in the navigation form.** Which forms should be opened? Which reports should be opened? Are there any tables or queries for which you need to create forms that can be opened in the navigation form?

- **Determine any special requirements for the way the tasks are to be performed.** When a form is opened, should a user be able to edit data, or should the form open as read-only? Should a report be exported or simply viewed on the screen?

- **Determine how to group the various tasks.** Should forms or reports simply be assigned to the tabs in the navigation form? Should they be grouped as buttons on a menu form? Should they be placed as options within an option group? (For consistency, you would usually decide on one of these approaches and use it throughout. In this chapter, one menu form uses command buttons, and the other uses an option group simply to illustrate both approaches.) As far as the navigation form is concerned, is a single set of horizontal tabs sufficient, or would you also like vertical tabs? Would you like two rows of horizontal tabs?

To Create a Menu Form Containing Command Buttons

You can create a menu form by adding command buttons to the form, just as you added command buttons to the form in Chapter 8 on pages AC 485 through AC 487. The following steps use this technique to create a menu form with three buttons: Open Client Master Form, Open Business Analyst Master Form, and Open Analyst Course Data. The actions assigned to each button will run a macro that causes the desired action to occur. For example, the action for the Open Client Master Form button will run the Open Client Master Form submacro, which in turn, will open the Client Master Form.

The following steps create a form in Design view and then add the necessary buttons.

1
- Display the Create tab.

- Click the Form Design button (Create tab | Forms group) to create a blank form in Design view.

- If a field list appears, click the Add Existing Fields button (Form Design Tools Design tab | Tools group) to remove the field list (Figure 9–17).

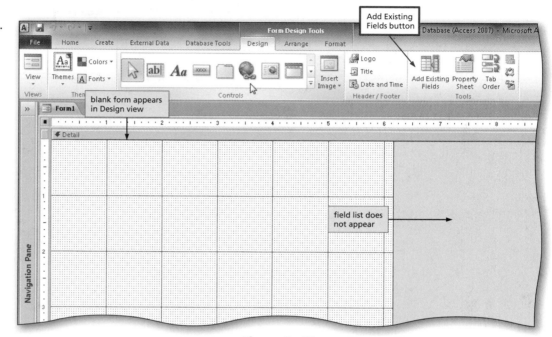

Figure 9–17

2
- Save the form using the name, Forms List.

- Make sure the Use Control Wizards button is selected.

- Click the Button tool (Form Design Tools Design tab | Controls group) and move the mouse pointer to the approximate position shown in Figure 9–18.

Figure 9–18

3

- Click the position shown in Figure 9–18 to display the Command Button Wizard dialog box.

- Click Miscellaneous in the Categories box, and then click Run Macro in the Actions box (Figure 9–19).

Figure 9–19

4

- Click the Next button to display the next screen in the wizard.

- Click Forms and Reports.Open Client Master Form to select the macro to be run (Figure 9–20).

Q&A

What does this notation mean?

The portion before the period is the macro and the portion after the period is the submacro. Thus, this notation means the Open Client Master Form submacro within the Forms and Reports macro.

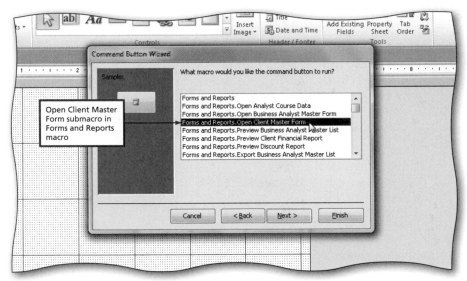

Figure 9–20

5

- Click the Next button to display the next Command Button Wizard screen.

- Click the Text option button.

Q&A

What is the purpose of these option buttons?

Choose the first option button to place text on the button. You then can specify the text to be included or accept the default choice. Choose the second option button to place a picture on the button. You then can select a picture.

- Type **Open Client Master Form** as the text (Figure 9–21).

Figure 9–21

- Click the Next button.

- Type `Open_Client_Master_Form` as the name of the button (Figure 9–22).

Q&A
Why do you include the underscores in the name of the button?

If you are working with macros or VBA, you cannot have spaces in names. One way to avoid spaces and still make readable names is to include underscores where you would normally have had spaces. Thus, Open Client Master Form becomes Open_Client_Master_Form.

Figure 9–22

- Click the Finish button to finish specifying the button.

- Use the techniques in Steps 1 through 6 to place the Open Business Analyst Master Form button below the Open Client Master Form button. The only difference is that the macro to be run is the Open Business Analyst Master Form submacro, the text is Open Business Analyst Master Form, and the name of the button is Open_Business_Analyst_Master_Form.

- Use the techniques in Steps 1 through 6 to place the Open Analyst Course Data button below the Open Business Analyst Master Form button. The only difference is that the macro to be run is the Open Analyst Course Data submacro, the text is Open Analyst Course Data, and the name of the button is Open_Analyst_Course_Data.

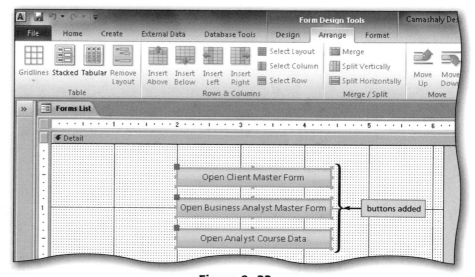

Figure 9–23

- Adjust the size and spacing of the buttons to approximately match those in Figure 9–23, using the Arrange tab, if necessary.

- Save the form.

Q&A
How can I test the buttons to make sure the macros work?

Right-click the Forms List form in the Navigation Pane and click Open. Click each of the buttons on the form. If there are errors in any of the macros, open the macro in the Macro Builder window and correct the errors.

Experiment

- Test each of the buttons on the form. Ensure that the correct form opens. If there are errors, correct the corresponding macro.

- Close the form.

To Create a Menu Form Containing an Option Group

You may decide to allow users to make a selection from some predefined options by including an option group. An **option group** is a rectangle containing a collection of option buttons. To select an option, you simply click the corresponding option button. The form you are creating contains an option group called Form Options. In this group, you select an option button to indicate either a report to preview or a report to export.

The following steps use the Option Group tool to create the Form Options option group.

- Display the Create tab.

- Click the Form Design button (Create tab | Forms group) to create a blank form in Design view.

- If a field list appears, click the Add Existing Fields button (Form Design Tools Design tab | Tools group) to remove the field list.

- Save the form using the name, Reports List.

- Click the More button (Form Design Tools Design tab | Controls group) to display the gallery of available tools (Figure 9–24).

Figure 9–24

- With the Use Control Wizards button selected, click the Option Group tool (Form Design Tools Design tab | Controls group) and then move the pointer to the approximate position shown in Figure 9–25.

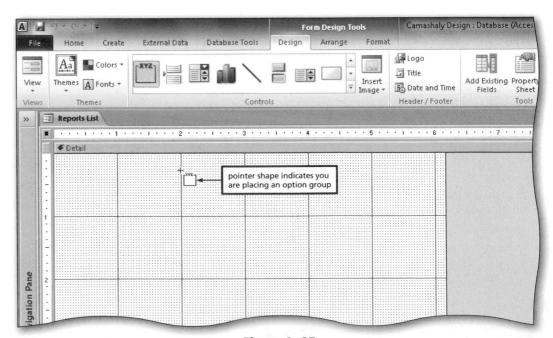

Figure 9–25

3

- Click the position shown in Figure 9–25 to place an option group and start the Option Group Wizard.

- Type **Preview Business Analyst Master List** in the first row of label names and press the DOWN ARROW key.

- Type **Preview Client Financial Report** in the second row of label names and press the DOWN ARROW key.

- Type **Preview Discount Report** in the third row of label names and press the DOWN ARROW key.

- Type **Export Business Analyst Master List** in the fourth row of label names and press the DOWN ARROW key.

Figure 9–26

- Type **Export Client Financial Report** in the fifth row of label names and press the DOWN ARROW key.

- Type **Export Discount Report** in the sixth row of label names and press the DOWN ARROW key (Figure 9–26).

4

- Click the Next button to move to the next Option Group Wizard screen.

- Click the 'No, I don't want a default' option button to select it (Figure 9–27).

Q&A What is the effect of specifying one of the options as the default choice?

The default choice will initially be selected when you open the form. If there is no default choice, no option will be selected.

Figure 9–27

5

- Click the Next button to move to the next Option Group Wizard screen and then verify that the values assigned to the labels match those shown in Figure 9–28.

 Q&A

How do I use the values that I have assigned?

You can use them in macros or VBA. You will use them in a macro later in this chapter.

Figure 9–28

6

- Click the Next button to move to the next Option Group Wizard screen, and then ensure that Option buttons is selected as the type of control and Etched is selected as the style (Figure 9–29).

 Experiment

- Click different combinations of types and styles to see the effects on the samples shown in the dialog box. When finished, select Options button as the type and Etched as the style.

Figure 9–29

7

- Click the Next button to move to the next Option Group Wizard screen and then type `Report Actions` as the caption.

- Click the Finish button to complete the addition of the option group (Figure 9–30).

Figure 9–30

Using an If Statement

You will create a macro that will take appropriate action when the user updates the option group, that is, when the user clicks an option button in the group. The macro will run the appropriate submacro, depending on which option the user has selected.

Because the specific actions that the macro will perform depend on the option button the user selects, the macro will contain conditions. The conditions will determine which action should be taken. If the user selects the first option button, Access should run the Preview Business Analyst Master List submacro. If, on the other hand, the user selects the second option button, Access should instead run the Preview Client Financial Report submacro. For each of the six possible option buttons a user can select, Access should run a different submacro.

To instruct Access to perform different actions based on certain conditions, the macro will contain an If statement. The simplest form of an If statement is:

```
If condition Then
  action
End If
```

If the condition is true, Access will take the indicated action. If the condition is false, no action will be taken. For example, the condition could be that the user selects the first option button, and the action could be to run the Business Analyst Master List submacro. No action would be taken if the user selects any other button.

Another form of the If statement contains an Else clause. This form is:

```
If condition Then
  first action
Else
  second action
End If
```

If the condition is true, the first action is taken; if the condition is false, the second action is taken. For example, the condition could be that the user selects option button 1; the first action could be to run the Preview Business Analyst Master list submacro, and the second action could be to run the Preview Client Financial Report submacro. If the user selects option button 1, Access would run the Preview Business Analyst Master list submacro. If the user selects any other option button, Access would run the Preview Client Financial Report submacro. Because there are six option buttons, the macro needs to use an If statement with multiple Else Ifs. This type of If statement has the form:

```
If first condition Then
  first action
Else If second condition Then
  second action
Else If third condition Then
  third action
End If
```

The first condition could be that the user selects the first option button; the second condition could be that the user selects the second option button; and the third condition could be that the user selects the third option button. The first action could be that Access runs the first submacro; the second action could be that it runs the second submacro; and the third could be that it runs the third submacro. This would work, except that in this case there are six option buttons and six submacros. For six conditions, as required in this macro, the If statement will contain five Else Ifs. The If statement along with five the Else Ifs will collectively contain six conditions: one to test if the user selected option 1, one for option 2, one for option 3, one for option 4, one for option 5, and one for option 6.

The expression that contains the option number is [Forms]![Client Master Form]![Form_Options]. Because this expression is fairly lengthy, the macro will begin by setting a temporary variable to this expression. A **variable** is a named location in computer memory. You can use a variable to store a value that you can use later in the macro. You will assign the name Optno (short for option number) as the variable name for the expression. This location can contain a value, in this case, the option number on the form. In each of the conditions, you can then use Optno rather than the full expression.

To Create a Macro for the Option Group

The following steps begin creating the macro and add an action to set the temporary variable to the desired value.

1

- With the option group selected, display a property sheet.

- If necessary, click the All tab.

- Change the name to Form_Options.

Q&A

Why this name?

The name Form Options reflects the fact that these are options that control the action that will be taken on this form. The underscore keeps the name from containing a space.

- Click the After Update property.

- Click the Build button to display the Choose Builder dialog box (Figure 9–31).

Figure 9–31

2

- With Macro Builder selected in the Choose Builder dialog box, click the OK button to create a macro.

- If necessary, click the Action Catalog button (Macro Tools Design tab | Show/Hide group) to display the Action Catalog.

- If necessary, collapse the Data Import/ Export category.

- Expand the Macro Commands action category.

- Double-click the SetTempVar action in the Action Catalog to add the SetTempVar action to the macro.

Figure 9–32

- Enter `Optno` as the value for the Name argument.

- Enter `[Form_Options]` as the value for the Expression argument (Figure 9–32).

Macro for Option Group

As mentioned previously, the macro contains six conditions. The first is [TempVars]! [Optno]=1, which simply means the value in the temporary variable Optno is equal to 1. In other words, the user selected the first option button. The action associated with this condition is RunMacro. The argument is the name of the macro. Because the macro to be run is a submacro, the name of the macro includes both the name of the macro containing the submacro, a period, and then the name of the submacro. Because the submacro to be run is Preview Business Analyst Master List and is contained in the Forms and Reports macro, the value of the Macro Name argument is Forms and Reports.Preview Business Analyst Master List.

The conditions and actions for options 2 through 6 are similar. The only difference is which submacro is to be run for each option button. The conditions, actions, and arguments to be changed for this macro are shown in Table 9–2. If the option number is 1, for example, the action is RunMacro. The argument to be changed for the RunMacro action is Macro Name argument. It is to be set to the Preview Business Analyst Master List submacro in the Forms and Reports macro. On the other hand, if the option number is 2, for example, the action is again RunMacro. In this case, however, the Macro Name argument is to be set to the Preview Client Financial Report submacro in the Forms and Reports macro. Similar actions take place for the other possible values for the Optno variable, that is, for the other option buttons the user could select. Because the temporary variable, Optno, is no longer needed at the end of the macro, the macro concludes with the RemoveTempVar command to remove this variable.

BTW

Adding Images to Reports
You can include a picture (image) on a report. To insert an image on a report, open the report in Design view or Layout view, click the Insert Image button (Design tab | Controls group), select the specific image, and place the image in the desired position on the report. You also can add images to forms.

BTW

Adding Background Images to a Report
You can use a picture (image) as the background on a report. To do so, open the report in Design view or Layout view, click anywhere in the report, click Background Image (Format tab | Background group), select the specific image, and place the background image in the desired position on the report. You also can add background images to forms.

Table 9–2 Macro for After Update Property of the Option Group

Condition	Action	Arguments to be Changed
	SetTempVar	Name: Optno Expression: [Form_Options]
If [TempVars]![Optno]=1		
	RunMacro	Macro Name: Forms and Reports.Preview Business Analyst Master List
Else If [TempVars]![Optno]=2		
	RunMacro	Macro Name: Forms and Reports.Preview Client Financial Report
Else If [TempVars]![Optno]=3		
	RunMacro	Macro Name: Forms and Reports.Preview Discount Report
Else If [TempVars]![Optno]=4		
	RunMacro	Macro Name: Forms and Reports.Export Business Analyst Master List
Else If [TempVars]![Optno]=5		
	RunMacro	Macro Name: Forms and Reports.Export Client Financial Report
Else If [TempVars]![Optno]=6		
	RunMacro	Macro Name: Forms and Reports.Export Discount Report
End If		
	RemoveTempVar	Name: Optno

To Add Actions to the Macro

The following steps add the remaining conditions and actions to the macro.

1

- Double-click the If element from the Program Flow section of the Action Catalog to add an If statement to the submacro and then type `[TempVars]![Optno]=1` as the condition in the If statement.

- With the Macro Commands category expanded, double-click RunMacro to add the RunMacro action.

- Click the drop-down arrow for the Macro Name argument and select the Preview Business Analyst Master List submacro within the Forms and Reports macro as the value for the argument (Figure 9–33).

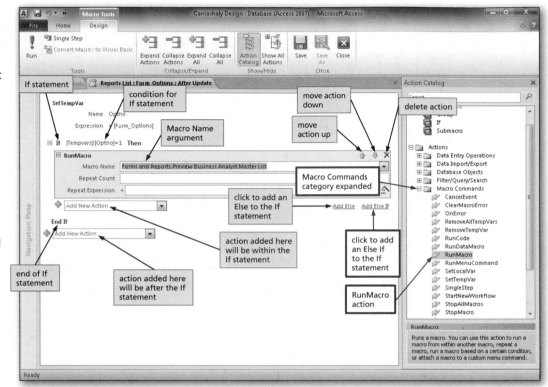

Figure 9–33

Q&A

What should I do if I add an action in the wrong position? What should I do if I add the wrong action?

If you add an action in the wrong position, use the Move Up or Move Down buttons to move it to the correct position. If you added the wrong action, click the Delete button to delete the action, and then fix the error by adding the correct action.

BTW

Macro Builder Window
The Macro Builder window in Access 2010 features IntelliSense. IntelliSense provides auto-completion of commands as well as context-sensitive lists and help.

2

- Click Add Else If to add an Else If clause to the If statement.

- Add the conditions and actions associated with options 2, 3, 4, 5, and 6 as described in Table 9–2 on page AC 561, and specify the arguments for the actions. Click Add Else If after adding each action except for the last one.

Q&A Do I have to enter all these actions? They seem to be very similar to the ones associated with option 1.

You can copy and paste the action for option 1. Right-click the action to select it and display a shortcut menu. Click Copy on the shortcut menu. Right-click the action just above where you want to insert the selected action and then click Paste. If the new action is not inserted in the correct position, select the new action and then click either the Move Up or Move Down buttons to move it to the correct location. Once the action is in the correct location, you can make any necessary changes to the arguments.

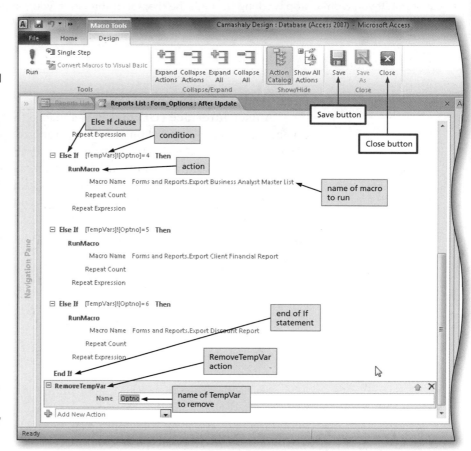

Figure 9–34

- Add the RemoveTempVar action and argument after the end of the If statement, as shown in Figure 9–34.

Q&A Do I need to remove the temporary variable?

Technically, no. In fact, if you plan to use this temporary variable in another macro and want it to retain the value you assigned in this macro, you would definitely not remove it. If you don't plan to use it elsewhere, it is a good idea to remove it, however.

- Collapse the Macro Commands action category.

3

- Click the Save button (Macro Tools Design tab | Close group) to save the macro.

- Click the Close button (Macro Tools Design tab | Close group) to close the macro and return to the form.

- Close the property sheet, save the form, and close the form.

Q&A How can I test the option group to make sure the macros work?

Right-click the Reports List form in the Navigation Pane and click Open. Click each of the buttons in the option group. If there are errors in any of the macros, open the macro in the Macro Builder window and correct the errors.

 Experiment

- Test each of the buttons in the option group. If you do not preview or export the correct report, correct the error in the corresponding macro. If you get an error indicating that the section width is greater than the page width, you have an error in the corresponding report. Correct the error using the steps shown on pages AC 371 through AC 372.

Break Point: If you wish to stop working through the chapter at this point, you can resume the project at a later time by starting Access, opening the database called Camashaly Design, and continuing to follow the steps from this location forward.

User Interface (UI) Macros

A **user interface (UI) macro** is a macro that is attached to a user interface object, such as a command button, an option group, or a control on a form. The macro you just created for the option group is thus a UI macro, as were the macros you attached to command buttons. A common use for UI macros is to associate actions with the clicking of a control on a form. In the navigation form shown in Figure 9–1a on page AC 538, for example, if you select the Client tab and then click the client number on a row in the datasheet, Access displays the data for that client in a pop-up form (Figure 9–1b), that is, a form that stays on top of other open objects, even when another object is active.

Recall that you can only use forms and reports for the tabs in a navigation form, but yet the Client tab appears to display the Client table in Datasheet view. You can make it appear as though you are displaying the Client table in Datasheet view by creating a datasheet form that you will call Client. It is in this form that you will create a UI macro. The UI macro that will be associated with the clicking of the client number on some record in the Client form will display the selected client in the Client Master Form.

To display the Client Master Form, the UI macro will use the OpenForm action. The Form Name argument of the OpenForm action needs to be set to the actual name of the form to be opened, Client Master Form. (Client View and Update Form is just the form caption.) Camashaly wants to prevent the user from updating data using this form, so the Data Mode argument is set to Read Only. The form is to appear as a pop-up, which is accomplished by setting the value of the Window Mode argument to Dialog.

The form should display only the record that the user selected. If the user clicks client number KD21 in the Client form, for example, the form should display only the data for client KD21. Restricting the record that appears in the form is accomplished by including the Where Condition argument. The condition needs to indicate that the Client Number in the form to be opened, Client Master Form, needs to be equal to the Client Number the user selected in the Client form.

In the Where Condition, you can simply refer to a control in the form to be opened by using its name. If the name has spaces, you would need to enclose it in square brackets. Thus, the name for the Client Number in the Client Master Form is simply [Client Number]. For any other form, you need to include both the name of the form and the name of the control, separated by an exclamation point. Thus, the Client Number in the Client would be [Client]![Client Number]. This declaration works correctly when you are programming a macro that simply opens the Client form. However, when you associate the Client form with a tab in the navigation form, the Client form becomes a subform, and the expression needs to be different. This means that a form that works correctly when you open the form may not work correctly when the form is assigned to a tab in a navigation form. A safer approach avoids these issues by using a temporary variable.

Table 9–3 shows the UI macro for the Client form. It is associated with the On Click event for the Client Number control. When a user clicks a Client Number, the UI macro will display the data for the selected client in the Client Master Form. The main function of the macro is to open the appropriate form using the OpenForm action.

Table 9–3 UI Macro Associated with On Click Event in the Client Form	
Action	**Arguments to be Changed**
SetTempVar	Name: CN Expression: [Client Number]
OpenForm	Form Name: Client Master Form Where Condition: [Client Number]=[TempVars]![CN] Data Mode: Read Only Window Mode: Dialog
RemoveTempVar	Name: CN

In the macro shown in Table 9–3, the first action, SetTempVar, assigns the temporary variable CN to the Client Number. The two arguments are: Name, which is set to CN, and Expression, which is set to [Client Number]. This refers to the Client Number in the Client form; recall that the completed macro will open the Client form. You can then use that temporary variable in the Where Condition argument. The expression is thus [Client Number]=[TempVars]![CN]. The [Client Number] portion refers to the Client Number in the Client Master Form. The [TempVars]![CN] portion is the temporary variable that has been set equal to the Client Number in the Client form.

The macro ends by removing the temporary variable.

Table 9–4 shows the macro for the Business Analyst form, which is very similar to the macro for the Client form.

Table 9–4 UI Macro Associated with On Click Event in the Business Analyst Form	
Action	**Arguments to be Changed**
SetTempVar	Name: BN Expression: [Business Analyst Number]
OpenForm	Form Name: Business Analyst Master Form Where Condition: [Business Analyst Number]=[TempVars]![BN] Data Mode: Read Only Window Mode: Dialog
RemoveTempVar	Name: BN

To Create Datasheet Forms that Incorporate UI Macros

The following steps create two datasheet forms, one for the Client table and one for the Business Analyst table. The steps also create the UI macro for the Client table shown in Table 9–3 and the UI macro for the Business Analyst table shown in Table 9–4.

- Open the Navigation Pane and select the Client table.

- Display the Create tab and then click the More Forms button (Create tab | Forms group) to display the More Forms menu (Figure 9–35).

- Click Datasheet to create a datasheet form.

- Save the form using the name, Client.

Q&A Is it acceptable to use the same name for the form as for the table?

Yes. In this case, you want it to appear to the user that the Client table is open in Datasheet view. One way to emphasize this fact is to use the same name as the table.

Q&A What is the difference between this form, Client, and the form named Client Form?

The Client Form is a simple form that displays only one record at a time. The form you just created displays the data in a datasheet.

- Click the Client Number (CL #) heading to select the Client Number column in the datasheet.

- Display the property sheet.

- Click the Event tab to display only event properties.

Q&A Why click the Event tab? Why not just use the All tab as we have before?

You can always use the All tab; however, if you know the category that contains the property in which you are interested, you can greatly reduce the number of properties that Access will display by clicking the tab for that category. That gives you fewer properties to search through to find the property you want. Whether you use the All tab or one of the other tabs is strictly a matter of personal preference.

Figure 9–35

Figure 9–36

- Click the On Click event mand then click the Build button (the three dots) to display the Choose Builder dialog box (Figure 9–36).

3

- Click the OK button (Choose Builder dialog box) to display the Macro Builder window.

- Add the SetTempVar action to the macro, enter `CN` as the value for the Name argument, and enter `[Client Number]` as the value for the Expression argument.

- Add the OpenForm action to the macro, select Client Master Form as the value for the Form Name argument, leave the value of the View argument set to Form, enter `[Client Number]=[TempVars]![CN]` as the value for the Where Condition argument, select Read Only as the value for the Data Mode argument, and select Dialog as the value for the Window Mode argument.

Figure 9–37

Q&A What does this expression mean?

The portion before the equal sign, [Client Number], refers to the Client Number in the form just opened, that is, in the Client Master Form. The portion to the right of the equal sign, [TempVars]![CN], is the temporary variable that was set equal to the Client Number on the selected record in the Client form. This Where Condition guarantees that the record displayed in the Client Master Form will be the record with the same Client Number as the one selected in the Client form.

- Add the RemoveTempVar action to the macro and enter `CN` as the value for the Name argument (Figure 9–37).

Q&A Why do you need to remove the temporary variable?

Technically, you do not. It has fulfilled its function, however, so it makes sense to remove it at this point.

4

- Click the Save button (Macro Tools Design tab | Close group) to save the macro.

- Click the Close button (Macro Tools Design tab | Close group) to close the macro and return to the form design.

- Close the property sheet.

- Save the form by clicking the Save button on the Quick Access Toolbar and then close the form.

- Use the techniques in Steps 1 through 4 to create a datasheet form for the Business Analyst table called Business Analyst, referring to

Figure 9–38

Table 9–4 for the actions. Create the macro shown in Figure 9–38 associated with clicking the Business Analyst Number (BA #) column.

5

- Click the Save button (Macro Tools Design tab | Close group) to save the macro.

- Click the Close button (Macro Tools Design tab | Close group) to close the macro and return to the form design.

- Close the property sheet.

- Save the form by clicking the Save button on the Quick Access Toolbar and then close the form.

To Create a Navigation Form

The following steps create a navigation form with horizontal tabs, save the form, and change the title.

1

- If necessary, open the Navigation Pane.

- Click the Create tab and then click the Navigation button (Create tab | Forms group) to display the menu of available navigation forms (Figure 9–39).

Figure 9–39

2

- Click Horizontal Tabs in the menu to create a form with a navigation control in which the tabs are arranged horizontally in a single row.

- If a field list appears, click the Add Existing Fields button (Form Layout Tools Design tab | Tools group) to remove the field list (Figure 9–40).

Figure 9–40

- Save the form using the name, Main Menu.

- Click the form title twice: once to select it and the second time to produce an insertion point.

- Erase the current title and then type **Camashaly Design** as the new title (Figure 9–41).

- Save the form.

Figure 9–41

To Add Tabs to a Navigation Form

To add a form or report to a tab in a navigation form, be sure the Navigation Pane is open and then drag the form or report to the desired tab. As a result, users can display that form or report by clicking the tab. For the Camashaly Design navigation form, you will drag four forms to the tabs. The Client form is a datasheet form that appears to display the Client table open in Datasheet view. Similarly, the Business Analyst form is a datasheet form that appears to display the Business Analyst table open in Datasheet view. The Forms List form contains three buttons users can click to display the form of their choice. Finally, the Reports List form contains an option group users can use to select a report to be previewed or exported. The following steps add the tabs to the navigation form. They also change the name of the Forms List and Reports List tabs.

- Scroll down in the Navigation Pane so that the Client form appears and then drag the Client form to the position to add a new tab (Figure 9–42).

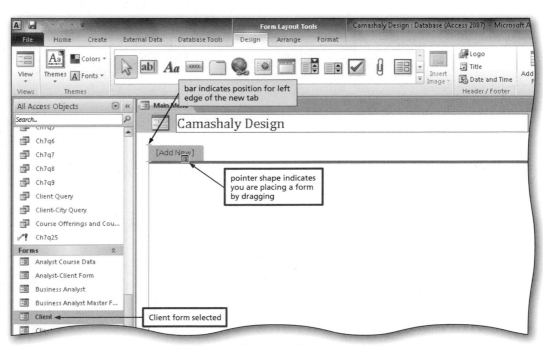

Figure 9–42

2

• Release the left mouse button to add the Client form as the first tab.

• Drag the Business Analyst form to the position to add a new tab (Figure 9–43).

The screen looks like a datasheet rather than a form. I thought you could only add forms or reports.

You are correct that you can only add forms or reports to the tabs in a navigation form. The reason it looks like a datasheet is that the form you added is a datasheet form.

What should I do if I made a mistake and added a form or report to the wrong location?

You can rearrange the tabs by dragging. Often, the simplest way to correct a mistake is to click the Undo button to reverse your most recent action, however. You can also choose to simply close the form without saving it and then start over.

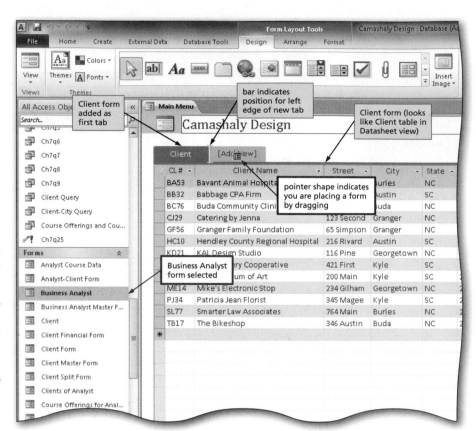

Figure 9–43

3

• Release the left mouse button to add the Business Analyst form as the second tab.

• Using the techniques illustrated in Steps 1 and 2, add the Forms List form as the third tab and the Reports List form as the fourth tab (Figure 9–44).

Figure 9–44

4
- Click the Forms List tab twice: once to select it and the second time to produce an insertion point.
- Change the name from Forms List to Forms.
- In a similar fashion, change the name of the Reports List tab from Reports List to Reports (Figure 9–45).

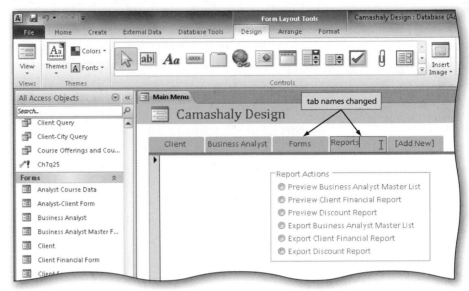

Figure 9–45

I created these two forms using the names Forms List and Reports List. Now I have changed the names to Forms and Reports. Why not call them Forms and Reports in the first place, so I would not have to rename the tabs?

Because the words, forms and reports, have specific meaning in Access, you cannot use these names. Thus, you needed to use some other names, like Forms List and Reports List. You can then rename the tabs to be called anything you want them to be.

5
- Save the form.
- Close the form.

Using a Navigation Form

The Main Menu navigation form is complete and ready for use. To use the navigation form, select the form in the Navigation Pane, and then click Open on the shortcut menu. The Main Menu form then will appear with the first tabbed object (see Figure 9–1a on page AC 538). To display the other forms, simply click the appropriate tab.

Data Macros

A data macro is a special type of macro that is associated with specific table-related events. The possible events are Before Change, Before Delete, After Insert, After Update, and After Delete. Data macros allow you to add logic to these events. For example, the data macro shown in Table 9–5 is associated with the Before Change event, the event that occurs after the user has changed the data but before the change is physically made in the database.

Table 9–5 Data Macro for Before Change Event		
Condition	**Action**	**Arguments to be Changed**
If [Hours Spent]>[Total Hours]		
	SetField	Name: [Hours Spent]
		Value: [Total Hours]
Else If [Hours Spent]<0		
	SetField	Name: [Hours Spent]
		Value: 0
End If		

Quick Styles for Controls

To make a navigation form more visually appealing, you can change the style of a command button and/or tabs. Quick styles change how the different colors, fonts, and effects are combined and which color, font, and effect is dominant. To change the style of a command button or tab, open the navigation form in Layout view. Select the control or controls for which you want to change the style and click Quick Styles (Form Layout Tools Design tab | Control Formatting group). When the Quick Styles gallery appears, select the desired style. You also can change the style of a control in Design view.

Data Macros
Data macros are similar to SQL triggers and are a new feature in Access 2010. You attach logic to record or table events and any forms and code that update those events inherit the logic. Data macros are stored with the table.

This macro will examine the value in the Hours Spent field. If the user's update would cause the value in the Hours Spent field to be greater than the value in the Total Hours field, the macro will change the value in the Hours Spent field so that it is equal to the value in the Total Hours field. Likewise, if the update would cause the value in the Hours Spent field to be less than zero, the macro will set the value in the Hours Spent field to 0. These changes take place before Access changes the value in the database.

There are other events to which you can assign data macros. The actions in a data macro associated with the Before Delete event will take place after a user has indicated that he or she wants to delete a record, but before the record is physically removed from the database. The actions in a macro associated with the After Insert event will take place immediately after a record is physically added to the database. The actions in a macro associated with the After Update event will take place immediately after a record is physically changed in the database. The actions in a macro associated with the After Delete event will take place immediately after a record is physically removed from the database.

To Create a Data Macro

Camashaly Design management wants to prevent users from entering invalid data into the database. The following steps create the data macro in Table 9–5, a macro that will be run after a user makes a change to a record in the Course Offerings table, but before the record is updated in the database.

- Open the Course Offerings table in Datasheet view and close the Navigation Pane.

- Display the Table tab (Figure 9–46).

What is the meaning of the events in the Before Events and After Events groups?

Actions in macros associated with the Before events will occur after the user has taken action to change or delete a record, but before the change or delete is made permanent in the database. Actions in macros associated with the After Events will occur after the corresponding update has been made permanent in the database.

Figure 9–46

2

- Click the Before Change button (Table Tools Table tab | Before Events group).

- Create the macro shown in Figure 9–47.

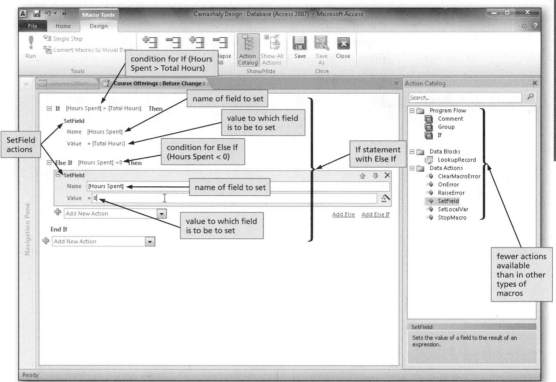

Figure 9–47

What happened to all the actions? In the previous macros we created, there seemed to be many more actions available.

There are only certain actions that make sense in data macros. Only those actions appear. The list of macros that appear is much smaller in a data macro than in other macros.

3

- Save the macro.

- Close the macro.

- Save and close the Course Offerings table.

Using a Table that Contains a Data Macro

If you update a table that contains a data macro, the actions in the data macro will be executed whenever the corresponding event takes place. If the data macro corresponds to the Before Change event, the actions will be executed after the user has changed the data, but before the change is saved in the database. With the data macro you just created, for example, if a user attempts to change the data in such a way that the Hours Spent is greater than the Total Hours (Figure 9–48a), as soon as the user takes an action that would require saving the record, Access makes Hours Spent equal to Total

BTW

Change the Shape of a Control
Command buttons and tabs have a default shape. For example, both command buttons and tabs have a rounded rectangle shape as the default shape. You can change the shape of a button or tab control on a navigation form. To do so, open the navigation form in Layout view. Select the control or controls for which you want to change the shape and click Change Shape (Form Layout Tools Design tab | Control Formatting group). When the Change Shape menu appears, select the desired shape. You also can change the shape of a control in Design view.

Hours (Figure 9–48b). Likewise, if a user attempts to set Hours Spent to a negative number (Figure 9–48c), as soon as the user takes an action that would require saving the record, Access will set Hours Spent to 0 (Figure 9–48d). This change will take place automatically, regardless of whether the user changes the values in Datasheet view, with a form, in an update query, or in any other fashion.

(a) Changing Hours Spent to a Value Greater Than Total Hours

(b) Hours Spent Set to Total Hours

(c) Changing Hours Spent to a Value Less Than Zero

(d) Hours Spent Set to Zero

Figure 9–48

Break Point: If you wish to stop working through the chapter at this point, you can resume the project at a later time by starting Access, opening the database called Camashaly Design, and continuing to follow the steps from this location forward.

PivotTables and PivotCharts

There are two alternatives to viewing data in Datasheet view or Form view. PivotTable view presents data as a **PivotTable**, that is, an interactive table that summarizes or analyzes data. PivotChart view presents data as a **PivotChart**, that is, a graphical representation of the data. PivotTables and PivotCharts allow you to view data in multiple dimensions, making them valuable tools for management decision making. For example, PivotTables and PivotCharts can be used to analyze past data and predict future patterns and trends, a technique known as **data mining**.

In a PivotTable, you can show different levels of detail, and you can change the organization or layout of the table by dragging items. You also can filter table data by checking or unchecking values in drop-down lists. In a PivotChart, just as in a PivotTable, you can show different levels of detail or change the layout by dragging items. You also can filter chart data by checking or unchecking values in drop-down lists. You can change the type of chart that appears as well as customize the chart by adding axis titles, a chart title, and a legend. In this section, you will create a PivotTable and a PivotChart. Both the PivotTable and the PivotChart can be based on queries.

PivotTables

Figure 9–49 shows a sample PivotTable. The rows in the table represent the courses. The columns represent the analyst numbers. Each column is subdivided into the total of the hours spent and the total of the hours remaining for courses for those clients assigned to the analyst. The Grand Total column shows the total of the hours spent and hours remaining for each course (row). The last row shows the grand total for items in each column.

Figure 9–49

To create the PivotTable, you place fields in predefined areas of the table called **drop areas**. In the PivotTable in Figure 9–49, the Course Number field has been placed in the row area, for example. The drop areas are listed and described in Table 9–6.

BTW

PivotTable and PivotChart Forms
You also can create PivotTable and PivotChart forms. To create a PivotTable or PivotChart form, select the table or query for the form in the Navigation Pane, display the Create tab, click the More Forms button (Create tab | Forms group) and select either PivotTable or PivotChart. Click the Field List button to display the field list and then use the steps shown in this chapter to create the PivotTable or PivotChart.

PivotTables and PivotCharts

PivotTables and PivotCharts can be based on either a table or a query. To view a table or a query in PivotTable view, click the PivotTable View button on the status bar. Click the PivotChart View button on the status bar to view the table or query in PivotChart view.

Table 9–6 PivotTable Drop Areas

Area	Purpose
Row	Data from fields in this area will appear as rows in the table.
Column	Data from fields in this area will appear as columns in the table.
Filter	Data from fields in this area will not appear in the table but can be used to restrict the data that appears.
Detail	Data from fields in this area will appear in the detail portion (the body) of the table.
Data	Summary data (for example, a sum) from fields in this area will appear in the detail portion (the body) of the table. Individual values will not appear.

Plan Ahead

Determine the organization of the PivotTable.
Once you decide that you should create a PivotTable, you need to make decisions on the organization of the PivotTable.

- **Determine the field or fields that will be used for the rows and columns.** What do you want the rows in the table to represent? What do you want the columns to represent? You can easily reverse the roles later if you want.

- **Determine the field or fields that will be summarized in the table.** Precisely what calculations are to be presented by the PivotTable?

- **Determine the field or fields that will be used to filter the data.** Are there any fields — in addition to the ones already identified — that will be used to filter the data?

To Create a PivotTable

Applying the steps in the Plan Ahead, Camashaly Design has determined that the rows will represent the Course Number field; the columns will represent the Business Analyst Number field; and the Hours Spent and Hours Remaining fields will be summarized in the grid. They also have determined that they may occasionally want to filter the data using the Client Number field. The following steps create the PivotTable using the PivotTable view of the Analysts and Course Offerings query and place fields in appropriate drop areas.

- Open the Navigation Pane, right-click the Analysts and Course Offerings query, click Open on the shortcut menu, and then close the Navigation Pane.

- Click the View button arrow to display the View button menu (Figure 9–50).

Can I just click the View button?

No. Clicking the View button would move to Design view of the query. You want PivotTable view.

Figure 9–50

2

- Click PivotTable View to switch to the PivotTable view of the query.

- If the PivotTable Field List does not appear, click the Field List button (PivotTable Tools Design tab | Show/Hide group) to display the field list.

- Click Course Number in the field list, and then ensure Row Area appears next to the Add to button (Figure 9–51).

Q&A If Row Area does not appear next to the Add to button, what should I do?

Click the Add to box arrow, and then click Row Area.

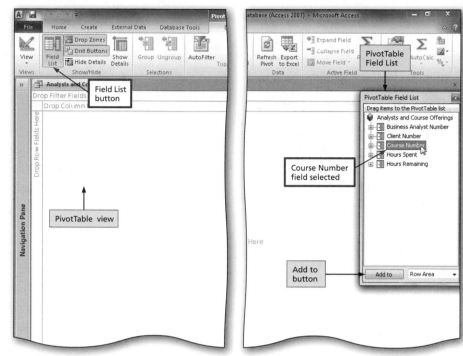

Figure 9–51

3

- Click the Add to button to add the Course Number field to the row area.

- Click the Add to box arrow to display the list of available areas (Figure 9–52).

Q&A Are the areas the same as drop areas?

Yes.

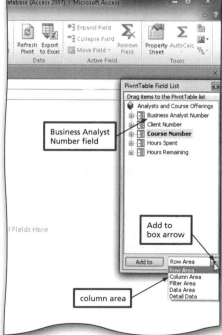

Figure 9–52

4

- Click Column Area, click the Business Analyst Number field in the field list, and then click the Add to button to add the Business Analyst Number field to the column area.

- Click the Add to box arrow, click Data Area, click Hours Spent, and then click the Add to button to add the Hours Spent field to the data area.

- Use the same technique to add the Hours Remaining field to the data area.

- Close the PivotTable Field List by clicking Field List button (PivotTable Tools Design tab | Show/Hide group) (Figure 9–53).

Figure 9–53

Other Ways

1. Click PivotTable View on status bar

To Change Properties in a PivotTable

You can use the property sheet for the objects in a PivotTable to change characteristics of the objects. The following steps use the appropriate property sheet to change the caption for Sum of Hours Spent to Spent and for Sum of Hours Remaining to Remaining in order to reduce the size of the columns in the PivotTable.

- Click the Sum of Hours Spent column heading to select it, and then click the Property Sheet button (PivotTable Tools Design tab | Tools group) to display a property sheet.

- Click the Captions tab in the property sheet (Figure 9–54).

2

- Delete the current entry in the Caption property box, type `Spent` as the new value for the Caption property, and then close the property sheet.

- Use the same technique to change the caption for the Sum of Hours Remaining box to Remaining.

Figure 9–54

To Save the PivotTable Changes

The following step saves the PivotTable changes.

 Click the Save button on the Quick Access Toolbar.

To Use a PivotTable

To view data using a PivotTable as well as to take advantage of the formatting and filtering that a PivotTable provides, you must open it. If the PivotTable is associated with a query, this would involve opening the query and then switching to PivotTable view. You then can click appropriate plus (+) or minus (–) signs to hide or show data. You also can click appropriate arrows and then check or uncheck the various items that appear to restrict the data that appears. You can drag items from one location to another to change the layout of the PivotTable. The following steps use the PivotTable view of the Analysts and Course Offerings query.

1

- If the query does not currently appear in PivotTable view, click the View button arrow and then click PivotTable View.

Q&A

What if I had closed the query? How would I get back in?

Right-click the query in the Navigation Pane and click Open on the shortcut menu.

- Click the plus sign (+) under analyst number 11 to remove the details for analyst number 11 (Figure 9–55).

Figure 9–55

2

- Click the minus sign (–) under analyst number 11 to again display data for analyst number 11.

- Click the Business Analyst Number arrow to display a list of available analyst numbers (Figure 9–56).

Figure 9–56

3

- Click the check box for analyst number 11 to remove the check mark and then click the OK button to remove the data for analyst number 11 (Figure 9–57).

🔑 **Experiment**

- Click the Business Analyst Number arrow and then try different combinations of check marks to see the effect of your choice.

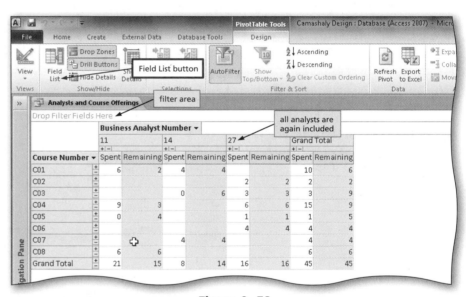

Figure 9–57

4

- Click the Business Analyst Number arrow, click the All check box to display all analyst numbers, and then click the OK button (Figure 9–58).

Figure 9–58

5

- Click the Field List button (PivotTable Tools Design tab | Show/Hide group) to display the PivotTable Field List. Click Client Number, click the Add to box arrow, click Filter Area, and then click the Add to button to add the Client Number field to the filter area.

- Click the Client Number arrow to display the client numbers (Figure 9–59).

Q&A

Why do I only see these clients and not the others?

These are the only clients who currently have courses.

Figure 9–59

6
- Click the check boxes in front of clients BA53 and CJ29 to remove the check marks and then click the OK button so that the data for these clients will not be reflected in the PivotTable.

- Close the field list (Figure 9–60).

 Experiment
- Click the Client Number arrow and then try different combinations of check marks to see the effect of your choice.

Figure 9–60

7
- Click the Client Number arrow, click the All check box, and then click the OK button to display data for all clients.

- Drag the Business Analyst Number field from the Column area to the Row area and then drag the Course Number field from the Row area to the Column area to reverse the organization (Figure 9–61).

Q&A I think I dragged to the wrong area. How can I fix it?

You should be able to redrag the fields into the correct areas. If you would rather start over, close the query without saving it, open the query, and then move to PivotTable view. You then can try again.

Figure 9–61

8
- Close the Analysts and Course Offerings query without saving your changes.

Q&A What if I save my changes?

The next time you open the query and move to PivotTable view, you will see the new organization. The roles of the rows and columns would be interchanged.

PivotCharts

BTW

Filtering PivotTables and PivotCharts
You can apply filters interactively to PivotTables and PivotCharts using the Filter area. This allows you to analyze your data more effectively. For example, applying a filter to the Analysts and Course Offerings PivotTable will help you analyze which clients are taking which courses. This knowledge can help you determine future course offerings.

Because you already created a PivotTable, your PivotChart for this query will automatically be based on the PivotTable. If you had not already created a PivotTable for a query or table, you could create a PivotChart for the query or table from scratch by placing fields in appropriate drop areas, just as you did when you created a PivotTable. The drop areas are shown in Figure 9–62. Their purpose is described in Table 9–7.

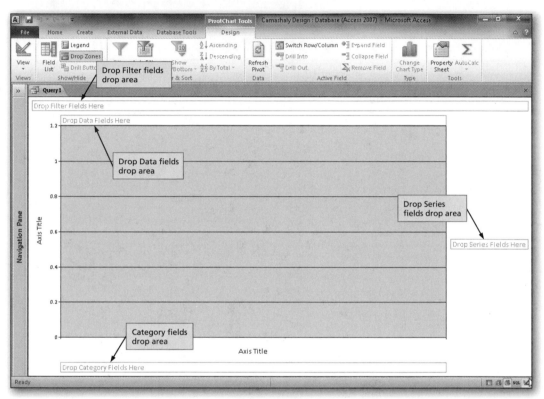

Figure 9–62

Table 9–7 PivotChart Drop Areas		
Area	**Purpose**	**Example**
Series	Data from fields in this area will appear as data series, which are represented by colored data markers such as bars. Related markers constitute a series and are assigned a specific color. The names and colors appear in the chart legend.	In the Camashaly Design PivotChart, the Series area contains the Course Number field. The course numbers and related colors appear in a legend.
Category	Data from fields in this area will appear as categories, that is, related groups of data. Category labels appear across the x-axis (horizontal area) of the chart provided the graph type selected has such an axis.	In the Camashaly Design PivotChart, the Category area contains the Business Analyst Number fields. The analyst numbers are listed across the x-axis.
Filter	Data from fields in this area will not appear in the chart but can be used to restrict the data that appears.	Camashaly does not currently use this feature in this PivotChart. If they decide they only want courses offered to certain clients, they would place the Client Number field in this area.
Data	Data from fields in this area will be summarized within the chart.	In the Camashaly Design PivotChart, Data areas are the Hours Spent and Hours Remaining fields. The sum of the values in these fields is represented by the bars in the chart.

Determine the organization of the PivotChart.

Once you decide that you should create a PivotChart, you need to make decisions on the organization of the PivotChart.

Plan
Ahead

- **Determine the field or fields that will be used for the series.** What field or fields will be represented as data series, that is, as colored data markers such as bars? Do you want these represented with a legend?

- **Determine the field or fields that will be used for the categories.** What field or fields will be represented as categories, that is, as related groups of data? Labels for these fields will appear across the *x*-axis in those chart types that have an *x*-axis.

- **Determine the field or fields that will be used for the data.** Which fields contain the data to be summarized in the chart?

- **Determine the field or fields that will be used to filter the data.** Are there any fields in addition to the ones already identified that will be used to filter the data?

- **Determine the type of chart.** What type of chart best represents the data? The most common types of charts are pie charts, line charts, and bar charts. A pie chart shows percentages as slices of pies. A line chart uses lines to connect dots that show ordered observations. A bar chart uses bars to show frequencies or values for different categories.

To Create a PivotChart and Add a Legend

If you are using the PivotChart view of a table or query and already have modified the PivotTable view, you have already done much of this work. Access will use the same information wherever possible. You can, of course, modify any aspect of the existing information to update the PivotChart. You can remove fields from drop areas by clicking the field name and then pressing the DELETE key. You can add fields to drop areas just as you did with the PivotTable. You also can make other changes, including adding a legend, changing the chart type, changing captions, and adding titles.

Camashaly Design has applied the steps in the Plan Ahead and determined that the Course Number field will be used for the series, the analysts will be used for the categories, the Spent and Remaining fields will furnish the data, and the chart type will be 3D Stacked Column.

The following steps create the PivotChart using PivotChart view of the Analysts and Course Offerings query and then add a legend.

1

- Open the Navigation Pane if it is currently closed.

- Open the Analysts and Course Offerings query.

- Close the Navigation Pane.

- Click the View button arrow, and then click PivotChart View.

- If the Chart Field List appears, close the field list by clicking the Field List button (PivotChart Tools Design tab | Show/Hide group) (Figure 9–63).

Q&A Where did the data come from?

Because you have already created a PivotTable, Access has represented the data in your PivotTable in the PivotChart. You can now make a variety of changes to this PivotChart.

Figure 9–63

2

- Click the Legend button (PivotChart Tools Design tab | Show/Hide group) to display a legend (Figure 9–64).

Figure 9–64

To Change the Chart Type

Several types of charts are available. You might find a pie chart more useful than a bar chart, for example. To change the chart type, use the Chart Type button, and then select the desired chart type. The following steps change the chart type to 3D Stacked Column.

1

- If the Change Chart Type button is dimmed, click the Chartspace (that is, the white space in the chart) (Figure 9–65).

Q&A

Does it matter where in the white space I click?

No.

Figure 9–65

2

• Click the Change Chart Type button (PivotChart Tools Design tab | Type group), and then, if necessary, click the Type tab to display the available chart types (Figure 9–66).

Figure 9–66

3

• Click the 3D Stacked Column type (row 2, column 3) to change the chart type.

 Experiment

• Click the Change Chart Type button and try other chart types to see how they present the data in the PivotChart. When done, select the 3D Stacked Column chart type.

• Close the property sheet (Figure 9–67).

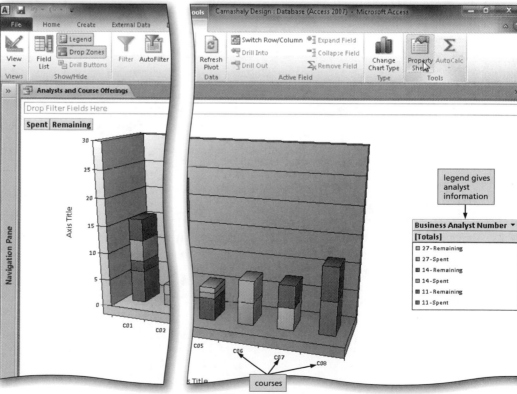

Figure 9–67

To Change PivotChart Orientation

The chart in Figure 9–67 has the course numbers along the horizontal axis and analyst numbers in the legend. The heights of the bars represent the total number of hours for each course. Within a bar, the colors represent the analyst and whether the amount represents hours remaining or hours spent (see legend). To change the chart orientation, you can click the Switch Row/Column button. The following step changes the orientation so the analyst numbers appear along the horizontal axis and the courses appear in the legend.

1
- Click the Switch Row/Column button (PivotChart Tools Design tab | Active Field group) to change the organization (Figure 9–68).

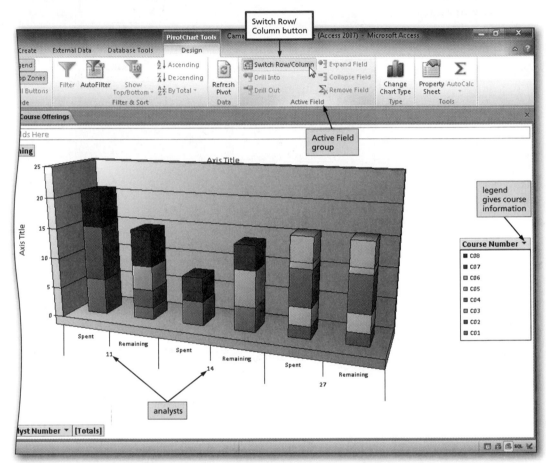

Figure 9–68

To Assign Axis Titles

You can assign titles to an axis by clicking the Axis Title box for the axis you want to change, displaying the property sheet, and then changing the Caption property to the title you want to assign. The following steps change the two axis titles to Hours and Business Analyst.

1

- Click the axis title to the left of the chart, and then display the property sheet.

- Click the Format tab in the Properties window, and then click the Caption box.

- Use the BACKSPACE or DELETE key to delete the old caption.

- Type **Hours** as the new caption (Figure 9–69).

2

- Close the property sheet to complete the change of the axis title.

- Use the same technique to change the other axis title to Analyst.

Other Ways

1. Right-click Axis Title box, click Properties on shortcut menu

Figure 9–69

To Remove Drop Areas

You can remove the drop areas from the PivotChart to give the chart a cleaner look. To do so, use the Drop Zones button on the Design tab. If you later need to use the drop areas to perform some task, you can return them to the screen by using the Drop Zones button on the Design tab a second time. The following step removes the drop areas.

1

- Click the Drop Zones button (PivotChart Tools Design tab | Show/ Hide group) to remove the drop zones (Figure 9–70).

Q&A

Why remove the drop zones? What if I want to use them later?

The PivotChart has a cleaner look without the drop zones (drop areas). You can always bring them back whenever you need them by clicking the Drop Zones button again.

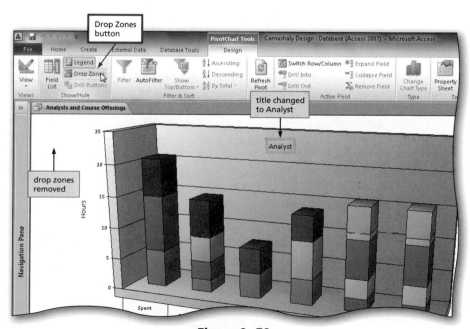

Figure 9–70

To Add a Chart Title

You can add a title to a PivotChart by clicking the Add Title button in the property sheet for the chart. You then can change the Caption property for the newly added title to assign the title of your choice. The following steps add a title to the PivotChart and then change the title's Caption property to Hours by Analyst and Course.

1

- Click anywhere in the Chartspace (the white space) of the PivotChart, display the property sheet, and then, if necessary, click the General tab.

- Click the Add Title button (Figure 9–71).

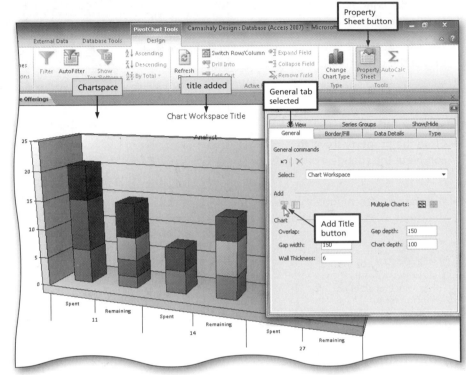

Figure 9–71

2

- Close the property sheet, click the newly added title, and then display the property sheet.

 Why did I have to change to a different property sheet?

The property sheet in Step 1 was the property sheet for the Chartspace. To change the title, you need to work with the property sheet for the title.

- Click the Format tab.

- Click the Caption box, and then use the BACKSPACE or DELETE key to erase the old caption.

- Type **Hours by Analyst and Course** as the new caption and press the ENTER key to change the caption (Figure 9–72).

Figure 9–72

3

- Close the property sheet (Figure 9–73).

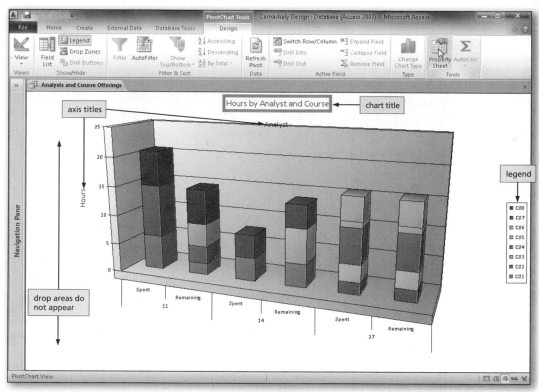

Figure 9–73

To Save the PivotChart Changes

The following step saves the PivotChart changes.

1 Click the Save button on the Quick Access Toolbar.

BTW

Certification
The Microsoft Office Specialist (MOS) program provides an opportunity for you to obtain a valuable industry credential — proof that you have the Access 2010 skills required by employers. For more information, visit the Access 2010 Certification Web page (scsite.com/ac2010/cert).

To Use a PivotChart

To use a PivotChart, you first must open the table or query with which it is associated and then switch to PivotChart view. You then can check or uncheck the various items that appear to restrict the data that appears. To do so, the drop areas must appear. If they do not, use the Drop Zones button on the Design tab to display them. You then can click the arrows. You also can drag fields to the drop areas.

You can make the same types of changes you made when you first created the PivotChart. You can change the chart type. You can change the orientation by clicking the By Row/By Column button. You can add or remove a legend. You can change titles. The following steps use the PivotChart view of the Analysts and Course Offerings query.

1

- Be sure the Analysts and Course Offerings query is open in PivotChart view.

- Click the Drop Zones button (PivotChart Tools Design tab | Show/Hide group) to display the drop areas (Figure 9–74).

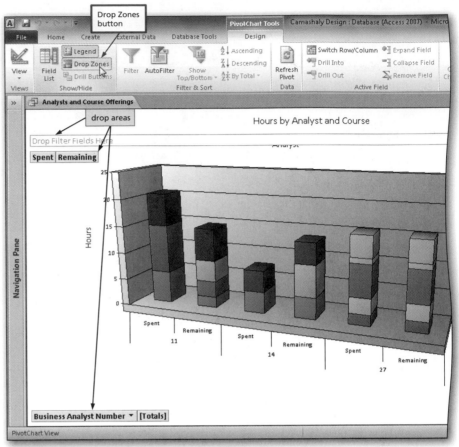

Figure 9–74

2

- Click the Business Analyst Number arrow to display the list of available analysts (Figure 9–75).

Figure 9–75

3

- Click the check box for analyst number 14 to remove the check mark and then click the OK button (Figure 9–76).

  Experiment

- Click the Business Analyst Number arrow and then try different combinations of check marks to see the effect of your choice.

4

- Close the PivotChart without saving your changes.

Q&A What would happen if I saved the changes?

The next time you view the PivotChart, the changes would be reflected. In particular, data for analyst 24 would not be reflected in the PivotChart.

Figure 9–76

To Quit Access

The following steps quit Access.

1 Click the Close button on the right side of the title bar to quit Access.

2 If a Microsoft Access dialog box appears, click the Save button to save any changes made to the object since the last save.

BTW **Quick Reference**
For a table that lists how to complete the tasks covered in this book using the mouse, Ribbon, shortcut menu, and keyboard, see the Quick Reference Summary at the back of this book, or visit the Access 2010 Quick Reference Web page (scsite.com/ac2010/qr).

Chapter Summary

In this chapter you have learned to create and use macros; create a menu form that uses command buttons for the choices; create a menu form that uses an option group for the choices; create a macro that implements the choices in the option group; create datasheet forms that utilize user interface macros; create a navigation form; add tabs to a navigation form; create data macros; create, customize, and use a PivotTable; and create, customize, and use a PivotChart. The following list includes all the new Access skills you have learned in this chapter.

1. Begin Creating a Macro (AC 543)
2. Add an Action to a Macro (AC 545)
3. Add Additional Actions to a Macro (AC 547)
4. Create a Menu Form Containing Command Buttons (AC 553)
5. Create a Menu Form Containing an Option Group (AC 556)
6. Create a Macro for the Option Group (AC 559)
7. Add Actions to the Macro (AC 562)
8. Create Datasheet Forms that Incorporate UI Macros (AC 565)
9. Create a Navigation Form (AC 568)
10. Add Tabs to a Navigation Form (AC 569)
11. Create a Data Macro (AC 572)
12. Create a PivotTable (AC 576)
13. Change Properties in a PivotTable (AC 578)
14. Use a PivotTable (AC 579)
15. Create a PivotChart and Add a Legend (AC 583)
16. Change the Chart Type (AC 584)
17. Change PivotChart Orientation (AC 586)
18. Assign Axis Titles (AC 586)
19. Remove Drop Areas (AC 587)
20. Add a Chart Title (AC 588)
21. Use a PivotChart (AC 589)

Learn It Online

Test your knowledge of chapter content and key terms.

Instructions: To complete the Learn It Online exercises, start your browser, click the Address bar, and then enter the Web address **scsite.com/ac2010/learn**. When the Access 2010 Learn It Online page is displayed, click the link for the exercise you want to complete and then read the instructions.

Chapter Reinforcement TF, MC, and SA
A series of true/false, multiple choice, and short answer questions that test your knowledge of the chapter content.

Flash Cards
An interactive learning environment where you identify chapter key terms associated with displayed definitions.

Practice Test
A series of multiple choice questions that test your knowledge of chapter content and key terms.

Who Wants To Be a Computer Genius?
An interactive game that challenges your knowledge of chapter content in the style of a television quiz show.

Wheel of Terms
An interactive game that challenges your knowledge of chapter key terms in the style of the television show *Wheel of Fortune*.

Crossword Puzzle Challenge
A crossword puzzle that challenges your knowledge of key terms presented in the chapter.

Apply Your Knowledge

Reinforce the skills and apply the concepts you learned in this chapter.

Figure 9–77

Creating Macros, PivotTables, and PivotCharts
Instructions: Start Access. If you are using the Microsoft Access 2010 Comprehensive text, open the Babbage CPA Firm database that you used in Chapter 8. Otherwise, see your instructor for information on accessing the files required in this book.

Perform the following tasks:
1. Create a data macro for the Accounts table. The macro will examine the value in the Hours Worked field. If the user's update would cause the value to be greater than 10, the macro will change the value to 8. If the user's update would cause the value to be less than 0, the macro will change the value to 0.

2. Create the navigation form shown in Figure 9–77. The purpose of the navigation form is to display three reports in the database as horizontal tabs. Name the form Report Menu and change the title to Reports for Babbage CPA Firm.

3. Create the PivotTable shown in Figure 9–78a and the PivotChart shown in Figure 9–78b. The PivotTable and PivotChart use the Bookkeepers and Accounts query created previously. In the PivotChart, the chart orientation has been changed. The chart type is 3D Stacked Column.

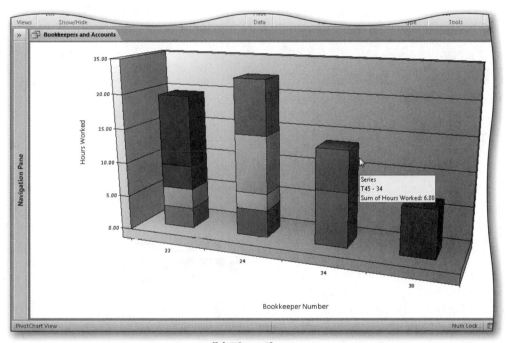

(a) PivotTable

(b) PivotChart

Figure 9–78

4. Submit the revised database in the format specified by your instructor.

Extend Your Knowledge

Extend the skills you learned in this chapter and experiment with new skills. You may need to use Help to complete the assignment.

Modifying Navigation Forms

Instructions: Copy the Camashaly Design database and rename the database to Chapter 9 Camashaly Design. Start Access and open the database that you copied and renamed.

Continued >

Extend Your Knowledge *continued*

Perform the following tasks:

1. Open the Main Menu form in Design view and expand the size of the form header. Add the current date to the form header. Add a command button to the form header that closes the form. Change the style of the command button to Colored Fill – Red, Accent 2. Change the background color of the Detail section to Light Gray 1 (row 2, column 1 of Standard Colors in the color palette). Save the changes and close the form.

2. Open the Reports List form in Design view. Select the Report Actions label, and change the font weight to semi-bold and the special effect to raised. You may need to enlarge the label slightly. Select all the option buttons and use the Size/Space menu to adjust the labels to the widest label. Save the changes and close the form.

3. Open the Forms List form in Design view. Add the title Form Actions to the form. Place a rectangle around the three command buttons. Make sure the back style is transparent and change the special effect for the rectangle to sunken. Save the changes and close the form.

4. Convert the Forms and Reports macro to Visual Basic code.

5. Open the Main Menu navigation form in Layout view. Change the shapes of the Forms tab and the Reports tab to Snip Single Corner Rectangle.

6. Submit the revised database in the format specified by your instructor.

Make It Right

Analyze a database and correct all errors and/or improve the design.

Correcting Macro Design Errors and Navigation Form Errors

Instructions: Start Access. Open the BikeDeliveries database. See the inside back cover of this book for instructions on downloading the Data Files for Students, or contact your instructor for more information about accessing the required files.

The BikeDeliveries database contains data for an organization that provides courier services using motorbikes. The owner of the company has created a datasheet form for the Customer table and a user interface macro that should open the Customer Update Form when a customer number is selected. When he tries to run the macro, he receives the error message shown in Figure 9–79.

The owner also forgot to set the Data Mode to Read Only for the form. He also created a navigation form for the database but forgot to add the Courier Master List as a tab, and he wanted to change the title on the form to BikeDeliveries. (*Hint:* To make changes to the navigation form, open the form in Layout view.)

Correct these errors and submit the revised database in the format specified by your instructor.

Figure 9–79

In the Lab

Design, create, modify, and/or use a database following the guidelines, concepts, and skills presented in this chapter. Labs are listed in order of increasing difficulty.

Lab 1: Creating Macros, a Navigation Form, and a PivotTable for the ECO Clothesline Database
Problem: ECO Clothesline would like an easy way to access the various tables, forms, and reports included in the database. This would make the database much easier to maintain and update.

Instructions: If you are using the Microsoft Office Access 2010 Comprehensive text, open the ECO Clothesline database that you used in Chapter 8. Otherwise, contact your instructor for more information about accessing the required files.

Perform the following tasks:

1. Create a macro named Forms and Reports that will include submacros to perform the following tasks:

   a. Open the Sales Rep Order Data form in read-only mode.

   b. Open the Sales Rep Master Form.

   c. Open the Customer Master Form.

   d. Preview the Sales Rep Master List.

   e. Preview the Customer Balance Report.

   f. Preview the Customer Discount Report.

   g. Export the Sales Rep Master List in PDF format.

   h. Export the Customer Balance Report in PDF format.

   i. Export the Customer Discount Report in PDF format.

2. Create the menu form shown in Figure 9–80. The command buttons should use the macros you created in Step 1 to open the Customer Master Form, the Sales Rep Master Form, and the Sales Rep Order Data form.

Figure 9–80

3. Create the menu form shown in Figure 9–81. The option group should use the macros you created in Step 1 to preview and export the three reports.

4. Create a datasheet form for the Customer table and name the form Customer. Create a UI macro for the Customer form. When a user clicks a customer number on a row in the datasheet, the Customer Master Form should appear in a pop-up form.

5. Create a datasheet form for the Sales Rep table and name the form Sales Rep. Create a UI macro for the Sales Rep form. When a user clicks a sales rep number on a row in the datasheet, the Sales Rep Master Form should appear in a pop-up form.

Figure 9–81

6. Create the navigation form shown in Figure 9–82 for the ECO Clothesline database. Use the same design for your navigation form as the one illustrated in this chapter. For example, the Customer tab should display the Customer form you created in Step 4, and the Sales Rep tab should display the Sales Rep form you created in Step 5. The Forms tab should display the Forms List form you created in Step 2, and the Reports tab should display the Reports List form you created in Step 3.

Continued >

In the Lab *continued*

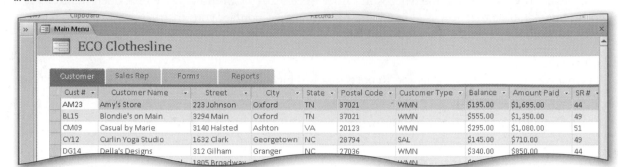

Figure 9–82

7. Submit the revised database in the format specified by your instructor.

In the Lab

Lab 2: Creating Macros and a Navigation Form for the Walburg Energy Alternatives Database

Problem: The management of the Walburg Energy Alternatives store would like an easy way to access the store's various tables, forms, and reports. This would make the database simpler to maintain and update.

Instructions: If you are using the Microsoft Office Access 2010 Comprehensive text, open the Walburg Energy Alternatives database that you used in Chapter 8. Otherwise, contact your instructor for more information about accessing the required files.

Perform the following tasks:
1. Create a macro that includes submacros to perform the following tasks:
   a. Open the Item Master Form.
   b. Open the Vendor Master Form.
   c. Open the Vendor Orders Data form in read-only mode.
   d. Preview the Inventory Status Report.
   e. Preview the Vendor Master Report.
   f. Preview the Item Discount Report.
   g. Export the Inventory Status Report in XPS format.
   h. Export the Vendor Master Report in XPS format.
   i. Export the Item Discount Report in XPS format. Name the macro Forms and Reports.

2. Create the menu form shown in Figure 9–83. The command buttons should use the macros you created in Step 1 to open the three forms. Be sure to include the title on the form.

3. Create the menu form shown in Figure 9–84. The command buttons should use the macros you created in Step 1 to preview and export the three reports. Be sure to include the title on the form.

Figure 9–83

4. Delete the Item form that is currently in the database. Create a datasheet form for the Item table and name the form Item. Create a user interface macro for the Item form. When a user clicks an item number on a row in the datasheet, the Item Master Form should appear in a pop-up form.

Figure 9–84

Figure 9–85

5. Create a datasheet form for the Vendor table and name the form Vendor. Create a user interface macro for the Vendor form. When a user clicks a vendor code on a row in the datasheet, the Vendor Master Form should appear in a pop-up form.

6. Create a navigation form for the Walburg Energy Alternatives database. Use the same design for your navigation form as the one illustrated in Figure 9–1a on page AC 538. For example, the Item tab should display the Item form you created in Step 4, and the Vendor tab should display the Vendor form you created in Step 5. The Forms tab should display the Forms List form you created in Step 2, and the Reports tab should display the Reports List form you created in Step 3.

7. Create the PivotTable shown in Figure 9–85. The PivotTable uses the Vendors and Orders query created previously. Change the caption for Sum of Numbered Ordered to Total Ordered.

8. Submit the revised database in the format specified by your instructor.

In the Lab

Lab 3: Creating Macros, a Navigation Form, a PivotTable, and PivotChart for the Philamar Training Database

Problem: Philamar Training wants an easy way to access the various tables, forms, and reports in the database. The company also wants the ability to easily change the way data concerning its classes and trainers is summarized and presented.

Instructions: Perform the following tasks: If you are using the Microsoft Office Access 2010 Comprehensive text, open the Philamar Training database that you used in Chapter 8. Otherwise, contact your instructor for more information about accessing the required files.

Instructions Part 1: Create a Forms and Reports macro that includes submacros to open the Client Update Form, the Trainer Master Form, and the Trainer Class Data form. The Trainer Class Data form should be read-only. The macro also should include submacros to preview and to export in PDF format

Continued >

In the Lab *continued*

the Client Status Report, the Clients by Trainer report, and the Trainer Master List report. Create a data macro for the Class Offerings table. The macro will examine the value in the Hours Spent field. If the user's update would cause the value to be greater than the Total Hours field, the macro will change the value to the value in the Total Hours field. If the user's update would cause the value to be less than 0, the macro will change the value to 0.

Instructions Part 2:   Create two menu forms, Forms List and Reports List, containing option groups. The first form, Forms List, should use the macros created in Part 1 to open each of the forms. The second form, Reports List, should use the macros created in Part 1 to preview and export the reports included in the macro. Create datasheet forms for both the Client table and the Trainer table. When a client number is selected in the datasheet form, the Client Update Form should open in a pop-up window as read-only. When a trainer number is selected in the datasheet form, the Trainer Master Form should open in a pop-up window as read-only. Create a navigation form for the Philamar Training database. Use the same design for your navigation form as the one illustrated in this chapter in Figure 9–1a. Include the Client form, the Trainer form, the Forms List form, and the Reports List form in the navigation form.

Instructions Part 3:   Create the PivotTable shown in Figure 9–86a and the PivotChart shown in Figure 9–86b. The PivotTable and PivotChart are based on the Trainers and Class Offerings query created previously.

Trainers and Class Offerings

Drop Filter Fields Here

Class Code	42 Spent	42 Remaining	48 Spent	48 Remaining	53 Spent	53 Remaining	67 Spent	67 Remaining	Grand Total Spent	Grand Total Remaining
C01	2	2	0	4					2	6
C02	0	4					2	2	2	6
C03			0	2	0	3			0	5
C04			3	3					3	3
C05			4	4					4	4
C06			4	12					4	12
C07							4	12	4	12
C08	3	9							3	9
C09	0	16							0	16
Grand Total	5	31	11	25	0	3	6	14	22	73

(a) PivotTable for Trainers and Class Offerings Query

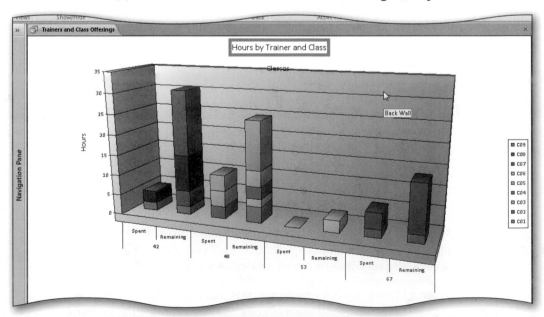

(b) PivotChart for Trainers and Class Offerings Query

Figure 9–86

Cases and Places

Apply your creative thinking and problem solving skills to design and implement a solution.

1: Creating Macros and a Navigation Form for the Chamber of Commerce Database

Academic

If you are using the Microsoft Access 2010 Comprehensive text, open the Chamber of Commerce database that you used in Chapter 8. Otherwise, see your instructor for more information about accessing the required files.

Your internship with the Chamber of Commerce is almost complete. The Chamber really appreciates the work you have done and is concerned that other employees will not be able to use the database as productively as you have. They have asked you to take on the task of creating macros and a navigation form. Use the concepts and techniques presented in this chapter to perform each of the following tasks:

a. Create a macro named CC Macros. The macro should include submacros to open the three forms: Advertiser Master Form, Ad Rep Master Form, and Ad Rep Account Data. The CC Macros macro also should include submacros to preview and export in PDF format the Ad Rep Master Report and the Advertiser Status Report. For the Ad Rep Account Data macro, select Read Only as the Data Mode.

b. Create a menu form for the three forms and a menu form for the two reports. Use command buttons for each form and include a descriptive title, such as Form Actions, on each form.

c. Create a datasheet form for the Advertiser table and name the form Advertiser. Create a user interface macro for the Advertiser form. When a user clicks an advertiser number on a row in the datasheet, the Advertiser Master Form should appear in a pop-up form.

d. Create a datasheet form for the Ad Rep table and name the form Ad Rep. Create a user interface macro for the Ad Rep form. When a user clicks an ad rep number on a row in the datasheet, the Ad Rep Master Form should appear in a pop-up form.

e. Create a navigation form for the Chamber of Commerce database. Use the same design for your navigation form as the one in Figure 9–1a. Include the Advertiser form, the Ad Rep form, the menu form for the forms, and the menu form for the reports.

Submit the revised database in the format specified by your instructor.

2: Creating Macros and a Navigation Form for the Consignment Database

Personal

If you are using the Microsoft Access 2010 Comprehensive text, open the Consignment database that you used in Chapter 8. Otherwise, see your instructor for more information about accessing the required files.

The volunteer group that manages the consignment shop would like to ensure that all volunteers can use the database easily. They have asked you to create macros and a navigation form for this purpose. Use the concepts and techniques presented in this chapter to perform each of the following tasks:

a. Create a macro named Consignment Macros. The macro should include macros to open the Item Master Form and the Seller Master Form, and to preview and export in XPS format the Available Items Report and the Item Sale Report.

b. Create a menu form that has two option groups: one for the two forms and one for the two reports. Name the menu form Forms and Reports.

c. Create a datasheet form for the Items table and name the form Items. Create a user interface macro for the Items form. When a user clicks an item number on a row in the datasheet, the Item Master Form should appear in a pop-up form.

Continued >

Cases and Places *continued*

d. Create a datasheet form for the Seller table and name the form Seller. Create a user interface macro for the Seller form. When a user clicks a seller code on a row in the datasheet, the Seller Master Form should appear in a pop-up form.

e. Create a navigation form for the Consignment database. The navigation form should be similar in design to the one created in this chapter. Include the Items datasheet form, the Seller datasheet form, and the Forms and Reports menu form.

Submit the revised database in the format specified by your instructor.

3: Creating Macros and a Navigation Form for the Senior Care Database

Professional

If you are using the Microsoft Access 2010 Comprehensive text, open the Senior Care database that you used in Chapter 8. Otherwise, see your instructor for more information about accessing the required files.

Senior Care is expanding rapidly, and several new employees will be using the database. These employees are not as familiar with Access as you are, so a navigation form would be beneficial. Use the concepts and techniques presented in this chapter to perform each of the following tasks:

a. Create a macro named SC Macros. The macro should include submacros to open three of the forms: Client Master Form, Helper Master Form, and Helper Service Data. They should also preview and export in XPS format the Helper Master Report and the Client Report. For the Helper Service Data macro, select Read Only as the Data Mode.

b. Create a menu form for the three forms and a menu form for the two reports included in the SC Macros macro. Use command buttons for both forms and include a descriptive title, such as Form Actions, on each form.

c. Create a datasheet form for the Client table and name the form Client. Create a user interface macro for the Client form. When a user clicks a client number on a row in the datasheet, the Client Master Form should appear in a pop-up form.

d. Create a datasheet form for the Helper table and name the form Helper. Create a user interface macro for the Helper form. When a user clicks a helper number on a row in the datasheet, the Helper Master Form should appear in a pop-up form.

e. Create a navigation form for the Chamber of Commerce database. Use the same design for your navigation form as the one illustrated in this chapter in Figure 9–1a on page AC 538. Include the Client datasheet form, the Helper datasheet form, and the menu forms that you created in Step b.

f. Create a PivotTable based on the Helpers and Services query you created previously. The rows in the PivotTable should be the Client Number, the columns should be the Helper Number, and the data area should contain the sum of hours worked. Create a PivotChart for the Helpers and Services query. Select the 3D Column Clustered type for the chart. Include a title for the chart and titles for both the *x*- and *y*-axes.

Submit the revised database in the format specified by your instructor.

10 | Administering a Database System

Objectives

You will have mastered the material in this project when you can:

- Create custom Quick Start fields
- Create a Web database and publish to Access Services
- Convert a database to and from earlier versions of Access
- Use the Table Analyzer, Performance Analyzer, and Documenter
- Create custom categories and groups in the Navigation Pane
- Use table, database, and field properties

- Create indexes
- Enable and use automatic error checking
- Encrypt a database and set a password
- Understand and use digital certificates
- Understand the purpose and use of options within the Trust Center
- Lock a database and split a database

10 Administering a Database System

Introduction

Administering a database system is an important activity that has many facets. These activities go far beyond the simple updating of a database's contents. They include activities to improve the usability, accessibility, security, and efficiency of the database.

Project —Administering a Database System

Camashaly Design realizes the importance of database administration, that is, the importance of administering its database system properly. Making a database available on the Web (Figure 10–1) is part of this activity. Another important activity in administering databases is the creation of custom templates, application parts, and data type parts. Application parts and data type parts are templates that you can add to your database to extend its functionality. Clicking an application part adds to your database a predetermined collection of objects such as tables, queries, forms, reports, and/or macros. Clicking a data type part adds a predetermined collection of fields to a table.

Camashaly management realizes that database administration encompasses a wide variety of activities (Figure 10–2). Database administration can include conversion of an Access database to an earlier version of Access. Database administration usually includes such activities as analyzing tables for potential problems, analyzing performance to see if changes are warranted to make the system perform more efficiently, and documenting the various objects in the database. It can include creating custom categories and groups in the Navigation Pane as well as changing table and database properties. It also can include the use of field properties in such tasks as creating a custom input mask and allowing zero-length

BTW

Q&As
For a complete list of the Q&As found in many of the step-by-step sequences in this book, visit the Access 2010 Q&A Web page (scsite.com/ac2010/qa).

BTW

BTWs
For a complete list of the BTWs found in the margins of this book, visit the Access 2010 BTW Web page (scsite .com/ac2010/btw).

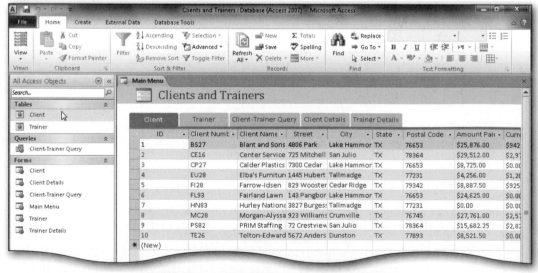

(a) Clients and Trainers Database in Access

Figure 10–1

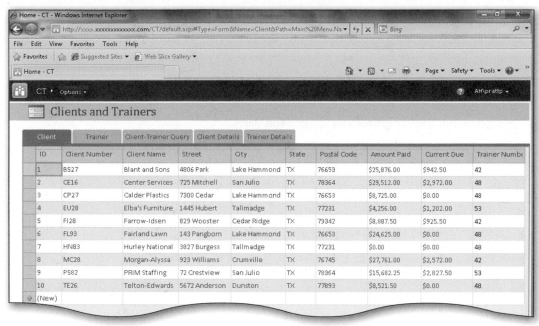

(b) Clients and Trainers Database on the Web

Figure 10–1

strings. It can include the creation of indexes to speed up retrieval. The inclusion of automatic error checking is part of the administration of a database system. Understanding the purpose of digital certificates and the Trust Center is critical to the database administration function. Another important area of database administration is the protection of the database. This protection includes locking the database through the creation of an ACCDE file to prevent unauthorized changes from being made to the VBA source code or to the design of forms and reports. Splitting the database into a front-end and a back-end database is another way to protect the functionality and efficiency of a database.

Figure 10–2

Overview

As you read through this chapter, you will learn how to administer a database by performing these general tasks:

- Create custom Quick Start fields.
- Create a Web database and learn how to publish the database to Access Services.
- Create and use templates and application parts.
- Learn how to convert databases to and from earlier versions of Access as well as how to use tools for analyzing and documenting Access databases.
- Create custom categories and groups in the Navigation Pane.
- Use table, database, and field properties as well as create indexes.
- Learn how to use automatic error checking.
- Understand digital certificates and the Trust Center.
- Lock a database and split a database.

BTW

Exporting XML Data
Database administration also may include responsibility for exchanging data between dissimilar systems or applications. **Extensible Markup Language (XML)** is a data interchange standard for describing and delivering data on the Web. With XML, you can describe both the data and the structure (schema) of the data. You can export tables, queries, forms, or reports. To export a database object, select the object and click the XML File button (External Data tab | Export group). Select the appropriate options in the Export XML dialog box.

Plan Ahead

Database Administration Guidelines

There are some special issues involved in administering a database. These issues are especially important when more than one person uses the database. As you make decisions about administering the database, you should follow these general guidelines:

1. **Determine whether a database needs to be able to be shared over the Web.** Do you have users who would benefit from being able to access a database over the Web? If so, you will need to create a database that is Web compatible and then publish the database to Access Services on a SharePoint site.

2. **Determine whether you should create any templates, application parts, or data type parts.** Is there a particular combination of tables, queries, forms, reports, and/or macros that you would like to enable users to easily include in their databases? If so, you could create a template and an application part containing the specific objects you want them to be able to include. Is there a particular collection of fields that you would like to enable users to include with a single click? If so, you could create a data type part containing those fields.

3. **Determine whether a database needs to be converted to or from an earlier version.** Do users of a previous version of Access need to be able to use the database? If so, you will need to be sure the database does not contain any features that would prevent it from being converted. Is there a database that was created in an earlier version of Access that you would like to use in Access 2010? If so, you can convert the database for use in Access 2010.

4. **Determine when to analyze and/or document the database.** Once you create a database, you should use the table and performance analyzers to determine if any changes to the structure are warranted. You also should document the database. You should perform these tasks whenever you change the structure.

5. **Determine the most useful way to customize the Navigation Pane.** Would it be helpful to have custom categories and groups? What objects should be in the groups? Would it be helpful to restrict the objects that appear to only those whose names contain certain characters? If so, you can customize the Navigation Pane to improve interaction with the database.

6. **Determine any table-wide validation rules.** Are there any validation rules that involve more than a single field? For example, a validation rule that states that the hours spent cannot exceed the total hours would involve both the Hours Spent and the Total Hours fields. Establishing such rules is a database administration function.

(continued)

(continued)

7. **Determine any custom database properties.** Are there properties that would be helpful in documenting the database and are not included in the list of database properties you can use? If so, you can add custom properties. For example, you may want a property called Status that indicates whether this database is a test version or the live version of the database. You may also want a property that indicates the date on which the database went into production.

8. **Determine indexes.** Examine retrieval and sorting requirements to determine possible indexes. Indexes can make both retrieval and sorting more efficient.

9. **Determine whether the database should be encrypted.** Encrypting a database is an excellent security feature. If you need to protect the security of the database's contents, you should strongly consider encryption. As part of the process, you also will set a password.

10. **Determine whether the database should be locked.** Should users be able to change the design of forms, reports, and/or macros? If not, you should lock the database to prevent such changes.

11. **Determine whether the database should be split.** It is often more efficient to split the database into a back-end database, which contains only the table data, and a front-end database, which contains other objects, such as queries, forms, and reports.

When necessary, more specific details concerning the above decisions and/or actions are presented at appropriate points in the chapter. The chapter also will identify the use of these guidelines in the administration of a database.

Plan Ahead

To Start Access

The following steps, which assume Windows 7 is running, start Access based on a typical installation. You may need to ask your instructor how to start Access for your computer.

1 Click the Start button on the Windows 7 taskbar to display the Start menu.

2 Type **Microsoft Access** as the search text in the 'Search programs and files' text box and watch the search results appear on the Start menu.

3 Click Microsoft Access 2010 in the search results on the Start menu to start Access.

4 If the Access window is not maximized, click the Maximize button next to the Close button on its title bar to maximize the window.

BTW

The Ribbon and Screen Resolution
Access may change how the groups and buttons within the groups appear on the Ribbon, depending on the computer's screen resolution. Thus, your Ribbon may look different from the ones in this book if you are using a screen resolution other than 1024 × 768.

To Open a Database from Access

The following steps open the Camashaly database from the Access folder in the CIS 101 folder on the USB flash drive.

1 With your USB flash drive connected to one of the computer's USB ports, click File on the Ribbon to open the Backstage view if necessary.

2 Click Open in the Backstage view to display the Open dialog box.

3 Navigate to the location of the file to be opened (in this case, the USB flash drive, then to the CIS 101 folder [or your class folder], and then to the Access folder).

④ Click Camashaly Design to select the file to be opened.

⑤ Click the Open button (Open dialog box) to open the selected file and display the opened database in the Access window.

⑥ If a Security Warning appears, click the Enable Content button.

Data Type Parts

Access contains data type parts that are available on the More Fields gallery. Some data type parts, like the Category part, consist of a single field. Others, like the Address part, consist of multiple fields. To insert all the fields in the part into your table, all you need to do is click the part. In addition to the parts provided by Access, you can create your own parts.

To Create Custom Data Parts

To create data parts in the Quick Start category from existing fields, you select the desired field or fields and then select the Save Selection as New Data Type command in the More Fields gallery. If you select multiple fields, the fields must be adjacent. If you have fields you do not want within the group of adjacent fields, you need to hide the fields you do not want before selecting the desired fields. The following steps create a Quick Start field consisting of the Last Name, First Name, Street, City, State, and Postal Code fields in the Business Analyst table. Once you have created this Quick Start field, users can add this collection of fields to a table by simply clicking the Quick Start field. Before creating this Quick Start field, however, you must hide the Phone Number field, because it appears between the State field and the Postal Code field.

- Open the Business Analyst table in Datasheet view and close the Navigation Pane.

- Right-click the Phone Number column heading to produce a shortcut menu (Figure 10–3).

Q&A

I see a Freeze Fields command on the shortcut menu. What does that command do?

The Freeze Fields command allows you to place a column or columns in the table on the left side of the table. As you scroll to the right, the column or columns remain visible. To freeze a column or columns, select the column(s), right-click and click Freeze Fields on the shortcut menu. To unfreeze fields, click the Unfreeze All Fields command on the shortcut menu. When you freeze a column, Access considers it a change to the layout of the table. When you close the table, Access will ask if you want to save your changes.

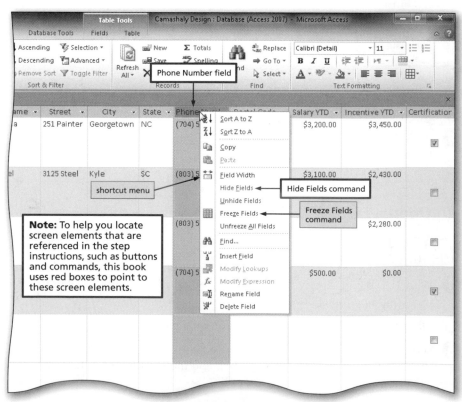

Figure 10–3

2

- Click Hide Fields on the shortcut menu to hide the Phone Number field.

 How do I unhide a field that I have previously hidden?

Right-click any column heading and then click Unhide Fields on the shortcut menu. You will see a list of fields with a check box for each field. The hidden field will not have a check mark in the check box. To unhide the field, click the check box for the field.

- Click the column heading for the Last Name field to select the field.

- Hold the SHIFT key down and click the column heading for the Postal Code field to select all the fields from the Last Name field to the Postal Code field.

- Display the Table Tools Fields tab.

- Click the More Fields button (Table Tools Fields tab | Add & Delete group) to display the More Fields gallery (Figure 10–4).

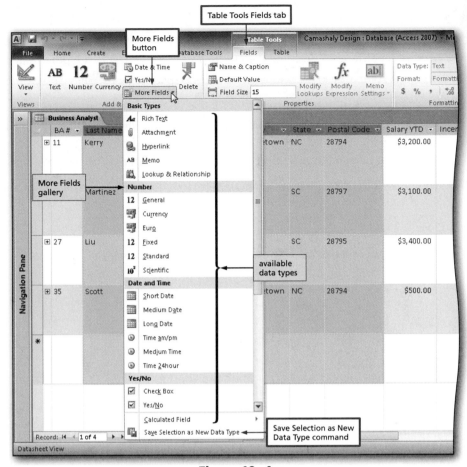

Figure 10–4

3

- Click Save Selection as New Data Type to display the Create New Data Type from Fields dialog box.

- Enter **Name-Address** as the name.

- Enter **Last Name, First Name, Street, City, State, and Postal Code** as the description.

 What is the purpose of the description?

When a user points to the Quick Start field you created, a ScreenTip will appear containing the description you entered.

- Click the Category drop-down arrow to display a list of available categories (Figure 10–5).

Figure 10–5

4

- Click Quick Start to indicate the new data type will be added to the Quick Start category.

Q&A

What is the difference between the Quick Start and User Defined Types category?

If you select the Quick Start category, the data type you create will be listed among the Quick Start data types that are part of Access. If you select the User Defined Types category, the data type you create will be in a separate category containing only those data types you create. In either case, however, clicking the data type will produce the same result.

- Click the OK button (Create New Data Type from Fields dialog box) to save the data type.

- When Access indicates that your template (that is, your Quick Start field) has been saved, click the OK button (Microsoft Access dialog box).

- Close the table.

- Click No when asked if you want to save the changes to the layout of the table.

BTW

SharePoint Services
SharePointServices 2010 offers users the ability to store data on the Web so that access to that data can be shared across a network. It is essentially a storage location that can be accessed collaboratively. No special software is required on the client side. SharePoint Services technology is particularly useful for sharing information across an intranet. SharePoint Services 2010 supports Access Services, which is the server-side support needed to host Access applications in SharePoint.

Web Databases

Posting a database to the Web enables other users to share the database. You can create a Web database in Access. A **Web database** is a database that is designed to be published to the Web on a SharePoint server, which is a technology that enables sharing of Microsoft Office documents and databases over the Web. Specifically, Web databases are published to a SharePoint server that is running Access Services. Access Services is a feature that supports the integration of Access 2010 with a SharePoint server.

You will find that there are restrictions in place when you create Web databases. You do not have access to Design view when creating a table; you must create the table in Datasheet view. Although you can change the name of the default autonumber primary key, you cannot change its data type. If you have a text field that you want to be the primary key, the best you can do is to specify that the field must be both required and unique. You cannot create relationships as you can do with a typical database. Rather, any relationships must be specified through lookup fields.

BTW

Forms and Reports in a Web Database
If you plan to use forms and reports in a Web database, you must create the forms and reports using Layout view.

Plan Ahead

Determine the design of the Web database.
If you decide to create a Web database, you must determine the design of the database. In particular, determine:

- The tables that make up the database. This process is similar to designing any other database, except that there are some restrictions on the primary key and on how you relate the tables.

- Any queries, forms, reports, or macros to include in the database.

- The main menu for the database. Determine the tabs that go on the navigation form that will be the main menu. If you would like a table to appear in Datasheet view on any tab, you will need to create a datasheet form for the table. You would then use the datasheet form on the tab.

To Create a Blank Web Database

The following steps create a blank Web database. Because it is a Web database, only those options appropriate for Web databases will be available.

- Click File on the Ribbon to open the Backstage view.

- Click the New tab.

- Click the 'Blank web database' button.

- Click the Browse button to display the File New Database dialog box, type **Clients and Trainers** as the name of the database file, navigate to the desired save location, and then click the OK button to return to the Backstage view (Figure 10–6).

Figure 10–6

- Click the Create button to create the database (Figure 10–7).

Figure 10–7

To Add Fields to the Table

The following steps add the Trainer Number, Last Name, First Name, Street, City, State, Postal Code, Commission Rate, and YTD Commission fields to a table. They designate the Trainer Number field as both required and unique. They add the Last Name, First Name, Street, City, State, and Postal Code as a single operation by using the Quick Start field created earlier. After adding the fields, they save the table using the name, Trainer.

- Click the Click to Add column heading and select Text as the data type.

- Type **Trainer Number** as the field name.

- Click the white space below the field name to complete the change of the name. Click the white space a second time to select the field.

- Change the field size to 2.

- Click the Required check box (Table Tools Fields tab | Field Validation group) to make the field a required field.

- Click the Unique check box (Table Tools Fields tab | Field Validation group) so that Access will ensure that values in the field are unique (Figure 10–8).

Figure 10–8

- Click under the Click to Add column heading to produce an insertion point in the next field.

- Click the More Fields button (Table Tools Fields tab | Add & Delete group) to display the More Fields gallery (Figure 10–9).

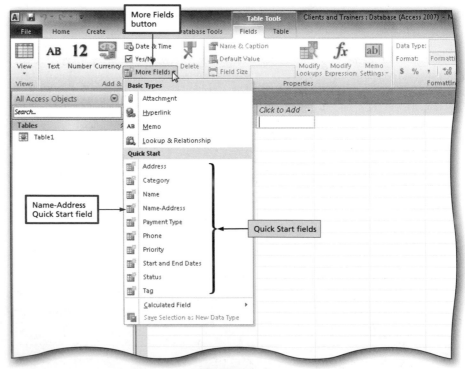

Figure 10–9

3

- Click the Name-Address Quick Start field that you created earlier to add the Last Name, First Name, Street, City, State, and Postal Code fields (Figure 10–10).

4

- Add the Hourly Rate and YTD Earnings fields as the last two fields. Both fields have the Currency data type.

- Save the table, assigning **Trainer** as the table name.

- Close the table.

fields added in one step; fields are based on the same fields from Business Analyst table

Figure 10–10

To Create a Second Table

The following steps create the Client table. They add a lookup field for Trainer Number to relate the two tables.

1

- Display the Create tab (Figure 10–11).

Q&A

What happened to the Table Design button?

The Table Design button creates a table in Design view. Design view is not available for Web databases.

Create tab

Table button

new table

Figure 10–11

2

- Click the Table button (Create tab | Tables group) to create a new table.

- Click the Click to Add column heading and select Text as the data type.

- Type **Client Number** as the field name.

- Click the white space below the field name to complete the change of the name. Click the white space a second time to select the field.

Figure 10–12

- Change the field size to 4.

- Click the Required check box (Table Tools Fields tab | Field Validation group) to make the field a required field.

- Click the Unique check box (Table Tools Fields tab | Field Validation group) so that Access will ensure that values in the field are unique (Figure 10–12).

3

- Click under the Click to Add column heading to produce an insertion point in the next field.

- Click the More Fields button (Table Tools Fields tab | Add & Delete group) to display the More Fields gallery (see Figure 10–9 on page AC 610).

- Click the Name-Address Quick Start field that you added earlier to add the Last Name, First Name, Street, City, State, and Postal Code fields.

Figure 10–13

- Right-click the Last Name field to produce a shortcut menu, and then click Delete Field to delete the field.

- Right-click the First Name field to produce a shortcut menu, click Rename Field to rename the field, and then type **Client Name** as the field name.

- Change the field size to 30 (Figure 10–13).

4

- Add the Amount Paid and Current Due fields. Both fields have the Currency data type.

- Save the table, assigning **Client** as the table name.

- Scroll, if necessary, so that the Click to Add column appears on your screen.

- Click the Click to Add column heading to display a menu of available data types (Figure 10–14).

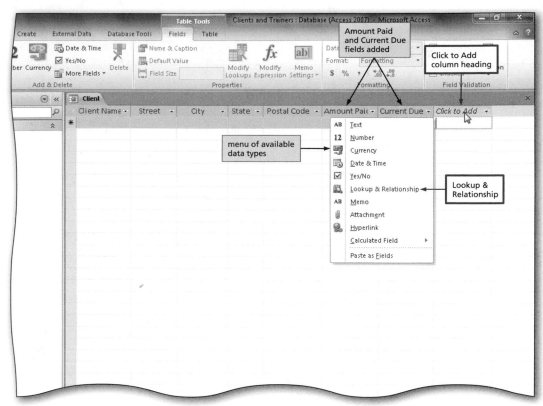

Figure 10–14

5

- Click Lookup & Relationship to display the Lookup Wizard dialog box (Figure 10–15).

Figure 10–15

6

- Ensure that the 'I want the lookup field to get the values from another table' option button is selected.

- Click the Next button to display the next Lookup Wizard dialog box, and then click the Trainer table to select it (Figure 10–16).

Figure 10–16

7

- Click the Next button, and then select the Trainer Number, First Name, and Last Name fields for the columns in the lookup field (Figure 10–17).

Figure 10–17

8

- Click the Next button, select the Trainer Number field for the sort order, and then click the Next button again (Figure 10–18).

Figure 10–18

9

- Ensure the 'Hide key column (recommended)' check box is selected, and then click the Next button.

- Type **Trainer Number** as the label for the lookup field.

- Click the Enable Data Integrity check box to select it (Figure 10–19).

Q&A

What is the effect of selecting Enable Data Integrity?

Access will enforce referential integrity for the trainer number. That is, Access will not allow a trainer number in a client record that does not match the number of a trainer in the Trainer table.

Figure 10–19

10

- Click the Finish button to add the lookup field.

- Save the table.

- Close the table.

To Import the Data

Now that the tables have been created, you need to add data to them. You could enter the data, or if the data is already in electronic form, you could import the data. The data for the Trainer and Client tables is included in the Data Files for Students as text files. The following steps import the data.

1 With the Clients and Trainers database open, display the External Data tab, and then click the Text File button (External Data tab | Import & Link group) to display the Get External Data–Text File dialog box.

2 Click the Browse button (Get External Data–Text File dialog box) and select the location of the files to be imported, for example, the folder called AccessData on drive E:. Select the Trainer text file and then click the Open button.

3 Select the 'Append a copy of records to the table' option button, select the Trainer table, and then click the OK button.

4 Be sure the Delimited option button is selected and then click the Next button.

5 Be sure the Comma option button is selected, click the Next button, and then click the Finish button.

6 Click the Close button to close the Get External Data – Text File dialog box without saving the import steps.

7 Use the technique shown in Steps 1 through 6 to import the Client text file into the Client table.

BTW

Rearranging Fields in a Query
If you add fields to a query in the wrong order, you can select the field in design grid, and drag it to the appropriate location.

To Create a Query Relating the Tables

The following steps create a query that relates the Client and Trainer tables.

1 Display the Create tab and then click the Query button (Create tab | Queries group) to create a new query.

2 Click the Client table, click the Add button, click the Trainer table, click the Add button, and then click the Close button to close the Show Table dialog box.

3 Double-click the Client Number, Client Name, and Trainer Number fields from the Client table. Double-click the First Name and Last Name fields from the Trainer table to add the fields to the design grid.

4 Click the Save button on the Quick Access Toolbar to save the query, type `Client-Trainer Query` as the name of the query, and then click the OK button.

5 Close the query.

BTW

Adding a Logo to a Form or Report
Many organizations require that all forms and reports include the company logo. It is the database administrator's job to ensure that all the organization's database policies are followed. To add a logo to a form or report, open the form or report in either Layout view or Design view. Click the Logo button (Design tab | Header/Footer group).

Creating Forms

There are several types of forms that need to be created for this database. The Client and Trainer detail forms show a single record at a time. The Client, Trainer, and Client-Trainer Query forms are intended to look like the corresponding table or query in Datasheet view. Finally, the main menu is a navigation form.

To Create Single-Item Forms

The following steps create two single-item forms, that is, forms that display a single record at a time. The first form, called Client Details, is for the Client table. The second form is for the Trainer table and is called Trainer Details.

1

• Select the Client table in the Navigation Pane and then display the Create tab (Figure 10–20).

Figure 10–20

2

- Click the Form button (Create tab | Forms group) to create a single-item form for the Client table.

- Click the Save button on the Quick Access Toolbar and then type **Client Details** as the name of the form (Figure 10–21).

3

- Click the OK button (Save As dialog box) to save the form.

- Close the form.

- Select the Trainer table, display the Create tab, and then click the Form button (Create tab | Forms group) to create a single-item form for the Trainer table.

- Save the form, using **Trainer Details** as the form name.

- Close the form.

Figure 10–21

To Create Datasheet Forms

The following steps create two datasheet forms, that is, forms that display the data in the form of a datasheet. The first form is for the Client table and is also called Client. The second is for the Trainer table and is also called Trainer. The steps also create macros that will display the data for a selected record in a single-item form, as you did in Chapter 9 on pages AC 566 through AC 568.

1

- Select the Client table and then display the Create tab.

- Click the Datasheet button (Create tab | Forms group) to create a datasheet form for the Client table.

- Click the Save button on the Quick Access Toolbar and then accept Client as the default name of the form.

- Click the column heading for the ID field to select the field.

- Display the property sheet and click the Event tab to display only the event properties (Figure 10–22).

Figure 10–22

2

• Click the Build button (the three dots) for the On Click event and then use the techniques on pages AC 559 through AC 563 in Chapter 9 to enter the macro shown in Figure 10–23.

3

• Click the Save button (Macro Tools Design tab | Close group) to save the macro and then click the Close button to close the macro.

• Close the property sheet.

• Save the Client datasheet form and then close the form.

Figure 10–23

4

• Use the techniques in Steps 1 and 2 to create a datasheet form for the Trainer table. Use **Trainer** as the name for the form. The macro for the On Click event for the ID field is shown in Figure 10–24.

5

• Save and close the macro.

• Close the property sheet.

• Save and close the form.

6

• Select the Client-Trainer Query.

• Create a datasheet form for the Client-Trainer Query. Save the form, using **Client-Trainer Query** as the form name.

• Close the Client-Trainer Query.

 Experiment

• Test each of the macros by clicking the ID number in the Client form or the Trainer form. Ensure that the correct form opens. If there are errors, correct the corresponding macro. When finished, close any form you have opened.

Figure 10–24

To Create a Navigation Form

The following steps create a navigation form containing a single row of horizontal tabs. The steps save the form using the name, Main Menu. They change the form title and add the appropriate tabs.

1
- Display the Create tab and then click the Navigation button (Create tab | Forms group) to show the menu of available navigation forms.

- Click Horizontal Tabs in the menu to create a form with a navigation control in which the tabs are arranged in a single row, horizontally.

- If a field list appears, click the Add Existing Fields button (Form Layout Tools Design tab | Tools group) to remove the field list.

Figure 10–25

- Save the navigation form, using **Main Menu** as the form name.

- Click the form title twice, once to select it and the second time to produce an insertion point.

- Erase the current title and then type **Clients and Trainers** as the new title (Figure 10–25).

2
- One at a time, drag the Client form, the Trainer form, the Client-Trainer Query form, the Client Details form, and the Trainer Details form to the positions shown in Figure 10–26.

- Save and close the form.

Q&A

What should I do if I made a mistake and added a form to the wrong location?

You can rearrange the tabs by dragging. Often, the simplest way to correct a mistake is to click the Undo button to reverse your most recent action. However, you can also choose to simply close the form without saving it and then start over.

Figure 10–26

To Select a Startup Form

If the database includes a navigation form, it is common to select the navigation form as a **startup form,** a form that appears when a user opens the database. The following steps ensure that the navigation form appears automatically when the Clients and Trainers database is opened. They also ensure the navigation form appears automatically when a user accesses the database on the Web.

- Click File on the Ribbon to display the Backstage view (Figure 10–27).

Figure 10–27

- Click the Options button.

- Click Current Database (Access Options dialog box) to select the options for the current database.

- Click the Display Form box arrow to display the list of available forms.

- Click Main Menu to select it as the form that will automatically be displayed whenever the database is opened.

- Click the Web Display Form box arrow to display the list of available forms.

- Click Main Menu to select it as the form that will automatically be displayed whenever the database is opened on the Web (Figure 10–28).

Figure 10–28

3

- Click the OK button (Access Options dialog box) to save your changes.

- Click the OK button (Microsoft Access dialog box) when Access displays a message indicating that you must close and reopen the database for the change to take effect.

- Close the database.

Break Point: If you wish to stop working through the chapter at this point, you can close Access now. You can resume the project at a later time by starting Access, and continuing to follow the steps from this location forward.

Templates

A **template** is a file that contains the elements needed to produce a specific type of complete database. You can select a template when you create a database. The resulting database will contains all the tables, queries, forms, reports, and/or macros included in the template. In addition, with some templates, the resulting database may also contain data.

Some templates are also available as **application parts**. Application parts are very similar to templates in that selecting a single application part can create tables, queries, forms, reports, and macros. The difference is that you select a template when you first create a database, whereas you select an application part after you have already created a database. The objects (tables, queries, forms, reports, and macros) in the application part will be added to any objects you already have created.

Access provides a number of templates representing a variety of types of databases (see Figure 10–6 on page AC 609). You also can create your own template from an existing database. When you create a template, you can choose to create an application part as well. In addition, you can choose whether or not to include data.

If you want to create a template from a database you plan to publish to Access Services, it is important to create the template before publishing the database. The publishing process turns the database into a Web application rather than a database, which prevents you from creating the template.

BTW

Templates and Application Parts
User-created templates and application parts are stored in the AppData folder. By default, this is a hidden folder in Windows.

To Create a Template

Before publishing the Clients and Trainers database to Access Services, the following steps create a template from the database. The steps also create an application part from the database.

1

- Open the Clients and Trainers database (Figure 10–29).

Figure 10–29

2

- Close the Main Menu form.

- Open the Backstage view.

- Click the Save & Publish tab.

- Click the Template button in the Save Database As area to indicate you are creating a template (Figure 10–30).

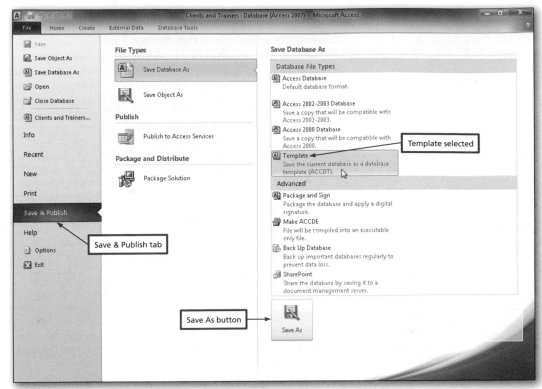

Figure 10–30

3

- Click the Save As button to display the Create New Template from This Database dialog box.

- Type **Clients and Trainers** as the name.

- Type **Database of clients and trainers with navigation form menu** as the description.

- Click the Application Part check box to indicate that you also want to create an application part.

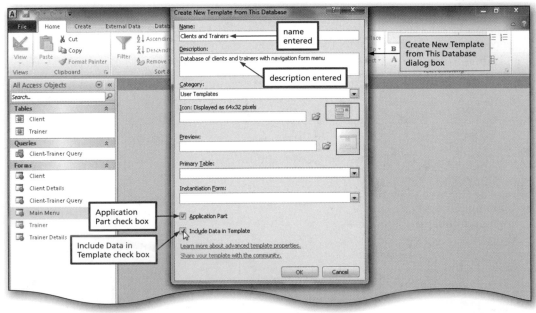

Figure 10–31

- Click the Include Data in Template check box to indicate you want to include the data in the database as part of the template (Figure 10–31).

Why include data?

When someone creates a database using the template, the database will automatically include data. This enables the users to see what any reports, forms, or queries look like with data in them. Once the users have the reports, forms, and queries the way they want them, they can delete all this data. At that point, they can begin adding the real data to the database.

4

- Click the OK button (Create New Template from This Database dialog box) to create the template.

- When Access indicates that the template has been successfully saved, click the OK button (Microsoft Access dialog box).

To Check Web Compatibility

Before publishing to Access Services, you should ensure that the database is compatible with the Web. To do so, you run the compatibility checker, which will tell you whether the database is compatible. If it is not, the compatibility checker will indicate the issues that prevent the database from being compatible. The following step ensures that the Clients and Trainers database is compatible with the Web.

1

- Open the Backstage view and then click the Save & Publish tab.

- Click Publish to Access Services in the Publish area and then click the Run Compatibility Checker button to check Web compatibility (Figure 10–32).

Q&A

What do I do if the database is not compatible with the Web?

Click the Web Compatibility Issues button to see the specific issues you would need to address. With each issue, there is a link to information on how to address the issue. The most difficult issues are relationships, which Web databases implement using lookup fields. To fix a relationship issue, you need to delete the relationship and then add the appropriate lookup.

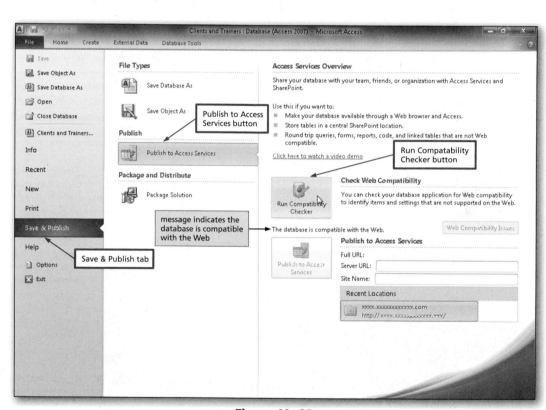

Figure 10–32

To Publish to Access Services

Because the Clients and Trainers database is now known to be compatible with the Web, you can create a Web database version of this database by publishing it to Access Services. Before doing so, you need to enter the URL of the server used to host this database, as well as a site name. The full URL for the Web database will be the combination of the server URL and the site name. You will need to obtain this information from your instructor.

Once you have entered the full URL, the Publish to Access Services button will be available. To complete the process, you click the Publish to Access Services button. You then establish the fact that you have authority to publish to the site by entering your user name and password.

NOTE: Do not complete the following section (pages AC 624 through 625) unless your instructor tells you to do so. Even if you are not completing the section, however, you should read it to make sure you understand the process.

The following steps publish the Clients and Trainers database to Access Services.

1
- Type `http://xxxx.xxxxxxxxxxxxxx.com` (the URL provided by your instructor) as the server URL.
- Type CT (or a name of your own choosing) as the site name (Figure 10–33).

Figure 10–33

2
- Click the Publish to Access Services button in the right-hand pane to publish the database to Access Services and display the Windows Security dialog box (Figure 10–34).

3
- Enter your user name and password and click the OK button (Windows Security dialog box).
- After Access indicates the outcome of your publication request in the Publish Access Application dialog box, click the OK button.
- Close the database.

Figure 10–34

To View the Web Database

The following step uses Internet Explorer to view the Web database.

1

- Start Internet Explorer and enter the URL for the Web database.

- Type your user name and password in the Windows Security dialog box and click the OK button to display the Web database (Figure 10–35).

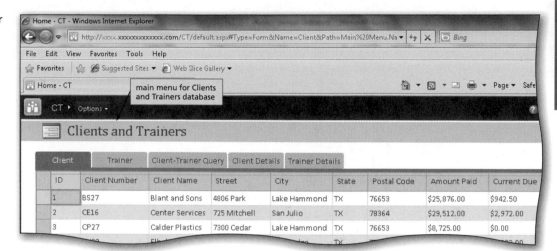

Figure 10–35

Using the Web Database

You can use the Web database just as you used the Access version of the database. You can update the data in the datasheets or forms. Any such updates will also be reflected in the corresponding Access database. In addition, if the Client tab is selected and you click the ID field on a record, you will see the details for that record appear in a pop-up form (Figure 10–36a). In the pop-up form, you cannot move to any other record, nor can you update the data.

(a) Data for Selected Client Appears in Pop-up Form

Figure 10–36

If you click the Trainer tab and then click the ID field on a record, you will see details for that trainer in a pop-up form (Figure 10–36b).

(b) Data for Selected Trainer Appears in Pop-up Form

Clicking the Client-Trainer Query tab shows the query results (Figure 10–36c).

(c) Client-Trainer Query Tab Selected

Figure 10–36

Clicking the Client Details tab shows the Client Details form (Figure 10–36d). Unlike the pop-up version of this form shown in Figure 10–36a, you can move from record to record. Another difference from the version shown in Figure 10–36a is that you can use this form to update the data.

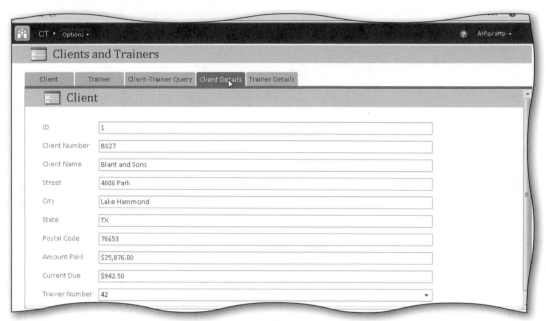

(d) Client Details Tab Selected

Clicking the Trainer Details tab shows the Trainer Details form (Figure 10–36e). As with the Client Details form, you can move from record to record and also update the data.

(e) Trainer Details Tab Selected

Figure 10–36

To Use the Template

You can use the template you created just as you would use any other template. The only difference is that, after clicking the New tab in the Backstage view, you need to click the My templates button (Figure 10–37).

Figure 10–37

You will then see any templates you created (Figure 10–38). You select the template you want.

Figure 10–38

Specifically, to use the template created earlier, you would use the following steps.

1. Select the New tab in the Backstage view.

2. Click the My templates button.

3. Click the desired template.

4. Enter a name and select a location for the database.

5. Click the Create button.

TO USE THE APPLICATION PART

To use the application part you created, you first need to create a database. After doing so, you click the Application Parts button (Create tab | Templates group) to display the Application Parts menu (Figure 10–39).

Figure 10–39

You can then click the application part you created, which will be located in the User Templates section of the Application Parts menu. If you have any open objects, Access will indicate that "all open objects must be closed before instantiating this application part" and ask if you want Access to close all open objects. After you click the Yes button, Access will add all the objects in the application part to the database (Figure 10–40). If you had already created other objects in the database, they would still be included.

Figure 10–40

BTW

Blank Forms Application Parts
The Blank Forms options in the Application Parts menu are pre-built objects that include controls and embedded macros. The available Blank Form application parts shown in Figure 10–39 are: 1 Right (one column of labels – add fields to the right); 1 Top (one column of labels – adding fields below); 2 Right (two columns of labels – add fields to the right); 2 Top (two columns of labels – add fields below); 5 Details (form with subform); 6 Dialog (dialog box), 7 List (list form); 8 Media (form with placeholders for media objects); 9 Msgbox (Message box); and 10 Tabs (form with tab control). All styles contain appropriate buttons.

BTW

Adding Blank Forms Application Part
To add one of the blank form application parts shown in Figure 10–39 to a database, click the Application Parts button (Create tab | Templates group) to display the Application Parts gallery, and then click the desired form. Access adds the form to the database using the name of the part type. For example, if you add a 1 Right form to the database, a form object with the name SingleOneColumn-RightLabels will appear in the Navigation Pane. You can open the form object in Layout view or Design view, and select the record source for the form. To add fields to the form after selecting the record source, click the Add Existing Fields button (Design tab | Tools group) to display the field list, hold down the CTRL key and drag the desired fields to the form. You can add labels, change the title, and make any other necessary changes to the form. You also can change the form name and caption.

Specifically, to use the application part created earlier, you would use the following steps.

1. Create or open the database for which you want to use the application part.
2. Display the Create tab and then click the Application Parts button (Create tab | Templates group).
3. Click the application part to be added.
4. If Access indicates that open objects must be closed, click the Yes button.

Break Point: If you wish to stop working through the chapter at this point, you can close Access now. You can resume the project at a later time by starting Access, and continuing to follow the steps from this location forward.

Converting Databases

Both Access 2007 and Access 2010 use the same file format, the .accdb format. The format is usually referred to as the Access 2007 file format. Thus, in Access 2010, you can use any database created in Access 2007. If you attempt to use Access 2007 to open a database created in Access 2010, however, there are certain restrictions. The following restrictions are the ones most likely to affect you:

1. You cannot use Access 2010 databases containing objects that have been published to the Web.
2. If the Access 2010 database contains data macros, any tables containing the data macros become read-only.
3. You cannot open any tables that contain calculated columns.

To Convert an Access 2007 Database to an Earlier Version

To convert an Access 2007 database to an earlier version, the database cannot contain any features that are specific to Access 2007 or 2010. These include attachments, multivalued fields, offline data, or links to external files not supported in earlier versions of Access. They also include objects published to the Web, data macros, and calculated columns. Provided the database does not contain such features, you can convert the database by clicking the Save & Publish tab in the Backstage view (Figure 10–41). You then can choose the appropriate format.

Specifically, to convert an Access 2007 database to an earlier version, you would use the following steps.

1. With the database to be converted open, click File on the Ribbon to open the Backstage view.
2. Click the Save & Publish tab.
3. With the Save Database As command selected, click the desired format, and then click the Save As button.
4. Type the name you want for the converted database, select a location, and click the Save button.

To Convert an Access 2000 or Access 2002–2003 Database to Default Database Format for Access 2010

To convert an Access 2000 or Access 2002–2003 database to the default database format for Access 2010, you open the database in Access 2010. Initially, the database is open in compatibility mode, where features that are new to Access 2010 and that cannot easily be displayed or converted are disabled. In this mode, the database remains in its original format. If you want to convert it so that you can use it in Access 2010, you use

Figure 10–41

the Access Database command on the Backstage view. Once the database is converted, the disabled features will be enabled. You will no longer be able to share the database with users of Access 2000 or Access 2002–2003, however.

Specifically, to convert an Access 2000 or 2002–2003 database to the default database format for Access 2010, you would use the following steps.

1. With the database to be converted open, click File on the Ribbon to open the Backstage view.

2. Click the Save & Publish tab.

3. With the Save Database As command selected, click Access Database and then click the Save As button.

4. Type the name you want for the converted database, select a location, and click the Save button.

Microsoft Access Tools

Microsoft Access has a variety of tools that are useful in analyzing databases. Analyzing a database gives information about how the database functions and identifies opportunities for improving functionality. You can use the Access analysis tools to analyze tables and database performance, and to create detailed documentation.

To Use the Table Analyzer

Access contains a Table Analyzer tool that performs three separate functions. This tool can analyze tables while looking for potential redundancy (duplicated data). The Table Analyzer also can analyze performance and check for ways to make queries, reports, or forms more efficient. Then the tool will make suggestions for possible changes. The final function of the analyzer is to produce detailed documentation describing the structure and content of the various tables, queries, forms, reports, and other objects in the database.

The following steps illustrate how to use the Table Analyzer to examine the Client table for **redundancy**, or duplicated data. If redundancy is found, the Table Analyzer will suggest ways to split the table in order to eliminate the redundancy.

- Open the Camashaly Design database.

- If necessary, close the Navigation Pane.

- Display the Database Tools tab (Figure 10–42).

Figure 10–42

- Click the Analyze Table button (Database Tools tab | Analyze group) to display the Table Analyzer Wizard dialog box (Figure 10–43).

Figure 10–43

- Click the Next button to display the next Table Analyzer Wizard screen (Figure 10–44).

Figure 10–44

- Click the Next button to display the next Table Analyzer Wizard screen.

- Select the Client table (Figure 10–45).

Figure 10–45

5

- Click the Next button.

- Be sure the 'Yes, let the wizard decide' option button is selected (Figure 10–46).

Figure 10–46

● Click the Next button to run the
 analysis.

● Drag the lower boundary of each
 field list down so that all fields in
 the lists are visible (Figure 10–47).

Q&A

I do not really want to put the city,
state, and postal code in a different
table, even though I realize that this
data does appear to be duplicated.
Do I have to follow this advice?

Certainly not. This is only a
suggestion.

Figure 10–47

To Use the Performance Analyzer

The Performance Analyzer will examine the database's tables, queries, reports, forms, and other objects in your
system, looking for changes that would improve the efficiency of database operations. These changes could include
modifications to the way data is stored, as well as changes to the indexes created for the system. (You will learn
about indexes later in this chapter.) Once the Performance Analyzer has finished, it will make recommendations
concerning possible changes. The following steps use the Performance Analyzer to identify possible areas for
improvement in the Camashaly Design database.

● Click the Analyze Performance
 button (Database Tools tab | Analyze
 group) to display the Performance
 Analyzer dialog box.

● If necessary, click the Tables tab
 (Figure 10–48).

Figure 10–48

2

- Click the Select All button to select all tables.

- Click the OK button to display the results (Figure 10–49).

Q&A What do the results mean?

Because both fields contain only numbers, Access is suggesting that you might improve the efficiency of the table by changing the data types of the fields to Long Integer. As the icon in front of the suggestions indicates, this is simply an idea — something to consider. For these particular fields, Text is a better type, however, so you should ignore this suggestion.

3

- Click the Close button to finish working with the Performance Analyzer.

Figure 10–49

To Use the Database Documenter

The Database Documenter allows you to produce detailed documentation of the various tables, queries, forms, reports, and other objects in your database. Hard copy documentation is required by many organizations. It is used for backup, disaster recovery, and planning for database enhancements. Figure 10–50 shows a portion of the documentation for the Client table. The complete documentation is much lengthier than the one shown in the figure.

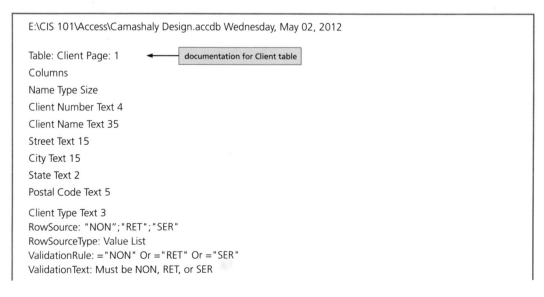

Figure 10–50 *(continued)*

(continued)

Services Needed 4
RowSource: "Ad";"Ban";"Bill";"Bus";"Enews";"Host";"Logo";"Mkt';"
News";"Pod";"SE";"Shop";"Soc"
RowSourceType: Value List

Amount Paid Currency 8

Current Due Currency 8
ValidationRule: >=0 And <=30000
ValidationText: Must be at least $0.00 and at most $30,000.00

Total Amount Currency (Calculated) 8
Expression: [Amount Paid]+[Current Due]

Contract Hours YTD Single 4

Business Analyst Number Text 2

Figure 10–50

Notice that the documentation of the Client Type field contains the row source associated with the Lookup information for the field. The documentation for both the Client Type and Current Due fields contains validation rules and validation text.

The following steps use the Database Documenter to produce documentation for the Client table.

1

• Click the Database Documenter button (Database Tools tab | Analyze group) to display the Documenter dialog box.

• If necessary, click the Tables tab and then click the Client check box (Figure 10–51).

BTW

Database Documenter
The Options button in the Documenter dialog box allows you to further specify what to include for each table and for each field in a table.

Figure 10–51

2

- Click the OK button to produce a preview of the documentation (Figure 10–52).

Q&A

What can I do with this documentation?

You could print it by clicking the Print button. You could create a PDF or XPS file containing the documentation by clicking the PDF or XPS button and following the directions. You could create a text file by clicking the Text File button and following the directions. Whatever option you choose, you may need to use this documentation later if you make changes to the database design.

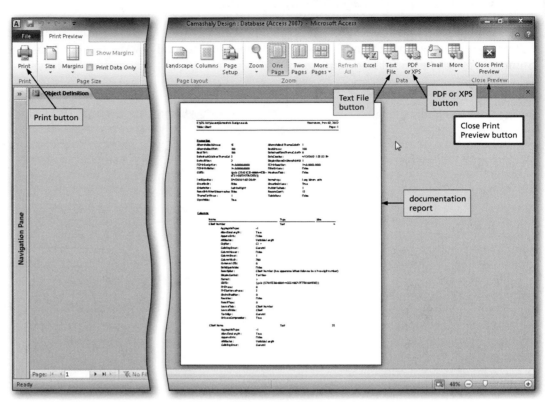

Figure 10–52

- Click the Close Print Preview button to close the preview of the documentation.

Experiment

- Try other options within the Database Documenter to see the effect of your choice on the documentation produced. Each time, close the preview of the documentation.

Navigation Pane

You already have learned how to customize the Navigation Pane by selecting the category and the filter as well as how to use the Search bar to restrict the items that appear in the Navigation Pane. You also can create custom categories and groups that you can use to categorize the items in the database in ways that are most useful to you.

Determine the most useful way to customize the Navigation Pane.
Determine the customization of the Navigation Pane that would be most helpful to your users. The types of issues to consider are the following:

- Is there a new category that would be useful?

- If so, are there new groups that would be useful to include in the new category?

- If you have created a new category and a new group, which items should be included in one of the new groups, and which should be left uncategorized?

Plan Ahead

To Create Custom Categories and Groups

You can create custom categories in the Navigation Pane and add custom groups to the categories. The following steps create a custom category called Financial Items. They then add two custom groups, Detailed and Summary, to the Financial Items category.

- Open the Navigation Pane.

- Right-click the Navigation Pane title bar to display a shortcut menu (Figure 10–53).

Figure 10–53

- Click the Navigation Options command on the shortcut menu to display the Navigation Options dialog box (Figure 10–54).

Q&A

What else could I do with the shortcut menu?

You could select a category, select a sort order, or select how to view the items within the Navigation Pane.

Figure 10–54

3

- Click the Add Item button to add a new category (Figure 10–55).

Figure 10–55

4

- Type **Financial Items** as the name of the category.

- Click the Add Group button to add a group and then type **Detailed** as the name of the group.

- Click the Add Group button to add a group and then type **Summary** as the name of the group (Figure 10–56).

Q&A I added the groups in the wrong order. How can I change the order?

Select the group that is in the wrong position. Click the Up or Down arrows to move the group to the correct location.

Q&A If I made a mistake in creating a new category, how can I fix it?

Select the category that is incorrect. If the name is wrong, click the Rename Item button and change the name appropriately. If you do not want the category, click the Delete Item button to delete the category and then click the OK button.

Figure 10–56

5

- Click the OK button to create the new category and groups.

To Add Items to Groups

Once you have created new groups, you can add existing items to the new groups. The following steps add items to the Summary and Detailed groups in the Financial Items category.

1

- Click the Navigation Pane arrow to produce the Navigation Pane menu (Figure 10–57).

Q&A

Do I have to click the arrow?

No. If you prefer, you can click anywhere in the title bar for the Navigation Pane. Clicking arrows is a good habit, however, because there are many situations where you must click the arrow.

Figure 10–57

2

- Click the Financial Items category to display the groups within the category. Because you created the Detailed and Summary groups but did not assign items, the table objects all appear in the Unassigned Objects area of the Navigation Pane.

- Right-click City-Analyst Crosstab to display the shortcut menu.

- Point to the 'Add to group' command on the shortcut menu to display the list of available groups (Figure 10–58).

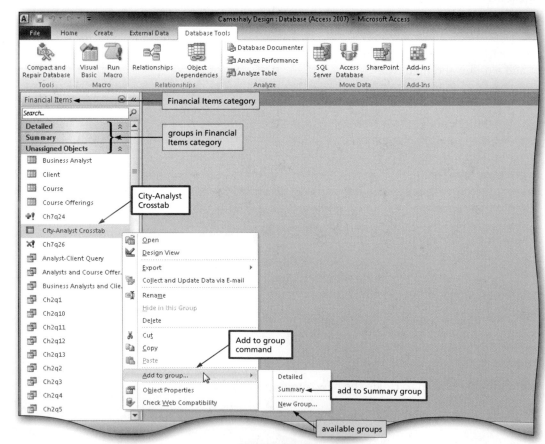

Figure 10–58

Q&A I did not create an Unassigned Objects group. Where did it come from?

Access creates the Unassigned Objects group automatically. Until you add an object to one of the groups you created, it will be in the Unassigned Objects group.

Q&A What is the purpose of the New Group on the submenu?

You can create a new group using this submenu. This is an alternative to using the Navigation Options dialog box. Use whichever approach you find most convenient.

3

- Click Summary to add the City-Analyst Crosstab to the Summary group.

- Using the same technique, add the items shown in Figure 10–59 to the Detailed and Summary groups.

Q&A What is the symbol that appears in front of the items in the Detailed and Summary groups?

It is the link symbol. You do not actually add an object to your group. Rather, you create a link to the object. In practice, you do not have to worry about this. The process for opening an object in one of your custom groups remains the same.

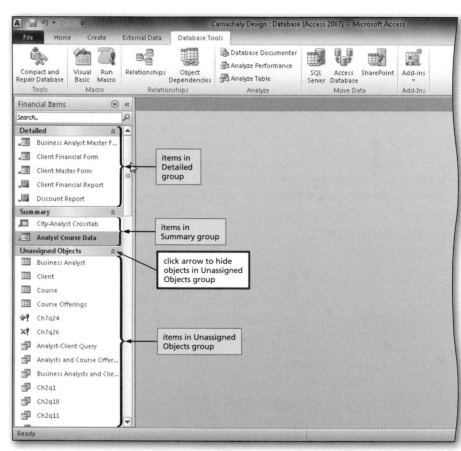

Figure 10–59

4

- Click the arrow in the Unassigned Objects bar to hide the unassigned objects (Figure 10–60).

Q&A Do I have to click the arrow?

No. Just as with the Navigation Pane, you can click anywhere in the Unassigned Objects bar.

Figure 10–60

Break Point: If you wish to stop working through the chapter at this point, you can close Access now. You can resume the project at a later time by starting Access, opening the Camashaly Design database, and continuing to follow the steps from this location forward.

Table and Database Properties

You can assign properties to tables. For example, you could assign a validation rule and validation text to an entire table. You also can assign properties to the database, typically for documentation purposes.

To Create a Validation Rule for a Table

Many validation rules apply to individual fields within a table. Some, however, apply to more than one field. In the Course Offerings table, you created a macro that would change the value of the Hours Spent field in such a way that it could never be greater than the Total Hours field. You can also create a validation rule that ensures this will never be the case; that is, the validation rule would require that the hours spent must be less than or equal to the total hours. This rule involves two fields, Hours Spent and Total Hours. To create a validation rule that involves two or more fields, you need to create the rule for the table using the table's Validation Rule property. The following steps create the appropriate validation rule for the Course Offerings table.

- If necessary, click the arrow for Unassigned Objects to display the objects in the Navigation Pane.

- Open the Course Offerings table in Design view and close the Navigation Pane.

- Click the Property Sheet button (Table Tools Design tab | Show/Hide group) to display the table's property sheet.

- Click the Validation Rule property and type **[Hours Spent]<=[Total Hours]** as the validation rule.

- Click the Validation Text property and type **Hours spent cannot exceed total hours** as the validation text (Figure 10–61).

Q&A

Could I use the expression builder to create the validation rule?

Yes. Use whichever method you find the most convenient.

Figure 10–61

- Close the property sheet.

- Click the Save button on the Quick Access Toolbar to save the validation rule and the validation text.

- When asked if you want to test existing data, click the No button.

- Close the Course Offerings table.

To Create Custom Properties

Custom properties are a collection of properties from which you can choose so you can supplement the general database property categories included in the property sheet. You can use custom properties to further document your database. If you have needs that go beyond the custom properties, you can create your own original or unique properties. The following steps **populate** the Status custom property; that is, they set a value for the property. In this case, they set the Status property to Live Version, indicating this is the live version of the database. If the database were still in a test environment, the property would be set to Test Version. The steps also create and populate a new property, Production, that represents the date the database was placed into production.

1
- Click File on the Ribbon to open the Backstage view.
- Ensure the Info tab is selected (Figure 10–62).

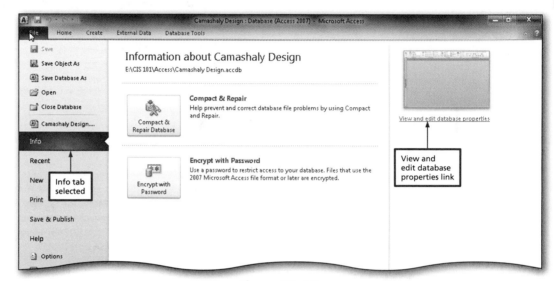

Figure 10–62

2
- Click the 'View and edit database properties' link to display the Camashaly Design.accdb Properties dialog box.
- Click the Custom tab.
- Scroll down in the Name list so that Status appears and then click Status.
- Ensure that the Type is Text.

Q&A
What if it is not?
Click the Type arrow and then click Text.

- Click the Value box and type **Live Version** as the value (Figure 10–63).

Figure 10–63

3

- Click the Add button to add the property.

- Type **Production** in the Name box.

- Select Date as the Type.

- Type **04/03/2012** as the value to indicate that the database went into production on April 3, 2012 (Figure 10–64).

Figure 10–64

4

- Click the Add button to add the property (Figure 10–65).

What if I add a property that I decide I do not want?

You can delete it. To do so, click the property you no longer want and then click the Delete button.

5

- Click the OK button to close the Camashaly Design.accdb Properties dialog box.

How do I view these properties in the future?

The same way you created them. Click File on the Ribbon, click the Info tab, and then click the 'View and edit database properties' link. Click the desired tab to see the properties you want.

Figure 10–65

Special Field Properties

Each field in a table has a variety of field properties available. Recall that field properties are characteristics of a field. Two special field properties, the Custom Input Mask property and the Allow Zero Length property, are described in this section.

Custom Input Masks

A way to prevent users from entering data that does not have a certain format is to use an input mask. You already have used the Input Mask Wizard to create an input mask. Using the wizard, you can select from a list the input mask that meets your needs. This often is the best way to create the input mask.

If the input mask you need to create is not similar to any in the list, you can create a custom input mask by entering the appropriate characters as the value for the Input Mask property. In doing so, you use the symbols from Table 10–1.

Table 10–1 Input Mask Symbols		
Symbol	**Type of Data Accepted**	**Data Entry Optional**
0	Digits 0 through 9 without plus (+) or minus (–) sign are accepted. Positions left blank appear as zeros.	No
9	Digits 0 through 9 without plus (+) or minus (–) sign are accepted. Positions left blank appear as spaces.	Yes
#	Digits 0 through 9 with plus (+) or minus (–) sign are accepted. Positions left blank appear as spaces.	Yes
L	Letters A through Z are accepted.	No
?	Letters A through Z are accepted.	Yes
A	Letters A through Z or digits 0 through 9 are accepted.	No
a	Letters A through Z or digits 0 through 9 are accepted.	Yes
&	Any character or a space is accepted.	No
C	Any character or a space is accepted.	Yes
<	Symbol converts any letter entered to lowercase.	Does not apply
>	Symbol converts any letter entered to uppercase.	Does not apply
!	Characters typed in the input mask fill it from left to right.	Does not apply
\	Character following the slash is treated as a literal in the input mask.	Does not apply

For example, to indicate that client numbers must consist of two letters followed by two numbers, you would enter LL99. The Ls in the first two positions indicate that the first two positions must be letters. Using L instead of a question mark indicates that the user must enter these letters; that is, they are not optional. If you had used the question mark, the user could leave these positions blank. The 9s in the last two positions indicate that the user can enter only digits 0 through 9. Using 9 instead of 0 indicates that the user could leave these positions blank; that is, they are optional. Finally, to ensure that any letters entered are converted to uppercase, you would use the > symbol at the beginning of the input mask. The complete mask would be >LL99.

BTW

Smart Tags
A smart tag is a button that appears in a table, query, form, or report that assists users in accomplishing various tasks, including connecting to the Web. Smart tags are available in other Office applications as well. To add a smart tag to a field in a table, open the table in Design view, click the row selector for the field to which you want to add a smart tag, click the Smart Tags text box to select it and then click the Build button. When the Smart Tags dialog box appears, select the appropriate smart tag and click the OK button.

To Create a Custom Input Mask

The following step creates a custom input mask for the Client Number field.

1

- Open the Client table in Design view and close the Navigation Pane.

- With the Client Number field selected, click the Input Mask property, and then type `>LL99` as the value (Figure 10–66).

Q&A What is the difference between the Format property and the Input Mask property?

The Format property ensures that data is displayed consistently, for example, always in uppercase. The Input Mask property controls how data is entered.

Figure 10–66

Q&A What is the effect of this input mask?

From this point on, anyone entering a client number will be restricted to letters in the first two positions and numeric digits in the last two. Further, any letters entered in the first two positions will be converted to uppercase.

Q&A In Figure 10–66, the Client Number field has both a custom input mask and a format. Is this a problem?

Technically, you do not need both. When the same field has both an input mask and a format, the format takes precedence. Because the format specified for the Client Number field is the same as the input mask (uppercase), it will not affect the data.

To Allow Zero Length

You can use zero-length strings to distinguish data that does not exist from data that is unknown. For example, in the Business Analyst table, you may want to set the Required property for the Comment field to Yes, so that users cannot forget to enter a comment. If the user does forget, Access will display an error message and not let the user add the record until he or she enters a comment. If, on the other hand, you find a certain analyst for whom no comment is appropriate, you can enter a zero-length string (" ") and Access will accept the record without generating an error message. A **zero-length string** is a string that contains no characters. To enter a zero-length string, you type two quotation marks with no space in between (" "). If you enter a zero-length string into a Text or Memo field whose Required property is set to Yes, Access will not report an error because entering a zero-length string is not the same as leaving the field blank.

If you want to ensure that data is entered in the field and that a zero-length string is not appropriate, you can set the Required property to Yes and the Allow Zero Length property to No. The following steps set the Allow Zero Length property for the Client Name field to No. (The Required property already has been set to Yes.)

1

- Click the row selector for the Client Name field to select the field.

- Click the Allow Zero Length property and then click the arrow that appears to display a menu.

- Click No in the menu to change the value of the Allow Zero Length property from Yes to No (Figure 10–67).

Q&A Could I just type the word, No?

Yes. In fact, you could type the letter, N, and Access would complete the word, No. Use whichever technique you prefer.

2

- Save your changes and click the No button when asked if you want to test existing data.

- Close the table.

Q&A What is the effect of this change?

If the value for the Allow Zero Length property is set to No, an attempt to enter a zero-length string ("") will result in an error message.

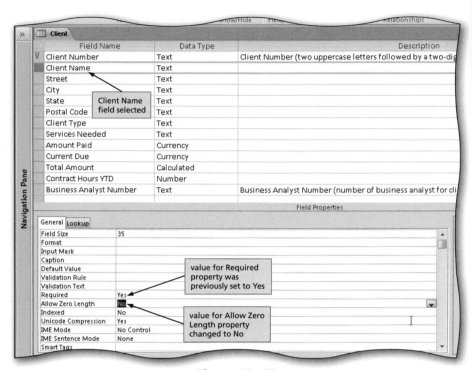

Figure 10–67

Creating and Using Indexes

You already are familiar with the concept of an index. The index in the back of a book contains important words or phrases along with a list of pages on which the given words or phrases can be found. An **index** for a table is similar. An index is a database object that is created based on a field or combination of fields. An index on the Client Name field, for example, would enable Access to rapidly locate a record that contains a particular client name. In this case, the items of interest are client names instead of keywords or phrases, as is the case in the back of this book. The field or fields on which the index is built is called the **index key**. Thus, in the index on client names, the Client Name field is the index key.

Each name occurs in the index along with the number of the record on which the corresponding client is located. Further, the names appear in the index in alphabetical order, so Access can use this index to rapidly produce a list of clients alphabetized by client name.

Indexes make the process of retrieving records very fast and efficient. With relatively small tables, the increased efficiency associated with indexes will not be as apparent as in larger tables. In practice, it is common to encounter tables with thousands, tens of thousands, or even hundreds of thousands of records. In such cases, the increase in efficiency provided by indexes is dramatic. In fact, without indexes, many operations in such databases simply would not be practical. They would take too long to complete.

Another benefit of indexes is that they provide an efficient way to order records. That is, if the records are to appear in a certain order in a database object, Access can use

BTW

Indexes
The most common structure for high-performance indexes is called a B-tree. It is a highly efficient structure that supports very rapid access to records in the database as well as a rapid alternative to sorting records. Virtually all systems use some version of the B-tree structure.

an index instead of physically having to rearrange the records in the database. Physically rearranging the records in a different order can be a very time-consuming process.

To gain the benefits of an index, you first must create one. Access automatically creates an index on the primary key as well as some other special fields. If, for example, a table contains a field called Postal Code, Access would create an index for this field automatically. You must create any other indexes you determine would improve database performance, indicating the field or fields on which the index is to be built.

Although the index key usually will be a single field, it can be a combination of fields. For example, you might want to sort records by amount paid within client type. In other words, the records are ordered by a combination of fields: Client Type and Amount Paid. An index can be used for this purpose by using a combination of fields for the index key. In this case, you must assign a name to the index. It is a good idea to assign a name that represents the combination of fields. For example, an index whose key is the combination of the Client Type and Amount Paid fields might be called TypePaid.

How Access Uses Indexes

Access creates an index whenever you request that it do so. It takes care of all the work in setting up and maintaining the index.

If you request that data be sorted in a particular order and Access determines that an index is available that it can use to make the process efficient, it will do so automatically. If no index is available, it still will sort the data in the order you requested; it will just take longer than with the index.

Similarly, if you request that Access locate a particular record that has a certain value in a particular field, Access will use an index if an appropriate one exists. If not, it will have to examine each record until it finds the one you want.

In both cases, the added efficiency provided by an index will not be apparent readily in tables that have only a few records. As you add more records to your tables, however, the difference can be dramatic. Even with only 50 to 100 records, you will notice a difference. You can imagine how dramatic the difference would be in a table with 50,000 records.

Plan Ahead	**Determine indexes.** Indexes in Access offer both advantages and disadvantages, so it is important to use them appropriately. Indexes improve efficiency for sorting and finding records. On the other hand, indexes occupy space on your disk. They also require Access to do extra work. Access must keep all the indexes that have been created up to date. The following guidelines help determine how and when to use indexes to their fullest advantage. Create an index on a field (or combination of fields) if one or more of the following conditions are present: 1. The field is the primary key of the table. (Access creates this index automatically.) 2. The field is the foreign key in a relationship you have created. 3. You frequently will need your data to be sorted on the field. 4. You frequently will need to locate a record based on a value in this field. Because Access handles Condition 1 automatically, you need only to concern yourself about Conditions 2, 3, and 4. If you think you will need to see client data arranged in order of current due amounts, for example, you should create an index on the Current Due field. If you think you will need to see the data arranged by amount paid within client type, you should create an index on the combination of the Client Type field and the Amount Paid field. Similarly, if you think you will need to find a client given the client's name, you should create an index on the Client Name field.

To Create a Single-Field Index

A **single-field index** is an index whose key is a single field. If you need to frequently locate clients by name, you would create a single-field index. The index key would be the Client Name field. In creating an index, you need to indicate whether to allow duplicates in the index key, that is, two records that have the same value. For example, in the index for the Client Name field, if duplicates are not allowed, Access would not allow the addition of a client whose name is the same as the name of a client already in the database. In the index for the Client Name field, duplicates will be allowed. The following steps create a single-field index.

- Open the Client table in Design view and close the Navigation Pane.

- Select the Client Name field.

- Click the Indexed property box in the Field Properties pane to select the property.

- Click the Down arrow that appears to display the Indexed list (Figure 10–68).

- Click the Yes (Duplicates OK) item in the list to specify that duplicates are to be allowed.

Figure 10–68

To Create a Multiple-Field Index

Creating **multiple-field indexes** — that is, indexes whose key is a combination of fields — involves a different process than creating single-field indexes. To create multiple-field indexes, you will use the Indexes button, enter a name for the index, and then enter the combination of fields that make up the index key. Assuming there is a need to sort records on the combination of Client Type and Amount Paid, you would create a multiple-field index whose key is the combination of the Client Type field and the Amount Paid field. The following steps create this multiple-field index and assign it the name TypePaid.

1

- Click the Indexes button (Table Tools Design tab | Show/Hide group) to display the Indexes: Client dialog box (Figure 10–69).

Figure 10–69

2

- Click the blank row (the row below Client Name) in the Index Name column in the Indexes: Client dialog box to select the position to enter the name of the new index.

- Type **TypePaid** as the index name, and then press the TAB key.

- Click the down arrow in the Field Name column to produce a list of fields in the Client table and then select Client Type to enter the first of the two fields for the index.

- Press the TAB key three times to move to the Field Name column on the following row.

- Select the Amount Paid field in the same manner as the Client Type field (Figure 10–70).

Figure 10–70

3

- Close the Indexes: Client dialog box by clicking its Close button.

- Click the Save button on the Quick Access Toolbar to save your changes.

- Close the Client table.

Automatic Error Checking

Access can automatically check for several types of errors in forms and reports. When Access detects an error, it warns you about the existence of the error and provides you with options for correcting it. The types of errors that Access can detect and correct are shown in Table 10–2.

Table 10–2 Types of Errors	
Error Type	**Description**
Unassociated label and control	A label and control are selected that are not associated with each other.
New unassociated labels	A newly added label is not associated with any other control.
Keyboard shortcut errors	A shortcut key is invalid. This can happen because an unassociated label has a shortcut key, there are duplicate shortcut keys assigned, or a blank space is assigned as a shortcut key.
Invalid control properties	A control property is invalid. For example, the property contains invalid characters.
Common report errors	The report has invalid sorting or grouping specifications, or the report is wider than the page size.

To Enable Error Checking

For automatic error checking to take place, it must be enabled. The following steps ensure that error checking is enabled and that errors are found and reported.

- Click File on the Ribbon and then click the Options button to display the Access Options dialog box.

- Click Object Designers to display the options for creating and modifying objects.

- Scroll down so that the error checking section appears.

- Ensure the 'Enable error checking' check box is checked (Figure 10–71).

Q&A

What is the purpose of the other check boxes in the section?

All the other check boxes are checked, indicating that Access will perform all the various types of automatic error checking that are possible. If there were a particular type of error checking that you would prefer to skip, you would remove its check mark before clicking the OK button.

- Click the OK button to close the Access Options dialog box.

- Close the database.

Figure 10–71

Error Indication

If an error occurs, a small triangle called an **error indicator** appears in the appropriate field or control. If you change the label for Business Analyst Number in the Client View and Update Form to include an ampersand (&) before the letter, N, the letter,

N, will be a keyboard shortcut for this control, which is a problem because the letter, N, is already a shortcut for Name to Find. If this happens, an error indicator appears in both controls in which the letter, N, is the keyboard shortcut, as shown in Figure 10–72.

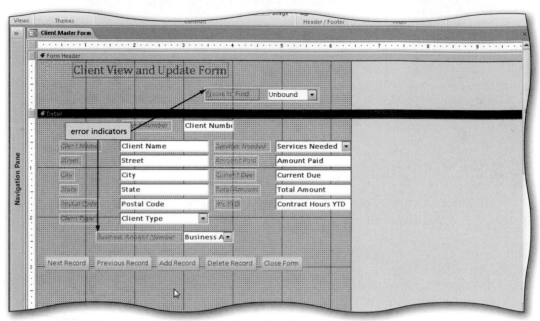

Figure 10–72

Selecting a control containing an error indicator displays an Error Checking Options button. Clicking the Error Checking Options button produces the Error Checking Options menu, as shown in Figure 10–73. The first line in the menu is simply a statement of the type of error that occurred, and the second is a description of the specific error. The Change Caption command gives a submenu of the captions that can be changed. The Edit Caption Property command allows you to change the caption directly and is the simplest way to correct this error. The Help on This Error command gives help

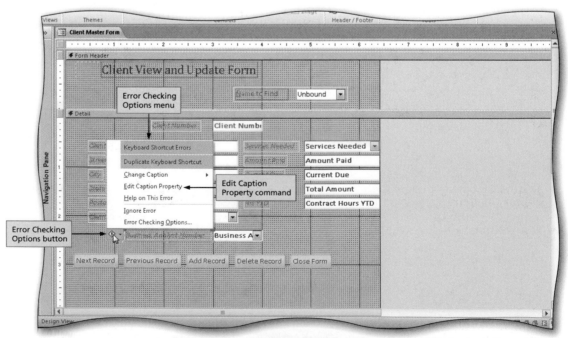

Figure 10–73

on the specific error that occurred. You can choose to ignore the error by using the Ignore Error command. The final command, Error Checking Options, allows you to change the same error checking options shown in Figure 10–71 on page AC 651.

The simplest way to fix this error is to edit the caption property. Clicking the Edit Caption Property command produces a property sheet with the Caption property highlighted. You could then change the Caption property to make another letter the shortcut key. For example, you could make the letter, B, the shortcut key by typing `&Business Analyst Number` as the entry.

Encrypting a Database

Encrypting refers to the storing of the data in the database in an encoded, or encrypted, format. Anytime a user stores or modifies data in the encrypted database, the database management system (DBMS) will encode the data before actually updating the database. Before a legitimate user retrieves the data using the DBMS, the data will be decoded. The whole encrypting process is transparent to a legitimate user; that is, he or she is not even aware it is happening. If an unauthorized user attempts to bypass all the controls of the DBMS and get to the database through a utility program or a word processor, however, he or she will be able to see only the encoded, and unreadable, version of the data. In Access, you encrypt a database and set a password as part of the same operation.

BTW

Passwords
Passwords should be eight or more characters in length. The longer the length of the password and the more random the characters, the more difficult it is for someone to determine. Use a combination of uppercase and lowercase letters as well as numbers and special symbols when you create a password.

NOTE: Once you have encrypted a database and set a password, you *must* remember the password to access your database. As a precaution, it is a good idea for you to make a backup copy of your database and store it in a secure location before performing this operation. That way, if you forget your password, you still can use the backup copy.

To Create a Database

The following steps create a blank database that you will encrypt. They then use the application part created earlier to add the same tables, query, and forms that were in the Clients and Trainers database. You will use this database in the upcoming steps in this chapter.

1 Create a blank database called AMK Trainers on your USB flash drive.

2 Click Create on the Ribbon, click the Application Parts button (Create tab | Templates group), and then click the Clients and Trainers user template that you created earlier in this chapter on pages AC 621 through AC 623.

3 When Access asks if you want Microsoft Access to close all open objects, click the Yes button.

To Open a Database in Exclusive Mode

To encrypt a database and set a password, the database must be open in exclusive mode; that is, no other user can access the database in any way. The following steps open the AMK Trainers database in exclusive mode in preparation for setting a password.

1 Close the open database by clicking File on the Ribbon and then clicking Close Database in the Backstage view.

2 With your USB flash drive connected to one of the computer's USB ports, click Open in the Backstage view to display the Open dialog box.

3 Navigate to the location of the file to be opened.

4 Click AMK Trainers to select the file name.

5 Click the Open button arrow to display the Open button menu (Figure 10–74).

6 Click Open Exclusive to open the database in exclusive mode.

Q&A What is the purpose of the other modes?

The first option, Open, opens the database in a mode so that it can be shared by other users. The second, Open Read-Only, allows you to read the data in the database, but not update the database. Other users can both read and update. The fourth, Open Exclusive Read-Only allows you to read but not update. Other users can also read the data, but they cannot perform updates.

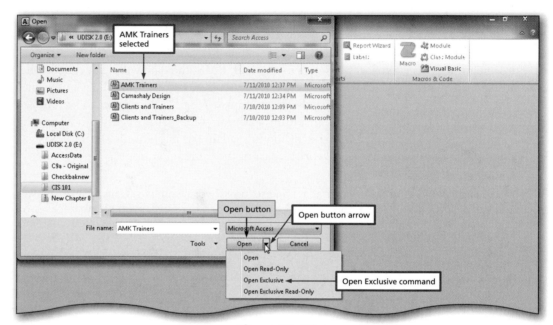

Figure 10–74

To Encrypt a Database with a Password

With the database open in exclusive mode, the following steps encrypt the database with a password. Be sure to remember the password that you type. You will use it again in the next sections.

1

• Click File on the Ribbon to open the Backstage view and ensure the Info tab is selected (Figure 10–75).

Figure 10–75

- Click the Encrypt with Password button to display the Set Database Password dialog box.

- Type a password in the Password text box in the Set Database Password dialog box.

- Press the TAB key and then type your password again in the Verify text box (Figure 10–76).

Figure 10–76

 What if I forget my password?

You will not be able to open your database. You would have to use the backup copy you made of your database.

Is the password case sensitive?

Yes, you must enter the password using the same case you used when you created it.

- Click the OK button to encrypt the database and set the password.

- If you get a message indicating that row level locking will be ignored, click the OK button.

- Close the database.

Opening a Database with a Password

When you open a database that has a password, you will be prompted to enter your password in the Password Required dialog box. Once you have done so, click the OK button. Assuming you have entered your password correctly, Access then will open the database.

To Decrypt the Database and Remove the Password

If you no longer feel the encryption and the password are necessary, you can decrypt the database and remove the password. The following steps accomplish this task.

- Open the AMK Trainers database in exclusive mode (see the steps on page AC 653), entering your password when requested.

- Display the Backstage view and ensure the Info tab is selected (Figure 10–77).

Figure 10–77

• Click the Decrypt Database button to display the Unset Database Password dialog box.

Q&A Why does clicking the Decrypt Database button display a dialog box that is called Unset Database Password?

The use of passwords and encryption are part of the same process, as the button you clicked earlier, Encrypt with Password, indicates. The same is true for decryption, even though the word, Password, does not appear on the button.

• Type the password in the Password dialog box.

• Click the OK button to remove the password and decrypt the database.

• Close the database.

BTW

Packaging
Packaging places the database in an Access Deployment (.accdc) file, signs the package, and then places the code-signed package at a location on the user's computer that you determine. Users then can extract the database from the package and work directly in the database (not the package file).

Digital Certificates

When you have created your database, you can convey to others that your database can be trusted by adding a **digital signature**, a stamp of authentication, which is contained within a **digital certificate**. To do so, you package and sign your database. You then can send the resulting package to others. The signature confirms that no one has tampered with the database. If the users trust the author, they then can enable the content of the database with confidence.

NOTE: Do not complete the following section (pages AC 656 through 659) unless your instructor tells you to do so. Even if you are not completing the section, however, you should read it to make sure you understand the process.

To Create a Self-Signed Certificate

To use a verified, authenticated digital certificate, you must obtain one from a trusted Microsoft partner certification authority (CA). If you do not have such a certificate, you can create your own digital certificate, known as a **self-signed certificate**. In the process, you are creating a certificate that can be used for personal macros only on the machine on which they were created. The following steps create a self-signed certificate.

• Open the AMK Trainers database.

• Click the Start button on the Windows 7 taskbar to display the Start menu.

• Click All Programs at the bottom of the left pane on the Start menu to display the All Programs list and then click Microsoft Office on the All Programs list to display the Microsoft Office list.

• Click Microsoft Office 2010 Tools on the Microsoft Office list to display the Microsoft Office Tools list.

• Click Digital Certificate for VBA Projects to display the Create Digital Certificate dialog box.

• Type your name in the 'Your certificate's name' text box (Figure 10–78).

Figure 10–78

2

- Click the OK button to create the certificate.

Q&A How will I know when it is created?

The SelfCert Success dialog box will appear, containing a message that indicates that you have successfully created a new certificate.

- Click the OK button in the SelfCert Success message box to close the message box.

Q&A Do I have to do this from within Access?

No. The digital certificate steps occur in a separate program.

To Package and Sign a Database

You can package, digitally sign, and distribute an Access database with a single operation. Access will save the result in the Access Deployment file format (.accdc). Other users can then extract the database from the package and use it. The following steps package and sign the AMK Trainers database, using the self-signed certificate you created earlier.

1

- Click File on the Ribbon to open the Backstage view.

- Click the Save & Publish tab (Figure 10–79).

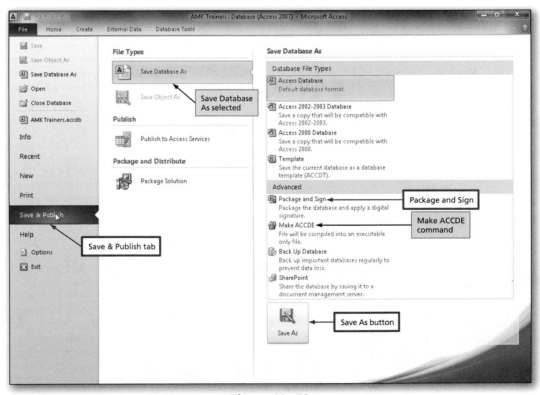

Figure 10–79

2

- With Save Database As selected, click Package and Sign in the Advanced area.

- Click the Save As button to display the Windows Security dialog box (Figure 10–80).

Q&A

What can I do with this dialog box?

You can confirm the certificate. You can also view the properties of the selected certificate.

Figure 10–80

3

- Click the OK button to confirm the certificate.

- Select the location where you will save the signed package and then accept the default name for the signed package (Figure 10–81).

Q&A

Did I need to select Microsoft Access Signed Package as the Save as type?

No. Access should do this for you automatically. If for some reason Microsoft Access Signed Package was not selected, you could select it yourself by clicking the arrow and then clicking the signed package in the list.

4

- Click the Create button to package and sign the database.

- Close the existing database.

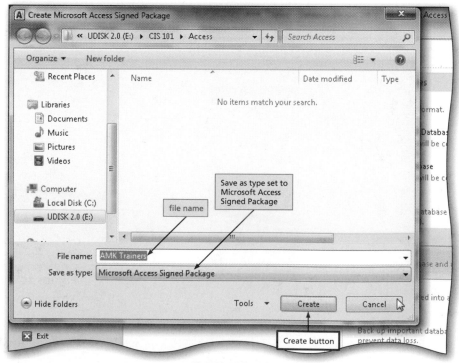

Figure 10–81

To Open a Signed Package

The following steps open the signed package you just created and then extract the AMK Trainers database from the package, giving it the name AMK Trainers New.

 1

- Open the Backstage view, and then click Open in the Backstage view to display the Open dialog box.

- Navigate to the location for the package and then change the file type by clicking the 'Files of type' box arrow and selecting Microsoft Access Signed Packages.

- Ensure the package you want to open is selected (Figure 10–82).

Figure 10–82

 2

- Click the Open button to open the package and, if there is a security concern detected, to display the Microsoft Access Security Notice dialog box (Figure 10–83).

 3

- Click the Open button to display the Extract Database To dialog box.

- Select your USB drive as the location and change the database name to **AMK Trainers New**.

- Click the OK button to extract the database.

- Because you will not be using this database, close the database and reopen the AMK Trainers.accdb database.

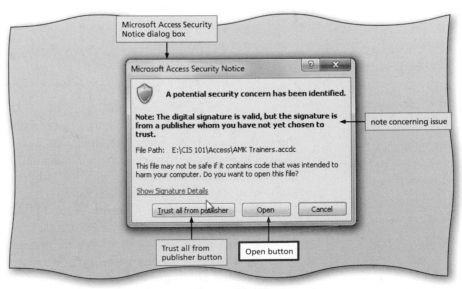

Figure 10–83

The Trust Center

The Trust Center is a feature within Access where you can set security options and also find the latest information on technology related to privacy, safety, and security. To use the Trust Center, you click File on the Ribbon and then click the Options button to display the Access Options dialog box. You then click Trust Center to display the Trust Center content (Figure 10–84). You then would click the Trust Center Settings button to display the Trust Center dialog box in which you can make changes in the following categories.

Figure 10–84

Trusted Publishers. Clicking Trusted Publishers in the Trust Center dialog box shows the list of trusted software publishers. Currently there are none. To view details about a trusted publisher, click the publisher and then click the View button. To remove a trusted publisher from the list, click the publisher and then click the Remove button. Users may also add trusted publishers.

Trusted Locations. Clicking Trusted Locations shows the list of trusted locations on the Internet or within a user's network. To add a new location, click the 'Add new location' button. To remove or modify an existing location, click the location and then click the Remove or Modify button.

Trusted Documents. You can designate certain documents, including database, Word, Excel, and other files, as trusted. For a trusted document, you will not be prompted when you open the document, even if the content of the document has changed. You should be very careful when indicating a document is trusted and only do so when you are absolutely sure the document is from a trusted source.

Add-ins. Add-ins are additional programs that you can install and use within Access. Some come with Access and are typically installed using the Access Setup program. Others can be purchased from other vendors. Clicking Add-ins gives you the opportunity to specify restrictions concerning Add-ins.

ActiveX Settings. You can determine the level of prompting when an Office application uses ActiveX controls.

Macro Settings. Macros written by others have the potential to harm your computer; for example, a macro could spread a virus. The Trust Center uses special criteria, including valid digital signatures, reputable certificates, and trusted publishers, to ensure a macro is safe. If the Trust Center discovers a macro that is potentially unsafe, it will take appropriate action. The action the Trust Center takes depends on the Macro setting you have selected. Clicking Macro Settings enables you to select or change this setting.

DEP Settings. You can enable or disable Data Execution Prevention Mode. Data Execution Prevention (DEP) is a feature that helps prevent damage from viruses and other security threats. It should normally be enabled.

Message Bar. Clicking Message Bar lets you choose whether the message bar should appear when content has been blocked.

Privacy Options. Clicking Privacy Options lets you set security settings to protect your personal privacy.

Managing Add-ins. You can manage add-ins by opening the Backstage view, clicking Options, and then clicking Add-ins. You can view details concerning existing add-ins. You also can manage existing add-ins or add new ones by selecting the add-in category in the Manage box and then clicking the Go button to start the Add-in Manager. You also can start the Add-in Manager by clicking Database Tools on the Ribbon to display the Database Tools tab and then clicking the Add-ins button.

Locking a Database

By **locking** a database, you can prevent users from viewing or modifying VBA code in your database or from making changes to the design of forms or reports. When you lock the database, Access changes the file name extension from .accdb to .accde. To do so, you would use the Make ACCDE command shown in Figure 10–79 on page AC 657.

TO CREATE A LOCKED DATABASE (ACCDE FILE)
To lock a database, you would use the following steps.

1. With the database to be locked open, click File on the Ribbon to open the Backstage view.
2. Click the Save & Publish tab.
3. Click Make ACCDE in the Advanced area.
4. Click the Save As button.
5. In the Save As dialog box, indicate a location and name for the ACCDE file.
6. Click the Save button in the Save As dialog box to create the file.

Using the Locked Database

You use an ACCDE file just as you use the databases with which you now are familiar, with two exceptions. First, you must select ACCDE files in the Files of type box when opening the file. Second, you will not be able to modify any source code or change the design of any forms or reports. If you right-clicked the Client Form, for example, you would find that the Design View command on the shortcut menu is dimmed, as are many other commands (Figure 10–85).

Figure 10–85

It is very important that you save your original database in case you ever need to make changes to VBA code or to the design of a form or report. You cannot use the ACCDE file to make such changes.

Record Locking

You can indicate how records are to be locked when multiple users are using a database at the same time. To do so, click File on the Ribbon, click the Options button, and then click Client Settings. Scroll down so that the Advanced section appears on the screen (Figure 10–86).

Figure 10–86

If you wanted the default open mode to be exclusive (only one user can use the database at a time) rather than shared (multiple users can simultaneously use the database), you could click the Exclusive option button. You can also select the approach you want for record locking by clicking the appropriate record locking option button. The possible approaches to record locking are shown in Table 10–3.

Table 10–3 Record Locking Approaches	
Locking Type	**Description**
No locks	When you edit a record, Access will not lock the record. Thus, other users could also edit the same record at the same time. When you have finished your changes and attempt to save the record, Access will give you the option of overwriting the other user's changes (not recommended), copying your changes to the Clipboard, or canceling your changes.
All records	All records will be locked as long as you have the database open. No other user can edit or lock the records during this time.
Edited record	When you edit a record, Access will lock the record. When other users attempt to edit the same record, they will not be able to do so. Instead, they will see the locked record indicator.

BTW

Certification
The Microsoft Office Specialist (MOS) program provides an opportunity for you to obtain a valuable industry credential — proof that you have the Access 2010 skills required by employers. For more information, visit the Access 2010 Certification Web page (scsite.com/ ac2010/cert).

Splitting a Database

You can **split** a database into two databases, one called the **back-end database** containing only the table data and another database called the **front-end database** containing the other objects. Whereas there only would be a single copy of the back-end database, each user could have his or her own copy of the front-end database. Each user would create the desired custom reports, forms, and other objects in his or her own front-end database, thereby not interfering with any other user.

Determine whether the database should be split.
The decision to split the database into a front end and a back end is based on several considerations.

- **Split the database when multiple users share a database, and individual users would like to develop their own custom forms, reports, queries, or other objects.** If this is the case and each user develops such custom objects, the database can become cluttered and confusing. Many reports, for example, could be developed by different users for different purposes. Further, unless some special action is taken, there is nothing to protect one user's object (for example, a report or form) from being modified by another user. Splitting the database solves this problem.

- **Split the database when size is an issue.** Splitting the database into a front end and a back end produces smaller databases.

Plan Ahead

To Split the Database

When splitting a database, the database to be split must be open. In the process, you will identify a name and location for the back-end database that will be created by the splitter. The following steps show how to split the AMK Trainers database.

1

- If it is not already open, open the AMK Trainers database and enable the content.

- Display the Database Tools tab.

- Click the Access Database button (Database Tools tab | Move Data group) to display the Database Splitter dialog box (Figure 10–87).

 The instructions say that I should make a backup copy of my database before splitting it. Should I do that now?

It is definitely a good idea to make a backup copy. Here, because you are using the AMK Trainers database, which is very easy to re-create if you need to, it is not necessary. If you have a problem, delete the AMK Trainers database and then follow the steps under To Create a Database on page AC 653 to create it a second time.

Figure 10–87

2

- Click the Split Database button to display the Create Back-end Database dialog box.

- Be sure the file name that appears in the Create Back-end Database dialog box is AMK Trainers_be.

- Select a location for the back-end database (Figure 10–88).

3

- Click the Split button to split the database.

- Click the OK button to close the dialog box reporting that the split was successful.

Figure 10–88

The Front-End and Back-End Databases

The database now has been split into separate front-end and back-end databases. The front-end database is the one that you would use. This database contains all the queries, reports, forms, and so on, from the original database. The front-end database only contains links to the tables, however, instead of the tables themselves (Figure 10–89). The back-end database contains the actual tables but does not contain any other objects.

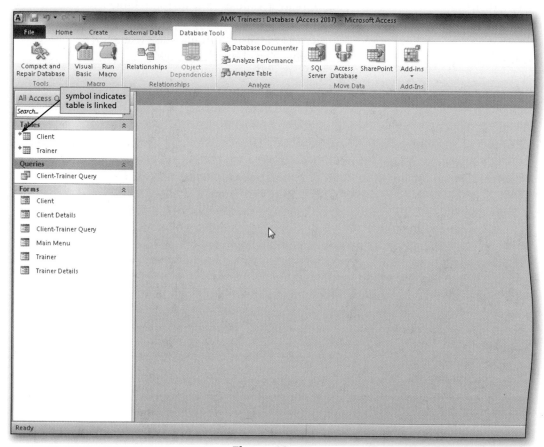

Figure 10–89

To Quit Access

The following steps quit Access.

1 Click the Close button on the right side of the title bar to quit Access.

2 If a Microsoft Access dialog box appears, click the Save button to save any changes made to the object since the last save.

BTW

Quick Reference
For a table that lists how to complete the tasks covered in this book using the mouse, Ribbon, shortcut menu, and keyboard, see the Quick Reference Summary at the back of this book, or visit the Access 2010 Quick Reference Web page (scsite.com/ac2010/qr).

Chapter Summary

In this chapter you have learned to create custom data parts, create a Web database and publish the database to Access Services, create and use templates and application parts, convert Access databases to and from earlier versions, use Microsoft Access tools to analyze and document an Access database, add custom categories and groups to the Navigation Pane, use table and database properties, use field properties to create a custom input mask and to allow zero-length strings, create indexes, use automatic error checking, encrypt a database and set a password, use digital certificates, use the Trust Center, lock a database, and split a database. The items listed below include all the new Access skills you have learned in this chapter.

1. Create Custom Data Parts (AC 606)
2. Create a Blank Web Database (AC 609)
3. Add Fields to the Table (AC 610)
4. Create a Second Table (AC 611)
5. Create Single-Item Forms (AC 616)
6. Create Datasheet Forms (AC 617)
7. Create a Navigation Form (AC 619)
8. Select a Startup Form (AC 620)
9. Create a Template (AC 621)
10. Check Web Compatibility (AC 623)
11. Publish to Access Services (AC 624)
12. View the Web Database (AC 625)
13. Use the Template (AC 628)
14. Use the Application Part (AC 629)
15. Convert an Access 2007 Database to an Earlier Version (AC 630)
16. Convert an Access 2000 or Access 2002–2003 Database to Default Database Format for Access 2010 (AC 630)
17. Use the Table Analyzer (AC 631)
18. Use the Performance Analyzer (AC 634)
19. Use the Database Documenter (AC 635)
20. Create Custom Categories and Groups (AC 638)
21. Add Items to Groups (AC 640)
22. Create a Validation Rule for a Table (AC 642)
23. Create Custom Properties (AC 643)
24. Create a Custom Input Mask (AC 646)
25. Allow Zero Length (AC 646)
26. Create a Single-Field Index (AC 649)
27. Create a Multiple-Field Index (AC 649)
28. Enable Error Checking (AC 651)
29. Encrypt a Database with a Password (AC 654)
30. Decrypt the Database and Remove the Password (AC 655)
31. Create a Self-Signed Certificate (AC 656)
32. Package and Sign a Database (AC 657)
33. Open a Signed Package (AC 659)
34. Create a Locked Database (ACCDE File) (AC 661)
35. Split the Database (AC 663)

 If you have a SAM 2010 user profile, your instructor may have assigned an autogradable version of this assignment. If so, log into the SAM 2010 Web site at www.cengage.com/sam2010 to download the instruction and start files.

Learn It Online

Test your knowledge of chapter content and key terms.

Instructions: To complete the Learn It Online exercises, start your browser, click the Address bar, and then enter the Web address **scsite.com/ac2010/learn**. When the Access 2010 Learn It Online page is displayed, click the link for the exercise you want to complete and then read the instructions.

Chapter Reinforcement TF, MC, and SA

A series of true/false, multiple choice, and short answer questions that test your knowledge of the chapter content.

Flash Cards

An interactive learning environment where you identify chapter key terms associated with displayed definitions.

Practice Test

A series of multiple choice questions that test your knowledge of chapter content and key terms.

Who Wants To Be a Computer Genius?

An interactive game that challenges your knowledge of chapter content in the style of a television quiz show.

Wheel of Terms

An interactive game that challenges your knowledge of chapter key terms in the style of the television show *Wheel of Fortune*.

Crossword Puzzle Challenge

A crossword puzzle that challenges your knowledge of key terms presented in the chapter.

Apply Your Knowledge

Reinforce the skills and apply the concepts you learned in this chapter.

Administering the Babbage CPA Firm Database

Instructions: Start Access. If you are using the Microsoft Access 2010 Comprehensive text, open the Babbage CPA Firm database that you used in Chapter 9. Otherwise, see your instructor for information on accessing the files required in this book.

Perform the following tasks:

1. Open the Client table in Design view and create an index that allows duplicates on the Client Name field. Zero-length strings should not be allowed in the Client Name field.

2. Create a custom input mask for the Client Number field. The first character of the client number must be an uppercase letter and the last two characters must be numerical digits.

3. Save the changes to the Client table.

4. Use the Database Documenter to produce detailed documentation on the Accounts table. Export the documentation to a Word RTF file. To export the documentation, right-click the Object Definition report in the Print Preview window, point to Export on the shortcut menu, and then click Word RTF File. Change the name of the file to LastName_Documentation.rtf where LastName is your last name.

5. Use the Table Analyzer to analyze the table structure of the Client table. Open the RTF file that you created in Step 4 and report the results of the analysis at the end of the file.

6. Use the Performance Analyzer to analyze all the tables in the database. Report the results of your analysis in your RTF file.

7. Populate the Status property for the database with the value, Apply Your Knowledge.

8. Create a custom property with the name, Due Date. Use Date as the type and enter the current date as the value.

9. Convert the database to an Access 2002–2003 database. Name the database Babbage CPA Firm_02_03.

10. Submit the revised Babbage CPA Firm database, the Babbage CPA Firm_02_03 database, and the RTF file in the format specified by your instructor.

Extend Your Knowledge

Extend the skills you learned in this chapter and experiment with new skills. You may need to use Help to complete the assignment.

Changing Access Options and Table Properties

Instructions: Copy the Camashaly Design database and rename the database to Chapter 10 Camashaly Design. Start Access and open the database that you copied and renamed.

Perform the following tasks:

1. Open the Client table in Design view and add a smart tag for the Client Name field. Select the Person Name action tag. (*Hint:* See the BTW on page AC 645 for help with smart tags.)

2. Add a custom input mask for the Postal Code field. Only digits are allowed in the field.

3. Save the changes to the Client table.

4. Open the Business Analyst Master List in Design view and add a logo to the report. You can create your own logo or use one of the sample pictures included with Microsoft Access. (*Hint:* See the BTW on page AC 616 for help with inserting a logo.)

Continued >

Extend Your Knowledge *continued*

5. Currently, when you open the Course table in Datasheet view, the table is ordered by Course Number. Change the property for the table so the table is in order by Course Description. (*Hint:* See the BTW on page AC 169). If necessary, resize the Course Description field so the entire description appears.

6. Add the Analysts and Course Offerings query to the Summary group in the Navigation Pane.

7. Submit the revised database in the format specified by your instructor.

Make It Right

Analyze a database and correct all errors and/or improve the design.

Correcting Table Design Errors

Instructions: Start Access. Open the Cleaning by Jenna database. See the inside back cover of this book for instructions on downloading the Data Files for Students, or contact your instructor for more information about accessing the required files.

The Cleaning by Jenna database contains data about a local business that provides cleaning services. The owner added the index shown in Figure 10–90 to the Customer table. The index is to sort records first by City and then by Balance, but she gets an error message when she tries to save the table change. Create the index correctly.

She also created an input mask for the Customer Number field. The input mask she created is shown in Figure 10–90; however, she found that it does not work correctly. It allows a user to input a customer number that does not include letters. The customer number must be two uppercase letters followed by two numbers. (*Hint:* There are two reasons why the input mask does not work.) Finally, she wants to change the macro settings for the database so that all macros except digitally signed ones are disabled, but she doesn't know how to do it.

Correct these errors and submit the revised database in the format specified by your instructor.

Figure 10–90

In the Lab

Design, create, modify, and/or use a database following the guidelines, concepts, and skills presented in this chapter. Labs are listed in order of increasing difficulty.

Lab 1: Administering the ECO Clothesline Database

Problem: ECO Clothesline has determined a number of database administration tasks that need to be done. These include creating a template, splitting the database, creating indexes, and adding table and field properties.

Instructions: If you are using the Microsoft Office Access 2010 Comprehensive text, open the ECO Clothesline database that you used in Chapter 9. Otherwise, contact your instructor for more information about accessing the required files.

Perform the following tasks:

1. Open the Open Orders table in Datasheet view and add the Quick Start Priority field to the table. Assign a High priority to orders for customers AM23 and JN34. Assign a Low priority to the order for TT21. All other orders have a Normal priority.
2. The Main Menu navigation form should display automatically when a user opens the database.
3. Open the Customer table in Design view and create custom input masks for the following fields: Customer Number, State, Postal Code, and Sales Rep Number. The Customer Number field should consist of two uppercase letters followed by two numbers. The State field should contain two uppercase letters. Both the Postal Code and Sales Rep Number fields only can contain numbers.
4. Create an index on the Customer Name field that does not allow duplicates. Create an index on the combination of Customer Type and Customer Name. Name the index TypeName.
5. Save the ECO Clothesline database as a template with data but not as an application part. Create a new database from the ECO Clothesline template. Name the database ECO New. Split the ECO New database.
6. Open the front-end database and add a logo to the Customer Master Form. You can create your own logo or use one of the sample pictures included with Microsoft Access. (*Hint:* See the BTW on page AC 645 for assistance with this task.)
7. Submit the revised databases in the format specified by your instructor.

In the Lab

Lab 2: Administering the Walburg Energy Alternatives Database

Problem: The management of the Walburg Energy Alternatives store would like to create a Web database of Items and Vendors.

Instructions: If you are using the Microsoft Office Access 2010 Comprehensive text, open the Walburg Energy Alternatives database that you used in Chapter 9. Otherwise, contact your instructor for more information about accessing the required files.

Perform the following tasks:

1. Open the Item table in Datasheet view and change the Required property for the Description field to No. (*Hint:* To change the property in Datasheet view, click the Required check box to remove the check mark.) Create a Quick Start data type that includes the Description, Cost, and Selling Price. Name the data type Desc-Profit.

Continued >

In the Lab *continued*

2. Open the Vendor table in Datasheet view and create a Quick Start data type that includes the Vendor Name and Phone. Name the data type Name-Phone.

3. Create a Web database named Items and Vendors.

4. Create a Vendor table that includes the Vendor Code field and the Name-Phone Quick Start data type. Vendor Code is a text field with a field size of 2. The field is required and unique.

5. Create an Item table that includes the Item Number and the Desc-Profit Quick Start data type. Item Number is a text field with a field size of 4. The field is required and unique. Vendor Code should be the last field in the Item table. Add this field as a Lookup & Relationship data type. Be sure to enable data integrity.

6. Import the Vendor.txt file into the Vendor table and the Item.txt file into the Item table. Because there is a relationship between the Vendor table and the Item table, you must import the Vendor.txt file first.

7. Create single-item forms for the Item table and the Vendor table. Name these forms Item Details and Vendor Details.

8. Create a datasheet form for the Item table. Create a macro for the On Click event that opens the Item Details form.

9. Create a datasheet form for the Vendor table. Create a macro for the On Click event that opens the Vendor Details form.

10. Create a navigation form similar to the one shown in Figure 10–1a on page AC 602 for the Items and Vendors database. Include the Item and Vendor datasheet forms and the Item Details and Vendor Details form. Name the form Main Menu.

11. Create a template and an application part from this database. Include data in the template. Name the template Items and Vendors.

12. Check the database to be sure that it is Web compatible.

13. If you have permission to do so, publish the Items and Vendors database to the Web.

14. Submit the revised Walburg Energy Alternatives database and the Items and Vendors database in the format specified by your instructor.

In the Lab

Lab 3: Administering the Philamar Training Database

Problem: Philamar Training has determined a number of database administration tasks that need to be done. These include creating indexes, setting startup options, creating input masks, allowing zero-length fields, customizing the Navigation Pane, and populating database properties.

Instructions: If you are using the Microsoft Office Access 2010 Comprehensive text, open the Philamar Training database that you used in Chapter 9. Otherwise, contact your instructor for more information about accessing the required files. Modify the database to make the changes described in the following instructions.

Instructions Part 1: The management of Philamar Training is concerned that as the database grows, it will take longer to retrieve information on client names. An index would speed up the retrieval process. Management also feels that an index on the last name and first name of the trainer would improve efficiency.

Instructions Part 2: The management wants to ensure that the client number field always contains two uppercase letters followed by two numeric digits. Also, errors are occurring because individuals are entering text instead of numbers in the Postal Code field of the Client table. In addition, empty strings should not be allowed in the Client Name field.

Instructions Part 3: Management wants the Main Menu navigation form to appear when the database is opened. They also want to populate the Status property with the value Current Version and create a custom property named Backup Date with a data type of Date. Populate the Backup Date property with the current date.

Instructions Part 4: Finally, management would like to add a validation rule to the Class table. They want to ensure that the value in the Increments field is equal to or less than the value in the Hours field.

Cases and Places

Apply your creative thinking and problem solving skills to design and implement a solution.

1: Administering the Chamber of Commerce Database

Academic

If you are using the Microsoft Access 2010 Comprehensive text, open the Chamber of Commerce database that you used in Chapter 9. Otherwise, see your instructor for more information about accessing the required files.

Your internship with the Chamber of Commerce is finished, but you have agreed to make some administrative changes. Also, in your Marketing class, you are part of a team whose assignment is to prepare for local retail businesses an innovative marketing plan targeted at young adults. The Chamber has agreed to let you export the name, address, and phone number data in the Chamber of Commerce database to contact retail businesses and ask them to critique your team's plan. Use the concepts and techniques presented in this chapter to perform each of the following tasks:

a. Create an index on the Advertiser Name field that does not allow duplicates. Create an index on the combination of the Advertiser Type and the Advertiser Name.

b. Create custom input masks for the Advertiser Number, Postal Code, and Ad Rep Number fields in the Advertiser table.

c. Run the Web Compatibility Checker for the database. If the database is incompatible with the Web, a Web Compatibility Issues table will be added to your database.

d. Create a query to find all advertisers that are retail organizations. Include the Advertiser Number, Advertiser Name, Address, Postal Code, and Telephone Number. Save the query as Retail Advertisers.

e. Export the query as an HTML document and as an Excel workbook.

f. Create a new database named Retail Contacts. Import the Excel file you created in Step e.

Submit the revised databases and the HTML document in the format specified by your instructor.

2: Administering the Consignment Database

Personal

If you are using the Microsoft Access 2010 Comprehensive text, open the Consignment database that you used in Chapter 9. Otherwise, see your instructor for more information about accessing the required files.

The volunteer group that manages the consignment shop has asked you to perform a number of administration tasks. Use the concepts and techniques presented in this chapter to perform each of the following tasks:

a. Change the Current Database options to ensure that the Main Menu opens automatically.

Continued >

Cases and Places *continued*

b. Customize the Navigation Pane by adding a custom category called Store Items. Then add two custom groups, Available and Reduced, to the Store Items category.

c. Add the Item Master Form and the Available Items Report to the Available group. Add the Item Sale Report, the Reduced Price Report, and the March Items Query to the Reduced group.

d. Back up the Consignment database.

e. If you have your instructor's permission, create a self-signed certificate for the Consignment database. Sign and package the database.

Submit the revised database, the backed-up database, and the signed and packaged database in the format specified by your instructor.

3: Creating a Web Database for Senior Care

Professional

If you are using the Microsoft Access 2010 Comprehensive text, open the Senior Care database that you used in Chapter 9. Otherwise, see your instructor for more information about accessing the required files.

Senior Care is expanding rapidly and now has branch offices in other cities. You and your partners would like to create a database that can be accessed using the Web. Use the concepts and techniques presented in this chapter to perform each of the following tasks:

a. Open the Client table in Design view and change the Required Property for the Last Name and the First Name fields to No. Save the changes. Create a Quick Start data type that includes all fields in the Client table except Services Needed and Helper Number. Save the data type as Basic Client Data.

b. Create a Quick Start data type that includes all fields in the Helper table except Comment. Save the data type as Basic Helper Data.

c. Create a Web database named Clients and Helpers.

d. Create a Helper table using the Basic Helper Data Quick Start data type.

e. Create a Client table using the Basic Client Data Quick Start data type. Helper Number should be the last field in the Client table. Add this field as a Lookup & Relationship data type. Be sure to enable data integrity.

f. Import the Helper.txt file into the Helper table and the Senior Client.txt file into the Client table. Because there is a relationship between the Helper table and the Client table, be sure to import the Helper.txt file first.

g. Create a query that joins the Client and Helper tables. Include the Helper Number, Helper Last Name, Helper First Name, Client Number, Client Last Name, and Client First Name. Save the query as Clients and Helpers.

h. Create single-item forms for the Client and Helper tables. Name these forms Client Details and Helper Details.

i. Create datasheet forms for the Client and Helper tables. Include an On Click macro in each form that opens the respective Details form.

j. Create a datasheet form for the Clients and Helpers query.

k. Create a navigation form similar to the one shown in Figure 10–1a on page AC 602. Include the datasheet forms and the detail forms.

l. Create a template and an application part for this database. Name the template Clients and Helpers.

m. Check the database to be sure that it is Web compatible.

n. If you have permission to do so, publish the Clients and Helpers database to the Web.

Submit the revised Senior Care database and the Clients and Helpers database in the format specified by your instructor.

11 | Database Design

Objectives

You will have mastered the material in this chapter when you can:

- Understand the terms entity, attribute, and relationship

- Understand the terms relation and relational database

- Understand functional dependence and be able to identify when one column is functionally dependent on another

- Understand the term primary key, and identify primary keys in tables

- Design a database to satisfy a set of requirements

- Convert an unnormalized relation to first normal form

- Convert tables from first normal form to second normal form

- Convert tables from second normal form to third normal form

- Represent the design of a database using diagrams

11 | Database Design

Introduction

This chapter presents a method for determining the tables and fields necessary to satisfy a set of requirements. The process of determining the particular tables and fields that will make up a database is known as **database design**. In designing a database, you must first identify the tables in the database, the fields in the tables, the primary keys of the tables, and the relationships between the tables.

The chapter begins by examining some important concepts concerning relational databases and then presents the design method. To illustrate the process, the chapter presents the requirements for the Camashaly Design database. It then applies the design method to those requirements to produce the database design. The chapter applies the design method to a second set of requirements, which are requirements for a company called Scryps Distributors. It next examines normalization, a process that you can use to identify and fix potential problems in database designs. The chapter concludes by discussing how to obtain information for database design from existing documents and also how to represent a database design with a diagram.

Project — Design a Database

This chapter expands on the database design guidelines presented in Chapter 1 on page AC 5. Without a good understanding of database design, you cannot use a database management system such as Access effectively. In this chapter, you will learn how to design two databases by using the database design process shown in Figure 11–1.

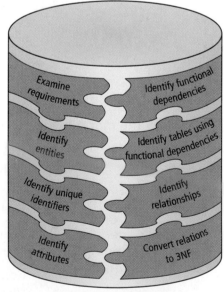

Database Design Process

Figure 11–1

You will design a database for Camashaly Design that is similar to the database you have used in the previous chapters. You also will design a database for Scryps Distributors, a distributor of energy saving and water conservation devices.

Overview

As you read this chapter, you will learn how to design databases using the method shown in Figure 11–1 by performing these general tasks:

- Examine database requirements.
- Identify entities.
- Identify unique identifiers.
- Identify attributes.
- Identify functional dependencies.
- Identify tables using functional dependencies.
- Identify relationships.
- Convert relations to 3NF.

BTW

Systems Analysis
The determination of database requirements is part of a process known as systems analysis. A systems analyst interviews users, examines existing and proposed documents, investigates current procedures, and reviews organizational policies to determine exactly the type of data needs the database must support.

Entities, Attributes, and Relationships

Working in the database environment requires that you be familiar with some specific terms and concepts. The terms *entity*, *attribute*, and *relationship* are fundamental when discussing databases. An **entity** is like a noun: It is a person, place, thing, or event. The entities of interest to Camashaly Design, for example, are such things as business analysts, clients, and courses. The entities that are of interest to a college include students, faculty, and classes; a real estate agency is interested in buyers, sellers, properties, and agents; and a used car dealer is interested in vehicles, customers, and manufacturers. When creating a database, an entity is represented as a table.

An **attribute** is a property of an entity. The term is used here exactly as it is used in everyday English. For the entity *person*, for example, the list of attributes might include such things as eye color and height. For Camashaly Design, the attributes of interest for the entity *client* are such things as name, address, city, and so on. For the entity *faculty* at a school, the attributes would be such things as faculty number, name, office number, phone, and so on. For the entity *vehicle* at a car dealership, the attributes are such things as the vehicle identification number, model, price, year, and so on. In databases, attributes are represented as the fields in a table or tables.

A **relationship** is an association between entities. There is an association between business analysts and clients, for example, at Camashaly Design. A business analyst is associated with all of his or her clients, and a client is associated with the one business analyst to whom the client is assigned. Technically, you say that a business analyst is *related* to all of his or her clients, and a client is *related* to his or her business analyst.

The relationship between business analysts and clients is an example of a one-to-many relationship because one business analyst is associated with many clients, but each client is associated with only one business analyst. In this type of relationship, the word *many* is used in a way that is different from everyday English; it might not always mean a large number. In this context, for example, the term *many* means that a business analyst might be associated with *any* number of clients. That is, one business analyst can be associated with zero, one, or more clients.

BTW

Entities
Camashaly Design could include many other entities in a database, such as entities for employees, hardware inventory, and software inventory. The decisions on which entities to include are part of the process of determining database requirements based on user needs.

BTW

Relationships
One-to-one relationships also can occur but they are not common. If one employee is assigned to a project and each project has only one employee working on it, a one-to-one relationship exists between employees and projects. To implement a one-to-one relationship, treat it as a one-to-many relationship. You must determine which table will be the one table and which table will be the many table. To do so, consider what may happen in the future. In the case of employees and projects, more employees could be added easily to a project. Therefore, the project table would be the one table and the employee table would be the many table.

There also is a relationship between clients and courses. Each client can be offered many courses, and each course can be offered to many clients. This is an example of a many-to-many relationship.

How does a relational database handle entities, attributes of entities, and relationships between entities? Entities and attributes are fairly simple. Each entity has its own table; in the Camashaly Design database, there is one table for business analysts, one table for clients, and so on. The attributes of an entity become the columns in the table. In the table for clients, for example, there is a column for the client number, a column for the client name, and so on.

What about relationships? Relationships are implemented through matching fields. One-to-many relationships, for example, are implemented by including matching fields in the related tables. Business analysts and clients are related, for example, by including the Business Analyst Number field in both the Business Analyst table and the Client table.

Many-to-many relationships are implemented through an additional table that contains matching fields for both of the related tables. Clients and Courses are related, for example, through the Course Offerings table. Both the Client table and the Course Offerings table contain Client Number fields. In addition, both the Course and the Course Offerings table contain Course Number fields.

Relational Databases

A relational database is a collection of tables similar to the tables for Camashaly Design that appear in Figure 11–2. In the Camashaly Design database, the Client table contains information about the clients to which Camashaly Design provides custom marketing services (Figure 11–2a). Note that, for simplification purposes, the tables in the figure do not include all the fields of the final Camashaly database in Chapter 10.

Client

Client Number	Client Name	Street	City	State	Postal Code	Amount Paid	Current Due	Business Analyst Number
BA53	Bavant Animal Hospital	134 Main	Burles	NC	28817	$0.00	$7,500.00	11
BB32	Babbage CPA Firm	464 Linnell	Austin	SC	28796	$1,500.00	$500.00	14
BC76	Buda Community Clinic	867 Ridge	Buda	NC	27032	$2,500.00	$750.00	11
CJ29	Catering by Jenna	123 Second	Granger	NC	27036	$3,000.00	$1,000.00	27
GF56	Granger Family Foundation	65 Simpson	Granger	NC	27036	$0.00	$6,500.00	11
HC10	Hendley County Regional Hospital	216 Rivard	Austin	SC	28796	$3,100.00	$1,200.00	27
KD21	KAL Design Studio	116 Pine	Georgetown	NC	28794	$6,000.00	$3,200.00	14
KG04	Kyle Grocery Cooperative	421 First	Kyle	SC	28798	$3,200.00	$0.00	11
KM03	Kyle Museum of Art	200 Main	Kyle	SC	28798	$0.00	$750.00	35
ME14	Mike's Electronic Stop	234 Gilham	Georgetown	NC	28794	$2,500.00	$1,500.00	27
PJ34	Patricia Jean Florist	345 Magee	Kyle	SC	28798	$0.00	$5,200.00	27
SL77	Smarter Law Associates	764 Main	Burles	NC	28817	$3,800.00	$0.00	11
TB17	The Bikeshop	346 Austin	Buda	NC	27032	$2,750.00	$1,200.00	27

(a) Client Table

Figure 11–2

Camashaly assigns each client to a specific business analyst. The Business Analyst table contains information about the analysts to whom these clients are assigned (Figure 11–2b).

Business Analyst								
Business Analyst Number	Last Name	First Name	Street	City	State	Postal Code	Salary YTD	Incentive YTD
11	Kerry	Cordelia	251 Painter	Georgetown	NC	28794	$3,200.00	$3,450.00
14	Martinez	Manuel	3125 Steel	Kyle	SC	28797	$3,100.00	$2,430.00
27	Liu	Jan	265 Marble	Byron	SC	28795	$3,400.00	$2,280.00
35	Scott	Jeff	1925 Pine	Georgetown	NC	28794	$500.00	$0.00

(b) Business Analyst Table

Figure 11–2

The Course table lists the specific courses that the analysts at Camashaly Design offer to their clients (Figure 11–2c). Each course has a number and a description. The table also includes the number of hours for which the course usually is offered and the course's increments; that is, the standard time blocks in which the course usually is offered. The first row, for example, indicates that course C01 is Using the Content Management System. The course typically is offered in 2-hour increments for a total of 8 hours.

Course			
Course Number	Course Description	Hours	Increments
C01	Using the Content Management System	8	2
C02	HTML Basics	4	1
C03	Digital Image Management	6	3
C04	Javascript Basics	12	3
C05	Understanding Social Networks	2	2
C06	Using Shopping Carts	4	2
C07	Understanding Cascading Style Sheets	8	2
C08	Podcasting	6	3

(c) Course Table

Figure 11–2

The Course Offerings table contains a client number, a course number, the total number of hours for which the course is scheduled, and the number of hours the client has already spent in the course (Figure 11–2d). The first record shows that client number BA53 currently has scheduled course C05. The course is scheduled for 2 hours, of which no hours have currently been spent. Note that the total hours is usually the same as the number of hours indicated for the course in the Course table, but it can differ. According to the Course table, the total number of hours for C01, Using the Content Management System, is 8. As indicated in the Course Offerings table, client KG04 opted to schedule C01 for 10 hours.

Course Offerings			
Client Number	**Course Number**	**Total Hours**	**Hours Spent**
BA53	C05	2	0
BB32	C01	8	4
CJ29	C03	6	3
HC10	C04	12	6
HC10	C05	2	1
KD21	C03	6	0
KD21	C07	8	4
KG04	C01	8	6
KG04	C05	2	0
KG04	C08	6	4
ME14	C06	4	2
PJ34	C06	4	2
SL77	C04	12	9
SL77	C08	6	2
TB17	C02	4	2

(d) Course Offerings Table

Figure 11–2

The formal term for a table is relation. If you study the tables shown in Figure 11–2, you might see that there are certain restrictions you should place on relations. Each column in a table should have a unique name, and entries in each column should match this column name. For example, in the Postal Code column, all entries should in fact *be* postal codes. In addition, each row should be unique. After all, if two rows in a table contain identical data, the second row does not provide any information that you do not already have. In addition, for maximum flexibility, the order in which columns and rows appear in a table should be immaterial. Finally, a table's design is less complex if you restrict each position in the table to a single entry, that is, you do not permit multiple entries, often called **repeating groups**, in the table. These restrictions lead to the following definition:

A **relation** is a two-dimensional table in which:

1. The entries in the table are single-valued; that is, each location in the table contains a single entry.

2. Each column has a distinct name, technically called the *attribute name*.

3. All values in a column are values of the same attribute; that is, all entries must correspond to the column name.

4. Each row is distinct; that is, no two rows are identical.

Figure 11–3a shows a table with repeating groups, which violates Rule 1. Figure 11–3b shows a table in which two columns have the same name, which violates Rule 2. Figure 11–3c shows a table in which one of the entries in the Course Description column is not a course description, which violates Rule 3. Figure 11–3d shows a table with two identical rows, which violates Rule 4.

In addition, in a relation, the order of columns is immaterial. You can view the columns in any order you want. The order of rows is also immaterial. You can view the rows in any order you want.

Course Offerings

Client Number	Course Number	Total Hours	Hours Spent
BA53	C05	2	0
BB32	C01	8	4
CJ29	C03	6	3
HC10	C04	12	6
	C05	2	1
KD21	C03	6	0
	C07	8	4
KG04	C01	10	6
	C05	2	0
	C08	6	4
ME14	C06	4	2
PJ34	C06	4	2
SL77	C04	12	9
	C08	6	2
TB17	C02	4	2

repeating group (more than one entry in a single table location)

two columns with the same name

Course

Course Number	Course Description	Hours	Hours	Increments
C01	Using the Content Management System	8	10	2
C02	HTML Basics	4	3	1
C03	Digital Image Management	6	5	3
C04	Javascript Basics	12	14	3
C05	Understanding Social Networks	2	3	2
C06	Using Shopping Carts	4	4	2
C07	Understanding Cascading Style Sheets	8	6	2
C08	Podcasting	6	8	3

(a) Course Offerings Table Violation of Rule 1 – Each Location in the Table Must Contain a Single Entry

(b) Course Table Violation of Rule 2 – Each Column has a Distinct Name

Course

Course Number	Course Description	Hours	Increments
C01	Using the Content Management System	8	2
C02	HTML Basics	4	1
C03	6	6	3
C04	Javascript Basics	12	3
C05	Understanding Social Networks	2	2
C06	Using Shopping Carts	4	2
C07	Understanding Cascading Style Sheets	8	2
C08	Podcasting	6	3

value does not correspond to column name; that is, it is not a course description

(c) Course Table Violation of Rule 3 – All Entries in a Column Must Correspond to the Column Name

Course

Course Number	Course Description	Hours	Increments
C01	Using the Content Management System	8	2
C02	HTML Basics	4	1
C03	Digital Image Management	6	3
C04	Javascript Basics	12	3
C02	HTML Basics	4	1
C05	Understanding Social Networks	2	2
C06	Using Shopping Carts	4	2
C07	Understanding Cascading Style Sheets	8	2
C08	Podcasting	6	3

identical rows

(d) Course Table Violation of Rule 4 – Each Row Is Distinct

Figure 11–3

A **relational database** is a collection of relations. Rows in a table (relation) often are called **records** or **tuples**. Columns in a table (relation) often are called **fields** or **attributes**. Typically, the terms *record* and *field* are used in Access.

To depict the structure of a relational database, you can use a commonly accepted shorthand representation: You write the name of the table and then within parentheses list all of the fields in the table. Each table should begin on a new line. If the entries in the table occupy more than one line, the entries that appear on the next line should be indented so it is clear that they do not constitute another table. Using this method, you would represent the Camashaly Design database as in Figure 11–4.

Client (Client Number, Client Name, Street, City, State, Postal Code,
    Amount Paid, Current Due, Business Analyst Number)

Business Analyst (Business Analyst Number, Last Name, First Name, Street,
    City, State, Postal Code, Salary YTD, Incentive YTD)

Course (Course Number, Course Description, Hours, Increments)

Course Offerings (Client Number, Course Number, Total Hours, Hours Spent)

Figure 11–4

The Camashaly Design database contains some duplicate field names. For example, the Business Analyst Number field appears in both the Business Analyst table and the Client table. This duplication of names can lead to possible confusion. If you write Business Analyst Number, it is not clear to which Business Analyst Number field you are referring.

When duplicate field names exist in a database, you need to indicate the field to which you are referring. You do so by writing both the table name and the field name, separated by a period. You would write the Business Analyst Number field in the Client table as Client.Business Analyst Number and the Business Analyst Number field in the Business Analyst table as Business Analyst.Business Analyst Number. Technically, when you combine a field name with a table name, you say that you **qualify** the field names. It is *always* acceptable to qualify field names, even if there is no possibility of confusion. If confusion may arise, however, it is *essential* to qualify field names.

Functional Dependence

In the Camashaly Design database (Figure 11–2 on pages AC 676 – AC 678), a given client number in the database will correspond to a single client because client numbers are unique. Thus, if you are given a client number in the database, you could find a single name that corresponds to it. No ambiguity exists. The database terminology for this relationship between client numbers and names is that Client Number determines Client Name, or, equivalently, that Client Name is functionally dependent on Client Number. Specifically, if you know that whenever you are given a value for one field, you will be able to determine a single value for a second field, the first field is said to **determine** the second field. In addition, the second field is said to be **functionally dependent** on the first.

There is a shorthand notation that represents functional dependencies using an arrow. To indicate that Client Number determines Client Name, or, equivalently, that Client Name is functionally dependent on Client Number, you would write Client Number → Client Name. The field that precedes the arrow determines the field that follows the arrow.

If you were given a city and asked to find a single client's name, you could not do it. Given Burles as the city, for example, you would find two client names, Bavant Animal Hospital and Smarter Law Associates (Figure 11–5). Formally, you would say the City does *not* determine Client Name, or that Client Name is *not* functionally dependent on City.

BTW

Functional Dependence
To help identify functional dependencies, ask yourself the following question. If you know a unique value for an attribute, do you know the unique values for another attribute? For example, when you have three attributes: Business Analyst Number, Last Name, and First Name and you know a unique value for Business Analyst Number, do you also know a unique value for Last Name and First Name? If so, then Last Name and First Name are functionally dependent on Business Analyst Number.

Client									
Client Number	Client Name	Street	City	State	Postal Code	Amount Paid	Current Due	Business Analyst Number	
BA53	Bavant Animal Hospital	134 Main	Burles	NC	28817	$0.00	$7,500.00	11	
BB32	Babbage CPA Firm	464 Linnell	Austin	SC	28796	$1,500.00	$500.00	14	
BC76	Buda Community Clinic	867 Ridge	Buda	NC	27032	$2,500.00	$750.00	11	
CJ29	Catering by Jenna	123 Second	Granger	NC	27036	$3,000.00	$1,000.00	27	
GF56	Granger Family Foundation	65 Simpson	Granger	NC	27036	$0.00	$6,500.00	11	
HC10	Hendley County Regional Hospital	216 Rivard	Austin	SC	28796	$3,100.00	$1,200.00	27	
KD21	KAL Design Studio	116 Pine	Georgetown	NC	28794	$6,000.00	$3,200.00	14	
KG04	Kyle Grocery Cooperative	421 First	Kyle	SC	28798	$3,200.00	$0.00	11	
KM03	Kyle Museum of Art	200 Main	Kyle	SC	28798	$0.00	$750.00	35	
ME14	Mike's Electronic Stop	234 Gilham	Georgetown	NC	28794	$2,500.00	$1,500.00	27	
PJ34	Patricia Jean Florist	345 Magee	Kyle	SC	28798	$0.00	$5,200.00	27	
SL77	Smarter Law Associates	764 Main	Burles	NC	28817	$3,800.00	$0.00	11	
TB17	The Bikeshop	346 Austin	Buda	NC	27032	$2,750.00	$1,200.00	27	

city is Burles; name is Bavant Animal Hospital

city is also Burles, but name is Smarter Law Associates (same city, but different client name)

Figure 11–5

Q&A In the Business Analyst table, is Last Name functionally dependent on Business Analyst Number?

Yes. If you are given a value for Business Analyst Number, for example 14, you will always find a *single* last name, in this case Martinez, associated with it.

Q&A In the Client table, is Client Name functionally dependent on Business Analyst Number?

No. A given Business Analyst Number occurs on multiple rows. Business Analyst Number 14, for example, occurs on a row on which the Client Name is Babbage CPA Firm. It also occurs on a row on which the Client Name is KAL Design Studio. Thus, analyst number 14 is associated with more than one client name.

Q&A In the Course Offerings table, is Hours Spent functionally dependent on Client Number?

No. There is a row, for example, on which the Client Number is KG04 and the Hours Spent is 6. There is another row on which the Client Number is KG04 but the Hours Spent is 0, a different number.

Q&A In the Course Offerings table, is Hours Spent functionally dependent on Course Number?

No. There is a row, for example, on which the Course Number is C05 and the Hours Spent is 0. There is another row on which the Course Number is C05 but the Hours Spent is 1, a different number.

Q&A On which fields is the Hours Spent functionally dependent?

To determine a value for Hours Spent, you need both a Client Number and a Course Number. In other words, Hours Spent is functionally dependent on the combination, formally called the **concatenation,** of Client Number and Course Number. That is, given a Client Number *and* a Course Number, you can find a single value for Hours Spent.

Q&A On which fields is the Total Hours functionally dependent?

Because the Total Hours for a given course can vary from one client to another, Total Hours is also functionally dependent on the combination of Client Number and Course Number.

Q&A On which fields would the Total Hours be functionally dependent if every time a course was scheduled, the Total Hours had to be the same as the number of hours given in the Course table?

In that case, to determine Total Hours, you would only need to know the course number. Thus, Total Hours would be functionally dependent on Course Number.

Primary Key

The **primary key** of a table is the field or minimum collection of fields — the fewest number of fields possible — that uniquely identifies a given row in that table. In the Business Analyst table, the analyst's number uniquely identifies a given row. Any analyst number appears on only one row of the table. Thus, Business Analyst Number is the primary key. Similarly, Client Number is the primary key of the Client table, and Course Number is the primary key of the Course table.

Q&A Is the Client Number field the primary key for the Course Offerings table?

No, because it does not functionally determine either Total Hours or Hours Spent.

Q&A Is the Course Number field the primary key for the Course Offerings table?

No, because, like Client Number, it does not functionally determine either Total Hours or Hours Spent.

Q&A What is the primary key of the Course Offerings table?

The primary key is the combination of the Client Number and Course Number fields. You can determine all other fields from this combination. Further, neither the Client Number nor the Course Number alone has this property.

Q&A Is the combination of the Course Number and Course Description fields the primary key for the Course table?

No. Although it is true that you can determine all fields in the Course table by this combination, Course Number alone also has this property. The Course Number field is the primary key.

The primary key provides an important way of distinguishing one row in a table from another. In the shorthand representation, you underline the field or collection of fields that make up the primary key for each table in the database. Thus, the complete shorthand representation for the Camashaly Design database is shown in Figure 11–6.

Client (<u>Client Number</u>, Client Name, Street, City, State, Postal Code, Amount Paid, Current Due, Business Analyst Number)

Business Analyst (<u>Business Analyst Number</u>, Last Name, First Name, Street, City, State, Postal Code, Salary YTD, Incentive YTD)

Course (<u>Course Number</u>, Course Description, Hours, Increments)

Course Offerings (<u>Client Number</u>, <u>Course Number</u>, Total Hours, Hours Spent)

Figure 11–6

Occasionally, but not often, there might be more than one possibility for the primary key. For example, if the Camashaly Design database included the analyst's Social Security number in the Business Analyst table, either the analyst number or the Social

Security number could serve as the primary key. In this case, both fields are referred to as candidate keys. Similar to a primary key, a **candidate key** is a field or combination of fields on which all fields in the table are functionally dependent. Thus, the definition for primary key really defines candidate key as well. There can be many candidate keys, although having more than one is very rare. By contrast, there is only one primary key. The remaining candidate keys are called **alternate keys**.

Database Design

This section presents a specific database design method, given a set of requirements that the database must support. The section then presents a sample of such requirements and illustrates the design method by designing a database to satisfy these requirements.

Design Process

The following is a method for designing a database for a set of requirements.

1. Examine the requirements and identify the entities, or objects, involved. Assign names to the entities. The entities will become tables. If, for example, the design involves departments and employees, you could assign the names, Department and Employee. If the design involves customers, orders, and parts, you could assign the names, Customer, Orders, and Part.

Note: The word, Order, has special meaning in SQL. If you use it for the name of a table, you will not be able to use SQL to query that table. A common approach to avoid this problem is to make the name plural. That is the reason for choosing Orders rather than Order as the name of the table.

2. Identify a unique identifier for each entity. For example, if one of the entities is parts, you would determine what it takes to uniquely identify each individual part. In other words, what enables the organization to distinguish one part from another? For a part entity, it may be Item Number. For a customer entity, it may be Customer Number. If there is no such unique identifier, it is a good idea to add one. Perhaps the previous system was a manual one where customers were not assigned numbers, in which case this would be a good time to add Customer Numbers to the system. If there is no natural candidate for a primary key, you can add an AutoNumber field, which is similar to the ID field that Access adds automatically when you create a new table.

3. Identify the attributes for all the entities. These attributes will become the fields in the tables. It is possible that more than one entity has the same attribute. At Camashaly Design, for example, clients and analysts both have the attributes of street address, city, state, and postal code. To clarify this in your planning, you can follow the name of the attribute with the corresponding entity in parentheses. Thus, Street (Client) would be the street address of a client, whereas Street (Business Analyst) would be the street address of an analyst.

4. Identify the functional dependencies that exist among the attributes.

5. Use the functional dependencies to identify the tables. You do this by placing each attribute with the attribute or minimum combination of attributes on which it is functionally dependent. The attribute or attributes on which all other attributes in the table are dependent will be the primary key of the table. The remaining attributes will be the other fields in the table. Once you have determined all the fields in the table, you can assign an appropriate name to the table.

BTW

Candidate Keys
According to the definition of a candidate key, a Social Security number is a legitimate primary key. Many databases use a person's Social Security number as a primary key. However, many institutions and organizations are moving away from using Social Security numbers as primary keys because of privacy issues. Instead, many institutions and organizations use unique student numbers or employee numbers as primary keys.

6. Determine and implement relationships among the entities. The basic relationships are one-to-many and many-to-many.

- **One-to-many.** You implement a one-to-many relationship by including the primary key of the "one" table as a foreign key in the "many" table. A **foreign key** is a field in one table whose values are required to match the *primary key* of another table. In the one-to-many relationship between business analysts and clients, for example, you include the primary key of the Business Analyst table, which is Business Analyst Number, as a foreign key in the Client table. You may have already included this field in the earlier steps. If so, you would simply designate it to be a foreign key. If you had not already added it, you would need to add it at this point, designating it as a foreign key.

- **Many-to-many.** A many-to-many relationship is implemented by creating a new table whose primary key is the combination of the keys of the original tables. To implement the many-to-many relationship between clients and courses, for example, you would create a table whose primary key is the combination of Client Number and Course Number, which are the primary keys of the original tables. Both of the fields that make up the primary key of the new table will also be foreign keys. The Client Number field, for example, will be a foreign key required to match the primary key of the Client table. Similarly, the Course Number field will be a foreign key required to match the primary key of the Course table.

Note: In the shorthand representation for the table containing the primary key, represent the foreign key by using the letters FK, followed by an arrow, followed by the name of the table containing the primary key. For example, to indicate that the Business Analyst Number in the Client table is a foreign key that must match the primary key of the Business Analyst table, you would write FK Business Analyst Number → Business Analyst.

You may have already identified such a table in the earlier steps, in which case all you need to do is to be sure you have designated each portion of the primary key as a foreign key that is required to match the primary key of the appropriate table. If you have not, you would add the table at this point. The primary key will consist of the primary keys from each of the tables to be related. If there are any attributes that depend on the combination of fields that make up the primary key, you need to include them in this table. (It is possible that no other fields are dependent on this combination. In that case, there will be no fields besides the fields that make up the primary key.)

The following sections illustrate the design process by designing the database for Camashaly Design. The next section gives the requirements that this database must support, and the last section creates a database design based on those requirements.

Requirements for the Camashaly Design Database

Systems analysts have examined the needs and organizational policies at Camashaly Design and have determined that the Camashaly Design database must support the following requirements:

1. For a client, Camashaly needs to maintain the client number, name, street address, city, state, postal code, amount paid, and the amount that is currently due. They also need the total amount, which is the sum of the amount already paid and the current amount due.

2. For a business analyst, store the analyst number, last name, first name, street address, city, state, postal code, year-to-date salary paid, and year-to-date incentive paid.

3. For a course, store the course number, course description, hours, and increments. In addition, for each offering of the course, store the number of the client for whom the course is offered, the total number of hours planned for the offering of the course, and the number of hours already spent in the course. The total hours may be the same as the normal number of hours for the course, but it need not be. This gives Camashaly the flexibility of tailoring the offering of the course to the specific needs of the client.

4. Each client has a single analyst to which the client is assigned. Each analyst may be assigned many clients.

5. A client may be offered many courses and a course may be offered to many clients.

Design of the Camashaly Design Database

The following represents the application of the design method for the Camashaly Design requirements.

1. There seem to be three entities: clients, analysts, and courses. Reasonable names for the corresponding tables are Client, Business Analyst, and Course, respectively.

2. The unique identifier for clients is the client number. The unique identifier for analysts is the analyst number. The unique identifier for courses is the course number. Reasonable names for the unique identifiers are Client Number, Business Analyst Number, and Course Number, respectively.

3. The attributes are:

> **Client Number**
> **Client Name**
> **Street (Client)**
> **City (Client)**
> **State (Client)**
> **Postal Code (Client)**
> **Amount Paid**
> **Current Due**
> **Business Analyst Number**
> **Last Name**
> **First Name**
> **Street (Business Analyst)**
> **City (Business Analyst)**
> **State (Business Analyst)**
> **Postal Code (Business Analyst)**
> **Salary YTD**
> **Incentive YTD**
> **Course Number**
> **Course Description**
> **Hours**
> **Increments**
> **Total Hours**
> **Hours Spent**

Remember that parentheses after an attribute indicate the entity to which the attribute corresponds. Thus, Street (Client) represents the street address of a client in a way that distinguishes it from Street (Business Analyst), which represents the street address of an analyst.

Q&A | Why isn't Total Amount included?

Total Amount, which is Amount Paid plus Current Due, can be calculated from other fields. You can perform this calculation in queries, forms, and reports. Thus, there is no need to include it as a field in the Client table. Further, by including it, you introduce the possibility of errors in the database. For example, if Amount Paid is $5,000, Current Due is $2,000, yet you set Total Amount equal to $8,000, you have an error. You also need to be sure to change Total Amount appropriately whenever you change either Amount Paid or Current Due. If it is not stored, but rather calculated when needed, you avoid all these problems.

Q&A | If including the Total Amount field is not appropriate, why did we include the Total Amount field in the Client table in Chapter 3?

With the most recent version of Access, Access allows calculated fields. Rather than storing a value, you simply indicate the calculation. Access will calculate the value when needed. This approach avoids the above problems, so you actually could include the field. Often, however, you will still decide not to include it. If you plan to use another database management system, for example, including an earlier version of Access, you should not include it. Also, if you are using Access but plan to use the database with SQL Server, you should not include it.

4. The functional dependencies among the attributes are:

> **Client Number → Client Name, Street (Client), City (Client), State (Client), Postal Code (Client), Amount Paid, Current Due, Business Analyst Number**

> **Business Analyst Number → Last Name, First Name, Street (Business Analyst), City (Business Analyst), State (Business Analyst), Postal Code (Business Analyst), Salary YTD, Incentive YTD**

> **Course Number → Course Description, Hours, Increments**

> **Client Number, Course Number → Total Hours, Hours Spent**

Q&A | Why is Total Hours listed with Client Number and Course Number rather than just with Course Number?

If the total hours were required to be the same as the number of hours for the course, then it would indeed be listed with Course Number, because it would not vary from one client to another. Because Camashaly wants the flexibility of tailoring the number of hours for which a particular course is offered to the specific needs of the client, Total Hours is also dependent on Client Number.

The client's name, street address, city, state, postal code, amount paid, and current due are dependent only on Client Number. Because a client has a single analyst, the analyst number is dependent on Client Number as well. The analyst's last name, first name, street address, city, state, postal code, salary YTD, and incentive YTD are dependent only on Business Analyst Number. A course description, the number of hours for the course, and the increments in which the course is offered are dependent only on Course Number. The total hours for a particular course offering as well as the hours already spent are dependent on the combination of Client Number and Course Number.

5. The shorthand representation for the tables is shown in Figure 11–7.

Client (<u>Client Number</u>, Client Name, Street, City, State, Postal Code,
Amount Paid, Current Due, Business Analyst Number)

Business Analyst (<u>Business Analyst Number</u>, Last Name, First Name, Street, City,
State, Postal Code, Salary YTD, Incentive YTD)

Course (<u>Course Number</u>, Course Description, Hours, Increments)

Course Offerings (<u>Client Number</u>, <u>Course Number</u>, Total Hours, Hours Spent)

Figure 11–7

6. The following are the relationships between the tables:

a. The Client and Business Analyst tables are related using the Business Analyst
Number fields, which is the primary key of the Business Analyst table. The
Business Analyst Number field in the Client table is a foreign key.

b. The Client and Course Offerings tables are related using the Client Number
fields, which is the primary key of the Client table. The Client Number field
in the Course Offerings table is a foreign key.

c. The Course and Course Offerings tables are related using the Course Number
fields, which is the primary key of the Course table. The Course Number field
in the Course Offerings table is a foreign key.

Q&A Isn't there a many-to-many relationship between clients and courses?

Yes. The Course Offerings table is precisely the table that will implement a many-to-many
relationship between clients and courses. You identified this table as part of the database
design process. If you had not, you would need to add it at this point.

Q&A In the Course Offerings table, the primary key consists of two fields, Client Number and
Course Number. There are two additional fields, Total Hours and Hours Spent. What if the
design requirements did not require these additional fields? Would we still need the Course
Offerings table?

Yes, because this table implements the many-to-many relationship between clients and
courses. It is perfectly legitimate for the table that implements a many-to-many relationship
to contain no columns except the two columns that constitute the primary key.

Q&A In the Course Offerings table, the primary key consists of two fields, Client Number and
Course Number. Does the Client Number field have to come first?

No. The Course Number could have come first just as well.

The shorthand representation for the tables and foreign keys is shown in Figure 11–8.
It is common to list a table containing a foreign key after the table that contains the
corresponding primary key, when possible. Thus, in the figure, the Business Analyst table has
been moved so that it comes before the Client table.

Business Analyst (<u>Business Analyst Number</u>, Last Name, First Name, Street, City, State, Postal Code, Salary YTD, Incentive YTD)

Client (<u>Client Number</u>, Client Name, Street, City, State, Postal Code, Amount Paid, Current Due, Business Analyst Number)
FK Business Analyst Number → Business Analyst

Course (<u>Course Number</u>, Course Description, Hours, Increments)

Course Offerings (<u>Client Number</u>, <u>Course Number</u>, Total Hours, Hours Spent)
FK Client Number → Client
FK Course Number → Course

foreign key designation

foreign key

table the foreign key must match

Figure 11–8

Scryps Distributors

The management of Scryps Distributors, a distributor of energy saving devices and water conservation devices, has determined that the company's rapid growth requires a database to maintain customer, order, and inventory data. With the data stored in a database, management will be able to ensure that the data is current and more accurate. In addition, managers will be able to obtain answers to their questions concerning the data in the database easily and quickly, with the option of producing a variety of reports.

Requirements for the Scryps Distributors Database

An analyst has interviewed users and examined documents at Scryps Distributors, and has determined that the company needs a database that will support the following requirements:

1. For a sales rep, store the sales rep's number, last name, first name, street address, city, state, postal code, total commission, and commission rate.

2. For a customer, store the customer's number, name, street address, city, state, postal code, balance, and credit limit. In addition, store the number, last name, and first name of the sales rep representing this customer. The analyst has also determined that a sales rep can represent many customers, but a customer must have exactly one sales rep. In other words, one sales rep must represent each customer; a customer cannot be represented by zero or more than one sales rep.

3. For a part, store the part's number, description, units on hand, the category the part is in, and the price.

4. For an order, store the order number, order date, the number and name of the customer placing the order, and the number of the sales rep representing that customer.

5. For each line item within an order, store the part's number and description, the number ordered, and the quoted price. The analyst also obtained the following information concerning orders:

    a. There is only one customer per order.

b. On a given order, each part is listed only as a single line item. For example, part DR93 cannot appear on multiple lines within the same order.

c. The quoted price might differ from the actual price in cases in which the sales rep offers a discount for a certain part on a specific order.

Design of the Scryps Distributors Database

The following steps apply the design process to the requirements for Scryps Distributers to produce the appropriate database design:

1. There appear to be four entities: reps, customers, parts, and orders. The names assigned to these entities are Rep, Customer, Part, and Orders, respectively.

2. From the collection of entities, review the data and determine the unique identifier for each entity. For the Rep, Customer, Part, and Orders entities, the unique identifiers are the Rep Number, the Customer Number, the Item Number, and the Order Number, respectively. These unique identifiers are named Rep Number, Customer Number, Item Number, and Order Number, respectively.

3. The attributes mentioned in the first requirement all refer to sales reps. The specific attributes mentioned in the requirement are the sales rep's number, last name, first name, street address, city, state, postal code, total commission, and commission rate. Assigning appropriate names to these attributes produces the following list:

> **Rep Number**
> **Last Name**
> **First Name**
> **Street**
> **City**
> **State**
> **Postal Code**
> **Commission**
> **Rate**

The attributes mentioned in the second requirement refer to customers. The specific attributes are the customer's number, name, street address, city, state, postal code, balance, and credit limit. The requirement also mentions the number, first name, and last name of the sales rep representing this customer. Assigning appropriate names to these attributes produces the following list:

> **Customer Number**
> **Customer Name**
> **Street**
> **City**
> **State**
> **Postal Code**
> **Balance**
> **Credit Limit**
> **Rep Number**
> **Last Name**
> **First Name**

There are attributes named Street, City, State, and Postal Code for sales reps as well as attributes named Street, City, State, and Postal Code for customers. To distinguish these attributes in the final collection, the name of the attribute is followed by the name of the corresponding entity. For example, the street for a sales rep is Street (Rep) and the street for a customer is Street (Customer).

The attributes mentioned in the third requirement refer to parts. The specific attributes are the part's number, description, units on hand, category, and price. Assigning appropriate names to these attributes produces the following list:

> **Item Number**
> **Description**
> **On Hand**
> **Category**
> **Price**

The attributes mentioned in the fourth requirement refer to orders. The specific attributes include the order number, order date, the number and name of the customer placing the order, and the number of the sales rep representing the customer. Assigning appropriate names to these attributes produces the following list:

> **Order Number**
> **Order Date**
> **Customer Number**
> **Customer Name**
> **Rep Number**

The specific attributes associated with the statement in the requirements concerning line items are the order number (to determine the order to which the line item corresponds), item number, description, the number ordered, and the quoted price. If the quoted price must be the same as the price, you could simply call it Price. According to requirement 5c, however, the quoted price might differ from the price. Thus, you must add the quoted price to the list. Assigning appropriate names to these attributes produces the following list:

> **Order Number**
> **Item Number**
> **Description**
> **Number Ordered**
> **Quoted Price**

The complete list grouped by entity is as follows:

> **Rep**
>
> > **Rep Number**
> > **Last Name**
> > **First Name**
> > **Street (Rep)**
> > **City (Rep)**
> > **State (Rep)**
> > **Postal Code (Rep)**
> > **Commission**
> > **Rate**

Customer

> **Customer Number**
>
> **Customer Name**
>
> **Street (Customer)**
>
> **City (Customer)**
>
> **State (Customer)**
>
> **Postal Code (Customer)**
>
> **Balance**
>
> **Credit Limit**
>
> **Rep Number**
>
> **Last Name**
>
> **First Name**

Part

> **Item Number**
>
> **Description**
>
> **On Hand**
>
> **Category**
>
> **Price**

Orders

> **Order Number**
>
> **Order Date**
>
> **Customer Number**
>
> **Customer Name**
>
> **Rep Number**

For line items within an order:

> **Order Number**
>
> **Item Number**
>
> **Description**
>
> **Number Ordered**
>
> **Quoted Price**

4. The fact that the unique identifier for sales reps is the Rep Number gives the following functional dependencies:

> **Rep Number → Last Name, First Name, Street (Rep), City (Rep), State (Rep), Postal Code (Rep), Commission, Rate**

This notation indicates that the Last Name, First Name, Street (Rep), City (Rep), State (Rep), Postal Code (Rep), Commission, and Rate are all functionally dependent on Rep Number.

The fact that the unique identifier for customers is the Customer Number gives the following preliminary list of functional dependencies:

> **Customer Number → Customer Name, Street (Customer), City (Customer), State (Customer), Postal Code (Customer), Balance, Credit Limit, Rep Number, Last Name, First Name**

Do you need to include the last name and first name of a sales rep in the list of attributes determined by the Customer Number?

There is no need to include them in this list, because they both can be determined from the sales Rep Number and are already included in the list of attributes determined by Rep Number. They will be removed in the next step.

The fact that the unique identifier for parts is the Item Number gives the following functional dependencies:

Item Number → Description, On Hand, Category, Price

The fact that the unique identifier for orders is the Order Number gives the following functional dependencies:

Order Number → Order Date, Customer Number, Customer Name, Rep Number

Do you need to include the name of a customer and the number of the customer's rep in the list of attributes determined by the Order Number?

There is no need to include the customer name and the rep number in this list, because you can determine them from the Customer Number, and they are already included in the list of attributes determined by Customer Number. They will be removed in the next step.

The final attributes to be examined are those associated with the line items within the order: Item Number, Description, Number Ordered, and Quoted Price.

Why aren't Number Ordered and Quoted Price included in the list of attributes determined by the Order Number?

To uniquely identify a particular value for Number Ordered or Quoted Price, Order Number alone is not sufficient. It requires the combination of Order Number and Item Number.

The following shorthand representation indicates that the combination of Order Number and Item Number functionally determines Number Ordered and Quoted Price:

Order Number, Item Number → Number Ordered, Quoted Price

Does Description need to be included in this list?

No, because Description can be determined by the Item Number alone, and it already appears in the list of attributes dependent on the Item Number.

The complete list of functional dependencies with appropriate revisions is as follows:

Rep Number → Last Name, First Name, Street (Rep), City (Rep), State (Rep), Postal Code (Rep), Commission, Rate

Customer Number → Customer Name, Street (Customer), City (Customer), State (Customer), Postal Code (Customer), Balance, Credit Limit, Rep Number

Item Number → Description, On Hand, Category, Price

Order Number → Order Date, Customer Number

Order Number, Item Number → Number Ordered, Quoted Price

5. Using the functional dependencies, you can create tables with the attribute(s) to the left of the arrow being the primary key and the items to the right of the arrow being the other fields. For tables corresponding to those entities identified in Step 1, you can simply use the name you already determined. Because you did not identify any entity that had a unique identifier that was the combination of Order

Number and Item Number, you need to assign a name to the table whose primary key consists of these two fields. Because this table represents the individual lines within an order, the name Line Item is a good choice. The final collection of tables is shown in Figure 11–9.

BTW

Line Items
A line item is a unit of information that appears on its own line. For example, when you purchase groceries, each grocery item appears on its own line. Line items also can be referred to as order line items or item detail lines.

Rep (<u>Rep Number</u>, Last Name, First Name, Street, City, State, Postal Code, Commission, Rate)

Customer (<u>Customer Number</u>, Customer Name, Street, City, State, Postal Code, Balance, Credit Limit, Rep Number)

Part (<u>Item Number</u>, Description, On Hand, Category, Price)

Orders (<u>Order Number</u>, Order Date, Customer Number)

Line Item (<u>Order Number</u>, <u>Item Number</u>, Number Ordered, Quoted Price)

Figure 11–9

6. You need to identify relationships between tables and understand the role each table plays in the database.

   a. The Customer and Rep tables are related using the Rep Number fields. The Rep Number field in the Rep table is the primary key. The Rep Number field in the Customer table is a foreign key.

   b. The Orders and Customer tables are related using the Customer Number fields. The Customer Number field in the Customer table is the primary key. The Customer Number field in the Orders table is a foreign key.

   c. The Line Item and Orders tables are related using the Order Number fields. The Order Number field in the Orders table is the primary key. The Order Number field in the Line Item table is a foreign key.

   d. The Line Item and Part tables are related using the Item Number fields. The Item Number field in the Part table is the primary key. The Item Number field in the Line Item table is a foreign key.

Q&A

Isn't there a many-to-many relationship between orders and parts?

Yes. The Line Item table is precisely the table that will implement a many-to-many relationship between orders and parts. You identified this table as part of the database design process. If you had not, you would need to add it at this point.

Q&A

In the Line Item table, the primary key consists of two fields, Order Number and Item Number. There are two additional fields, Number Ordered and Quoted Price. What if the design requirements did not require these additional fields? Would we still need the Line Item table?

Yes, because this table implements the many-to-many relationship between orders and parts. It is perfectly legitimate for the table that implements a many-to-many relationship to contain only the two columns that constitute the primary key.

The shorthand representation for the tables and foreign keys is shown in Figure 11–10.

Rep (<u>Rep Number</u>, Last Name, First Name, Street, City, State, Postal Code, Commission, Rate)

Customer (<u>Customer Number</u>, Customer Name, Street, City, State, Postal Code, Balance, Credit Limit, Rep Number)
   FK Rep Number → Rep

Part (<u>Item Number</u>, Description, On Hand, Category, Price)

Orders (<u>Order Number</u>, Order Date, Customer Number)
   FK Customer Number → Customer

Line Item (<u>Order Number</u>, <u>Item Number</u>, Number Ordered, Quoted Price)
   FK Order Number → Orders
   FK Item Number → Part

Figure 11–10

Sample data for the Scryps Distributors database is shown in Figure 11–11.

Rep

Rep Number	Last Name	First Name	Street	City	State	Postal Code	Commission	Rate
20	Kaiser	Valerie	624 Randall	Georgetown	NC	28794	$2,542.50	0.05
35	Hull	Richard	532 Jackson	Kyle	SC	28797	$3,216.00	0.07
65	Perez	Juan	1626 Taylor	Byron	SC	28795	$2,487.00	0.05

Customer

Customer Number	Customer Name	Street	City	State	Postal Code	Balance	Credit Limit	Rep Number
148	Al's Hardware Store	2837 Greenway	Oxford	TN	37021	$2,550.00	$7,500.00	20
282	Brookings Direct	3827 Devon	Ashton	VA	20123	$431.50	$2,500.00	35
356	Ferguson's	382 Wildwood	Georgetown	NC	28794	$2,785.00	$7,500.00	65
408	The Energy Shop	1828 Raven	Granger	NC	27036	$1,285.25	$5,000.00	35
462	Walburg Energy Alternatives	12 Polk	Walburg	NC	28819	$1,412.00	$2,500.00	65
524	Kline's	838 Ridgeland	Oxford	TN	37021	$3,762.00	$7,500.00	20
608	Conservation Foundation	372 Oxford	Ashton	VA	20123	$106.00	$5,000.00	65
687	CleanPlanet	282 Evergreen	Lowton	TN	37084	$2,851.00	$5,000.00	35
725	Patricia Jean's Home Center	282 Columbia	Walburg	NC	28819	$248.00	$7,500.00	35
842	The Efficient Home	28 Lakeview	Pineville	VA	22503	$4,221.00	$7,500.00	20

Figure 11–11

Orders

Order Number	Order Date	Customer Number
12608	4/3/2012	148
12610	4/3/2012	356
12613	4/4/2012	408
12614	4/4/2012	282
12617	4/6/2012	608
12619	4/6/2012	148
12623	4/6/2012	608

Part

Item Number	Description	On Hand	Category	Price
AT94	Air Deflector	50	General	$5.45
BV06	Energy Saving Kit	45	Energy	$42.75
CD52	Fluorescent Light Bulb	65	Energy	$4.75
DL71	Low Flow Shower Head	21	Water	$8.75
DR93	Smoke Detector	38	General	$6.10
DW11	Retractable Clothesline	12	General	$13.25
FD21	Water Conservation Kit	22	Water	$13.45
KL62	Toilet Tank Water Saver	32	Water	$3.35
KT03	Programmable Thermostat	8	Energy	$34.25
KV29	Windows Insulator Kit	19	Energy	$4.95

Line Item

Order Number	Item Number	Number Ordered	Quoted Price
12608	AT94	11	$5.45
12610	DR93	5	$6.10
12610	DW11	3	$12.50
12613	KL62	10	$3.35
12614	KT03	6	$33.00
12617	BV06	2	$40.25
12617	CD52	20	$4.25
12619	DR93	12	$6.00
12623	KV29	8	$4.95

Figure 11–11 (continued)

Normalization

After you create your database design, you should analyze it using a process called
normalization to make sure the design is free of potential update, redundancy, and
consistency problems. This process also supplies methods for correcting these problems.

The normalization process involves converting tables into various types of **normal forms**. A table in a particular normal form possesses a certain desirable set of properties. Several normal forms exist, the most common being first normal form (1NF), second normal form (2NF), and third normal form (3NF). The forms create a progression in which a table that is in 1NF is better than a table that is not in 1NF; a table that is in 2NF is better than one that is in 1NF; and so on. The goal of normalization is to take a table or collection of tables and produce a new collection of tables that represents the same information but is free of problems.

First Normal Form

A table that contains a **repeating group**, or multiple entries for a single row, is called an **unnormalized table**. Recall from the definition of relation that an unnormalized table actually violates the definition of relation.

Removal of repeating groups is the starting point in the goal of having tables that are as free of problems as possible. In fact, in most database management systems, tables cannot contain repeating groups. A table (relation) is in **first normal form (1NF)** if it does not contain repeating groups.

In designing a database, you may have created a table with a repeating group. For example, you might have created a Course Offerings table in which the primary key is the Client Number and there is a repeating group consisting of Course Number, Total Hours, and Hours Spent. In the example, each client appears on a single row and Course Number, Total Hours, and Hours Spent are repeated as many times as necessary for each client (Figure 11–12).

Course Offerings

Client Number	Course Number	Total Hours	Hours Spent
BA53	C05	2	0
BB32	C01	8	4
CJ29	C03	6	3
HC10	C04	12	6
	C05	2	1
KD21	C03	6	0
	C07	8	4
KG04	C01	10	6
	C05	2	0
	C08	6	4
ME14	C06	4	2
PJ34	C06	4	2
SL77	C04	12	9
	C08	6	2
TB17	C02	4	2

fourth row indicates that client HC10 is being offered both course C04 and course C05

Figure 11–12

In the shorthand representation, you represent a repeating group by enclosing the repeating group within parentheses. The shorthand representation for the Course Offerings table from Figure 11–12 is shown in Figure 11–13.

Course Offerings (<u>Client Number</u>, (Course Number, Total Hours, Hours Spent))

Figure 11–13

Conversion to First Normal Form

Figure 11–14 shows the normalized version of the table. Note that the fourth row of the unnormalized table (Figure 11–12) indicates that client HC10 currently is being offered both course C04 and course C05. In the normalized table, this information is represented by *two* rows, the fourth and the fifth. The primary key for the unnormalized Course Offerings table was the Client Number only. The primary key for the normalized table now is the combination of Client Number and Course Number.

Course Offerings			
Client Number	**Course Number**	**Total Hours**	**Hours Spent**
BA53	C05	2	0
BB32	C01	8	4
CJ29	C03	6	3
HC10	C04	12	6
HC10	C05	2	1
KD21	C03	6	0
KD21	C07	8	4
KG04	C01	10	6
KG04	C05	2	0
KG04	C08	6	4
ME14	C06	4	2
PJ34	C06	4	2
SL77	C04	12	9
SL77	C08	6	2
TB17	C02	4	2

fourth row indicates that client HC10 is being offered course C04

fifth row indicates that client HC10 is being offered course C05

Figure 11–14

In general, when converting a non-1NF table to 1NF, the primary key typically will include the original primary key concatenated with the key of the repeating group, that is, the field that distinguishes one occurrence of the repeating group from another within a given row in the table. In this case, Course Number is the key to the repeating group and thus becomes part of the primary key of the 1NF table.

To convert the table to 1NF, remove the parentheses enclosing the repeating group and expand the primary key to include the key to the repeating group. The shorthand representation for the resulting table is shown in Figure 11–15. Notice that the primary key is now the combination of the Client Number field and the Course Number field.

Course Offerings (<u>Client Number</u>, <u>Course Number</u>, Total Hours, Hours Spent)

Figure 11–15

Second Normal Form

Even though the following table is in 1NF, problems may exist that will cause you to want to restructure the table. In the database design process, for example, you might have created the Course Offerings table shown in Figure 11–16.

Course Offerings (<u>Client Number</u>, Client Name, <u>Course Number</u>, Course Description, Total Hours, Hours Spent)

Figure 11–16

This table contains the following functional dependencies:

Client Number → Client Name

Course Number → Course Description

Client Number, Course Number → Total Hours, Hours Spent

This notation indicates that Client Number alone determines Client Name; Course Number alone determines Course Description, but it requires both a Client Number and a Course Number to determine either Total Hours or Hours Spent. Figure 11–17 shows a sample of this table.

name of client HC10 occurs more than once

description of course C05 occurs more than once

Course Offerings

Client Number	Client Name	Course Number	Course Description	Total Hours	Hours Spent
BA53	Bavant Animal Hospital	C05	Understanding Social Networks	2	0
BB32	Babbage CPA Firm	C01	Using the Content Management System	8	4
CJ29	Catering by Jenna	C03	Digital Image Management	6	3
HC10	Hendley County Regional Hospital	C04	Javascript Basics	12	6
HC10	Hendley County Regional Hospital	C05	Understanding Social Networks	2	1
KD21	KAL Design Studio	C03	Digital Image Management	6	0
KD21	KAL Design Studio	C07	Understanding Cascading Style Sheets	8	4
KG04	Kyle Grocery Cooperative	C01	Using the Content Management System	10	6
KG04	Kyle Grocery Cooperative	C05	Understanding Social Networks	2	0
KG04	Kyle Grocery Cooperative	C08	Podcasting	6	4
ME14	Mike's Electronic Stop	C06	Using Shopping Carts	4	2
PJ34	Patricia Jean Florist	C06	Using Shopping Carts	4	2
SL77	Smarter Law Associates	C04	Javascript Basics	12	9
SL77	Smarter Law Associates	C08	Podcasting	6	2
TB17	The Bikeshop	C02	HTML Basics	4	2

Figure 11–17

The name of a specific client, HC10 for example, occurs multiple times in the table, as does the description of a course. This redundancy causes several problems. It is certainly wasteful of space, but that is not nearly as serious as some of the other problems. These other problems are called **update anomalies**, and they fall into four categories:

1. **Update.** A change to the name of client HC10 requires not one change to the table, but several: You must change each row in which HC10 appears. This certainly makes the update process much more cumbersome; it is more complicated logically and takes longer to update.

2. **Inconsistent data.** There is nothing about the design that would prohibit client HC10 from having two or more different names in the database. The first row, for example, might have Hendley County Regional Hospital as the name, whereas the second row might have Northwest Regional Hospital.

3. **Additions.** There is a real problem when you try to add a new course and its description to the database. Because the primary key for the table consists of both Client Number and Course Number, you need values for both of these to add a new row. If you have a client to add but there are as yet no courses scheduled for it, what do you use for a course number? The only solution would be to make up a placeholder course number and then replace it with a real course number once the client requests a course. Certainly this is not an acceptable solution.

4. **Deletions.** In Figure 11–17, if you delete course C05 from the database, you would need to delete all rows on which the course number is C05. In the process, you will delete the only row on which client BA53 appears, so you would also *lose* all the information about client BA53. You would no longer know that the name of client BA53 is Bavant Animal Hospital.

These problems occur because there is a field, Client Name, that is dependent on only a Client Number, which is just a portion of the primary key. There is a similar problem with Course Description, which depends only on the Course Number, not the complete primary key. This leads to the definition of second normal form. Second normal form represents an improvement over first normal form because it eliminates update anomalies in these situations. To understand second normal form, you need to understand the term nonkey field.

A field is a **nonkey field**, also called a **nonkey attribute**, if it is not a part of the primary key. A table (relation) is in **second normal form (2NF)** if it is in first normal form and no nonkey field is dependent on only a portion of the primary key.

Note that if the primary key of a table contains only a single field, the table is automatically in second normal form. In that case, there could not be any field dependent on only a portion of the primary key.

Conversion to Second Normal Form

To correct the problems, convert the table to a collection of tables in second normal form. Then name the new tables. The following is a method for performing this conversion.

1. Take each subset of the set of fields that make up the primary key and begin a new table with this subset as its primary key. The result of applying this step to the Course Offerings table is shown in Figure 11–18.

(<u>Client Number,</u>

(<u>Course Number,</u>

(<u>Client Number, Course Number,</u>

Figure 11–18

2. Place each of the other fields with the appropriate primary key; that is, place each one with the minimal collection of fields on which it depends. The result of applying this step to the Course Offerings table is shown in Figure 11–19.

(<u>Client Number</u>, Client Name)

(<u>Course Number</u>, Course Description)

(<u>Client Number</u>, <u>Course Number</u>, Total Hours, Hours Spent)

Figure 11–19

3. Give each of these new tables a name that is descriptive of the meaning of the table, such as Client, Course, and Course Offerings.

Figure 11–20 shows samples of the tables.

name of client HC10 occurs only once

Client

Client Number	Client Name
BA53	Bavant Animal Hospital
BB32	Babbage CPA Firm
BC76	Buda Community Clinic
CJ29	Catering by Jenna
GF56	Granger Family Foundation
HC10	Hendley County Regional Hospital
KD21	KAL Design Studio
KG04	Kyle Grocery Cooperative
KM03	Kyle Museum of Art
ME14	Mike's Electronic Stop
PJ34	Patricia Jean Florist
SL77	Smarter Law Associates
TB17	The Bikeshop

description of course C05 occurs only once

Course

Course Number	Course Description
C01	Using the Content Management System
C02	HTML Basics
C03	Digital Image Management
C04	Javascript Basics
C05	Understanding Social Networks
C06	Using Shopping Carts
C07	Understanding Cascading Style Sheets
C08	Podcasting

Figure 11–20

Course Offerings			
Client Number	Course Number	Total Hours	Hours Spent
BA53	C05	2	0
BB32	C01	8	4
CJ29	C03	6	3
HC10	C04	12	6
HC10	C05	2	1
KD21	C03	6	0
KD21	C07	8	4
KG04	C01	10	6
KG04	C05	2	0
KG04	C08	6	4
ME14	C06	4	2
PJ34	C06	4	2
SL77	C04	12	9
SL77	C08	6	2
TB17	C02	4	2

Figure 11–20 (continued)

The new design eliminates the update anomalies. A client name occurs only once for each client, so you do not have the redundancy that you did in the earlier design. Changing the name of a client is now a simple process involving a single change. Because the name of a client occurs in a single place, it is not possible to have multiple names for the same client in the database at the same time.

To add a new client, you create a new row in the Client table, and, thus, there is no need to have a course offering already scheduled for that client. Also, deleting course C05 has nothing to do with the Client table and, consequently, does not cause client BA53 to be deleted. Thus, you still have its name, Bavant Animal Hospital, in the database. Finally, you have not lost any information in the process.

Q&A

Can I reconstruct the data in the original design from the data in the new design?

Yes. The following SQL query would produce the data in the form shown in Figure 11–17:

```
SELECT [Client].[Client Number], [Client Name],
   [Course].[Course Number], [Course Description],
   [Total Hours],[Hours Spent]
FROM [Client],[Course],[Course Offering]
WHERE [Client].[Client Number]=[Course Offerings].
   [Client Number]
AND [Course].[Course Number]=[Course Offerings].
   [Course Number];
```

Third Normal Form

Problems still can exist with tables that are in 2NF, as illustrated in the Client table whose shorthand representation is shown in Figure 11–21.

Client (<u>Client Number</u>, Client Name, Street, City, State, Postal Code,
Amount Paid, Current Due, Business Analyst Number, Last Name, First Name)

Figure 11–21

The functional dependencies in this table are:

Client Number → Client Name, Street, City, State, Postal Code, Amount Paid, Current Due, Business Analyst Number

Business Analyst Number → Last Name, First Name

As these dependencies indicate, Client Number determines all the other fields. In addition, Business Analyst Number determines Last Name and First Name.

Because the primary key of the table is a single field, the table is automatically in second normal form. As the sample of the table shown in Figure 11–22 demonstrates, however, this table has problems similar to those encountered earlier, even though it is in 2NF. In this case, it is the last name and first name of an analyst that can occur many times in the table; see analyst 11, Cordelia Kerry, for example. (Note that the three dots represent fields that do not appear due to space considerations.)

name of analyst 11 occurs more than once

Client

Client Number	Client Name	...	Amount Paid	Current Due	Business Analyst Number	Last Name	First Name
BA53	Bavant Animal Hospital	...	$0.00	$7,500.00	11	Kerry	Cordelia
BC76	Buda Community Clinic	...	$2,500.00	$750.00	11	Kerry	Cordelia
GF56	Granger Family Foundation	...	$0.00	$6,500.00	11	Kerry	Cordelia
KG04	Kyle Grocery Cooperative	...	$3,200.00	$0.00	11	Kerry	Cordelia
SL77	Smarter Law Associates	...	$3,800.00	$0.00	11	Kerry	Cordelia
BB32	Babbage CPA Firm	...	$1,500.00	$500.00	14	Martinez	Manuel
KD21	KAL Design Studio	...	$6,000.00	$3,200.00	14	Martinez	Manuel
CJ29	Catering by Jenna	...	$3,000.00	$1,000.00	27	Liu	Jan
HC10	Hendley County Regional Hospital	...	$3,100.00	$1,200.00	27	Liu	Jan
ME14	Mike's Electronic Stop	...	$2,500.00	$1,500.00	27	Liu	Jan
PJ34	Patricia Jean Florist	...	$0.00	$5,200.00	27	Liu	Jan
TB17	The Bikeshop	...	$2,750.00	$1,200.00	27	Liu	Jan
KM03	Kyle Museum of Art	...	$0.00	$750.00	35	Scott	Jeff

Figure 11–22

This redundancy results in the same set of problems described previously with the Course Offerings table. In addition to the problem of wasted space, you have similar update anomalies, as follows:

1. **Updates.** A change to the name of an analyst requires not one change to the table, but several changes. Again the update process becomes very cumbersome.

2. **Inconsistent data.** There is nothing about the design that would prohibit an analyst from having two different names in the database. On the first row, for example, the name for analyst 11 might read Cordelia Kerry, whereas on the third row (another row on which the analyst number is 11), the name might be Theresa Peters.

3. **Additions.** In order to add analyst 39, whose name is Tati Angelo, to the database, she must have at least one client. If she has not yet been assigned any clients, either you cannot record the fact that her name is Tati Angelo, or you have to create a fictitious client for her to represent. Again, this is not a desirable solution to the problem.

4. **Deletions.** If you were to delete all the clients of analyst 14 from the database, then you also would lose all information concerning analyst 14.

These update anomalies are due to the fact that Business Analyst Number determines Last Name and First Name, but Business Analyst Number is not the primary key. As a result, the same Business Analyst Number and consequently the same Last Name and First Name can appear on many different rows.

You have seen that 2NF is an improvement over 1NF, but in order to eliminate 2NF problems, you need an even better strategy for creating tables in the database. Third normal form provides that strategy.

Before looking at third normal form, you need to become familiar with the special name that is given to any field that determines another field, like Business Analyst Number in the Client table. Any field or collection of fields that determines another field is called a **determinant**. Certainly the primary key in a table is a determinant. Any candidate key is a determinant as well. (Remember that a candidate key is a field or collection of fields that could function as the primary key.) In this case, Business Analyst Number is a determinant, but it certainly is not a candidate key for the Client table shown in Figure 11–22, and that is the problem.

A table is in **third normal form** (3NF) if it is in second normal form and if the only determinants it contains are candidate keys.

Conversion to Third Normal Form

You now have identified the problem with the Client table: It is not in 3NF. You need a way to correct the deficiency in the Client table and in all tables having similar deficiencies. Such a method follows.

First, for each determinant that is not a candidate key, remove from the table the fields that depend on this determinant, but do not remove the determinant. Next, create a new table containing all the fields from the original table that depend on this determinant. Finally, make the determinant the primary key of this new table.

In the Client table, for example, Last Name and First Name are removed because they depend on the determinant Business Analyst Number, which is not a candidate key. A new table is formed, consisting of Business Analyst Number as the primary key, Last Name, and First Name. Specifically, you would replace the Client table in Figure 11–22 with the two tables shown in Figure 11–23.

BTW

3NF
The definition given for third normal form is not the original definition. This more recent definition, which is preferable to the original, is often referred to as *Boyce-Codd normal form (BCNF)* when it is important to make a distinction between this definition and the original definition. This text does not make such a distinction but will take this to be the definition of third normal form.

Client (<u>Client Number</u>, Client Name, Street, City, State, Postal Code, Amount Paid, Current Due, Business Analyst Number)

Business Analyst (<u>Business Analyst Number</u>, Last Name, First Name)

Figure 11–23

Figure 11–24 shows samples of the tables.

Client						
Client Number	Client Name	...	Amount Paid	Current Due	Business Analyst Number
BA53	Bavant Animal Hospital	...	$0.00	$7,500.00	11
BC76	Buda Community Clinic	...	$2,500.00	$750.00	11
GF56	Granger Family Foundation	...	$0.00	$6,500.00	11
KG04	Kyle Grocery Cooperative	...	$3,200.00	$0.00	11
SL77	Smarter Law Associates	...	$3,800.00	$0.00	11
BB32	Babbage CPA Firm	...	$1,500.00	$500.00	14
KD21	KAL Design Studio	...	$6,000.00	$3,200.00	14
CJ29	Catering by Jenna	...	$3,000.00	$1,000.00	27
HC10	Hendley County Regional Hospital	...	$3,100.00	$1,200.00	27
ME14	Mike's Electronic Stop	...	$2,500.00	$1,500.00	27
PJ34	Patricia Jean Florist	...	$0.00	$5,200.00	27
TB17	The Bikeshop	...	$2,750.00	$1,200.00	27
KM03	Kyle Museum of Art	...	$0.00	$750.00	35

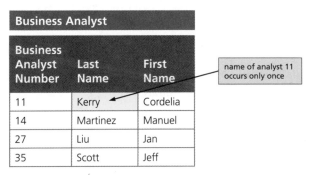

Business Analyst		
Business Analyst Number	Last Name	First Name
11	Kerry	Cordelia
14	Martinez	Manuel
27	Liu	Jan
35	Scott	Jeff

name of analyst 11 occurs only once

Figure 11–24

This design corrects the previously identified problems. An analyst's name appears only once, thus avoiding redundancy and making the process of changing an analyst's name a very simple one. It is not possible with this design for the same analyst to have two different names in the database. To add a new analyst to the database, you add a row in the Business Analyst table so it is not necessary to have a pre existing client for the analyst. Finally, deleting all the clients of a given analyst will not remove the analyst's record from the Business Analyst table, so you retain the analyst's name; all the data in the original table can be reconstructed from the data in the new collection of tables. All previously mentioned problems have indeed been solved.

Q&A

Can I reconstruct the data in the original design from the data in the new design?

Yes. The following SQL query would produce the data in the form shown in Figure 11–22:

```
SELECT [Client Number], [Client Name], [Street],
   [City], [State], [Postal Code], [Amount Paid],
   [Current Due], [Client].[Business Analyst Number],
   [Last Name], [First Name]
FROM [Client],[Business Analyst]
WHERE [Client].[Business Analyst Number]=
   [Business Analyst].[Business Analyst Number];
```

Special Topics

In addition to knowing how to design a database and how to normalize tables, there are two other topics with which you should be familiar. First, you may be given a requirement for a database in the form of a document the database must be capable of producing, for example, an invoice. In addition, you should know how to represent your design with a diagram.

Obtaining Information from Existing Documents

Existing documents can often furnish helpful information concerning the database design. You need to know how to obtain information from the document that you will then use in the design process. An existing document, like the invoice for the company named Scryps Distributors shown in Figure 11–25, will often provide the details that determine the tables and fields required to produce the document.

The first step in obtaining information from an existing document is to identify and list all fields and give them appropriate names. You also need to understand the business policies of the organization. For example, in the order shown in Figure 11–25, the information on Scryps Distributors is preprinted on the form, and it is not necessary to describe the company. The following is a list of the fields you can determine from the order shown in Figure 11–25.

BTW

Existing Documents
Other examples of existing documents would be purchase orders, procedural manuals, organizational policy manuals, inventory lists and so on.

> **Order Number**
> **Order Date**
> **Customer Number**
> **Customer Name**
> **Street (Customer)**
> **City (Customer)**
> **State (Customer)**
> **Postal Code (Customer)**
> **Rep Number**
> **Last Name (Rep)**
> **First Name (Rep)**
> **Item Number**
> **Description**
> **Number Ordered**
> **Price**
> **Total**
> **Order Total**

Scryps Distributors

555 Main Street
San Rita, TX 78364
Phone 512-555-0190 Fax 512-555-0191

INVOICE

preprinted invoice
information

ORDER: 12617
DATE: APRIL 12, 2012

TO:
Customer: 462
Walburg Energy Alternatives
12 Polk
Walburg, NC 28819

SALES REP: 65
Juan Perez

ITEM NUMBER	DESCRIPTION	NUMBER ORDERED	PRICE	TOTAL
BV06	Energy Saving Kit	2	40.25	80.50
CD52	Fluorescent Light Bulb	20	4.25	85.00
	TOTAL			165.50

Make all checks payable to Scryps Distributors
Total due in 15 days. Overdue accounts subject to a service charge of 1% per month.

Thank you for your business!

Figure 11–25

Next, you need to identify functional dependencies. If the document you are examining is unfamiliar to you, you may have difficulty determining the dependencies and may need to get all the information directly from the user. On the other hand, you can often make intelligent guesses based on your general knowledge of the type of document you are studying. You may make mistakes, of course, and these should be corrected when you interact with the user. After initially determining the functional dependencies, you may find out additional information. The following are possible initial functional dependencies:

Customer Number → Customer Name, Street (Customer), City (Customer), State (Customer), Postal Code (Customer), Rep Number, Last Name (Rep), First Name (Rep)

Item Number → Description, Price

Order Number → Order Date, Customer Number, Order Total

Order Number, Item Number → Number Ordered, Price, Total

You may find, for example, that the price for a particular item on an order need not be the same as the standard price for the item. If that is the case, Price and Total are functionally dependent on the combination of Order Number and Item Number, not just Item Number alone. You may also decide to change the field name to Quoted Price to indicate the fact that it can vary from one order to another.

For the same reasons that you did not include Total Amount in the Camashaly Design database, you would probably not want to include either Total or Order Total. Both can be computed from other data. The other correction that you should make to the functional dependencies is to realize that the last name and first name of a rep depend on the data in the Rep Number field.

Given these corrections, a revised list of functional dependencies might look like the following:

Rep Number → Last Name, First Name

Customer Number → Customer Name, Street (Customer), City (Customer), State (Customer), Postal Code (Customer), Rep Number

Item Number → Description, Price

Order Number → Order Date, Customer Number

Order Number, Item Number → Number Ordered, Quoted Price

After you have determined the preliminary functional dependencies, you can begin determining the tables and assigning fields. You could create tables with the determinant — the field or fields to the left of the arrow — as the primary key and with the fields to the right of the arrow as the remaining fields. This would lead to the following initial collection of tables shown in Figure 11–26.

Rep (<u>Rep Number</u>, Last Name, First Name)

Customer (<u>Customer Number</u>, Customer Name, Street, City, State, Postal Code, Rep Number)

Part (<u>Item Number</u>, Description)

Orders (<u>Order Number</u>, Order Date, Customer Number)

Line Item (<u>Order Number</u>, <u>Item Number</u>, Number Ordered, Quoted Price)

Figure 11–26

Adding the foreign key information produces the shorthand representation shown in Figure 11–27.

Rep (<u>Rep Number</u>, Last Name, First Name)

Customer (<u>Customer Number</u>, Customer Name, Street, City, State, Postal Code, Rep Number)
    FK Rep Number → Rep

Part (<u>Item Number</u>, Description)

Orders (<u>Order Number</u>, Order Date, Customer Number)
    FK Customer Number → Customer

Line Item (<u>Order Number</u>, <u>Item Number</u>, Number Ordered, Quoted Price)
    FK Order Number → Orders
    FK Item Number → Part

Figure 11–27

At this point, you would need to verify that all the tables are in third normal form. If any are not in 3NF, you need to convert them. If you have not created the functional dependency of Last Name and First Name on Rep Number, for example, you would have had Last Name and First Name as fields in the Customer table. These fields were dependent on Rep Number, making Rep Number a determinant that is not a primary key, violating third normal form. Once you converted that table to 3NF, you would have the tables shown in Figure 11–27.

You may have already created some tables in your database design. For example, you may have obtained financial data on customers from the Accounting department. If so, you would need to merge the tables in Figure 11–27 with those tables you already created. To merge tables, you combine tables that have the same primary key. The new table contains all the fields in either individual table and does not repeat fields that are present in both tables. Figure 11–28, for example, illustrates the merging of two tables that both have the Customer Number field as the primary key. In addition to the primary key, the result contains the Customer Name and Rep Number fields, which are included in both of the original tables; the Street, City, State, and Postal Code fields, which are only in the first table; and the Balance and Credit Limit fields, which are only in the second table. The order in which you decide to list the fields is immaterial.

Merging

Customer (<u>Customer Number</u>, Customer Name, Street, City, State, Postal Code, Rep Number)

and

Customer (<u>Customer Number</u>, Customer Name, Balance, Credit Limit, Rep Number)

gives

Customer (<u>Customer Number</u>, Customer Name, Street, City, State, Postal Code, Balance, Credit Limit, Rep Number)

Figure 11–28

Diagrams for Database Design

You have now seen how to represent a database design as a list of tables, fields, primary keys, and foreign keys. It is often helpful to also be able to represent a database design with a diagram. If you have already created the database and relationships in Access, the Relationships window and Relationships report provide a helpful diagram of the design. Figure 11–29 shows the Access relationship diagram and report for the Camashaly Design database discussed in this chapter. In these diagrams, rectangles represent tables. The fields in the table are listed in the corresponding rectangle with a key symbol appearing in front of the primary key. Relationships are represented by lines with the "one" end of the relationship represented by the number, 1, and the "many" end represented by the infinity symbol (∞).

BTW

Certification
The Microsoft Office Specialist (MOS) program provides an opportunity for you to obtain a valuable industry credential – proof that you have the Access 2010 skills required by employers. For more information, visit the Access 2010 Certification Web page (scsite.com/ac2010/cert).

(a) Access Relationship Diagram for Camashaly Design Database

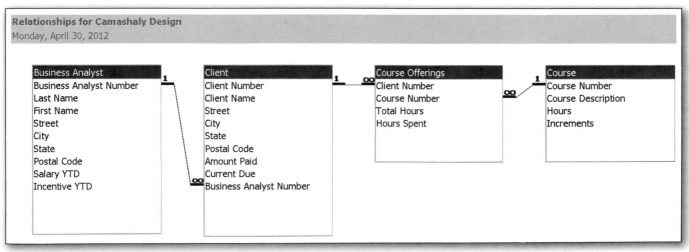

(b) Access Relationship Report for Camashaly Design Database

Figure 11–29

Figure 11–30 shows the Access relationship diagram and report for the Scryps Distributors database.

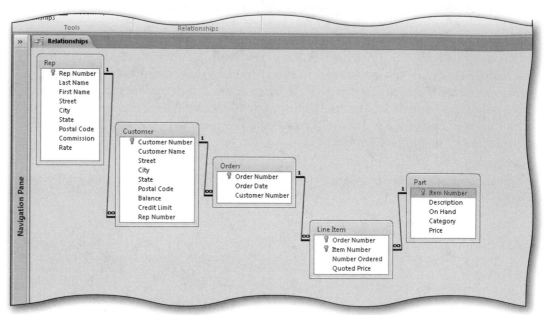

(a) Access Relationship Diagram for Scryps Distributors Database

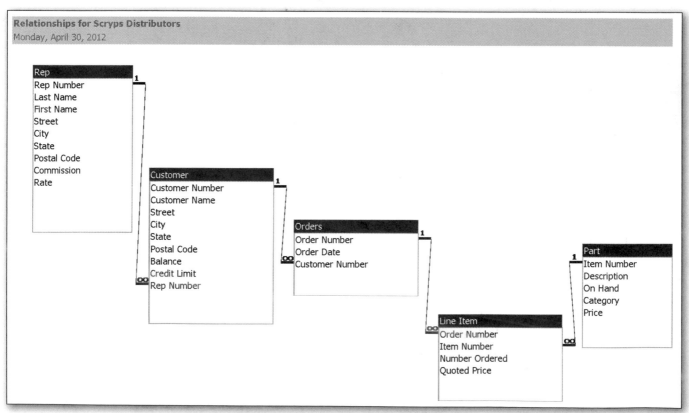

(b) Access Relationship Report for Scryps Distributors Database

Figure 11–30

Access Chapter 11

Another popular option for diagramming a database design is the **entity-relationship diagram (ERD)**. Figure 11–31 shows an ERD for the Camashaly Design database. In this type of diagram, rectangles represent the tables. The primary key is listed within the table above a line. Below the line are the other fields in the table. The arrow goes from the rectangle that represents the many part of the relationship to the one part of the relationship.

BTW

Quick Reference
For a table that lists how to complete the tasks covered in this book using the mouse, Ribbon, shortcut menu, and keyboard, see the Quick Reference Summary at the back of this book, or visit the Access 2010 Quick Reference Web page (scsite.com/ac2010/qr).

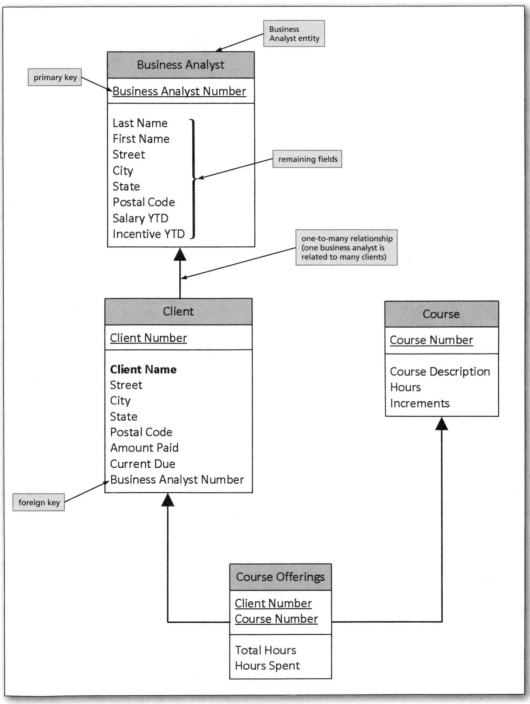

Figure 11–31

Figure 11–32 shows a similar diagram for the Scryps Distributors database.

Figure 11–32

Many options are availabe for such diagrams. Some options include more detail than shown in the figure. You can include, for example, such details as data types and indexes. Other options have less detail, showing only the name of the table in the rectangle, for example. There are also other options for the appearance of the lines representing relationships.

Chapter Summary

In this chapter, you have learned the following concepts.

1. An entity is a person, place, thing, or event. An attribute is a property of an entity. A relationship is an association between entities.

2. A relation is a two-dimensional table in which the entries in the table are single-valued, each column has a distinct name, all values in a column are values of the same attribute (that is, all entries must correspond to the column name), and each row is distinct.

3. In a relation, the order of columns is immaterial. You can view the columns in any order you want. The order of rows is also immaterial. You can view the rows in any order you want.

4. A relational database is a collection of relations.

5. Rows in a table (relation) often are called records or tuples. Columns in a table (relation) often are called fields or attributes. Typically, the terms record and field are used in Access.

6. If you know that whenever you are given a value for one field, you will be able to determine a single value for a second field, then the first field is said to determine the second field. In addition, the second field is said to be functionally dependent on the first.

7. The primary key of a table is the field or minimum collection of fields that uniquely identifies a given row in that table.

8. The following is a method for designing a database for a set of requirements.

    a. Examine the requirements and identify the entities (objects) involved. Assign names to the entities.

    b. Identify a unique identifier for each entity.

    c. Identify the attributes for all the entities. These attributes will become the fields in the tables.

    d. Identify the functional dependencies that exist among the attributes.

    e. Use the functional dependencies to identify the tables.

    f. Identify any relationships between tables by looking for matching fields where one of the fields is a primary key. The other field will then be a foreign key. In the shorthand representation for the table containing the primary key, represent the foreign key by using the letters FK, followed by an arrow, followed by the name of the table containing the primary key.

9. A table (relation) is in first normal form (1NF) if it does not contain repeating groups.

10. To convert a table to 1NF, remove the parentheses enclosing the repeating group and expand the primary key to include the key to the repeating group.

11. A field is a nonkey field (also called a nonkey attribute) if it is not a part of the primary key. A table (relation) is in second normal form (2NF) if it is in first normal form and no nonkey field is dependent on only a portion of the primary key.

12. To convert a table to 2NF, take each subset of the set of fields that make up the primary key and begin a new table with this subset as its primary key. Place each of the other fields with the appropriate primary key; that is, place each one with the minimal collection of fields on which it depends. Give each of these new tables a name that is descriptive of the meaning of the table.

13. Any field (or collection of fields) that determines another field is called a determinant. A table is in third normal form (3NF) if it is in second normal form and if the only determinants it contains are candidate keys.

14. To convert a table to 3NF, for each determinant that is not a candidate key, remove from the table the fields that depend on this determinant, but do not remove the determinant. Create a new table containing all the fields from the original table that depend on this determinant and make the determinant the primary key of this new table.

15. An entity-relationship diagram (ERD) is a diagram used to represent database designs. In ERDs, rectangles represent tables and lines between rectangles represent one-to-many relationships between the corresponding tables. You can also diagram a database design by using the Access relationship window.

 If you have a SAM 2010 user profile, your instructor may have assigned an autogradable version of this assignment. If so, log into the SAM 2010 Web site at www.cengage.com/sam2010 to download the instruction and start files.

Learn It Online

Test your knowledge of chapter content and key terms.

Instructions: To complete the Learn It Online exercises, start your browser, click the Address bar, and then enter the Web address `scsite.com/ac2010/learn`. When the Access 2010 Learn It Online page is displayed, click the link for the exercise you want to complete and then read the instructions.

Chapter Reinforcement TF, MC, and SA
A series of true/false, multiple choice, and short answer questions that test your knowledge of the chapter content.

Flash Cards
An interactive learning environment where you identify chapter key terms associated with displayed definitions.

Practice Test
A series of multiple choice questions that test your knowledge of chapter content and key terms.

Who Wants To Be a Computer Genius?
An interactive game that challenges your knowledge of chapter content in the style of a television quiz show.

Wheel of Terms
An interactive game that challenges your knowledge of chapter key terms in the style of the television show *Wheel of Fortune*.

Crossword Puzzle Challenge
A crossword puzzle that challenges your knowledge of key terms presented in the chapter.

Apply Your Knowledge

Reinforce the skills and apply the concepts you learned in this chapter.

Instructions: Answer the following question in the format specified by your instructor.

Understanding Keys and Normalization

1. Figure 11–33 contains sample data for parts and for suppliers who supply those parts. In discussing the data with users, you find that part numbers — but not descriptions — uniquely identify parts, and that supplier names uniquely identify suppliers. Multiple suppliers can supply the same part. For example, air deflectors can be purchased from either Asterman or JMZ Technologies. Convert this relation into an equivalent set of relations in third normal form (3NF).

Item				
Item Number	**Description**	**Supplier Name**	**Address**	**Unit Cost**
1234	Air Deflector	Asterman	Georgetown	5.00
		JMZ Technologies	Buda	4.50
5678	Energy Saving Kit	Scryps Distributors	San Rita	3.00
		Asterman	Georgetown	2.00
		JMZ Technologies	Buda	3.75

Figure 11–33

2. Figure 11–34 contains sample data for an Employee table. Use this figure to answer the following:
   a. Is the table in first normal form (1NF)? Why or why not?
   b. Is the table in second normal form (2NF)? Why or why not?
   c. Is the table in third normal form (3NF)? Why or why not?
   d. Identify the candidate keys for the table.

Employee				
SSN	**Emp_ID**	**Name**	**Manager SSN**	**Manager Name**
1111	123-678B	Bruce	8888	Bob
2222	345-890S	Sue	9999	Meg
3333	432-789T	Teresa	7777	Mary
4444	654-342L	Lee	8888	Bob

Figure 11–34

Extend Your Knowledge

Extend the skills you learned in this chapter and experiment with new skills. You may need to use Help to complete the assignment.

Modifying a Database Design and Understanding Diagrams

Instructions: Answer the following questions in the format specified by your instructor.

1. Using the shorthand representation, indicate the changes that you would need to make to the Camashaly Design database design shown in Figure 11–8 on page AC 688 in order to support the following requirement: A client does not necessarily work with one business analyst but can work with several business analysts.

2. Using the shorthand representation, indicate the changes that you would need to make to the Scryps Distributor database design shown in Figure 11–10 on page AC 694 in order to support the following requirement: The price for a part does not change but is the same for all customers.

3. Use the Access Relationship report for the Regional Books database shown in Figure 11-35 to answer the following:
   a. Identify the foreign keys in the Book table.
   b. What is the purpose of the Book Order table?
   c. What is the primary key of the Book Order table?
   d. Identify the foreign keys in the Book Order table?

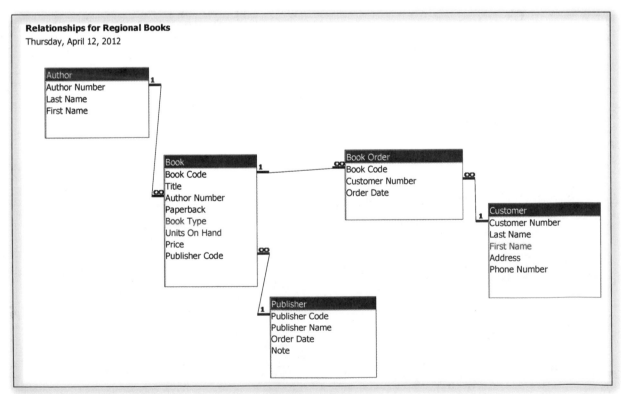

Figure 11–35

Make It Right

Analyze a database and correct all errors and/or improve the design.

Correcting a Database Design

Instructions: Answer the following questions in the format specified by your instructor.

1. List four relational table characteristics that are violated in the table shown in Figure 11–36.

Orders			
Date	Item Num	Number Ordered	Date
04/01/2012	AX12	11	04/12/2012
04/01/2012	BT04	1	04/09/2012
	BZ66	1	Friday
04/03/2012	CB03	4	04/13/2012
04/03/2012	CX11	2	04/12/2012
04/04/2012	AZ52	2	04/12/2012
	BA74	4	$182.91
04/04/2012	BT04	1	04/15/2012
04/03/2012	CX11	2	04/12/2012
04/04/2012	CZ81	2	04/13/2012

Figure 11–36

2. The following table is a student's first attempt to create a database design:

   Student (<u>StudentID</u>, Student Name, Credit Hours, AdvisorID, Advisor Name, (Course ID, Course Name, Grade))

   a. Identify the functional dependencies.

   b. Convert this table to an equivalent collection of tables in third normal form (3NF).

In the Lab

Design, create, modify, and/or use a database following the guidelines, concepts, and skills presented in this chapter. Labs are listed in order of increasing difficulty.

Lab 1: Designing a Database for Phil's Limousine

Instructions: Consider the following set of requirements for Phil's Limousine Service:

- For each driver, the company keeps track of the driver's name (first name and last name), driver's address (street, city, state, postal code), driver's license number, home telephone number, and cell telephone number.

- For each limousine, the company keeps track of a unique limousine ID number, limousine license number, limousine color, and number of passengers the limousine can hold.

- A driver can be assigned to more than one limousine. A limousine will have multiple drivers but only one driver at a time.

continued

STUDENT ASSIGNMENTS

In the Lab *continued*

Based on these requirements, do the following:

1. Identify and list the entities and the attributes of those entities.

2. Identify and list the functional dependencies.

3. Create a set of 3NF relations using the shorthand notation given in the chapter. Be sure to identify all primary keys and foreign keys appropriately.

Submit your database design in the format specified by your instructor.

In the Lab

Lab 2: Normalizing a Patient Relation

Instructions: Answer the following questions in the format specified by your instructor.

Consider the following relation:

> Patient (Patient#, PatientName, BalanceOwed, DoctorId, DoctorName, ServiceCode, ServiceDesc, ServiceFee, ServiceDate)

This is a relation concerning data about patients of doctors at a clinic and the services the doctors perform for their patients. The following dependencies exist in Patient:

> Patient# → PatientName, BalanceOwed
> DoctorId → DoctorName
> ServiceCode → ServiceDesc, ServiceFee
> Patient#, DoctorId, ServiceCode → ServiceDate

1. Convert Patient to 1NF based on the functional dependencies given.

2. Next, convert to a set of relations in 3NF.

In the Lab

Lab 3: Designing a Student Activities Database

Instructions: Design a database to meet the following requirements.

1. A database at a local high school that offers multiple sports activities must support the following requirements:

    a. For an activity, store its number and name, for example, 084, Tennis. Each activity has a cost associated with it.

    b. For a student, store his or her number, first name, and last name as well as the name, home telephone number, and cell telephone number of the parent or guardian primarily responsible for the student.

One student can enroll in many activities, and one activity can include many students. One parent/guardian can have many students.

2. Based on these requirements:

    a. Identify and list the entities and the attributes of those entities.

    b. Identify and list the functional dependencies.

    c. Create a set of 3NF relations using the shorthand notation given in the chapter. Be sure to identify all primary keys and foreign keys appropriately.

Submit your database design in the format specified by your instructor.

Cases and Places

Apply your creative thinking and problem solving skills to design and implement a solution.

1: Designing a College Database

Academic

Instructions: The instructor for your database course thinks that an excellent way to understand database concepts is to apply them to a situation with which all students are familiar. Use the concepts and techniques presented in this chapter to design a database to meet the following requirements.

1. A database for a college must support the following requirements:

   a. For a department, store its name.

   b. For an advisor, store his or her number, last name, first name, and the department number to which the advisor is assigned.

   c. For a course, store its code and description, for example, CIS 101, Introduction to Computers.

   d. For a student, store his or her number, first name, and last name. For each course the student takes, store the course code, the course description, and the grade earned.

   e. Also store the number and name of the student's advisor. Assume that an advisor may advise any number of students, but that each student has just one advisor.

Use your own experience as a student to determine any functional dependencies.

2. Based on these requirements:

   a. Identify and list the entities and the attributes of those entities.

   b. Identify and list the functional dependencies.

   c. Create a set of 3NF relations using the shorthand notation given in the chapter. Be sure to identify all primary keys and foreign keys appropriately.

Submit your database design in the format specified by your instructor.

2: Designing a Movie DVD Database

Personal

Instructions: You have a growing collection of movie DVDs and realize that you need to keep better records of your collection. Use the concepts and techniques presented in this chapter to design a database called Movie DVD.

1. The Movie DVD database must support the following requirements:

   a. For each movie, list its number, title, the year the movie was made, the date the DVD was purchased, its type — for example, documentary, comedy, drama, and so on — and the length of the movie in minutes. You also rate movies according to your own rating system.

   b. For each movie star, list his or her number, first name, and last name.

   c. For each director, list his or her number, first name, and last name.

A movie star can appear in many movies, and one movie can have many stars. A director can direct many movies, but a movie can only have one director.

2. Based on these requirements:

   a. Identify and list the entities and the attributes of those entities.

   b. Identify and list the functional dependencies.

   c. Create a set of 3NF relations using the shorthand notation given in the chapter. Be sure to identify all primary keys and foreign keys appropriately.

Submit your database design in the format specified by your instructor.

continued

Cases and Places *continued*

3: Designing a Dog Walkers Database

Professional

Instructions: You have just started a dog walking business. You want to create a database to keep track of your customers and their dogs. Use the concepts and techniques presented in this chapter to design a database to meet the following requirements.

1. The Dog Walkers database must support the following requirements:

   a. For each dog, list the dog ID, dog name, breed name — for example, Dalmatian, mixed, collie and so on — size (large, medium, small), gender, number of times walked per day, and owner's first name and last name as well as cell telephone number.

   b. For each customer, list the customer ID, the customer's first name, last name, address (street, city, postal code), home telephone number, cell telephone number, current amount due, and amount paid.

   c. The database also must store the cost per walk. The cost to walk each dog depends on both the dog and the customer.

A dog belongs to only one breed, but a breed can have many dogs. An owner also can have many dogs.

2. Based on these requirements:

   a. Identify and list the entities and the attributes of those entities.

   b. Identify and list the functional dependencies.

   c. Create a set of 3NF relations using the shorthand notation given in the chapter. Be sure to identify all primary keys and foreign keys appropriately.

Submit your database design in the format specified by your instructor.

NOTES

NOTES

NOTES

NOTES

Appendix A

Project Planning Guidelines

Using Project Planning Guidelines

The process of communicating specific information to others is a learned, rational skill. Computers and software, especially Microsoft Office 2010, can help you develop ideas and present detailed information to a particular audience.

Using Microsoft Office 2010, you can create projects such as Word documents, PowerPoint presentations, Excel spreadsheets, and Access databases. Productivity software such as Microsoft Office 2010 minimizes much of the laborious work of drafting and revising projects. Some communicators handwrite ideas in notebooks, others compose directly on the computer, and others have developed unique strategies that work for their own particular thinking and writing styles.

No matter what method you use to plan a project, follow specific guidelines to arrive at a final product that presents information correctly and effectively (Figure A–1). Use some aspects of these guidelines every time you undertake a project, and others as needed in specific instances. For example, in determining content for a project, you may decide that a chart communicates trends more effectively than a paragraph of text. If so, you would create this graphical element and insert it in an Excel spreadsheet, a Word document, or a PowerPoint slide.

Determine the Project's Purpose

Begin by clearly defining why you are undertaking this assignment. For example, you may want to track monetary donations collected for your club's fund-raising drive. Alternatively, you may be urging students to vote for a particular candidate in the next election. Once you clearly understand the purpose of your task, begin to draft ideas of how best to communicate this information.

Analyze Your Audience

Learn about the people who will read, analyze, or view your work. Where are they employed? What are their educational backgrounds? What are their expectations? What questions do they have?

PROJECT PLANNING GUIDELINES

1. DETERMINE THE PROJECT'S PURPOSE
Why are you undertaking the project?

2. ANALYZE YOUR AUDIENCE
Who are the people who will use your work?

3. GATHER POSSIBLE CONTENT
What information exists, and in what forms?

4. DETERMINE WHAT CONTENT TO PRESENT TO YOUR AUDIENCE
What information will best communicate the project's purpose to your audience?

Figure A–1

Design experts suggest drawing a mental picture of these people or finding photos of people who fit this profile so that you can develop a project with the audience in mind.

By knowing your audience members, you can tailor a project to meet their interests and needs. You will not present them with information they already possess, and you will not omit the information they need to know.

Example: Your assignment is to raise the profile of your college's nursing program in the community. How much do they know about your college and the nursing curriculum? What are the admission requirements? How many of the applicants admitted complete the program? What percent pass the state board exams?

Gather Possible Content

Rarely are you in a position to develop all the material for a project. Typically, you would begin by gathering existing information that may reside in spreadsheets or databases. Web sites, pamphlets, magazine and newspaper articles, and books could provide insights of how others have approached your topic. Personal interviews often provide perspectives not available by any other means. Consider video and audio clips as potential sources for material that might complement or support the factual data you uncover.

Determine What Content to Present to Your Audience

Experienced designers recommend writing three or four major ideas you want an audience member to remember after reading or viewing your project. It also is helpful to envision your project's endpoint, the key fact you wish to emphasize. All project elements should lead to this ending point.

As you make content decisions, you also need to think about other factors. Presentation of the project content is an important consideration. For example, will your brochure be printed on thick, colored paper or posted on the Web? Will your PowerPoint presentation be viewed in a classroom with excellent lighting and a bright projector, or will it be viewed on a notebook computer monitor? Determine relevant time factors, such as the length of time to develop the project, how long readers will spend reviewing your project, or the amount of time allocated for your speaking engagement. Your project will need to accommodate all of these constraints.

Decide whether a graph, photo, or artistic element can express or emphasize a particular concept. The right hemisphere of the brain processes images by attaching an emotion to them, so audience members are more apt to recall these graphics long term rather than just reading text.

As you select content, be mindful of the order in which you plan to present information. Readers and audience members generally remember the first and last pieces of information they see and hear, so you should place the most important information at the top or bottom of the page.

Summary

When creating a project, it is beneficial to follow some basic guidelines from the outset. By taking some time at the beginning of the process to determine the project's purpose, analyze the audience, gather possible content, and determine what content to present to the audience, you can produce a project that is informative, relevant, and effective.

Appendix B

Publishing Office 2010 Web Pages Online

With Office 2010 programs, you use the Save As command in the Backstage view to save a Web page to a Web site, network location, or FTP site. **File Transfer Protocol (FTP)** is an Internet standard that allows computers to exchange files with other computers on the Internet.

You should contact your network system administrator or technical support staff at your Internet access provider to determine if their Web server supports Web folders, FTP, or both, and to obtain necessary permissions to access the Web server.

Using an Office Program to Publish Office 2010 Web Pages

When publishing online, someone first must assign the necessary permissions for you to publish the Web page. If you are granted access to publish online, you must obtain the Web address of the Web server, a user name, and possibly a password that allows you to connect to the Web server. The steps in this appendix assume that you have access to an online location to which you can publish a Web page.

To Connect to an Online Location

To publish a Web page online, you first must connect to the online location. To connect to an online location using Windows 7, you would perform the following steps.

1. Click the Start button on the Windows 7 taskbar to display the Start menu.

2. Click Computer in the right pane of the Start menu to open the Computer window.

3. Click the 'Map network drive' button on the toolbar to display the Map Network Drive dialog box. (If the 'Map network drive' button is not visible on the toolbar, click the 'Display additional commands' button on the toolbar and then click 'Map network drive' in the list to display the Map Network Drive dialog box.)

4. Click the 'Connect to a Web site that you can use to store your documents and pictures' link (Map Network Drive dialog box) to start the Add Network Location wizard.

5. Click the Next button (Add Network Location dialog box).

6. Click 'Choose a custom network location' and then click the Next button.

7. Type the Internet or network address specified by your network or system administrator in the text box and then click the Next button.

8. Click 'Log on anonymously' to deselect the check box, type your user name in the User name text box, and then click the Next button.

9. If necessary, enter the name you want to assign to this online location and then click the Next button.

10. Click to deselect the Open this network location when I click Finish check box, and then click the Finish button.

11. Click the Cancel button to close the Map Network Drive dialog box.

12. Close the Computer window.

To Save a Web Page to an Online Location

The online location now can be accessed easily from Windows programs, including Microsoft Office programs. After creating a Microsoft Office file you wish to save as a Web page, you must save the file to the online location to which you connected in the previous steps. To save a Microsoft Word document as a Web page, for example, and publish it to the online location, you would perform the following steps.

1. Click File on the Ribbon to display the Backstage view and then click Save As in the Backstage view to display the Save As dialog box.

2. Type the Web page file name in the File name text box (Save As dialog box). Do not press the ENTER key because you do not want to close the dialog box at this time.

3. Click the 'Save as type' box arrow and then click Web Page to select the Web Page format.

4. If necessary, scroll to display the name of the online location in the navigation pane.

5. Double-click the online location name in the navigation pane to select that location as the new save location and display its contents in the right pane.

6. If a dialog box appears prompting you for a user name and password, type the user name and password in the respective text boxes and then click the Log On button.

7. Click the Save button (Save As dialog box).

The Web page now has been published online. To view the Web page using a Web browser, contact your network or system administrator for the Web address you should use to connect to the Web page.

Appendix C

Microsoft Office 2010 Specialist and Expert Certifications

What Are Microsoft Office Specialist and Expert Certifications?

Microsoft Corporation has developed a set of standardized, performance-based examinations that you can take to demonstrate your overall expertise with Microsoft Office 2010 programs, including Microsoft Word 2010, Microsoft PowerPoint 2010, Microsoft Excel 2010, Microsoft Access 2010, and Microsoft Outlook 2010. When you successfully complete an examination for one of these Office programs, you will have earned the designation as a specialist or as an expert in that particular Office program.

These examinations collectively are called the Microsoft Office 2010 Specialist and Microsoft Office 2010 Expert certification exams. The information in Table C–1 identifies each of these examinations.

Table C–1 Microsoft Office Specialist and Expert Certifications			
Certification Exam	**Description**	**Requirement**	**Credential Earned**
Microsoft Word 2010 Specialist	Indicates you have proficiency in using at least 80 percent of the features and capabilities of Word 2010	Successfully complete Exam 77-881	Microsoft Office Specialist: Microsoft Word 2010
Microsoft Word 2010 Expert	Indicates you have proficiency in using Word 2010 at the feature and functionality levels, together with advanced features of Word 2010	Successfully complete Exam 77-887	Microsoft Office Specialist: Microsoft Word 2010 Expert
Microsoft PowerPoint 2010 Specialist	Indicates you have proficiency in using PowerPoint 2010 by creating complex slide shows using sophisticated data presented in visual formats	Successfully complete Exam 77-883	Microsoft Office Specialist: Microsoft PowerPoint 2010

Table C–1 Microsoft Office Specialist and Expert Certifications *(continued)*			
Certification Exam	**Description**	**Requirement**	**Credential Earned**
Microsoft Excel 2010 Specialist	Indicates you have proficiency in using at least 80 percent of the features and capabilities of Excel 2010	Successfully complete Exam 77-882	Microsoft Office Specialist: Microsoft Excel 2010
Microsoft Excel 2010 Expert	Indicates you have proficiency in using Excel 2010 at the feature and functionality levels, together with advanced features of Excel 2010	Successfully complete Exam 77–888	Microsoft Office Specialist: Microsoft Excel 2010 Expert
Microsoft Access 2010	Indicates you have proficiency in using Access 2010 by creating, modifying, and extending functionality of basic database objects	Successfully complete Exam 77–885	Microsoft Office Specialist: Microsoft Access 2010
Microsoft Outlook 2010	Indicates you have proficiency in using Outlook 2010 by formatting message content, creating contact records and appointments, scheduling meetings, and sharing schedules	Successfully complete Exam 77–884	Microsoft Office Specialist: Microsoft Outlook 2010

You will notice in Table C–1 that Word and Excel have an Expert certification. The other programs do not.

Microsoft provides one other level of Office certification: 2010 Microsoft Office Master certification. To be certified as a 2010 Microsoft Office Master, you must successfully complete the following exams:

- 77-887: Word 2010 Expert
- 77-888: Excel 2010 Expert
- 77-883: PowerPoint 2010

and either

- 77-885: Access 2010

or

- 77-884: Outlook 2010

Why Should You Be Certified?

Microsoft Office 2010 certification provides a number of benefits for both you and your potential employer. The benefits for you include the following:

- You can differentiate yourself in the employment marketplace from those who are not Microsoft Office Specialist or Expert certified.
- You have proved your skills and expertise when using Microsoft Office 2010.
- You will be able to perform at a higher skill level in your job.
- You will be working at a higher professional level than those who are not certified.
- You will broaden your employment opportunities and advance your career more rapidly.

For employers, Microsoft Office 2010 certification offers the following advantages:

- When hiring or promoting employees, employers have immediate verification of employees' skills.
- Companies can maximize their productivity and efficiency by employing Microsoft Office 2010 certified individuals.

Taking the Microsoft Office 2010 Certification Exams

The Certiport Company administers the Microsoft Office 2010 Specialist and Expert certification exams. You can contact Certiport at 888-999-9830 x138 or at the Web site, http://www.certiport.com. On the Web site, click the Microsoft Office 2010 Specialist link. Be sure to explore the links on these Certiport pages to obtain a thorough understanding of the Microsoft Office 2010 certification exams.

To take an exam, you must register and pay a fee. The fee varies depending on the test and the testing center. Each exam requires that you complete specified tasks using the program on which you are being tested, that is, tasks you would perform while at work. Remember — these are performance-based exams, so you will be using the software, not answering questions about the software.

You can find testing centers by following the links on the Certiport Web site and then clicking Find a Testing Center.

How Do I Prepare for the Microsoft Office 2010 Specialist Exam?

The Shelly Cashman Series offers Microsoft-approved textbooks for the certification exams listed in Table C–1 on pages APP 5 and APP 6. These textbooks can be found by visiting the Web site, www.cengagebrain.com, and then entering the search topic, Shelly. Using any of the approved textbooks will prepare you to take and pass the indicated Microsoft Office 2010 Specialist or Expert exam. For a list of skill sets specific to this book, see Table C–2 on pages APP 8 through APP 11. The use of all appropriate Shelly Cashman Series Office 2010 textbooks will prepare you for the 2010 Microsoft Office Master certification.

For further information from Microsoft regarding Microsoft Office 2010 certification, please visit http://www.microsoft.com/learning/en/us/certification/mos.aspx and http://office.microsoft.com/en-us/word-help/should-you-become-a-microsoft-office-specialist-HA001211101.aspx.

Table C–2 Specialist-Level Skill Sets and Locations in Book for Microsoft Access 2010

Skill Set	Page Number
Managing the Access Environment	
Create and manage a database.	
Use Save Object As	AC 47, AC 84, AC 88, AC 426, AC 544
Use Open	AC 27, AC 653, AC 655, AC 659
Use Save and Publish	AC 61, AC 62, AC 614, AC 615, AC 622–AC 623, AC 630–AC 631, AC 649, AC 653, AC 657, AC 661
Use Compact & Repair Database	AC 61
Use Encrypt with Password commands	AC 654–AC 656
Create a database from a template	AC 14, AC 628, AC 653
Set Access options	AC 37, AC 58, AC 420, AC 421, AC 457, AC 527, AC 620–AC 621, AC 651, AC 660
Configure the Navigation Pane.	
Rename objects	AC 62, AC 447
Delete objects	AC 62
Set Navigation options	AC 14, AC 127–AC 128, AC 232, AC 638–AC 641
Apply Application Parts.	
Use Blank Forms	AC 629
Use Quick Start	AC 282, AC 606–AC 608, AC 610–AC 611, AC 612, AC 629
Use user templates	AC 629, AC 653
Building Tables	
Create tables.	
Create tables in Design View	AC 33–AC 37, AC 344
Create and modify fields.	
Insert a field	AC 17–AC 20, AC 155, AC 159–AC 161, AC 278–AC 279, AC 282, AC 610–AC 615
Delete a field	AC 20, AC 155, AC 282, AC 612
Rename a field	AC 17, AC 20, AC 282, AC 612
Hide or Unhide fields	AC 606–AC 607
Freeze or Unfreeze fields	AC 606
Modify data types	AC 18, AC 155, AC 156–AC 158
Modify the field description	AC 18, AC 35
Modify field properties	AC 16–AC 19, AC 33–AC 37, AC 165–AC 168, AC 344, AC 610, AC 612, AC 645, AC 646–AC 647, AC 649–AC 650
Sort and filter records.	
Use Find	AC 144–AC 146
Use Sort	AC 193–AC 195
Use Filter commands	AC 148–AC 154
Set relationships.	
Define Primary Keys	AC 16–AC 18, AC 34, AC 343, AC 344, AC 347
Use Primary Keys to create Relationships	AC 185–AC 189, AC 346–AC 347, AC 613–AC 615
Edit Relationships	AC 188, AC 189, AC 342, AC 346–AC 347
Import data from a single data file.	
Import source data into a new table	AC 38–AC 41, AC 345
Append records to an existing table	AC 39–AC 41, AC 345
Import data as a linked table	AC 345–AC 346

Table C–2 Specialist-Level Skill Sets and Locations in Book for Microsoft Access 2010 *(continued)*	
Skill Set	**Page Number**
Building Forms	
Create forms.	
Use the Form Wizard	AC 243–AC 244
Create a Blank Form	AC 325, AC 326
Use Form Design Tools	AC 246–AC 248, AC 293, AC 295, AC 296, AC 299–AC 300, AC 301–AC 302, AC 307, AC 308, AC 309, AC 310–AC 315, AC 472–AC 483, AC 490, AC 497–AC 498, AC 503–AC 507, AC 510
Create Navigation forms	AC 568–AC 571, AC 619
Apply Form Design options.	
Apply a Theme	AC 238–AC 240, AC 241, AC 375
Add bound controls	
Text box	AC 221, AC 358–AC 360, AC 503–AC 505
Drop down	AC 475–AC 480, AC 488–AC 489
Format Header/Footer	AC 246–AC 248, AC 301, AC 312–AC 313, AC 484
View Code	AC 551
Convert Macros to Visual Basic	AC 494, AC 551
View Property Sheet	AC 311, AC 313, AC 481–AC 482, AC 490, AC 494, AC 497, AC 506, AC 560, AC 566
Add Existing Fields	AC 251–AC 252, AC 293–AC 294, AC 297–AC 299, AC 473–AC 474
Apply Form Arrange options.	
Use the Table functions	
Insert	AC 521
Merge	AC 522
Split	AC 522
Move table	AC 522, AC 525
Use Reposition/Format controls	
Anchor	AC 255, AC 526
Padding	AC 230, AC 524
Margins	AC 230, AC 524
Apply Form Format options.	
Reformat Font in form	AC 312–AC 313
Apply background image to form	AC 485
Apply Quick Styles to controls in form	AC 571
Apply conditional formatting in form	AC 230
Creating and Managing Queries	
Construct queries.	
Create Select query	AC 74, AC 78–AC 79, AC 102–AC 103, AC 163, AC 164, AC 501, AC 616
Create Make Table query	AC 165
Create Append query	AC 164
Create Crosstab query	AC 123, AC 124–AC 126
Manage source tables and relationships.	
Use the Show Table command	AC 78–AC 79, AC 90, AC 102–AC 104, AC 347, AC 348, AC 501, AC 616

Table C–2 Specialist-Level Skill Sets and Locations in Book for Microsoft Access 2010 *(continued)*

Skill Set	Page Number
Use Remove Table command	AC 79
Create ad hoc relationships	AC 102
Manipulate fields.	
Add field	AC 80–AC 81, AC 85, AC 90, AC 98, AC 103, AC 116
Remove field	AC 80, AC 95
Rearrange fields	AC 94, AC 616
Use Sort and Show options	AC 85–AC 86, AC 94, AC 96, AC 98–AC 100
Calculate totals.	
Use the Total row	AC 119–AC 122
Use Group By	AC 122–AC 123, AC 444–AC 445
Generate calculated fields.	
Perform calculations	AC 115, AC 116–AC 118, AC 119–AC 122, AC 348–AC 349, AC 434, AC 441, AC 443, AC 501–AC 502
Use the Zoom box	AC 116–AC 118, AC 349, AC 501–AC 502
Use Expression Builder	AC 115, AC 159–AC 161, AC 348–AC 349, AC 394
Designing Reports	
Create reports.	
Create a Blank Report	AC 238
Use Report Design Tools	AC 351–AC 352, AC 354–AC 355, AC 358–AC 370, AC 387–AC 392, AC 394
Use the Report Wizard	AC 106–AC 108, AC 215, AC 232–AC 235
Apply Report Design options.	
Apply a Theme	AC 238–AC 240, AC 240–AC 241
Add calculated controls	
Total report records	AC 57–AC 58, AC 221–AC 223, AC 387–AC 392
Group report records	AC 216, AC 217–AC 219, AC 220–AC 221, AC 352–AC 353, AC 387–AC 388
Add bound/unbound controls	
Text box	AC 358–AC 360, AC 388–AC 390, AC 394
Hyperlink	AC 357
Drop down	AC 357
Graph	AC 357
Insert page break	AC 357, AC 381
Header/Footer	
Insert page number	AC 378–AC 379, AC 398
Insert logo	AC 616
Reorder tab function	AC 519
Apply Report Arrange options.	
Use the Table functions	
Insert	AC 230, AC 521
Merge	AC 230, AC 522
Split	AC 230, AC 522

Table C–2 Specialist-Level Skill Sets and Locations in Book for Microsoft Access 2010 *(continued)*

Skill Set	Page Number
Move table	AC 230, AC 522
Reposition/Format records	
Padding	AC 230, AC 523–AC 524
Margins	AC 230, AC 523–AC 524
Align report outputs to grid	AC 394
Apply Report Format options.	
Rename label in a report	AC 54, AC 55, AC 356, AC 360, AC 389, AC 397
Apply background image to report	AC 485, AC 561
Change shape in report	AC 573
Apply conditional formatting in report	AC 224–AC 227
Apply Report Page Setup options.	
Change page Size	AC 399–AC 400
Change page orientation	AC 175–AC 177, AC 232–AC 235, AC 399–AC 400
Sort and filter records for reporting.	
Use the Find command	AC 147, AC 231
Use Sort command	AC 217–AC 219, AC 351–AC 353, AC 392
Use Filter commands	AC 228–AC 229
Use view types	AC 53, AC 54–AC 58, AC 216, AC 217–AC 219, AC 351–AC 356, AC 361, AC 392–AC 393

Index

Quick Reference Summary

Microsoft Access 2010 Quick Reference Summary

Task	Page Number	Mouse	Ribbon	Shortcut Menu	Keyboard Shortcut
Advanced Filter/Sort, Use	AC 153		Advanced button (Home tab | Sort & Filter group), Advanced Filter/Sort		
All Fields in Query, Include	AC 79, AC 80	Double-click asterisk			
Alternate Row Colors, Change in Datasheet	AC 181, AC 182		Select table, Alternate Row Color button arrow (Home tab | Text Formatting group), select color OR Datasheet Formatting Dialog Box Launcher (Home tab | Text Formatting group)		
Append Query, Use	AC 164		Append button (Query Tools Design Tab | Query Type group)		
Application Part, Use	AC 621		Create database, click Application Parts button (Create tab | Templates group), click application part to use		
Ascending Button, Use to Order Records	AC 194		Select field, Ascending button (Home tab | Sort & Filter group)	Right-click field name, click Sort A to Z or Sort Z to A	
Axis Title, Assign	AC 586	Click default axis title, open property sheet, change caption text		Right-click axis title, property sheet, change caption text	
Background Image, Add to Form or Report	AC 485		Click anywhere in form or report, click Background Image button (Format tab | Background group)		
Blank Web Database, Create	AC 609	In Backstage view, click New tab, click Blank web database button			
Border Style, Change	AC 398		Select controls, Property Sheet button (Report Design Tools Design tab | Tools group), click Border Style property box, select style	Select controls, right-click a control, click Properties, click Border Style property box, select style	

Microsoft Access 2010 Quick Reference Summary *(continued)*

Task	Page Number	Mouse	Ribbon	Shortcut Menu	Keyboard Shortcut
Calculated Field in Query, Create Using Expression Builder	AC 348		Builder button (Query Tools Design tab | Query Setup group)	Right-click field row, Build	
Calculated Field in Query, Use	AC 116			Right-click field row, Zoom	
Calculated Field, Add to Form	AC 503		Text Box tool (Form Design Tools Design Tab | Controls group), click in form, click in text box, enter expression in text box		
Calculated Field, Create	AC 159	In Design view, create new field, click Data Type box arrow, click Calculated			
Can Grow Property, Change	AC 373, AC 386		Select control, Property Sheet button (Report Design Tools Design tab | Tools group), change Can Grow property to Yes	Right-click control, click Properties, change Can Grow property to Yes	
Caption, Change in Query	AC 118		Property Sheet button (Query Tools Design Tab | Show/Hide group), Caption box	Right-click field in design grid, click Properties on shortcut menu, Caption box	
Cell, Split in Form or Report	AC 522		Click cell to be split, Split Vertically button (Arrange tab | Merge/Split group) to split vertically OR Split Horizontally button (Arrange tab | Merge/Split group) to split horizontally		
Cells, Merge in Form or Report	AC 522		Select all cells to be merged, Merge button (Arrange tab | Merge/Split group)		
Chart Title, Add	AC 588	Click Chartspace, display property sheet, click General tab, click Add Title button, close property sheet, click title, display title property sheet, click Format tab, change caption text			
Chart Type, Modify	AC 514			Display chart in Design view, right-click chart, point to Chart Object, click Edit, right-click chart, click Chart Type, click desired chart sub-type	

Microsoft Access 2010 Quick Reference Summary *(continued)*

Task	Page Number	Mouse	Ribbon	Shortcut Menu	Keyboard Shortcut
Chart, Format	AC 517			Right-click chart, point to Chart Object on shortcut menu to display chart Object submenu, click Edit on the Chart Object submenu	
Charts, Insert	AC 510		More button (Form Design Tools Design tab | Controls group), click Chart tool, click in form to display Chart Wizard		
Close Object	AC 23	Close button for object		Right-click object tab, Close	
Collection of Legal Values, Specify	AC 167	In Design view, enter criterion specifying legal values in Validation Rule property box in Field Properties pane			
Column Headings, Modify for Report	AC 54	Click twice in column heading to display insertion point, erase current heading, type new heading			
Column, Delete in Form or Report	AC 521		Click any control in the column, Select Column (Arrange tab | Rows & Columns group), DELETE		
Column, Insert in Form or Report	AC 521		Select any control in column to right or left, Select Column button (Arrange tab | Rows & Columns group), Insert Left button (Arrange tab | Rows & Columns group) to insert blank column to left OR Insert Right button (Arrange tab | Rows & Columns group) to insert blank column to right		
Column, Resize	AC 54, AC 55	Double-click right boundary of field selector in datasheet OR drag right boundary		Right-click field name, Field Width	
Combo Box	AC 475		More button (Form Design Tools Design tab | Controls group), Combo Box tool (Form Design Tools Design tab | Controls group), click in form		
Command Buttons, add to Form	AC 485		With Use Control Wizards button selected, click the Button tool (Form Design Tools Design tab | Controls group), click in form		

Microsoft Access 2010 Quick Reference Summary *(continued)*

Task	Page Number	Mouse	Ribbon	Shortcut Menu	Keyboard Shortcut
Common Filter, Use	AC 150			Click arrow for field, point to filter	
Comparison Operator, Use	AC 91	Create query, enter comparison operator in criterion			
Compound Criterion Involving AND, Use	AC 92	Place criteria in same row			
Compound Criterion Involving OR, Use	AC 93	Place criteria in separate rows			
Conditional Value, Assign	AC 394		Text Box tool (Report Design Tools Design tab | Controls group), select text box, click Property Sheet button (Report Design Tools Design tab | Tools group), click Control Source property, click Build button, assign condition using Expression Builder dialog box		
Control for a Field, Add to Form Design	AC 293	Drag field from field list to form			
Control Margins, Change	AC 524		Select any cell in layout, Select Layout button (Arrange tab | Rows & Columns group), Control Margins button (Arrange tab | Position group), select desired margin setting		
Control Padding, Change	AC 524		Select layout, Control Padding button (Arrange tab | Position group), select desired padding setting		
Control Shape, Change	AC 573		Select control or controls, Change Shape (Form Layout Tools Design tab | Control Formatting group), on Change Shape menu, select desired shape		
Control, Anchor in Form or Report	AC 526		Select control or controls, Anchoring button (Arrange tab | Position group), select desired Anchoring option from Anchoring gallery		
Control, Change Format	AC 248		Select control, Form Layout Tools Format tab, select formatting option from Font group		
Control, Move	AC 249	Point to control, drag with four-headed mouse pointer			
Controls, Align	AC 295		Click+SHIFT to select controls, Align button (Form Design Tools Arrange tab | Sizing & Ordering group), select alignment style		

Microsoft Access 2010 Quick Reference Summary *(continued)*

Task	Page Number	Mouse	Ribbon	Shortcut Menu	Keyboard Shortcut
Controls, Conditionally Format	AC 224, AC 230		Conditional Formatting button (Format tab | Control Formatting group), Conditional Formatting Rules Manager dialog box, specify rule		
Controls, Move in Control Layout	AC 249	Select labels and controls for fields, drag to desired location			
Convert Earlier Access Database to Access 2010	AC 630	With database to convert open, click File, click Save & Publish tab, select Save Database As command, click Access Database, click Save As button, specify name and location for database, click Save button			
Convert to Earlier Version of Access	AC 630	With database to convert open, click File, click Save & Publish tab, select Save Database As command, click desired format, click Save As button, specify name and location for database, click Save button.			
Criteria, Use in Calculating Statistics	AC 121		Totals button (Query Tools Design Tab | Show/Hide group), Total box arrow, click calculation		
Criterion, Use	AC 46	Right-click query, Design View, enter criterion in Criteria row			
Crosstab Query, Create	AC 124		Query Wizard button (Create tab | Queries group), Crosstab Query Wizard		
Custom Categories and Groups, Create	AC 638			Right-click Navigation Pane menu bar, Navigation Options command, Add Item button (Navigation Options dialog box), specify category and group names, OK button	
Custom Data Parts, Create	AC 606	Open table in Datasheet view, select column headings, click More Fields button (Table Tools Fields tab | Add & Delete group), click Save Selection as New Data Type			

Microsoft Access 2010 Quick Reference Summary *(continued)*

Task	Page Number	Mouse	Ribbon	Shortcut Menu	Keyboard Shortcut
Custom Input Mask, Create	AC 646	In Design view, select field for mask, click Input Mask field property, enter mask symbols			
Custom Properties, Create	AC 643	In Backstage view, click Info tab if necessary, click 'View and edit database properties' link, click Custom tab			
Data Macro, Create	AC 572	Open table in Datasheet view, click Before Change button (Table Tools Table tab | Before Events group), create macro in Macro Builder			
Data, Enter in Attachment Field	AC 289			Right-click field for attachment, Manage Attachments command, Add button	
Data, Enter in Date Fields	AC 285	In Datasheet view, click field, type date			
Data, Enter in Hyperlink Field	AC 291			Right-click hyperlink field, Hyperlink command, Edit Hyperlink, enter Web address, click OK button	
Data, Enter in Memo Fields	AC 285	In Datasheet view, click field, type data			
Data, Enter in OLE Object Field	AC 287			Right-click object field, Insert Object command, Browse button, navigate to file to insert	
Data, Enter in Yes/No Fields	AC 284	In Datasheet view, click check box to indicate Yes value			
Data, Enter Using an Input Mask	AC 283	In Datasheet view, type data into field			
Data, Export to Excel	AC 111		Excel button (External Data tab | Export group)	Right-click object, click Excel on Export menu	
Data, Import	AC 38, AC 345		Button for imported data format (External Data tab | Import & Link group)	Right-click object, click selected format on Import menu	
Data, Sort in Query	AC 96		Select field in design grid, click Sort row, click Sort row arrow, select order		
Database Documenter	AC 635		Database Documenter button (Database Tools tab | Analyze group)		

Microsoft Access 2010 Quick Reference Summary *(continued)*

Task	Page Number	Mouse	Ribbon	Shortcut Menu	Keyboard Shortcut
Database Properties, Change	AC 59		'View and edit database properties' link (File tab | Info tab)		
Database, Create	AC 13		Blank database button (File tab | New tab)		
Datasheet Form with UI Macro, Create	AC 565		More Forms button (Create tab | Forms group), click Datasheet, name and save form, select column heading in form, display property sheet, click Event tab, click On Click event, click Build button, click OK button, create macro in Macro Builder		
Datasheet Form, Create	AC 617	Select table in Navigation Pane, click More Forms, click Datasheet			
Date, Add	AC 246		In form, click Date and Time button (Form Layout Tools Design tab | Header/Footer group), select format, OK button		
Decrypt Database	AC 655	Open database in exclusive mode, in Backstage view, click Info tab if necessary, click Decrypt Database button, type password, click OK button			
Default Value, Specify	AC 167	In Design view, select field in upper pane, enter value in Default Value property box in Field Properties pane			
Delete Query, Use	AC 163		Delete button (Query Tools Design tab | Query Type group)	Right-click any open area in upper pane, point to Query Type on shortcut menu, click Delete Query	
Design Grid, Clear	AC 95	In Design view, select all columns, DELETE	Advanced button (Home tab | Sort & Filter group), Clear Grid		
Drop Area, Remove	AC 587		Drop Zones button (PivotChart Tools Design tab | Show/Hide group)		
Duplicate Records, Find	AC 193		Query Wizard button (Create tab | Queries group), Find Duplicates Query Wizard		
Duplicates, Omit	AC 97		In Design view, click first empty field, Property Sheet button (Query Tools Design tab | Show/Hide group), click Yes in Unique Values property box	Right-click first empty field, click Properties on shortcut menu, click Yes in Unique Values property box	

Microsoft Access 2010 Quick Reference Summary *(continued)*

Task	Page Number	Mouse	Ribbon	Shortcut Menu	Keyboard Shortcut
Encrypt Database	AC 654	In Backstage view, click Info tab, if necessary, click Encrypt with Password button, type a password (Set Database Password dialog box), click OK button			
Error Checking, Enable	AC 651	In Backstage view, click Options tab, click Object Designers, click 'Enable error checking' check box, click OK button			
Field Contents, Change	AC 146	In Datasheet view or Form view, click in field, enter data			
Field in Query, Add	AC 79	Double-click field in upper pane			
Field in Query, Rearrange	AC 94	Click column selector for field and drag			
Field List, Move	AC 297	Drag field list title bar			
Field, Add New	AC 155		In Design view, Insert Rows button (Table Tools Design Tab | Tools group)		Design view, INSERT
Field, Add to Form	AC 251		Add Existing Fields button (Form Layout Tools Design tab | Tools group), drag fields from field list to form		
Field, Add to Report	AC 175		In Layout view, Add Existing Fields button (Report Layout Tools Design tab | Tools group), drag field from field list to desired location		
Field, Delete	AC 155	In Design view, click row selector for field, DELETE	Delete Rows button (Table Tools Design tab | Tools group)		
Fields, Add to Form Design	AC 473	Drag fields from field list to form			
Fields, Freeze	AC 606			In Datasheet view, select column(s), right-click, click Freeze Fields	
Filter and Sort Using Form	AC 253		Advanced button (Home tab | Sort & Filter group), Advanced Filter/Sort command, add field names to design grid, select sort order and specify criteria in design grid, Toggle Filters button		
Filter by Form, Use	AC 152		Advanced button (Home tab | Sort & Filter group), Advanced button, Filter by Form		

Microsoft Access 2010 Quick Reference Summary *(continued)*

Task	Page Number	Mouse	Ribbon	Shortcut Menu	Keyboard Shortcut
Filter by Selection, Use	AC 148		Selection button (Home tab | Sort & Filter group), select criterion		
Filter, Clear	AC 150		Advanced button (Home tab | Sort & Filter group), Clear All Filters		
Filter, Toggle	AC 150		Toggle Filter button (Home tab | Sort & Filter group)		
Font Color, Change in Datasheet	AC 181		Select table, Font Color button arrow (Home tab | Text Formatting group), select color		
Font Size, Change in Datasheet	AC 181		Select table, Font Size box arrow (Home tab | Text Formatting group), select size		
Font, Change in Datasheet	AC 181		Select table, Font box arrow (Home tab | Text Formatting group), select font		
Form Background Color, Change	AC 480		Background Color button arrow (Form Design Tools Format tab | Font group), select color from palette		
Form Controls, Format	AC 481		Property Sheet button (Form Design Tools Design tab | Tools group), change properties		
Form for Query, Create	AC 109		Select query, Form button (Create tab | Forms group)		
Form Label, Change	AC 308	In Design View, click twice to produce insertion point, edit text			
Form Title, Add	AC 484		Title button (Form Design Tools Design tab | Header/Footer group)		
Form Title, Modify Appearance	AC 312		In Design view, select control, Property Sheet button (Form Design Tools Design tab | Tools group)	Right-click control, click Properties	
Form with Datasheet, Create in Layout View	AC 325		Blank Form button (Create tab | Forms group), display field list, click Show all tables, expand "one" table and drag fields to desired locations, expand "many" table and drag first field onto form, drag remaining fields		
Form with Tab Control, Create	AC 503		Form Design button (Create tab | Forms group), select entire form, display property sheet for form; with All tab selected, click Record Source property, click arrow that appears, click table to serve as record source		

Microsoft Access 2010 Quick Reference Summary *(continued)*

Task	Page Number	Mouse	Ribbon	Shortcut Menu	Keyboard Shortcut
Form, Create	AC 48		Form button (Create tab | Forms group)		
Form, Create in Design View	AC 292, AC 472		Select table, Form Design button (Create tab | Forms group)		
Form, Create Using Form Wizard	AC 243		Select table, Form Wizard button (Create tab | Forms group)		
Form, Use	AC 315	Open Form in Form view, view records using navigation buttons, manipulate data using form fields			
Form, View in Form View	AC 305		View button (Home tab | Views group)		
Format Painter, Use	AC 482		In form, click format source control to copy, double-click Format Painter button (Form Design Tools Format tab | Font group), click each control to apply formatting		
Format, Specify	AC 168	In Design view, select field, click Format property box, type format			
Gridlines, Change in Datasheet	AC 180		Gridlines button (Home tab | Text Formatting group)		
Group and Sort in Report	AC 217		Open report in Layout view, Group & Sort button (Report Layout Tools Design tab | Grouping & Totals group), Add a group or Add a sort button		
Group, Sort and Total Pane, Remove	AC 223	Close Grouping Dialog Box button	Group & Sort button (Design tab | Grouping & Totals group)		
Grouping, Use	AC 122	Create query, select Group By in Total row, select field to group by			
Image, Add to Form or Report	AC 501		Insert Image button (Form Design Tools Design tab | Controls group), place image in desired position		
Input Mask Wizard, Use	AC 280	In Design view, click Input Mask property box in Field Properties pane, Build button, select desired mask			
Items, Add to Groups	AC 640	Navigation Pane arrow, click category, right-click object, point to 'Add to group' command, click desired group			

Microsoft Access 2010 Quick Reference Summary *(continued)*

Task	Page Number	Mouse	Ribbon	Shortcut Menu	Keyboard Shortcut
Join Properties, Change	AC 105			In Design view, right-click join line, click Join Properties	
Labels, Create	AC 255		Labels button (Create tab | Reports group)		
Layout, Create for Form or Report	AC 520		Select controls, Stacked button (Arrange tab | Table group) for stacked layout OR Tabular button (Arrange tab | Table group) for tabular layout		
Layout, Move in a Form or Report	AC 525		Click any cell in layout, Select Layout button (Arrange tab | Rows & Columns group), drag layout to new location		
Layout, Remove for Form or Report	AC 520			Right-click any control, point to Layout, Remove Layout	
Layout, Split in a Form or Report	AC 525		Select all cells to move to new layout, Stacked button (Arrange tab | Table group) to place cells in Stacked layout OR Tabular button (Arrange tab | Table group) to place cells in tabular layout		
Lock Database	AC 661	With database to be locked open, click File tab, click Save & Publish tab, click Make ACCDE, click Save As button, specify location and name for ACCDE file (Save As dialog box), click Save			
Logo, Add to Form or Report	AC 616		Open form or report in Layout view or Design view, Logo button (Design tab | Header/Footer group)		
Lookup Field, Create	AC 156	In Design view, click Data Type column for field, Data Type box arrow, Lookup Wizard			
Macro, Add Action	AC 545	Double-click Submacro element in Action Catalog, enter actions in Macro Builder			
Macro, Convert to VBA Code	AC 551		In Macro Builder window, Convert Macros to Visual Basic button (Macro Tools Design tab | Tools group), in Convert Macro dialog box, select appropriate options, click Convert		

Microsoft Access 2010 Quick Reference Summary *(continued)*

Task	Page Number	Mouse	Ribbon	Shortcut Menu	Keyboard Shortcut
Macro, Create	AC 543		Macro button (Create tab | Macros & Code group)		
Macro, Save as a VBA Module	AC 544	In Backstage view, click Save Object As, in Save As dialog box, click Module in the As text box, click OK			
Macro to VBA Code, Convert	AC 494		Convert Form's Macros to Visual Basic button (Form Design Tools Design tab | Tools group)		
Make-Table Query, Use	AC 165		Make Table button (Query Tools Design tab | Query Type group)		
Menu Form with Command Buttons, Create	AC 553		Form Design button (Create tab | Forms group), remove field list if necessary, with Use Control Wizards button selected, click Button tool (Form Design Tools Design tab | Controls group), click form to place command button and display Command Button Wizard dialog box		
Menu Form with Option Group, Create	AC 556		Form Design button (Create tab | Forms group), remove field list if necessary, More button (Form Design Tools Design tab | Controls group), with Use Control Wizards button selected, click Option Group tool (Form Design Tools Design tab | Controls group), click form to place option group and display Option Group Wizard		
Multipage Form, Create Using Tab Controls	AC 505		Tab Control tool (Form Design Tools Design Tab | Controls group), click form to place tab control, format tab properties		
Multiple Keys, Sort on	AC 98	Assign two sort keys in design grid			
Multiple-Field Index, Create	AC 649		Indexes button (Design tab | Show/Hide group), click blank row in Indexes: *(Table)* dialog box		
Multitable Form Based on Many Table, Create	AC 326		Blank Form button (Create tab | Forms group), Add Existing Fields button		

Microsoft Access 2010 Quick Reference Summary *(continued)*

Task	Page Number	Mouse	Ribbon	Shortcut Menu	Keyboard Shortcut
Multitable Report, Create	AC 232		Select table, Report Wizard button (Create tab | Reports group), add fields for first table in Report Wizard, select second table, add fields for second table		
Multivalued Field, Query Showing Multiple Values	AC 183	Create query with specified fields			
Multivalued Lookup Field, Use	AC 172	In Datasheet view, click field, click check boxes, click OK button			
Navigation Form, Add Tabs	AC 569	With navigation form open, drag tab object from Navigation Pane to tab			
Navigation Form, Create	AC 568		Navigation button (Create tab | Forms group), click desired command, remove field list if necessary		
Navigation Pane, Customize	AC 127	Navigation Pane arrow			
Number Criterion, Use	AC 90	Create query, select table, add field(s) to query, enter criterion in field grid			
Object Dependencies, View	AC 319		Select table, Object Dependencies button (Database Tools tab | Relationships group), 'Objects that depend on me' option button		
Open Database	AC 27	In Backstage view, Open button (File tab) OR Recent tab, *file name*			
Open Table	AC 24	Double-click table in Navigation Pane		Right-click table in Navigation Pane, click Open in shortcut menu	
Package and Sign Database	AC 657	In Backstage view, click Save & Publish tab, Save Database As command, click Save As button, click OK button, click Create button			
Parameter Query, Create	AC 87		In Design view, type parameter in square brackets in criterion row of field grid, View button (Query Tools Design tab | Results group)		
Performance Analyzer	AC 634		Analyze Performance button (Database Tools tab | Analyze group)		

Microsoft Access 2010 Quick Reference Summary (continued)

Task	Page Number	Mouse	Ribbon	Shortcut Menu	Keyboard Shortcut
PivotChart Orientation, Change	AC 586		Switch Row/Column button (PivotChart Tools Design tab | Active Field group)		
PivotChart, Create	AC 583	Open query, click View button arrow, click PivotChart View			
PivotChart, Use	AC 589		Open query in PivotChart view, Drop Zones button (PivotChart Tools Design tab | Show/Hide group), click drop area arrows, hide or display data as desired		
PivotTable, Create	AC 576	Open query, click View button arrow, click PivotTable View, display field list, add desired fields to row and data areas			
PivotTable, Use	AC 579	Display query in PivotTable view, click plus (+) and minus (–) signs to change data displayed			
Place Controls in a Control Layout	AC 245		Open form in Layout view, Form Layout Tools Arrange tab, select form controls, select control style from Table group		
Preview or Print Object	AC 31		Print or Print Preview button (File tab | Print tab)		CTRL+P, ENTER
Publish to Access Services	AC 624	In Backstage view, click Save & Publish tab, in Publish to Access Services area, enter URL and site name, click Publish to Access Services button			
Query, Create in Design View	AC 78, AC 347		Query Design button (Create tab | Queries group)		
Query, Create Using Simple Query Wizard	AC 43		Query Wizard button (Create tab | Queries group)		
Query, Export	AC 111, AC 113, AC 114		Select query in Navigation Pane, application button (External Data tab | Export group)	Right-click query in Navigation Pane, point to Export	
Quick Styles, Change	AC 571		Select control or controls, Quick Styles (Form Layout Tools Design tab | Control Formatting group), in Quick Styles gallery, select desired style		

Microsoft Access 2010 Quick Reference Summary *(continued)*

Task	Page Number	Mouse	Ribbon	Shortcut Menu	Keyboard Shortcut
Range, Specify	AC 166	In Design view, select field, enter criterion specifying range in Validation Rule property box in Field Properties pane			
Record, Add	AC 28	New (blank) record button in Navigation buttons	New button (Home tab | Records Group)		CTRL+PLUS SIGN (+)
Record, Delete	AC 147	In Datasheet view, click record selector, DELETE	Delete button (Home tab | Records group)		
Record, Search for	AC 144, AC 231		Find button (Home tab | Find group)		CTRL+F
Record, Update	AC 146	In Form view or in Datasheet view, change desired data			
Records in a Join, Restrict	AC 115	In Design view, enter criterion for query			
Records, Filter in Report	AC 228		Selection button (Home tab | Sort & Filter group)	Right-click field, select filter	
Rectangle, Add to Form	AC 490		More button (Form Design Tools Design tab | Controls group), click Rectangle tool		
Referential Integrity, Specify	AC 186, AC 346		Relationships button (Database Tools tab | Relationships group), add tables, click Enforce Referential Integrity check box (Edit Relationships dialog box)		
Remaining Fields in Table, Define	AC 19	In Datasheet view, click Click to Add field (Fields tab)			
Report Filter, Clear	AC 229			Right-click field, Clear filter from menu option	
Report Margins, Change	AC 400		Margins button (Report Design Tools Page Setup tab | Page Size group)		
Report, Add a Combo Box	AC 357		More button (Report Design Tools Design tab | Controls group), click Combo Box tool (Report Design Tools Design tab | Controls group), click in report		
Report, Add a Date	AC 378		Date and Time button (Report Design Tools Design tab | Header/Footer group)		
Report, Add a Graph	AC 357		More button (Report Design Tools Design tab | Controls group), Chart tool (Report Design Tools Design tab | Controls group), click in report to display Chart Wizard		

Microsoft Access 2010 Quick Reference Summary (continued)

Task	Page Number	Mouse	Ribbon	Shortcut Menu	Keyboard Shortcut
Report, Add a Group	AC 352		Group & Sort button (Report Design Tools Design tab | Grouping & Totals group)		
Report, Add a Hyperlink	AC 357		Hyperlink tool (Report Design Tools Design tab | Controls group), enter hyperlink in Address text box (Insert Hyperlink dialog box)		
Report, Add a Page Break	AC 381		More button (Report Design Tools Design tab | Controls group), Insert Page Break tool (Report Design Tools Design tab | Controls group), click in report		
Report, Add a Page Number	AC 378		Page Numbers button (Report Design Tools Design tab | Header/Footer group)		
Report, Add a Sort	AC 353		Group & Sort button (Report Design Tools Design tab | Grouping & Totals group), 'Add a sort' button		
Report, Add a Subreport	AC 368		More button (Report Design Tools Design tab | Controls group), click Subform/Subreport tool		
Report, Add a Text Box	AC 358		Text Box tool (Report Design Tools Design tab | Controls group)		
Report, Add a Title	AC 378		Title button (Report Design Tools Design tab | Header/Footer group)		
Report, Add Additional Fields	AC 385	Drag field from field list to report			
Report, Add Fields	AC 354, AC 382, AC 385		Add Existing Fields button (Report Design Tools Design tab | Tools group)		
Report, Add Totals and Subtotals	AC 387		Group & Sort button (Report Design Tools Design tab | Grouping & Totals group)		
Report, Create	AC 52		Report button (Create tab | Reports group)		
Report, Create in Design View	AC 351		Report Design button (Create tab | Reports group)		
Report, Create in Layout View	AC 236		Blank Report button (Create tab | Reports group)		
Report, Create Involving Join	AC 106		Select query, Report Wizard button (Create tab | Reports group)		

Microsoft Access 2010 Quick Reference Summary *(continued)*

Task	Page Number	Mouse	Ribbon	Shortcut Menu	Keyboard Shortcut
Report, Group Controls	AC 362		Select controls, Size/Space button (Report Design Tools Arrange tab | Sizing & Ordering group), click Group		
Report, Publish	AC 381		PDF or XPS button (External Data tab | Export group)	Right-click report, click PDF or XPS on Export menu	
Required Field, Specify	AC 166	In Design view, select field, Required property box in Field Properties pane, box arrow, Yes			
Row and Column Size, Change	AC 286	In Datasheet view, drag field selector edge for column and drag row selector edge for row			
Row, Delete in a Form or Report	AC 521		Click any control in row, Select Row (Arrange tab | Rows & Columns group), DELETE		
Row, Insert for a Form or Report	AC 521		Select any control in row above or below, Select Row button (Arrange tab | Rows & Columns group), Insert Above button (Arrange tab | Rows & Columns group) to insert a blank row above selected row OR Insert Below button (Arrange tab | Rows & Columns group) to insert blank row below selected row		
Rows, Move in Form or Report	AC 522		Select any cell in row, Select Row button (Arrange tab | Rows & Columns group), Move Up button (Arrange tab | Move group) to move row up one row OR Move Down button (Arrange tab | Move group) to move row down one row		
Save Object	AC 21	Save button on Quick Access Toolbar OR in Backstage view, File tab, Save			CTRL+S
Self-Signed Certificate, Create	AC 656	Open database, Start button on Windows 7 taskbar, All Programs, Microsoft Office, Microsoft Office 2010 Tools, Digital Certificate for VBA Projects, type certificate name, click OK button, with Save Database As selected, click Package and Sign			

Microsoft Access 2010 Quick Reference Summary *(continued)*

Task	Page Number	Mouse	Ribbon	Shortcut Menu	Keyboard Shortcut
Signed Package, Open	AC 659	In Backstage view, click Open, navigate to file location, click 'Files of type' box arrow, select Microsoft Access Signed Packages, select package to open, click Open button, click Open button again, rename database if necessary, click OK button			
Simple Form with a Datasheet, Create	AC 323	Select "one" table, Form button (Create tab | Forms group)			
Single or Multivalued Lookup Fields, Modify	AC 161	In Design view, select field, click Lookup tab in Field Properties pane, change list in Row Source property to desired list			
Single-Field Index, Create	AC 649	In Design view, select field, change Indexed field property to Yes			
Single-Item Form, Create	AC 616	Select table in Navigation Pane, save and name form			
Size Mode, Change	AC 309		Click control, Property Sheet button (Form Design Tools Design tab | Tools group), Size Mode property		
Split Database	AC 663		Access Database button (Database Tools tab | Move Data group), click Split Database button, click OK button		
Split Form, Create	AC 142		Select table, More Forms button (Create tab | Forms group), Split Form		
Startup Form, Select	AC 620	In Backstage view, click Options tab, click Current Database (Access Options dialog box), click Display form box arrow, select form to display			
Statistics, Calculate	AC 119		Create query, Totals button (Query Tools Design tab | Show/Hide group), click Total row in design grid, click Total box arrow, select calculation		
Subdatasheet, Use	AC 191	In Datasheet view, click plus sign in front of row			

Microsoft Access 2010 Quick Reference Summary *(continued)*

Task	Page Number	Mouse	Ribbon	Shortcut Menu	Keyboard Shortcut
Subform, Add	AC 506		More button (Form Design Tools Design tab | Controls group), with Use Control Wizards button selected, click the Subform/Subreport tool (Form Design Tools Design tab | Controls group), click in form to start SubForm Wizard		
Subform, Place on a Form	AC 301		More button (Form Design Tools Design tab | Controls group), Subform/Subreport tool, click in form to launch SubForm Wizard		
Subform, Resize	AC 509	In Design view, drag a form sizing handle			
Summary Report, Create	AC 242		Open report in Layout view, Hide Details button (Report Layout Tools Design tab | Grouping & Totals group)		
Tab Order, Change on Report	AC 519		In Design view, Tab Order button (Form Design Tools Design tab | Tools group), use Tab Order dialog box to change order		
Tab Stop, Change	AC 314		In Design view, select control, Property Sheet button (Form Design Tools Design tab | Tools group), All tab, change Tab Stop property to No		
Table Analyzer, Use	AC 631		Analyze Table button (Database Tools tab | Analyze group)		
Table, Create in Design View	AC 33, AC 343		Table Design button (Create tab | Tables group)		
Table, View in Design View	AC 21		View button arrow (Table Tools Fields tab | Views group), Design View		
Tables, Join	AC 102		Query Design button (Create tab | Queries group), add field lists for tables to join, add desired fields to design grid, view query		
Template, Create	AC 621	Open database, click File tab, click Save & Publish tab, click Template button, click Save button			
Template, Use	AC 628	In Backstage view, click New tab, click My templates button, click desired template, enter name and location for database, click Create button			

Microsoft Access 2010 Quick Reference Summary *(continued)*

Task	Page Number	Mouse	Ribbon	Shortcut Menu	Keyboard Shortcut
Text Data Criterion, Use	AC 80	Enter text as criterion in Criteria row of design grid			
Theme, Assign to a Single Object	AC 241		Open object in Layout view, Themes button (Design tab | Themes group), right-click theme in Theme picker, click the Apply Theme to This Object Only command		
Theme, Assign to All Objects	AC 240		Open object in Layout view, Themes button (Design tab | Themes group), select theme from Theme picker		
Title, Add to a Form	AC 301		Title button (Form Design Tools Design tab | Header/Footer group)		
Top Values Query, Create	AC 99		In Design view, Return box arrow (Query Tools Design tab | Query Setup group)		
Totals and Subtotals, Add	AC 221		Select field, Totals button (Report Layout Tools Design tab | Grouping & Totals group)	Right-click column header, click Total	
Totals, Add to a Report	AC 57		Totals button (Report Layout Tools Design tab | Grouping & Totals group)		
Totals, Include in a Datasheet	AC 177		In Datasheet view, Totals button (Home tab | Records group), click Total row, click arrow		
Totals, Remove from a Datasheet	AC 179		Totals button (Home tab | Records group)		
Unmatched Records, Find	AC 193		Query Wizard button (Create tab | Queries group), Find Unmatched Query Wizard		
Update Query, Use	AC 162		Create query, Update button (Query Tools Design tab | Query Type group), select field, click Update To row in design grid	Right-click any open area in upper pane, point to Query Type on shortcut menu, click Update Query on Query Type submenu	
Validation Rule for Table, Create	AC 642		In Design view, click Property Sheet button (Table Tools Design tab | Show/Hide group) click Validation Rule property, enter rule		
VBA Code for Forms or Reports, View	AC 551		Open form or report in Design view, View Code button (Report Design Tools Design tab | Tools group) for reports OR View Code button (Form Design Tools Design tab | Tools group) for forms		

Microsoft Access 2010 Quick Reference Summary *(continued)*

Task	Page Number	Mouse	Ribbon	Shortcut Menu	Keyboard Shortcut
Web Compatibility, Check	AC 623	In Backstage view, click Save & Publish tab, click Publish to Access Services, click Run Compatibility Checker button			
Web Database, View	AC 625	Launch browser, enter URL for Web database			
Wildcard, Use	AC 83	In Design view, click Criteria row in design grid, type criterion including wildcard			
Zero Length, Allow	AC 646	In Design view, select field, change Allow Zero Length field property value to Yes			